International Library of Psychology
Philosophy and Scientific Method

Plato's Theory
of Ethics

International Library of Psychology Philosophy and Scientific Method

GENERAL EDITOR : . . . . C. K. OGDEN, M.A.
(Magdalen College, Cambridge).

Plato's Theory of Ethics

THE MORAL CRITERION AND
THE HIGHEST GOOD

By
R. C. LODGE

*Professor of Logic and History of Philosophy
in the University of Manitoba, and Visiting
Lecturer in Philosophy at Harvard University*

LONDON
KEGAN PAUL, TRENCH, TRUBNER & CO., LTD.
NEW YORK: HARCOURT, BRACE AND COMPANY

1928

PRINTED IN GREAT BRITAIN BY THE DEVONSHIRE PRESS, TORQUAY

CONTENTS

ANALYSIS

PREFACE

IT is necessary to explain my use of the term " platonism "
and the method of interpretation which I have applied
to the Dialogues. In Plato himself, the fourth-century
Athenian, in the obscure problems connected with his
personal history, in the motives which led him to write, in the
intentions behind the publication of Dialogues so very different
as the *Protagoras* and the *Parmenides*, and in the personal evolution of his views—in short, in all the questions which especially
interest philologists[1]—I take little interest. What Plato the
Athenian personally supposed or wished his words to mean is a
very delicate enquiry which I prefer to leave to those who have
faith that their methods will enable them to pursue it successfully. There is no lack of such faith, and never has been.
But, until such students succeed in coming to reasonable
agreement *inter se*, it would be absurd for one who is primarily
a dialectician to believe that he can attain to significant
convictions. I take Burnet's text—quite arbitrarily—as a
starting-point, and select all the passages bearing directly or
indirectly upon each topic which I study. These I approach
without any *a priori* bias which I can detect, other than the
supposition that, handled dialectically, they are likely to
yield a significant message which will prove to be more or
less consistent with messages similarly extracted from all the
passages which refer to allied topics. The conclusion which
I seek, the " one " which gives meaning to this " many,"
would be a single system of dialectically consistent meanings
which would throw a very clear light upon the meaning of
any passage in the Dialogues which fell within the general
field of investigation. Such a system would, of course, be
different from what a reader would find fully expressed in
any single passage ; for it would represent the concentrated
essence of all relevant passages, with a large fringe of associations covering the variations with which that meaning-essence

[1] *Cf.* Wilamowitz-Moellendorff, *Platon*[2], 1920, Vol. I., pp. 3-9.

is expressed in individual contexts. It would represent the essential meaning which is " platonism," somewhat loosed from the individual contexts of the particular Dialogues ; in such a way that the Greek texts would represent the fluctuating phenomena of which this systematic whole would represent the " idea." Of the fluctuating phenomena, from this standpoint, no exact and final science would be possible, except, possibly, of the philological type which I (arbitrarily) presuppose as attained by Burnet. But each of my chapters would represent an inductive approach towards the ideal system from the standpoint of some particular aspect of that system. For example, " Chapter I " is an attempt to ascertain the nature of the ideal moral judge ; " Chapter II " is an attempt to ascertain the nature of the objective element in goodness, *etc.*, so that, after the final chapter it should be possible to turn back again, and, in the light of the " unhypothetical first principle," to explain deductively the various platonic discussions of the highest good.

An important point in method should, perhaps, be cleared up. I have stated that passages from the Dialogues are handled " dialectically." The term " logically " might have been misapprehended. What is usually thought of, when this term is used, is logic of the traditional type, or modern improvements upon this type, in which the elements which enter into the reasoning process are " reduced to logical form " as abstract identities, and are handled by the absolute *sic et non* of the formal law of contradiction. This method has led to strange conclusions. Passages taken out of the contexts in which they occur, and then subjected to the manipulations of formal logic, can, of course, be interpreted in ways which would yield a single system of meanings, but the result might be a mere travesty upon what the interpreter was proposing to explain. So well understood is this source of error, that interpreters nowadays sometimes err in the opposite direction, and become sticklers for contextual interpretation in a sense which precludes any attempt to understand " platonism " as a whole. " Dialectic " expands the implications of each passage in relation to its context, but finds, in fact, that these original contexts and their expansions, when compared, seem to present different fragments of a single pattern, and, when put together, do, in point of fact, indicate the presence of a single thought-pattern which does

not violate the contextual implications of the individual
passages, but throws considerable light upon the fringe of
meaning which belongs to such passages.[1] The dialectician
arranges such passages in a series, passing from the more
superficial to the more profound, and developing their systematic implications in accordance with the platonic hints
for practising the dialectical art. There is a danger, even here,
of losing sight of the original contexts, but the danger can
be met, faced, and overcome.

A second danger, which besets all interpreters without
exception, is of reading one's own philosophical notions,
whether innate or acquired, into the passages studied. Where
there is more than one possible interpretation of a context
or group of contexts, it is natural for any interpreter to take
up into his own mind only the interpretation which fits in
with the natural or acquired workings of that mind. Examples
of this danger are only too well known. Plato has been interpreted as a utilitarian of the type of J. S. Mill, as an idealist
of the Marburg school, as an academic realist of the mediaeval
type, or as a neo-realist of the most up-to-the-minute brand.
All this is well known, and it is only to be expected that the
Dialogues will be understood according to the measure of
their interpreter. It is possible that deliberate avoidance
of the excessive subjectivism associated with the name of those
who (still) follow the path opened by Schleiermacher, in
favour of a rigorous dialectical method, will somewhat lessen
this danger ; but the history of platonic interpretation indicates beyond reasonable doubt that each interpretation is
itself one more phenomenon of the ideal world, and
contains elements which are personal and peculiar to the
interpreter. It is thus not to be expected that the present
writer has escaped entirely this kind of error ; for it is precisely
this " constant " error of the " personal equation " which
tends to remain constant, in spite of self-criticism. And,
in spite of scientific method, is not all interpretation an art
rather than an exact science ?

In conclusion, it should be stated that the evidence from
the Dialogues indicates that Plato would himself like his
writings to be understood as phenomena of the ideal realm,

---

[1] Cf. the comparison of the idea of beauty in the Symposium
with the idea of good in the Republic.

phenomena coloured in his case also by subjective prejudice, by considerations of space and time, by particularities of context, etc.; but still as phenomena of a reality which the sifting method of the dialectician can, perhaps, succeed in uncovering, at least in its fundamental outlines. He would also, I think, insist that only in so far as his writings can be used to reveal this ideal reality, are they of fundamental significance to humanity. They do not so much contain a " system " as indicate a certain standpoint ; but this standpoint has systematic implications ; and it is these which constitute the essence of platonism.[1]

I am indebted to the editors and publishers of the Philosophical Review and of the International Journal of Ethics, and of " Philosophical Essays Presented to John Watson " for permission to reprint chapters or portions of chapters which they have published during the last seven or eight years. To the University of Minnesota I am indebted for a series of small grants for clerical assistance. To Plato-students, past and present, I am, of course, indebted to an extent far greater than can be indicated by footnote references. But my chief debt is, equally of course, to Plato himself. Like most Plato-students, I have learnt far more from living with the five or six volumes associated with his name than from any other source ; and this source seems, to me as to other *epigoni*, to remain inexhaustible.

---

[1] *Phaedr.* 265c-266cm, 275c-277a, 277e-278e ; *cf.* 249e-250b ; *cf. Epist.* 341c-e. *Cf.* Fouillée, *La philosophie de Platon*, p. 15 ; Shorey, The Interpretation of the Timaeus : *Am. Jour. Philol.*, Vol. IX., p. 401.

INTRODUCTION

HISTORIANS of philosophy assert with one voice that the supreme achievement of ancient ethical reflection was the determination of the conception of a highest good, and that the fundamental outlines of that determination were drawn once for all, by Plato. On a subject of such importance, we should expect modern scholarship to have probed the evidence and to have come to a unanimous verdict, so that the case might well be regarded as closed. But when we turn to the literature, and examine, sympathetically but critically, the method, scope, and results of the treatises, general and special, which deal with this subject, what do we find?

In the first place, we find that modern scholars generally adopt towards Plato the attitude, not of a pupil, but of a judge. The stage is set beforehand, usually by reference to Kant's distinction between a complete and a highest good, and Plato's text is compelled to answer the questions of a definitely alien interpreter. This at once imports a certain foreign element into the modern reconstruction ; and whether it is the standpoint of Kant, or of Hegel, or of Mill, which is adopted by the interpreter, the result is necessarily a more or less distorted platonism.

In the second place, the special method of approach is usually to set forth (1) the views of other Greek writers, from Homer to Antisthenes, on the highest good ; (2) the various reflections of these views opposed in the platonic Dialogues ; and (3) Plato's " own " views, especially as revealed in the *Philebus*. In practice, however, it is found difficult to separate (1) and (2) in such a way as to do no injustice to the other Greek writers, and to separate (2) and (3) without doing severe injustice to Plato. The treatment of (1) and (2) lends itself to uncritical insistence upon identities in the form of expression, without much reference to

underlying differences of thought, while the treatment of
(3) lends itself, in practice, to a certain narrowness and undue
confinement of the platonic genius.

In the third place, we note that the treatment, even
of the platonic writings, reveals a certain restriction of outlook. While other dialogues always receive honourable
mention, it is usual, in practice, to confine the arts of strict
analysis to (a) that portion of the *Republic* which deals with
the " idea of good," and (b) the *Gütertafel* of the *Philebus*.   In
spite of scrupulously accurate treatment of details, such
deliberate narrowing of the field of vision inevitably induces
intellectual myopia, and brings with it a certain incompleteness of insight which diminishes the general significance of
the results of even persistent inquiry.[1]

Finally, if we look at the results, we find diversity more
in evidence than agreement.   So far as these results can be
reduced to brief definitions, by disregarding or slurring over
minor disagreements, we find " Plato's *summum bonum* "
declared to be some one or two or three of the following :—

1. Pleasure, or pleasures organized into a system.[2]
2. Happiness, or a life founded upon, and participating
   in, the harmonious life of the universe.[3]
3. Virtue, or the life of active citizenship in the ideal
   community, under the guidance of science and
   philosophy.[4]
4. The co-ordination of all individual purposes into a
   single system patterned upon the " idea of good."[5]
5. The intellectual or rational life.[6]
6. Contemplative wisdom, or the intuitive vision of the
   definitely transcendental " idea of good."[7]
7. Beatitude, or complete subordination of self to God
   until one becomes like God or unified with God.[8]

These definitions refer to the highest good considered
relatively to man.   Considered absolutely, without especial
reference to humanity, Plato's highest good is declared to be :

8. Absolute unity.[9]
9. Conformity to law.[10]
10. The idea of good.[11]
11. The self-identity of thought.[12]
12. Absolute Mind, or God.[13]

To a reader unfamiliar with the detailed qualifications found in the literature, it might appear that these definitions, so far from being mutually exclusive, emphasize various aspects of a single underlying conception ; and the hope might well arise that, by combining all these definitions, a little logical ingenuity might succeed in formulating the whole truth about Plato's highest good. But to the student who is more at home with the literature, it is only too apparent that very few of the scholars concerned would consent to accept even the modest degree of *rapprochment* implied in grouping them together at all, and that most of them would unhesitatingly reject all definitions of the highest good except the definition characteristic of their own group. For example, those who define the highest good as " pleasure " explicitly exclude from their definition such attributes as " participation in objective harmoniousness " or " virtue " or " transcendental intuition," except in so far as these may be regarded as means to the great end of producing pleasure as a state of somebody's consciousness. On the other hand, those who believe in " harmony " or " virtue " or " intuition " reject pleasure as " subjective " and almost beneath contempt. In the same way, the partisans of " the intellectual or rational life " mean life here on earth, and explicitly reject " intuition " and " transcendence," on the ground that these are ultimately irrational. On the other hand, the partisans of " contemplative wisdom " refuse, with equal lack of hesitation, to regard as " highest " any " good " restricted to this mortal sphere. To such writers the restriction would degrade Plato to the level of " an eagle chained." It is thus the divergences, rather than the agreements, which stand out after closer scrutiny.

In the face of these divergences in the results attained by scholars whose completeness no one would dream of questioning, the only possible conclusion is that the subject is perhaps somewhat more complex than the eclectic and deliberately narrowed concentration of the special monographs has realized, and the hope therefore remains that a new investigation which is strictly empirical and as complete as possible may succeed in penetrating beneath verbal forms and accidental contextual implications to the deeper strata of platonic reflection. We shall study the subject of the highest good, not with reference to Kant or Mill, but in the kind of setting in which it is found in the platonic Dialogues, and shall study it, as far as possible, in its relation to the whole thought of Plato.

What is the setting of the highest good in the Dialogues ? If we look over the passages in which the twenty-odd candidates for the position of highest good are mentioned or discussed—pleasure, wealth, health, power, happiness, immortality, etc.—we observe that the " highest " good is often so named as being the highest point on a " scale " or " ladder " of goods, and that there are many such scales scattered up and down the different dialogues. This necessitates a special study of such scales, as a vital part of the concrete setting of the highest good in Plato's thought. And further : an attempt to discover the principles which govern the construction of such scales leads inevitably to consideration of the general principles or criteria by which Plato distinguishes good in general from bad in general. A special investigation, then, of the general criteria in question properly precedes consideration of the specific value-scales, as this in turn precedes consideration of the various specific candidates for the position of highest good.

In accordance, then, with this principle of division—a principle derived from the empirical study of the Dialogues, and not read into the subject *a priori*—the present investigation consists of three main parts : (1) the moral criterion, (2) scales of goods, and (3) highest goods. In each of these sections an attempt is made to be reasonably complete, and to be as just as possible to the deeper significance of each passage studied.

One further question of method remains to be discussed. It is frequently asserted that the only scientific approach to the study of Plato is that which follows the *Werdegang* of his thought, and studies the Dialogues in a certain order. It is further claimed that nowadays it is unnecessary to follow the " subjective " and " unscientific " arrangement of Schleiermacher and his spiritual successors—an arrangement, or rather a series of diverse arrangements, based upon purely internal evidence—but that we can accept at least the main results of the " objective science of stylometry " founded by Lewis Campbell. On the other hand, many distinguished scholars assert that it makes little difference in what order we read the Dialogues, provided that we read them *all*, and that at present, at any rate, considerations based primarily upon the " Epistles " and upon some special arrangement of the Dialogues, tend to be of a highly speculative character. A still further difficulty arises from the insistence of scholars of the highest repute upon a rather sharp distinction between " platonism proper "—*i.e.*, the content of Plato's academic lectures, known to us obscurely from the polemical hints of his pupil, Aristotle—and the content of the Dialogues, which is regarded as, in large part, extra-platonic socraticism, and in any case unsafe as a source for the construction of Plato's " own " thought.[14] These contentions, if proven, would seem to register a *caveat* against any investigation of the philosophical contents of the Dialogues taken as a whole, or at least against calling the result either scientific or specifically platonic. Historically, of course, it is precisely such investigations to which the name of " platonic " has been, and still is, applied, and it is in this historical sense that the term is used in the present study.

The present investigation attempts, in the first place, to lay down completely and accurately what the various criteria are, what the various scales are, and what the various highest goods are, according to the discussions which we find in the Dialogues. Until this has been determined, it is impossible to arrange them in any order whatever, whether supposed to represent their order of development in Plato's *philosophische Entwickelung*, or with some other object in view. There are, in effect, two lines of treatment, both equally admissible. On the one hand, we may attempt to construct the general background of the thoughts expressed in the Dialogues, by combining, in accordance with the ideal of unity and consistency, all the leading pronouncements on each particular point investigated, without much reference to the question of the particular order in which the different dialogues may (or may not) have been written. This is a *logical* problem, and deals, not so much with what a given speaker in a given context happens to say, as with the system of thoughts implied by the contexts to which we are introduced in the Dialogues taken as a whole, *i.e.*, with what is historically known as " platonism." On the other hand, it is no doubt possible, by arranging the same thoughts in an order dictated by stylometrical or other philological considerations, to establish, at least to some extent, the order in which these same ideas came to be effectively taken up into the focus of the philosophical consciousness of Plato the Athenian. This problem is *psychological* and genetic, and deals, not so much with platonism as a systematic whole—which is what, historically, platonism has meant, at least to philosophers—as with the various strata of platonism found embedded at different dates in a single concrete example. For a full understanding of the specifically genetic problem, some prior solution of the logical problem seems essential, and we shall accordingly devote ourselves primarily to the logical or dialectical arrangement of the thoughts which are to be found in the Dialogues, *i.e.*, to the construction of the ethical portions of platonism.

PART I

THE MORAL CRITERION IN PLATONISM

IF we read the Dialogues in the spirit of a pupil rather than of a judge, we find many avenues of approach to the question of the distinction between good and evil, and to the tests or criteria by which that distinction is established. In the first place, in view of the great diversity of opinion as to good and evil—a diversity to which the Dialogues do full justice—it seems necessary to settle the question as to who is entitled to pass judgment, and to select a group of experts whose verdict will be in accordance with the evidence and will give us the whole truth and nothing but the truth. This problem occupies an important position in platonic reflection upon ethics, and is, in general, an attempt to answer the question, " *Who* is the judge ? " In the second place, we have the attempt to answer the question, " *How* does the judge pass judgment ? " That is to say, by reference to what objective features of the cases before him does he arrive at his decisions ? In the third place, we have the attempt to answer the question, " What *standards* does the judge apply ? " In the fourth place, we have a psychological analysis of the moral judgment, an attempt to answer the question, " How, in a *psychological* sense, does the judge come to make his decisions ? " That is to say, (a) what elements in his nature are behind his judgment ?, and (b) what is the genesis, the history of the development of his powers of judgment ? Finally, in the fifth place, we have the more metaphysical attempts to explain the *validity* of moral judgments in the universe in general. There are a number of minor problems which also touch upon the topic of the moral criterion, but in the main there seem to be these five chief lines along which the discussions of this subject in the Dialogues pass, and, if we wish to be just to the discussions as we find them, we must study them in this way, completely, and without *a priori* bias. In the five chapters which follow, an attempt is made to deal dialectically with the passages which discuss these five fundamental questions, and finally, in the sixth chapter, to sum up the results of our enquiry, so far as these results directly concern the general distinction between good and evil.

CHAPTER I

WHO IS THE JUDGE ?

IN answer to the inquiry, Who is the judge in ethical questions ?, the platonic dialogues furnish a number of replies :—(1) Everyone, (2) The many, (3) The interlocutor, (4) The good man (just man, man of character and moral education, etc.), (5) The experienced man, (6) The wise man, (7) The philosopher (dialectician, man of knowledge, understanding, or reason), (8) The legislator or guardian. Under these eight heads is concentrated all the evidence relative to the question, and it should be possible, by proceeding inductively and taking somewhat in detail the various answers grouped under each head, eventually to arrive at a point where the general platonic answer to the main question—if there *is* any such general question and general answer—can be formulated, and, when formulated, also definitely verified. Such somewhat detailed examination with the hope of discovering the general outlines of the Platonic position on this question, is the aim of the present chapter.

1. Everyone.

In the first place, it is frequently stated, sometimes by Socrates, sometimes by his interlocutors, that some form of moral sense is universal, that " everyone " is rightly regarded as a judge in matters of conduct. Just what is Plato's attitude on this point ? Stated negatively, Plato seems to mean that moral judgment is not a matter for a few technical experts. It does not require a long apprenticeship or elaborate specialized education, such as is necessary to acquire sound judgment in architecture, shipbuilding, etc. It is not a prerogative of noble birth and social position, and is entirely independent of economic status.[1] More positively, a moral sense is strictly universal. Every citizen possesses it, and, like language, it is an attribute of humanity as such. We all have the root of the matter in us, an " eye of the soul," a sense of honour and justice.[2] We all foster its development, in our contemporaries and especially in the rising generation, by word and deed, by public law, and by all the devices of a general, non-technical education.[3] Absenee of such a sense of honour and justice is unnatural, pathological, the worst of diseases, a sign of subnormality, an insanity indicating a state of mind less than human, a " lie in the soul " abhorred alike of men and gods.[4]

As evidence that moral judgment is not a matter for experts, the practice of the Athenian assembly is adduced —where experts are consulted on technical questions, but on questions of general policy *any* citizen is given a hearing.[5] In support of the contention that moral judgment is not the product of a specialized system of education, emphasis is again and again laid upon the fact that men like Themistocles, Pericles, and Thucydides—like Lord Chesterfield in more modern times—failed signally in pedagogic experiments upon their sons or friends among the rising generation.[6] Finally it is urged that universality of this sense of honour and justice is a *sine qua non* of civilized life. Men simply could not live together in cities, could not form a true community, unless they could at least trust one another,[7] and it is a divine law that the subnormal or morally diseased, if hopelessly incurable, should be put to death.[8]

In saying, then, that everyone is a judge in matters of conduct, Plato means that we all have the root of the matter in us. He does not mean that our judgment is infallible, or that it is fully developed in each one of us. Differences of moral opinion are only too glaring, in his eyes,[9] and on the question of development of moral judgment, it is one of the main points of dispute between him and the sophists, whether the ordinary institutions of Greek life are capable of developing reliable moral judgment (whether supplemented or not by the services of a professional tutor), or whether a new method of reflection, the liberal, non-technical art of dialectic, is not essential to the development of a judgment which shall rise above the contradictions, perplexities, and blindness of every-day, conventional morality.[10]

2. The many.
That " the many "—*i.e.*, the numerical majority—

should be regarded by Plato as judges in ethical questions, may seem strange to the reader who has derived from the dialogues the impression that Plato is an intellectual aristocrat who looks down with snobbish superiority upon democratic tendencies of all sorts. And it remains true that he by no means accepts their judgments as final.[11] But a careful examination of the instances shows that, while often dissenting from their conclusions, he by no means denies them the right and the capacity to judge questions of conduct. Their judgment may not, perhaps, rise much above the level of conventional morality, and may thus come into conflict with his own more highly reflective ethical beliefs, but on the whole it is not the moral judgment of the many as such, of which Plato disapproves, but rather the noise and exaggeration with which it tends to be accompanied in the general assemblies, and the unreasoning violence with which decisions superficially arrived at are carried out.[12] It is, in other words, the unreasoning and conservative, anti-progressive tendencies of the many, to which the philosopher takes exception. It is not that they judge, but that they so soon cease to judge and proceed at once to hasty action, that he finds worthy of censure—not that they judge, but that they do not judge more. It is, in fact, an essential element in his social philosophy that the many should be regarded as capable of recognizing ethical truth when they meet with it, and his one hope for the salvation of society is that they should come to appreciate the value of a "good pilot,"[13] and trust themselves to the rule of the philosopher-king[14]—a contingency which he regards as by no means impossible.[15] It is, in fact, the social duty of the philosopher who has seen the vision, to return to the cave and educate his less well educated brethren—the many, or at any rate the best of the many.[16] The many, then, are judges in ethical questions, though not, of course, final judges.

How does this position compare with the statement that "everyone" is a judge in such questions? There is, of course, no contradiction. "Everyone" meant, as we saw, any and every normal human being, as such. "The many" means a group of such individuals contributing towards the formation of a group judgment, and the group-judgment which these individuals form in their various assemblies, whether professional or political, or simply at the gymnasium

or theatre, would seem to constitute an advance upon the
isolated judgments of the same individuals apart from
society.[17] At the same time, it is plain that for further
advance Plato expects the many to rise superior to the methods
of the theatre, the club, or the political assembly. The
highest degree of enlightenment is hardly to be looked for in
such circumstances.

3. The interlocutor.

In the third place, it is universally assumed in the
dialogues that in the discussion of philosophical questions
in general, and of ethical questions in particular, one or both
of the parties to the discussion possess sufficient judgment
to give some kind of decision. At times, this is even stated
explicitly, especially in passages where the method itself
is under discussion.[18] But it is throughout assumed, not only
that one of the parties to the discussion is competent to give
some sort of answer, but also that the interlocutor is capable
of examining the validity of such answers, when given. This,
too, is frequently explicitly recognized.[19] This capacity of
the interlocutor does not seem to be confined to the specific
respondent in the discussion, but extends to the bystanders
also, whether these in turn take some part in the discussion
and thus become respondents—as especially in the *Protagoras*,
Gorgias, and *Republic*—or whether they remain silent and
appreciative listeners, as in the case of auditors who repeat
the whole dialogue at which they were present without taking
active part. It is possible also that this capacity is intended
to extend to readers or hearers of the dialogues, who also in
some sort take part in the discussions.[20]

From this brief review of the question, it looks as though
under the head of " interlocutor " is included everyone-who-
takes-part-in-ethical-discussions. Does Plato's position here
differ at all from his position when he regards " everyone "
without qualification as a judge, or when he regards " the
many " as judges ?

In answer to this question we must at once recognize
that there are at least certain differences of emphasis. In
the unqualified statement that " everyone " is a judge,
stress is laid upon the non-technical character of the moral
judgment and upon its social value in cementing the bonds
of civic life. In saying that " the many " are judges, stress

is laid upon certain characteristics of Greek public life, and upon the unfavourable nature of such conditions for developing the very highest type of judgment. In saying that the interlocutor is a judge, we pass at once into a different sphere of discourse. Stress is laid here upon the characteristic standards of truth-as-reached-by-two-investigators-working-together—*i.e.*, upon sincere introspection, upon analysis and gradual synthesis, upon consistency and systematic coherence. Socrates *ex professo* does not know the true answer to his questions, but he has a grasp upon the demands of scientific method, and can proceed, with the co-operation of his inter-locutor, to extend the intellectual context of a given answer and examine the consistency of the statement considered in its wider implications, following the argument whither-soever it may lead.[21] From the point of view, then, of emphasis and immediate context, to say that " everyone " is the judge, or that " the many " are the judges, is different from the statement that the interlocutor is the judge. But from a point of view which enables us to see further than questions of immediate emphasis, there is no doubt a funda-mental unity underlying the three different positions. Every-one has a moral sense, and it is by becoming an interlocutor —*i.e.*, by taking part in ethical discussions which go a little urther than mere acceptance of tradition or convention, and are free from the irrational elements which attend a public debate on political issues—that he develops this moral sense. There is no doubt that practically everyone is regarded by Plato as a possible interlocutor.[22] In none of these cases, however, is the immediately resulting judgment regarded by Plato as in any sense final. The interlocutor is capable of judging, capable—at least in many cases—of becoming a good judge. But just because he is an inter-locutor and is capable of this development, it does not follow that he has already completed the process of " becoming " and has already, in some sense, summed it to infinity.[23]

4. The good man.

The man of good moral character is always regarded by Plato as a judge whose decisions in matters of conduct are peculiarly trustworthy. It is a principle in the production of such a character that, when young, the good man has undergone no contamination from personal acquaintance with evil.[24] For evil-doing warps the judgment and gives it a pathological twist. The honourable mind which is to form a healthy judgment must be free from everything pathological, and will be formed upon the pattern of honesty. As Plato expresses it, such a character has in itself the pattern of honesty[25]—i.e., is a personification of the moral standard —and the judgments of such a character result from the direct and immediate application of the moral standard. Hence their accuracy and trustworthiness. In all forms of pleasure,[26] in all forms of art,[27] in all questions of education,[28] and generally speaking in all questions of moral values, his judgment is to be accepted. The man of good moral character is the measure of all things. What he judges to be good, *is* good, and what he judges to be evil, *is* evil.[29] His judgments, unlike those of the ordinary man, are in no sense capricious or subjective. They are objective—in touch with reality— and are through and through rational.[30]

How does the good man compare, as a judge, with the cases previously considered ? Like " everyone " and " the many," he has, of course, a sense of right and wrong. But, unlike them, he is utterly uncontaminated, entirely free from any taint of evil which might warp his judgment and obscure the moral standard. He represents human nature at its best, as it can be and as, under a proper system of education, it should be,[30] always true to itself and always in vital contact with the reality of things. As compared with the interlocutor, it may be said that the good man takes peculiar pleasure in philosophical discussions and is peculiarly convinced of their value.[31] He may, in fact, be regarded as an interlocutor with an especially fine character. The emphasis, however, is usually upon his moral, rather than upon his intellectual characteristics, and he would not *necessarily* be regarded as a speculative philosopher, but rather as a good citizen.[32] He is, however, always in close sympathy with speculative philosophy.

5. The experienced man.

On the necessity of a practical experience of men for the judge whose decisions are to be regarded as mature, Plato is very definite. An idealistic education and environment may implant correct sentiments, true taste, and thoroughly moral habits of thought and action. But this alone is in sufficient to fit a man to give judgments in matters of conduct —at least in a way which could be regarded as in some sense final. Youthful enthusiasts trained in idealistic habits of thought are the easiest people in the world to deceive, and, without practical knowledge of the world and worldly ways, the graduate of the seminary is apt to make very false judgments in matters of conduct.[33] The ideal judge can thus not possibly be a very young man. Experience—usually referred to by Plato as the experience of a long life—the experience which comes with years—gradually gives us the eye to see rightly, an appreciation of the facts of life and of the limitations of theory.[34] It is an experience essentially cognitive in character, containing, as it does, a study and understanding of evil and all forms of vice—subjects which must receive a purely external and objective investigation, if they are not to creep into the mind and poison the judgment.

How does this compare with the previously considered case ? The judgment of worldly experience does not always agree with the judgment of the man of moral character, as no one knows better than Plato, and the two are frequently contrasted—usually to the discredit of " experience."[36] There are, in fact, two kinds of experience recognized by Plato, and it is only one of these which is of value for moral judgment. There is, on the one hand, the practical experience which sharpens the wits and opens the eyes, but is pre-eminently non-moral—if not immoral—in character. This is the experience of the legal trickster, of the seeker after immoderate wealth, of the devotee of power infinite, who, with all their experience, are the most miserable of mortals.[37] For experience of this kind, Plato has nothing but condemnation, touched sometimes with pity, and it is only with this kind of experience that the judgment of the man of moral character comes into sharp conflict. On the other hand, there is the late ripening experience of the moral man himself, the man who has within himself the true standard and the correct moral sentiments. He makes practical mistakes at first, no doubt, but it is this man, and no other, to whom experience gives the eye to see rightly.[38] The judge, then, of whom Plato here approves, is the moral man, or man of character, with practical experience superadded.

6. The wise man.

Just what does Plato understand by the wise man, as a judge in problems of conduct ? He means, in the first place, the well-balanced man, the man whose nature represents a harmonious balance of its various elements—the various instinctive and emotional impulses—under the rule of reason.[39] The concept of the wise man thus corresponds, in large measure, to the concept of the man of moral education, whose ways of thinking and acting have been organized along ethical lines, but with this difference, that here rather more stress is laid upon the element of reason, intelligence, insight, calculation, scientific method.[40] The conception here is something like Bishop Butler's conception of the enlightened self-interest which deliberates dispassionately in a cool hour upon the plan of life. The wise man is pre-eminently reasonable and prudent. He takes counsel for the good of the *whole* self—not merely for the strictly rational side of our nature[41]— and takes care to maintain the harmonious and well-balanced condition of the mind which is the effect of justice,[42] and thus leads directly to the securing of that rational satisfaction which is true happiness.[43]

In the second place, wisdom involves rational deliberation, with all which this implies. The wise man is " good in counsel," and good counsel can be given only in respect of things concerning which the counsellor has accurate knowledge—something more than mere opinion.[44] This does not, however, mean that the wise man is a narrow specialist, in the sense in which a technical expert is a specialist. His is the knowledge which advises, not about some particular thing as such, but about the life plan or policy of the man as a whole, or—in political life—of the state as a whole.[45] For this purpose, however, it is necessary to know what is for the true interest of the whole and for each of the parts or elements of factions within the whole.[46] In the light of this well-developed sense of values, the wise man develops a certain unswerving singleness of aim, in a way which is typically Platonic.[47]

In the third place, the element of " reason," which is so especially characteristic of wisdom, is regarded as divine— *i.e.*, as non-materialistic and metaphysical—and to be developed, not by habit and bodily *askesis*,[48] but by dialectic alone. The concept of the wise man here tends to pass over into the concept of the dialectician.

The wise man, then, is essentially reasonable, sees life whole, and plans for it as a whole. He is no blind opportunist, but has a single well-thought-out plan, in accordance with the nature of the universe in general. This plan, however, is not static, but can be applied in a plastic way to the changing detail of life so characteristic of fourth century Greece.[49] As compared with the man of moral character, the wise man is more speculative, but not less ethical. As compared with the man of experience, he is more consciously scientific and methodical, though not less mature in judgment. He is a man of high moral character who is also experienced and has developed the divine light of reason within him by becoming an interlocutor, a philosophical participant in discussing the fundamental values. The end-goal of his development, and typical form into which the concept is always tending to pass in Plato's hands, is that of the philosopher-king, the personality which unites dialectical ability with practical power in a political sense.[50]

7. The philosopher.

In stating that the philosopher is a judge in matters of conduct, Plato draws a somewhat sharp distinction between the actual and the ideal. He emphatically does not mean that the actual votaries of philosophy in his own time—composed, as he believed, largely of men who had strayed into philosophy from other pursuits, and without much natural aptitude or sound training—are to be regarded as authorities in ethics.[51] It is rather the ideal philosopher—a definite construction of his own[52]—whom he has in mind, and there can be no doubt that, as constructed by Plato, the ideal philosopher and the ideal judge in matters of conduct ultimately coincide in all respects. Born under conditions eugenically ideal,[53] of ideally perfect physique[54] and ideally perfect mental[55] and moral qualities,[56] educated in an ideally perfect environment[57] and with due attention to the requirements of practical experience as well as of intellectual development,[58] the resultant dialectician studies the most perfect methods of solving philosophical problems,[59] until he has penetrated to the utmost bounds of the *mundus intelligibilis*[60] and has grasped the unhypothetical first principle of things, the Idea of Good, which is at once the *ratio cognoscentis*, the *ratio cognoscendi*, and the *ratio essendi*, and explicitly transcends the world of existence.[61] From this absolute or final standpoint, human problems fall into their proper perspective,[62] and are judged by the spectator of all time and existence with impartial and unerring accuracy. The instrument of his thought is pure reason, liberated once for all from the misleading influences of instinct, sense-perception, and emotion, and with his new powers of division, classification, and deduction, the dialectician, remaining always within the sphere of pure thought,[63] can reach adequate solutions of any and every question which can arise. His judgments are final, for he sees as God sees, and has an adequate grasp upon the nature of ultimate reality.[64]

How does the philosopher, as a judge, compare with the cases previously considered ? Like " everyone," he has, of course, the normal human sense of honour and justice, but unlike everyone, he has received an exceptionally liberal education, especially designed to free him from the misleading influences of instinct, emotion, and prejudice of all sorts, and to turn the eye of the soul towards the light, so that it will see freely and fully. Like " the many," he has all the advantages which can be derived from social intercourse. But, unlike them, his social experiences, being derived chiefly from a highly select group of peculiarly valuable associates, are peculiarly valuable, and are free from the meannesses and degrading prejudices which resulted in the general levelling down of characters and ideals in the democracy of Plato's own time.[65]

Again, the philosopher is an " interlocutor," but a peculiarly well developed interlocutor, a genuine dialectician, no amateur, but a finished master in this most liberal of all arts, with all the natural ability and all the training which the mind of Plato can imagine as helpful. Again, the philosopher has a moral character of the very highest order, partly natural, partly developed by a system of training which selects, by special tests, only the very finest characters for the higher reaches of education.[66] He has practical experience equal to the practical experience of any other citizen, and superior in value, for some men get more out of their experiences than others, and he is already such a man as to extract, from his experiences, the utmost possible value.[67]   Again, he is wise, with a well-balanced character which is organized, not according to chance or caprice, but according to a single principle which is identical with the principle of value in the universe—the Idea of Good.[68] Finally, he is more than wise in a merely practical sense ; for he also possesses the finest speculative insight, and fully understands the principle which underlies his own character no less than the universe.[69]

In a word, the concept of the philosopher sums up all that is valuable in the other cases considered, and carries those elements of value still further, grounding them in their principle.   This the philosopher apprehends in a way which raises him almost beyond the highest levels attainable by humanity.   He represents the Platonic conception of the Superman, and remains the supreme ideal of Greek philosophy.[70]

8. The legislator.

Who is the legislator, whom Plato regards as a judge in matters of conduct ?   Like the philosopher, he is an ideal construction of Plato's own.   He is, in fact, the philosopher himself, when, the highest vision having been attained, he sets himself, from a sense of duty, to rule the state and to educate the most promising of the younger generation so that they, too, in their turn may become guardians.[71]   As a guardian and ruler of the state, he makes laws, and, in the form of legislative enactment, expresses his own moral judgments, with special adaptations to meet the special type of case considered.   Thus expressed in the form of laws, his judgments are not final in any static or absolute sense, for they are special applications of general principles to a concrete and admittedly imperfect stage of social evolution.   As social evolution of itself brings about new conditions, his judgments—the written laws—will become out of date, and the new generation of law-givers and guardians, acting in his spirit, and with the same grasp of principle, will make new adjustments to fit the new conditions.[72]   These laws, being the standard in accordance with which the censor, in matters of art,[73] and the judge in his law-court[74] render their decisions, sufficiently indicate that the speculative philosopher, when he turns his attention to matters of government and administration, becomes a judge and an inspiration to judges, in a very literal sense. In fine, the guardian or legislator sums up all that is of importance in the characters previously considered, and gives out, in the form of administrative and legal decisions, his judgments on matters of conduct. He is the philosopher become practical.

SUMMARY

To sum up, then, the results of our inquiry :—We have seen that, while at first sight there appeared to be no less than eight groups of candidates for the position of judge in matters of conduct, yet, when we examine the cases more closely, there is a certain unity underlying all eight groups. Every normal human being has at least the *Anlage* for moral judgment, and indeed a little more than the *Anlage*. Social and political intercourse, co-operation in the work of the army, the law-courts, religion, the theatre, and the various other institutions of Greek social life, develop the moral sense in a way which, so far as it goes, is genuine and valuable. Practical experience of all sorts, when it is the experience of a man of fundamentally sound character, develops this sense to a much higher degree. Add to these qualities a certain type of intellectual education—by dialectical discussion—and we have the wise man, who, with yet further and more intensive intellectual training, passes over into the philosopher. Finally, the philosopher as ruler gives laws to his state and expresses his moral judgments in the way which is most helpful to his country as well as to himself. There is something of philosophy in every normal human being. Environmental stimulus and dialectical training will bring this out and develop it. This is the principle of unity which entitles members of each one of the eight groups to the position of judge-in-matters-of-conduct. So far as their judgment is philosophical, so far it is valuable.

It might be inferred from the above treatment, that every normal human being without exception is capable of developing into a philosopher-king—as though it were purely a matter of the appropriate social and educational milieu. This is, however, far from being the case. Men are born unequal. Some belong to the copper class, others to the silver class. Very few belong by birth to the golden class, and extremely few can pass into it by especial merit from one of the lower classes.[75] And not only is birth—*i.e.*, natural capacity—in favour of small numbers. When it comes to the philosophical education, a still more rigidly selective process takes place. Development is strictly continuous, it is true ; but only for those who actually develop. At every step of the educational ladder, psychological tests are applied,[76] and out of the select few who begin, there are very few indeed who reach the higher rungs. Wise men are very few, and of philosophers competent to rule Plato hardly counts on very many, even in his ideal state.[77]

Our conclusion, then, must be that for Plato, while every normal human being without exception is competent to give some sort of judgment on ethical questions, the judge in the fullest sense of the word is the philosopher, and more particularly the philosopher who has definitely devoted himself to tasks of administration, the guardian or philosopher-king.

CHAPTER II

THE OBJECTIVE BASIS OF THE MORAL JUDGMENT

THE aim of the present chapter is to discover, so far as possible, what elements in the cases before the philosophical judge are made the basis of his judgment. In the dialogues, the philosophical judge is represented sometimes by the Platonic Socrates, sometimes expressly by the dialectician or the legislator. We shall therefore proceed to examine a number of typical cases of such moral judgments, with the aim of discovering what the elements are, in such cases, which lead Plato to regard them as " good." In order to cover the whole field of " goods," we shall examine the following sample cases :—(1) Health, (2) money and possessions, (3) pleasure, (4) right opinion, (5) good memory, (6) intellectual acumen, (7) courage, (8) self-control, (9) justice, (10) art, (11) law, (12) philosophy. We shall then sum up our detailed results, and compare them with Plato's general attitude on the subject of goodness, and also with his general attitude on the subject of evil, in order to reach a sufficiently valid general conclusion.

1. Health.

Bodily[1] health is spoken of by Plato sometimes simply as health, but most frequently as the product of the medical art, as the " good " produced by medicine.[2] In order to form a concrete idea of its meaning in the Platonic dialogues, we shall therefore commence with the concept of disease—such opposites being intelligible only in this kind of cross-reference[3]—and shall then consider briefly the transition to a state of health. When we have in this way obtained a concrete acquaintance with the Platonic concept of health, we shall proceed to ask, in virtue of what characteristic it is regarded as " good."

Disease, for Plato, is emphatically what we should call

degeneration.   He thinks of the body as composed of fire, water, earth, and air,[4] in certain relations proportionate to one another.[5]   If this proportion becomes disturbed— usually by excess of one of these elements,[6] which excess may have been produced by excessive indulgences in bodily pleasures[7]—then the elements which are contiguous in the affected part of the body no longer harmonize well, but fight with one another[8] and produce inflammations, *etc.*, loosening the bonds which normally hold that portion of the body together, and producing a dissolution of " kindred " elements.[9] The flesh comes away from the bones, the marrow of the bones disintegrates,[10] and death, in such extreme cases, tends to result.[11]   Disease, then, is viewed by Plato as an upsetting of the balance, a disturbance of the mean[12] or due proportion which holds the body together.   It is a dis- solution, a literal falling to pieces, of the body.

How does the physician face this situation, and effect a cure ?   He has two methods : (1) physical, (2) psycholo- gical.   In the first method (1) he deals directly with the body of the patient.   By surgery and cautery,[13] or by emetics and cathartics,[14] he removes, as soon as may be, the ex- cessive element which is the primary physical cause of the disturbance, [15] and thus remedies the disproportion, restoring the " mean."[16]   The inferior sort of physician employs no other method,[17] and it is a method eminently suitable for the treatment of slaves.[18]   But in dealing with free-born patients, the better sort of physician employs, as a further method (2), what we should call a bed-side manner, which has a soothing effect upon the mind.[19]   He discusses the situation, reasons upon causes and effects, philosophizes in fact, and educates the patient,[20] because he believes that the correct mental attitude exercises valuable influence upon the bodily state.[21]   The essence of the cure, then, con- sists in restoring the mean or due proportion to the bodily elements, *plus* a rational state, a sense of the meaning of the situation, to the mind.

Thus produced, health is a state of the body in which the various elements cease to work against one another, and function naturally and harmoniously together.[22]   The body is now a whole, a single organism to the life of which each element contributes its part.[23]   It is held together by the " limit," " mean," or principle of proportion, with a unity resembling that of a musical composition.[24] This normal and correct state once given, the internal equilibrium of the bodily forces continues of itself.[25]

Such being the nature of health, in what sense is it regarded by Plato as a " good " ?   The physician naturally regards it as the greatest of human goods,[26] and the patient also naturally longs for it and regards it as the most desirable of goods.[27]   This experience becomes generalized, and the value of physical well-being receives almost universal recognition.[28]   But are the judgments of the physician, the patient, and " the many " *valid ?*   Would the philosopher or legislator concur with this popular judgment ?   There is no doubt that he would not.[29]   For Plato, no simple answer is possible. In order to discover whether physical well-being is really good, we must go beyond the standpoint of the physician. He aims at producing health—that is his *raison d'être*, the object of his art, his " good."   But whether, when he has restored his patient to health, he has performed an action which, in that particular case, is good for the patient, or good for society—*that* it transcends his ability to say.[30]   There are many men who had better be dead than alive, even for their own sakes.[31]   Whether health is or is not a good, it lies outside the province of medicine to decide.   So too with the judgment of the patient.   The judgments of sick men are often unsound,[32] and on such a subject as health, peculiarly unsound.   All that the patient understands by the " health " which he so ardently desires, is freedom from present suffering—a neutral state.[33]   Of the positive value which may, in certain circumstances, attach to bodily well-being, he is not in a position to form an adequate conception.

What, then, is the judgment of the philosopher and legislator, the rational conclusion of unprejudiced and thorough deliberation ?   Harmony of body is valuable, because and in so far as, it subserves the symphony of the soul.[34]   What the philosopher and the legislator regard as especially valuable—the contemplation of pure being by means of pure thought[35]—is out of the question if the body, by reason of some excess or defect, is in a state of physical pain, and thus constantly attracts attention to itself and its needs.[36]   Sickness is an evil, precisely because it interferes with higher pursuits.   Health is a good, precisely so far as it prevents interference with the higher studies.   In other words, health is a good to men who have the character and intelligence to put it to the right use, and who make it play its part in the higher life.[37]

What is the main characteristic of bodily health, in virtue of which it can be put to such use ? Partly, no doubt, the physical vigour and robustness, the reserves of strength and energy, which usually accompany health,[38] but chiefly the presence of the " limit "—*i.e.*, of unity and law, on account of the presence of which, excellence of body is regarded as directly analogous to excellence of soul.[39] The " goodness " of the *corpus sanum*, so far as it *is* good, depends, then, upon the presence of measure, organization, law.

2. Money and possessions.

Money may be obtained in various ways, *e.g.*, (1) by inheriting, by receiving gifts, by finding, or even by pure chance.[40] It may also be acquired (2) by making wealthy marriages, by forming irregular sexual connections, by fleecing young men, by lending money at usurious rates of interest, by violating trusts, and in various other ways which are either technically within the law, or at least difficult of detection.[41] A further way is (3) by methods definitely outside the law, such as highway robbery, burglary, *et hoc genus omne*.[42] Yet another way is (4) by economizing, spending as little as possible on one's own needs and particularly avoiding opportunities of contributing to public service.[43] All these are ways of making money without furnishing much equivalent in the form of service. A still further way of making money is (5) by honest work, by performing some definitely recognized form of service, such as retail or wholesale trading, and particularly such forms of service as are of a troublesome character, such as tilling the soil or teaching the young, or even dangerous, such as skippering a Greek sailing vessel.[44]

Money is not good *per se*, independently of the way in which it has been acquired.[45] It is almost universally recognized that only as obtained by methods which are at least not dishonest, is it to be regarded as a " good."[46] But still, in the popular consciousness, robbery on a grand scale, which culminates in making a man general dictator in his state, tends to be regarded as a good.[47] As a rule, however, property acquired by reasonably honest means is regarded as a good, while property obtained by dishonest means is not so regarded.

This represents the general Greek attitude on the subject. What is the attitude of the representatives of philosophical insight in the Dialogues ? The popular judgment, that the method by which wealth is acquired is important, is accepted and confirmed by a study of the psychological effects of money-making. There is even a demonstration *a priori* that immoderately large fortunes cannot have been acquired by strictly honest means :—When it comes to receiving money, the just and honourable citizen will make moderate gains by scrupulously honest dealings, whereas the man who is bent upon amassing a fortune will make as much as he can by any and every form of business dealing which will bring in money.[48]   So too when it comes to paying out money, the honourable citizen will contribute his fair share—perhaps even a little more—to public service, while the money-maker will expend the absolute minimum, whether upon himself or upon others.[49]   It follows that the larger fortunes will inevitably be obtained by the money-grubbers, while the honourable citizen will, perhaps, at most slightly increase his patrimony.[50]   Immoderate wealth is thus a reflection upon the character of its possessor, implying that his ethical standards are not of the highest, however much he may have kept within the law of the state.

In actual practice, Plato feels towards the acquisitive instinct much as Kant feels about the " heteronomy of the will." Money-making—the impulse to acquire without limit —is a passion which absorbs the whole man, and gives his character a twist and a bias which distorts his whole sense of values.[51] He becomes one-sided, *banausic*, thoroughly worthless as a citizen, and almost unfit for human companionship.[52] Reason and ambition becomes the slaves of his passion for more,[53] and if he obtains political power, his absorption in his private interests simply ruins the state by engendering, on the one hand, luxury and idleness with all their accompaniments, and, on the other, pauperdom with its characteristic vices and characteristic dangers for the state.[54] Out of the dissensions among the rich, and the great gulf between rich and poor,[55] arises, step by step, a revolutionary tendency which results ultimately in the complete overthrow of the constitution and the death or exile of the plutocrat and his adherents.[56]   The passion for wealth is thus, in the end, self-destructive, that is to say, contradictory and unreasonable.

In the above criticisms, Plato is far from viewing money, as such, as bad in its effects upon character.   It is the passion for *excessive* wealth, the desire which knows no limits, no respect for order, no appreciation of values higher than more-and-more-of-this-world's-goods, which is self-contradictory.   His objection to money is only to money posing as the chief or exclusive good, absorbing the *whole* energies of its worshippers.   In its proper place, as an element in a life which has a well-developed sense of higher values, money is a genuine good.[57]   There is a certain minimum, below which the citizen must never fall, if he is to continue to perform his civic duties.[58]   Above this minimum, the possession of moderate means, the acquisition and expenditure of which is directed wisely,[59] and with a due regard to the relative values of money, bodily well-being, and spiritual development,[60] will be a genuine good and will form an important element in the highest kind of life.[61]   Certain of the uses of money mentioned with approval are, its expenditure upon education, physical and mental,[62] and upon various forms of public services, such as entertaining distinguished foreign guests who are visiting the state in order to study its institutions.[63]

What are the characteristics of worldly possessions, in virtue of which they can thus contribute to the good life ? In itself, money is, as we have seen, neither good nor bad. Here, as in the previous case, the conception of the " mean " or " limit " is prominent.   It is so far as it is moderate in amount, and acquired by just and lawful means, and expended in a judicious and moderate manner, as an element in a kind of life which respects restraint, orderliness, and reasonableness, that money is a good.   It is a good only to men who have the character and intelligence to use it wisely and moderately.[64]   Stated briefly, it is the presence of measure, restraint, a sense of law and reasonable limits, which makes wealth regarded by the philosophic judgment as sometimes a good.[65]

3. Pleasure.

Pleasure is as universal as life and consciousness.   Wherever we have perception, wherever we have activity of any kind, there we have some kind of feeling-tone, some degree of the pleasure-pain experience. In all kinds of bodily movement, from a twitch of the limbs to the articulate use of the voice,[66] in all forms of sensation, from the simplest vision and audition to the complex organic sensation of bodily well-being,[67] in all the activities which lead to the satisfaction of instinctive wants, such as hunger, thirst, and the sex-appetite,[68] we experience a simple and immediate feeling of pleasure. This feeling of pleasure in bodily activity we have in common with the rest of the animal kingdom. It is universal, and it is fundamental.[69]

Certain forms of pleasure, however, are confined to human beings. No other animal has our sense of rhythm and harmony, our feeling for the ordered recurrence of beats and periods, our appreciation of measure, order, law.[70] The pleasures which arise in the enjoyment of Art are thus specifically human. All animals naturally take pleasure in *any* sort of movement, however wild and spasmodic. Man alone takes pleasure in the orderly measures of the choric dance, of the song, and of poetry in its various forms.[71] Rhythm and harmony are akin to something deep down in our nature, and stir us as no other form of experience does. Artistic pleasures are peculiarly human, and their influence upon our conduct is almost incalculably profound.[72]

Other forms of pleasure, resting, like the artistic pleasures, upon our human appreciation of law, and indeed hardly to be distinguished from the aesthetic pleasures even in language,[73] are the ethical and intellectual pleasures. We take pleasure in all forms of organic unity, in all adaptation of means to ends, whether in economic, in social, or in intellectual experience. The well-ordered life of ethical self-control, the restraint and sense of proportion which characterize the true student, not only are extremely pleasant to the individuals who live such lives,[74] but also impart genuine pleasure to others who contemplate, in them, realizations of their own ideals.[75] So too the intellectual life, from its delight in the neatness of a specific solution to a perplexing problem, to the calm enjoyment of philosophic contemplation of first principles, is peculiarly pleasant to a rational being, and may indeed be regarded as the most satisfying of all forms of human activity.[76]

To Greek reflection in the time of Plato, the very universality of pleasure presented a perplexing problem for practical ethics. That pleasure, as such, is good, is, to the typical Greek mind no less than to John Stuart Mill, self-evident. It is desirable, because it is desired. Every human being aims at securing a maximum of pleasure and a minimum of pain. This is elementary, and no one but an ignorant idealist, utterly deficient in practical experience, could doubt it.[77] But we can obtain pleasure from any and every form of activity—including sources which are mutually contradictory.[78] Hence the perplexity. How are we to choose ? Are we to say that some pleasures are inherently good, and others inherently bad[79]—or that all pleasure, *qua* pleasure, is good,[80] and that the ethical disapproval associated with certain types of pleasure is a matter of " convention " ? In the latter case, our rationalism, in recognizing the " convention " for what it is—man-made, arbitrary, and without rational justification—makes way for the release of desire, and our ideal becomes the life of the *viveur*, tasting any and every kind of experience without distinction and with a cynical disregard for *bourgeois* judgments of right and wrong.[81] Between these two attitudes, of the old-fashioned moralist on the one hand, and the modern cynic on the other, the typical Greek of Plato's time hung, in uneasy suspension.[82]

Faced with this dilemma, Plato adopts, in different passages, standpoints which seem, at first sight, different. In the first place, he adopts the premises of hedonism, but draws consequences disconcertingly inconsistent with the position of the *viveur*. Assume, if you please, that the only element of genuine value in life is some form of pleasurable consciousness—what is the deduction ? The use of wine gives pleasure. Can we therefore argue that the use of much wine gives much pleasure ? No. The facts of experience show but too plainly that excessive indulgence in the pleasures of appetite, whatever the appetite, bring disease and pain, and, in extreme cases, even death.[83] For the moment, such indulgence is pleasant, but in the long run violent pleasures bring violent pains, and the game is not worth the candle. The life of the *viveur* is thus self-contradictory, without inner unity, and incapable of giving permanent satisfaction.[84] There is a limit, beyond which pleasure passes over into pain, at least in the long run. If we desire to be consistent hedonists, with a claim to be considered reasonable and wise in a practical sense, we must recognize the presence of this limit. The life which recognizes law, order, and measure as primary, is the pleasant life, and the life which aims at securing momentary satisfactions from any and every source without discrimination, is nasty, brutish, and short.[85]

The argument just set forth shows that the pursuit of pleasure without regard to its limitations is self-contradictory. Another line of reasoning endeavours to prove that bodily pleasure, at best, is negative rather than positive in character. Pleasure is, as a rule, the satisfaction of desire. But desire is want, lack, emptiness, a falling short of the normal, and indicates that the natural equilibrium of the body has become upset, much the same as in disease.[86] There is, in fact, something pathological about desire, especially in its more violent forms,[87] and the pleasure which results from satisfying such cravings is little more than freedom from pain. Such restoration of equilibrium lulls the pain to sleep for the time being, and frees us from the immediate pressure of the stimulus. But its function ceases there. It has no positive value.[88] Plato's position here is identical in principle with the more modern argument that indulgence of the bodily appetites turns them into cravings, and that in proportion as the stimulus increases in force, the positive pleasure resulting from its satisfaction decreases until it sinks to zero—if indeed it rises so high—and the life of the pleasure-seeker oscillates between the strings of desire and the *ennui* which results from absence of stimulation.[89]

The further development of this line of reasoning consists in differentiating pleasures into kinds in terms of a sharp distinction between body and soul.[90] Just as sensory experience of a cognitive kind—experience in which the body has an unmistakable share—is illusory, whereas the experience of " pure " reason—*i.e.*, of reason without interference of any sort from the body—alone gives us true knowledge,[91] so sensory or bodily pleasures are illusory, while intellectual pleasures, which are experienced in the world of true being— the world in which the philosopher is at home—are alone pure and genuine.[92] Sensory experience, whether with a cognitive or with an affective reference, is a *genesis*, and, as such, belongs to the world of mere appearance.[93] Intellectual experience alone enters the world of true existence, on its affective no less than on its cognitive side,[94] and it is accordingly so far as the rational elements of our nature are developed at the expense of the more animal and less rational elements, that we enjoy the genuine kind of pleasure.[95]   This antithesis of sense and intellect, of body and soul, is emphasized by Plato with such religious fervour, that the philosopher is said to regard his body as a kind of prison or tomb, from which he is seeking to escape, and his ruling passion is for physical death, so that, freed from the fetters of the body, he may live eternally in the heaven of pure ideas.[96]

These three lines of reasoning, different as they may seem at first sight, are closely connected in Plato's thought.   His view may be summed up briefly as follows :—In intellectual experience alone are we in contact with reality, and the pleasures which attend upon such experience are alone truly satisfying.   The body and all its concerns are relatively unreal.   The most we can ask of them is that they shall not interfere with higher pursuits.   The chief bodily appetites must be gratified just so far as to keep them quiet, and to keep the body generally in a state of health, so as to leave us undisturbed and free for the intellectual life.[97].   If we ask, how far bodily pleasure is a good, the answer is, pleasure in excess is bad, pleasure in moderation, as an element in the higher life, is a good in precisely the same sense as health, i.e. so far as, being obedient to reason, law, and order, it furthers, rather than interferes with, intellectual life.[98]   If we ask further, what it is in *intellectual* pleasure which makes it a good, the answer is, that it is its close connection with the world of ideas, with reason, law, and order, which makes it a good.[99]   In a word, pleasure is not morally good in its own right.[100]   What makes it morally good at any time is the presence in it of the " mean," of law, orderliness, reason.[101]

4. Right opinion.

Just precisely what Plato means by *doxa* and kindred forms of expression, it is very difficult to state in terms of modern psychological theory.   Such expressions seem to refer to a very wide class of cognitive experiences, which have in common little more than the characteristic of falling short of scientific knowledge, although from a practical point of view the information which they give may be sufficiently reliable. Certain thought processes of an obscure nature, which take place presumably in the form of subliminal associations,[102] in relative independence of the control of outer experience,[103] may terminate (1) in mere fancies, associated with mental imagery, (2) in opinions, also associated as a rule with imagery, or (3) in logical judgment—imageless apprehension of the Ideas.[104] Only the last of these gives us knowledge in the strict sense. To both of the less perfect forms the term *doxa* is explicitly applied, though more frequently to the second form (2).[105] " Opinion " thus represents the conclusion of a cognitive mental process, and seems to be a superficial and insufficiently grounded form of judgment.[106] It is a mental reconstruction of elements which have an objective reference,[107] but is without intellectual grasp of the law of synthesis, i.e. without adequate understanding of the principle involved. The state of mind to which Plato refers is that of the child, the student, or the juror, accepting information upon the dogmatic authority of the parent, teacher, or advocate, without independent examination of the evidence, and without adequate consideration of the rational principles involved.[108]

As compared with the clear light of knowledge, this is a twilight state of mind,[109] and as contrasted with the firm assurance and permanence of a system of scientific truths, it is wavering and transitory, liable to come and go—much as our opinions on certain subjects vary according to the last book we have been reading.[110] It is, in brief, the state of mind characteristic of the empirical groping after truth, the method of trial and error, but without grasp of the requirements of scientific method which converts empirical groping into empirical science. For instance, by putting together many cases of a phenomenon, it is possible to extract the identical element from the many differing examples, i.e. it is possible to extract the universal, the law or Idea.[111] But the man whose mind is in a state of *doxa* is incapable of the analysis and synthesis involved, and cannot, as a rule, even follow the steps by which the scientist establishes his conclusions.[112] " Opinion " is, in a word, an essentially immature state of mind.

Immature as it may be, it is not, however, necessarily false. There is, it is true, such a thing as *false* opinion, mistaken prejudice, a mental construction which, when brought to the test, fails to connect with the realities of life.[113] But there is also such a thing as *right* opinion, in which the mind is in a state of truth, i.e. in which the mental reconstruction does actually reproduce the essential characteristics of the reality to which it refers, in spite of the inadequate grasp of principle.[114] It may result from a guess, a blind shot in the dark. But the guess may be right, the shot may hit the mark.[115] In such a case, we are in a state of *right* opinion. With children, and indeed with the majority of people, this is the best mental condition of which they are capable. Next to having scientific knowledge of how things are constituted, it is of importance to the best conduct of life, that we should have a belief or faith or opinion which—however regrettably ungrounded—is at least correct.[116] It is especially in regard to ethical convictions that Plato emphasizes the importance and absolutely fundamental value of right opinion.[117] In his ideal state, the magistrates and all candidates for the higher education are chosen from those who, when tested, are shown to have taken firmly and indelibly the dye of right opinion.[118] For the highest positions of all in the state, this twilight condition of mind is, of course, insufficient. The *full* guardians must have thorough insight into principle.[119] But the full guardians are few in number ; and for the rest, steadfast loyalty to the correct opinions inculcated by the laws established by the guardians, represents an ideal of the highest value.[120]

If we ask what it is in right opinion which makes it a " good," the answer is surprisingly simple. Right opinion is always good. Opinion is morally good precisely in so far as it is intellectually right or true. It is bad only so far as it is false.[121] The man who has right opinion, is in a " true " state of mind. His thought is objective, in touch with reality, and he accordingly shares in all the advantages which belong to such a mental condition.[122] In fact, from a practical point of view, he is almost as well off as if he had scientific knowledge. The two states of mind are closely akin, and from the point of action are hardly to be distinguished.[123]

If we ask what these advantages are, we find that, in a general way, they are the advantages which attach to knowledge as opposed to ignorance, to truth as opposed to falsity, to sanity as opposed to insanity.[124] More definitely, from the standpoint which considers ethical values, the adoption of a correct viewpoint makes sense of life, makes us at home in the universe, gives us a measured calmness and dignity of spirit, enables us to see things in their proper proportions, frees us from vulgar temptations of all descriptions, and, in a word, fits us for living the higher life.[125]

As compared, however, with scientific knowledge, there are certain drawbacks which attach to the state of mere opinion, however correct and true this may be. Knowledge is permanent. When we know, we know, and there's an end on't. Opinion, however, is wavering, transitory, changeable, anything but permanent.[126] Having no firm root, and resting as it does on mere associations, the attacks of sophistry, or indeed any considerable extension of our narrow range of experience, can easily shake it.[127] One of the very first effects of intellectual study, and especially introspective study, upon the adolescent mind, in the puppy-dog stage of dialectic, is to shake its convictions in the case of all traditional standards,[128] however correct in principle these may, in the end, prove to be,[129] and the resulting scepticism tends to have regrettable ethical concomitants, when we no longer know what to think upon such subjects. Such a state of mind, wavering and in conflict with itself, an easy prey to the arts of sophistry and to the seductions of pleasure in its more primitive forms,[130] is anything but desirable, and Plato has, in his ideal state, regulations expressly designed to prevent its occurrence.[131]

Such drawbacks, however, belong to opinion as such. It is the nature of opinion to be unstable. So far as opinion is *right* or true, and so long as we are in this true state of mind, so far—in spite of its instability—our mental condition is desirable. It is not the *highest* good, but, so far as it goes, it helps us to understand life, and to live in the best possible way. It may not *know* what the goal of life is, but it aims unconsciously at such a goal. It strives persistently towards a Better, and feels a natural affinity with the life of law, orderliness, and reverence for ideals.[132] It is this " truth," this appreciation of the objectivity and fundamental value of law, order, and measure, which makes right opinion regarded as a " good."

5. Memory.

What does Plato understand by memory ? It is a continuation of certain processes involved in sensory experience, and is not to be understood apart from a study of sense-

perception.[133]   Such processes are not purely psychical, but
are intimately associated with processes which are definitely
of a physical character.   Let X and Y be two purely physical
bodies, and let Z be a physical body which is also the body of
a living organism endowed with consciousness : and let
X, Y, and Z be in physical interaction.   Motion of X—let
us call it s_1—will affect both Y and Z, and will provoke in both
" vibrations," reactions of a physical type.   Let us call the
Y-vibrations p_1 and the Z-vibrations p_2.   Such production
of p_1 and p_2 by s_1 represents the working of a general physical
law.   With certain kinds or degrees of stimulation s_1, the
physical vibrations p_1, and the physical vibrations p_2 are
generically indistinguishable.   That is to say, the fact that a
consciousness happens to be associated with Z makes no
difference to the Z-vibrations, and the Z-vibrations in question
make no difference to that consciousness.   The vibrations
are in both cases purely physical, and if we *must* speak of a
Z-consciousness in connection with this exclusively physical
process, we must call it *un*consciousness.[134]

On the other hand, with certain other kinds or degrees of
stimulation s_2, Y and Z behave differently.   In both cases
physical vibrations p_3 and p_4 result as before ; but with Y
there is nothing more, while with Z certain further processes
q_1, mental in character, make their appearance.   In Z there
are now taking place two kinds of vibratory process, p_{4a},
p_{4b}, p_{4c} . . . which are physical, and q_{1a}, q_{1b}, q_{1c} . . .
which are psychical.   These two processes p_4 and q_1 are
specifically distinct, and yet contain certain elements in common.   As we might say, they partially overlap or coincide.[135]
So far as they do not coincide, the physical vibrations p_{4a} fall
outside consciousness—i.e. behave precisely like p_1, p_2, and
p_3, considered above.   Similarly certain mental vibrations
q_{1a} fail to connect with the physical vibrations, and remain,
perhaps ἐν τόπῳ νοητῷ—we are not further concerned with
them.   So far, however, as the remaining vibrations fall
together, we have in pq not merely two series of vibrations,
but mind and matter come together, and the Z-consciousness
has become cognitively aware of the physical body X.   This
experience is sense-perception, and is a definitely psycho-
physical process.[136]

By memory, Plato understands the retention of this psycho-
physical process pq, the conservation of the X-percept.   So

far as his metaphors can be translated into scientific terminology, we can state that pq is retained in the sub-consciousness of Z,[137] in a relatively permanent form.   Sensation is a process in which the element of " flux " is peculiarly prominent.[138] In memory, the element retained appears to have been withdrawn from the flux-process, and from now on remains relatively fixed.[139]   Further change takes place chiefly as pq becomes associated—subliminally for the most part—with other elements, such association becoming stronger with age.[140] These retained processes can be centrally aroused, i.e. can be recalled to consciousness by the non-physical, or purely mental, process of recollection.[141]   Retention itself, however, is a psycho-physical process, in which mechanical elements continue to play their part.[142]

What is a good memory ?   The chief excellences of memory are (1) strength of the association, involving duration of the retention, (2) clearness and distinctness of the retained element, and (3) adaptability to speedy and accurate recall.[143]   These characteristics depend largely upon physiological factors of an obscure kind.   The most that we can safely infer from Plato's hints and metaphors is that excellence of memory is analogous to excellence of bodily condition generally, and depends upon the proper organization of the physiological factors concerned—i.e. upon the presence of order, law, and the " mean," and upon the absence of excess or defect of any kind.[144]

What is it that makes an efficient memory morally valuable ?   In itself, of course, efficiency of memory is like any other natural endowment, and lies outside of moral approval or disapproval.   Whether it becomes a good or an evil depends wholly upon how it is used.   Employed in the service of folly and vice, it is an evil.   Employed by the good man under the guidance of reason and wisdom, as an element in the higher life, it is a good.[145]   And it is an indispensable element in the intellectual life of the philosopher.   From memory *plus* sense-perception arises " opinion," and whether opinion is true or false, depends in no slight degree upon whether the memory is or is not efficient.[146]   Upon the truth or falsity of opinion, as we have already seen, turns the whole question of the attainability of knowledge in the higher sense. This can be reached only by the methodical sifting of opinions which are, at least in large numbers, true.[147]   The higher know-

ledge, upon attainment of which the salvation of mankind
rests, thus depends in large measure, upon efficiency of
memory, and such a memory is a good, precisely because it
is an indispensable element in the philosophic life.[148]   What
makes it morally valuable is thus (1) its efficiency, which
as we have seen, depends upon the presence of law and order,
and (2) its being guided by wisdom and reason.   That is to
say, what makes memory a " good " is the presence in it of
law, order, reason.

6.   Intellectual acumen.

Intellectual acumen is found only in those who possess
what we should call a sound nervous system.   The anatomical
and physiological basis of intelligence is much the same as
the basis of a good memory, which we have already considered,
and like it involves the presence of orderliness, proportion, and
law.[149]   If the sensory impressions are " pure " and un-
confused, we are quick at understanding them, i.e. at taking
them in and classifying them appropriately with reference
to the question under consideration.[150]   Quickness of apprehension, however, is not the sole characteristic of intellectual
acumen ; to this quality we must add a certain accuracy and
objectivity, in virtue of which our understanding follows the
processes of nature[151] and, indeed, by means of the method
of classification, grasps the law of these processes and apprehends their Idea.[152]   Intellectual acumen is thus the faculty
which from sensory and associational experiences develops
" opinion " and, in the end, scientific knowledge.[153]   It
represents a wide-awake state of mind, and is capable of solving
problems above the ordinary degree of difficulty, from making
a new discovery in mathematics to devising a complete system
of education, or indeed a complete philosophy of life.[154]
It is especially developed by mathematical studies of all sorts,[155]
and is exemplified in the more or less actual characters of
Theaetetus and Dion,[156] and in the more definitely ideal
characters of the younger guardians and rulers in the *Republic*
and *Laws*.[157]

Thus considered, intellectual acumen is specifically
intellectual, as the study of mathematics is intellectual, i.e.
is, as nearly as possible, a specifically non-moral process.   It
is possible to possess this characteristic and still to be a villain,
i.e. to employ one's powers of intellect in the pursuit of ends

which are morally reprehensible.[158]   It is accordingly not to be regarded as good in itself.   Whether it does or does not become a good, depends wholly upon the situation and the way in which it is used.   Used by the good man, in the service of ends deliberately chosen after rational reflection, it is a good.[159]   Its quickness and objectivity, for example, are indispensable elements in the philosophic life.   The accuracy with which it penetrates to the essential laws underlying the phenomena of experience is a *sine qua non* of philosophic study, and without a certain natural quickness of apprehension no one is qualified for the arduous mental discipline which results in giving us the finished dialectician.[160]   As an element in such a life—a life spent in research and administration in the service of the state—intellectual acumen is a good.   As an element in a life in which illiberality, excessive love of money, self-seeking, and other vicious characteristics are prominent, it results in giving us the finished villain,[161] and is so far an evil.   It is thus not a " good " in its own right, but is good so far as the quickness and accurate grasp of underlying law— which are its chief characteristics—enable it to be used as an indispensable element in the higher life.

7.   Courage.

The basis of courage is an innate psychophysical disposition which manifests itself, on the physiological side, in accelerated heart-beat, in more rapid breathing and blood-flow, in certain typical muscular contractions, etc., the whole being controlled from a definite section of the nervous system.[162] This disposition is found in the higher animals no less than in man, and is regarded as instinctive in character.   It corresponds fairly closely in principle to what, in our modern textbooks of psychology, is known as the instinct of pugnacity.[163]

This instinctive or physical courage is susceptible of further development, to some extent in the higher animals, but especially in man.[164]   A certain toughness and ability to endure hunger, cold, and pain without wincing can be developed by certain hardening processes well understood in the Spartan discipline,[165] and a more human system of gymnastics, which will educate the mind as well as the body, can carry this development to a higher level.[166]   Such education consists essentially in subjecting the natural disposition to the control of personal and social ideals of life in such a way that the instinctive sympathies of generous youth are enlisted upon the side of community ideals among which he has grown to manhood.[167]   Such direction of pugnacity by " right opinion " is the beginning of that control of instinct by reflection which is the essence of the higher morality.[168]   The further stages are developed in proportion as the youth learns to substitute for right opinion, " knowledge," or a more rational conception of what is of fundamental value in the community life, and thus becomes a fully developed, ethically self-controlled individual. In the light of this intelligent loyalty, what was once instinctive pugnacity becomes righteous indignation, the resolution and force of character which supports every worthy cause, and keeps down what is unworthy, whether in the world of men without or in the world of brute desires within.[169]   In modern terminology, the element of " conation " which received a specific direction in the instinct of pugnacity, has become transmuted into the higher complex known as " will," which, in the ethically self-conscious individual, functions in the service of reason and of the higher life.[170]

For Greek thought, the typical situation in which such courage is seen at its best, is on the battle-field, when the courageous man stands fast in the ranks, obeying his officers, and enduring death in the service of the community and its ideals, rather than accepting defeat or slavery.[171]   But Plato never fails to point out the presence of this same spirit in other situations of life, in sickness, in poverty, on ship-board,[172] in political, judicial, and philosophical life, and generally, in the presence of temptation and pleasure no less than in the presence of fear and pain.[173]   His position is, that every sort of life needs courage, or cheerful resolution and loyalty, and that this courage is properly the ally of reason—not the reason of the technical expert, of the professional soldier or sailor who is unafraid just so long as his science tells him no real danger is present[174]—but the reason of the more general and philosophical kind, which consists in an objective appreciation of the values of things.   This leaves its possessor undaunted and resolute in the face of social disapprobation and contempt no less than of physical danger and death, provided only that he can hold fast to what his reason convinces him is the right.[175]   It is, in fact, the rational conviction that the most fundamental value in the universe is the Idea of Good, which

is the philosophical basis and intellectually sustaining element
in the reflective virtue of courage.[176]

How far is courage a good ? The natural instinct of
pugnacity is, of course, of no moral value in itself. Unless
guided by reason, it is liable to be harmful to its possessor and
to the community. Its value depends wholly upon how it is
used. Employed in the service of irrational or anti-social
ends, it is an evil.[177] Used as the staunch ally of reason,
as an element in the higher civic and philosophical life, in the
service of law and order, whether civic or philosophical, it
is a good. Stated briefly, it is the presence of law, order,
and rational insight which make, of the natural instinct of
pugnacity, something morally valuable, a " good."[178]

8. Temperance or self-control.

The basis of temperance is a certain innate disposition,
a natural tendency towards quietness, orderliness, obedience
to law, and minding one's own business.[179] This is associated
with a certain slowness and steadiness both of mind and of
body,[180] an evenness of temper and a certain freedom from
passion and the promptings of appetite,[181] and a marked
tendency towards pacifism or even fatalism, in private no less
than in public relations.[182] Mistrusting impulse, and abhor-
ring excitement in any shape or form, it shrinks from the
unruly spontaneity of pleasure-seeking and of the *joi de vivre*,[183]
no less than from the rough-and-tumble competition of
business or of public life.[184]

Gentleness, refinement, tender-mindedness—what has such
a retiring disposition to do in our work-a-day world, in the
stern business of living ? For Plato, the answer depends
wholly upon the degree of intellectual insight with which this
disposition is associated. Such a disposition leans naturally
and inevitably upon something stronger, something more
robust than itself. In the lower stages of enlightenment, it
tends to look outside itself for the vigour and guidance which
it lacks, tends to look to the more dominant will and unhesi-
tating command of other men. At this level, it practically
invites aggression and exploitation in the struggle for existence.[185] At a higher stage of enlightenment—the stage of
right opinion—it seeks this strength in the laws and usages of
the community, co-operating in every possible way with the
government, and seeking from the wisdom of political superiors

that rule of life which it still fails to find for itself.[186] At the highest stage—the level at which right opinion becomes transmuted into " knowledge " or philosophical insight—respect for the law of the community becomes reverence for the moral law which is found within,[187] and those who have attained to this stage of enlightenment, while still retaining their sense of community values, become ethically mature, self-conscious and self-controlled personalities.[188]

This level once reached, development does not, however, come to a stop. The insight which philosophy brings makes it impossible for the temperate man to continue to retain the one-sided refinement and shrinking from public life, which have hitherto been his most pronounced characteristics. By associating with these feminine characteristics somewhat manlier qualities, he learns gradually to overcome his natural diffidence,[189] and undertakes, from a profound sense of duty and of the needs of the community, the functions of leadership in public life,[190] withdrawing only when the approach of old age justifies such retirement, to the philosophical contemplation which he loves and in which he feels most completely at home.[191]

Where, in this gradual development, does the natural disposition pass over into the reflective virtue of temperance ? The transition takes place at the level of right opinion. In view of the distinction between right opinion and philosophical insight, Plato does, indeed, at times speak of *two* virtues of temperance, the one at the lower level, the level of acceptance, docility, obedience, co-operation with the directions of superior insight,[192] the other at the higher level at which insight involves the duty of imposing upon oneself the burdens of leadership. At this higher level, Plato emphasizes more especially the problems connected with " self-knowledge " —by which he seems to mean largely a knowledge of one's own capacities and limitations[193]—and the two aspects of (1) obedience and (2) self-knowledge seem at first sight disparate. But for the maturer thought of Plato, both are intimately connected. The bond which unites them is the service of the community, and from this standpoint, Plato tends to speak of temperance as the virtue, not of one section of the community, not exclusively of those who accept the burdens of leadership, nor in any special sense of those who accept the principle of taking their orders from above, but rather as the harmony and agreement of the whole community on this point—the intelligent acceptance of control on the one hand, and the intelligent imposition of control on the other—in the interest, in both cases, of the community as a whole. This is the essence of the civic virtue of temperance.[194]

What is it about temperance which makes it a good ? In the first place, the disposition itself has in it tendencies which, for Greek feeling, inevitably make for happiness and the higher life. Its moderation, its sense of the value of orderliness and law, makes it ready to accept naturally and at the level of feeling, the truths which a more intellectual insight will some day discover, and it is thus physically attuned to the nature of a universe in which law and order are the most pronounced characteristics.[195] Again, such a disposition is docile, and lends itself to the higher education. Indeed, without a certain degree of submissiveness and acceptance, the higher development which education brings would be out of the question.[196] These two elements, then, (1) the natural kinship with reason, and (2) the docility, the willingness to accept what reason brings, are elements of virtue in the disposition itself.

What is important here, is not the readiness to accept the leadership of others as such. For that may be mere weakness, and may lead to the exploitation and eventual enslavement of the community.[197] It is rather the objectivity of the disposition, its kinship with the rational law which is at the basis of things, its willingness to recognize and accept what *reason* brings, which makes the disposition itself of ethical significance. Not the tendency to accept guidance, but the tendency to follow an opinion which is *right*, is the basis of its value. It is, in other words, not the mere presence of a sense of law and order which makes the disposition valuable from an ethical standpoint, but rather the presence of a sense of values which is *guided by reason*, whether this is at the level of right opinion or at the more advanced level of philosophical insight. Plato even goes so far as to state that only at the level of philosophical insight can we be truly and completely temperate.[198] But, as a rule, his position is that temperance is a good, and leads towards the higher kind of happiness, precisely so far as it is an element in the life in which our sense of the value of law and order is enlightened by reason.[199] We cannot all be leaders, but we can all be temperate, and can devote ourselves to the control of instinct by reason, and to the intelligent organization of the community life.

(9) Justice.

Man is essentially gregarious. He has an instinctive feeling for herd or group life, with all that this involves. This feeling is universal. Every member of the group shares it to some degree,[200] and if there are any members in whom it is very weak, these are universally regarded as pathological, abnormal, and, as militating against the existence of group life, are rightly put to death at the hands of the group.[201] This elementary sense of the value of group life furnishes the raw material out of which the cardinal virtue of justice is gradually developed.

How does this development take place ? Stated roughly and in general terms, it takes place in proportion as knowledge becomes substituted for instinctive feeling—that is to say, in proportion as the relations between members of the group to one another and to the group as a whole—relations implicit in the feeling for herd-life—become explicitly recognized and definitely stamped as essential elements of social value. In this process two levels are to be noticed, the levels of right opinion and of knowledge in the strict sense. Right opinion, consisting mainly in an acceptance of social tradition and in the development of a conservative moral sense which judges in accord with the general ideals of the group,[202] is inculcated, not merely by public education in the state schools, but by all the devices by which society enforces social standards, including at the one extreme what we may call the spirit of the community or the general social atmosphere, and at the other the definitely organized technical instruments of indict-ment in the law-courts.[203] At this level, justice appears to be closely connected with the laws and the law-courts. Each community passes laws in the interest of the group as a whole,[204] and the courts which administer and enforce such laws are the outward and visible manifestation of justice.[205] Just action, for the individual, consists in conforming to the laws,[206] and the final repositories of community standards and real moral educators of the community are the judges who interpret the laws.[207]

A higher level is attained when, for " opinion " of this sort, knowledge in the strict sense is substituted. When we know, with the certainty of the finished dialectician, that the relations of members of a group to one another and to the group as a whole *must*, in consistency, be of such and such a kind—

i.e. when we realize what is involved in the ideal of a genuine community—e.g. that every member is to have his due and no more than his due, and that his " due " is relative, not only to his service but especially to the needs of the community as a whole, and that he lives his true life only as a loyal member of the social organism[208]—we are not far from the end. This end is reached when we realize that the principle of organic unity, which we perceive to be essential to community organization,[209] is also of cosmic significance, and that the universe as a whole is based upon this principle, the Idea of Good[210]— then indeed we have seen the ultimate vision, and cannot but devote ourselves to making real in human life also, so far as may be, the principle of rational order which we have beheld.[211] This is justice in the higher sense, the only sense which is truly objective and final.[212]

If we ask how far, and for what reasons, justice is regarded as a good, we must make certain distinctions. Mere gregariousness is, in itself, neither good nor bad. Whether, in certain circumstances, it is capable of becoming morally valuable, depends wholly upon the degree of enlightenment with which it is associated.[213] At the level of right opinion, such enlightened social feeling is regarded as a good much as medicine is regarded as a good.[214] It is a *sine qua non* of social life that men should voluntarily refrain from anti-social acts, and we would all choose an ordered social existence in preference to the war of all against all.[215] But there is much of the old Adam in each one of us. Our natural instincts are adapted to a more primitive stage of civilization, and seek only their own immediate satisfaction. We all naturally desire to be supermen, acting, like Gyges with his ring, without regard to what *le bon bourgeois* calls good and evil.[216] The ring being, however, unfortunately mythical, bitter experience has taught a race of weaklings that it is better to exercise a measure of control over such instincts, and to agree to accept a conventional standard to maintain community existence. The principle recognized in this social contract, the principle which presides over the ordered life in the group, is justice. The value of justice is thus medicinal, as the value of a strict diet is medicinal. We all hunger after forbidden pleasures, but for fear of unpleasant consequences agree to follow the regimen prescribed by reason. Justice is thus good, not in itself, but purely for its consequences.[217]

The above represents the state of mind of the ordinary good citizen, who does not rise above the level of right opinion. He has a feeling which bids him obey the laws and do the right thing by the community, but he lacks knowledge, and his theory is unsound. The theory, of itself, would fall back into the sophistic deification of Might, and would thus be inconsistent with any sound theory of Right.[218] At the higher level which is attained by philosophic insight, justice is seen to be a good, not only because it is, in the long run, the best policy, nor merely because it is fundamental for every human virtue—on the ground that activities essentially social must logically be based upon the principle which makes social life possible[219]—but especially because it is the ultimate principle upon which God has constructed the universe, in making it in His own image.[220] What makes justice a good is thus, not only its regard for law and order, but especially its objectivity, its regard for a law and order which are the Divine law and the Divine order, a law and an order which are absolutely final.[221]

(10) Art.

All animals delight in motion. Frisking, gambolling, the twitching of limb or tail, the exercise of the vocal cords—all such motions, however spasmodic and chaotic, give pleasure, express and intensify the animal joy in living, in a way which is primitive, instinctive.[222] Regulated motion, motion governed by measure, rhythm, and recurring accent, the control of instinct by a feeling for law and order, is not found in all animals. The disposition to control the joyous *abandon* of animal motility, to reshape it in terms of measure and rhythm, of harmony and balanced order, is specifically human, and is regarded by Plato as the basis of art in all its forms.[223] First comes the choric dance, the general community expression of community feeling,[224] then the more specialized art-forms : —music, whose proper function is to follow the words of the chant and mark the beat of the dance ;[225] poetry, now severed from its connection with music and dancing, and appearing in the complex forms of the drama and epic ;[226] pictorial art, the representation in colour-patterns or in sculptured forms of the scenes and figures which appeal to the artist ;[227] and the other arts, great and small. As life has become more complex, the older, simpler art-forms have ceased to satisfy, and the specialized development of music, poetry, and painting has led to a search for new rhythms and harmonies, bizarre combinations and fantastic art-patterns,[228] until the art of our moderns has become estranged from its original function of enhancing community feeling in the choric dance.

Nor is this entirely to be wondered at. The artist is not a being of superior insight, understanding what he does and why he does it.[229] Artistic creation is not a matter of sober planning, of rational deliberation.[230] The artist is possessed, inspired. He is under the influence of enthusiasm, passion, a frenzy akin to delirium,[231] and follows his feeling whithersoever it may lead. He is freakish, unaccountable, irresponsible. The really responsible entity is the community itself.[232] Art is a social product. In the patriarchal village, art expresses itself in songs and dances of an Arcadian simplicity, hymns of praise and worship, the reflection of the traditions, hopes, and aspirations of the group.[233] In our luxurious modern age, when there is no longer any true unity in the state, and our modern citizens have lost their old-time single-mindedness towards virtue,[234] art also becomes decadent, emphasizing the ridiculous, effeminate, and base in human conduct, imitating the senseless noises of animals, and even reproducing the utterly meaningless sounds and sights of inanimate nature.[235]

The artist is thus an irresponsible imitator of the sounds and sights around him, possessed of the singular gift of enhancing and intensifying for the feeling of his audience whatever his hand has touched. Reduced to the non-artistic form of unpretentious narrative prose, the significance of his creations is often paltry enough.[236] But rhythm and harmony have a charm for our feelings, whether our reason approves or not,[237] and under the spell of the artist's wizardry we may be led to say and do many things at which our sober common sense would look askance.[238] Art is thus a dangerous weapon, and may react upon the community which permits untrammelled artistic creation, with fatal results. Simple and innocent-appearing innovations may have consequences of wide-reaching importance,[239] and may intensify and accelerate the tendency towards disruption and disunion which is so marked a feature of fourth-century democracies.[240]

What is the attitude of the philosopher towards this child-like but dangerous figure ? Plato seems to hesitate between two main attitudes. At times, impressed by the enormous power of art, and of its potential danger to the community which yields to its charm, he is for banishing forever the whole tribe of artists from his ideal state. That way, and that way alone, safety lies.[241] But this, after all, is a somewhat crude way of loosening the Gordian knot, and in general Plato prefers another method.[242] The artist can create, but cannot judge the value of his creations.[243] The philosopher-statesman has an accurate sense of values, but cannot create.[244] Let the statesman, then, apply his standards of value to the creations of the artist, permitting some and suppressing others in accordance with these standards, and the problem is solved.[245] A strict censorship will see to it that only art-works which enhance community feeling and emphasize the fundamental values of community life, shall see the light of day.[246] As an educative influence, art can so train the feelings of the young that they will welcome virtue as a thing of beauty, and reason as an old and trusted friend.[247] So too for the older citizens, art can make them realize the charm of civic duty and the glory of defensive war.[248] Such, and such alone, is the function of art in the ideal state. Anything which enhances community values is to be encouraged ; anything which tends towards innovations and the following after strange art patterns, is to be suppressed.[249] For the philosopher alone knows what are the true patterns of life, and will see to it that these, and these alone, are intensified and made beautiful by art.[250]

If we ask, then, how far art is a good, the answer is simple. Art has an enormous power over men for good or ill, but in itself is strictly non-moral. As such, it must either be banished from the ethical community, or must be made to serve community ends. As an element in the good life, regulated by the law and order recognized by philosophic insight as objective and final, it is a good. It is the presence of such law and such order alone, which makes it good.[251]

11. Law.

Law is a *sine qua non* of group life. Every social group, in the course of the natural struggle for existence, is called upon to face certain problems :—(a) problems arising out of the struggle with the natural environment, such as the never-ending battle with disease and the maintenance of an adequate food-supply for the group ; (b) problems arising out of the competition of other social groups, such as the exchange of commodities in the way of trade, or the establishment of settled relations by diplomacy or war ;[252] (c) problems arising within the group itself from the inherent difficulty of enforcing co-operation in the interests of the group as a whole, upon units whose diverse and competing interests tend towards the disruption of the group, e.g. economic problems produced by disparity of possessions, and the whole mass of problems produced by the lust for power on the part of individual would-be supermen.[253] Such problems force themselves upon the social group, and inevitably set their stamp upon the organization of the community. War, famine, and disease, no less than party-feuds or economic competition, express themselves by producing within the group a definite structure in the form of habits, customs, and explicit laws, called forth to meet the situation,[254] and eventually constituting, in their totality, a concentrated expression of the history and evolution of the group as a whole.[255]

So far considered, law, in its main outlines, is not subjective, artificial, or arbitrary, but reflects, in the civic structure and centralized authority within the group, the working of great natural forces, and is to be regarded as objective, natural, and even Divine.[256] As the civic group, however, gradually attains self-consciousness, law ceases to be the natural reaction to an objective situation, and becomes a matter of deliberate experimentation on the part of individuals or groups, a definite attempt to regulate community organization and manipulate the authority of law in the interest of certain ideas.[257] In this process we can distinguish two levels, the level of " opinion," and the level of knowledge or philosophic insight. At the lower level, the opinion seems to prevail that, as the function of law is to maintain the unity of the group, the first duty of government—the centralized authority arising naturally in the struggle for community existence—is to preserve itself. Party and class legislation is legislation in the interest of the governing body, and—at the level of " opinion "—this seems the natural and proper way of preserving the unity of the group as a whole.[258] Legislation seems thus properly expressive of the interest of the stronger or ruling caste, and ordinary political opinion in fourth century Greece does not appear to have been capable of rising above this conception.[259]

At the higher level, however, such a notion of the function of legislation is seen to be hopelessly inconsistent with the maintenance of the unity of the whole group. Disregard of the rights of minorities is one of the chief causes of disruption in states, and class-legislation is regarded by Plato as a main factor in the decadence which was spreading so rapidly over the faction-torn cities of his own time.[260] For the philosopher, the only proper function of deliberate legislation is to ensure the unity of the group as a whole, not by passing laws in the interest of a single class or caste,[261] but by so educating all classes of the community that they come to be permeated by a common spirit, the spirit of social service, to be realized precisely by means of the diversity of interests and powers which each individual citizen can learn to direct to the common good.[262] This philosophic ideal is sketched in the *Republic* and *Laws*, and its details are too numerous even to mention. But the general principle underlying the philosophic idea of the function of law is, clearly and beyond doubt, the interest of the community as a whole, and that interest is understood as co-partnership with God in establishing upon earth laws modelled after patterns which are objective and Divine in the highest sense.[263]

Law, then, arises as a natural reaction against forces, whether external or internal, which threaten the existence of the community. In the more primitive stages of social development, it is almost wholly unreflective ; but as political self-consciousness evolves, laws become man-made attempts to alter the constitution of the group in the interest of individuals or of principles. Class-legislation is inconsistent with the continued existence of the group, but legislation based upon rational and objective principles ensures to the citizens the highest development of which they are capable. Thus understood, how far is law a " good " ?

Not all laws are good. Indeed, so little love has Plato for lawyers and law-making,[264] that his thought may be thrown into the form of a dilemma. Either the citizens are at the level of opinion, or they have reached the level of philosophic insight. If they are at the level of opinion, no amount of tinkering with the details of the constitution will ever succeed in producing results of permanent value,[265] while for those who have attained to philosophic insight laws are a simple impertinence, if not directly harmful.[266]

E

In either case, they seem to be useless. But where the citizens are not all at one and the same level of development, the leaders who have insight can use the institution of law as a kind of *pis aller*, to educate the mass of their fellow-citizens and lead them gradually in the direction of virtue. Human nature being what it is, no real progress towards right living is possible apart from law.[267] But this must be law interpreted and enforced by men of genuine insight, if the results are to be of moral value. Only so far as the specific enactments are modelled after the Divine patterns, and are perpetually reshaped to meet changing circumstances, can law be regarded as a force which makes for morality. It is a good precisely so far as it expresses the structure of the ideal community, which is rational, objective, and truly Divine.[268]

12. Philosophy.

Man naturally desires to know. He reaches out after new experiences, new sounds, new sights, new tastes. Anything which stimulates retina or tympanum, anything which titillates the palate or nostril, awakens into activity cognitive processes whose mere functioning, as such, is associated with an immediate and instinctive satisfaction.[269] This itch to handle for himself, to look at and listen to everything in his environment which arouses cognitive interest, is what we call curiosity, and is the instinctive basis of all further development of a specifically intellectual character.[270]

The natural urge of curiosity leads primarily to the enlargement of experience at the sensory level. It is seeing, feeling, handling, etc., i.e., simple experiences of a sensory kind, which gives the most primitive and the most universal satisfaction of this impulse.[271] But the satisfaction which they yield is not final. The cognitive disposition is synthetic. There is in us something which expects and demands orderliness, consistency, and rationality in our experiences, and so far as our new sensations conflict with one another and refuse to settle down into a single cognitive system, our expectation of orderliness receives a shock. The shock to our natural demand that the world and the idealizing tendencies of our own minds shall be in pre-established harmony, constitutes an obstacle to our cognitive impulse, throws us back upon ourselves and awakens resistance, an acceptance of the challenge, a determination to decide the conflict before

some higher court than that of mere sensation.[272]   The desire
to know is thus raised above the merely sensory level, and
reaches the higher levels of ideation and reason.   At the
ideational level, the level of " opinion," most men remain
satisfied.   With the large majority of mankind, the cognitive
impulse can no further go.[273]   It remains largely sensory—
for what is " opinion " but sub-consciously synthesized
sensation ?—and conceals its ultimate failure to solve our
obstinate questionings by a great busy-ness, a plunging into
a vast multiplicity of half-developed theories and partially
organized masses of experience, making up in breadth what
it lacks in depth, and keeping steadily outside of real philosophy.[274]   With a few chosen mortals, however, the cognitive
impulse goes further.[275]   As sensations and memories were
synthesized into opinions,[276] so opinions in their turn become
synthesized into " ideas,"[277] and finally the systems of ideas
or laws which constitute the special sciences become synthesized, at least in outline and in terms of their most fundamental
presuppositions, so as to compose a single system which is
ultimate, inasmuch as it organizes the whole field of possible
knowledge by means of a single all-pervading principle, a
principle which is not merely convenient as a means of
introducing unity and system into the presuppositions which
underlie our jostling sciences, but is also objective, the
ultimate principle in accordance with which God has constructed the universe.[278]   Thus to penetrate to the utmost
bounds of the *mundus intelligibilis* and, in the light of the
ultimate principle, the Idea of Good, to devote oneself to
the task of working over and re-organizing the whole of
human experience, theoretical and practical,[279] is to live the
life which is the life of philosophy, the highest and most
blessed life possible to man, the life which substitutes intellect
for sensation, and reflective reason for animal instinct, and
makes of man a self-knowing and deliberate co-worker with
God.[280]

To ask how far such a life is to be regarded as a good,
may seem, on the face of it, absurd.   And yet, there is a
point in asking such a question.   For if we look at the actual
facts of experience, it seems doubtful whether the most
esteemed and valuable citizens are to be sought in the ranks
of professional students of philosophy.[281]   For the individual
and for the state, devotion to philosophy may constitute

a real danger, and instinct, habit, and acceptance of the conventions approved in the experience of the race may well
seem a safer guide than speculative research.[282]   For ordinary
educated opinion in fourth-century Greece, withdrawal
from practical life for the purpose of philosophic study is
admittedly valuable during the adolescent period. A little
philosophy opens the mind and broadens the range of interests.[283]   But there is such a thing as too much training,
and an unduly protracted adolescence unfits the seminarist
for the active business of life. Practical life needs quick
decisions, and prolonged pondering over the eternal questionings which, after all, lead nowhere, makes the student *gauche*,
unpractical, immature, useless both to himself and to the
community.[284]   Young men with the qualities of character
and intellect which lead to success in such studies, should
not be allowed to fritter away their potential value to the
community. The crying need of the age is for trained leaders
and men who possess the qualities for such leadership should
be compelled to enter public life as soon as their training is
reasonably complete. Nothing but physical unfitness or
some disqualifying one-sidedness of character is acceptable
as an excuse for continuing academic studies beyond the
adolescent period.[285]

To this appeal to the facts of experience, what is Plato's
answer ? He accepts the premisses, admits the justice of
the reasoning, but denies the conclusions. It is true that many
of the devotees of philosophy are eccentric, immature in
judgment, unfitted for leadership, useless to themselves and
to the community.[286]   But the fault lies, not with philosophy
as such, but rather with the character of the actual professionals or with the social environment, or both. Strong
social pressure in the direction of practical affairs means
deserting theoretical studies too early and throwing oneself
into the illiberal influences of party politics.[287]   What public
life lacks is not half-trained leaders, but leaders whose training
has been carried much further—far enough at least to overcome the will to power and to realize the worthlessness of
personal ambition to individual and community alike.[288]
For the rest, Plato devises means to provide practical experience and avoid the admitted ills of unduly protracted
study, and recognizes the right of the community to compel
its trained students to enter public service, though at an

age much later than that required by ordinary opinion.[289] Safeguarded by proper tests for candidates—tests of character as well as tests of intelligence[290]—and with proper provision for practical experience as well as for theoretical studies, most of the dangers are averted, and the life which fits the student for the transvaluation of traditional values[291] and the guidance of the community towards the city of God, is of the utmost worth both to himself and to the community.

What is it which makes philosophy a good ? Curiosity, of itself, has no particular moral value, and " opinion," as we have seen, is good only so far as it is right or true, i.e., so far as it approximates to philosophic insight. It is, then, philosophy itself which is good, and what makes it a good is precisely its insight into the Idea of Good. In studying great principles, something of their greatness enters our lives and frees us from vulgar temptations.[292] We learn gradually to re-shape our lives and the lives of those entrusted to our charge in terms of these ideal principles, and by means of such studies the Idea of Good comes to have a habitation in our personal lives and in the social group in which we are leaders.[293] Philosophy is thus a good, precisely because it is *par excellence* the realization of the ideal life, the making real, in human experience, of ideals or laws which are not only inspiring to the imagination, but are objective and Divine in a literal sense, the ultimate laws which express the true nature of the Real.[294]

Summary.

So far we have considered somewhat in detail examples representative of the whole field of recognized goods, with the aim of discovering, in each case taken by itself, what are the special features which commend it to the philosophic judgment. We should now be in a position to sum up our individual conclusions, in order to discover, if possible, what precisely are the objective elements present throughout the range of such cases, what attributes are common to all goods, what characteristics are apprehended by philosophic insight as justly entitling phenomena which possess these characteristics to be regarded as members of the class, " goods."

As we look over the cases studied, one result stands out with unexpected clearness.[295] All goods have this one feature in common, the expression of measure, organization, proportion, law.   Thus Health is the harmony resulting from a certain organization of the four bodily elements, Wealth is good so far as it is acquired and spent with a certain regard for law and order and the system of social values, Pleasure is good so far as our hedonic feelings take on a certain stable structure in accordance with the laws discovered by intellect. Again, what is Memory but organized sensory experience, consisting of elements abstracted from the flux of sensation and taking on the beginnings of that organization which gives us Opinion ?   So too Intellectual Acumen is the efficient grasp of the laws revealed by methodic organization of experience, and Right Opinion is characterized especially by its orderly reproduction of the system of social and cosmic values.   So also with the moral virtues.   Courage represents the organization of instinctive pugnacity in terms of a system of values, Temperance is a passive disposition which takes on the colouring and structure of law and order, and Justice is the herd-instinct re-organized so as to reproduce, in community life, a structure patterned upon the final system of values which is dominated by the Idea of Good. Again, Art—essentially the introduction of measure, proportion, law, into our sensory experience—is good from a moral standpoint precisely as it is the beauty of systematic and orderly living, and of right community values, which it intensifies and enhances.   So too Law is a civic structure of a systematic kind, and Philosophy—the final vision of the Ideas—leads to the complete re-organization of experience in terms of law and order.

Law and order, then, are essential objective elements in everything regarded as good.   Law and order—*any* law and *any* order ?   Is there something about " law and order " *as such*, which constitutes them elements of objective value ? Let us consider.   This can hardly be the case, at least without further qualification.   Health of body, for all its law and order, is no absolute or unconditioned good.   It is only to the man who is himself good, and exercises a certain degree of insight into higher values, that health is of moral worth. Soo too with money and possessions, with pleasure, with memory and intellectual acumen.   These are of moral worth only to men of character and insight into higher values. So also of courage, temperance, art and law : it is insight

into higher values alone which gives these ethical worth—
the kind of insight which distinguishes the man of right
opinion and, above all, the philosopher.

What does it mean, this qualification—that it is only
to men of character and insight that what the world regards
as " goods " are of genuine moral worth ?   Men of character
presumably use these goods in the service of right ends,
and men of insight know how to use them, know what ends
are right.   It is as elements in the " higher " life, the life of
moral and intellectual excellence—as elements in the service
of community values, in a community which makes a maximum
of moral and intellectual life possible for its members—that
these goods, health, money, art, and the rest, are of genuine
worth.   That is to say, one thing, and one thing alone, is
of value : moral and intellectual life.   Bodily health, artistic
refinement, a sufficiency of this world's goods—all such
things are secondary, good only as means to the life of philosophic insight with all which this involves.   This life, however,
the life of philosophic insight, is good without further
qualification, good in itself.

Good in itself—why ?   What is it about philosophy
which makes it good without qualification ?   What are the
objective features which make it supremely valuable ?
Philosophy is insight—insight into what ?   Insight into
values ?   Such a procedure is circular.[296]   It is a vicious
circle, if we explain value in terms of insight, and insight
in terms of value.   No.   What is of importance for us is the
nature of the world in which we live, the nature of the objective, the real.   It is insight into the nature of reality which
is valuable, and it is valuable precisely because it enables
us to get in touch with reality in a practical way, to take
reality up into our lives and make them real, to re-organize
our experience in terms of patterns which are not man-made,
arbitrary and subjective, out of touch with things-as-they-
are, matters of chance and fashion, the fluctuating opinions
of a Protagoras or a Heraclitus, or the ideas of a ruling caste
swept up from the underworld of party politics into a brief
span of mis-spent power, blind leaders of the blind—but
patterns which are permanent, eternal, real, genuine, because
they are elements of *what is*.   Philosophic insight is insight
into the genuine laws of the real world, and the philosophic
life is the re-organization of human experience, both of the

individual and (under favourable conditions) of society, in terms of these laws, a making real upon earth of the ideal city whose pattern is laid up in heaven, the city of God.

Let us apply this general conclusion to the particular "goods." Intellectual acumen, art, law, temperance, and the rest, are of moral value so far as they bring us into closer contact with the nature of reality. Just what does this mean in detail ?   It means that Law, for example, is of genuine worth only in proportion as the civic structure in which it is embodied reproduces the general structure of the ideal patterns in accordance with which the cosmos was framed, in such a way that the frame-work of society, so far as that rests upon law, *is* the objective system of ideal patterns, translated into civic structure.   So too Art is of genuine significance only so far as it is the Divine patterns—whether in the natural or in a social environment which has been formed upon those patterns—which, in terms of colours, tones, and rhythms, are revealed to men as the sources of all that partakes of true beauty.   Again, it is only so far as the structure and colouring which they take on are the structure and colouring of the Divine order, that Temperance acquires genuine meaning, that Courage places its stores of energy and resolution at the service of the eternal values, that Justice, the principle of social union, comes to represent, in the social group, the objective system of inter-related elements all working towards the realization of the Idea of Good. So too with Pleasure, Memory, Health—these are of genuine worth only so far as they take on a structure expressive of values which derive from the eternal order ; and finally, Intellectual Acumen, Right Opinion, and Philosophy, obtain their whole value and significance from the objective order which they make their study and with which they bring us into cognitive contact.

For Platonism there is, on the one hand, Reality, a system of Ideas organized around the Idea of Good, a system which is perfect, self-sufficient, final.   On the other hand, there is Man, a being imperfect, dependent, weak and needing support.   The good for man consists in seeking that support where alone final support is to be found—in learning to understand the Divine order, and to make over human life in terms of the Divine patterns, to take reality up into human nature, to become real and Divine, so far as this is possible for man.[297] Man is a bundle of instincts, reachings out after experiences of all sorts. Of themselves, these instinctive gropings lead nowhere. Out of touch with the one thing which supremely matters, all the lesser goods of life—wealth, power, and the rest—are simply unmeaning, and a life spent in the pursuit of pleasure, wealth, etc., is a life utterly devoid of value and significance.

One thing alone matters : to get in touch with reality, and thus become real; to make over sense-perception, memory, opinion, and intellect, until these are at home in the world of Ideas ; to make over the social instincts and habits until we have virtues, trained habits of choice which follow after ideals of objective significance ; to make over the institutions of society, creative art, the administration of law and politics, etc., until these also come to partake of the ideal patterns in which alone there is reality and true being. The way to do this, to obtain insight into the workings of reality and to translate these workings into principles of direct and immediate significance for human life, is by philosophy, and by philosophy alone. To the selection and training of the ablest minds for this task, the whole energies of society are to be devoted, and for the Platonist it is true to say that philosophy is the way and the life.

What, then, is our final conclusion ? The elements of objective value in the various " goods " are the elements of objectivity, reality, ideality. The system of Ideas alone truly *is* ; and it is so far as the various goods of life partake of the Ideal system, that they are objective, real, and of ethical significance.

CHAPTER III

THE MORAL STANDARDS

SO far we have considered what are the objective features of actions and situations, upon which the judge fixes his attention with a view to discovering whether they are or are not of moral value. In the present chapter, our aim is to consider what are the standards of judgment, the principles or criteria which the judge applies in coming to his decision as to the ethical value of such actions and situations. With this aim, we shall proceed to examine inductively and without prejudice the various norms mentioned now and again in the dialogues, one by one, until, after all have been investigated, we find ourselves in a position to come to some general conclusion as to Plato's main standpoint—if there *is* any main standpoint—on the general question.

The actual norms or standards definitely mentioned in the dialogues as criteria which help us to distinguish between good and evil are :—(1) Universal assent, (2) The writings of the legislator, (3) Quantity of pleasure, (4) Æsthetic quality, (5) Expediency or benefit, especially to individuals, (6) Contribution towards the life of the *whole*, (7) Orderliness, (8) Adequacy and self-sufficiency, (9) Consistency, (10) Objectivity. Under these ten heads is concentrated all the evidence from the dialogues which bears upon the question of the moral norms or standards. We shall proceed to examine this evidence, taking one item at a time.

1. Universal assent.

With Plato it is almost axiomatic that all normal men agree on certain general questions in ethics, and that their agreement establishes certain general norms of conduct. All percipient beings whatever desire and hunt after good, and take no interest in the attainment of anything which is not accompanied by good. Good is the universal object of desire, the final end which every living being pursues, refusing to be put off with mere appearances, and insisting always upon establishing contact with reality.[1] This universal sense of honour and justice remains, however, very general in character, and can be appealed to only to settle very general questions, such as the characteristics which must be ascribed to a chief or perfect good in order to make it universally eligible.[2] As soon as questions of detail come up for discussion, although dialecticians like Socrates and distinguished teachers like Protagoras or Gorgias can come to some agreement on ethical questions somewhat in advance of contemporary ethical opinion, and exceptionally gifted students in exceptionally favourable circumstances can be led to understand and accept detailed applications of general principles, yet in general, assent ceases to be strictly universal, and dissent and dispute seem in fact to be the rule.[3] The use of this criterion or standard is thus limited to the most general questions.

2. The writings of the legislator.

A definite group of norms, establishing concrete detailed standards of right and wrong, is furnished by the written laws of the community. These arise largely, as we saw in the preceding chapter, from the experience of the group itself in the course of its struggle for unity and continued existence in an environment only partially favourable to such existence. But as the group develops, it tends to make a definite study of the laws of other social groups, testing out by experience such as can be adapted to its own needs, and eventually incorporating these, so far as possible, in its own legal system.[4] This body of social and civic norms is kept up to date by each new generation of legislators,[5] and is of the utmost value, not only in deciding questions of justice and injustice between man and man,[6] but also as furnishing certain standards of community values which can be used, e.g. to determine what writings are fit or unfit to be put into the hands of youth for purposes of education,[7] or to instruct adults as to how they may make the most out of social life or test the quality of their own moral development and see clearly in what direction they are trending.[8] The general body of law thus furnishes a standard which is primarily of value for the ordinary citizen. If we are inquiring what are the norms by reference to which the philosopher or legislator himself comes to his decisions, while this is, of course, partly a matter of precedent and acceptance of the experience of the race in general and of the group in particular, yet the fact that written laws of themselves tend to lag behind the moral evolution of the community, while the legislator himself keeps, if anything, slightly in advance of the times,[9] sufficiently indicates that for the *original* standards which guide the legislator himself in giving expression to norms which reflect and at the same time guide what is best in the experience of the community, we must look further.

3. Quantity of pleasure.

Pleasure and pain are the first perceptions of children, according to Plato, and are the forms under which virtue and vice are originally present to them.[10] For most men the use of pleasure as a standard for measuring the value of actions is retained through life, and so general is its acceptance as such a standard, that it can almost claim the authority of universal assent. But, as in other cases of universal assent, so here ; it is only in cases of the simplest kind that such a standard is found perfectly satisfactory. As soon as problems of any degree of complexity make their appearance, certain restrictions and qualifications are at once found to be inevitable. Thus, pleasure can be derived from diverse sources, some of which are mutually inconsistent ; men are said to be led astray by being overcome by pleasure ; certain pleasures are thought to be bad and certain pains are thought to be good, etc.[11] In the face of such problems, the difficulty of which is a matter of almost universal experience, it is found necessary to introduce certain distinctions, which lead gradually further and further away from the basis of simple sense-pleasure. Thus, the first and most widely acceptable of these distinctions is the distinction of pleasures in terms of quantity. Everyone believes that a greater quantity of pleasure is to be preferred to a smaller quantity. But this distinction becomes clearly intelligible only if we think of pleasures as reduced to a unit basis, e.g. in respect of intensity and duration, so as to admit of arithmetical computation.   A thoroughly scientific hedonistic calculus, erected upon this basis, would be of immense value as an intellectual standard by which to check the misleading influences of appearances—i.e. of our ready-made, " snap " judgments, whether in ethics proper or in the calculation of a merely psychological maximum of enjoyment—and could, indeed, well be regarded as the saving principle of human life.[12]   The standard has thus begun to shift from the field of experienced pleasure to the field of scientific, mathematical calculation, i.e., from the sphere of sensation to the sphere of intellectual evaluation. In the *Protagoras*, scientific hedonism is left, without further qualification, as the formulation of the moral standard which meets with acceptance from the whole group of professional teachers of ethics,[13] and there are, in the other dialogues also, many traces of this position.[14]   But mathematical calculation, for Plato, is always merely a first step upon the long road of intellectual development which ends in the vision of the Ideas, and especially of the Idea of Good, as the final source of the reality of our experiences,[15] and in dialogues where the question is discussed more deeply than in the *Protagoras*, the shift from sense to intellect, which we have already noted as furnishing the norm or standard of pleasure, is carried further, and as the sense-pleasures drop out of sight as unworthy of the genuine philosopher,[16] the scientific calculation of such pleasures also vanishes, and its place is taken by intellectual insight into the objective sources of real value. The saving principle of human life thus becomes less a matter of " nicely calculated less and more," and more a matter of getting in touch with the objective sources of permanent satisfaction, so that quantity of pleasure cannot be regarded as a final standard of moral value.[17]

4. Aesthetic quality.

The close connection between beauty and symmetry on the one hand, and moral excellence on the other, is always clearly recognized in Plato.   It is, indeed, sometimes stated simply and without qualification, that the good *is* the beautiful, and arises from the presence of symmetry.[18]   At other times it is stated more figuratively that virtue is the beauty of the soul, that grace and harmony are the twin sisters of goodness and virtue, etc.,[19] and a certain parallelism between the vision of absolute beauty and the Idea of the Good has frequently been noted by modern Plato-students.[20]   How far such a general connection is to be regarded as furnishing a definite norm or standard, so that the moral worth of a man or of an action could be decided by consideration of such aesthetical characteristics, is, however, not quite so clear. It is definitely stated that the good man is superior to the evil man in beauty,[21] and a thorough training in " music " and art generally forms a considerable portion of the early education which is to develop moral character ; but if we push our questions, and insist on knowing, e.g. whether the presence of aesthetical qualities may always be regarded as reliable evidence of the presence of ethical qualities, we come upon certain difficulties. We find, e.g. on the whole, that aesthetical qualities are in themselves regarded as specifically non-moral, and that they derive whatever moral value they may come to possess for certain educational purposes, solely from imitating or participating in ideas which are moral in their own right.[22] Although beauty and symmetry are reckoned high in the list of goods,[23] there can be no question that the moral significance of aesthetical quality is fundamentally dependent on " a rightly and nobly ordered mind and character," and that in general the beautiful is to be weighed by the sole standard of the good,[24] so that Plato's settled conviction appears to be that aesthetical quality, in spite of its frequent connection with moral quality, cannot, as such, be used legitimately as a norm or standard for determining moral excellence.

5. Expediency or benefit.

By the expedient or beneficial, Plato as a rule means something opposed to and contrasted with the harmful. By harmful, he normally understands something which destroys or impairs the peculiar excellence of anything, i.e. that in virtue of which it functions in its own specific way, and thus makes it inferior ; e.g. in the case of a man, justice being regarded as his peculiar excellence, in virtue of which he functions as a specifically human being, to " harm " him is to make him lose his specific excellence and become less just, less fit to take his place in a society which is struggling towards closer co-operation and organization.[25] To " benefit " a man, then, is to confirm and strengthen him in respect of his peculiar excellence, to make him a better man, more just, better fitted to play his part in the forward march of humanity,[26] and it is peculiarly characteristic of good men, whether as private citizens or as leaders and guardians in the community, that they are beneficial to their fellow-citizens in this way, and give advice and pass laws which are expedient for the group

as a whole.[27]   What makes good men capable of being beneficial in this way is partly (1) their ethical characteristics, which
bring them into especial favour with the Gods, who will not
suffer men who resemble Them to fall permanently into misfortune or error of any kind,[28] partly also (2) their intellectual
insight, which enables them in an especial sense to acquire
an appreciation of the true values of things and to get in touch
with what really matters, with the nature of the Real and the
Idea of Good.[29]   Hence the advice they give to their fellow-
citizens, and the laws which they pass, being based upon the
ultimate sources of value, tend to be of genuine and permanent
benefit to the community of which they are members.

How far can expediency or benefit be regarded as a standard by reference to which we can decide questions of moral
value ?   Let us consider.   Bodily health is sometimes expedient or beneficial, sometimes harmful to the individual ; is
it a good so far as it is beneficial, and an evil so far as it is
harmful ?   Plato says, Yes, and adds, that it is beneficial so
far as it is guided by genuine insight into values and used in
the service of such values.   So also of strength, good looks,
money, temperance, justice, manliness, magnificence, intellectual acumen, sound memory, etc., in a word, of all the
excellencies of body and mind : these are all " goods " so far
as they are beneficial, and evils so far as they are harmful.
But it is added that in themselves they are neither beneficial
nor harmful.   What makes them beneficial, is the way in
which they are employed in specific concrete situations ; and
the value of the way in which they are thus employed depends
wholly upon philosophic insight into values, into the nature
of things.[30]   So too poetry is regarded as an evil, to be banished from the ideal community, largely because it is harmful
and able to make even good men inferior as citizens ; though
even in such cases it is because it is deficient in insight, out
of touch with things-as-they-are, that poetry produces this
effect.[31]   So again it is stated that the one thing of supreme
importance is to choose between the good and the evil life,
using as a sole criterion the quality of making the soul more
just, i.e. expediency or benefit.[32]   But here also, as in the other
cases, it is philosophic insight into objective values which is
finally decisive, and the emphasis tends to shift, from expediency or harmfulness as such, to the objective nature of
reality as the real standard.

6. Contribution towards the life of the *whole*.

In the ethical community the well-being of the whole group is one of the supreme values. Law, art, science, commerce, agriculture, politics and diplomacy—in all of these it is the interest of the group taken as a whole which is, and which should be, the ruling principle.[33] So too in the case of the virtues of manliness, self-control, wisdom, and justice ; it is especially their social or civic side whose value is constantly stressed by Plato,[34] and even in the case of dialectic or technical philosophy, it is its value to the community as a whole which tends to be placed in the foreground.[35] So again in such social institutions as friendship and family life, or in the more individual pursuit of power, wealth, and happiness, it is always the interest of the group as a whole which should predominate.[36] In fact, for Plato the civic ideal is always a united, firmly organized group, the members of which live, as far as possible, a common life, educated from the cradle in common nurseries and schools, eating and drinking at common tables, exercising in common, and having, as far as may be, common objects of joy and grief on all occasions of life.[37] The " enemy " is excessive individualism, the pursuit of private well-being, exclusive power, exclusive wealth, exclusive pleasures,[38] whether such individualism assumes the collective form, which pursues the interest of a specially favoured group, such as an industrial class, a political faction, or an aristocratic club,[39] or assumes the more extreme form which produces the superman or tyrant. Tendencies in such directions disrupt the community, cause it to disintegrate, to separate into its component elements, so that the flower of civilization perishes.[40] Individualism is thus the root of all evil, and communism[41] is the root of all good.

That the life of the social *whole* furnishes a norm, an explicit rule or standard by reference to which the philosopher or legislator guides himself in estimating the ethical value of actions and situations, is frequently stated and yet more frequently implied in the Dialogues. Thus the question as to the happiness of the guardian class is explicitly determined by reference to this principle,[42] and when it is a question of justifying almost any element in the social organization of the state, it is to this standard that the appeal is almost invariably made.[43] So too the immoderate pursuit of wealth, on the one hand, and the life of political faction with all its consequences, on the other, are condemned, precisely because they divide the city and cause it to fall apart.[44] Finally, it is more than hinted that the principle is of more than practical significance, and has an ultimate or metaphysical justification.[45]

This last statement leads naturally to a further question. Is the judgment that actions and situations are " good " because and in so far as they contribute to the life of the whole, final—or is it only a proximate standard, itself in need of further, metaphysical justification ? The answer can be in no doubt. The organized ethical community, with all the subordinate elements contained in its idea, certainly furnishes a standard, and a high standard, by reference to which a large group of difficult questions concerning ethical values can definitely be settled. But it does not furnish a final or absolute standard. It has its place in the world of ideas which furnish standards for human life. But its use as a standard cannot be final, until it has been transformed and justified by being grounded in the ultimate principle of the ideal world—the Idea of Good.[46] Only when transmuted in the light of this final principle, is its use as a standard, by which to decide ethical questions without possibility of error, legitimate. In itself, it is a high standard or norm, but not the highest.

7. Orderliness.

That orderliness is a characteristic of virtue and disorderliness or lack of orderliness is a characteristic of vice, is a commonplace in Greek philosophical literature ever since it found embodiment in the Pythagorean table of opposites. So too in the Platonic writings. Whether in opposition to the sophistic glorification of systematic *pleonexia*,[47] or to the man of the world's pursuit of pleasures,[48] or to the well-known Syracusan habits of luxury,[49] the reference to orderliness as the test of virtuous living is clear and unmistakable.

Just exactly what does Plato understand by orderliness ? In the first place, he understands by it a certain innate quietness of disposition, a temperamental tendency in the direction of moderation and self-control in the satisfaction of impulses and appetites. The virtuous man is temperate, orderly, and self-restrained, free from sudden excitements, without violent passions, not liable to fall into temptation, and simply and naturally quiet and self-controlled in all things.[50]

F

In the second place, by orderliness Plato understands a tendency to accept without question the direction of those in authority, not only to conform to the actual legislative enactments of the community, but also a certain willingness to co-operate in a more general spirit with the government in its effort to regulate conduct in the interest of the group as a whole. This represents a higher stage of ethical development than the mere natural disposition, as here the temperament is, at least to a certain degree, directed and controlled by reason. The reason, however, by which the virtuous man is here guided, is reason at a comparatively low level, the level of " right opinion."[51]

In the third place, something beyond respect for the opinions of men is understood. The orderliness of which Plato speaks is regarded as having a certain cosmic significance. The movements of the planets betray the presence of a certain immutable and Divinely established order. Not only the system of sunrises and sunsets, but the orderly movements of the whole physical universe, are here in Plato's mind. It appears to him to be impossible to study astronomy and other branches of physical science without something of the order in the object studied sinking into the soul of the student and making it orderly and attuned to this cosmic orderliness. This represents a still higher stage of ethical development, as it raises the reason of the student above the level of mere opinion, and of reliance upon the guidance of others, to a level at which he seeks and attains for himself a certain dispassionate insight into law and order.[52]

In the fourth place, Plato understands by the term a certain ideal orderliness, an ideal only very partially realized in the measured dance of the planets, and in the motions of the world which we can touch and see. It is the same ideal which is partly realized in the legal institutions of men, and even in the mere physical disposition towards quietness and moderation. The home of this ideal orderliness is in the realm of ideal patterns generally, and the final source and pattern of orderliness is the highest of these ideals, the Idea of Good.[53] From this standpoint, Plato speaks of things or actions as morally valuable, so far as they are partakers in the ideal patterns and resemble these, so far, that is, as they conform to their own idea or realize their own law. This is expressed perhaps most characteristically in his doctrine of the " mean " or

" limit," actions which exemplify this being orderly and tidy, rather than disorderly and sprawly, and representing, in the form of a microcosm, or small organized system, a portion of the macrocosm or complete ideal system itself.[54]

Thus understood, in what sense is orderliness to be regarded as a standard or criterion, by which we can determine whether an action is good or bad ? The first and lowest level, the stage of innate disposition, does not, when we come to examine Plato's meaning, furnish us with such a criterion. While it may be true that all virtuous men are orderly and quiet in this sense, it cannot be urged that all men who are un-aggressive by nature, and who readily accept orders from those in authority, are virtuous. At the two lower levels of temperament and opinion, those who possess this ingrained tendency towards obedience practically invite aggression and exploitation on the part of less scrupulous and less tender-minded neighbours, and may thus be the cause of evil, rather than good, to the community. This Plato regards as culpable weakness, rather than virtue, and at this level, orderliness can thus not be treated as a test which would serve to distinguish good from bad.[55] So too at the next level, the level of opinion, it is not because action is controlled by opinion that the action can be regarded as good. Action controlled by false opinion is bad, and is bad precisely in proportion as the opinion is false. It is so far as the guiding opinion is right or true, i.e. in accordance with the truths discovered by philosophic insight, that the resulting action can be designated good. It is not the mere orderliness or controlledness of action which makes it good, but the rationality and objective validity of the principle in accordance with which it is ordered and controlled, which make it good.[56] So too the cosmic orderliness, the orderliness of the observed movements of the phenomena of nature, is not morally valuable in its own right. Its moral significance resides wholly in its providing a training-ground for the developing intelligence so as to distract it from the merely actual and sensuous, and to assist it in its progress towards acquiring insight into the ideal of a strictly rational, more than phenomenal, realm.[57] When, however, we come finally to the orderliness of this realm of ideas, knowledge of which arises only as we succeed in obtaining insight into the Idea of Good, then indeed we seem to have come upon an orderliness which may be used as a standard by which to

measure actions and decide whether they are good or evil.
Action patterned upon the ideal order, and guided by insight
into its orderliness, is virtuous.   Action not so guided is not
virtuous, but may be either morally insignificant or—if
opposed to the ideal order—vicious.[58]   In this sense, then,
orderliness *is* a criterion.   But it must be noted that, understood in this sense, orderliness either coincides fully with
criteria such as consistency and objectivity, or at least overlaps
to such an extent as to be practically indistinguishable from
these criteria.   Further consideration of ideal orderliness,
then, must await consideration of these further criteria.

8. Adequacy and self-sufficiency.

When Socrates sums up the discussion in the *Philebus* by
attributing to the *summum bonum* the distinguishing characteristics of adequacy, perfection, and self-sufficiency,[59] he is
simply repeating, so far as the words used are concerned, what
is an accepted commonplace in Greek philosophical literature
and life.   It is universally admitted that the good is something
final, something which everyone seeks as a basis which shall
give to his life meaning and value ; that he who is in possession
of the good is in some sense superior to the unenlightened mass
of humanity ; and that he has access to some hidden source
of power, which makes of him a master of life, independent
of other men and indifferent to the sudden reversals of fortune
which were so marked a feature of fourth-century political
existence.[60]

So far as the words used are concerned, this is the merest
commonplace, and there is no one to oppose it.   *Cadit quaestio.*
But when we come to consider the content of the terms, we
note a great difference, which corresponds to the difference
between opinion and philosophic insight.   For the average
educated Greek, and indeed for the sophists from whom the
Greek gentleman obtained his higher education, as well as
for the general public opinion, the highest good was regarded
as consisting in political power.[61]   Based, as was actual fourth-
century life, upon the distinction between free-born citizen
and slave, and upon further distinctions of caste or wealth
within the free-born class, it seemed natural, and indeed
inevitable, that the basis for living a free, independent existence should be a matter of wealth and power.   The man without means and without powerful friends was exposed, not only

to neglect, but to calumny and even direct insult, against which he had no effective remedy. The obvious way to raise his life above this quasi-slavish level, was to seek power, by acquiring wealth and powerful friends, linked together in a political club. Thus secured, he could not be insulted with impunity.[62] Carried to its extreme conclusion, the ideal of the independent life seemed to the average educated Greek to be represented in the person of the unconstitutional dictator or " tyrant," who exercised supreme power in the community, and was accountable to none.[63] And this seemed reasonable, for the tyrant-ideal appeared to exhibit in unmistakable form all the characteristics of the *summum bonum*. The tyrant lived a complete, spacious, well-rounded life, surrounded with art and luxury, and, in a word, with all external goods. Raised above the opinion of the world, and self-sufficient to the highest degree, he was also the fount of honour, and the chief immediate source of values in the community ; for could he not elevate his friends to positions of eminence, and exile his enemies and confiscate their goods, where he did not go further and actually take away their lives ? Dazzling and glorious, an object of envy to all beholders and all hearers, supreme power appeared to be the most satisfying of all earthly goods, the sweetest bliss and sole fruition, the highest and most assuredly valuable of human ideals.[64]

To this ideal, so cunningly interwoven out of strands which are partly true and only partly false, the representatives of philosophic insight in the Dialogues oppose varying objections, from empirical generalizations to a mathematical demonstration of the complete misery of the established tyrant. The exercise of political power is never accepted as the highest of human activities, and never regarded as satisfying to the highest degree the demands of such standards as adequacy, finality, and self-sufficiency. From this standpoint there is one kind of activity which is indubitably more satisfactory and demonstrably more raised above possible criticism : the life of philosophic contemplation.[65] But society cannot allow its finest intellects to enjoy this life to the full ; for it cannot afford to allow such men and women to withdraw wholly from the pressing problems of the community. Accordingly men and women with the aptitude and training for this higher life are compelled to descend into the arena and accept the task of political administration, not as

a highest good, as something desirable and an object of com‑
petition, but as a form of service, as something which they
accept as a social duty.[66]   Thus, to the popular ideal of the
unconstitutional despot, Plato opposes his ideal figure, the
philosopher-king.

The opposition is not, however, between a power-ideal and
a knowledge-ideal, between force and philosophy, or between
Might and Right, as such.   The contrast is rather between
two fillings-in of one and the same power-ideal : between
power directed by instinct, and the same power directed by
reason.   The despot of popular admiration is, when all is
said and done, devoid of vision, a blind leader of the blind,
a man who uses his power, however acquired, merely in ex‑
ternal things, to heap up riches for himself at the expense of
others, to satisfy his desires at the expense of others, in a word,
to exploit the people, to pull down what others have built.   The
struggle for power, in this sense, is always regarded by Plato
as hopeless, unprogressive, leading nowhere, a confused motion
back and forth, which is essentially meaningless.[67]   All that
the tyrant can do with his power is to satisfy his instinctive
cravings, his " unnecessary " appetites.   Additional power
brings him no accession of insight, and his habitual cravings
merely become stronger, more unreasonable, harder to control
and harder to satisfy.   There is no saving grace in him.[68]

Certain elements, then, in the popular ideal, Plato rejects.
But certain other elements he unhesitatingly accepts.   He
accepts, with certain reservations, the high value ascribed to
political power.   He accepts, and indeed insists upon, the
necessity of economic independence, as a *sine qua non* of a
socially valuable career.[69]   He anticipates admiration and
willing obedience to the philosophic wielder of power on the
part of the citizens, hearty co-operation, and the greatest
success, not only in domestic policy, but also in the foreign
relations of the city-state.[70]   He accepts, and indeed empha‑
sizes, the characteristic of " superiority " for his guardians.
But it is not merely as raised above the opinion of others,
in a political sense, that they are to be esteemed superior to
the ordinary run of humanity.   They regard no human thing
as of serious importance, and despise the honours of the present
world, and think nothing of misfortune or even death.[71]   The
reason for this is that in the life of philosophic contemplation,
to which they return at frequent intervals, they have another

and a better life than that of an administrator. With their eyes fixed upon true being, and as spectators of all time and existence, they contemplate and derive continual refreshment and inspiration from the eternal ideas of right and justice, taking up into their souls something of the strength and permanence of the Divine order, and regarding themselves as co-workers with God, when they set in order their own city.[72] Not the exploitation, but the salvation of humanity, is their ideal, and they possess the knowledge and training to realize this ideal.

From the new standpoint of philosophic insight, just what does Plato understand by adequacy and self-sufficiency ? In the first place, he understands a certain all-roundness. The concept of adequacy or completeness means wholeness as opposed to something which falls short of wholeness.[73] In the second place, a systematic, organized wholeness is meant, a wholeness which has been put together out of particular experiences in accordance with a single principle.[74] In the third place, this principle, in accordance with which character-elements are organized into a well-rounded whole, is a rational principle, a principle discovered by philosophic insight and by opinions which are true or objective. That is to say, the character which is adequate or complete is one which is based upon and guided by the philosophic element in the soul, and from this standpoint, to say that the good is adequate or complete is to say that it possesses the characteristic of being a totality organized upon a principle which is not only rational and intelligible, but also is " true " or objective, grounded upon the nature of the universe.[75]

The good is " self-sufficient." More negatively, this means that the good man is peculiarly independent of resources which are mainly external, such as wealth, powerful relatives, and friends, and is superior to mischance and even death.[76] More positively, this freedom from external wants and consequent independence upon others, arises from the fact that the good man contains within himself whatever is necessary for a happy life. That is to say, his character, as such, is based upon philosophic insight into values, an insight which enables him to live at the level of the " real Above," a life which partakes of true being and real existence.[77] Self-sufficiency, then, like adequacy, is a consequence of wholeness, i.e. of a totality organized in accordance with a principle which is not only intelligible but also of objective significance.

Thus understood, to what extent can adequacy, perfection, and self-sufficiency be regarded as *criteria*, as touchstones by which to distinguish good from bad ?   Whatever is good is adequate, perfect, and self-sufficient ;   whatever is bad is inadequate, incomplete, and lacking in many ways.[78]   Assuming this to be established, can we go further, and say that whatever possesses the characteristics of adequacy and self-sufficiency is morally valuable, and that whatever is without these characteristics is evil, or at least morally unsound ?   As we read the Platonic Dialogues, it would seem so, at least at first sight.   The presence and absence of these attributes are frequently used to distinguish characters and actions as good and bad.   Thus the tyrant is regarded as positively evil, on the ground that he is so weak in respect of internal organization and internal resources, and so wholly dependent upon others and upon resources which, like wealth, are external, and because even these resources have little objective significance, his friends, for example, being almost wholly untrustworthy.[79]   But when we examine such cases more closely, we gradually come to see that these characteristics of adequacy and independence, while symptomatic of moral value, are not in themselves final tests or criteria.   It is as indicating that a character under discussion is in genuine contact with the nature of things, i.e. is based upon a rational principle which is identical with the principle in accordance with which the genuine universe, the world of Ideas, is constructed, that adequacy and self-sufficiency can be used to characterize the good and to distinguish it from what is evil. So too it is as showing that the opposite character is out of touch with things-as-they-are, insignificant because blind to the ideal realm, that inadequacy, weakness, and incompleteness or fragmentariness can be used to assist in recognizing the presence of moral evil.[80]   The real test is what lies behind the proposed criteria, and is brought out by the question, is such and such a character real and objective, in touch with things-as-they-are, i.e. with the ideal world, or is it the reverse ? The further consideration of this criterion leads to a consideration, therefore, of the two further criteria of consistency and objectivity.

9. Consistency.

Consistency is, in the first place, understood by Plato in a logical sense, as a standard of scientific method, or a principle governing the research of philosophical interlocutors, as they experiment in common and observe the logical sequences of an argument, following it whithersoever it may lead.[81] If the various consequences of a given position contradict one another, that is a sure sign that there is some logical flaw in the position itself, and that the position in question must, by all who accept the standards involved in the dialectical method, be abandoned.[82] If, on the other hand, all the logical consequences of a given position meet in a single point, or tend in one and the same direction, i.e. are harmonious and consistent, they not only confirm one another, but strengthen, and indeed, in the end, prove the truth of the position under discussion.[83] The ideal of method is thus that scientific thinking should exhibit the characteristics of identity of direction, concentration of evidence upon a single point, harmony and systematic unity.[84]

The reason for accepting consistency as a standard for methodical or scientific thinking is that consistency is a fundamental characteristic of the object of such thinking. The aim of scientific or methodical thinking is to discover a law, to disentangle the Idea from its sensory environment, its "appearances," and study it by the clear light of intellect, not only in its own nature, but also in its relations to other Ideas.[85] Thus discovered, the Idea is found to be a "one in many," i.e. to exhibit the characteristic of identity in diversity, or of consistency and systematic unity, and in their relations to one another the Ideas as a whole constitute precisely such a system.[86] Each Idea is different from each other Idea, but the ideal realm as a whole exhibits in the clearest possible way the attributes of unity in diversity, consistency, systematic harmony.[87] The object of thought thus possesses the characteristic of consistency in the highest degree, and can be approached cognitively only by a method which is capable of taking on this characteristic. Man possesses innately a certain kinship with reality. He has an *Anlage* in his mind which is identical in principle with the most fundamental law of objects. The problem is, so to develop his *Anlage* that the mind can fully apprehend its natural objects.[88] Not every activity of mind will do ; e.g. sense-perception, which many regard as the proper instrument of knowledge, is hopelessly inadequate. Fluidity, instability, impermanence—its prevailing characteristics—are as such incapable of taking on fixity and permanence. Sensory experience and the world of ideal relationships are thus disparate, and no amount of using our eyes and ears will ever give us scientific knowledge.[89] So again of emotional and artistic experience, commonly regarded as the pathway to Truth. This goes somewhat further, for the artist feels his kinship with reality, and is actually capable, when truly inspired, of certain intimations and partial revelations of the ideal world. To these momentary visions he gives powerful expression in the form of rhythms and symbols, and his influence upon mankind is incalculably great. But intense feeling and enthusiasm are uncertain guides, and whether his individual visions are true or false, the artist, as such, does not know. In the absence of a consistent method and a scientific criterion, he frequently, in practise, selects the inferior and less valuable types of experience for artistic embellishment, and such failures in selection sufficiently indicate that following one's feelings is not the best way to seek knowledge of the ideal realm.[90] For the building up of scientific knowledge, then, sensory and emotional experience are inadequate, and it is necessary to seek a method which will develop to the full the human *Anlage*, and thus remain identical in principle with the object to be investigated. This method is to be found in strict analysis and synthesis, and the scientist uses this method, which is the embodiment of consistency, because, by its means, he is enabled to take up into his mind the systematic unity and consistency which are the most fundamental characteristics of the ideal world, i.e. of the objects whose nature he desires to investigate.

It is not, however, in a merely " formal " sense that Platonic consistency is to be understood. Megarian logic has solved its problem when it has succeeded in establishing bare identities and bare differences. Not so with the Platonic dialectician. He rather investigates how far, and in what specific ways A is identical with, or different from, other elements B, C. D . . . in the ideal world. It is not so much the abstract as the concrete universal, which is under observation.[91] The Platonic scientist does not satisfy the demands of his method by establishing, e.g. the proposition that A is A (or B or C) but develops the concept which forms his subject of discourse by expanding its intellectual context, i.e. by expanding its concrete meaning in accordance with the demands of consistency. An example will explain what is meant. Let our subject of discourse be the concept of " the philosopher." The philosopher is, by definition, a lover of truth. This means (1) that he loves *truth*, that he refuses to rest satisfied with appearances and opinions, but presses on until he reaches the end of the intellectual world, and apprehends truth in its own nature.[92] It means further (2) that he loves *all* truth, that he refuses to remain satisfied with a kind of knowledge which is accurate enough as far as it goes but does not cover the entire field, but he loves the *whole*.[93] It means further (3) that he *loves* the truth, that there is something in him that responds to its appeal, that he desires to possess it, to possess it eternally, to realize the fruits of it in his life, in his life as a private citizen or, if he finds himself in the right kind of state, also in the lives of those around him who willingly accept him as their leader.[94] This example illustrates, perhaps, sufficiently how scientific method expands the concrete significance of an Idea in accordance with the demands of consistency. Understood in this concrete sense, consistency is a characteristic of every concept so far as it is an Idea, so far, that is, as it genuinely constitutes an element in the Ideal world, and the function of scientific analysis and synthesis consists precisely in unfolding the meaning and relationships in the ideal world which belong to the particular Idea which happens to be the subject under investigation.

From this it follows that moral Ideas also, e.g. the Ideas of Justice, Courage, Temperance, etc., possess this characteristic of being a one in many, of forming parts of a single consistent system, and are capable of intellectual expansion at the hands of the scientific student of ethics.[95] But it should be noted that it is not in virtue of any specifically ethical quality that they are expansible—mathematical and aesthetical ideas are equally expansible—but in virtue of their being Ideas and constituting portions of the Ideal system. It is their ethical quality which gives them their moral significance, their impressiveness and importance for the conduct of life ; but it is from their more general, metaphysical or ideal quality that they derive their consistency and expansibility. When, then, it is demonstrated that what is commonly accepted as a moral idea—e.g. money-making, power-seeking, or the pursuit of pleasure as the goal of life and the supreme good—falls apart, in the hands of the scientific analyst, into elements which are disparate, i.e. leads, when consistently expanded, to consequences which contradict one another, the argument proves not so much that the ideal in question is lacking in ethical quality as that it is lacking in logical quality.   Thus, when it is shown that the ideal of money-making leads to a plutocratic and oligarchic constitution, and that a state ruled by oligarchs eventually destroys itself, so that the ideal of money-making leads not to success in money-making but to financial ruin, if not to death, what is directly proved is that this popular ideal contradicts itself and is thus irrational, is not an Idea at all, cannot be regarded as forming part of the Ideal system.[96]   It follows from this, of course, that it is not a *moral* Idea either ; but the point of the argument is, primarily, to deny that it is an Idea at all, in any final sense.   So too of the argument against Thrasymachus.   The point made is that systematic *pleonexia*, which *can* take place only under the presupposition of a stable social order, is inconsistent with the order which it presupposes, and leads inevitably to the disruption of all social order, in this way destroying its own possibility.   As an ideal for social leadership, it is thus self-contradictory, and thus cannot possibly constitute an element in the ideal system, of which consistency is so prominent an attribute.[97]   From this it follows that it is not a *moral* ideal either, but the argument is directed, primarily, against its claim to be regarded as rational or as one of the ideal patterns which together constitute reality.   It is with a clear consciousness of this that the Platonic Socrates sums up the discussion with the statement that so far as the specific nature of the moral idea (justice) under discussion is concerned nothing definite has been discovered.[98]   So too in the argument with Callicles, he states that he himself knows nothing as to the specific moral truths involved—here the idea of temperance is under discussion—but that he is convinced that such a position as has been maintained by Callicles is contradictory and irrational.[99]

From these and other similar instances it follows that, for Plato, consistency is a criterion, not so much of the morality, as of the ideality of certain situations or proposed actions.

It tests their right to be accepted as ideals at all, i.e. as fitted to take their place in the ideal system which constitutes reality, and to be regarded as fully rational. Thus understood, the term is employed in two main senses : (1) logical, i.e. as one of the standards necessarily involved in the dialectical method. Two or more interlocutors, in order to come to grips with each other, in order to discuss at all, necessarily observe the requirements of consistency. In this sense consistency is used to test whether a given subject of discourse—e.g. the Parmenidean " one," or pleasure or power claiming to be the chief good—can be discussed consistently at all, or whether it leads to contradictions which make discussion itself ludicrous and absurd.[100] The second sense (2) is more metaphysical, less a law of thought, and more a law of ultimate entities, a law expressing the relationship to one another of elements in the metaphysically real world of Ideas.[101] In this sense consistency tests the right of a proposed course of action to be regarded as " real " rather than as illusory, i.e., tests the objective validity of the subject of discourse.[102] This sense seems to be the more final for Plato. Interlocutors observe the requirements of consistency, not merely in order to discuss with one another, but especially in order that, by means of such discussion, they may establish contact with the ideal world which constitutes reality. In our search for the Platonic criterion which distinguishes between good and evil, we thus pass from the study of " consistency," in the logical sense, to its profounder sense, in which it coincides with " objectivity."

10. Objectivity.

From the time of Thales to the time of Plotinus, the reference to the objective or the real as a final standard by which to determine the value of actions is characteristic for Greek thought. Everywhere around him, in the eclipses of the heavenly bodies, in the calms and sudden storms of the Aegean, in the rapid social and political developments from Magna Graecia to Persia, the Greek saw change, instability, a bewilderingly kaleidoscopic movement of life. On the outskirts of the Greek world, e.g. among the Heracliteans of Asia Minor and the Sophists of the North and West, there was a tendency to see in life nothing but a struggle of conflicting wills-to-power, each equally arbitrary and subjective, a kind of atomistic individualism, in which might made right, and intelligence was a convenient instrument in the hands of the unconstitutional dictator for the Machiavellian deception of his less clever subjects as well as of his competitors for power. In Greece itself, under the influence of a historically successful imperialism, this doctrine found a measure of acceptance among the aspiring and half-educated scions of noble and wealthy families ; but for the typically Greek thinker Change always constitutes a challenge to seek for some underlying Permanent, a Reality of which the changing phenomena are but the Appearances, and the chief solution of the problem along these lines is found in the Dialogues of Plato.

The problem is, starting from the changing phenomena of experience, somehow to penetrate beneath the surface and discover the underlying reality, a reality which shall satisfy the demand of reason for unity, consistency, and meaning. The only way in which this problem can be solved is by using a method which will sift the phenomena so as to extract from them all of their content which can satisfy the ideal of consistency and systematic unity. This is the dialectical method, and in the hands of Plato it is used, with clear self-consciousness, for precisely this purpose.[103]

All experience, however illusory, however much a matter of " appearance," is at least partly objective, contains some references to reality, although its reference to the final reality, the system of Ideas, may be indirect and implicit. For example, sensory experience, however fluctuating and illusory, does convey information concerning the physical object which stimulates eye or ear,[104] and the physical object certainly partakes of the reality which Plato ascribes to all objects which can act upon others.[105] Scientific method cannot, however, extract from sensory experience any kernel of reality which, while remaining at this level—i.e., remaining a matter of direct sensory experience—will also satisfy the demands of the method for system, consistency, unity. There is no possibility of erecting a structure which shall be both of sensory and of scientific value. For in the hands of the dialectician sensory experience inevitably develops inconsistencies of all sorts, and the problems thus raised cannot be solved until we rise above the level of sensation.[106] Judged, then, by reference to the standard of objectivity, sensory experience, so far as it remains sensory, fails to satisfy the demands of reason.

Unsatisfactory, however, as it is in this form, sensation yet furnishes the basis upon which something a little more helpful can be erected. Freed from fluctuations, made more permanent and, as it were, standardized in the form of memories, such experiences,[107] when synthesized with yet further sensations, can give us " opinion "—a kind of experience which expresses, in condensed and concentrated form, the meaning-elements common to many memories and sensations.[108] Opinion, however, is not only less fluctuating than sensation. Containing, as it does, the elements common to many experiences of the same type, it tends to be also more consistent than the single sensory experience, and thus more nearly satisfies the demands of scientific method. And yet, there is a reason which prevents it from ever being fully satisfactory. Analysis and synthesis of our opinions, resulting in something which still remains opinion, leave us with a certain deficiency, a deficiency inherent in the nature of opinion as such. Opinion may be correct and true, objective and sound, and, so far, from a strictly practical standpoint, e.g. as a guide to specific action, is satisfactory enough. If the opinion, on the basis of which we act, is itself based upon reality, then our action reflects the true nature of the reality in question ; e.g. if we wish to reach a certain place, and if our opinion as to the route which should be followed is correct, we shall reach the place.[109] But the difficulty is that opinion, as such, is merely opinion, and contains in itself no criterion of its own correctness. It may thus, equally well, be false, out of touch with things-as-they-are. If our opinion as to the route to be followed is false, we shall not reach the place.[110]

Opinion, then, may be true, or it may be false. If opinions are false, no scientific manipulations can extract from them objectively valid conclusions.[111] Even if we imagine two false opinions " accidentally " so opposed to one another as to cancel out in such a way as to leave a statement which happened to be true, this result itself could be no more than an ungrounded belief, *right* opinion, possibly, but still only *opinion*, without insight into its own truth or falsity, and thus, as such, unsatisfactory from a theoretical standpoint. If opinions are true, however, or at least largely true, Plato thinks it possible, by comparing them carefully, by a thorough analysis and synthesis, to cancel out the false elements and to retain the positive element common to all the true opinions, and this method of sifting does actually result in giving us something satisfactory, for it gives us the Idea itself.[112]   But so long as we remain at the level of opinion, the reality undoubtedly contained within the opinion cannot be extracted in such a way as to fulfil the requirement of the scientist. The reality which is finally extracted has raised us above the level of opinion, to the level of the Idea.

To the level of the Idea. Yes, but not to the level of the Idea conidered in its full nature as ideal. At the present level, which we may perhaps characterize as the higher level of opinion or the lower level of knowledge, the level of the special or departmental sciences,[113] the idea is still an empirical generalization. It is raised above the mere groping which precedes science, and has won its way through to a certain degree of clearness, but it is still empirical, still closely bound up with the masses of opinion from which it has been with difficulty extracted. That is to say, it is still grounded in sensory experience, still verified by reference to sensory experiments. It may be compared with other ideas which fall within its own group, and may thus be slightly further loosed from its moorings in an experience which is still, in the end, sensory ; but so long as these other ideas are at its own level, no amount of intellectual manipulation can make this level more than the level of departmental knowledge, a type of knowledge which is still partly " blind," i.e., still devoid of the highest insight.[114]   The standpoint and con-clusions of the departmental sciences, resting, as these do, upon assumptions, upon something accepted, taken for granted, still retain to a certain degree the nature of " opinion," and it is only when, by a still wider synthesis of these assumptions themselves, the element which has been taken for granted is finally grounded, and grounded in a principle which is itself ideal and completely permeable to reason, that we reach the stage of perfect system, perfect unity, perfect consistency, perfect intelligibility. Reality is now envisaged as a system of all the Ideas unified and made intelligible in their interrela-tions   by   the   supreme   principle   of   their   nature   and organization, the Idea of Good, and in this vision the demands of consistency and objectivity are fully satisfied. The prob-lem has been solved.[115]

This ideal vision is difficult for the individual to realize. But when and so far as realized, it is not something tenuous, formal, abstract, less vital than the ordinary human experiences at the level of sensation or opinion. On the contrary, these more elementary experiences are fragmentary, contradictory, overlaid with misleading associations which obscure what sources of insight we do possess.[116] The result of the sifting method of dialectic is to give us the genuine elements of reality which underlie the tissue of associations which constitute "common" sense, and these elements, separated out and apprehended in their interrelations, are concrete, rich and vital in the highest degree. The experience of the dialectician is not a convenient epistemological arrangement of formal patterns expressive of unity and diversity, but is a rational, clear-cut experiencing of the actual, concrete structure of reality itself.[117] The Permanent underlying Change, the Real which underlies Appearance, has been finally discovered, and the source of superficiality, irrelevance, and deception has been finally removed.

When, therefore, it is stated that the value of conduct and character should be estimated by reference to the degree of "objectivity" which they manifest, what is meant is that conduct organized and directed by insight into the genuine structure of reality is not a house of cards, or the baseless fabric of a dream-illusion, but is firm as reality, is itself real and an organic portion of reality itself.[118] A character which is formed upon the ideal patterns, takes up into itself, as constituent elements in its own structure, the principles discovered by scientific method. In fact, the philosopher gradually becomes the embodiment of the ideal system, each pattern which he discovers in the universe having its counterpart in his own mind, so that the macrocosm and the microcosm are, at least in principle, identical, the visible universe and the knowing mind being two expressions of one and the same system of Ideas.[119] It is because the philosopher has the root of the matter in him, that he is capable of understanding the universe, and the process of philosophic study is thus at one and the same time (1) development of insight into the ideal patterns and their interconnection in the universe, and (2) the development in his own character of structural lines corresponding precisely to the patterns and their interconnections which his insight

G

is discovering. The character and conduct of such a man escape subjectivity and fallacy, and are rational and objective in the highest sense.[120] When, then, it is stated that objectivity is a moral standard, what is meant is that actions and characters are of value precisely so far as they express the genuine nature of a rational universe, and of a universe which is not only rational, not only satisfactory to the intellect, but is also existence, *the* universe which *is*, and is rational. This certainly constitutes a standpoint for deciding upon the value of actions, and it is impossible to conceive of one which could be more final. As Plato puts it, we have come to the end of the intellectual realm. For the philosophic judge, i.e., for the finest and most highly trained reason, such a standard is final, absolutely true.

So far we have considered, separately and in detail, the evidence upon which universal assent, written law, pleasure, benefit, social solidarity, etc., are regarded as furnishing us with moral standards, with criteria upon which we can rely in our attempts to distinguish good from evil. We should now be in a position to put together the results of these separate investigations, and, by summing up the evidence in a more general way, to come to a final conclusion as to Plato's general attitude on the moral standard.

As we look over the results of our separate studies, we note that nearly all the proposed moral standards have one thing in common : it is from the standpoint of opinion rather than of knowledge, that they are accepted at their face value as moral standards. As opinion deepens into knowledge or philosophic insight, they are seen to be inadequate and partial, pointing beyond themselves to another standard as more final, a standard which alone gives to them what moral significance they possess. In our more general summary of the evidence, we can thus take this as our single point of comparison, and can ask, in each case, what this final standard is, to which, by the verdict of philosophic knowledge, the special standard seems to point.

Let us begin with " universal assent." If we ask what is the exact content common to all opinions on moral subjects, and whence derived, we find that the content itself is highly general and vague, amounting to little more than agreement that there *is* a distinction between good and evil, that the distinction is of great practical importance, and that the good possesses characteristics such as independence upon externals, adequacy, desirability, etc. If we ask upon what this universal assurance is grounded, we find that it rests upon the general experience of the race, especially upon general social experience, and that this is the gradually sifted-out residuum of countless fluctuating sensations and associations. So far as these matters of universal opinion are correct—and Plato believes that, at least on these general points, they *are* correct—this means that in the general experience of the race, a certain amount of reality has become sifted out from appearances, and that these general opinions are right and true, as being based upon the reality which is experienced even in the less valuable forms of sensation and association. The final standard, then, by reference to which the value of universal assent as a criterion is decided, is its objectivity, the degree to which the content of universal assent corresponds to the nature of the real, i.e. the ideal world.

So too legal enactments represent, to a large extent, the workings, upon the community, of forces such as hunger, disease, war, trade, etc., which are a part of physical nature— so much so, in fact, that the institutions of law derive a large portion of their objectivity from the objectivity of these great natural forces.[121] The highest kind of law, however, is not an unreflective reaction to the stimulation of the environment, but is a deliberate attempt, on the part of the philosophic legislator, to reshape the constitution, so as to reproduce, in its structure, the structure of the system of Ideas, and, so far as he is successful,[122] law has not only the objectivity of nature, but shares also in the very essence of objectivity, the *ratio essendi* itself. The measure of his success, and in consequence the final standard by which the value of law itself is judged, is the objectivity of the result, i.e., the extent to which legal enactments reproduce the structure of the ideal system.

So also with pleasure. Plato's position is that pleasure, which accompanies the functioning of our action-systems, is actually more pleasant, more intense and more permanent, according as it is more objective, more real. That is to say, the organization of our action-systems upon the ideal patterns which together constitute the metaphysically real world, is accompanied by a pleasure which is more real and genuine, not only in a metaphysical sense, but actually as experienced pleasure, than any pleasures which could accompany action-systems organized upon some plan which is not attuned to the nature of the universe. For these, being out of touch with things-as-they-are, would tend to be narrow and thus unsatisfactory and in some conflict with themselves, as well as ill-adjusted to their environment, and their hedonic tone would thus inevitably be inferior. Quantity of experienced pleasure, then, depending upon and thus representing the structure of the ideal world, can be used as a moral standard, as a test of the objective value of the different ends which men pursue. The final moral standard, however, which gives to " quantity of pleasure " its significance as an index to values, is objectivity, or the degree to which the organization of character corresponds to the organization of the real world of Ideas.

The case of aesthetical quality is not, perhaps, so clear. Essentially a matter of rhythms and balances and ordered recurrences of accent, in a word, the introduction, into sensuous experience, of an intellectually apprehensible principle of order (symmetry) in such a way as to bring about a relatively intense emotional reaction, aesthetical quality is, of course, an attribute of whatever exhibits these characteristics. Ethical character, for instance, is an organization of sensuous experience in terms of an intellectually apprehensible principle ; it is orderly, balanced, and harmonious, and makes a certain appeal to the emotions ; it thus possesses aesthetical quality, and this is fully recognized by Plato. On the other hand, just as pleasure may be obtained from many sources, some of which are mutually exclusive,[123] so also of aesthetical pleasure ; and a study of the actual situations and character-types enhanced by the wizardry of the artist leads Plato to the conclusion that ethically inferior characters and situations, into which the element of contrast and conflict—an element ideally absent from the ethical character—enters, admit of a greater degree of aesthetical quality. There is therefore a difference between pleasure and aesthetical quality. For while different situations, $a, b, c, \ldots n$, all give pleasure to certain corresponding characters, $A, B, C, \ldots N$, a maximum of pleasure is produced by situations which are ethical, so that the pleasure experienced by the ethical character is demonstrably superior to that of the others. But with aesthetical quality, while *any* situations which are orderly in such a way as to stimulate emotion, have this quality, actually the maximal emotional reaction is produced, not by ethical situations and characters, i.e. not by what is orderly as such, but rather by what is emotionally exciting. Maximal artistic experience is compatible with a comparatively small amount of objective orderliness,[124] and thus consistency—absence of contrast and conflict—as well as objectivity, is of less importance, in dealing with aesthetical quality, than in dealing with pleasure. There is thus no direct correlation between moral and aesthetical quality. It remains true that the " rightly and nobly ordered mind and character " will always possess aesthetical quality ; but it cannot be inferred that, because a given character is beautiful and affects the beholder like a work of art,[125] it is also of high ethical quality. Aesthetical quality is always an accompaniment, never a condition of ethical quality ; and as it accompanies it only as a necessary consequence of the orderliness of the ethical character, which orderliness in turn is dependent upon and representative of the ideal order, it follows that it is really the ideal order, or objectivity, which gives to aesthetical quality whatever meaning it possesses as confirmatory evidence of moral quality. The final standard, then, to which the occasional use of aesthetical quality in this way points, is objectivity, or the extent to which a given character or situation reproduces the orderliness of the ideal world.

The case of expediency or benefit is more plain. To benefit a man is to help him to realize his own Idea, to become more fully a man, more fully the embodiment of Justice and of the other qualities which go to make up the ideal of humanity, i.e. to assist him to take up reality into his own life and thus become more nearly the embodiment of the ideal or ultimately real system. When, therefore, it is stated that expediency or benefit constitute a standard by reference to which we can estimate the value of actions and characters, what is meant is that the degree to which an action realizes the ideal, embodies the objective and metaphysically real system of Ideas, is the final standard of value, and that anything which helps to bring this about, or is " beneficial," derives its value from this final standard of objectivity or realization of the ideal world.

The case of " contribution to the life of the social whole " is no less clear.   While, at the level of opinion, it is possible to support class legislation, to aim at the interest of the stronger or governing class, through thick and thin, with complete honesty of purpose, but with a certain deficiency of insight, at the higher level of knowledge it is beyond doubt that the ideal for the social group is to be fully representative of the virtues of wisdom, courage, temperance, and justice, so that the individual citizen realizes his own Idea in harmony with the Ideas of all citizens who belong ideally to the group, and the group as a whole realizes, as completely as possible, the system of ideal patterns laid up in heaven, the City of God.   The valuable thing here is undoubtedly the realization of the ideal system, and when it is asked, Does such and such an action contribute towards the life of the social whole ? what is meant is, Does it contribute to realize the ideal life, to make empirically real on earth what is ideally real in heaven ?   The final standard here is thus undoubtedly objectivity, or realization of the ideal patterns which together constitute ultimate reality.

The case of orderliness can similarly be in no doubt. At the level of opinion, the orderliness of a psychic disposition, of obedience to the powers that be on earth, of the starry heaven, etc., can be mistaken for trustworthy moral standards, though in themselves these may be, in spite of their relative orderliness, of but slight moral significance.   But at the level of knowledge it becomes clear that it is ideal orderliness, the orderliness which is found in the mutual relations of the ideal elements which together constitute ultimate reality, which gives whatever moral significance and value attaches to human and physical laws.   The final standard is thus clearly objectivity, i.e. the extent to which the orderliness of an institution or character corresponds to and embodies the ideal orderliness, the orderliness of the final reality.

So too with adequacy and self-sufficiency.   While opinions may go so far astray as actually to invest the concept of the unconstitutional despot with these attributes of the highest good, from the higher standpoint of knowledge, to say that something is adequate and independent, means that it constitutes an organized whole, and that its principle of organization is identical with the principle which underlies the ideal or ultimately real system.   It is thus objectivity, or its reproduction of the structure of reality, which makes the ethical character adequate and independent, and it is objectivity which, here also, is the real standard of the value-judgment.

Finally, consistency is understood by Plato, not merely as a logical principle or law of thought, but also as a law of things, a law which expresses the inter-relationship of the Ideas, and it is used, as we have seen, to test, not so much the morality, as the ideality of a proposed line of action, i.e. to test its objectivity or correspondence with the ideal system which constitutes ultimate reality. The final standard, then, here also, is objectivity.

We are now in a position to sum up our conclusion briefly. The final standard of value, in every case, has turned out to be objectivity, or the degree to which a proposed course of action, or a character under investigation, is patterned upon the ideal principles which, for Plato, constitute reality. These principles are organized in terms of a single principle, the Idea of Good, i.e. the principle of Value as such, value and reality being identified ; and a character or an action has value, precisely to the degree in which it is based upon and tends to realize the principle of Value itself. Understood in the light of this final principle, i.e. as expressions of ultimate Value or of the essence of Reality, universal assent, written law, quantity of pleasure, expediency, consistency, etc., can safely be used as proximate standards, by which to measure the value of actions and characters in particular situations and from particular standpoints. It is in this sense that they are used by the Platonic dialectician. But apart from such transvaluation in the light of this principle, they belong to the region of opinion, the region of twilight and moral blindness, and cannot safely be used as moral standards at all. It is insight into Reality, or the ideal realm and its principle, alone, which enables the philosophic judge to make value-judgments which are reliable and valid.

CHAPTER IV

THE PSYCHOLOGICAL ASPECT OF THE MORAL JUDGMENT, (a) ANALYSIS ; (b) GENESIS

SO far we have investigated the questions, (1) Who is entitled to pass judgment in matters of ethics ? (2) What are the objective elements common to all situations judged to be ethical ? (3) What are the standards which the judge applies in coming to a decision ? It is now incumbent upon us to pass from the objective to the subjective aspect, and to investigate the moral judgment itself. We wish to discover how the judge comes to his decisions, (a) what it is in his mind or personality which actually makes the judgment, i.e. what are the psychological elements involved in the moral judgment as such, and (b) how these elements become fused together in the case of the recognized authority on moral questions, i.e. to trace the development of the moral judgment. These two problems belong (a) to analytic, and (b) to genetic, psychology, respectively. After completing these two inquiries, we should then be in a position to sum up our results, and answer clearly and fully, what it is in the character and personality of the moral judge, which enables him to come to his decisions, i.e. what really does the judging.

(a) Analysis of the moral judgment.

If we attempt to put together the very various hints and statements in the Dialogues as to the psychological basis of the moral value-judgment, we find that these fall, naturally and inevitably, under three main heads. These are :—(1) Nature—i.e. original psychological equipment for making value-judgments *überhaupt ;* (2) Experience—i.e. a development of the " natural " equipment in accordance with repeated social experience, so as to attain a new equilibrium at the level of social habit ; (3) Reason, or the spirit of philosophy— i.e. a development of the natural equipment in accordance with insight into ultimate reality. Under these three heads is grouped together for special consideration all the evidence found in the Dialogues. We shall proceed to consider this evidence, inductively and without prejudice,[1] under these three heads.

1. Nature.

A value-sense of some sort is universal, and is found, not only among human beings, who possess reason, but among animals generally. All beings which have perception have, as such, a quasi-instinctive interest in satisfactions as opposed to dissatisfactions.[2] Conation as such, even in its widest and most elementary sense, is bound up with satisfactions and dissatisfactions.[3] Wherever we have any form of the pleasure-pain sense, we have the basis and rudimentary beginnings of the value-judgment.[4] Finally, as this pleasure-pain sense functions in connection with (a) all forms of sensation without exception, from the simplest vision and audition to the complex organic sensation of bodily well-being,[5] (b) all kinds of bodily movement as such, from a simple twitch of limb or tail to the articulate use of the voice,[6] (c) all activities whatever which lead to the satisfaction of instinctive wants such as hunger, thirst, and the sex-appetite,[7] we can conclude that the value-sense also is as universal as life and consciousness. So far as any activity is pleasant, it is sought after, and regarded as a good. So far as it is unpleasant, it is avoided, and regarded as an evil.[8]

This, then, is the primitive and universal type of experience upon which all elementary value-judgments rests. At this level, man is a bundle of quasi-instinctive wants, each of which seeks its own satisfaction independently of the rest. The general result is somewhat chaotic, inconsistent and confused, a matter of conflicting and unintelligent special interests.[9] Out of this confusion, however, there gradually emerge certain groups of satisfaction-seeking tendencies which drift together, and thus give rise to distinct types of value-judgment. In the first place (a), man is distinguished from other animals by taking pleasure, not merely in any and every kind of movement, in movement as such, but especially in ordered, rhythmic movement, in sequences and recurrences appropriately accentuated and stressed.[10] This feeling after law and order in the sphere of movement and kinaesthetic sensation, expressing itself primitively in the choric dance, is the basis of art in all its forms,[11] and thus, even at the natural or quasi-instinctive level of a feeling after the rhythmical, and avoidance of the unrhythmical, furnishes us with the rudimentary beginnings of taste or the *aesthetic* value-judgment.[12]   In the second place (*b*), the group of gregarious or herd instincts, including the natural dispositions at the bottom of physical courage and quietness or moderation,[13] when associated with this human feeling after law and order, results in some kind of instinctive analogon of Justice, a set of dispositions which seek satisfaction in a social life of law and order, with all the social standards which this inevitably involves.[14]   This feeling after satisfaction in the sphere of orderly social life furnishes us with the beginnings of moral sentiment and the *ethical* value-judgment.   In the third place (*c*), under the urge of what we may, perhaps, designate as curiosity, the instinctive reaching-out after novel experiences, primarily of a sensory kind,[15] the human feeling after law and order seeks a certain satisfaction in cognitive experience as such, from neat solutions of specific puzzles and problems[16] to the creation of systems of philosophy, and thus, in the satisfaction which it takes in what hangs together consistently, gives us the beginnings of the *logical* value-judgment.[17]   In the fourth place (*d*), the feeling after satisfaction as such contains the germ of a distinction between apparent and real satisfaction, and the search for a genuine satisfaction, something more permanent and more fundamentally satisfying than our ordinary experience, is also universal.[18]   This feeling after reality is not exhausted in art, social conduct, and science, but seeks a satisfaction which shall be less specialized, more fundamental and more universal.   In certain of its forms this tendency becomes a reaching out after God and a yearning to become like him, and thus gives rise to the feeling of reverence, the beginnings of the *religious* value-judgment.[19]   In its more intellectual forms, i.e. when raised out of the level of mere feeling to the more logical level of a feeling after truth and the methodical, scientific search for reality,[20] the ideal of " assimilation to God " becomes the ideal of attaining knowledge of ultimate reality, and the feeling of pleasure which underlies this research magnificent furnishes us with what we may perhaps designate as the beginnings of the *metaphysical* value-judgment, the most fundamental of all our senses of value, and the most universal, linking together again, at the upper *limen*, as it were, of our value-sense, the specialized forms of the value-judgment in art, social conduct, and science, which were originally also linked together at the lower *limen* of the general feeling after satisfaction and pleasure as such.

While the specialization referred to is not complete, so that the aesthetical, the ethical, and the logical standpoints at times overlap and partially coincide, they are, in virtue of the feeling for law and order common to them all, frequently in the Dialogues opposed to the more general feeling after the pleasant as such, on the ground that they are more definite and consistent, less chaotic and uncontrolled, less animal and more rational, more human, more Hellenic.[21] But the general and unspecialized feeling after satisfaction as such is also opposed to them, in respect of their specific and narrow exclusion of value-in-general in favour of art-values, science-values, and social-conduct values. In the final case of the metaphysical standpoint, the special forms, as such, are transcended, and it is only the element of value as such, common to all value-judgments without exception, which is extracted by the dialectician and, in the form of the Idea of Good, accepted as absolute and unconditioned value.[22] That is to say, the metaphysical value-judgment accepts the general element present in the universal pleasure-pain experience as such, and transcends the specific distinctions between art, social conduct, and logic—upon the retention of which distinctions the specialized forms of the value-judgment depend—and thus attains to the universal essence of value, which was present from the first, though obscurely, in the feeling after satisfaction as such. The specialized forms are, in fact, at the level which Plato regards as clearer than " opinion " but less clear than " science," and need to be transcended if the dialectician is ever to get at the full truth which is present, however obscurely, at the natural, or quasi-instinctive level. The identity between the elementary value-sense and the final discoveries of philosophic insight is brought out in such passages as those in which Plato maintains that " love " is essentially " love of the good,"[23] or elaborates the conception of the " eye of the soul," which is present in every normal human being. It is true that the eye of the soul requires a special education to free it from the influence of sensation, emotion, and prejudice, but, once set free, the primitive value-sense described under this term passes by an absolutely continuous development into the final insight of the philosopher-king.[24]

The natural level thus contains, in its feeling after satisfaction, and especially in the specifically human feeling after *orderly* satisfaction, an *Anlage* or germ may become differentiated and integrated again in such a way as to furnish the beginnings of the aesthetical, the ethical, the logical, the religious, and the metaphysical value-judgment. But in itself, and left to itself, the natural level is not likely to develop beyond the merest beginnings of these value-judgments. The eye of the soul is there, it is true, but it is darkened and overlaid by all sorts of coverings and obscuring elements. In all of us there is a lawless, wild-beast element which belongs to our animal nature as such, and these animal passions are like leaden weights which keep us down and prevent us from soaring aloft into the upper realm.[25] Or, by another analogy, our nature is like a tender plant, which requires very special treatment if it is to attain the full development of its potentialities, and not to be stunted, feeble, and withered.   Under purely " natural " conditions, as in the case of a wild plant, Plato is doubtful if the human plant can ever attain its ideal development.[26]   It needs help, and the help must, in the first place, come from " heaven."   There are, he believes, in every large community a few " divinely inspired " men who have developed a high sense of values,[27] and the advice of such men, even though they are themselves at the level of inspiration, i.e. of an " opinion " which, though right or true, is ungrounded and not yet reduced to strict science, as in the well-known cases of Themistocles, Pericles, and Cimon,[28] is of the utmost value to the community which needs their leadership.   For, *qua* inspired and " friends of God,"[29] they establish or confirm already established institutions in such a way as to reflect the nature of reality and thus to be of genuine and permanent assistance to the community in its upward struggle towards the higher life.[30]   So too it is only with especially fine natures that even the educational system of his ideal community can do anything,[31] and these exceptionally fine natures as such are regarded as " divinely inspired,"[32] as well as somewhat rare.[33] On the average, human nature runs after sense-pleasures and private, exclusive enjoyments, and remains obstinately blind to the higher things of life,[34] and in general we must admit that, while every man undoubtedly contains the germ of all sorts of value-judgments, he is not likely, apart from an especially fortunate disposition and an unusually excellent environment, to rise above the instinctive and associated level, the level of unassisted nature, the level of ordinary sensual humanity.

2. Experience.

Social experience, arising from the grouping of men together in their civic life, and especially in the social institutions of the gynmasium, theatre, law-court, and assembly,[35] develops a standard set of community values, values into which the young citizen grows up and which he accepts because they have become, through education, a part of himself.[36] He takes pleasure in activities which give pleasure to the majority of his fellow-citizens, and is pained at activities which grieve them, and this social or community value-sense is further developed until it becomes second nature, not only as a result of constant social pressure, but also, if necessary, of the more technical device of indictment in the courts if he ventures to think otherwise than as the many-headed beast thinks in such matters.[37] This level of acceptance of social standards represents the level at which most men, even in the ideal community, are to be found, the level, not of insight and scientific knowledge, but of " opinion," a value-judgment grounded in the pleasure-pain sense of numbers, masses of humanity, a kind of greatest common measure of human valuations.

In itself, this constitutes a certain advance upon the unstandardized reaction of the individual. In both cases we have a somewhat simple reaching out after satisfaction as such, an elementary and unspoiled sense of the value of a maximum of pleasure and a minimum of pain, a feeling for the harmonious, consistent, and permanent balancing of all human activities in such a way as to keep these functioning successfully for as long a time as possible. But as compared with the value-sense of the unaided individual, the standardized value-sense of public opinion represents a further development. It is based upon a wider range of experiences, and the organization of these, with the cancelling out of whatever is contradictory and the concentration in a single direction of whatever tendencies are mutually harmonious and consistent, necessarily penetrates further into the sources of empirical satisfaction.   Greater breadth and greater depth : these are the characteristics which distinguish the social value-sense from the primitive value-sense of the mere individual.[38]

In the case of the aesthetical value-judgment, this distinction is strongly marked.   Left to themselves, the opinions of individuals as to the aesthetic value of works of art differ and conflict with one another,[39] and the effect of artistic surroundings upon the characters and judgment of those who select those surroundings only on the basis of individual pleasure, is to confirm them in their diversity, and thus to tend to disrupt the community, as well as to make the artists themselves hardly fit for membership in the ethical polity.[40] But under the influence of the herd-instinct, a certain uniformity begins to make its appearance.   The individual accepts the agreement of his fellows as a standard of artistic appreciation, and learns to conform to this standard.   What the majority regard as beautiful, he comes to regard as beautiful, and what they regard as ugly, he also comes to regard as ugly.   The clamour of the spectators or audience, whether by way of applause or by way of condemnation, necessarily influences his own judgment, especially where that judgment is not already formed,[41] and his individual value-sense thus becomes enlarged to the capacity of the community judgment *re* aesthetic values.

So too in the case of the moral value-judgment.   Individuals differ enormously in their estimation of the moral value of particular actions and situations,[42] chiefly, perhaps, because they are carried away in diverse directions by their exclusive interest in pleasure-pain experiences, an interest which makes it difficult for them to realize the value of public good, good in which all can share, as opposed to private and exclusive good, good which only one can enjoy to the exclusion of other competitors.[43]   Because of this individualism, they find it hard to co-operate in the task of building up the community, and exhibit, in many ways, a tendency towards social disruption.[44]   But, as in the case of the aesthetic value-judgment, so here : the influence of public opinion is so great, especially as expressed in such community-institutions as the gymnasium, law-court, and assembly, that no amount of private thinking or even of private training will really enable the individual to stand up against an overwhelming flood of popular opinion.[45]   He inevitably accepts, at least in their main outlines, the traditional community value-judgments, and comes to have the notions of good and evil which the public in general has, and not only to act, but also to think and feel, as the public acts and thinks and feels.[46] When further we remember that in matters which affect the community values directly, there is not only the general social atmosphere, but the law of the state to be reckoned with as well, with its very definite and explicit system of penalties for non-conformity, we realize that the part played by social experience in the total value-judgment in matters of morality is of extreme importance.[47]

In the case of the logical value-judgment, i.e. the feeling for consistency and for the enlargement of experience by some kind of scientific method, something of the same sort is to be noted. This is brought out with especial clearness in the frequent contrasts between the methods of the professional teachers of higher education on the one hand, and of Socrates, with his new instrument of thought, the clear-cut concept, on the other. The professional teachers of the day are at the level, not of knowledge, but of opinion, and give to their students a reflection of the opinions of the social group in a slightly more vivid and slightly more consistent form than their students could obtain from their non-professional friends and teachers.[48] In this they are influenced, primarily, not so much by abstract logical standards as by the economic interest in a cash remuneration for their services, which practically confines them to reproducing the prejudices of the wealthy and powerful classes. And yet, owing to the need of their students for training in public speaking, there is a certain pressure which tends to develop the feeling for logical consistency,[49] and in particular for a professional method which will aid in piecing together scraps of individual experience so as to produce a harmonious texture and pattern in the form of set speeches.[50] This function of social pressure in developing a certain demand for consistency and scientific method is further brought out by Plato's proposal for State endowment of research in the neglected field of solid geometry.[51] The precise effect of this social pressure upon the logical value-sense of the individual is two-fold. In the first place, it stresses not only vigour, but also continuity of thought, thus stimulating persistent and systematic thinking, as opposed to laconic *aperçus*,[52] and in the second place it directs this systematic thinking into channels which lead towards social service rather than to merely personal advancement.[53]

In the case of the religious value-sense, the influence of social experience expresses itself chiefly in the formation of certain institutions, the function of which is to care for the religious interests of the group as such, and for individuals mainly as members of the group.   Such institutions are found in the Orphic cult and the Mysteries on the one hand,[54] and civic and national cults on the other,[55] with their organized forms of worship and their definite aims and spheres of influence.   The tendency is thus towards a certain uniformity and orthodoxy, enforced primarily by social custom, but at times— as in the notorious case of Socrates himself—also by the extreme force of the law.   It is to be noted that in his ideal community Plato himself believes in the legal enforcement of orthodoxy on cardinal points of doctrine,[56] as well as in the influence of general social pressure on subordinate points.[57] The religious value-sense thus developed is primarily a *group* value-sense, and the function of the Mysteries or of the cult of ancestral or civic Divinities, while these do assist individuals to satisfy a certain yearning, a reaching out after some form of " blessedness," is primarily to render assistance to individuals not as such, but as initiates, as citizens, as members of a particular social organization.

In all these ways, then, the individual ceases to think and act as a mere individual, and begins to think and act as the group thinks and acts.   In place of individual value-judgments, we have public opinion, the value-judgment of the group as such, giving a certain impulse towards community art, group-morality, state-regulated research and teaching, group-religion.   The individual thus comes to look for the reality, the firmly grounded and entirely trustworthy values of experience, in social solidarity, in unity of thought and feeling with the great masses of his fellow-men, in moving, as we say, with the crowd.   The highest value is social solidarity as such, class-consciousness and a sense of community in satisfactions and dissatisfactions alike.   This community of pleasure-pain experiences binds the members of the group to one another, and Plato even states roundly that there can be no higher good to the community than this common feeling.[58]   In itself, however, this unity of feeling is at the level of " opinion." The crowd sticks together, it is true, and treats with penalties, from social ostracism to an ignominious death, those who seek to pursue their own path.[59]   But the crowd is blind.   Devoid of genuine insight into the nature of reality, its art is blind, a copy of a copy, and thus three degrees removed from the archetypal reality.[60]   Its politics are blind, a meaningless struggle for power and a confused conflict over mere images and shadows of justice.[61]   Its science is unenlightened, overly departmentalized and content with attaining something less than the truth.[62]   Its religion is blind, an impious mixture of foolish cupidity and unreasoning superstition, in grievous need of reform.[63]   In a word, social experience, while of overwhelming importance for the individual in the formation of his value-judgments—for it inevitably sets its own stamp and its own system of values upon the individual seeker after satisfaction and thus forces him into the common social mould, so that he comes to seek satisfaction mainly in what satisfies the group as a group, i.e. in group art, group morality, group science, and group religion—is not, and cannot become a final and trustworthy guide to permanent and genuine satisfaction. In following the crowd, the individual may be on the right path, or he may, equally well, be on the wrong path.   He has given up his own individual value-sense, and has received in exchange the same value-sense, writ large and endlessly multiplied in the value-judgments of his fellows, more forceful but no whit less confused, more compelling but leaving him with his restless craving for a true and abiding good still unsatisfied.   Neither his fellow-seekers, nor those who study in more scientific fashion the moods and movements of the social organism,[64] can solve the problem.   Everywhere there is movement, stir, complexity, change.   But whether the movement is leading anywhere, whether the change and complexity are significant or utterly meaningless, whether the satisfactions which men seek in groups are, in the end, more genuine than the satisfactions which men seek as individuals, social experience—human force, concentrated but essentially blind—does not know and cannot tell.

3. Reason.

So far we have considered the value-judgments of men as (1) a function of the feeling after individual satisfaction, and (2) a function of the struggle for group satisfaction, in which the value-judgment comes to express, in condensed and concentrated form, the value-experiences of the social group, at the level of opinion, as opposed to knowledge. It remains to consider (3) the element of knowledge or reason, or the spirit of philosophy itself, and the part which this plays in the value-judgment.

This third element is comparatively rare. Most men remain contented with the level of sensation and association and the acceptance of social convention.[65] But the cognitive urge cannot be fully satisfied with " opinions " however far reaching and however widely accepted. Just as the individual's groping after satisfaction is less satisfactory than the group struggle after satisfaction, because the individual's experience is narrower and less consistent, less standardized, than the experience of the social group, and thus the various action-tendencies, being in conflict with one another, defeat their own end, of obtaining for the organism a satisfaction which shall be permanent and secure[66]—so also the standards thus attained, the opinions and conventions of the group, are themselves inconsistent, in conflict with one another, and thus also defeat their own purpose. The traditional conventions and standards can easily be shown, whether by sophist or dialectician, to be inconsistent with one another, if not with themselves,[67] and are thus " blind," based indeed upon masses of actual experience, but upon experience only very partially sifted out and resting, in the end, upon beliefs or convictions which are inadequate and inconsistent. The conventional value-judgments of the social group are thus in need of further standardization, and the ideal gradually emerges of a kind of value-judgment which shall be satisfactory for all social classes and members of the group, not merely for the ruling caste, or for the drones or paupers and radicals, but of judgments acceptable to an ideal social group, a group which shall constitute a true unit, as opposed to a miscellaneous crowd,[68] a group which shall represent a perfect fusion of diverse interests in the single direction of moral and intellectual development, so as to enable every member of the group to realize the ideal life.[69]

This is a rational ideal, and the " rational " element therein consists in an analysis and synthesis which omits the fluctuating and contradictory elements contained in social opinion, and concentrates and urges in a single direction all the elements in social opinion which are harmonious and consistent with one another.[70] In virtue of its superior method, this re-organization of the elements concerned tends to penetrate yet further into the nature of reality, in the first place in the form of the departmental sciences, but finally transcending the limitations and presuppositions even of these, and penetrating to the final principle of all, the Idea of Good.

This vision once attained, we can see that reason is apprehension of reality. Objectively, it is a grasp upon the nature of the real. Subjectively, it is the building up, in the instinctive and habitual mechanisms of the individual, of an organization which reproduces the essential lines of the world of Ideas, the essential structure of ultimate reality. The rational individual has in his soul the patterns of Justice, Temperance, etc., i.e. has his various action-tendencies organized in such a way as to reproduce the organization which characterizes the world-soul. He becomes the embodiment, so far as this is possible for a human being, of the idea of Good,[71] a co-worker with God, a channel for the infiltration of Divinity upon this earthly experience, so that his judgments come to represent the concentration, upon each problem which arises, of the whole of wisdom and insight into the final nature of reality.

Let us consider what this means in the case of the specialized value-judgments. The satisfaction in ordered sequences, which had become a satisfaction in such ordered sequences as were approved by the social group, becomes transformed into satisfaction in such rhythms and sequences as reproduce the patterns which reason apprehends as constituting reality. That is, the rational individual seeks satisfaction in art-works which have a deeper significance than the appeal of " popular " art to the superficial and untrained reactions of the individual, or to the only partly trained reactions of the citizen, the member of an orderly group—in art-works which express, in forms adapted to trained human comprehension in an ideal group,[72] the orderliness and inter-relations of the Ideas, the Divine patterns which in their totality constitute ultimate reality, the reality upon which the ethical community, the ideal human group, is striving to model its own life. The value-judgment of the rational individual thus takes on the forms and structure apprehended by reason, and it is the rhythms and patterns of the rational and true universe in which he now seeks and finds complete aesthetical satisfaction, and which furnish him with a final standard of art-values. Only when this stage is reached are the true and the beautiful apprehended as being one and the same.[73]

In the case of the ethical value-judgment, a similar process of change is more clearly brought out in the Dialogues. Our natural dispositions of (1) pugnacity, (2) quietness, and (3) the gregarious or herd instinct, etc., become transformed, under the influence of group life, into the civic virtues of courage, temperance, and justice, respectively, remaining, however, always at the level of " opinion." As reason and the higher insight, as opposed to mere opinion, make their appearance, these socialized dispositions become transformed yet further, so as to take on the shape of reflective virtues, trained habits of intelligent choice, (1) the manly resolution and force of character which supports every worthy cause and keeps down whatever is unworthy, whether in the world of men without, or in the world of brute desires within, and is the natural ally of the values apprehended by reason ;[74] (2) the feeling for the value of law and order as these are revealed to reason, a feeling partly of docility and acceptance, partly of co-operation in the enforcement of rational principles by the personal assumption of the burdens of leadership in the community, a feeling corresponding in principle to what, at the present day, we should call an appreciation of the value and need of intelligent social social service ;[75] (3) the acceptance of the value of social living as such, especially in the ethical community, the group which, in its institutions and concrete ways of living, reproduces, so far as is humanly possible, the institutions and structure of the world apprehended by reason, the kingdom of ideal patterns organized around the Idea of Good.[76] It is *qua* taking on the structure of the ideally real world, that our natural dispositions finally become transformed into rational virtues, and the ideal patterns revealed to us by philosophic insight furnish us with an absolutely reliable standard for the transvaluation of traditional values and the formation of a sound ethical value-judgment.

The same process is at work in the case of the logical value-judgment also. The confused groping after harmony and consistency which characterized the individual, and the greater emphasis in the same direction which characterized the social group, become transformed, under the influence of a reason which has worked its way through to self-consciousness, into the clear-cut method of dialectic, a method of conceptual analysis and synthesis which definitely disengages the Idea from its sensuous environment and makes a special study of the inter-relations of the elements of the ideal world and of their dependence upon the Idea of Good. As following lines of cleavage which are of objective significance,[77] the dialectician reaches the end of the intellectual realm and apprehends ultimate reality in its own nature. His mental processes become standardized and transformed until they take on entirely the form and structure of the ideal world, and this, when fully apprehended, comes to provide him with a final standard for the criticism and evaluation of theoretical constructions.

So too with the religious value-judgment. The groping after something which, amid the chances and changes of this mortal life, should be fixed, permanent, vital, and of human significance—a groping which in the social group had taken on the forms of Orphic beliefs and initiation into Mysteries, on the one hand and of the worship of ancestral and civic Divinities, on the other—is entirely transformed under the influence of the developing reason. In place of superstitious cults and of observances which are, in the main, primitive and unworthy of a more enlightened humanity, the rationalist in religious matters picks out what is essential, i.e. what expresses in clear and unmistakable form the nature of the ideal realm, and concentrates his attention upon this as a nucleus for the transmutation of the rest, refining and pruning the traditional observances until he brings them into some sort of conformity with the principles revealed by reason.[78] The standard for the development and gradual reformation of the religious value-judgment, and for the construction of a system of observances which shall appeal to and satisfy what is deepest in man, is furnished by the ideal realm into which the higher development of reason brings insight.

In this way we come to realize that it is the metaphysically real world, the system of Ideas organized around the Idea of Value as such, which constitutes the essence of reason and makes our human minds rational, i.e. is the *ratio cognoscentis* as well as the *ratio cognoscendi* and *ratio essendi*. It is only when we have won our way clear through the mists of sensuous perception and social convention, to the complete liberation of that element in us which is identical with the principle of intelligibility in that which has being, so that our cognitive nature is completely formed upon the Idea of Value, that we become truly rational. The metaphysically real world, to insight into which we have now won our way, furnishes us with a final standard of value in all the departments of value-judgment. Our aesthetical value-judgment becomes a consideration of rhythmic forms in the field of tones or colours, etc., in order to see how far these are expressive of the ideal patterns. Our moral value-judgment becomes an estimation of human plans as approximations towards the realization, in the medium of human actions and institutions, of the same realm of ideal values. Our logical value-judgment becomes an appreciation of the inter-relations of human concepts, in so far as these correspond to the inter-relations of the elements in the world of Ideas ; and our religious value-judgment becomes an estimation of religious observances and institutions as of value in so far as they also, in their own peculiar medium, express the nature of ultimate reality. The new standard revealed by reason is thus universal, as well as final. What makes experience, in any of its typical forms, valuable, is the extent to which it takes on the structure and relations of the ideal realm, which alone truly *is*, the extent to which it becomes purified of all irrelevant and superfluous elements, and is thus transmuted, directly and immediately, into Value itself, the Reality which is fundamental, permanent, and vital.

We should now be in a position to sum up clearly, if still somewhat provisionally, what has been brought out in our analysis of the value-judgment.

Our problem was, to discover just how the moral judge arrives at his decisions, what psychological elements in his own nature are brought into action, what it is in him which does the judging. Our analysis has shown that the fundamental form or law of all value-judging is a vague but universal feeling after satisfaction, an impulsive reaching out after something real, permanent, and vital, in our experiences. The first and most universally acceptable concrete filling-in of this form is supplied by our pleasure-pain sense. To the average sensual man, whatever brings sensory pleasure is satisfactory and is received as " good " ; whatever brings pain produces dissatisfaction and is so far regarded as " evil." Sensory pleasures, however, can arise from sources which are contradictory, and many other genuine puzzles occur at this level, which are beyond the average man's powers of solution.[79]

The sensory pleasure-pain experience is thus not entirely satisfactory, does not completely fulfil the value-requirements of the organism.

A second, and almost universally acceptable concrete filling-in of the value-seeking form is provided by the norms and conventions which arise in social experience, embodying, as these do, the experience of the race, or at least of large masses of humanity, as to what yields permanent and abiding satisfaction. The norms and standards of this group-morality are of overwhelming importance for the individual member of the group, but, representing, as they do, an experience which, though massive, has been only partially sifted out and reduced to order, remaining at the level of " opinion "—i.e. of an experience still grounded largely in sensation rather than in reason—these also, as intelligence develops, are seen to be in many ways contradictory and inadequate, incapable of fully satisfying the value-needs of the organism.

The third candidate for the fulfilment of our value-needs is philosophy, rational insight into the nature of ultimate reality, with all its main laws and principles apprehended in their relation to the final principle of law and order, the Idea of Good, i.e. the principle of value as such. Once this vision has been attained, its function is to serve as a nucleus for the complete reorganization of the whole organism. The reverent contemplation of the principles of value and being inevitably impels us to assimilate them, to embody them in the habits of thought, feeling, and will, of the organism itself in the first place, and, in the second place, to extend the understanding and reverent appreciation of them throughout the social environment, until all who are capable of the higher development are taking up reality and the true and genuine values into their lives, and are co-operating in the realization, upon earth, of the city whose pattern is laid up in heaven, the city of God. This is to convert the natural organism into a medium for the realization and transmission of the highest values, to form it upon reality, to make it real in the highest sense, permanent, and endowed with supreme vitality. No higher kind of satisfaction is even conceivable. The problem has been solved, and the life which is genuinely and permanently satisfying, the final and absolute fulfilment of the value-seeking needs of the organism, is entering upon the process of complete attainment.

If we consider briefly the inter-relation of these three elements in the value-judgment, in order to discover "what does the judging," we realize that they are not mutually exclusive, from a psychological standpoint, but are rather three stages of development, in diverse directions, of psychological elements which remain identical throughout, each advance being due to a reorganization of the elements present at the lower stage. The group value-judgment, for example, is simply the greatest common measure of the individual gropings after pleasure, reorganized and facing in a new direction by making the satisfaction of the group, as such, dominant, so that the individual comes to seek satisfaction only in what gives satisfaction to the group. The pleasures of eating, e.g. become the pleasures of eating-in-common, at common tables, in the common spirit of service to the community. So also with the pleasures of drinking, which have the added function of serving as tests of character and value to the community.[80] The pleasures of love similarly become transformed into something of almost religious significance in the service of the community. And so also with the other instinctive and habitual sources of satisfaction. They are not excluded from the personality by the advances to the new stage, but are retained in a form which has been transfigured by the new group-spirit, the spirit of social service.

So too in the case of the highest stage of all, the stage at which the life of instinct and habit becomes transmuted into the life of reason. The concrete instincts and habits are not repressed and driven below the threshold of conscious, purposeful, living, but are made over and reorganized by the new spirit, the spirit which seeks assimilation to the highest values ; and the philosopher-king who has seen the vision when he sets himself to introduce these principles into the lives and institutions of his willing fellow-citizens, does so not by negating and destroying their instinctive and habitual tendencies, but by reorganizing their ways of thinking, feeling, and willing, by turning the eye of their souls towards the light.[81]

If we ask, then, what it is in the moral judge which actually does the judging, the answer is, and must be, that it is the whole of his experiences, so far as these exert influence upon cognition, reorganized by being based upon principles which constitute reality, and that a particular value-judgment

—e.g. as to the comparative worth-whileness of the life which pursues knowledge, in contradistinction to the pursuit of personal honour or of personal riches—is a function of the whole experience of the organism, sifted out until each factor is given its full value, and brought to bear in concentrated form upon the problem in such a way as to reproduce, so far as is humanly possible, what would be the judgment of a complete experience, of omniscience combined with omnipotence, of ultimate reality itself, upon the problem in question. Not negation, but fulfilment ; not exclusion, but complete and harmonious satisfaction of all the elements which fuse together to make human personality—this is the relation of reason to instinct and habit, in the judgment by which moral and other values are estimated in the case of the trained mind which alone is finally capable of passing such judgment.

B. Genesis of the moral judgment.

We now approach the moral judgment from the genetic side, studying its development in the ideally perfect moral judge, in order to discover, clearly and distinctly, all the elements which go to the make-up of the perfect moral judgment. We study the ideally perfect judge, because the character of the average man, who falls short of the ideal, contains only some of the elements which are found in the character of the man who has gone through the complete process of moral evolution, and also tends to contain certain elements which distort and warp the judgment. Finally, in virtue of these positive and negative deficiencies, the elements which go to make up the character of the average man are likely to exhibit some form and arrangement which is different from the organization which is to be observed in the perfect character. But it is this organization and these elements which we wish to discover.

We begin, following as far as possible the actual treatment in the *Republic*, with the birth and childhood of the future judge. The general aim of the regulations which surround the process of conception is the perfection of the coming generation, not as an end in itself, but as a means to the continuance of the ethical community, as a means to its preservation and maintenance in a condition approximating to human perfection. The coming generation is to be, if possible, not only more excellent from a moral standpoint, but also more useful, of greater value to the community, than the preceding generation. With this aim, only adults who excel both morally and physically will be especially encouraged towards undertaking for the State the service of parentage.[82] The first element, then, which at birth itself enters the nature of the future moral judge, is physical strength and excellence, with a corresponding tendency towards that natural " good temper " which depends upon health and strength,[83] *plus* a certain moral background, consisting partly in the general moral atmosphere which is the natural consequence of a good civic constitution,[84] partly in the more special atmosphere of service towards the community, which surrounds the whole business of parentage, and partly in a direct tendency to inherit the moral as well as the physical characteristics of the parents.

Once born, the first three years of the child's life are to be devoted primarily to physical development, i.e. to nutrition, physical growth, and mastery of the simpler movements and physical adjustments to the environment. The nutrition is provided for, partly by the mothers, partly by especially suitable nurses, who relieve the actual mothers of much of the trouble which, in less well-planned cities, too often falls to their lot in dealing with very young children.[85] The education during this period is not, however, exclusively physical. Not only is the general moral atmosphere and the attitude towards social service much the same after birth as before, but certain special tendencies which begin to show themselves at this time require moral direction. Young children, like the rest of mankind, seek satisfaction and avoid dissatisfaction. With them, this general tendency expresses itself in a desire for simple sense-pleasures and an avoidance of pain. During the first three years, they tend to express these wants by crying, so as to attract the notice and assistance of parents and attendants. This tendency to cry whenever the child is afraid, or wants anything, may easily, if unchecked, lay the physical foundations for dispositions which, if further developed, will become the vicious habits of excessive timidity, querulousness, and " bad temper."[86] The task of parent and nurse, during this period, is to prevent the formation of such habits. They must endeavour to develop in their charges a feeling not directed wholly towards the attainment of pleasure, nor wholly towards the avoidance of pain, but rather a general attitude towards attaining the " mean," i.e. moderation in the realm of pleasure-pain experiences, and especially to foster such habits of feeling and action as tend towards the acquisition of manliness, self-control, and serene good temper.[87] The elements contributed by this stage towards the building up of character in the future moral judge are thus, in addition to the more vague and undefined attitude towards social service, physical strength and dexterity, *plus* a strong disposition towards overcoming obstacles and acquiring the rudiments of manliness and good temper.

The next stage is somewhat indefinite in extent, beginning, presumably, with the third or fourth year, and continuing without absolute limit. It is characterized especially by the beginnings of education proper, still, at first, at the hands of mother or nurse, and later at the hands of professional teachers.[88] At this stage, education through the medium of literature and music is introduced. The literature consists chiefly of such poetry and prose as embodies the history and nobler traditions of the race ; the music consists chiefly of very simple accompaniments, upon such instruments as the lyre and guitar, to be used in connection with the songs and dances taught to the children.—The immense influence of music and literature upon the habits and dispositions of the growing child is fully recognized,[89] and the consequence is strictly drawn that only such art is to be permitted and encouraged for educational purposes as is calculated, in the opinion of the best judges, to develop and strengthen such natural dispositions as friendliness, religious sense, dignity, self-mastery, manliness, justice, singleness of aim, love of the beautiful in every shape and form, and also certain tendencies which prepare the mind for the gradual development of reason.[90] What is contributed towards the formation of the moral value-judgment by this training is thus love of the beautiful, the good, and the true, a sense of acceptance and of familiarity with all that is of permanent value in life, a basis in the habits of feeling and willing for a lofty type of idealism.

Starting a little later than the education in literature and music, but, like it, beginning in early childhood and continuing indefinitely,[91] comes physical training, including hygiene. This aims, first and foremost, at developing a sound bodily constitution and at strengthening its powers of resistance to disease, by prescribing a very simple and moderate diet and mode of living generally.[92] The special moral aim to be kept in view throughout this process of physical training is to develop manliness and self-confidence in the growing child, taking care to correct and tendency towards roughness by the counterbalancing influence of music.[93] The more general contribution towards the formation of a perfect moral judgment is stated to be the reserves of health and strength which are a useful, and indeed indispensable, basis for the arduous mental studies which come later. The physical training is thus surrounded by a general atmosphere of preparation for future social service.[94]

Starting a little later than physical culture, but still beginning in childhood and continuing indefinitely throughout life, with especial emphasis at the entrance upon physical maturity,[95] comes intellectual education proper, the definite and continuous endeavour, by means of special studies, to liberate the intellect from a too narrow preoccupation with the sense-perceivable world, and to direct its powers gradually towards its own peculiar province, towards the apprehension of the intelligible world, the world of Ideas. This education falls into two parts. The preparatory portion, which constitutes a sort of prelude to the final hymn of dialectic, is a matter partly of moral, partly of specifically intellectual training. On the moral side, it is necessary to liberate the whole conative system of action-tendencies which originate in instinct and are cradled in habit, from their natural propensity towards excessive preoccupation with the world of sense-perception, with its inevitable interest in sensual satisfactions, the " leaden weights " which prevent the soul from soaring into the upper regions.[96] This liberation is accomplished, to a slight extent by the moral influences which we have already considered, but to a greater extent by the deliberate application of a policy of strict selection, only those who show unusual proficiency in moral development, in the control of instinctive and habitual action-tendencies by ideas —at this stage, of course, the ideas inculcated by their parents and teachers—as well as in such intellectual qualities as love of study, intellectual acumen, and sound memory, being permitted to enter upon the specifically intellectual portion of this period of training.[97] This testing of character as well as intelligence, and the steady elimination of the morally, as well as of the intellectually, unfit, ensures that intellectual and moral qualities shall develop hand in hand in the select group of students who are being trained for leadership.

The intellectual training which belongs to this period of preparation, proceeds by means of a peculiar study of arithmetic, geometry (plane and solid), astronomy, and harmonics. These different subjects are studied contemporaneously, though harmonics is not commenced until the student has made some progress in astronomy, astronomy is not commenced until the student has made some progress in solid geometry, solid geometry similarly presupposes a certain acquaintance with plane geometry, and this again presupposes a certain acquaintance with arithmetic. Up to the age of twenty, these subjects are studied separately, so as to give the student a certain grounding in each. After that age, they are studied more in their inter-relations, and with an explicit and avowed interest in their epistemological and ontological significance.[98]

The peculiar element in this study is due to the object with which these sciences are cultivated. The aim of the educator here is not to turn out mathematicians and astronomers as such, but rather to use these studies as a means for effecting a certain revolution in the intellectual outlook of the students, as well as to develop their general intellectual ability. The usual interest in the sciences is practical. It is with the aim of solving some practical difficulty in the actual world revealed by sense-perception, that the average student enters upon theoretical studies. The military commander requires a sure grasp of the elements of arithmetic and geometry, if he is to solve the problems of military organization which are certain to arise. The naval officer requires a certain knowledge of mathematics and astronomy, if he is to keep on his course during the night. The musician who is to be more than the merest empiric, must have some grasp of the principles of harmonics, and so with the other professions.[99] Theoretical investigation thus arises in connection with practical difficulties, and is directed mainly if not entirely to the removal of those difficulties. The problem once solved, the theoretical interest quickly subsides.[100] In the new system of education advocated by Plato, while the same general relation between theory and practice is present, the " revolution " consists in a very much greater interest in theory, and in the postponement of the more important practical problems until a much later period, when the theoretical training is, at least in principle, complete. This involves using practical difficulties in the world of sense-perception mainly as intellectual irritants, as concrete situations specially adapted for the awakening and continuous stimulation of intellectual activity, an activity which does not culminate in the first practical solution of the problem, but is itself fruitful in arousing still further intellectual interest, until the scientific habit of mind is fully formed, and the intelligence of the youthful inquirer begins to feel genuinely at home in the world of laws and relations which can be apprehended only by the trained intelligence.[101] This preparatory stage terminates in a sustained investigation of the inter-relations of the various sciences which have been studied, and is followed by a further stage of severe and sustained reflection upon the principles which underlie the moral and religious life also, as a final step preceding entrance upon the highest stage of dialectic.[102]

We must further note, during this preparatory period, the important social influence exercised by the students upon one another. The members of this leadership class constitute always a highly select group. The basis of selection is always physical, moral, and intellectual excellence, with the physical element dropping more and more into the bachground, as a constant presupposition, and the emphasis passing more and more to moral and intellectual characteristics. The members of this group thus enjoy all the advantages which attach to continued association and friendship with what we should call super-normal children, and to absence of association and familiarity with average and sub-normal children. In the ideal community, they have no home-ties,[103] but associate always with one another and with older members of the same special group, consecrated to the same special task, the development of the qualities requisite for leadership. On the negative side, just as they are kept apart from anything imperfect and defective in their curriculum, so they are kept separate from the masses, with their pitifully dwarfed and stunted souls and bodies, their vices and their tricky cleverness, their unreasoning hatred of things intellectual, their aimless wallowings in sensual pleasure and their meaningless ambitions and reachings after miscalled " power."[104] On the positive side, the whole of their social life, with its common meals, common exercises, common studies, common dangers, and common joys, is concentrated upon the growth and development of a special morale or community spirit, a spirit appropriate to the " golden " class, with its ideal of service rather than ambition, and its sincere and flawless love of truth, goodness, and beauty.[105] The effect of this comparative seclusion from the world, during their carefully sheltered childhood and youth, is to keep them a little child-like and unsuspicious on the one hand, somewhat easily deceived by an unscrupulous artist in lying,[106] but on the other hand, this openness of spirit fits them for that higher insight into values which is denied to those who have played with pitch and drunk life to the dregs.[107] Their social life thus confirms them in their habits of manliness, self-mastery, and social considerateness, on the one hand, and, on the other, in their sheer joy in the keen play of intellect, in learning, and in all spiritual excellence.

One further element which is of great importance during this period of preparation, is especially noteworthy. This is the element of practical experience. Plato has no intention to permit his select group to degenerate into seminarists, idealists who are ignorant of the practical things of life and *gauche*, unable to mix easily with their fellow-men and to act as real leaders. On the contrary, he makes especial provision, while always retaining their organization as a separate class, for practical, as well as theoretical training. In childhood and early youth, they are trained in field-sports, such as hunting, racing, and military exercises,[108] at first in play, and as spectators, but with the avowed aim of fitting them in later life to defend their country and its institutions in earnest, if necessary. The years from seventeen to twenty are given over almost wholly to these exercises, and certain military duties are performed as need arises until the age of thirty.[109] Then, after an interval of five years devoted to continuous reflection upon moral and religious problems,[110] they are, at the age of thirty-five, again " sent down into the cave " and are compelled to hold such offices as befit young men, such as certain magistracies and positions of military command, until they are fifty years old. The explicit aim of this performance of civic and military duty is that they may keep up with their neighbours in practical address,[111] and may fit themselves completely for what is to follow. Finally, after the age of fifty, when their training is complete, they accept, when their turn comes, the hard duties of the highest public office in the commonwealth, and devote themselves to the work of admin-istration, regulating their country, their fellow-citizens, and themselves, after the pattern of the Idea of Good, and super-vising the education of the rising generation of leaders, so as to leave trained successors to fill their place when they are called away.[112] What this element contributes towards the final character and personality of the moral judge, is experience in leadership, in administration, in handling men as well as in solving practical problems, complete freedom from any awkwardness and hesitation, and, on the moral side, the com-plete permeation of the action-systems with the spirit of social service, until it becomes second nature.

It now remains to consider the final intellectual training, the training which raises the student out of the class of auxiliaries or junior guardians, who, while holding various positions as magistrates, are still at the level of " opinion," into the class of full guardians, whose actions are based upon the insight and knowledge which comes upon complete achievement of the philosophic quest. This last stage of training is undertaken at the age of fifty, and only by an exceedingly small group, whose moral and intellectual equip-ment is of the very highest, and all of whose experiences, including the intensive study of moral and religious questions from the age of thirty to the age of thirty-five, have fitted them to take this final step.[113]

What has been accomplished during this period of pre-paration is the gradual making over of the whole nature of the students, so that their characters have come to be based, so far as this is possible at the level of opinion, upon the Ideas, and are thus already representative of the universe of values. The Ideas of manliness, self-mastery, and justice, have become, by long habituation and moral practice, constituent elements in their nature, and the Idea of wisdom has similarly, by means of their scientific training and philosophical reflection, become a central element in their personality.[114] Furthermore, these Ideas do not remain in isolation from one another, enclosed in morally water-tight compartments, but have been associated together since early childhood, and so have become insepar-able. So much for the influence of habit. On the side of reflection, the leaders have already become accustomed to think over the interrelation of the sciences as pathways to reality, and have spent some years of intensive study also in the consideration of moral and religious problems, so that not only has their whole nature become an earthly habitation for the Ideas which together constitute reality, but there has also been some attempt at feeling after some integration of the Ideas, in their embodiment in human nature, so as to convert the human copy into the reflex of reality, assimilating, not only its elements, but also its organization, a feeling after some principle which shall transcend the limitations and oppositions of Ideas embodied at the level of habit and opinion, and from its new standpoint unify them and bring them into perfect harmony with one another. And this feeling has begun to rise towards the level of reflection and of persistent, conscious search for such a principle. Only men who have developed a character and personality which already *is* the Ideas in their interconnection and, at least to some extent, also in their relation to the Idea of Good, can really take this last and greatest step from their slumbering and quasi-twilight vision to full self-consciousness, so as to apprehend in a final way the inner meaning of reality, the principle which makes all their life clear and beautiful and one with the essence of value.

While the preparation is thus largely a matter of development of personality, of moral as well as intellectual training, consisting of the unconscious or semi-conscious assimilation of character to the structure of ultimate reality, the last and final step, which leads to the vision of the Ideas as forms of the Idea of Good, is severely intellectual, without direct assistance either from bodily habit or from an apprehension depending directly upon the activities of the bodily sense-organs. It is necessary to use as starting-points the masses of organized experience which constitute the departmental sciences, and perhaps also the moral and religious institutions developed in the course of human evolution,[115] which have already been studied in some relation to one another, and endeavour, after ascertaining the presuppositions, the accepted principles on which each science, as a separate department of action or investigation, rests, to transcend them, to convert what has been hitherto accepted into matter of inquiry, to seek further for its ground in a higher and more rational principle, a principle resting, not on sense-perceivable fact, but on intellectually apprehensible Ideas. Hitherto the Ideas have been apprehended as empirical generalizations, as laws which bring together large masses of sensory experience and are verified by reference to that experience.[116] The aim is now, to rise above this empirical basis, and endeavour to apprehend the Ideas in their full nature as Ideas, set free from the narrowing limitations of sensory experience, of the accidents of the here and now and of the personal equation, and apprehend them as true universals, as Ideals which can be appreciated only when considered as members of an ideal and purely rational realm, to which any embodiment in a merely physical nature, a nature apprehensible by animal and human sense-organs, is and can be only a faint approximation.[117]

Human concepts are dual in nature. On the one hand, they are matters of sensory and associational experience ;[118] on the other, they participate in an ideal nature, in some principle which, at least partly, converts them into Ideas proper, members of the Ideal Realm. When we abstract from the conditions of sensory experience, and set out upon the dialectical quest, the only path of investigation which remains is to consider what this principle is, upon which their nature as Ideas depends, the principle of ideality as such. . For this alone is what is common to all Ideas, whatever the department of inquiry in which they have been discovered, and this alone can suffice to give them, considered as a systematic group in relation to its own law or principle, an absolute grounding, a grounding which does not point beyond itself to something yet higher, but transcends the questionings which attach to the merely bodily and human conditions of inquiry, and gives a final, ideally sufficient answer to the dialectical problem, an answer which will satisfy, not merely the intellect with its feeling for logical values, but also the moral, aesthetical, and religious aspirations of humanity, and furnish an absolute basis for the whole spiritual life of man.[119]

That some such answer would fully satisfy the deepest spiritual needs of man, may perhaps be admitted. And further, that the principle of ideality and value can be adequately realized, if at all, only when the complete experience of the individual has been trained and developed somewhat as Plato prescribes, may perhaps also be admitted. But we could all wish that the inquiry should proceed further, and enable us, at least to some extent, to enter the completed experience of the dialectician. And this wish can be, at least partly, satisfied. The matter does not necessarily remain vague and incomplete, hanging in mid-air.[120] Certain things which the philosophical investigator will discover about the Idea of Good can be stated at least in a formally correct way, even though the full concrete realization of their truth and meaning may have to be left for the man whose whole life has prepared him to experience this final vision.

Thus, in the first place, the dialectician will assuredly discover that this principle is of assistance to him in his search after knowledge. There is a certain correspondence, as we have seen, between the mental structure of the junior guardian and the laws of the ideally real world, and it is in virtue of this admittedly imperfect correspondence that the guardian, at this level of opinion and with the help of merely human concepts, of ideas which represent only the reorganization of large masses of an experience shot through with elements which satisfy sensation rather than the uncompromising demands of intellect, has been able to build up any semblance of genuine knowledge. The reason for this inadequacy is the imperfect nature of the correspondence in question. There is a gap between the system of Ideas on the one hand, and the distorted reflection of this which gradually emerges, through the medium of human sensation, in our own minds. The resulting structure, which we dignify by the name of empirical science, is, as Plato puts it, more clear than mere opinion, but more obscure, less completely permeable to intelligence, than a true or ideal knowing would be.[121] If, then, by concentrating upon the strictly intellectual and formal element in knowledge, it becomes possible to perfect the form, to withdraw for a season from further sensory experience, and to think out in abstraction the formal ideal of systematic consistency which would completely satisfy the intellect, it will be possible to use this ideal as a standard, by reference to which the previous cognitive experiences of the individual can be rearranged, in spite of their frequent omissions and inadequacies, so as to correspond, in their main lines, to the main lines of the new pattern, and can thus be made to yield their utmost of knowledge-value. The ideal once clearly grasped, and the nature of the gap between sense and intellect once clearly understood, the dialectician can set out, with a mental structure which has been reformed so as to be now identical in principle with the structure of the ideal world, to make over and reorganize his sensory experiences, to extract from them everything which in any way measures up to the ideal, and to arrange the elements, thus extracted, in accordance with the arrangement of the ideal pattern, so that his labours will gradually reveal to him in detail, as well as in principle, the nature of the laws which constitute reality. From this point of view, the ideal principle may be described as the *ratio cognoscentis*, the principle which makes knowledge possible for the individual knower.[122]

In the second place, the dialectician will discover that this highest principle is of immense assistance for the conduct of life. The psychological springs of action are furnished by the large instinctive needs for such " goods " as food, protection, companionship, and sex-satisfaction, as well as by innumerable minor impulses.[123] Under the pressure of ordinary social living, these originally somewhat diverse and chaotic impulses have become hammered into some conventional semblance of principle and orderliness. But the semblance is a mere veneer, and beneath the surface there is a fierce riot of seething passions, each waiting for a chance to satisfy itself without much regard for the rest or for social conventions. This lawless, wild-beast element in our nature can be kept under, to some extent, by the force of law and of social opinion, in the case of the average citizen, if not in the case of the successful despot.[124] But suppression of a problem by force is no adequate and final solution of the very real and very pressing difficulty. The difficulty arises from the fact that both individual impulse and social convention oppose one another as rivals for the same position : each claims to represent " reality," to be actual and genuine, the other being regarded as " mere appearance." The partisan of lawless living and the complete release of desire believes with a whole-hearted faith in Pan. For him, the instincts are alone real and according to the order of nature, while social and political norms are of merely " conventional " significance, an un-natural imposition upon the imperious and self-justified needs of powerful individuals.[125] On the other hand, the partisan of law and order is profoundly convinced that these are of a higher, more ideal nature, and that they have a more rational claim to satisfaction than the brute instincts and unnecessary appetites. For him, the State is more significant, more truly representative of reality, than the isolated individual, even when the individual is successful as a superman, and his will to power rises superior to all human checks.[126] Finally, he believes that, the universe being essentially and ultimately rational, a genuine, harmonious, and permanent satisfaction, not only of the social and gregarious instincts, but of the whole instinctive and emotional side of human life, is possible only when the ruling force in life is reason, with its powers of organization on the one hand, and its kinship with ultimate reality on the other.[127]

Both sides thus claim for themselves the authority of nature and reality ; and that there is some degree of truth in both claims, no candid inquirer can altogether deny. There is thus, so long as the level of opinion remains untranscended, no way of solving the deadlock. Each side is convinced that it is right, and neither will give way, whether in the case of the individual man, or in the case of the State, which is but the individual writ large. If the conflict is to be decided at all, some higher court is needed than that of instinct, passion, and convention. And a higher court can be reached. Both sides have something in common, viz. the straining after an ideal of human life which shall be not superficial and futile, but shall be truly in contact with reality, the genuine, final, ultimate, highest reality. The only possible pathway towards a solution of the conflict, towards the attainment of a point of view which shall be perfectly just to the complete facts of the situation on both sides, is to be found by abstracting, for the time being, from the fierce passions and instinctive impulses aroused on both sides, including the passionate conviction of rightness, of being already in touch with truth and reality, which each partisan possesses, and in investigating, dispassionately and humbly, the element which both possess in common, in order to determine by an appeal to strictly rational standards the full nature of the ideal of social living, the ideal or principie which shall reconcile the opposing elements and make them friends,[128] a higher principle at which both were fundamentally aiming, though by different paths, a principle expressive of the true and ultimate nature of reality in a form which can be used as a standard for social living, a standard which every rational being, as such, can accept openly and without qualification. By withdrawing from the immediate pressure of practical needs, and by reflecting continuously and by an abstract method upon the nature of this social ideal, the seeker comes to realize that community of aim, community of final, underlying purpose, is the only principle

which can unite and harmonize the diverse instincts in the
individual, and the diverse individuals in the commonwealth.
Co-operation, each element, whether in the individual or in the
community, doing all that it can for the service of the whole—
i.e. for the service of others as well as of itself, considered all
as members of one and the same organism—is the only possible
way of constructing a harmony which will work, which will
bring into effective functioning all the diverse elements, and
will thus build up a totality, whether in the case of the individual personality or in the case of the commonwealth, which
will express and bring out whatever of positive content, whatever of reality, is to be found in the impulses and sources which
push towards effective action.[129]

This ideal is based upon a conception of reality as a totality
of elements which are all positive, though not devoid of
" othernesses," i.e. differences and diversities which, unless
all are properly organized with reference to this one possible
principle of satisfying all harmoniously in relation to the
totality as such, would negate one another.[130]   This conception of the real universe as a complex organism, wherein every
element has its own function, contributing somehow to the
life of the whole, and finding its own deepest and most abiding
satisfaction, can be applied in a very direct way as a standard
for the reorganization of our social living, as well as for the
solution of our own more individual problem of attaining a
united and vigorous personality.[131]   Upon this conception
depends immediately the ideal of a State which shall be a
genuine organism, every element therein contributing all it
can to the service of the State as a whole ; and this ideal
contains the two important principles of (1) social service as
the true spirit of the citizen, and (2) every citizen doing his
own work, realizing his own potentialities, fulfilling completely
his own natural and proper function, and finding, in loyal
service of the ideal community which includes himself as one
of its members, serenity of spirit and perfect satisfaction.
Diverse functions involving specialization, united by the common spirit of service to a common ideal, the elimination of
waste and useless conflict, and the development of the full
resources of every member of the community—principles such
as these bring out the full value, the utmost positive contribution to the enrichment of life, the closest approximation
to the ideal reality of things, which we can conceive.   It is

in this sense that the Idea of Good is declared to be the pattern by which the philosopher-king will guide not only himself, but also the community, in the complex business of social living.[132]

It is not only in solving his own personal problem, his search after a unified, concentrated life which shall develop in a vigorous, consistent, and useful way all the elements of power and value contained in his organism, that the dialectician will find the principle of ideality and value to be of supreme assistance. Not only does it furnish him with a standard for the improvement of social living and the advancement of scientific truth. It is also of the utmost help to him in art and religion. In art—not in artistic creation as such, for that is a matter of inspiration, of surging emotion and uncritical frenzy[133]—but in artistic criticism, in estimating the value of art-works. The conception of the ideal universe as a vision which realizes the utmost possible of positive beauty, the "science of beauty everywhere," becomes a standard by which he can estimate the greatness of artistic creations. The senseless embellishment of elements which are superficial and devoid of real significance, is put in its place,[134] the claim of the artist who is merely a bold and skilful player upon our human feelings, to be accepted as the interpreter of the deeps of life, is roughly rejected,[135] and great art is recognized as the representation, in its own medium of rhythmic movements, whether free, as in the dance, or arrested, as when embodied in colours, tones, or words, etc., of the interplay of elements which together constitute the highest reality, the world of Ideas united under the Idea of Good. In this form it is the natural ally of science and morality, and elevates those who are susceptible to its fascination and wizardry, out of the fragmentariness and littleness of the common places of life to an appreciation of their genuine and underlying unity with the depths, with the perennial sources of freshness and inspiration, the true beauty and reality of things.[136]

So too in religion. The withdrawal for a space from the warring creeds and from the unworthy promises too often held out to the believer who will surrender himself wholly, and the sustained philosophical reflection upon the idea of the God and Father of all, gradually leads to the development of the conception of a Spirit who is the living counterpart of the principle of ideality, who is in very sooth the universe in which we live and move, but is no mere concept or bloodless category, but a living Spirit, the Spirit of goodness, beauty, truth, knowledge, and power, the Spirit who is reality in its own living.[137]   This conception once attained, the dialectician will be able to set about the reform of received creeds, which worship the Father of all in forms and ceremonies into which superstition, self-seeking, and folly have gradually found their way, and will regard as the essence of true religious worship and self-surrender, the yearning after assimilation to God, the sustained attempt to live a God-like life here on earth, and the hope of hereafter living a more perfect, more real and God-like life in heaven.[138]

Such, then, is the nature of the Idea of Good, and such are some of the principles which the trained seeker after the wisdom which comes from a knowledge of ultimate reality will discover. But the discovery is no tenuous abstraction, no withdrawal from life to monastic seclusion.   It is the living completion of the years of preparation through which the student has passed, the culmination of his living, the continuation, with complete self-consciousness, of the life which he has been living already in the lower phase of incomplete awareness.   It is in his life, in every pulse and throb of his blood, in his brain, heart, and hand, in his planning, his feeling, and his acting, that the Idea of Good has come to have its local habitation, and, through him, in the community also which has trained him to lead them into the right way.   The final principle which he discovers is thus the true life of the community itself, the human copy of that higher, complete, and absolute life which is reality itself, the life of God.

This vision realized, we may now ask what this final stage of training has added to the elements which go to make up the moral judgment.   In the first place, it has taken away the blindness, the groping, the baffled feeling inseparable from the stage of opinion, and has substituted for it a clearness of outlook, a sureness of grasp upon moral criteria, a breadth and depth of insight, which are illuminating to the highest degree and bring with them a measured calmness of spirit, a peace and certainty with regard to the issues of life, which make the philosopher finally at home in a universe to which he now not only feels, but knows, himself to be spiritually akin.   In the second place, the new experience is a deepening of self-consciousness, an awareness of his own deepest Self, an under-standing of what has been slowly developing within him through the long years of preparation, a recognition of his great powers and an acceptance of the great responsibilities which these powers entail, a full comprehension of his place and function in the scheme of things, including not only his relation to his fellow-men, but also his relation to God and the unseen world of Ideas. What is new, then, is this deeper and clearer knowledge of Self and of the Universe, and, in the light of this new knowledge, a more profound understanding of life, and a key by the help of which he can solve the problems of conduct, not only for himself, but also for the community, and can thus enter, with others, into the higher life, into the peace and joy (*eudaimonia*) which come to those who walk steadfastly in the pathway which they know, with every fibre of their being, to be right.

His training is now complete, and the guardian can pro-ceed to make moral judgments in the full sense. Just what elements enter into his judgment ? What is it in him which does the judging ? The first and simplest answer is, that he does the judging himself, and that the elements which enter into his judgment are the elements which have truly entered into his Self. These are the physical, moral, and mental elements already considered, the instincts, habits, and intelli-gence, so trained and ripened by social and educational influences as to have taken on the form and pattern of the ideal world, and to have become, so far as this is possible in an organism which retains to the end something of its animal origin, the human habitation and embodiment of the Ideas of Manliness, Temperance, Justice, and Wisdom, in the full harmony and unity which comes with attainment of the Idea of Good also. What " does the judging " is thus the whole nature of the individual man, together with all the influences which have made his nature what it has come to be, the influence of literature, art, science, and religion, the history, traditions, and aspirations of the community, the whole welded together and transmuted into an adequate reflex of that Experience which we designate as Absolute. The judgment of such a man represents, then, not the chance reaction to a chance stimulation, but the rich experience of the whole race, sublimated and idealized until it represents, so far as this is humanly possible, the complete experience which is the life and thought of God. What does the judging is thus the Absolute Experience itself, so far as the human organism can become a channel for Its expression, and what is judged is the human problem. The judging consists in analyzing the human situation which provides the problem, in comparing it with the Divine standard so as (1) to make clear its deficiencies, its falling short of that standard, and also (2) to point out the remedy and the solution, the steps which will re-form its elements and bring our human actions into closer approximation to that Experience which furnishes the Absolute Pattern for human living.

The conclusion of our synthetic examination thus confirms the conclusion of our analysis of the moral value-judgment. In both cases we have discovered that it is the total experience of the individual which, according to Plato, is concerned in passing judgment, the physical and instinctive basis, the social training and habituation to community ideals, the rational insight which forms the key-stone of the arch and makes clear to consciousness the kinship of humanity to Divinity. These elements are worked over, sublimated and transmuted, but not discarded, and the Divine Experience, which ultimately passes judgment, does so through the medium of the human organism, when this has been so trained under Divine favour[139] as to become expressive of the whole experience of humanity in its responsiveness to and reflection of the Ideal Experience which is God.

CHAPTER V

VALIDITY OF THE MORAL JUDGMENT

THAT human judgment upon moral issues is liable to error, has only to be stated in the Platonic Dialogues to meet with universal acceptance. The fact of conflict and dispute in such cases, whether we consider the direct recognition of this fact by such interlocutors as Euthyphro or Glaucon, or whether we note its exemplification in the sharply divergent opinions of Socrates on the one hand, and, on the other, of such thinkers as Thrasymachus or Callicles, is so obvious, that human fallibility in questions of moral valuation forces itself upon our attention and constitutes a genuine problem.

Moral judgments, then, are in some cases certainly and beyond doubt invalid ; in other cases, they may possibly be accepted as valid. Upon what conditions does their validity or invalidity depend ? Are there any tests which a careful thinker might apply in order to determine their degree of validity ?

For Plato, the answer to this question is largely a matter of discovering a moral criterion or standard in the form of the moral law, the law accepted by the perfect moral judgment. This ideal law furnishes a standard, comparison with which sufficiently indicates the extent to which a particular moral judgment approximates to, or falls short of, the law, and thus serves to measure, with a fair degree of accuracy, the validity or invalidity of the moral judgment in question.[1] If we ask what the ideal principle accepted by the perfect moral judgment is, we have, in the Dialogues, various answers, e.g. universal assent, written law, quantity of experienced pleasure, expediency, self-sufficiency, consistency, and objectivity. If we then proceed to examine these answers, we find that, in the end, they all resolve themselves into a single answer. The final standard of value, in every case, turns out to be objectivity, or the degree to

123

which a proposed course of action, or possibly a character under investigation, is patterned upon the ideal principles which, for Plato, constitute reality. These principles are expressions of a single ultimate principle, the Idea of Good, i.e. the principle of Value or Ideality as such, value and ideal or ultimate reality being identified. A character or an action thus comes to have value, precisely to the degree in which it is based upon and tends to realize the principle of Value itself. Understood in the light of this final principle, i.e. as expressions of ultimate Value or of the essence of Reality, universal assent, written law, expediency, consistency, etc., can safely be used as proximate standards, by which to measure the value of actions and characters in particular situations and from particular standpoints. It is in this sense that they are used by the Platonic dialectician. But apart from such transvaluation in the light of this principle, they belong to the region of " opinion," the region of twilight and moral blindness, and cannot safely be used as moral standards at all. It is insight into Reality, or the ideal realm and its principle, alone, which enables the philosophic judge to make value-judgments which are reliable and valid.[2]

From a more psychological point of view, the moral judgment can be considered as representative of a certain quantity and quality of experience, and if we consider its evolution in the case of the perfect moral judge, we construct the ideal of a judgment so comprehensive and so profound, as to transcend the sensory experiences of a single individual, and eventually to represent the concentration, upon the question at issue, of the whole of human experience, refined and idealized as far as is humanly possible. The elements which enter into the moral judgment are thus the elements which have truly entered into the Self of the perfect moral judge. These are the physical, moral, and mental elements discussed in the Platonic theory of education, the instincts, habits, and intelligence, so trained and ripened by social and educational influences as to have taken on the form and pattern of the ideal world, and to have become, so far as this is possible in an organism which retains to the end something of its animal origin, the human habitation and embodiment of the Ideas of Manliness, Self-control, Justice, and Wisdom, in the full harmony and unity which comes with attainment of the Idea of Good also. What actually does the judging is thus the whole nature of the individual man, together with all the influences which have made his nature what it has come to be, the influence of literature, art, science, and religion, the history, traditions, and aspirations of the community, the whole welded together and transmuted into an adequate reflex of that Experience which we designate as Absolute. The judgment of such a man represents, then, not the chance reaction to a chance stimulation, but the rich experience of the whole race, sublimated and idealized until it represents, so far as humanly possible, the complete experience which is the life and thought of God. This ideal furnishes a standard, comparison with which shows with reasonable clearness how far a particular moral judgment approximates to, or falls short of, its completeness and organized concentration.[3]

In both cases, the ideal judgment of the perfect moral judge is understood, epistemologically, as a sufficiently valid apprehension of the nature and structure of ultimate reality, whether that reality is conceived rather as a system of laws and values, or chiefly as an ideal Experience. It is thus ultimate reality which furnishes the final touchstone of human value-judgments. So far as the human judgment corresponds to the nature of *what is*, the human judgment expresses the nature of reality, expresses the Divine judgment to which it has, by training and grace, gradually become responsive, and so far the human judgment is metaphysically valid. So far, on the other hand, as it falls short, or diverges from the path, it deviates necessarily into insignificance and futility, and so far as it goes further and contradicts the nature of *what is*, it not only stultifies itself, but invokes against itself the higher forces of the universe. The ultimate standard, then, of the validity of the moral judgment, is furnished by comparison with the structure of ultimate reality.

All this has been brought out in the preceding chapters, and it has been recognized that Plato's position is at least formally satisfactory. The structure of ultimate reality would undoubtedly furnish an ultimate standard for testing the validity of our human attempts at moral judgment, at seeing as God sees. From the standpoint of God, one could judge finally and without appeal. But while formally correct, a further question at once arises, as to the substantial and material correctness of the view of ultimate reality which is furnished by Plato. The structure of reality furnishes the touchstone. Well and good. But what, precisely, in principle and, if possible, also in detail, is the structure of reality ? How, if at all, can we be assured of the soundness of the Platonic theory of Reality ? It is of vital importance to know this, and to realize clearly how far Plato's teaching on this point can be accepted, and how far it has its limitations. The investigation of the validity of the Platonic metaphysic of morals is thus the object of the present chapter.

Reality, according to Plato, consists of entities of a peculiar kind, the Ideas or conceptual essences, and the structural pattern of reality is thus constituted by the relations of these entities to one another, a relatedness controlled by a single ultimate principle, the Idea of Good, i.e. the principle of ideality or essentiality as such. We shall therefore begin our investigation by making out a roughly classified list of the entities which constitute these conceptual essences, and shall then proceed to study the inter-relations of these essences, including in our study, not only their relations to one another, but also their relation to the highest principle, the principle of essentiality. Having in this way discovered, as far as possible, the nature and structure of ultimate reality, as Plato conceives it, we shall then proceed to determine the validity of his conception in relation to possible human experience.

The entities definitely recognized in the Dialogues as " ideas," i.e. as conceptual essences which in some sense constitute the ultimately real, fall naturally into groups, representing the essences of :

    (1) natural phenomena (hair, clay, dirt, water, fire, heat, cold, etc.).

    (2) organisms (man, horse, ox, etc.).

    (3) artefacts (bed, table, shuttle, awl, etc.).

    (4) goods of body (health, strength, disease, weakness, good looks, pleasure, pain, etc.).

    (5) social and political goods (high or low birth, wealth, poverty, private or public station, the ideal state, tyranny, etc.).

    (6) goods of mind (cleverness, dullness, knowledge, ignorance, etc.).

(7) moral ideals (good, evil, justice, injustice, temperance, wisdom, all virtues and their opposites).

(8) aesthetical ideals (beauty, ugliness, " the musical," " the unmusical," etc.).

(9) the essential form of life, death, mortality, immortality, the perishable and the imperishable, etc. (*Phaedo* 105d f).

(10) categories and ideas of relation (one, other numbers, many, oddness, evenness, identity, difference, likeness, unlikeness, greatness, smallness, equality, motion, rest, being, not-being, wholeness).

(11) the idea of good.

The above eleven groups are intended to cover the whole field of Being, from the realities inadequately exemplified in the world of sense-perceivables to the realities more adequately expressed in the realm of moral, aesthetical, and religious valuings, and more adequately apprehended by non-sensuous, intellectual processes, culminating in the apprehension of the " idea of good," the principle of reality itself. Nothing which *is*, is intentionally omitted from the list,[4] and it may consequently be regarded as, at least in intention and in principle, complete.

Before proceeding to discuss the relations of group to group, it is advisable to consider briefly each group by itself, in order to discover clearly and unambiguously upon what grounds it is placed in the Dialogues among the conceptual essences in which reality consists.

(1) the first group, of natural phenomena, is considered in relation to a distinction between (a) absolute Ideas and (b) the phenomena which " partake of them," the Idea being consistently regarded as transcendent or " apart from " the phenomena. The question is raised, whether there is an absolute essence of such natural phenomena as fire or mud, etc., distinct from and " apart from " the actual phenomena with which we come into sensory contact, or not. The platonic Socrates expresses a certain doubt and hesitation. On the one hand, he is inclined to attribute to sensuous phenomena none but a phenomenal existence, a reality purely sensuous, fluctuating and relative to our sense-organs, and entirely devoid of ideal essence.[5] On the other hand, however, when he reflects further, he is inclined to believe that nothing which has any kind of existence can be without

an Idea, in which case even sensuous phenomena would partake of some kind of ideal essence, would be the appearance of some underlying reality. The sequel to this discussion seems to indicate that, in spite of the Socratic hesitation, the second view is, on the whole, accepted by Plato.[6] Our general conclusion, then, regarding this group is that there are absolute, transcendent Ideas of natural phenomena, conceptual essences abstracted from sensuous phenomena, such notions as Water-as-such, Clay-as-such, Fire-in-itself, as distinct from actually experienced concrete examples of water, clay, fire, etc., which only partially and imperfectly represent the ideal nature of such objects—much as a physical experiment, intended to " demonstrate " the law of the conservation of energy, falls short of its complete ideal.[7]

(2) The second group, which includes at least all organic bodies, is considered partly in the same context. Socrates expresses a certain indecision as to whether, over and above all actual human creatures, and " apart from " them, there is such an entity as Man-as-such.[8] Here also the sequel appears to imply with reasonable certainty that, in spite of the Socratic indecision, Plato himself would decide the question in the affirmative. This is supported by the discussion in the *Philebus* as to the existence of such entities as Man-as-such, Ox-as-such, etc. It is there implied, with sufficient clearness, that such entities retain a permanent core of individuality, " apart from " changes in the realm of generation and destruction.[8] Here also, then, our general conclusion must be that of organisms such as man, ox, etc., there exists, as expressed in the class-name, a principle which holds the class together as a unity, a conceptual unity distinguished from and contrasted with the multiplicity of sensuous particulars in the phenomenal world.[9]

(3) Concerning the third group, which consists of at least the Ideas of artefacts, e.g. such objects as beds and tables made by the carpenter, Plato is very definite. The Ideas of such objects are given as examples of unity-in-multiplicity, a group which includes all artefacts and, indeed, extends far beyond them.[10] Wherever there is a collection of phenomena, a " many " which can be grouped together as examples of a common principle, there is also the principle of organization, the " one " or the Idea which is at least partially expressed in every member of the group. This is more than a mere

class-name. It expresses rather the ideal partially realized in the concrete embodiments which can be touched and seen. It is the ideal table, and the ideal bed, whose patterns are laid up in heaven, the principle of table-ness or bed-ness, which the carpenter endeavours to realize in wood or iron, and which the true artist should also endeavour to portray in his own medium, instead of contenting himself with copying the product of the carpenter's art. It is sharply distinguished from the particular concrete objects which, in the phenomenal world, only partially and imperfectly express the ideal nature.

(4) The fourth group, representing what Plato frequently classes together as " goods of the body," e.g. health, strength, good looks, and their corresponding opposites, is nowhere in so many words stated to be transcendent, absolute Ideas, constituents of ultimate reality. However, in view of the undoubted facts, that (1) they come under the one-in-many principle just explained, i.e. represent the common principle in terms of which many individuals can be grouped together as " healthy," " strong," etc., and (2) they constitute ideals for human choice, and are thus " patterns " strikingly similar to the two great patterns of choice in the *Theaetetus*—which are certainly absolute Ideas—it seems reasonable, at least tentatively and unless we discover reasons which might incline us to take the contrary view, to regard them as Ideas.[11] The case of Pleasure presents, however, at least at first sight, a certain difficulty, inasmuch as it is at times apparently regarded as a *genesis* rather than an *ousia*.[12] But further investigation shows that this is a temporary, not a permanent point of view, and in view of the facts that (1) pleasure is frequently referred to as a typical life-ideal,[13] (2) the question is seriously discussed, whether or not pleasure is to be identified with " the good "—which is quite certainly an absolute Idea,[14] (3) the " *Ideas* of Pleasure " i.e. the subordinate type-forms of pleasure—are discussed and to some extent subjected to the analysis of the dialectician, whose function consists in analyzing and synthesizing *Ideas*,[15] and (4) the unity-in-multiplicity principle seems to apply to it, inasmuch as pleasurableness is the element common to all the various examples of the pleasure-experience—in view of all these facts, it seems necessary to recognize a certain ideality about pleasure also, especially, perhaps, in its purer forms. Taking,

then, the class, "goods of the body," as a whole, we shall in what follows, at least provisionally, regard the members of this class as constituting ideal patterns which have a genuine existence, which may be distinguished from and contrasted with the particular concrete experiences of healthiness, pleasure, etc.

(5) The fifth group, which is constituted by social and political goods, is also nowhere as a whole stated to belong definitely to the world of absolute Ideas, as opposed to phenomenal realities. But, so far as wealth, birth, power, etc., are concerned, the same arguments apply which we found convincing in the case of the fourth group : (a) Each of these entities is a one-in-many, as wealthiness is a characteristic common to all members of the class " wealthy," (b) wealth, power, etc., constitute typical life-ideals, patterns of choice,[16] and (c) the inter-relations and consequences of the members of this group, in their effect upon human character, constitute the subject-matter of moral science,[17] i.e. form part of the study of the dialectician, and are thus certainly to be regarded as Ideas ; e.g. the life of the tyrant, as contrasted with the life of the philosopher-king in respect of happiness, is even represented mathematically, i.e. as an Idea, for all numbers possess ideal quality ;[18] and the political ideals, which are somewhat similarly contrasted with one another, are also presumably to be regarded as possessing ideal quality, for it is definitely stated of one of them, the Platonic ideal city, that there exists a pattern of it set up in heaven, i.e. that it is a transcendent Idea.[19]   We shall therefore, at least provisionally, regard this group also as consisting of conceptual essences apprehended as ideal type-forms underlying the various phenomena of social life, and as contrasted with the particular lives actually lived.

(6) The sixth group is in a somewhat similar situation. The various qualities of mind exemplified above constitute a portion of the subject-matter studied by the moral scientist, who, whether as a departmental scientist, or as a dialectician who has realized the final vision of the Idea of Good, presumably studies only Ideas. Knowledge, again, is subjected to a thorough-going dialectical analysis, and the results of the analysis, i.e. subordinate types of knowledge, are definitely referred to as Ideas, and frequent attempts are made to define its " nature " or essence, so that we appear to be

justified in regarding it as possessing ideal quality.[20]   These qualities of mind also come under the one-in-many principle, and furnish one of the typical life-ideals, the life of knowledge, or the contemplative, philosophic life, so that, in spite of the undeniable fact that Plato nowhere refers directly and un-ambiguously to this group as a whole as a group of trans-cendent Ideas, it seems reasonable, at least at the present stage, to regard this group as furnishing conceptual essences or ideal type-forms, which are apprehended as underlying the varied phenomena of the intellectual life, exemplified, perhaps to an especial degree in the life of the ideal philosopher, and more or less adequately realized in the actual lives of educated individuals.

(7) Concerning the seventh group, there can be no possible doubt. Good and evil, justice and injustice, temperance, wisdom, and all the virtues and vices are referred to, again and again, individually and collectively, as absolute Ideas.[21] They are contrasted sharply with the realm of phenomena perceptible by the senses, as being unitary, permanent, and intelligible, as opposed to the manifoldness, the transitori-ness, and the fluctuating quality of sense.[22] In a word, they are, one and all, transcendent essences, ideals of Reason, infinitely superior to the actual, concrete experiences of sensation, instinct and habit.

(8) So too of the eighth group, which consists of aesthetical ideals, from the beauty or ugliness of personal appearance, through the beauties of science and conduct, to the ultimate science of beauty everywhere, with its ennobling influence upon human life.[23] Here also there is no shadow of doubt. Beauty is referred to, again and again, as an ideal essence far transcending the particular examples which may be observed in the phenomenal realm. It is the essence of beauty as such, the principle, participation in which makes all particular beautiful things beautiful, but is not exhausted, or even adequately expressed, in any particular object, or in any group of particular objects. It has the higher kind of reality, the " greater share of pure being " which belongs to the ideal as such, and is sharply contrasted with the meaner realities (such as they are) which can be touched and seen.[24]

(10) So far as the tenth group is concerned, the very nature of the objects referred to is such that no one could possibly confuse them with sense-perceivables. Unity,

duality, triplicity, oddness, evenness, likeness, identity, etc.—
such entities are obviously apprehensible only by the intellect. They are of the mind, mental, and are used by the
intellect in organizing sensory phenomena into systematic
groups, groups characterized, e.g. by some underlying
" identity " of sense-quality, which is " different " from the
" identity " of sense-quality underlying some " other "
group. Each of these " identities," again, is " one," and
taken together they are " two," and, while " different,"
they may be either " alike " or " unlike," and, whether alike
or unlike, they are one and all equally " beings." Plato
expresses their nature by saying that these entities are
universal elements common to all sense-perceivables, and
apprehended, not by sense, but by " the soul herself," i.e.
by reason or intellectual intuition.[25] They represent what
we should call categories and ideas of relation, and are plainly
ideal in character, i.e. non-sensory elements apprehensible
only by the intellect. They have also the characteristic
of being one-in-many, or universals.

(11) Concerning the Idea of Good, it is perhaps not
necessary to state much here. It is the highest of all Ideas,
and is apprehended last of all, and only after a special training,
and even then only with a great effort. When apprehended,
it is recognized as the ultimate principle which makes clear
every object of spiritual aspiration, and leads to a certain
transvaluation of what was previously, in every department
of experience, accepted as valuable. From the standpoint
of science, it is the clear vision of truth, the adequate realization of the true form of knowledge, transcending the
limitations of the special sciences, and pointing the way
towards their final unification in a single, purely intelligible
system of Ideas. It is the principle which makes knowledge
possible for the individual knower, the supreme law of thought.
It is also the principle which makes objects knowable, the
supreme formal principle of things, the ideal of perfect logical
consistency, expressing the cognitive inter-relationship of
all knowable entities in the light of a single ultimate principle.[26]
From the standpoint of conduct, it is the ideal of perfect
social living, the formal principle which expresses the co-
operation of every element in the social group, in such a way
that each element contributes its all to the common good,
the complete well-being of the group as a whole, and in so

doing, finds its own completeness and most harmonious development, its own perfect well-being and final satisfaction.[27] From the standpoint of art, it is the realization, in the medium of rhythmic movements, expressed, it may be, in tone and colour-patterns, of the ideal elements everywhere underlying our experiences, the "science of beauty everywhere," which does so much to transform our living and make it more nearly what it might be, a thing of beauty, a universalized aesthetic joyousness.[28] So too from the standpoint of religion, the Idea of Good is the supreme object of worship, the supreme principle of reality conceived, not as an impersonal principle, but as a living God, the Father of all, to whom men endeavour reverently to assimilate themselves, the living ideal of the God-like life, inadequately depicted in the various religious creeds of the world, but the true and ultimate source of whatever meaning those creeds possess.[29] That is to say, the Idea of Good, in general, is the principle of ideality, the principle which gives value and significance to our experiences, the principle which lifts them above the level of passing phenomena, changes devoid of meaning, and endows them with something of permanent and abiding import, something of its own Reality. As such, it is a transcendent, absolute Idea, contrasted with the impermanence, the fluctuation, and the insignificance, of particular, sensory experiences.

By "Idea," then, in general, Plato understands the one as opposed to the many, the universal as opposed to the particular, the intelligible as opposed to the sensory, the absolute as opposed to the relative, the meaningful as opposed to the insignificant, the idea as opposed to the actual, the ultimately Real as opposed to the phenomenal. The true life of the spirit is the life which rises above the barren trivialities of instinct, habit, and convention, to the full realization of the potentialities of humanity, the realization which comes with the development of reason, of the apprehension of the ideal, the permanent and abiding elements of value within experience, the realization of man's co-partnership with God in transforming the actual into the semblance of the ideal, in making real upon earth the ideal city whose pattern is laid up in heaven, the city in which science, art, and religion combine to enlighten conduct and thus to bring about the salvation of humanity from within, so that men

at last come to live lives which are truly real, elevated above
the particular, the mechanical, the sensory, and the trivial,
to the true home of the free spirit, the dwelling-place of the
Ideas, the City of God.

So much, then, for what Plato understands by the Idea.
That there are everywhere within experience ideal elements
pointing beyond the limitations of our immediate experiences,
such as these are, and that there arises inevitably before the
eye of the soul the vision of a transmuted, ideally complete
Experience, in which every element of value finds its place,
all tending towards the living development of the Whole,
and each realizing its full potentialities in complete harmony
and fellowship with all the rest—this vision of the ideal life
has furnished forth the substance of the faith of philosophers,
of the interpreters of the thoughts of humanity, throughout
the ages, and has been the comfort and the inspiration of
leaders in art, science, and religion, and concerning its general
validity for humanity there can be little serious question.
Our immediate inquiry, however, for the present, is as to how
Plato fills in the outlines, how he views the interconnection
of the ideal elements in experience, what kind of pattern he
weaves as his final expression of the structure of absolute
reality.

That the various Ideas recognized by Plato must have
some relation to one another, will be apparent from a glance
at the list we have given above. Some of the Ideas, for
example, fall into one and the same group; e.g. the Ideas
of hair, dirt, and clay, etc., fall into the group of natural
phenomena, the Ideas of temperance, justice, wisdom, etc.,
fall into one and the same group, representative of moral
ideals, the Ideas of identity and difference, likeness and unlikeness, etc., fall into one and the same general group, which
we have called " Ideas of relation." So, too, each of the
departmental sciences studies all that falls within the scope
of some one general Idea ; but what it studies, even in relation
to sense-perceivable phenomena, is always Ideas ; e.g. it is
the ideal diameter, the ideal square, etc., which the mathematician studies by means of his sense-perceivable figures,[30]
so that it is a group of Ideas which, as studied from the standpoint of a particular science, falls within the scope of the
general Idea of that science. It is, then, at once evident
that certain of the Ideas have something in common, in

virtue of which they come under a wider, more inclusive Idea.

A further glance at the list will reveal the widespread presence of another relationship, the relationship of opposition. Though falling within one and the same group, certain members of the group are sharply distinguished from, and opposed to, other members of the group. Thus goodness, temperance, and justice, are sharply distinguished from, and contrasted with, evil, intemperance, and injustice, although these " opposites " are also recognized as Ideas and as falling within the same general group of moral ideals.[31] So also identity, likeness, greatness, and being, are opposed as logical contraries to difference, unlikeness, smallness, and not-being ; and yet, though " opposites," they are explicitly recognized as Ideas, and as belonging, just as much as identity, likeness, etc., to the same group, which we have named Ideas of relation.[32] So also in the Platonic view of scientific investigation, it is usually and normally maintained that " opposites " fall within the scope of a single science, i.e. fall under a single general Idea.[33] And a further glance at our list of Ideas will show that this kind of difference and opposition is sufficiently evident in the other groups also.

The relations just noted, which we may, perhaps, regard as relations of identity and difference, or, as Plato sometimes calls them, sameness and otherness, fall within the field of some one of the eleven groups which compose our list, considered apart from the other ten groups, in reference only to its internal organization. But it will also be sufficiently obvious that the groups themselves, when considered in relation to one another, either as wholes or as aggregates, are also related by way of identity and difference. By way of identity— for, as Ideas, i.e. as examples of the principle of ideality, whether in direct relation to the Idea of Good, or in relation to the diverse phenomena which they sum up and whose meaning they express, the groups as wholes, and also all examples of each group, have certain formal elements in common. They are, e.g. *one* as opposed to many, *universal* as opposed to particular, *conceptual* as opposed to sensuous, etc. By way of difference—for the group expressing Ideas of relation is clearly different from the group of social goods, or of goods of the body, or from natural phenomena or artefacts. Formally, then, all Ideas whatever, whether considered as individual Ideas or as groups naturally falling together under a single " higher Idea," are to some extent interrelated. Is it possible to go further, and to urge that, just as the individual Ideas which fall under one and the same higher Idea (e.g. justice, temperance, wisdom, etc., as falling under the higher Idea of virtue) are related in respect of content as well as of general form, so also some of the groups are related to one another in content as well as in general form ?

All the above points of relationship are noted incidentally by Plato, and the question of the general inter-relationship of Ideas and groups of Ideas is definitely discussed in the *Sophist*. There it is declared that the dialectician who has learned to analyse correctly—i.e. following lines of cleavage established in the nature of things—will discover :[34]

a. One form pervading a scattered multitude ;

b. Many forms, existing only in separation and isolation ;

c. Many forms, knit together into a single whole and contained under one higher form ;

d. Some classes having communion with only a few other forms ;

e. Some classes having communion with many other forms ;

f. No reason why there should not be some classes which have communion with *all* forms.

A brief study of these distinctions is necessary in order to ascertain clearly what is intended. The first division (a) is apparently a description of the general function of the Idea as such. Each and every Idea is a one-in-many, a single form pervading and uniting an otherwise scattered multitude of particular examples, as e.g. " furniture " might be regarded as a general term pervading and uniting miscellaneous particular specimens of furniture in an auction sale, or as the medical term " bile " or " biliousness " serves to unite under a single head many symptoms which, in appearance, at any rate, seem diverse and disconnected.[35]

The second division (b) seems to give rise to a serious difficulty, for, if the separation and isolation of the Ideas in this division is taken absolutely, we have a clear contradiction to the division of universally pervasive forms (f), and there is also a lack of harmony with the well-known platonic position, maintained in this dialogue also, that the isolation and separation of conceptual elements is the negation of all discourse and all reasoning.[36]   But in actual fact, if we may judge by the sequel, he understands the separation and isolation as relative, as motion and rest, e.g. logically exclude one another, or as sameness and otherness logically exclude one another. The distinction is, then, a relative distinction, and is not intended to imply that Ideas can be absolutely isolated, separated into logically water-tight compartments.

The third division (c) recognized by the dialectician would be exemplified by any of the departmental sciences, e.g. by geometry, which studies such ideal elements as the point, line, surface, diameter, square, etc., in their inter-relations, as coming under a single comprehensive principle and thus as being knit together into a single whole.[37]   Another example would be the grouping together of such Ideas as greatness, smallness, equality, etc., identity, differences, similarity, dissimilarity, etc., so as to constitute a single class, included within the higher, more comprehensive notion of " universals apprehended as common to all sense-perceivables," or, as the discussion in the *Sophist* and *Parmenides* indicates, common also to many Ideas.   Yet a third example would be furnished by moral science, which investigates the inter-relations of such Ideas as noble birth, wealth, high station, etc., and studies their effect upon character, according as they are variously combined in varying circumstances, thus knitting together into a single complex totality all these Ideas.[38]   An even more common example in the Dialogues would be the example of the various " parts of virtue," viz. Justice, Piety, Temperance, Fortitude, etc., each of which is certainly regarded as an Idea, but all of them are certainly regarded, in spite of difficulties, as linked together under the higher and more comprehensive single Idea of Virtue.[39]

The fourth and fifth divisions become much clearer (d and e) if we consider concretely, in relation to definite examples, what is meant.   Artefacts, for example, such as beds and tables in the ideal sense, have " communion with " other Ideas in a relatively small degree.   That is to say, they have certain points of contact which link them up with other groups of Ideas, but only to a limited extent.   The Idea of Bed, for example, has certain points of contact with the Idea of Wood, or of Metal—or even with the Ideas of Hair, Dirt, Water, Fire, etc.—but such connections are obviously super-

ficial, unessential. So again, the Idea of Bed has some points
of contact with the group constituted by the Ideas of organisms, e.g. with the Idea of Man. It has extremely superficial
and unimportant points of contact with the Ideas grouped
together as goods of the body or with the social-goods class,
still more superficial and insignificant points of contact with
the goods-of-the-mind class, or with the moral-ideals class.
To the aesthetical-ideals class it bears a slightly more recognizable relation, and has a number of relations to such Ideas as
greatness, smallness, motion, and rest, and is of course connected with the Idea of Good. Such an Idea as Bed or Table
may be regarded as an example of the fourth division (d).
On the other hand, as an example of the fifth division (e),
such Ideas as the mathematical Ideas, and such Ideas as
likeness and unlikeness, seem to have a more universal connection, or, as Plato expresses it, have communion with many
other forms. These examples indicate, briefly but perhaps
adequately, what is meant by the intercommunion of forms,
which furnishes so much of the subject-matter to be investigated by the dialectician.

The sixth division (f) is exemplified, in the discussion which
takes place in the *Sophist*, primarily by such " higher Ideas "
as Motion, Rest, Identity and Difference (or, as these last two
Ideas are treated in the discussion, relative Being and Otherness), and also, perhaps, by such Ideas as absolute Being and
the Idea of Good. The upshot of the discussion appears to
be that motion and rest are not strictly universal, but that
identity and difference (or relative being and otherness, or
relative not-being) belong to each and every example of
ideality, the notion of absolute being, which is perhaps to be
identified with the Idea of Good, apparently falling outside
the discussion. It will be noted, however, that the universals
which remain within the discussion have only a " relative
being," i.e. have meaning and reality mainly in relation to
one another ; e.g. as good and evil are correlated in the
Theætetus, so likeness and unlikeness are correlated in the
Parmenides, and sameness and otherness in the *Sophistes*.
The notion of absolute Being, however, i.e. of ideal Being,
the form or principle of Being itself, which is presumably to
be equated with the Idea of Good, is apparently to be understood as a single form which has communion with all forms,
precisely so far as they are forms, i.e. on their formal side,

as the principle of formality or ideality which necessarily underlies each and every individual form or Idea.

So far, then, we have discovered that, from the ideal standpoint, the whole of reality is akin. The ideal qualities apprehended by the dialectician as everywhere underlying our experiences, constitute an interconnected totality, a single ideal system. But as soon as we attempt to look more closely into the system, and probe into the interconnection itself, we come upon a certain difficulty, which is disguised, perhaps, rather than elucidated by the statement that there is an " intercommunion of forms " and that it is a large part of the dialectician's task to investigate this intercommunion, with little more to guide him than the formal certainty that some forms are universally present, others less universally —in a word, that he may expect to discover any and every degree of intercommunion, from totality to zero.

In this difficulty let us, for the moment, leave the text of the *Sophistes* and *Politicus*, and construct, from what we have learnt from the other Dialogues, the general ideal theory, in order to see if it will throw any light upon the precise significance of this difficulty of the inter-relatedness of the ideal qualities discovered by the dialectician.

Each and every Idea, as such, is, as we have repeatedly observed, in the first place, an empirical generalization, i.e. is a group of sensuous experiences so analyzed and synthesized as to become telescoped, concentrated, idealized, raised to a higher, supra-sensuous, power in the form of a concept, as, e.g. the conception of the ideal bed-quality arises out of a number of empirical bed-experiences, by processes of abstraction, comparison, etc., resulting in a certain symbolization and standardization of the experiences in question, and giving us, in the " bed-ness " concept, something which the mind can grasp as an intelligible unity, something elevated above the sensuous flow of consciousness, a conceptual essence of meaning, colourless, shapeless, intangible, as Plato puts it.

In this process, nothing of genuine importance has been omitted. The fluctuation, impermanence, uncertainty, and chaotic plurality of the sensuous experiences are gone, but every element of ideal quality anywhere contained in those experiences has been extracted by the dialectician and taken up into the final concept. The meaning of the sensuous experiences, and the meaning expressed in the concept, are not two meanings. They are identical, with however this difference, that in the concept the meaning finds expression in a clear-cut form which not merely can be felt vaguely, as a part of the living stream of conscious experience, but, while still felt, is also known, distinctly apprehended by the intellect, the " pilot " of the soul.

Suppose, now, we take a second ideal quality, the Idea of Comfort,[40] and let us assume that this concept has been obtained from a number of empirical experiences, partly of beds, partly of chairs, partly of clothing, etc., in such a way that the bed-experiences, at any rate, are identical with the bed-experiences in the first case considered. This concept also is obtained by abstraction, comparison, etc., and results in an intellectualized, colourless, shapeless, intangible essence, which is not merely felt (*erlebt*) as part of the living-process, but is also grasped distinctly by the intellect.

If we proceed to compare these two Ideas in order to investigate in the dialectical manner how far they have " inter-communion," we discover that in a certain regard they are not different from one another, but are identical. Both arise from sensuous experiences which are analyzed, synthesized, telescoped, and concentrated in such a way as to omit the fluctuation, impermanence, and uncertainty which are inevitably bound up with the sensuous mode of experiencing, and to retain, in consistent and harmonious inter-relationship within the limits of a single ideal unity, all the elements of meaning-value which could be extracted from the original, relatively more sensuous experiences. And further : this, which both have in common, is common to all Ideas without exception. One and all, they represent attempts at extracting from sensuous experience all relevant elements of meaning-value, and at inter-relating these elements in such a manner as to secure harmony, consistency, unity, and the maximal development of ideal quality within the limits of the conceptual totality, the Idea, which results from these operations.

That is to say, all Ideas without exception are examples of one and the same law, the principle of Ideality, the demand that every conceptual unity, as such, shall exhibit the maximum of ideal quality which is capable of being extracted from sensuous experience and expressed in consistently organized, systematic unity. But this principle of Ideality is, as has been pointed out elsewhere,[41] what Plato calls the Idea of

Good, so that every particular Idea is a particular determination of the Idea of Good, is, on its ideal side, identical
with the Idea of Good, taken, however, not universally in its
full and final sense, but as being limited by being applied to
a particular, limited group of sensuous experiences.

Let us consider briefly but more precisely what this
means. The Idea of Good is, as we have seen from a logical
point of view, the principle of completeness and consistency,
the scientific ideal of including within one and the same consistent system every element of positive knowledge-value
within experience. From the ethical and social point of view
it is the ideal of a social organism which calls out the complete
development of every member in harmony with the complete development of every other member, each contributing
its all to the common good. From the metaphysical point
of view the Idea of Good is the conception of an ideal reality
in which the positive significance of each element which exists
is fully brought out in harmonious relationship with everything of positive significance throughout the rest of existence ;
it is the conception of an ideal existence consisting of the
fullest and richest development of the potentialities of the
universe in a single, self-supporting system, with a complete
absence of conflict, waste, privation, and negation.

Let us now take a particular Idea, e.g. the Idea of Bedness,
and compare it with the Idea of Good. The Idea of Bedness
represents an attempt to extract from certain sensuous experiences everything which has bed-quality, and to organize
the elements so extracted into a single harmonious system,
representing the complete systematic development of all
relevant elements of meaning-value. That is to say, it is
the principle of the Idea of Good, applied, however, not to
the whole universe, but to a particular section of sensuous
experience. The difference, then, between a particular Idea
and the Idea of Good is the difference between the more
particular and the more universal, i.e. more comprehensive
and more thorough-going, application of one and the same
principle, the principle of ideality. Every Idea is, then,
in principle identical with the Idea of Good, the principle of
ideal or ultimate reality ; but, as being narrow and without
comprehensiveness in its application, or as being superficial
rather than profound, i.e. with the process of idealization only
partially carried through as at the level of " opinion," it

falls short of being a complete expression of the ideally trans-muted Experience which is ultimate Reality.

In the final analysis, then, there is only one Idea, the Idea of Good, the Absolute or Divine Experience. But between this and the lower limit of experience which is wholly sensuous, are to be found various stages of human attempts at idealiza-tion, such as are noted in the theory of the " four stages of intelligence " in the *Republic*. Some of these, empirical generalizations at the level of opinion, are hardly to be called Ideas at all as they are more closely related to sensuous than to intellectual experience. But they pass by imperceptible gradations into Ideas at the higher level of opinion or lower stage of knowledge which is represented by the generalizations studied in the departmental sciences.[42] These need to be still further idealized by abstracting from their sensuous basis and gradually making them over in accordance with the formal demand for the complete and systematic development of all that is positive in their conduct until they are truly permeable to intelligence and have become transformed from proximate into ultimate reality. They are then Ideas in the strict or final sense, and it is with the ideal vision attained in this way, i.e. with the vision of the complete idealization of human experience, the transmuting of all its baser elements into elements of beauty and glory, each realizing itself in its true place as related to the other elements which together make up the absolute totality, that the philosopher-guardian proceeds to make over the whole of our experience, working into our social institutions the principle of the Idea, and elevating our experience gradually, and so far as is possible for an experience which retains to the last elements of human imperfection, to the level of insight at which we become co-partners with God in the real work of the world, the full development of potentiality, and the onward march of human-ity towards the progressive realization of the Idea.

We are now in a position to ask how upon these premises one Idea is related to another, i.e. how certain sensuous processes partially idealized are related to certain other processes partially idealized, or to the same processes, perhaps, idealized from a different point of view, e.g. how the Idea of Comfort is related to the Idea of Bed.[43] The answer depends primarily upon the standpoint of the questioner. From the standpoint of " opinion " or ordinary education, Ideas, though all admittedly "ideal," and thus resembling one another, are, on the whole, rather sharply distinguished from one another, and even a thinker like the Socrates of the *Parmenides* has not adequately realized the gap which separates an empirical generalization like "likeness," "unlikeness," "greatness," "smallness," etc., from an Idea in the full sense. From this standpoint it is assumed that each Idea is itself and is sharply distinct from every other Idea, and it is not understood that an element of "difference" or "multiplicity" is retained in every such generalization. This position is not quite consistent with the belief, expressed in the *Sophistes*, that the Ideas "intercommunicate," i.e. that, in spite of each Idea being distinct from each other Idea, they possess certain elements in common so as partly to overlap and coincide ; for if they possess certain elements in common they cannot possibly be quite as distinct as is assumed in the *Parmenides*. In fact, a great part of the purpose of the *Parmenides* as a dialogue appears to be, to convince " Socrates " that in the Ideas as he understands them there is contained a fringe or margin of difference or multiplicity analogous to the diversity and manifoldness which he recognizes as present in sensuous experience, and that accordingly, in the empirical generalizations which he accepts as complete idealizations, there is much of the contradictoriness and fluctuation which is, to his mind, as much a paradox in the ideal realm as it is a commonplace in the realm of sensation.[44] That is, the truth emphasized by the *Parmenides* in this connection is, that the Socratic " Ideas " are not Ideas in the highest sense, not complete idealizations, but retain, in that portion of their content which has been only imperfectly abstracted from its empirical beginnings, a mass of experience which remains sensuous, unidealized, and admitting of all the logical difficulties which are accepted as the inevitable attributes of untransmuted sensuous experience.

At this level, then, which appears to correspond to the " third stage of intelligence," Ideas seem to be sharply distinct from one another, and a question may well be raised as to their inter-relationship, as in more modern times a conflict has been recognized between groups of experience organized under such headings as " Science " and " Religion," or " Art " and " Morality," or between such organizing principles as " Mechanism " and " Teleology," and the inter-relations of such pairs of Ideas have been subjected to prolonged and systematic investigation. It is, in fact, largely to this method, viz. of investigating the inter-relations of such comprehensive generalizations, that the Platonic dialectician looks for success in rising out of and beyond the third stage of intelligence into the fourth,[45] i.e. to the realization that these generalizations are not complete or final idealizations, and to the discovery of the unhypothetical first principle which underlies experience in general, and especially experience as partly reorganized in these wide generalizations.

When this final stage of philosophic insight has been reached it becomes sufficiently clear that each Idea (e.g. Science, Religion, Art, Morality, etc.) now represents the whole of philosophic insight turned in a particular direction, and it becomes plain that, whatever the direction, it is one and the same insight which is represented in each of these cases, so that the difference and conflict which were noted at the lower stage of reflection cease, at the higher standpoint, to have any meaning, and the complete harmony in which the various aspects of experience now inter-penetrate and throw light upon one another, has so transformed them all that there is now only one continuous experience. In this single experience, the different Ideas, such as Art, Morality, etc., represent different directions of thought, different reference-points for the concentration of the whole of experience, and are related to one another as different lines of interest, i.e. with the freest possibilities of overlapping, interacting, etc. From this higher standpoint the dialectician is made free of the whole intellectual realm of Ideas, and can pass at pleasure from any one direction of thought to any other, secure in the insight into the Idea of Good, which illumines each pathway and enables him to surmount what, at the lower stage of reflection, constituted serious obstacles for his thought, opaque and impermeable to his intelligence.[46]

If we now proceed to inquire what, from the standpoint thus attained, is the structure of ultimate reality, we discover that the question has little meaning.[47] The difficulties concerning the inter-relation of Ideas which appeared distinct and opposed to one another, vanish of themselves when it is realized that such difficulties subsist only between incomplete idealizations, i.e. at a stage of philosophic reflection lower than the one now reached. From the new and final standpoint, reality is envisaged as completely intellectualized, completely ideal, and consequently as possessing only the structure which belongs to the nature of the intellectualized and ideal, as such.   That is to say, ultimate reality is identical with the Idea of Good, and its structural form is consequently nothing more or less than the form of organization.   It is the ideal of unity-in-multiplicity applied upon the widest possible scale, viz. to the whole of experience, the ideal of comprehensiveness and consistency, the ideal of a totality of harmoniously inter-penetrating contents, or rather, the ideal of a single unified richness which is Experience itself, raised above the sensuous to the intellectual level, and completely idealized, expressed in the form of a single, all-comprehensive and all-expressive judgment, in which every content of possible experience finds its true and final place in relation to all other possible contents, and all differences, conflicts, and oppositions, which at the lower, more empirical level are so painfully apparent, are transcended.   They are overcome in the transmutation effected by the new unification, the bringing of all experiences into a togetherness, an inter-penetration, in the name of the single supreme principle of Totality.[47]

This, then, is the Platonic view of ultimate, ideal reality. In order to make sufficiently clear its concrete application as a criterion in questions of moral evaluation, we shall follow Plato's example, and shall begin with the individual writ large, i.e. with the community organized into a city-state, before passing on to consider the moral judgments of the individual citizen as such.   The first characteristic of the ethical state which is to be noted, is its unity.   Made up, as it is, of different individuals and classes, a strong natural tendency of the social group is towards disruption, towards the development of group-interest, of class-consciousness and class-legislation, expressing itself in the life of political faction which was so marked a feature of civic living in fourth-century Greece.   Such groups, as Plato never wearies of pointing out, constitute not one community but a plurality of cities, related to one another by way of hostile neutrality if not of open warfare, and their notions of justice and virtue are simply unmeaning.[48]   But disruption, in every shape and form, is " the enemy," and, in opposition to this state of things, the ethical community aims at true spiritual unity, in spite of the diversity of civic activities, and, in and through that diversity itself, uniting the members of the state in the common bonds of social service and co-operation in citizenship.

Each citizen is to realize his full potentialities. The cobbler is to make shoes and to turn himself into a better cobbler. The farmer is to cultivate the soil and make two blades of corn grow where one grew before. The potter is to turn himself into a better potter, the weaver into a better weaver, each realizing his " idea." But this is not to be understood in a too narrow and technical sense. The ethical community does not consist of a loose federation of diversely-interested, competitive groups of farmers concerned only in the production and sale of wheat, of carpenters concerned only with the ideals of a carpenters' trade union, etc., of manufacturers of agricultural implements concerned only with the production and sale of their wares, each competing against all the rest for higher wages, better working conditions, etc. On the contrary, it is only as genuinely inter-related, as belonging to a wider totality which unifies all its members, that the farmer, carpenter, etc., realize their full potentialities. It is as citizens of one and the same community, as workmen who perform all that they do in the spirit of service of the common-weal, that true co-operation develops, without which spirit the highest development of the farmer, weaver, etc., is impossible. The highest civic good is a certain community of feeling, a sense of belonging together for good or ill, not a matter of cold, logical or economical calculation, but a warm, living sense of unity, such as is found in the best kind of family life.[49] This is realized with peculiar vividness in the case of the guardian caste. For this is welded together by a certain *morale*, developed by the common work, common play, common social life, and common aspirations of the select group of community leaders. But right through the commonwealth runs a bond of unity which binds together leaders and followers, the agreement, namely, as to which shall lead and which shall follow, the civic virtue of temperance or self-determination.[50] And throughout the whole group runs the living sense of community, of belonging together, the herd-instinct idealized into the social virtue of justice, so developed that each citizen contributes his best to the common stock, secure in the realization that each of his fellow-citizens is doing the same. This applies not only to guardians and auxiliaries but also to farmers, weavers, and potters.[51] All alike are linked together in spiritual brother-hood, in virtue of their habitual sense of the Whole to which they belong, the ideal State in which they have their being, and to whose service they owe their full development as in-dividual citizens.

So far as a social group exhibits the characteristics of unity and full harmonious development of the most diverse abilities in the service of the community as a whole, we have a phenomenon which corresponds to the Idea of Good, i.e. the ideal conception of ultimate reality.[51a] So far, on the other hand, as we have groups which exhibit diversity, as when the central ideal pursued is not the well-being of the community as a whole, but the amassing of wealth, the en-joying of sensuous pleasure, or the expressing of an anarchic sense of " freedom "—we have a manifest falling away from the ideal. When considerable masses of citizens organize against their fellow-citizens in order to secure a disproportion-ate share of the wealth of the community, or when large numbers of the well-to-do refuse to regard themselves as belonging to the group as a whole and thus as bound to serve its interests, but insist that they should be free to get from the service of others whatever appears to their narrow, anti-social egoism to be desirable, the community ceases, in fact, to exist. We have no longer one city, but rather a plurality of cities, not at peace among themselves, but competing for goods which they cannot enjoy in common, and riddled with conflicts, oppositions, and contradictions. Faction-torn, divided against themselves, unstable, an easy prey to assaults from without and the forces of disruption within, they lead, by clearly marked and inevitable gradations, to the last and most miserable state of any social group, complete and tyranni-cal despotism.

It is in some such way as this that the Platonic view of ultimate reality can be used as a criterion or standard, by comparison with which we can decide whether a given con-stitution is making for unity of civic spirit, for an idealism which will develop each citizen to the full, and will bring to the community as a whole the free, ungrudging, joyous service of every citizen, or whether, on the other hand, self-seeking, the egoistic grasping after power and opportunity, the futility of party strife, and a cynical disregard of public good, is slowly but inevitably tearing the group to pieces and unfitting it to contribute anything free, noble, and worthy towards the onward march of humanity.

As with the State, so with the individual. Each one of us consists of a number of tendencies which are at war with one another and threaten to disrupt the personality. Along with the sense for law and order which distinguishes human beings from the other animals,[52] and furnishes the basis for so much which is characteristically human in our lives— e.g. Art, Law, Morality, Science—goes what Plato designates as a lawless, wild-beast element, which, even in the best-regulated personalities, peers out in the dream-life, disregarding our most sacred conventions and rejoicing in trampling upon our most cherished social convictions.[53] This " concupiscent element " is usually at daggers drawn with the more rational elements of our nature, seeking satisfaction for its instinctive needs with an absolute disregard for anything but the immediate satisfaction of those needs. It is especially and peculiarly opposed to the virtue of temperance or self-control, whether at the instinctive level or at the more rational levels of opinion and philosophical insight, and endeavours to convert reason into its minister, so as to make money which will procure satisfaction for its lawless desires, and by force and fraud to seek power in the community, in order, not only to discover means to its ends, but also to indulge its appetites with impunity.[54] Its last and final aim is to induce a self-sophistication of the reason which poisons our religious intuitions at the source, by spreading the belief that, out of the gains of systematic wrong-doing in the service of " desire," the Gods themselves can be bribed into acquiescence.[55] This spirit of materialistic self-seeking is thus a strong, lawless tendency, directly opposed to our ethical, religious, and rational impulses, and the source of a fundamental conflict in our nature.

Into this conflict a third element of major importance may enter, the " spirited element," with its tendencies towards pugnacity, vigour, and " character." This is capable of taking sides with either party, and of acting energetically either against the concupiscent impulses or against our more rational tendencies.[55a] And even as some sort of moral organization begins to develop, all kinds of conflict tend to make their appearance. Thus the dispositions (1) towards pugnacity and (2) towards tender-mindedness, quietness, and sobriety, are opposed, not only at the level of instinctive or unreflective disposition, but also at the level of opinion, i.e. even when they have taken on something of the nature of the two virtues of courage and temperance.[56]   And, finally, our intellectual nature itself, rational though it is, may be led so as to serve ends mutually contradictory, as in the case of the burglar, or rascally lawyer, whose intelligence is an instrument of evil,[57] as opposed to the case of the philosopher-king, in whom it is an instrument of good.

Thus we see that our human nature contains a multiplicity of impulses which are at variance with one another, so that the individual is naturally and almost inevitably at war with himself, not one man but two men or more, with diverse interests and diverse characters, oscillating between different and opposed lines of conduct, unstable equilibrium personified, swaying now towards reason and philosophy, now towards poetry and the fine arts, now towards wealth and grasp of power, and now towards sensuous enjoyment, a many-sidedness scintillating and dangerous, fascinating, dazzling, peculiarly Hellenic.[58]

Amid these conflicting impulses, however, there tends to arise, in the individual, some dominating group, some complex of impulses which acts together as a unit and functions as a kind of nucleus, introducing its own type of organization among the other impulses, and eventually converting them all into more or less reluctant ministers to its own type of satisfaction.   In certain cases, the ruling complex consists of those impulses which are concerned with the acquisition of wealth.   When this complex becomes dominant in an individual, it converts every other impulse in his nature into a means for acquiring wealth, or at least into something which is not a hindrance to that pursuit.   Thus, in respect of his various bodily appetites, he will, of deliberate choice, satisfy only such as are indispensable for the support of life, and these too only in such ways as assist to strengthen him in his pursuit of riches.   For example, so far as hunger and thirst are concerned, which are " necessary " appetites, he will satisfy these with plain fare, such as bread, meat, and water, rather than with the costly viands sometimes seen at the rich man's table, partly because he shrinks from paying out money, and partly because simple food is better for his health, and leaves him free to work hard.[59]   It must not be supposed, however, that he has no craving for tasty and expensive dishes. On the contrary, he lusts after any and every kind of satisfaction, and does not hesitate for a moment to gratify his desires, provided that someone else will pay the cost. His self-restraint is exercised only when gratification would cost him money, and his motives are entirely sordid and ignoble. Appetites which are not essential to the maintenance of life, and, so far from being of assistance in money-making, are actually a source of considerable expense—these he will keep down by violent constraint, because and in so far as they contradict his dominant motive of spending nothing himself. The constraint is unreasoning, a battle between opposed lusts, between which there can be only a patched-up truce, temporary at best, as questions of virtue and reason do not enter into the conflict at all.[60] Again, from a civic point of view, he is entirely devoid of public spirit, and not only steadily refuses to compete for distinction and office, for fear of encouraging his own expensive appetites under the stimulus of rivalry and the struggle for civic victory,[61] but evades the payment of taxes, impoverishes his fellow-citizens by the practice of usury, and, in general, devotes his great powers of work always to profit and hoarding, making mean and petty savings, from any and every source.[62]

His mode of living carries with it certain fatal consequences. The appetites which he refuses to gratify at his own expense, are, indeed, expelled for the time being, driven, as we should put it nowadays, below the threshold of consciousness. But, as there is no attempt to alter or educate them, they remain beyond the threshold, craving satisfaction. Eventually they tend to become unified in virtue of their common expulsion, and thus gradually and inevitably build up a rival complex, which in the end tends to get control of the organism, and thus finally destroys the well-organized but narrow complex of parsimonious impulses. The effort at dominance on the part of the wealth-seeking impulses thus results, after a temporary ascendency, in the creation of a powerful rival which ultimately succeeds in overthrowing it, and the individual tends to lapse into an unrestrained and chaotic satisfaction of diverse appetites, one after another, a condition which differs from the original state of the individual mainly in that the lack of restraint now tends to be deliberate.[63]

Let us consider, as a second example of one-sided development of character, the case in which love of " freedom," of lack of restraint, becomes dominant. In this case, the function of the dominant complex is the somewhat neutral one of allowing free play to any and every impulse without distinction. In fact, the organizing complex equates all impulses in respect of satisfaction-value,[64] and restricts its regulatory function to seeing that no one impulse, whatever its strength, succeeds in dominating the others for longer than a brief period. Like Dryden's Zimri, such an individual is an epitome of all sorts of man and is deliberately devoid of unity, everything by starts, and nothing long. First, all for music, then for gymnastic training ; now he idles, now he throws himself into philosophical investigation. Now he devotes himself to public life, adopting a political or a military career ; now he turns trader, and worships commercial success which can be measured in cold cash, with a marked tendency to make light of the laws and of all constituted authority. [65]

To the individual who lives this highly sophisticated kind of life, it appears to be, not one-sided, but many-sided, as he allows free play to every side of life in turn, as chance stimulates now this interest, now that. But as it is a matter of chance rather than of rational control, and as, in the kaleidoscopic changes and alterations of interest, all tendency towards permanent organization of character is deliberately eschewed, the controlling complex gradually deteriorates in power, and the individual, thus self-weakened, falls inevitably under the dominion of some one of the " terrible appetites " which, whatever its relative satisfaction-value, is more than equal to the other appetites in strength, and, once firmly in the saddle, is not easily unseated. As appetites which, when once released and entirely loosed from moral and rational control, develop to such a terrible extent, Plato names sex-desire, the craving for intoxicants, and other tendencies which he classes together as definitely pathological.[66] The deliberate purpose of maintaining neutrality and setting free any and every impulse without distinction, results in its own negation. For it inevitably delivers the individual, with diminished powers of resistance, into the hands of some one of the great demons which it has succeeded in unchaining, so that the path to freedom via many-sidedness leads to slavery and one-sidedness after all.[67]

By disorganization, then, and sophistication it is not possible to realize true freedom and the development of every natural impulse. Let us proceed to consider, not complexes motivated by ambition, or lust of power, which, after a brief and hectic ascendency, similarly fall victims to the rival complexes which their one-sidedness has called into being, but the attempt at organizing character in terms of reason and virtue. The training here consists, not in violent constraint, as in the case of avarice or anarchism or ambition, but in reasoning, in appealing to the rational element inherent even in our appetites.[68] We seek to convince appetites A, B, C, that it is to their own advantage, as appetites which seek their own satisfaction, to give up the irrational attempt at obtaining satisfaction by a system of internecine rivalry, and to substitute for this senseless and suicidal struggle a consistent attempt at rational co-operation, at the development of a harmonious life-ideal which will find room for every impulse which tends to develop and enrich a comprehensive personality. Where an appetite needs to be restrained in the interest of the totality of which it thus forms a part, it is possible to appeal to our sense of the part-whole relationship, and thus to persuade an appetite that it is to its own interest to accept and impose upon itself a certain degree of restraint. This kind of training not only welds together our various impulses in harmonious co-operation, but welds them together in terms of the rational element which is common to all of them, and considers what is, upon the whole, advantageous for each, so that, in a life-ideal so formed, not only is there no permanent conflict of interests, but the rational element rules, and rules over willing subjects, which are themselves rationalized and fully taken up into the strongly organized rational personality which represents their ideal result.

Their union thus represents, not a loosely organized federation of interests essentially competitive, a union external and liable on any occasion to disrupt and lapse into open coflict, but an inner, spiritual, unity in which each element, originally separate to some extent, has grown together with the others into a single closely-organized nature, which acts as one, feels and thinks as one, and *is* a genuine, living, spiritual unity.[69] Each of the elements originally separate, with a separateness capable of accentuation in the competitive struggle and one-sided development described above, comes to lose its one-sidedness and exclusiveness, and takes on something of the nature of the other elements which are all growing together in the interest of the personality as a whole. An instinctive impulse, originally capable of developing into a " terrible appetite," by co-operating with the other impulses in rational living becomes transmuted into an organic portion of the forces which are gradually building up a strong personality which will take its part in the onward march of humanity, and thus reflect the nature of the ideal which is by these means being realized.

In this transmuted form, it is precisely in the higher type of personality, so organized upon ethical and spiritual principles as to take on the nature of ideal reality, that every human impulse and appetite comes to realize its own highest potentialities, and thus attains to true inward freedom. The organization which develops by taking up into itself what is of positive value in every element in our nature is not something which acquires an external and temporary ascendency at the expense of creating some rival complex which will eventually overcome and enslave it. On the contrary, it grows stronger, more liberal and free, more permanent and assured, with each forward step it takes towards realizing the ideal, until at last each element has freely contributed its best and highest towards building up the personality of the philosopher-king, the strongest and most valuable personality possible for a human being, which reflects the whole value-experience of the race in its long upward struggle, and worthily assumes the position of leadership in the community.

The development of a personality of this type is definitely to be regarded as a gradual approximation to the nature of ultimate, ideal reality. This may be clearly seen in two ways. In the first place, as representing the utmost possible development of each natural impulse in the interest of the social organism as a whole, and thus as the maximal development of the potentialities of the organism thus harmoniously attuned to social service, it approximates to the nature of the Idea as such, to the Idea of Good which constitutes ideal reality. In the second place, a study of the genesis of the highest type of character from birth to the age of fifty[70] sufficiently shows how the natural organism gradually becomes responsive to the Ideas of courage, temperance, justice, beauty, piety and wisdom. By taking these up into its nature, it furnishes a human habitation for the highest Ideas, and fills in the outlines under the influence of the best literature, art, science, philosophy, and religion. Literature depicts in worthy form the noblest traditions of the race. Art fosters the growth of insight into the ideal which everywhere underlies the actual, and thus transforms our sensuous experience into the symbolic apprehension of the highest realities.[71] Art possesses the further function of training our habits of feeling and thinking along the noblest lines until the ideal has sunk into the inmost recesses of our being.[72] Science disengages the intelligence from its sensuous envelope and prepares it to traverse the intellectual realm of Ideas from one end to the other.[73] Philosophy enables the trained scientist and dialectician to raise his intellectual vision to the contemplation of the Idea of Good itself ; and finally religion enables the living spirit of man to realize its kinship with the living Spirit which is the universal Ideal, the God and Father of all, and, in the illumination which comes of this fusion of living faith and knowledge, to live the new life of assured blessedness, the peace and joy (*eudaimonia*) which come to those who have found their true and assured place in the bosom of Reality, as co-workers with their Divine Archetype.

The development of a personality of this type represents, then, an approximation to ideal reality. Other types of personality, which exhibit the dominance of some particular complex of impulses, such as the thirst for wealth, honour, or power, appear, in the light of this comparison, as one-sided perversions, tragically beside the point. So also the entirely mistaken attempt to be just to every natural impulse by equating the claims upon our good-will of each and every desire, and permitting each impulse to dominate in turn, as chance stimulates it into activity, giving up all positive attempt at central guidance and control,[74] represents a distinct falling away from the ideal. For in these cases, in place of completeness, we have one-sidedness, over-development here, under-development there. In place of harmony, we have conflict, open or disguised, culminating in the futility of self-contradiction. In place of steady, forward growth, we have a period of ascendency followed by conflict, disruption, and the ascendency of some rival complex. In place of peace and joy we have uneasiness, scheming, unrestrained savagery in victory, and abject fear in defeat. Of these one-sided tendencies, some are more orderly, more organized than others, and thus come nearer to the ideal. Others are more definitely weak, more obviously a prey to the blind forces of chaos, and are thus further removed from the ideal.

The consideration of such comparisons indicates with sufficient clearness how the conception of ideal or ultimate reality is used in Platonism as a criterion or standard by which to test the value of the individual personality.[75] It remains to make clear how the conception is used in moral judgment generally, and thus to discover upon what the metaphysical validity of moral judgments, in general, depends.

Moral judgment consists in asking, in the case of a character or an action presented for evaluation, how far does it approximate to this ideal standard? That is, does the action in question do full justice to the situation, does it bring out the maximal positive harmonious development of the organism in the service of the wider social and physical whole of which the organism constitutes a portion?[76] That is to say, does the action or character in question, as a microcosm, reproduce the structure of the ideal macrocosm which is reality? So far as it does, the action or character under consideration approximates to the ideal and is judged to be morally valuable. So far, on the other hand, as it exhibits looseness of organization, one-sidedness, contradiction, tendencies towards disruption and anarchy, it fails to exhibit the essential characteristics of the Idea, and is judged to be morally inferior, out of touch with the ideal reality of things.

So much for the technical nature of moral judgment. But if we are to penetrate to Plato's full meaning, we must look deeper, and realize that a moral judgment is always the decision of the moral judge. Not any and every person is capable, immediately and without a long process of development, of applying the moral standard in a way which will be valid. The moral judge, ideally speaking, is always understood by Plato to be a person born and trained under ideal moral, social, physical, and intellectual conditions. His training gives him the mental and moral outlook of the finished administrator and dialectician, with a personality which adequately reflects the ideal nature of ultimate reality, so far as this is possible for a human being with the mechanism provided by the normal animal organism. The judgment of such a personality sums up all that has gone into his training, and thus represents the concentration, upon the point at issue, of the whole of human experience, organized and refined, idealized and transmuted, until it approximates to the judgment of God. Such an individual realizes fully his own kinship to reality, and appreciates the spiritual significance of reality with every fibre of his being. His judgment is thus no external, coldly intellectual comparison between (a) a formal statement of the nature of the moral ideal and (b) an action or character submitted for judicial investigation, for an investigation which would take the form of cold intellectual analysis, methodical and complete, unsparingly impersonal. On the contrary, his judgment represents, so far as humanly possible, the warm personal appraisal of the action or character in the light of a complete experience, an experience which is not narrow or superficial, not merely sensuous or emotional, not merely intellectual, but broad and deep as humanity itself. And it is not merely comprehensive. It is an organized spiritual experience, as completely unified as may be, and reflects, in its judgments, the judgments of humanity as a whole, at its highest and best, in an idealized form which approximates to the living Standard of value, the Supreme Ideal of Experience which we designate as Absolute, as God.

We should now be in a position to sum up the result of our investigations and give a sufficiently clear and definite answer to the question which furnished the problem studied in the present chapter. Our question was, given the diversity of moral opinions, and given the demand that comparison with the nature of reality shall decide as to the validity of these opinions, upon what does the validity of the specifically Platonic theory of reality and of its application to questions of moral value depend ? To answer this question we shall re-state the results of our inquiries in two forms, (1) starting from the empirical, human side, and (2) starting from the transcendent, absolute side, so as to make our answer as clear, concrete, and adequate as possible.

On the empirical side, every human judgment represents the concentration, upon some subject of interest, of the relevant experiences of the individual. Experience concentrated in intellectual form is generalization, i.e. a certain stage in the development of what Plato calls an Idea. Judgment is thus the study of some subject of discourse in the light of an Idea, i.e. of the experience of the individual concentrated and raised to the intellectual level which omits the fluctuation, vagueness, etc., of sensation, emotion, etc., but retains the full conceptual essence of the experience in question. A moral judgment thus always represents the acceptance or rejection of some proposed action, or other object of moral approval or disapproval, in the light of the idealized experience of the individual judging. The Idea used in moral judgment is thus never a cold, bloodless category, but always the full, living experience of a personality.

Moral judgments on one and the same issue differ, according as the idealized experiences of different individuals differ, or possibly as an individual makes a hasty, superficial judgment, instead of bringing to bear, in condensed form, *all* that is of significance in his relevant experiences. Empirical, reflective comparison of such differing judgments in respect of their strong, as well as of their weak, points gives rise to the ideal of an experience which shall be (a) comprehensive and (b) adequately concentrated rather than superficial. For example, an experience which could sum up the history of humanity and be representative of the sum of human wisdom would be wider, more comprehensive than the hasty judgment of the moment, and also more profound, more highly concentrated, more nearly expressive of the nature of the Idea.

When we further remember that, for Plato, all experience is experience-of-reality, we appreciate the Platonic position that reality enters into our experience in more certain and unmistakable form, according as we leave the hasty, superficial, fluctuating, and vague level of sensuous and emotional experience, and enter into the more concentrated, higher reaches of experience which are expressed as Ideas apprehended by reason. Reality enters into all our experiences, even the most superficial. But it enters more comprehensively and more profoundly, when that experience has been purified of irrelevant and misleading elements, and raised more nearly to the ideal level which expresses adequately the nature of reality. In its most ideal form, we think of experience as being fully responsive to reality, pulsating with the pulse of reality, in the closest and most intimate interaction.

So far, then, as reality is in this way taken up into our experience, it follows that it is reality itself that passes judgment, accepts or rejects proposed courses of action, etc. So far as our experience, in the light of which we judge, has become widened and deepened, idealized until it takes on something of the character of Absolute, Ideal Experience, the moral judgments which we pass express the final nature of reality, the knowledge and wisdom of God, and are metaphysically satisfactory. Elevated as such an ideal is, concerning its concrete and empirical, human *status* there can be no doubt, as no item in its content is other than strictly a matter of human experience.

Let us now approach the question from the more transcendental side. Absolute or ultimate reality is regarded by Plato as God or the Idea of Good, the living essence of ideality and value, the Supreme Pattern of the ideal world, an ideal expressed in determinate and limited form in every concrete Idea and ideal, but not, of course, exhausted in any one such determination. From the transcendental standpoint, each Idea is itself absolute, i.e. represents the concentration in a single determinate direction, of the whole, completely organized, absolute Experience, experience organized to infinity. We can obtain a symbolic conception of what is meant, by comparing various human ideas with the absolute Idea representing the " judgment of Zeus." Consider e.g. the idea of a city. Human ideas, derived from our limited and imperfectly organized experiences of cities, represent the civic idea as a balance of diverse interests, held together by common needs, common fears, and a strong government. Such government we regard as representing powerful interests, and as furnishing, in its great opportunities for self-aggrandisement, an object of envy to all would-be supermen.[77] In such a community, political faction, organized, continuous group struggles, in addition to sporadic individual efforts to obtain the chief power, may well appear inevitable. A certain amount of crime, a great deal of futile, energy-and-time-consuming conflict, endless misunderstanding, hatred, and malice, seem inextricably bound up with such an existence. With concrete knowledge of actual constitutions, such as the Spartan, Theban, Athenian, and Cretan, it is possible, after comparison, to work out the main lines of an ideal constitution. In such a construction, it should be theoretically possible to overcome many of the actual obstacles to progress, and to release, at least to a considerable extent, the energies of the citizens for more fruitful pursuits than industrial and political bickerings. But still, however great the good-will, and however exact the experience and knowledge of the individual, such a construction would represent only an approximation to a truly ideal constitution. If we imagined the whole experience of the human race concentrated and brought to bear upon the question in idealized form, the result would probably be more satisfactory, but even in that case there would still arise before the eye of the soul a formal demand for something yet more satisfactory, for something which should do more than approximate to the ideal, a demand for the ideal itself. Such a final ideal, representing the judgment of ideal Omniscience, is what is understood by the absolute or transcendental Idea, the Idea of the City which is "laid up in heaven."[78] The absolute Idea, then, in every case, is the Idea of Good, the living principle of absolute value, in some especial and particular reference, and thus furnishes inevitably a final and absolute standard, a highest and last court of appeal, for judgments which involve reference to ideals.

It is misleading to regard the individual absolute Idea as "a thought in the mind of God." Such a formula is at once too narrow and too subjective in colouring. To adopt the language of the formula, God's Mind does not, for Platonism, consist of a plurality of thoughts. It is one thought, supremely complex, but also supremely organized, supremely one. Each Idea, e.g. the Idea of Bed, or the Idea of City, in the absolute sense, is the whole of God's Mind. That is why it is theoretically possible for the finished dialectician to pass from one Idea to another, once he has, by adequate contemplation of the Idea of Good, become free of the whole intellectual realm.[79] But the formula is not only too narrow. It is also too subjective. An Idea is never a mere thought. It is objective reality, entering into and giving significance to the mental processes of sifting, comparing, concentrating, etc., which have resulted in the human generalization which corresponds to the Idea. But the Idea itself, absolutely regarded, is reality in its own living essence, supreme reality, the *ens realissimum*, an entity which has, indeed, full cognitive quality, but is far more than merely cognitive. It is fully spiritual and fully objective, real in the realest sense conceivable. It is the ideal element in existence, and indeed may be said to transcend existence, being, as it is, the supreme essence, of which existence is a more or less empirical copy.[80] As such, it constitutes, always and inevitably, the final Pattern to which a judgment which wishes to be of objective significance, in spiritual contact with reality, will seek to conform and assimilate itself. When, therefore, the philosopher-king, with a personality which has been developed until it represents a human analogon to the Divine Personality, passes moral judgment in the form of laws establishing civic, judicial, and educational institutions it is ultimately the Divine Personality, that ultimate reality, to which he has gradually made every fibre of his being, flesh, sinews, heart, and brain, organically responsive, which is passing judgment, and, through the instrumentality of his legislative activities, passes over into the world of concrete human institutions, the empirical realities of social living.

Upon what does the validity of this view rest? Its first appeal is to experience, ordinary, human experience, and it cannot be denied that the appeal is upheld, not only by our hopes, but also by the evidence of our senses in actual, every-day experience. We try, each one of us, to make sense of life by generalizing, comparing, and abstracting the more universal elements in our experience, and regarding these as more fundamental, more essential, more trustworthy guides to action than the fluctuating sensations and emotions of the moment. We see in experience the working of general, universal laws and principles, and the only hope we have of making life better, settling it upon a more secure basis, is in the scientific manipulation of our experiences, the methodical sifting which results in verifying and substantiating our tentative hypotheses as to the nature of these fundamental, universal, permanent aspects of experience. The hope that, by such investigations, we are gradually coming into closer contact with reality, and learning to take up reality into our lives to a greater degree than without such inquiries, is definitely substantiated by the appeal to experience. This becomes plain, not only if we reflect upon our own individual sensuous experiences, but even more clearly if we glance at the history of scientific discovery within the last three generations. The improved means of transportation, of lighting, of mechanical power, of intercommunication, and also of destruction, which have resulted from scientific investigation of the more universal elements in experience, have transformed, and are in process of transforming, the daily lives of each one of us, affecting us, as they do, at so many points, economic political, social, religious, moral, that human life has become infinitely more complex. Life has become vastly more able to develop its resources and hidden potentialities, so as to be able to devote the results to the enrichment of humanity, and the forward march of the civilized nations of the world. It is true that the moral, political, and religious development still lags behind the more technical advances; for these depend upon the use of discoveries which have been made, for the most part, not by ourselves, but by a very few out-standing individuals. It is, however, to be supposed that improvements in general education will follow which, in their turn, will also develop these potentialities for civilization, for better social living, to the utmost. The appeal to every-day, sensuous and emotional experience, then, largely supports the Platonic claims.

The second appeal is to logic, i.e. to experience, no longer accepted at the sensuous level, but refined, standardized, formalized, and raised to a level which admits of intellectual proof and disproof, a level at which inconsistencies can hardly remain hidden from the scrutiny of the trained investigator. Here also the appeal is evidently upheld. The identity in principle between all actual stages of human generalization on the one hand, and the ideal of generalization on the other, is sufficiently evident. The ideal is to extract from the experiences generalized every element of positive content, and so to synthesize these elements in relation to each other that they come to constitute a true, harmonious unity, in which each element supports and is supported by each other element, all working in one and the same direction, the direction of that totality which they help to form. The Idea of Good, the aspirations of humanity, and the generalizations from sensuous experience, from the highest to the lowest, are logically akin, and are clearly recognized as such by the Platonic dialectician.[81] From the logical standpoint, then, as well as from the standpoint of sensuous experience, the Platonic metaphysic of morals appears to be justified.

One gap remains, a gap clearly and sharply emphasized by Plato himself. Human logic, after all, is itself only

M

generalized experience, and between (1) the ideals constructed by our intelligence in conformity with logical standards, out of the materials with which we first become acquainted in sensuous perception, ideals which inevitably retain a certain empirical element, and (2) the absolute Ideas which Platonism conceives as constituting the essence of ultimate reality, a reality which lies partly within, and partly beyond our narrow human experience, there is a certain *hiatus*. So far as reality enters into our experience, both sensuous and logical, we can deal with it in a way which, from the human point of view, is satisfactory enough. But the absolute Idea which furnishes, as we have seen, the last and highest court of appeal, the ideal Experience which we conceive under the form of God, the Father of All, transcends our experience, even at its best and deepest. Our experience enters into the ideal Experience, and draws from it whatever significance our human thought and life come to possess ; but it does not, and cannot exhaust the significance of the ideal Experience. The absolute ideal, on the one hand, and its highest reflection in idealized human experience, on the other, remain, in the last resort, disparate.[82]

It is the recognition of this which makes the philosopher, at times, tend to despair of his task, the task of embodying the Idea in human institutions. He has himself a correct grasp of the Idea, correct, that is, so far as it goes. But while formally correct, it is, and can be, correct in content only so far as the content of human experience reaches, and this has not, he seems to think, reached far enough. Our modern sense of the value of evolution, and the hope of indefinite progress, of indefinite development in approximating to the Idea, of building up a science and a civilization which shall know no final limitations, makes us still, in the main, hopeful. But Plato himself has not our historical perspective and our faith in the continuity of historical progress. He seems rather to think that the highest points are reached by a few individuals in a single generation, and have to be re-discovered in subsequent generations. Of that continuity, whereby later generations can so build upon the heritage of the past as to advance still further, he appears to have no real sense.[83] He therefore tends, at times, to despair, and to magnify the importance of the gap which, no doubt, exists and has never yet been completely bridged.

Containing, however, as it does, an at least sufficient admission of the existence of this gap between the humanly realizable and the nature of the absolute Idea, an adequate recognition of the substantial identity of human generalization and the fundamental nature of reality, and an insistence that only by founding our thinking and acting upon this reality in methodic, scientific fashion can the highest moral development of the potentialities of humanity be attained—this view, the Platonic metaphysic of morals, must be regarded as satisfying, not only our aspirations, nor only our logic, but also our every-day experience, sensuous, emotional, and practical. That is to say, from every standpoint which seems relevant and legitimate, his theory appears to be, fundamentally and in principle, valid.

CHAPTER VI

CONCLUSION : THE MORAL CRITERION

THE aim of the present chapter is to sum up the results established in the preceding studies in such a manner as to focus every ray of illumination upon the question of the moral criterion, the distinction between good and evil. As we look over what we have discovered, we note that three main concepts stand out as affording an adequate basis for distinguishing good from evil. These are (1) the concept of idealized human experience ; (2) the concept of ultimate reality ; and (3) the concept of value expressed in the principle of ideality. What we have discovered concerning each one of these, considered apart from the other two, we shall now put together. We shall then proceed to sum up the three conclusions thus established, in order to see whether there is a single more fundamental conception which can express the truth established in each of our three investigations, and thus exhibit the final view of Platonic thought concerning the moral criterion.

1. Idealized human experience.

Again and again in the course of the preceding studies, we have met with the view that human experience, in idealized form, constitutes the court of appeal in moral questions, whatever is consistent with moral and intellectual development being regarded as good, and whatever tends towards lower levels of acting and thinking being regarded as evil.[1] All normal human beings have some kind of moral sense, and the moral judge *par excellence*, the philosopher-guardian, is only a man, born and educated under conditions so ideal that he comes to represent human potentiality at its best. His judgments, then, which in questions of right and wrong are accepted as beyond question valid, express human experience in idealized form. These judgments are published in the form of written laws, and these written laws are definitely used as criteria of good and evil. Not only the judges in civil and criminal cases, and not only the censors in the matters of art, refer to these laws as standards, but the average citizen uses them as a kind of moral yard-stick, by which to measure the extent and direction of his own ethical development.[2] These laws are not absolutely final, but need to be revised from time to time, as conditions change. But it is the philosophical guardian alone who is competent to carry through the revision. He is regarded by Plato as a personification of the moral standard, and as definitely superior to any non-living, non-human, impersonal statement of the moral criterion.[3]

So too, in inquiring what it is about pleasure, wealth, etc., which makes men regard them as " good," we discovered that, in Plato's opinion, it is only to men of character and insight that they are really goods. In the hands of men who are perverted or stupid, wealth and the other objects of human endeavours are evils. It is philosophic insight, the insight of human experience at its finest and best, which transforms these means-to-ends into organic elements in moral and intellectual living, and thus gives them true moral significance. That is to say, the standard here, by which the value of the so-called " goods of life " is determined, is the living standard of moral and intellectual experience. So far as they are taken up into the higher life, pleasure, money, etc., are morally valuable ; so far as they are hindrances to the higher development and tend to make us look downward, away from the ideal, they are evil.[4]

Again, in investigating the concepts regarded by Plato as moral standards, we saw that " expediency or benefit " was frequently treated as furnishing such a standard. But this means that whatever tends to make men better as men, to raise human experience more nearly to the ideal level, as contrasted with what harms them as men, makes them less fit to play their part in the onward march of humanity, is of moral value, and the standard here is clearly the more ideal kind of life, the life of moral and intellectual development. That is to say, the criterion here also is what we have called idealized human experience.[5]

Yet again, in analysing the character of the moral judge, and in putting together, in the order of their development the various elements which gradually make a strong character capable of making valid moral judgments, we saw in principle, and to some extent also in detail, precisely how human experience becomes idealized. We saw how the instinctive dispositions, the natural equipment which man possesses for making value-judgments, gradually turn away from the immediate satisfaction of impulse, towards developing a group sense of value, and thus become responsive to the demands of the social group as such. We saw further, how these socialized dispositions gradually developed in the direction of rationality and philosophic insight, clothing themselves in Ideas and thus becoming truly idealized. In the final result, we observed how the whole knowledge and wisdom of the group, the history, traditions, and aspirations of the race, its science, art, and religion, all enter into the personality of the judge, until his judgments become representative of the highest and deepest thought of humanity, refined and idealized into some sort of reflex of the absolute ideal towards which we men, in our long drawn out social evolution, have been slowly feeling our way.[6]

Finally, in investigating the validity of the Platonic value-judgment, we discovered that it is its appeal to experience which constitutes its strongest claim. The appeal is always to human experience, especially in the form of philosophic insight, i.e. in idealized form, which expresses the universal reason, in which all classes of the community share, in proportion to the degree of their insight.[7]

When, then, it is stated that idealized human experience embodies the moral standard, the experience referred to is, in the first place, human experience, instinctive, emotional, and practical, the impulses and social conventions which have made their appearance in the course of human evolution. In the second place, this experience is idealized, worked over and transformed in two ways, (a) by condensation and concentration, so as to abstract from the fluctuating impulse or mood of the moment, to look before and after, and sum up the whole history and wisdom of the race, to express all that has been achieved by humanity ; (b) by sublimation and transmutation, by forming the structure of experience, as far as possible, upon absolute models, by transplanting into the growing life the ideal principles of manliness, self-determination, social considerateness, love of truth, beauty, and God until, in the new form, human experience comes to express, not only the past achievements of humanity, but also its ideals and aspirations, its soul and essence, looking steadfastly beyond its achievements to the Source of whatever illumination has come to the race, looking to God, the Father of all. In the third place, even when idealized, the experience remains human and personal, no cold intellectualism, but a warm, living realization of human experience in its many-sided evolution, transmuted indeed, but in its transmuted form retaining whatever of value can be contributed, not only by science, but also by instinct, emotion, social convention, artistic and religious feeling, human experience at its deepest and best. As a human touchstone of human values, what higher or more valid form of judgment can be conceived ?

2. Ultimate reality.

The distinction between appearance and reality is fundamental for Greek thought, and the characteristic work of Greek philosophy from the very first has been the search for the reality which underlies the changing phenomena of nature and of human experience. It is therefore not surprising that this reality should be regarded as the rock upon which humanity should seek a firm basis, and should thus be used as a final touchstone of value.

Understood in this sense, the concept of ultimate reality as a criterion has made its appearance again and again in the course of our investigations. Thus practical moral experience has been praised as giving a reliable appreciation of the facts of life and the limitations of mere theorizing.[8] So too the man of moral character has been recognized as a sound judge, on the ground that, as personifying the moral standard, his judgments are not subjective and capricious, but are objective, in touch with reality. Finally, the philosopher, as an essential part of his training, studies the *ratio essendi*, the ultimate nature of reality, and definitely makes this his standard in his characteristic work of remodelling human institutions. We have also, after somewhat detailed study, discovered that it is precisely the extent to which human institutions embody and express ultimate reality, which gives value and significance to art, law, and science on the one hand, and on the other to such natural endowments as good looks, a sound bodily constitution, the possession of adequate means, etc. Left to themselves, the instinctive dispositions which constitute our natural equipment, pugnacity, timidity, the herd-instinct, curiosity, etc., are of merely subjective significance. They work themselves out, bringing more or less satisfaction for the moment in the process. But if out of touch with the one thing that matters, reality, they remain mere gropings, reachings-out which terminate in themselves and lead nowhere. It is only in proportion as they are made over and transformed in such a way as to acquire objective significance, that they acquire value. For then they enable us gradually to transcend the stage of mere groping. The aim of life is to found itself upon reality, to take up reality into every phase of life and make it real, objective, an organic portion of the cosmos. When made over by the philosophical guardian, in the light of his vision of ultimate reality, every element in human life can be utilized towards this end, and become worth while because, it can be transmuted into a channel for expressing reality itself.[9]

So too in our study of the moral standards discussed in the Dialogues, we discovered that it is objectivity, or the degree to which the structure of reality is reproduced in a character or situation, which is the decisive moment in each one of the standards such as universal assent, pleasure, expediency, etc. We saw that all human experience, even the most superficial and sensory, contains some objective reference, and that the method of analysis and synthesis, (a) in the factual form of memory and association, and (b) in the logical form which disengages the Idea, gradually concentrates and emphasizes the objective reference in question, until ultimately the concept of Reality itself as the final standard and court of appeal, summing up the essence of experience and its aspiration, becomes clear to the philosopher, and is thenceforward used consciously, as the highest standard of value.[10]

Again, in our inquiry into the psychological basis of the value-judgment, we noted, in the universal tendency to seek satisfaction, even at the sensory level, a certain distinction between appearance and reality, and a consequent feeling after reality. This is deepened by social experience, and the social estimate of values penetrates somewhat more reliably into the nature of reality than does the satisfaction-seeking tendency of the isolated individual. Further deepening takes place as the rational ideal develops of seeking for a satisfaction which shall be acceptable, not merely to individuals or to dominant social groups, but to an ideal society, a universally acceptable satisfaction. The new method of analysis and synthesis employed in the realization of this ideal penetrates still further into the nature of reality, and finds, in the reality which it discovers, a final standard for the guidance of our human search for satisfaction, in art, in social living, in scientific investigation, and in religious aspiration. Throughout our moral development, then, it is reality which represents the goal of our effort and the final standard of value.[11]

Finally, we made a special study of the Platonic conception of reality, and discovered that ultimately the real and the ideal are regarded as coinciding, everything which experience in any sense accepts as real being related to everything else which experience accepts as real, and all being, in the last analysis, determinate expressions of the principle of reality itself. Ideal or ultimate reality is envisaged as a consistent system of elements, organized in such a way as to secure the utmost positive realization of potentiality on the part of each element, in full harmony with the positive realization of potentiality on the part of each other element, the whole becoming fused together as a living totality, an *ens realissimum* containing, in complete inter-penetration, all fact and all value, and expressing, fully and finally, the principle of essentiality and value. Thus understood, the Platonic conception of ideal or ultimate reality is applied in a very practical way as a standard of value, asking, as it does, whether x (the situation to be evaluated) does or does not bring out the full realization of the potentialities of every element in the situation, in harmonious relationship with the fundamental values of life, whether it is consistent with wider social aims, and with the facts and values of the universe in general.[12]

3. The Idea of Good.

That the conception of value expressed in the principle of ideality furnishes a chief standard or criterion for estimating the moral value of actions or situations, we have discovered again and again. It will perhaps be sufficient in this place to sum up in systematic form the conclusions reached in our earlier studies.

In the first place, in relation to the development of personality, e.g. the ideal personality of the moral judge. Every human idea is a generalization, a condensation of a number of human experiences in such a way as to bring out their essence, i.e. to extract every relevant element of positive significance, and connect it with every other element of positive significance within the experiences of the individual, so as to bring them all together within the unity of a single complex idea. Moral development takes place (a) by the formation of habits, i.e. by the repetition of certain types of reaction until the type, e.g. the courageous type, the temperate type, the socially considerate type of reaction, becomes an organic part of the mechanisms of the individual. This means that at the mechanical level certain generalizations in the field of reaction-tendencies are taking place ; (b) by the formation of habitual ways of thinking, the acceptance of social convention, i.e. of certain generalizations based upon the experience of the group ; (c) by sustained reflection upon the *rationale* of social habits and social ways of thinking, i.e. by an intellectual analysis and synthesis which liberates the mind from the restraining influence of habit and convention, now that these have served their purpose of implanting in the mind a certain generalized structure, and considers clearly and consistently the principles by whose aid an ideal structure can be developed, a structure which will embody, in concentrated form, the whole essence of the values attained in human evolution. In this process of embodiment, the habits of the individual are made over, and also our social ways of feeling, thinking, and acting, until we come to realize, consistently and thoroughly, the essential principle of value, and make our life more nearly ideal than it could be without this re-organization. In this way, then, first in the mechanism of our simpler action-systems, then in our more complex habitual ways of social thinking and acting, and finally in a thorough-going philosophical reflection, in the light of which we completely re-organize our habits of thinking and acting, we learn to take up into our gradually developing personality[13] the essence, the concentrated values of experience, the Ideas of courage, self-determination, social considerateness, and wisdom, fused together into a living, intelligent unity in the light of our apprehension of the principle of ideality and value, the Idea of Good. Our personality thus furnishes a human habitation for the Ideas and their principle, and becomes, so far as humanly possible, a living expression of the Idea of Good, the principle of realizing, in thought and in action, the utmost of value-essence which experience contains, and realizing it in rich, harmonious, concentrated unity.

In the second place, in relation to the conception of reality. Each Idea represents the gathering together of the relevant elements within experience, thus deepening the significance of the experience in question. As experience, for platonism, is always experience of reality, the Idea is a clearer and more profound experiencing of reality than is the vacillating and shifting sensuous and emotional type of experiencing. The Idea, then, by condensing the sense of our scattered and superficial experiences, brings us into closer and more reliable knowledge-contact with reality; or, as this may also be expressed, reality, which is always to some extent present even in our most superficial experiences, expresses itself in our lives more clearly and significantly in the form of the Idea. In the highest Idea of all, the principle which expresses in a single, all-comprehensive, unity the whole meaning of experience, reality expresses itself most clearly and most significantly. That is to say, the final conceivable reality and the final essence of experience meet together in the Idea of Good. Ultimate reality is the essence of experience, and experience, at its deepest, is essentially and fundamentally reality in its own living. There is, however, a certain gap in practice between reality as humanly experienced, even at its highest and best, and reality as ideally, completely and finally experienced in the absolute Experience which we designate as God. Our human experience is not completely idealized, and there always rises before our mental vision the notion of a completely, perfectly idealized Experience, which contains, indeed, the full truth of our human experience, but transcends it in dignity and power. This is the Idea of Good in the absolute sense, which coincides with the conception of absolute or ultimate reality, the conception of God.[14]

Thus understood, the Idea of Good, as a standard of significance and value, is clearly final. It is not possible to conceive of a more perfect and more ultimate standard. The reality of things, the underlying truth and significance of human experience, and, further, the transcendent ideal of an absolute experience which contains the full meaning of human experience in a way which goes beyond our human powers of comprehension and fulfills the demands of the absolute ideal—such a standard for distinguishing between good and evil is final. This " judgment of Zeus " decides without appeal whether an action or character is or is not patterned upon the principle of extracting from experience its utmost of positive significance, its utmost of reality ; so far as it succeeds in so doing, an action or character is of real significance, of moral value. So far as it falls short of the ideal, it is devoid of meaning and reality, and sinks into futility and insignificance, and is weak, pathological, degenerate, wretched, stupid, evil.

So far we have seen that there are, in the Dialogues, three main concepts which stand out as moral criteria :— (a) idealized human experience, (b) ultimate reality, and (c) the Idea of Good. We have set forth what we have discovered about each of these, considered apart from the others. It now remains to compare them, and to see whether it is not possible to sum up the truth which they express, in their different ways, in a single formula which will state the essence of the platonic position *re* the moral criterion.

One thing comparison shows us at once : these are clearly different ways of expressing a single essential meaning, however this should be formulated. Idealized human experience is (a) human and empirical ; but it is also (b) experience of reality. Reality enters into it, and as it becomes more completely idealized, the reality which enters into it approximates to the reality which we have recognized as ultimate. Finally (c) it is idealized as far as possible, i.e. expresses in living, human form the Idea of Good itself. That is to say, regarded as a criterion of moral excellence, human experience at its best is, so far as humanly possible, identical with ultimate reality and the Idea of Good. We must, however, admit it is identical with them, not in their final or absolute completeness, but only so far as they can be *humanly* realized.

So too ultimate reality and the principle of ideality are conceived by platonism as identical, and they are certainly thought of as expressing the full reality of human experience at its best. The only difference, so far as we can recognize difference here, is that ultimate reality and the Idea of Good are thought of as transcending the empirical reality of human experience and the extent to which an ideal can be realized by human beings. They represent rather the empirical reality of human experience summed to infinity, idealized beyond the highest point to which we, with our bodily mechanisms, can reach, a transcendent ideal. At the same time, we must conceive the ideal in question as not impersonal, a mere law or concept, but a living ideal, a complete and final Experience, which is more truly experience than are our human fragmentary attempts at experiencing, Experience in its finally idealized form, the Experience which is God.

In attempting, then, to sum up the whole teaching of platonism on this point, we must include experience, recognizing that the Idea is experience in its most vital form, and also reality, appreciating the position that experience, especially in its higher condensation as Idea, is reality, and that reality is Idea, is living experience. A single formula which would sum up the truth of platonism on this point would be, e.g., the ideal life, provided that we understand by this the Divine Living (a) in itself, as the ultimately real and as the principle of all reality and all knowing, feeling, and willing which is of genuine significance, and (b) as the ideal for human aspiration, for one human attempt at making over our bodily mechanisms, our habits of feeling, acting, and thinking, until they approximate to the absolute standard (*homoiosis theoi*). Understood in this sense, then, *the Platonic criterion of moral value is the ideal life*; the life which expresses the living principle of the Idea of Good, the life which is a channel for pouring forth what is ultimately real, reality in its own living, the life of God. Whatever constitutes an organic portion of this, is real, significant, and morally valuable. Whatever fails to constitute an organic portion of the ideal life is so far unreal, insignificant, and morally worthless. This is the platonic criterion of good and evil.

PART II

THE MORAL CRITERION AND THE HIGHEST GOOD

SCALES OF GOODS IN PLATONISM

INTRODUCTION

S O far we have studied the general moral criterion in Platonism, the standard for distinguishing between good and evil. The object of the present investigation is, remaining within the field of goods which are recognized as such and conform to the criterion already discovered, to examine the relations of " higher " and " lower " accepted in this field. This investigation of the various scales or ladders of goods discussed in the Dialogues is preliminary to a final investigation of the " highest " goods recognized by Plato, which are, for the most part, related to one or another of these scales.

If we approach the Dialogues wholly in the empirical spirit of inductive inquiry, we find between two and three hundred passages which refer to such scales, and about fifty more or less distinct scales. Very many of these scales have at least one term in common, such as " wisdom " or " justice " or " pleasure," but, as the other terms differ, such scales must be regarded as distinct. Distinct as they are, however, many of them are so clearly inter-related, that we can treat them together as distinct groups, especially in the case of scales which seem to be fundamental for Platonism, and occur again and again, in the greatest variety of contexts, i.e., are of more central and universal significance. Such grouping naturally occurs (1) in relation to a scale consisting of soul-body-wealth, (2) in relation to a scale of virtues, from wisdom, justice, temperance, etc., down to physical well-being, good looks, etc., (3) in relation to a distinction between public and private goods, (4) in relation to a distinction between mind or intelligence, and all other goods, and (5) in relation to a distinction between divine and human goods. We shall proceed by making each of these groups the object of a separate, particular study, and, after having thus covered the entire field in detail, shall put together the results of our separate investigations, and draw whatever conclusions as to the scales and their significance for the Platonic ethics seem to be justified.

CHAPTER VII

SOUL—BODY—WEALTH

ONE of the most frequently mentioned scales of goods, a scale not only current throughout the Hellenic world, but definitely accepted by Plato and emphasized as of the first importance for moral living, is the scale of soul-body, or soul-body-wealth. In the present chapter we shall first attempt to discover precisely what Plato understands by " soul " and " body," so as to realize upon what grounds the one is ranked higher than the other in the scale of values,[1] and shall then consider " wealth " in relation to the soul-body scale. Finally we shall attempt to consider more thoroughly its significance for Platonism by relating it to a number of the other scales accepted by Plato.

By " soul," then, in the first place, Plato, like any other Greek, understands life, i.e. the vital principle manifested in all entities which are regarded as living, such as plants, animals, human beings, higher orders of beings.[1a] Not all these living entities have quite the same functions, and for the purpose of studying the value-scale in Platonism it is, at present, seldom necessary to leave the central point in the above list of entities endowed with life, i.e. human beings. As the chief functions of such organisms, according to Plato, are (1) biological, (2) social, and (3) cognitive, we shall proceed to investigate the nature of the vital principle in relation to these vital functions.

1. The biological functions.

These are summed up in the terms nutrition and reproduction. We shall first investigate the meaning of these terms for Plato, and shall then ask what the soul does in relation to these biological functions. For Plato these are the most universal functions of the living organism, and are uniformly regarded as reactions of an instinctive nature. Hunger, thirst, and sex are "necessary" appetites, fundamental instincts.[2] As forces which impel to action, they are without equal in respect of intensity, and so wide is the scope of their interest, that they are declared to constitute the largest portion of the soul.[3]

Let us take nutrition first. Food is, of course, essential to the continued existence and development of the organism, and, as such, has a proper place among human interests. But the preparation of food, and the attempt to satisfy the impulsion of hunger, give endless trouble. The student is drawn from his studies and compelled, for the time being, to leave philosophic contemplation and turn the eye of his soul downwards. There is even serious danger to temperance and self-control in our strong natural interest in eating. Gluttony, one of the commonest of vicious habits, is easily acquired, and is incompatible with the higher development of the organism.[4] So much for the individual. For the group, there are further complications. To secure a continued and adequate food supply for the group, measures are necessary which leave a very definite stamp upon the laws and structure of the community. Agriculture on the one hand, markets and retail trade on the other, together with all the supervision and regulations which these necessarily involve ; the wholesale exchange of commodities with other communities, with the corollary of a transportation system on the one hand, and, on the other, a probable development in the direction of diplomacy if not of war with competing groups ; such are a few of the elements which necessarily impress themselves upon the laws and civic structure of the community in relation to this one requirement of food.[5]

So also with thirst. In itself, this is a " necessary " appetite, and its reasonable satisfaction, like the reasonable satisfaction of our hunger-instincts, is subservient to health and the higher development of the organism. The Hellenic habit, however, of holding symposia—a practice observed perhaps in the Platonic Academy itself[6]—tended to lead, not merely to regulated drinking, but also to intoxication ; and while the value of intoxication on such occasions as a test of character is debated at great length and decided, apparently, in the affirmative,[7] there can be little doubt, on the whole, that the danger of hard drinking to both health and character is more prominent in Plato's mind, and that it is usually regarded as a dangerous foe to temperance and self-control, and as incompatible with the higher moral and intellectual life.[8]

So again with sex. In itself, the sex-interest is mainly a phenomenon of adolescence and physical maturity, and leads naturally to the reproduction of the species. This is its proper function, and, as such, has a definite and central place in the life of the community. So powerful, however, and so unreasoning is its instinctive appeal, that it overflows its banks and spreads into neighbouring territories. From this invasion no part of human life is entirely safe. Physical and military efficiency are liable to be impaired by an interest in the professional damsels of Corinth.[9] The dignity and respect which should attach to family life and social living may be utterly ruined by erotic passion.[10] The expense entailed by self-indulgence tends to break down habits of honesty, and, speaking generally, all respect for law and order, whether civil or religious, tends to give way under the continued pressure of this instinctive urge.[11] Even in the man of strong ethical character, it seeks fulfilment in forbidden wish-dreams,[12] and in the case of men who abandon themselves to its sway, it leads to the complete ruin of character. Licentiousness is an unholy thing.[13] On the other hand excessive control and repression have evils no less marked,[14] and, while strongly condemning perversities of all sorts, Plato does full justice to the ethical influence of the sex-interest. Under proper conditions, it is capable of stimulating and strengthening the idealistic tendencies of later adolescence. The lover makes a better warrior, a better student, a better philosopher, and in the ideal state expression, not repression, is to be the rule. Sex-interest, then, should be (a) an awakener of idealism,[15] (b) a stimulus to greater effort in serving the community,[16] and (c) an almost religious expression of the ideals of community living.[17] Its importance, whether for good or for ill, can hardly be exaggerated.

These, then, are the chief biological functions recognized by Plato. It might easily be supposed that they are concerned with the body rather than with the soul, and it remains true that the organism, on the side of its chief instinctive reactions, is functioning in a way which is largely mechanical rather than spiritual. The function of these mechanisms of the organism, is, however, in Plato's opinion, confined to providing the setting, the occasion, the concrete situation. The stimulus, mechanical though it may seem, penetrates to the soul, and the resulting reaction, though taking place through the medium of mechanical motions possible for the particular organism, is not itself mechanical, but spiritual. It is always the soul which actually apprehends the force of the stimulus and initiates the reaction. E.g. the body is empty, but it is the soul which feels hungry or thirsty, as the case may be, and experiences the not-yet-realized mental image of a satisfactory drink, and initiates the movements which will procure the reality which the image suggests.[18] So too, when Socrates' body is in the condemned cell, it is his soul which reflectively considers the whole situation, and holds fast to an idea which keeps the bones and muscles of his body in a sitting position, and does not accept the mental image (suggested by the words of Crito) of rapid movement in the direction of Megara.[19]

While our actions are always psycho-physical in the sense indicated, it is, however, possible for mechanical impulses to exert a preponderating influence upon the soul, or for spiritual impulses to exercise a preponderating influence upon the body. There is a very wide margin of difference. A reaction which is instinctive may be, e.g. brutish, almost wholly unenlightened by reason. The case of sex-interest at its lowest development furnishes an obvious example,[20] as also does intoxication. The spiritual is there, but it is obscured, covered over and enslaved by the mechanical.[21] On the other hand, the reaction may be partially enlightened by reason, at the level of "opinion," as so many of our more habitual bodily reactions to hunger, thirst, and sex-attraction are controlled by social convention.[22] Finally, the reaction may be wholly enlightened by reason, i.e. by the Idea of Good, in which case our reaction represents what, in the light of thorough-going knowledge, is judged to be best for the organism as a whole, considered in relation to the total situation. Psycho-physical reaction, then, of the type indicated represents the attempt to realize the Idea of Good with the mechanical means at the disposal of the organism, and within the circle of choice provided by the concrete situation.[23] Our conclusion is that, in all these biological reactions, the function of the soul is to appreciate the full force of the biological situations, and so to guide the action-systems of the body as to realize, as far as possible, in, and by means of those action-systems, the principle of ideality, of co-operating with God so as to bring into existence the utmost possible of reality and value.

2. The social functions.

The functions of an organism in relation to other members of a social group are necessarily of three main types. If there is to be a social group at all, the units which compose it must, in the first place, exhibit restraint, forbearance, an absence of aggression towards each other ; i.e. they must have a natural quietness of disposition, a marked tendency to refrain from interference with other units. In the second place, each unit, in order to be itself, to continue to function in its own characteristic way and thus make its characteristic contribution to the life of the group, must have a certain power of resistance, a forcefulness of disposition, which will not only confirm and strengthen it in pursuing its own proper path, but will also repel interference and undue influence on the part of other units. In the third place, presupposed in all social grouping is some sort of desire for group living ; all the units concerned must prefer to live in some sort of community rather than in isolation, otherwise no group would form, but something like Hobbes' " State of Nature " would be the rule : a social atomism which might well subsist in a sparsely-populated country, but hardly under other conditions. We shall proceed to investigate these functions as we find them in the human organism, and shall then inquire what part is played by the soul in relation to these social functions.

Corresponding to these three functions, which are necessarily involved in the conception of community living, we find, in social organisms such as man, three fundamental types of instinctive reaction. In the first place, we find an instinctive quietness of disposition, a tendency to mind one's own business and refrain from any aggressiveness or self-assertion, a shrinking from noise, publicity, and excitement in every shape and form.[24] In an unfavourable social environment, this instinct of itself tends to invite aggression and exploitation on the part of powerful and unscrupulous neighbours, but if circumstances are more favourable, it may develop gradually, along with certain other instinctive dispositions, into the cardinal virtue of temperance or self-determination.[25] In the second place, we find an instinct which man shares with many of the animals, the instinct of pugnacity, the disposition to react to unwelcome stimulation with unreasoning violence, kept up until one of the two parties is *hors de combat*.[26] Under unfavourable circumstances, this tends to make of the pugnacious organism a violent and unpleasant neighbour, and, unless tempered by something of the opposite tendency to mind one's own business, inevitably provokes a protective combination among the victims, which may easily result in the slavery or death of the assailant. Under more favourable circumstances, however, this disposition may be developed into the cardinal virtue of manliness or courage which constitutes an essential part of the best kind of character, whatever the life one chooses to lead.[27] In the third place, we find an action-tendency which at the present day would be called the herd-instinct, the disposition to seek and cleave to one's kind, to live in groups, gregariously, and to avoid isolation. This disposition furnishes the basis which may, under favourable circumstances, develop into the cardinal virtue of justice, which is regarded by Plato as the social virtue *par excellence*.[28] In fact, justice, which consists essentially, according to Plato, in doing all one can for society as a whole, as such involves both (a) the energetic development of self, the resolution contained in the idea of courage or manliness, and (b) minding one's own business, refraining from interfering with others, i.e. the characteristic of temperance or self-determination. It is also easy to see that courage and temperance, as social virtues, presuppose a tendency towards community living, and thus to suspect that the three virtues, in their higher development, provide a case of almost complete interpenetration.

As in the case of the biological, so also in the case of the social functions, we notice three stages of development. The lowest stage is at the instinctive level, at which the organism reacts unreflectively to various social situations by (a) timidity and shrinking, or by (b) pugnacity, the unreasoning attempt to remove obstacles by all the forces of the organism which can be called into action, while always at the same time (c) retaining an unreflective consciousness of kind, a sense of the value of group living, with some feeling of what this involves in the way of conduct.

The second stage is at the level of social habit and convention, at which the instinctive reaction-tendencies of the individual are controlled by ideas, mainly by the force of public opinion, i.e. by the half-reflective mass-tendencies of the social group. This control may be " blind," but it is certainly powerful.[29] At this level, the individual accepts the beliefs of the group as representing enlightenment and truth. His disposition to timidity and quietness becomes uncritical acceptance of the direction of his political superiors and obedience to the powers that be, mainly because they are the powers that be, without further investigation as to whether might and right always coincide. His disposition to resist aggression is directed into the orthodox channel of military service, the enemy being always accepted as the group designated as " the enemy " by his officers. At this level he is in truth a good watch-dog, obedient to his masters and ready to fly, when so commanded, at any stranger.[30] So, too, his gregarious disposition is fully converted into acceptance of the ideals of his group, and " justice " for him consists in obedience to the established laws, which are identi-fied with the ideal. He is thus a model citizen, though not, of course, one of the leaders.[31]

The third stage arises when, in place of unreflective instinct and habitual acceptance of the conventions of the social group, the individual makes philosophic insight into reality the organizing principle of his conduct. This means that he takes reflective cognizance of the logic of the social situation, and appreciates from a rational standpoint what action is necessarily involved for one who chooses deliberately to be a member of an ideal community. The repression or sublimation of all one-sided and disruptive tendencies, whether in himself or in others, the development of a well organized personality which will contribute its all freely to the good of the community as a whole, co-operation with all who are similarly attempting to realize the higher ideals of life,[32] these become his guiding principles. As Plato puts it almost technically, he keeps his eye steadfastly upon the principle of realizing the maximal possible value, upon the Idea of Good, in governing himself and the community which willingly accepts his leadership, and so co-operates with God in doing the real work of the world.[33]

In all these social reactions, whether at the instinctive, the habitual, or the intelligent level, it is the soul which appreciates the situation and initiates the reaction. The body, in physical interaction with the physical environment, carries through to the soul the various features of the concrete social situation, and thus functions as an instrument which assists, indeed, in supplying and furthering information, but is, in itself, incapable of appreciating, judging, and acting. These functions belong specifically to the soul, with its spiritual principle of judging and acting, the principle of ideality, with the help of which it selects and puts together all that is of value and significance in the concrete situation, and, in the light of the wider situation envisaged by the idealizing imagination, rectifies these empirical generalizations until they approximate more closely to their Ideas, the patterns in accordance with which the soul is endeavouring to re-shape its social no less than its individual living. At the more instinctive level, this function of the soul is overlaid and almost escapes notice ; but as the appreciation of social conventions develops, it becomes more prominent, for even " opinion " is reaching out after the apparent good,[34] and when finally the rational level is reached, the Idea of Good is clearly apprehended and deliberately used as a standard of thinking and acting.

3. The cognitive functions.

These functions of the organism are dealt with mainly under the names of sense-perception, memory, imagination and opinion, and a whole group of intellectual operations classed together as dialectic or reason. We shall first investigate the Platonic meaning attached to these terms, and shall then ask what the function of the soul is in relation to cognition. As the first three of these, sensation, memory, and opinion, have been dealt with in sufficient detail elsewhere,[35] it will only be necessary, in the present context, to sum up our results and apply them to the present situation.

Sense-perception is regarded by Plato as a psycho-physical process in which, by means of physical vibrations from a physical body X, there are set up in Z, a physical body endowed with consciousness, two kinds of vibration, (1) p, which are physical in character, a direct transmission of the X-vibrations, and (2) q, which are psychical in character. The two series of vibrations, p and q, partly remain separate, p remaining physical and q remaining, perhaps, in the " intellectual place " ; but in part they overlap and coincide, so that in pq we have the physical and psychical coming together, and, in place of two independent series of vibrations, have the consciousness of the physical body, the sensory apprehension by Z of X. This psycho-physical process is " vibratory," i.e. fluctuating and elusive, anything but fixed, static, and permanent. In memory, however, we have something more permanent, viz. the retention of the X-percept in a form which is withdrawn from the sensory flux, a pq severed from the vibratory process, cut off and relatively fixed, residing in what we should perhaps call the sub-consciousness. Even in this state, however, it is somewhat elusive and easily confused with other percepts similarly withdrawn from the sensory vibration. Like sensation, then, memory is definitely psycho-physical, but it is less liable to change, less elusive, relatively more permanent. It represents the persistence of the result of sense-perception, withdrawn from the changing play of competing and succeeding sensations and preserved in a central storehouse.

In this central region, the memory-image pq is liable to certain definite changes. In the first place, it becomes associated with other memory-images and thus, in virtue of the new connections thus formed, tends to lose something of its particular original connection with peripheral sensation. In the second place, as the central region represents the *terminus ad quem* of the sensory process, it tends to become associated also with newly arriving associations, and thus to acquire new peripheral relations. This association of memories with sensations gives rise to a new sub-conscious synthesis to which Plato gives the name of " opinion," which as representing the elements common to many memories and sensations, is more permanent and less fluctuating than the individual memories and sensations which are thus fused together, more cut off from particular sensations, and liable to further modification mainly as further sensations and memories are taken up into the synthesis. Opinion thus represents what, in modern logical terminology, would be called an elementary or unreflective judgment, a " judgment of perception " (Kant), or an approximation to a " judgment of (direct) experience " (Erdmann), with a tendency, however, to remain on the hither side of the fence, among the *Denkvorgänge* (Erdmann, Wundt) rather than among the full-fledged logical judgments.

By dialectic or reason, something further is understood. This is a deliberate, methodical process of analysis and synthesis which seeks out the true universal and disengages the Idea from its sensory envelope. The ideal to which, in every department of inquiry alike, it endeavours to approximate, is the absolute ideal of truth, the systematic concentration of every element of relevant meaning in a single, consistent, and completely intelligible totality, an interpenetrating and unitary apprehension of the ultimate essence of things, an approximation to the knowledge and wisdom of Omniscience.[36] When the dialectician has won his way through to a grasp of this ideal, the principle of ideality itself, and has thus reached the end of the intellectual realm, he proceeds to work over the results achieved in every department of investigation, seeking to convey these results, which are still largely empirical and sensuous, into an ever closer approximation to the ideal form, a form more completely permeable to reason, more transcendently satisfying. He thus endeavours to idealize the whole of experience, whether sensuous, or stored in memory, or partially generalized in "opinion," until he shall have converted it into the reflex of truth itself, the counterpart of the system of Ideas.[37]

Here, as in the case of the biological and social functions, we may observe the presence of three levels : (1) the instinctive level of mere curiosity, (2) the conventional level at which the thirst after knowledge is more or less satisfied with large draughts of "opinion," retailed in the schools and more or less accepted by society as a whole, and (3) the level of philosophic insight, which, when attained, is found transcendently satisfying, complete and final.

In all these cognitive processes, the function of the soul is not difficult to grasp. The body, with its physical mechanism underlying sensation, memory, and imagination, is an instrument for placing the soul in varying degrees of cognitive contact with the physical situation. Through this instrumentality, the soul receives the physical stimulus and appreciates its meaning and cognitive significance, at first in the fluctuating forms of sensuous experience, in which mechanical elements play an almost overwhelming part, so that the spiritual element seems to be hardly master of the situation.[38] But as the various forms of generalization develop in their deeper aspects, the function of the soul becomes gradually more prominent, more clearly dominant. Its function is, to select the meaningful elements of experience, through whatever mechanism these are attained, and to put these together, to concentrate, synthesize, and generalize so as to extract in unitary and harmonious, systematic form, the full cognitive significance of the experiences in question. At the highest level of philosophical self-consciousness, the soul becomes aware of the essential identity of this function with the principle of ideality itself, and sets itself deliberately, so far as humanly possible, to realize this principle.[39]   Stated briefly, then, the cognitive function of the soul is to idealize experience, to use the standard of ideality for the reorganization of its sensations, memories, opinions, and scientific investigations, so as to approximate, in its reorganized experience to the final ideal of the Absolute Experience which is both truth and reality.

So far we have studied the function of soul in relation to (a) the biological, (b) the social, and (c) the cognitive functions of the organism, considered separately and apart from one another.   We shall proceed to put together these results, and consider the function of soul in relation to body in a more general way, penetrating, if possible, rather more deeply beneath the level of phrases used in different contexts up and down the Dialogues.   In general, then, we conclude that the body is regarded by Plato as an instrument of the soul, a mechanism which is used by spiritual forces, and receives whatever significance it comes to possess from the degree to which it is penetrated by spiritual forces.   Thus penetrated, it comes to express, not the merely physical functioning of a merely physical mechanism, but the physical realization of a meaning which is essentially and fundamentally spiritual, one with the spiritual essence and meaning of the universe itself, so far as this is possible for an organism which still retains elements not entirely permeated with spirit.

In this relation of soul and body, there are three points which should receive strong emphasis.   In the first place, the body is an instrument.   It is never a piece of meaningless mechanism, but is adapted, as far as possible for a piece of mechanism which has its limitations, to serve as an instrument for the expression of spiritual values.   That is to say, it is not entirely alien to the principle of value itself, the Idea of Good.   We have duly noted that, on the cognitive side, the sense-organs are mechanical means of selecting stimuli and concentrating them, bringing them to a common focus so as to generalize and thus stress the visual or auditory elements in the environment which are of significance for the organism. In the same way, it is not difficult to realize that hunger, thirst, and sex-interest are mechanical means of selecting and focussing certain types of stimulus, and indeed further, of concentrating the reaction-systems of the organism so that they all work together for a common end. So also we can realize that the various forms of the herd-instinct function in such a way as to select and concentrate the more social types of stimulus, and to bring to a single, generalizing focus, a large number of otherwise disparate reaction-tendencies, so that the forces of the organism, so far as these are social-regarding, all work together harmoniously, as means to bring about the end, viz. community living.

This mechanical adaptation to the principle of ideality is, then, not difficult to understand in these instances. But it goes deeper, and reaches into the details of the circulatory and respiratory system, and indeed into the disposition and functioning of muscles, sinews, bones, and flesh. Whatever the modern biologist may think of the scientific details of the Platonic anatomy and physiology, the philosophical reader of the *Timaeus* cannot fail to note the general principle which lies behind the whole of Plato's " mythology," the principle of regarding the various bodily elements as physically, in their natural reaction-systems, so put together as to tend to concentrate all the forces of the organism in a single, co-operative type of reaction which will satisfy all the needs of the various parts of the organism, and will at the same time give harmonious expression to the complex organism regarded as a totality. Down to every detail, then, the body, with its instincts, sense-organs, muscles, flesh, bones, and marrow,[40] constitutes a mechanism which is physically attuned, as far as this is possible at the natural, biological level, to the nature of universe which is, in its ultimate principle, ideal, spiritual. It thus constitutes an instrument in the full sense of the word, and is adapted, as far as this is possible for an instrument which, as such, remains physical, devoid of life and insight into values, to follow the guidance and direction of a spirit which consciously, or at least half-consciously, thinks and acts in terms of genuine insight into the principle of ideality.

In the second place, the function of soul in relation to body conceived in this way as instrument, is, of course, to use it, to make the fullest and best use of it, to call out all its powers into harmonious co-operative activity, to direct all its energies into the most valuable channel. This means (a) that every fundamental instinct and every element in the body shall receive appropriate recognition, so that the soul will, to some extent, be limited by the mechanism with which it has to deal, will be, as Spinoza puts it, the ideai of the body, the mental side of the various processes which, in their totality, make up the mechanical side of the organism. And it remains true that, however much the soul, in the use to which it puts its instrument, may modify and reorganize the mechanical systems contained in the natural body, it is always and inevitably limited by the ultimate potentialities of the instrument. The ideals which it is endeavouring to realize physically, to bring into being in the world which we can touch and see, must be physically realizable, capable of being brought into effective relation to the mechanical action-systems to the use of which it is confined.

On the other hand, however, (b) Plato is no materialist. The soul is not restricted to the action-systems which it finds ready-made in the body. Of themselves, these systems are blind, devoid of insight, mere mechanism. But they can be directed, guided, developed, and modified in ways which may produce the very greatest changes in the mechanism. Thus, by becoming socialized, altered and developed in relation to the obvious requirements of social living, such individual instinctive dispositions as timidity and pugnacity, which in extreme form entirely unfit a man for social living, may be developed into the social virtues of civic self-determination and military morale, respectively, and while, as individual instincts, contrarily opposed to one another, they may be so developed as to constitute complementary, harmonious, and perfectly consistent elements of character in the citizen.[41] In these, and in very many others ways, the body, while still, of course, consisting of bones, flesh, blood, and instinctive action-patterns, becomes so reorganized, so made over in respect of its habitual reaction-systems, as to become an instrument for expressing community living, rather than a mechanical congeries of purely mechanical forces. It is true to say that the body has come to express, still somewhat at the level of unenlightened and conventional habit, the community idea, i.e. has become, to some extent, the home of the Ideas of temperance, courage, justice, and holiness. But it is when the higher cognitive development takes place, that the difference between mechanical origins and mechanical-spiritual ends becomes most marked. Moral and spiritual development consists, in the first place, of a reorganization of the bodily mechanisms so that these come to express, in ever closer approximation, the Ideas of temperance, courage, justice, etc. But the higher cognitive development, with its study of mathematics, physics, astronomy, etc., raises the personality above the merely social and conventional level. From the study of natural law and the impersonal, inevitable sequences of the planets, something of the calm, the serenity, the impersonality of the scientific spirit inevitably enters the soul of the student. He cannot avoid assimilating himself, to some extent, to that which he reverently contemplates,[42] and, by plunging into the world of objective law, discovers a cure for impatience, moodiness, the hundred and one wayward urges of subjectivity which characterize an instrument attuned, perhaps, to social demands, but not yet in perfect harmony with the austere beauty of the universe itself. The bodily mechanisms change gradually, adapting themselves to the new interest. His actions become more quiet, dignified, and controlled, more purposive, more concentrated, more objective. Finally, after many years spent in the new studies and the new activities, he achieves the dialectical quest, and contemplates, with his growing insight, the principle of ideality and value itself, a principle imperfectly manifested in the starry heavens, in the laws and institutions of man, in the moral habits which he has been slowly developing in his own personality, and implicit from the beginning in his own gradually unfolding intellectual powers. When he eventually discovers this principle, which reveals the inner meaning of life and of the universe, the ultimate essence of his own soul in its identity with the ultimate essence of the universe, the last and final reorganization takes place, and the bodily mechanisms become, so far as humanly possible, instinct with spirituality, entirely responsive to the principle of ideality, and his body is an instrument for expressing and realizing in the phenomenal realm the maximum of significance and value in the various concrete situations which arise.[43]

The function, then, of soul in relation to body, is so to use this instrument as not only to give full play to its various mechanisms, but especially to reorganize these, to build up mechanisms very imperfectly adapted, in their natural state, for the ideal life, into an instrumentality more adequately responsive to and expressive of the principle of ideality or ultimate reality. In this way the bodily mechanisms not only receive all the physical development of which they are capable, but also become of moral, social and metaphysical significance, an organic portion of the ideal universe which alone is ultimately real.

The treatment of the above two points, viz. (1) the nature of body as instrument, as adapted to spiritual purposes, and (2) the function of soul as director of the body to the spiritual ends to which it is adopted, and as developing the spiritual potentialities of body to the utmost, is thoroughly Platonic. It is also reasonably consistent, soul and body being regarded as correlates, as complementary aspects of the living organism. The theory thus appears to be complete, and we should now proceed to ask how far, and for what reasons, Plato ranks " soul " higher in value than its correlate, " body "—if it were not for a startling and disconcerting fact. Every student of Plato has noted, up and down the Dialogues generally, but especially in the *Phaedo*, traces of a different theory of the nature and inter-relation of soul and body, and this new theory seems incompatible with that we have just constructed. We shall therefore pause for a while, in order to study this second theory more minutely.

The difficulty arises in connection with the vast difference between the *terminus a quo* and the *terminus ad quem* of the development outlined above. The difference between a mechanism very imperfectly adapted to spiritual ends, and the same mechanism when transmuted into spirituality towards the close of the development, is so great that an opposition inevitably arises between the earlier and the later stages, and this opposition is very strongly felt by Plato.

Let us consider more closely how this opposition develops. On the one hand, the instinctive needs of the body for food, drink, and sex-satisfaction are crude and primitive. They represent mechanisms which are naturally so strong as to resist vigorously all attempts at their development and sublimation. Plato expresses this by stating roundly that, so far as these needs are concerned, the organism is incapable of appreciating the claims of reason.[44] These mechanisms constitute " leaden weights " which hold the soul down and interfere with the higher moral and intellectual development.[45] They are like a strong and unruly steed which will not obey the charioteer.[46] They endeavour to pervert reason itself to the uses of mechanism, enmeshing it in the pleasures of gluttony and sensuality, and so enslaving it that our rational powers are employed only in discovering means to ends which are instinctive, set by these strong, but lower, needs of the organism. The individual thus comes to use his powers of calculation in the service of the body, making money to procure satisfaction for his lower appetites, and employing every device of cunning and perverted dexterity to escape the consequences, physical and social, of continued indulgence.[47] So also in the community, on the wider stage of public life, many insidious forces are at work to corrupt and enslave the man of genuine ability in leadership, so as to interfere with any development towards idealism, and to divert into mere flattery of the baser appetites of the mob and of his own body, powers which might otherwise be used for reformation of the many-headed beast and its guidance towards the higher life.[48]

On the other hand, reason, in its upward struggle towards the light, easily comes to regard the bodily mechanisms which are holding it down, not as an integral part of the personality, which should be developed by rational processes as a harmonious whole, but as a constant drag, and even as a deadly enemy, which should be fought against, preached against, philosophized against, overcome, and destroyed. Body and soul are contrasted and distinguished until, at times, they seem to be regarded as entirely separate, having nothing in common[49] except a mysterious, external, and undesirable connection during this life on earth, in which the body is so much dead lumber, or, in Pythagorean language, is the prison or tomb of the soul, the source of all evil and of all hindrances to a completely satisfactory soul-life.[50]

From this standpoint, the soul is regarded as the only genuine concrete expression of the essence of life.[51] It lives in its own right, entirely apart from any union with the body, and enjoys, before such union, a free and unfettered soul-life, a life of ethical, aesthetical, cognitive, and religious completeness, in the eternal realm of Ideas.[52] This pure soul-life is, to a varying extent, impaired by any connection with a body, with its cognitively narrowing sense-organs, its irrational love of pleasure, and its incomprehensible, soul-perverting instincts.

The true function of the soul is to withdraw from the enforced connection with the body as far as possible, to neglect the sense-organs and their message, to let the instincts become atrophied, to free itself from emotion, and to carry through, as far as humanly possible, an artificial but complete separation, living consistently its own life of contemplation of the Ideas.[53] Finally, when the welcome separation comes to pass in the order of nature, at physical death, the soul which has preserved its own mode of living, pure from all bodily contamination, soars aloft to its eternal home, and again takes up its ideal soul-life,[54] while the body sinks into the nothingness, the " not-being " from which it came. The individual who has attained to this religious standpoint, is contemptuously superior to all earthly changes, has as little as possible to do with his fellow-men, with their petty politics and soul-destroying interest in bodily satisfactions, and seeks to remain aloft in his sphere. The true life, for him, negates everything which belongs to the mechanical side of his nature, instinct, emotion, habit, and convention, and consists in the deliberate and continuous contemplation of Ideas which are kept rigidly " apart from " all other human interests.[55] So pronounced is this yearning after separation, that the connection, external and enforced but essentially irrational, constitutes a serious problem. Why should the immortal, immaterial, knowledge-loving soul have been united with a body which is its exact antithesis, mortal, material, and sensual ; is not such union a contradiction in terms ? The only solution suggested, in passages which are explicitly non-scientific, and yet are written with all the seriousness of religious conviction, is the notion of a " fall," which has to be followed by a long period of trial and purification, until the soul, if successful in every trial, gradually attains the reward of eternal bliss, the recovery of its state before the fall.[56]

We have, then, in Plato's thought, two strata which are logically incompatible. An attempt might conceivably be made to keep them apart : to maintain that (a) metaphysically and religiously, our life on earth is an insignificant moment in eternity, and that the true soul-life is with the stars and the world-soul, but that (b) ethically and practically, while here on earth, we should endeavour to realize, with the bodily instruments provided for the purpose, the idealization of the environment, the true and natural life of the soul. In some

o

such way we might seek to combine an empirical idealism with a transcendental realism. But a study of the Dialogues shows convincingly that in Plato's own thinking the two standpoints, incompatible as they are, are not kept distinct. They are combined, and their combination is present in his most fundamental conceptions. We will consider one, as an example. The philosopher-king, as a concept, represents the combination of (1) ideal contemplation with (2) political power. But the combination remains, in Plato's thinking, a postulate, and the elements remain irreconcilable. For while, on the one hand, the philosophic training is calculated to make the guardian absolutely at home in the whole universe, on its practical and moral no less than on its metaphysical and religious side, we cannot help noting the presence of the *weltflüchtige Stimmung* already discussed. The member of the caste which is trained for this life of service is from the beginning superior to all mundane affairs. For him, empirical science is a delusion, the efforts of his fellow-men in art, religion, politics, and even philosophy are worthless, if not pernicious. His tendency, strongly reinforced by most of his training, is away from human sympathy, away from active life, with its noise and confusion, its madness and irrational dangers. Like the modern academically-minded man, he naturally seeks to abstain wholly from politics and let the rest of the world go by, while he preserves himself uncontaminated in the shelter of his college walls, and finds an austere but solitary enjoyment in the contemplation and discovery of truth.[57] The philosopher is thus naturally a recluse, and to induce such a man to enter the political arena requires external compulsion.[58] So conscious of the difficulty is Plato, that he allows his guardians frequent opportunities of withdrawal to their "higher" life, for repose and spiritual refreshment before they again descend into the underground den and again take up the ungrateful task of converting the beasts into some semblance of humanity, if not of divinity.[59]

The only satisfactory way out of this difficulty would be to insist that the complete interpenetration of Idea and action-systems represents the highest human life, and that the withdrawal of the philosopher into the "higher" realm of mere contemplation represents a natural, but mistaken aberration, to be explained, perhaps, out of the circumstances of Plato's life[60] and regarded as a religious *Stimmung* which, at times, comes over all of us but is not to be taken as serious philosophical doctrine. If, however, we desire to follow, on this point, the chief authority on Platonism, we shall refrain from satisfying the demands of logic, further than explicitly recognizing the inconsistency, and shall conclude that, for Platonism, there are *two* theories of the relation of soul to body.

According to the first of these theories, which we shall call the more empirical, " body " and " soul " represent correlative aspects of the empirical, living organism, both equally present at every stage of development, from the most instinctive to the most ideal. It is from this standpoint that certain writers regard the immortality doctrine as an expression of the ideal life, rather than mere temporal continuity of existence, even in interpreting the *Phaedo*, and the Idea of Good as a merely regulative principle for the control and development of empirical science, rather than as a transcendent, constitutive principle of existence.[61] According to the second theory, which we shall call the more transcendental, the body belongs to the realm of not-being, which can, at best, only be apprehended by pseudo-cognitive processes, true life consisting in contemplation of the Ideas, in complete logical independence of any bodily organism, whether before, during, or after any enforced connection with such a nonentity. We shall endeavour then, keeping these two theories as distinct as possible, to discover on what grounds the soul is ranked higher than the body in the Platonic scale of values.

From the empirical standpoint, the distinction of " lower " and " higher " is introduced in the following way : The body-soul organism exhibits its powers in varying degrees of development. At the lowest level it is, in modern terminology, polymorphous perverse. That is to say, it consists of a loosely federated set of instinctive tendencies, each with a soul-side as well as a mechanical side, and each endeavouring to realize its own potentialities and satisfy its own needs. As these tendencies are not brought into any sort of effective interrelation, the life of the organism at such a level is unstable and inconsistent, full of unresolved problems and conflicts, a prey to any strong impulse, and devoid of even an approximation to inner unity and individuality.[62] Affectively unpleasant on the whole, cognitively a confused jumble of fluctuating sensations and inconsistent opinions, on the side of action such an organism exhibits the fierce wavering and futile self-negating which inevitably result from contradictory action-tendencies. The organism at this level is exemplified in the more or less actual characters of Callicles and Thrasymachus, and in the abstract ideal construction of the " tyrant " in the *Republic*, who represents the opposite extreme to the equally ideal, though perhaps less abstract, construction of the philosophic guardian.

At a higher level, the federation is less loose, and the organization is more close and consequently, on the whole, more stable. Various potentialities are knit together so as to constitute vast complexes of thought, feeling, and action, each being more or less consistent within itself, but not in any well-defined degree consistent with other rival complexes. At this level, the level of " opinion," the organism is for the time being in the control of some one of the chief appetites, such as love of pleasure, love of wealth, love of honour, etc. As long as this one is dominant, the organism remains relatively stable ; but as, while the units competing for control are larger than in the previous case and are far less numerous, they are none the less competing ; here also there is no permanent stability, no inner unity and individuality.[63] Feelings, thoughts, and actions at this level are more forcible, because better organized. But their inner inconsistency is exhibited again and again in the Socratic overthrow of the representatives of this level of development, Protagoras, Polus, Polemarchus, and most of his interlocutors in the earlier Dialogues.

At a still higher and more ideal level, the potentialities of the organism are thought of as all harmoniously developed, each so related to all the rest as to present the closest possible approximation to unity and genuine individuality. In their increasing interpenetration, each side of our nature co-operates with all the rest, and shares in the new vigour, persistency, and stability which organization brings. On the side of thought, rivalry disappears, and each and all of our cognitive processes are regulated and unified by the ideal of perfect consistency. On the side of action, competition disappears, and our various conative tendencies are controlled and unified by the ideal of efficient, concentrated purposiveness, in harmony with what philosophic insight accepts as the major purposes of human life, of external nature, and of the spiritual forces which have made and are progressively re-shaping the universe. At this level, the organism as a whole becomes an efficient instrument in the hands of cosmic and more than cosmic forces, with its various potentialities developed to their utmost capacity in the service of the whole.[64]

From the empirical standpoint, then, we recognize the presence of different levels, to which the distinction of " lower " and " higher " seems to apply. Upon what does the application of this value-distinction rest ? A little consideration shows that it is a question of the degree to which the organism is penetrated, the penetration going right down to its constituent elements, by the principle of maximal efficiency, the principle of realizing the maximum of potentiality in a systematic way, which Plato calls the Idea of Good. At the lowest level we have what amounts to disease in body and in soul. Bodily disease is consistently regarded by Plato as disintegration, a dissolution of the fire, water, earth, and air which as elements constitute the material of the body.[65] Mental and moral disease are regarded in the same way : inconsistency and conflict destroy the principle of unity, and under their influence the soul tends to fall to pieces, though without apparently entirely ceasing to exist. The lowest level then is definitely pathological.[66] The second level, at which the great mass of mankind are to be found, represents a partial penetration into our potentialities, of the principle of maximal efficiency. While complete insight is not reached, there is still a feeling after " the Better," a groping after the guiding principle which alone brings significance and objective validity to our efforts.[67] The third level, exemplified in the ideal construction of the philosophic guardian, represents the complete permeation of the organism by the higher principle, the complete re-organization of our forces by the Idea of Good. This, the perfect soul in a perfect body, is spoken of as the true health of the organism, a genuine approximation to the principle of the Idea.[68]

This distinction of " lower " and " higher " is thoroughly Platonic, and is even of empirical significance at the present day. But what we must especially note in this place is that it cannot in any sense be made to coincide with a distinction between " body " and " soul." We might be tempted to regard the lowest level as mechanical or bodily, and the highest level as spiritual, as expressing the true nature of the soul, and it is not disputed that Plato himself sometimes writes as if this were the case. But if we are to hold fast to what we find in the Dialogues we must insist that, from the standpoint which we have distinguished as empirical, the temptation must be resisted. At the lowest level the soul-side of the organism is pathological, as we have seen ; but so is the bodily side also, and for a similar reason. At the highest level the soul-side is at its best, and expresses, as we have seen, its true nature ; but so is the body-side also. The ideal is to have " a perfect soul *in a perfect body*," a single organism approximating to perfection from every point of view.[69] Again, it is frequently maintained that the bodily potentialities can be well used, or misused ; but it is also maintained in the same general contexts,[70] that the mental and even moral potentialities can be well used, or also and equally misused. In both cases the reason is the same. The distinction of " lower " and " higher," applied in proportion as the Idea of Good is less or more nearly realized, respectively, applies, in fact, to the organism as a whole, and not to " body " as opposed to " soul " or to " soul " as opposed to " body." From this empirical standpoint, then, there is nothing especially sacrosanct about " soul " *per se* any more than there is anything especially vile about " body " *per se*. There is no value-distinction between them, but both are judged in relation to the degree of their development as established by reference to one and the same ideal standard of measurement. A more minute study would seem to indicate that the physical and spiritual sides of the organism develop, in spite of certain variations, approximately *pari passu*. The value-judgment, then, by which " soul " is ranked higher than " body," is not applicable from the empirical standpoint which we find in Platonism.

From the more transcendental standpoint, however, it is not difficult to realize why the soul is regarded as higher than the body. Considered in itself and apart from the body, to which it is in every sense prior,[71] the soul is always a being of a higher order. In its own nature it is essentially reason, the living apprehension of ultimate reality, the Ideas. With these it lives and moves and has its being in the intellectual place beyond the heaven of the fixed stars.[72]

Its " living " is fundamentally a knowing, a contemplative vision of the natures of justice, beauty, goodness, greatness, etc.,[73] a vision in which there is no sensuous admixture, but the entities envisaged are devoid of colour, shape, or tangible quality, and the whole vision is specifically intellectual, a matter of " pure " reason, an apprehension of the universal essences which constitute ultimate reality.[74] This apprehension, however, is not coldly intellectual, but is essentially joyous, a feast of reason, a replenishment of the soul, its proper food, in which the soul rejoices and is made glad.[75]

The " moving " of the soul is analogous to the movement of a circle which turns upon its own axis.[76] It is self-moved, i.e. obeys its own internal principle, which is choice of the best, the best being determined by reference to the ideal pattern, of which it has so clear a vision.[77] It thus, in its own self-movement, realizes the Ideas of wisdom, temperance, justice, etc.,[78] as far as this is possible. As we are now considering it apart from the actual or phenomenal realm, its realization of these Ideas is restricted to intellectual vision, and the movement of the soul is thus a continuous, un-changing contemplation of the unchanged Ideas, an immortal intuition.[79]

The " being " of the soul, considered apart from the body, is equally simple. It participates in the being of the ideal realm which it contemplates, and is divine ; but its participation takes the form of active intellectual vision, the actualization of its own divine potentiality for such contemplation, so that the " being " of the soul coincides with its " living " and " moving," and is simply a joyous knowing.[80]

When we compare this formulation of the pure essence of the philosophic spirit with our earlier more concrete conclusions, re the empirical function of an embodied, human spirit, where soul and body appear to be correlative, we at once become aware of the abstract, mythical, and unreal, one-sided nature of the transcendental standpoint in Platonism. In actual fact, it is only in relation to body that the soul, as its principle of life, has any concrete meaning. It is only in relation to body that the soul is created " co-eval with the heavens." It is only in relation to body that the soul's function is defined as " to have the care of (otherwise) inanimate being everywhere." It is only the embodied soul which can " use its vision of the unchanging laws of the ideal realm so as to order the laws concerning justice, temperance, and holiness here below." It is indeed in relation to embodied existence that the soul is said to have acquired its vast knowledge of the ideal realm.[81] Even after physical death, when the soul goes aloft to rule a star, it is in relation to a body (the star) that its " ruling " has significance. In short, if we persist in considering the soul in its divine essence, apart from the bodily world, we can, if we will, regard it as a being " akin to the Ideas and likest to them," i.e. as the principle of ideality engaged in the deathless and changeless process of self-contemplation ; but how inferior does this divine essence appear as a mere potentiality when compared with the full realization of that potentiality under the material conditions[82] of actual existence ! There is the further difficulty that, apart from the empirical world, it seems hardly possible for the Platonic metaphysician to distinguish one divine essence from another divine essence, or even from the essence of Divinity itself, and that there appears to be absolutely no reason for the creation of soul-substances, and no justification for their being endowed with the functions ascribed to them. In fact, the strict separation of " soul " from " body " and their contrast from the transcendental standpoint, appear to be an example of " the philosopher's fallacy " *par excellence*, viz. the hypostatization of abstractions under the influence of ethical and religious emotion.[83]

One small point remains to be explained. The soul is sometimes spoken of as having " parts," and as being subject to a " tripartite division into reason, spirit, and appetite." With certain variations, this general kind of division is found in many Dialogues. Thus in the *Timaeus* there is even a psycho-physical correlation between reason, spirit, and appetite on the one hand, and the cerebral, thoracal, and abdominal segments of the " spinal marrow " on the other, respectively. In the *Republic*, certain analogous distinctions rest upon the basis of analytic psychology, and in the *Phaedrus* we are introduced to certain mythical and poetical separations of a corresponding type. In all these cases there is an absence of complete clearness, but on the whole, the distinction seems to apply only to the embodied soul. From the transcendental standpoint, with which we are at present concerned, the soul is always regarded as a strict unity, coinciding approximately and in principle with the " rational " segment of the embodied soul.

Once soul and body have been separated by abstraction, and have been hypostatized into two opposed and contrasted extremes, the relation of the first to the second is always in terms of the distinction of higher and lower in Platonism. Thus, the soul has the care of inanimate being, while the body has to be cared for ;[84] the soul rules and gives orders to the body, while the body has to obey.[85] So, too, the soul is the source of life and motion, whereas the body merely receives and transmits motion ;[86] the soul is simple and stable, whereas the body is multiform and unstable.[87] Finally, the soul is rational and acts from choice of the best, while the body is motivated by appetitive principles which are often at variance with reason and indeed are hardly amenable to strictly rational considerations.[88] In fact, so diverse do they appear that at times they are roundly stated to have nothing in common.[89] From the transcendental standpoint, then, the soul is always superior to the body, because it is akin to the ideal principles which constitute ultimate reality, and is thus the source of whatever value the body at any time comes to possess. The body is always inferior to the soul, because it belongs essentially to the realm of not-being, and only takes on a borrowed and partly spurious value from its temporary association with a soul which stoops from its heavenly home.

So far, we have considered only two of the three divisions of the value-scale which is the subject of the present chapter. It remains to investigate the third, viz. wealth and material possessions. For Platonism it is almost axiomatic that material objects, considered merely as such, fall entirely outside the value-scale. Being lifeless and devoid of consciousness, their motions, in which they are always passive transmitters and never originators, possess no value for themselves. Whatever value they can come to possess thus necessarily depends upon their being brought into relation to some system of conscious purposes, wants, desires, and plans, the thwarting of which occasions pain, or negative value, and the furthering of which occasions pleasure, or positive value. It is the soul, or at least the soul-body organism, which is the source of motion and change in material objects, and these acquire value, positive or negative, according as they further or hinder the wants, desires, and plans which characterize the activity of soul or of the soul-body organism.[90]

The chief human needs are for food, drink, clothing, and shelter,[91] and it is in relation to such instinctive requirements that material objects first come to acquire value-significance. In this relation they assume the form of possessions or property, such as land and implements for agriculture, clothing and buildings of various types. Again, out of the dependence of men upon one another, some devoting themselves to agriculture, others to cloth-making, others to the manufacture of agricultural implements, others to the manufacture of pots and pans for the preparation of food, etc., arises a sort of communal association around a common geographical centre, and out of this association arises inevitably the need for some medium of exchange, in terms of which the farmer, weaver, potter, and carpenter can exchange the surplus products of their labour upon some equitable basis. This medium of exchange takes the form of a currency, i.e. material objects stamped with some conventional symbol which makes them of recognized value for the exchange purposes of the community.[92] Further expansion, also inevitable, in the direction of a central market, with wholesale and retail trade, and in the yet further direction of export and import relations with neighbouring communities, involves the creation of a transportation system, of an international currency, and of commissions of various sorts which will represent and protect the interests of the community, partly at home and partly in its foreign relations. Step by step there thus arises a highly complex system of social purposes, in relation to all of which material possessions, and especially the impersonal symbol of their exchange-value, money, come to acquire a most important significance for the individual member of such a group. In every social relation money now seems valuable, whether it is a matter of purchasing food, drink, clothing, shelter, and tools, whether it is a matter of disposing of the surplus products of one's labour either in the home market or in foreign markets, or whether it is a matter of contributing in some way to the support of the central commissions which maintain order and an equitable exchange at home, and effect satisfactory relations, commercial, diplomatic, and military, with other communities.[93]

Money, then, represents in a conventional way the exchange-value of the products of the labour of the community, which is thought of as partly rural and partly urban. The very first problem which arises in such a community is the problem of equitable exchange. On what basis of com-

parative value should the rural producer and the city distributor exchange their services? Should a citizen be permitted and encouraged to accumulate property beyond his
own immediate uses? And what should be done with a
citizen whose earning power is insufficient to procure satisfaction for his vital needs? The Platonic solution of such
difficulties is simple in theory. The cost of government is
to be borne by the community as a whole, but the governing
commissions are to be so highly trained that their services
will more than balance the cost, partly in view of the security
to life and property which they guarantee, partly in view of
the increased efficiency which comes from educating all who
are capable of genuinely profiting from higher education,[94]
but mainly because the trained insight with which the highest
officials direct the whole life of the community keeps every
citizen in the closest possible contact with the deeper sources
of value, material and spiritual.

After the cost of the various commissions has been
subtracted from the general surplus of production over
consumption, the currency which represents the exchange-
value of what remains, is used by the citizens in their private
transactions. When the surplus is small, the actual amount
paid for the products of labour is slight, but in proportion as
the surplus increases, the remuneration of individuals, i.e.
the actual amount of currency which they obtain for the
products of their labour, will also increase, so that all will
share in the growing prosperity of the community.[95] As to
the actual amount which is to be paid for agriculture as
opposed to manufacturing, or to distributing as opposed to
agriculture, etc., that is determined in accordance with the
following principle. The rewards of agriculture are to be
such as to keep the farmer on the farm, and to keep him
interested in making himself a better farmer. The rewards
of industry are to be such as to encourage the manufacturers
to stick to their particular manufacturing, and for each
shoe-maker, cloth-maker, etc., to keep on trying to improve
himself in his particular industry. Every member of the
community is to continue, as far as possible, to improve the
quality of his own particular product, and also, and especially,
is to remain throughout interested in remaining a member
of the community.[96] The general principle involved here
is the maximal development of the potentialities of each

and every member of the community, consistently with the continued existence and prosperity of the group as a whole. What is to be guarded against is some extreme, some one-sidedness in the way of excess or defect, which would interfere with the functioning of this principle.

Let us consider what this means. Suppose that in the case of *A*, *B*, and *C*, consumption exceeds earning capacity, so that they are reduced to poverty. This inevitably means inadequate tools, inadequate training of apprentices, and generally, poor workmanship, with diminished production-value. The poverty-stricken farmer or workman goes from bad to worse, and such progressive deterioration of the types of citizen necessary to the well-being of the community inevitably diminishes the wealth and importance of the community as a whole. Below a certain minimum, the poverty-stricken citizen ceases to function as a citizen at all. That is to say, he ceases to make his characteristic contribution, as farmer, carpenter, etc., to the welfare of the community as a whole, and becomes at best a parasite upon the resources of the group, and at worst joins the idle and discontented proletariate, who are more or less actively plotting against the propertied classes and are developing gradually but inevitably into an actual menace to the constitution.[97]

So too with the other extreme. Excessive wealth tends to unfit a man for citizenship. The farmer who has " made money " retires prematurely, and joins the moneyed classes. That is to say, he ceases to enrich the community by the products of his labour, and thus becomes a consumer instead of a producer. His tendency is then to join the ranks of those who " make money make money " by devices other than productive labour. The class which he has joined is interested in keeping the labouring classes from becoming too powerful, and as against the impoverished classes, whose numbers their financial operations tend to increase, they use trickery, legal and illegal, and where necessary, as a last resort, force, the force employed by hired guards and illegal convictions.[98] The immoderately wealthy, then, by ceasing to contribute anything positive to the well-being of the community, tend at best to become parasites upon the work of the labouring classes, and at worst to increase pauperism, and to widen the gulf between capital and labour, until the social group ceases to be a single community in anything but name.[99]

How would Plato hinder the operation of these disruptive tendencies ? The answer is, partly by education, partly by direct legislation. Education so trains the value-sense, that money and material possessions gradually lose that fascination which they seem to have for the half-educated,[100] and the legislative precautions are as complete as Plato can make them. The two highest classes, from whose ranks are drawn all the officials without exception, educational and judicial, military and administrative, are not only trained in the spirit of public service, but are strictly public servants, supported entirely by the community and forbidden to own private property in any shape or form.[101] In their case, then, by the general economic conditions of their class, extreme poverty and immoderate wealth are absolutely excluded, and no problem arises.

In the case of the productive classes, a certain subsistence-minimum and a certain maximum are established for all such members of the community by law. The minimal subsistence-requirement is guaranteed in the following way. In the ideal community, the basic industry is agriculture, and the governing commission determines, as carefully as possible, how many families can reasonably be supported by the produce of the available territory, allowing, not only for the bare subsistence of the family, but also for all civic and religious dues and taxes. The territory is then subdivided into a corresponding number of lots, and the holding of a lot constitutes the minimal basis for citizenship. The lots remain fundamentally in the possession of the community, though their cultivation-value is granted, subject to continued good behaviour as citizens, to a particular family in perpetuity.[102] In this way, the number of productive citizenships, as it were, will remain the same, even though the actual holders of these citizenships from time to time will be subject to all the natural causes of alteration in the population. War, disease, and crime will thin the ranks of the lot-holders, while the natural development of families, by birth, marriage, or adoption, may tend to multiply the numbers who are on the waiting-list, as we should put it, for appointment to the citizenships.[103] The aim of all such regulations in Platonism is not primarily in the interest of individual men as such, but rather to preserve from poverty the citizenships which constitute the community, much as a modern university consists of scholarships and professorships which are held only by individuals who are properly qualified, in order that the characteristic work of the university may proceed with maximal efficiency. As a further measure to preserve the community from poverty, all younger sons who do not become lot-holders by adoption or marriage into families where there is a vacant citizenship, and all persons who, as individuals, become seriously impoverished, are disposed of by the standard Hellenic remedy for such cases, viz. government-encouraged emigration into some newer and less developed region, where they will be able to make a new start.[104]

On the other hand, in order to preserve the community from the evils of wealth, where the incomes of some citizens are so great as to unfit them for good citizenship, a certain maximum is established, and the acquisition of property of any sort in excess of this maximum—which is established as equivalent to four times the minimum—is checked by the simple device of confiscatory legislation.[105] In these ways then, by education, by the control of population—partly by birth-control,[106] partly by emigration or, if necessary, immigration,[107]—and partly by establishing minimal and maximal qualifications for citizenship, Plato endeavours to preserve the community from falling into the extremes of poverty and wealth. He is not himself convinced that his plan will always work with individual men and women,[108] and it must be borne in mind that it is not so much for human beings as individuals, as for the community as a whole that he is legislating, and that his measures do not descend into the region of the particular, but stop short at the artificial entity which we have called the citizenship.

Material possessions, then, acquire value-significance for human beings partly in relation to their primary vital needs, but especially in relation to the complex system of social purposes which we find in the complete community. The social ideal is that of a human hive, in which every citizen devotes himself to the utmost development of his capacities in the way of service to the community as a whole, and all share in the products of the labour of the group in such a way as to maintain, if not to improve, the quality[109] of their service. It is in so far as money constitutes an indispensable means to the realization of this ideal, i.e. as a medium of exchange in both home and foreign markets, with all which this involves, that money is of genuine value. In excess, however, of the very moderate amount required for civic life, money constitutes a serious danger. It may be expended upon the thoughtless gratification of impulse, upon the undiscriminating indulgence of bodily appetites, and may thus strengthen the already vigorous human tendencies to seek mere pleasure, and will thus result in a kind of private living in one's feelings, rather than in a life oriented in the socially useful direction of public-spirited citizenship.[110] Or, again, it may be hoarded, and may develop the more avaricious tendencies of the individual, again with the result of withdrawing him altogether from a useful life of civic activity,[111] or possibly with the even worse result of inducing him to seek office as a means of enriching himself at the expense of the public.[112] In short, it is only men of character and insight who can, under any circumstances, wisely be entrusted with power, and in their case Plato insists that, while they direct public expenditure, they shall not be permitted, in the ideal community, to own private property at all.[113]

So far, we have investigated the nature and value of material possessions. It remains to compare them with the organic body, with the body-soul organism as a whole, and with the soul considered as independent of the bodily organism, in order to discover for what reasons material possessions receive a position lower than these on the value-scale. The organic body and human possessions of all kinds are both mechanical, and their value is instrumental, i.e. depends upon the extent to which they can be used as means to ends which fall outside themselves. For example, " making money make money " as such merely increases the quantity of the means which *may* acquire value by being used to promote purposes which are valuable in their own right, but is not, in itself, a valuable pursuit. The instrumental value of property is thus a secondary kind of value, and derives its worth from the intrinsic value of the ends to which property serves as a means. In relation to the body, money can be expended indiscriminately upon the satisfaction of any and every bodily appetite—a procedure which would tend to result in disease and bodily deterioration,[114] or it can be expended in ways which are more controlled and rational, in purchasing the necessities of life, food, drink, clothing, shelter, etc. The well-being of the body consists in the harmonious satisfaction of the various " necessary " bodily wants, and money can thus be spent as one of the means to the healthy functioning of the bodily organism as a whole. The first kind of expenditure, by ruining the body, i.e. the purposes in relation to which property has value-significance, is ultimately self-destructive and contradictory,[115] but expenditure as a means to the end of health shares in the value which attaches to bodily wellbeing. Health, or the good of the body, is thus prior to wealth, which is a mere means to this good. Again, as health results directly from exercise and the moderate satisfaction of bodily impulses according to a certain rule,[116] whereas money is only indirectly and conventionally instrumental in contributing towards such exercise and such satisfaction, the value of material possessions, even as a means to health, is only partial, indirect, and conventional. Further, in the ideal community healthy citizens are always regarded as of more value than wealthy citizens, for health and citizenship are consistent and indeed aid one another, but great wealth and citizenship are inconsistent with one another,[117] and great wealth and physical well-being also tend to be inconsistent with one another.[118] It is, then, only under regulations which keep money and property generally in a strictly subordinate place in the scale of civic values, that they can be regarded as at all constituting a genuine good to their possessors, and even then, they are always less important than bodily well-being.

We can now pass to a comparison of material possessions with the soul-body organism. The ideal to which this organism aspires is, as we have seen earlier,[119] the maximal harmonious development of its various potentialities, physical, moral, and mental, so that it can express and help to realize in this world the Idea of Good. It follows, then, that money and property generally will be of value precisely so far as they assist in that development, and that, so far as they hinder the full development of the soul-body organism, they are definitely harmful, For example, the expenditure of money upon education, physical, moral, and mental,

obviously assists in that development, and is therefore
mentioned with approval.[120] Further, as the aim of the
ideal community is the maximal development of its various
members, material possessions, so far as they contribute
directly or indirectly to the maintenance of the ideal community, are a means to the maximal development of soul
and body. Thus, the use of a currency in connection with
the necessary commercial activities of the citizens assists in
building up a surplus wealth which can be expended upon the
further development of resources, upon the maintenance of
commissions which assist in the development of community
ideals, upon research in the natural and social sciences,[121]
and upon the whole of the higher education generally. And
again, so far as material possessions contribute to the maintenance of the necessary subsistence-minimum for citizenship, upon which the whole higher structure, economically
speaking, is based, they are also and equally approved.
Finally, the governors who apply to the amelioration of
human conditions the insight which education brings, apply
that insight in the form of legislation which is largely concerned with material possessions and their influence upon
the development of the average citizen. The whole life of
the community rests, economically speaking, upon labour,
and in translating the crude results of labour into a means
of realizing the highest good both for the individual and
for the community, possessions and a currency constitute
an indispensable element.[122] But the value of labour resulting in the building up of a surplus which is translated into
property is always strictly subordinate to the higher development of the soul-body organism as a whole. Money-
making is, as we have seen, subordinate to health, and
physical health is always subordinate to moral development,
so that, as a good, property is always subordinate to the
moral virtues, the virtues of the body-soul organism.[123]
In this higher development, material possessions certainly
play their part in the ideal community. But they are only
one of the means to such development, and are only to a
very slight extent strictly essential, and again, on the other
hand, the currency-mechanism in social life easily lends
itself to the gravest abuses, developing acquisitiveness and
an interest in private, as opposed to public good, an interest
which is disruptive of individual character as well as of the

P

social group as a whole.[124] It is thus not difficult to see why it is only in a strictly qualified sense that property is regarded as a genuine good at all, and why, even then, it is a good only as a means to the greater good consisting in the development of the soul-body organism as a whole.

In the above considerations, we confined ourselves to the empirical standpoint, treating the soul in the closest relation to the bodily organism. It remains to take the transcendental standpoint, and treat the soul as independent of and superior to bodily considerations. From this standpoint, the true life of the soul consists in wisdom, i.e. in philosophical contemplation, an activity in which the body and all its concerns have, directly at any rate, no conceivable share. To such a soul, apart from its temporary and enforced union with a body, money and material possessions mean absolutely nothing. It is wholly immaterial, and is interested in remaining so, any connection with the material being regarded as a serious lapse.[125] To such a soul, then, it is only in relation to its life on earth, entombed in the body, that material possessions can be regarded as in any sense desirable and valuable.

As thus entombed, the characteristic danger of such a soul is to forget its transcendental origin and to remain entombed in the flesh, drawn downward by sensuous enjoyment and by a soul-destroying interest in acquiring means to the furtherance of such enjoyment. Money is easily used as a help in indulging the bodily appetites, in riveting the soul to the body and preventing it forever from realizing its supreme mission.[126] This being so, is there any definite way in which property, with all which it implies, can ever be anything but a real drag upon the soul ?

Let us consider. The aim of the transcendental soul, when thus united to a body, is to free itself, as far as may be, from the fetters of the flesh, to withdraw itself wholly from the life of instinctive gratification, to withdraw wholly from the vulgar struggle for wealth, position, and power, to liberate itself from the senses and sensuous emotions, and to become all mind, pure reason, as nearly as possible a disembodied intellect.[127] Money and material possessions generally it naturally regards with contempt, if not with hostility,[128] and there is, logically speaking, only one conceivable way in which such things could be of value. If they could somehow be used to assist towards this liberation and withdrawal of the spirit, they would so far be instrumental in realizing the ideals towards which the soul aspires, and would so far share in the value of those ideals.

How far can this be done ? We have already noted that property and a currency are indispensable in the development of a social system which makes state education possible, and that such education, physical, moral, and mental, is of value to the organism consisting of body as well as soul, assisting it to develop its powers to the utmost. Is there any sense in which such education is of value to the transcendental soul in its characteristic struggle to escape from the body ? Let us see. Physical education results in bodily health. From our present standpoint, bodily health is of value in so far as it frees the soul from the bodily impediments to contemplation—such as headaches and other consequences of a sedentary life—i.e. in so far as it eliminates bodily concerns from the contemplative consciousness altogether.[129] Moral education results in temperance, courage, and justice, as social habits of the empirical body-soul organism. From our present point of view, these virtues are valuable to the transcendental soul in so far as they free it from the pernicious influences of acquisitiveness and exclusive pleasure-pain interests,[130] and eliminate instinctive and emotional interests entirely from the philosophic consciousness. So too mental education, beginning with mathematics and culminating in dialectic, is of value as freeing the transcendental soul entirely from the misleading influences of sensuous experience, and making it possible for this soul to develop its own organ of pure reason, by which alone it can hope to envisage the Ideas and thus begin, even on earth, to enter upon its rich heritage of wisdom.[131]

So far, then, as money can be expended upon an education which will liberate the eye of the soul from the " outlandish slough " in which it is buried by our bodily interest in material things, it is of value to the soul in its characteristic effort after withdrawal from this mundane sphere and all its concerns. But it must be noted that it is only very indirectly and indeed, in the end, by contradicting its own downward tendency towards materialism, that such a material thing as money can be made to serve the idealistic purposes of the transcendental soul. If we were pure spirits, we should have no material needs. If we had no material needs, we should not require an income. If we set ourselves to acquire an income, we are in danger of becoming blind to higher things. Having, however inexplicably, bodies with powerful material needs, we must set ourselves to acquire an income. The danger of losing our own souls is to be avoided only in one way. We must interest ourselves in acquiring an income which will exactly counterbalance the various bodily needs, procuring food, drink, and shelter sufficient in quantity and quality to keep the body from obtruding its wants upon the soul, and carefully avoiding any kind of stimulation which would develop the body unduly.[132] The aim is thus to balance and eliminate the body, and so far, our aim is merely negative. We must further, however, acquire an income sufficient to provide the higher education, the education which will liberate our minds from the materialism of the half-educated. Along with this education comes insight into the limits to the value of money, and we shall refuse to take the slightest interest in increasing our income beyond the level thus reached, and shall acquiesce in the wisdom of confiscatory legislation in respect of higher incomes.[133] The value of property, as compared with the value of spiritual life, is thus strictly limited, and is confined to what we might regard as the operation of short-circuiting all bodily interests, in such a way as to give adequate play to those interests, but to prevent them from in any way interfering with spiritual life, which is, from the transcendental standpoint, the only life possessing genuine value.[134]

So far we have investigated the scale of soul—body—wealth. In the Dialogues this is sometimes presented merely as a result of the philosophic value-judgment, without much regard to its possible application,[135] but at other times it is explicitly treated as a standardized norm used by the ideal legislator in establishing or revising a system of concrete laws.[136] It now remains to examine further a number of scales of somewhat similar general import, but varying from the above standard, and appearing more in the form of value-judgments, and less in the guise of definite norms for concrete application. In what immediately follows we shall first consider very briefly all other value-scales in which " soul " has a place, then all in which " body " has a place, and then all in which " wealth and material possessions " have a place. After this, we should be in a position to conclude the present investigation by summing up finally what we have discovered concerning the nature and value-relation of soul, body, and wealth.

"Soul," as a value, is never clearly compared, in the Platonic Dialogues, with anything but "body" or "wealth." But there are quite a number of value-scales in which souls of higher value are compared and contrasted with souls of lower value. These are, briefly, as follows :—

1. World-soul—Planetary souls—Human souls—Animal souls—Plant-souls.[137]
2. Souls ranked in accordance with the degree of their moral development :—
   a. Orderly soul—Disorderly soul.[138]
   b. Virtuous soul which has never been vicious—Virtuous soul delivered (by punishment) from vicious condition — Vicious soul (remaining unpunished)[139].
   c. Just (and temperate) soul—Unjust (and intemperate) soul.[140]
   d. Soul which masters its sensuous feelings—Soul which is mastered by its feelings.[141]
3. Souls ranked in accordance with degree of mental development :—
   a. Soul with its " eye " turned towards the light—Soul with its " eye " still dimmed by materialistic environment.[142]
   b. " Winged " soul—" Wingless " soul.[143]
   c. Wise soul—Foolish and ignorant soul.[144]
   d. Soul perfected by mental education—Imperfect soul.[145]

In the first of the above value-scales, the value-ranking seems to depend on two different principles. The first three members of the scale have the same (Divine) origin, but the " materials " out of which the " soul-seeds " of the planetary and human souls are constructed are said to be " less pure " than the materials (otherwise identical) of which the world-soul is formed. On the other hand, while the first three souls are essentially rational and capable of apprehending the Ideas, the world-soul apparently does so perfectly, the planetary souls more perfectly than the human souls, but less perfectly than the world-soul, and the human souls with difficulty, because the motions of the bodies in which their soul-seeds are implanted are less orderly than the motions of the planets. The difference thus seems to be, from this standpoint, a matter of the orderliness of the body in which the soul-seed has been implanted, and it is perhaps a continuation of the same principle which ranks the animal soul (which does not attain to a vision of the Ideas, but is capable of some degree of courage and temperance, as well as of self-movement and nutrition) as lower in value, and the plant-soul (which has no self-movement, but retains only the nutritive and reproductive functions) as lowest of all soul-possessing entities. The superior souls, then, are those in which the intellectual principle has the greatest development, and the inferior souls are those which are most nearly reduced, by the conditions of their material environment, to the least intelligent and most purely instinctive level of conscious existence. The value-scale, then, is closely akin to the soul-body scale considered from the more transcendental standpoint, and has so far been adequately taken into account in that connection.

The scales which fall within the second group can similarly be reduced to the soul-body scale considered from the more transcendental standpoint, for the various moral virtues are emphatically bodily habits, enlightened, in their higher development, by that insight into the Ideas which characterizes the soul at its best, but retaining always elements which remain material.[146] Similarly the leaden weights which hold down the soul and hinder it from entering upon the higher development, are definitely of a material nature, so that this scale, being reducible in principle to the soul-body scale, has already received sufficient consideration.

So too of the scales which make up the third group. It is the body with its instinctive feeling after sensuous pleasure, which dims the intellectual vision of the Ideas and thus hinders the eye of the soul from looking to the true " above." It is the body which drags down the soul towards earth, so that it loses its wings, the pinions which bear it aloft towards the plains beyond the heavens, where abides the true food which nourishes the transcendental soul. So too the " wisdom " of the soul consists in transcendental contemplation of the Ideas, and the " folly " and " ignorance " of the soul, which stand in the way of such contemplation, are sensuous hindrances which come from our bodily nature. And finally, the mental education which perfects the otherwise imperfect soul, is explicitly a matter of training the soul to withdraw its attention from the world of sensuous experience, and gradually to make itself at home in the ideal realm in which the light-and-life-giving source is the Idea of Good. The scales of this group, then, are also reducible, without remainder, to the soul-body scale considered above, and the principle of value, the standard by which the winged and wise soul is declared to be of greater value-significance than the wingless and ignorant soul, is ultimately the degree of intellectual vision attained by the soul under consideration, the closeness of its approximation to the principle of ideality, the Idea of Good.

We now pass on to consider the other scales in which " body " has a definite place. In Platonism, " body " is never compared, from the standpoint which is interested in values, with anything but " soul " on the one hand, and " material possessions " on the other. But there do exist in the Dialogues a few value-scales in which bodies of higher value are contrasted with bodies of lower value. These are as follows :—

1. The body of the universe—Human bodies,[147]
2. Bodies which grow up in the best and straightest manner—Bodies which grow too fast and are insufficiently exercised,[148]
3. Body with sound constitution—Diseased body.[149]

Human and animal bodies are composed of fire, water, earth, and air, which are also the elements out of which the body of the universe is composed ; but in the universe-body they are perfect, or at least as perfect as possible, but in our bodies they are inferior in quality and in strength and in every way less " beautiful "—i.e. less well proportioned and less well adapted and adjusted to one another. The human and animal body is thus a less perfect instrument, a mechanism less well adapted to realize the soul's purposes, than is the case with the universe-body, which is the almost perfect instrument of the world-soul. This contrast between an efficient and an inefficient mechanism is at the basis of the physically trained body as contrasted with the inadequately trained body, with the additional thought that the motions employed in physical training are akin to the regular motions of the planets, and serve to overcome the disorderly movements of the untrained body and attune it, as it were, to the general nature of the cosmos. So too with the healthy, as opposed to diseased body, the point of the contrast is that an inefficient mechanism will hinder the soul in its upward endeavour, while the *corpus sanum* can be used in the service of temperance and justice, and thus assist the soul in its higher development. In every case, no value is attached to healthy states of the body *per se*, but always in relation to the purposes of the soul, which can realize the Idea of Good more adequately with an efficient than with an inefficient mechanism. The value-scales considered here, then, fall under the general value-scale of body—soul—wealth, and have therefore been discussed sufficiently above.

Wealth and material possessions are found explicitly mentioned in the following value-scales :—

1. Virtue as a whole—Wealth (or other benefit) separated from virtue.[150]
2. Justice in the soul—Wealth.[151]
3. Philosophy—Honour—Wealth.[152]
4. Reason—Wealth.[153]
5. Wisdom—All lesser goods (including wealth).[154]
6. Divine goods—Human goods (including wealth).[155]
7. Public goods—Private goods (including wealth).[156]
8. Wealth—Means to wealth.[157]

Cursory inspection of the above scales shows that they all presuppose some such value-scale as " Intellectual vision—Moral development—Physical development—Wealth—Means to wealth," which would be a complex form of the soul-body scale investigated above, and so far as they are variants of this scale, they have already received sufficient consideration But 1, 2, 3, and 5 will be more in place in relation to the scale of virtues which forms the subject-matter of Chapter VIII, and 7 is to be made the subject of a special study in Chapter IX, and 4 and possibly 5 seem to come more appropriately under the heading " mind, as contrasted with other goods," which is to be the subject investigated in Chapter X, and finally 6 is to be treated at length in Chapter XI. After duly noting, then, that 8 (wealth—means to wealth) comes under the general principle of instrumentality, the means deriving their value from the ends to which wealth is instrumental, which are such ends as education of the soul-body organism—so that 8 comes under the general soul-body-wealth scale—we shall postpone further discussion of the other scales until we come to them in their most appropriate contexts.

CHAPTER VIII

THE VALUE-SCALE : WEALTH, STRENGTH, BEAUTY, HEALTH, COURAGE, JUSTICE, TEMPERANCE, WISDOM

AMONG the value-scales discussed in the different Dialogues, we find a great variety of brief formulations which partly overlap and are almost entirely included in other, longer, formulations. The most inclusive, and at the same time the longest, of these formulations is officially adopted in the *Laws* as a pattern to be used in guiding legislation, and is thus of fundamental significance for Platonism. Starting with wealth, i.e. with money and material possessions, the scale proceeds upwards to muscular strength, then to bodily health, then—with some recognition of the magnitude of the step—to courage, then to justice, then still higher to temperance, and finally to wisdom or philosophical insight.[1] Our object in the present chapter will be to discover, in the first place, just why each of these values receives the particular position assigned to it on the scale, and, in the second place, what principle or principles govern the composition of the scale as a whole. Finally, by comparing the principles thus discovered with the principles underlying kindred value-comparisons in other contexts, we shall attempt to find out the ultimate meaning and value of such scales for the Platonic philosophy in its deeper aspects.

We begin, then, with wealth, ranked as lower than strength, and ask, why this valuation ? In the last chapter, we saw that money and material possessions acquire value-significance only as means to ends which are valuable *per se*, or at least approximate to such ends. The value of wealth is thus always instrumental, not intrinsic. In relation to the body, money can be used as a means to satisfying bodily wants, so that the body with its wants is the end, the value, towards the attainment of which, money is instrumental. The body is thus prior in the order of value to money, and lends to money a large portion of the value-significance which this may come to possess. In the second place, bodily needs can not be satisfied directly with current coin of the realm. Hunger and thirst require food and drink, and it is only in a state of society so organized as to use a currency as a medium of exchange, that money can procure the desired satisfaction. It is therefore only an indirect and conventional means of satisfying bodily wants. In the third place, money, of itself, contains no guiding principle, no insight which can utilize it for helpful ends. It can be spent upon gratifications which are harmful, and may thus destroy the body, in relation to the needs of which it acquires so much of its significance. In such a case, it is destructive of what value it might conceivably have acquired. For these three reasons, then, money and material possessions are valued as lower than the body as a whole. It remains to apply these conclusions to the special case of physical strength.

Physical strength, for Plato, is largely a matter of bodily fitness, and is conditioned chiefly by diet and methodical exercises in the gymnasium and in field-sports.[2] It is one of the excellencies of the body,[3] and is almost universally regarded as a value in itself.[4] At its lowest, when unaccompanied with much intelligence, it still has a definite market-value in the community which depends upon labour,[5] and at a higher level of development its value for athletic and military contests is so well understood that every Greek city tends to have its professional " strong men,"[6] who make the cultivation of physical strength one of their main ends. Plato, however, disapproves of the professional regimen which develops the muscles at the expense of bodily and mental health, and substitutes for it a training of a more wiry and military type, in the spirit of service of the community as a whole.[7] This training is given, not to a few champions, but to every member of the guardian caste.

Money and material possessions are of value, for Plato, *qua* providing for this caste the leisure, the food, and the gymnasia for this training.[8] Apart from this, they are not only valueless, but are regarded as a source of danger, and the military caste is not allowed to own private property in any shape or form.[9] The value of material possessions is thus, at best, secondary. It is admitted only so far as such possessions are instrumental to the development of the approved type of strength, in due subordination to physical well-being and to mental and moral progress.

The next highest " good " on the value-scale is good looks or physical beauty. Good looks and physical strength are very frequently mentioned by Plato in the closest connection. The same general conditions control the development of both of these bodily excellencies. Apart from the turn of a nose or ear, which are largely accidental, good looks, like strength, depend upon general bodily fitness, i.e. upon proper food and proper exercise, and Plato's treatment of these in the case of good looks is the same as in the case of physical strength.[10] We note particularly the use of a principle of balance and symmetry in the exercises which are to develop the body so that it will be good looking,[11] but in all other respects the bodily conditions are identical.

Why should good looks be ranked higher than physical strength ?[12] The answer is nowhere to be found stated in so many words, but seems to be implied beyond reasonable doubt in the *Phaedrus* and *Republic*. Good looks have a certain emotional appeal which does not attach to strength, as such. They awaken affection and love, the desire to create, in community with the beloved, objects of beauty. Symbolic of ideal beauty in a sense surpassing in the directness of its appeal the ideal symbolism of other material copies of the Ideas, they stimulate and develop the innate idealism of the soul to an especial degree, with an intensity and at the same time a universality which has no equal.[13] Practically everyone reaches the level of " opinion," at which he loves beautiful objects as such, and a few are stimulated to advance still further, and in the end apprehend the Idea of Beauty itself, which transforms the whole meaning and value of life. There is, then, about good looks a peculiar charm, a poetry, which kindles the idealistic fires of the soul, and thus starts a process of development which may lead to the loftiest heights attainable by humanity. It is this which renders it of greater value than physical strength, although both have a similar physical basis in bodily fitness.

The next good on the scale is health, physical well-being as such. Strength and good looks are both, as we have seen, based upon bodily fitness, that is to say, all three goods alike are dependent upon proper nourishment and proper exercise, and also, where necessary, upon medical treatment, in the form of emetics, and carthartics, cautery and surgery, etc.[14] Health and its consequences are often spoken of together as perfections of the body, and as opposed in value to mere money-making, but of the three goods, health, beauty, and strength, health is universally regarded as a higher kind of good, not only by the other interlocutors in the Dialogues, but also by Socrates and other representatives of philosophic insight.[15] What, then, are the grounds upon which physical well-being is ranked as superior in value to strength and good looks ? Plato appears, in the first place, to be influenced by the fact that strength and good looks are, in Aristotelian terminology, accidentally rather than essentially connected with physical well-being. Professional devotees of muscular development tend to sleep too long and eat too much for perfect health,[16] and the culture of a beauty which is only skin-deep[17] is accompanied by temptations to activities and passivities which are not calculated to develop the wiry endurance of which Plato approves. Health is thus a deeper and more universal sort of thing than muscular strength and an attractive appearance. Consisting essentially of a balanced harmony of the various bodily elements, it contains a principle of self-continance,[18] and is thus in a high degree self-sufficient, i.e possesses a characteristic which belongs to higher, rather than to lower goods.[19]

In the second place, he is very much influenced by the fact that a sound bodily constitution is essential to the higher development of the mind. The judgments of sick men tend to be unsound, even in matters of simple sense-perception,[20] and the physical pain which tends to accompany disease is perpetually attracting attention to bodily concerns, and thus effectively interferes with philosophic contemplation of pure being by means of pure thought.[21] Physical well-being is of permanent value, precisely because it eliminates the occasion of such interference with the higher studies in which philosophical living consists.[22] On both these grounds, then, physical well-being appears to be a more valuable possession than physical good looks or muscular development.

The goods so far considered are frequently grouped together as " goods of the body " and are somewhat sharply contrasted with the higher goods which remain to be studied, or at least to the principle of these higher goods. It is denied that the bodily goods are valuable in their own right. Money, strength, good looks, health, and even life itself, may be employed to further purposes which are vicious rather than virtuous : in which case it is pointed out that, on the principle of *corruptio optimi pessima*, the possession of such " goods " leads directly to ruin.[23] In any average social environment, such excellences are accompanied by inherent tendencies to misuse,[24] and their value is thus plainly of a secondary order. As Plato expresses it, such excellences are really valuable only when their possessors are men of character and intelligence, who convert them into organic portions of the philosophic life.[25] These lower goods " depend upon the soul, and the soul depends upon wisdom," so that it is only when the higher goods, symbolized by wisdom, are present, that the lower goods become of genuine value.[26]

Among these higher goods, the lowest in rank, and, therefore, from our present standpoint, the first to be considered, is courage. Physical courage, as we have seen in an earlier chapter, consists of instinctive impulses which concentrate the bodily powers in the direction of removing or destroying by violence any aggressor ; i.e. it is what is nowadays called the instinct of pugnacity.[27] Enlightened by social convention, these pugnacious tendencies assume the form of morale, and are directed mainly against the enemies of the community, in the orthodox channels of military and police service in defence of the community and its ideals. As controlled by reflection and directed towards the support of ideals which have a value of their own, the pugnacious impulses begin to assume something of the nature of value, and are recognized as a " good," although not of the primary kind, which is valuable *per se*, but rather of the secondary, instrumental kind, which receives its value from the ideals supported and maintained.[28] When yet further enlightened by reason, these same pugnacious impulses take their place as elements in that resolution and strength of character which supports every cause recognized by reason as worthy, and keeps down whatever is regarded as unworthy, whether in the world of brute force without, or in the world of brute desire within, the organism. Courage in this sense represents the reorganization of all the bodily forces so that they rally, with one accord, to the support of the Idea of Good in the ideal life.[29]

So far as courage is regarded at all as a good, i.e. at the two higher or enlightened levels of social and philosophical excellence, this virtue is consistently treated as a higher kind of thing than physical health or indeed any of the bodily goods from wealth up. The distinction seems to be almost one of kind. The higher goods generally, from courage up to wisdom, are regarded as " divine," i.e. as inherently valuable, whereas the lower or "human" goods are of value only to persons who already possess the higher goods.[30] On further examination, however, we can see that the distinction is, after all, only one of degree, if we remember that courage, no less than health, has a definitely physical basis. Without the pugnacious dispositions which constitute physical courage, the higher virtue simply cannot be developed,[31] and to that extent, while neither health nor pugnacity possess value in themselves, both are at least *sine quibus non* in relation to the higher development. So too it is only when enlightened by wisdom that either physical courage or physical well-being become of genuine value. The distinction seems to depend mainly upon the fact that, while health, resulting from the right amount of eating, drinking, exercising, and sleeping, is a *sine qua non* of the higher development, the activities of which it is the resultant can hardly be idealized beyond a certain point. These activities remain primitive, and cannot quite take on the higher attributes which would make them an integral portion of the life of pure reason.[32] Courage, however, although largely, like health, a corporeal affair, seems capable of further idealization. It can readily be converted into morale, and can indeed gradually be transmuted, without much remainder, into force of character, and thus undoubtedly takes on more of the spiritual nature and significance of the Idea of Good. Thus transmuted by wisdom, it becomes an organic portion of the higher life itself, and thus assists positively, and not merely (like health) negatively, as a *sine qua non*, in raising experience as a whole towards the higher, more ideal level. This seems to be the main reason why it is ranked consistently as a higher kind of thing than physical well-being.

The next good to be considered is justice. At its lowest, this is what we nowadays call gregariousness, the herd-instinct, a consciousness of kind, i.e. a somewhat undiscriminating sense of the value of group living, with some slight feeling of what this involves in the way of conduct.[33] Under the continued pressure of social living, it becomes a relatively enlightened respect for the laws and the government in its outward and visible form, and thus becomes associated with the virtues of courage and temperance, at this social or con-

ventional level.[34] As enlightenment develops still further
and finally reaches the level of wisdom or philosophical
insight into values, justice becomes the social virtue *par
excellence*, the virtue which realizes the highest possibilities
of social living. Courage and temperance, which were still,
at the conventional level, antagonistic to one another, become
synthesized and transmuted in the service of the new community ideal.[35] In fact, Plato gives as a formula for justice
in this sense "wisdom *plus* temperance *plus* courage."[36]
Each citizen is to develop all his potentialities to the utmost
and to realize fully his Idea, as farmer, carpenter, merchant,
student, soldier, or statesman.[37] But further, he is to contribute the results of his activities to the community, receiving
in return the results of the activities of other citizens. As
Plato puts it, justice is to be found somewhere in the mutual
exchange of the products of these activities.[38] And finally,
having reached the level of reflective insight, the citizen is to
realize that only by dedicating himself to the service of the
ideal community does he fully develop his own potentialities.
His function as a man thus consists in realizing on earth, in
the social environment to which he owes his education and all
his opportunities, the main characteristics of the ideal city
which he envisages as "in heaven" and of which he now
conceives himself to be a citizen.[39] With equally reflective
determination, he reproduces gradually in his own character,
so far as possible, a structure and organization patterned upon
the same model, so that justice in the higher sense is realized
when the individual and the community, no less than the
starry heavens controlled directly by God's hand, come to
express the ideal principle of the maximal consistent development of potentiality, the Idea of Good.[40]

Thus understood, it is not difficult to realize why justice
is ranked as higher than courage. Like courage, it has a
physical basis developed into social value largely by habituation, i.e. by the unremitting pressure of the social environment.[41] But it is of a less one-sided and more universal nature
than courage ; so much so, that it is only as comprehended
within justice that courage reaches its highest and most
valuable level of development. Justice, then, is the most
comprehensive of the virtues hitherto discussed. Courage,
at best, becomes indeed an organic portion of the ideal life,
and is the natural ally of justice. But justice is the ideal life

itself, considered on its social side, i.e. is a far more comprehensive portion of this ideal life, if not the whole of it.[42]

On the scale which we are considering, temperance or self-
control is the next highest step. At its lowest, this is the
natural disposition towards quietness and sobriety, towards
minding one's own business and avoiding excitement and the
rough-and-tumble side of life. It thus contains an element
of timidity as well as of refinement.[43] Under the steady
pressure of social living, it develops into the docility inseparable from obtaining the benefits of education, an attitude of
acceptance and obedience towards duly constituted authority,
whether spiritual or temporal, what has been called " followership " in relation to leadership, the ideal attitude, from a
certain point of view, for the average citizen.[44] It is thus
sometimes regarded as the virtue *par excellence* of the civilians
who devote their lives to mercantile pursuits,[45] but on the
whole is treated by Plato as an essential element in the character which is to attain the highest human development.[46]
As the insight which comes from the higher education begins
to control the organism, the somewhat feminine qualities which
belong to temperance at the level just considered become
tinged with something of the more robust and manly qualities
of character,[47] and the student seeks in himself and his own
reason the authoritative source of rules for the direction of
life, rather than in the stronger wills of aggressive personalities
or in the organized force of civic and military institutions.
Temperance thus becomes *self*-control. The element of
docility, acceptance and followership remains, but receives a
new orientation. It is the authority of reason, rather than
the dominant will of man or of " the government," towards
which the docility is now directed, and in the light of reason,
i.e. with his eye fixed upon the ideal pattern of " the good,"
the individual modestly but firmly begins to set his own house
in order.[48] So too on the wider field of political action.
Plato's candidate for leadership is reluctant to push forward
and grasp the reins of power. He retains always this element
of modest withdrawal, and has to be persuaded, if not almost
forced, to take the highest administrative office in the community. He governs, when he does govern, in the spirit of
service, and because he realizes, not only that the community
has, by training and educating him for this responsibility,
placed him in its debt,[49] but also that, if he declines, the power

will fall into hands more avid, indeed, of high position, but less well qualified to direct the destinies of the community beneficially and wisely.[50]. At its highest, then, temperance or self-control means modest but unflinching activity in the spirit of the highest idealism, an activity based upon contemplation and issuing in action.

So much for the meaning of temperance as a virtue. It remains to ask, on what grounds it is ranked higher than justice. At first sight we should be inclined to say that, according to the general tenor of Platonism, it ought to be ranked somewhere at the same level as courage. Courage represents the masculine, temperance the feminine side of character. Only out of their complete synthesis and interpenetration under the influence of philosophical insight does the complete development occur. But this complete virtue is unmistakably stated to be justice, and there can be no doubt that justice should rank higher than either of the two one-sided elements which enter into its composition. This seems to be the lesson of the *Politicus*, and indeed of the very passage of the *Laws* in which temperance is ranked as higher in value than justice.[51] While recognizing the value of this reasoning, let us, however, look more deeply into Plato's meaning. Courage and temperance are each one-sided, contrasted elements of character. This is undoubted. But it does not follow that they should be ranked as equal in value, except, possibly, at their lowest and most instinctive level. Courage is the natural ally of reason, but temperance stands in a much closer relation to the development of wisdom,[52] and is thus more intimately and organically a part of the philosophic life. Without docility, no education, no sound feeling for values. Docility is the student's attitude *par excellence*, and enters inextricably into the life of contemplation and research. Whole-souled devotion to the cause of truth, joyous acceptance of the laws which reason discovers, the transformation of the whole organism into an instrument attuned to the ideal harmonies, what is this but the life of philosophy itself ? In that rapturous contemplation of the eternal Ideas, in which the soul knows itself, with every fibre of its being, to be the co-partner of God in the work of regenerating itself and the world, docility, self-control, and the highest wisdom are fused together into the unity which is the ideal life itself.

From the standpoint thus reached, it is not difficult to realize why it is that, for Platonism, temperance ranks higher than courage. But how about its value-relation to justice ? Let us pursue the argument a little further. Justice is, after all, the complete social virtue, the virtue of the administrator who attempts to realize, in the social environment, the Idea of Good by means of legislative enactments of an essentially temporal and imperfect character.[53] Law-making is always a *pis aller*, and above the life of the administrator one always, in reading Plato, finds the life of the philosopher, the life of wisdom unimpeded by earthly clogs and fetters. The administrator is permitted to retire, at times, to this higher life, in search of inspiration and spiritual replenishment, and it is an axiom for the Platonist that good administration is possible only where the administrator has this higher life, the life of contemplation and research, always open to him.[54] But this is the life of the student, in which docility and self-control constitute an important portion, while the life of administration is felt to be a definitely lower thing. For all that the *Republic* insists upon practical training for the guardians,[55] there is something contrary to Plato's spirit, something forced and unnatural about this. The student leaves his studies for a number of years, to hold various magistracies and positions of military command. But how irksome this is, we can see from the fact that the motive is merely to avoid the besetting sin of the seminarist, *gaucherie* and deficiency in practical address. The practical training is regarded as an enforced descent into the underground den. What the student longs for, and what Plato seems to regard always with a similar longing, is to withdraw to academic contemplation, and, from behind college cloisters, to let the madness of the many take care of itself. It is only external and practical necessities which force the student to desert, for a season, his beloved cloister and undertake the ungrateful task of administration. But it is in this higher life of contemplation that he seeks inspiration, and to which he must be allowed to withdraw at frequent intervals, if the quality of his administration is not to suffer. Justice, in fact, is a virtue which contains mechanical elements, and without repeated returnings to the plain of truth, on which grows the nutriment of the highest part of the soul, the spirit of idealism flags and droops.[56] This life of contemplation is always higher than the life of action in the phenomenal world. But temperance, at its finest, is peculiarly bound up with this life of contemplation ; so much so, that it appears to be part and parcel of the life of wisdom itself, whereas justice is rather the application of the visions of that life to the mundane sphere in which visions, if not frequently renewed, grow dim.[57] There is much of the mystic in Plato, and in this ranking of temperance as higher than justice, of contemplation as higher than administration, we see something of the spirit which we have traced in the " transcendental " theory of the soul's nature and destiny. From the human or empirical standpoint, justice should, no doubt, be ranked as higher than temperance. From the transcendental standpoint, i.e. for one who regards the soul as a plant, not of earthly, but of heavenly origin and destiny,[58] temperance, as more closely associated with the life of philosophical contemplation, inevitably ranks higher.

Finally we come to wisdom or insight, which, on the scale under consideration, ranks as higher than temperance, justice, and courage. If we ask what, precisely, Plato understands by wisdom or insight, we find certain variations of meaning in different contexts. These variations seem to fall into two main groups. At times, wisdom is understood as equivalent to the specifically intellectual side of life, the insight which solves problems of any and every description. It proceeds by the method of analysis and synthesis, extracting from any situation under investigation the maximum of cognitive significance, i.e. the Idea,[59] and passes over, without any violent transition, into dialectic and metaphysics. Understood in this sense, intellectual excellence is not necessarily and intimately associated with moral excellence, but is admitted to exist even in characters of a definitely vicious stamp,[60] i.e. is altogether independent upon habit and social convention. It tends to be regarded by Plato as entirely independent upon material antecedents, as a " divine spark " which in origin and value transcends all empirical acquisitions, such as the virtues and vices, and indeed lends to all such growths the significance and value which they come to possess for us.[61] Ultimately, wisdom consists in the principle of idea-ness, the principle which organizes into cognitive unity all elements of consistent meaning-value which can be found in any given situation.[62] While expressing itself, here on earth, in and through the formation of empirical unity-complexes, it is essentially a transcendent, non-empirical principle, the teleological principle in accordance with which God constructed the cosmos. That is to say, wisdom is ultimately identified in principle with the Divine activity,[63] to which, as creatures of heavenly origin on our rational side, we endeavour to approximate in elevating ourselves to the rational level of pure contemplation of the Ideas.[64]

In other contexts, wisdom appears to have a more empirical basis and function. We have instinctive feelings of curiosity, a tendency to see, hear, and manipulate for ourselves, a natural impulse in the direction of sensory experience.[65] But each sense-organ is a mechanical instrument for selecting and bringing to a common focus certain stimulations, visual, auditory, etc., i.e. is an instrument for carrying through a kind of rudimentary generalization.[66] When simple sensory experience breaks down in its tendency towards generalization, e.g. by falling into illusions and contradictory experiences which refuse to come to a single focus, the generalizing impulse seeks satisfaction by rising above the level of direct sensation to the level of opinion, i.e. of complex sensory experience, the massive organization of sensory and memory images which, with the vast majority of men, does duty for cognitive experience.[67] Such empirical generalizations are more satisfactory than direct but unorganized sensory experiences, for they are drawn from a wider field of observation, and are more constant, less fluctuating and contradictory, while still remaining sufficiently close to direct sensation to seem familiar truths to most men. For such men, they naturally pass for wisdom. But for Platonists, the true wisdom of life is to be sought somewhat more deeply. A prolonged study of something more profound than mere social experience, e.g. a study of mathematical and physical science, is necessary. This, in turn, is to be followed by logical and metaphysical reflection upon the ideal of generalization itself, the method of research followed in these scientific investigations. When the nature of idealization thus comes to be understood, the new rational insight into the Idea of Good, the principle of organizing into a single consistent system all elements of experience, is used for making over the whole of our human attempts at knowledge and faith.[68] It is in this task of idealization, of reorganizing sensory and practical experience so as to bring out its utmost of meaning and value, that wisdom is finally held to consist, in co-operation with God in applying the teleological principle innate in reason to all the details of human problems. In this way alone we can assimilate human life to the Divine, and can realize here upon earth, out of human materials, the ideal city whose pattern is laid up in heaven.[69]

These two conceptions of wisdom, (1) the turning away from everything sensory and empirical to the transcendent contemplation of the eternal Ideas, and (2) the transmutation of the mechanical and empirical into the ideal and spiritual, correspond to the two theories of the soul which we have previously found to exist in Plato's thought. Yet whether the world is disdained and rejected, or whether it is lovingly and patiently transformed, it is not difficult to see why wisdom, in whichever of the two senses we understand it, is ranked as higher in value than temperance and justice. For, on the one hand, wisdom is the complete life of which temperance and justice are mere fragments, and is thus superior to them as the whole is superior to its parts in completeness and self-sufficiency. Again, on the other hand, wisdom is the life of reason itself ; but it is reason which elevates temperance and justice to the highest level of their development. Accordingly, it is rational insight which really gives meaning and value to temperance and justice, i.e. raises them above the level of mere bodily dispositions to the position of organic portions of the life of idealism.[70] They are thus to be regarded either as means to an end, as contributory elements towards the rational life, or as resultants of the application of wisdom to the life of study or to social life generally, i.e. as the rational life itself in certain particular applications.

So far, we have examined the detailed comparisons out of which the value-scale has grown. It remains to consider the scale as a whole, penetrating beneath the phrases incident to particular contexts and to the interests of particular Dialogues, to the deeper meaning of Platonism as a whole, which has given life and meaning to the varying expressions which we find in the different contexts.

If, then, we consider the scale as a whole, the general principle upon which the comparative valuations rest seems easy to determine. The philosophic life, the life of wisdom or insight, constitutes the standard of value, and the position of each and every step on the ladder of values is apparently determined by the closeness of its approximation to this standard. Thus, the life of wisdom is itself the highest step. Immediately next to it, as most completely absorbed in the life of wisdom, and most nearly coinciding with it, comes the virtue of temperance or self-control, considered as the virtue of the student. The third step from the top is constituted by the virtue of justice, which, as complete social virtue, while still containing mechanical elements which cannot entirely be sublimated,[71] almost coalesces with the ideal life of insight, if we consider this on its practical side, as regenerating society and the individual. The fourth step down is constituted by the virtue of courage, the concentration of all the available forces at the disposal of the organism in the service of social and spiritual ideals. Somewhat narrower in scope than justice, and retaining always certain elements which remain mechanical, this manly resolution and righteous indignation constitutes a virtue of a very high order, which to a very large extent passes over into the adventurousness and persistency which distinguish the philosophic life.[72]

The fifth step is appreciably lower. For physical well-being, which is found at this level, owes its position mainly to the fact that it does not impede the higher development. The body must be in a healthy condition, if it is not to interfere with the higher moral and mental development. But, except in respect of the reserves of energy which support the forceful persistence of the soul in its arduous philosophic quest, it does not enter at all into the higher life, and its constituent elements, viz. eating, sleeping, and taking physical exercise, necessarily remain somewhat primitive, incapable of transmutation into philosophy. Health of body, with its three good meals *per diem*, is perhaps a *sine qua non* of the idealistic spirit ; but it remains, in very large part at any rate, obstinately bodily rather than spiritual.[73]

The sixth step down is constituted by physical good looks, regarded largely as a minor consequence of the bodily activities whose complete goal is physical well-being generally. The value of good looks depends upon a number of conditions, which are not often fulfilled. Good looks normally stimulate sex-interest, a physical interest in physical charms. But the rapture which sweeps lovers off their feet may raise them above the level of the senses to an appreciation of higher beauties, and this kindling of the idealistic spirit may lead, by definite gradations, to the full life of philosophy. Physical beauty is symbolical of ideal beauty, and its highest function is to awaken the innate idealism of the soul. But, once awakened to the ideal vision, the soul, entranced by the ideal realities which promise a newer and truer life, neglects the material symbol which originally stimulated the growth of its wings, and soars away to its spiritual home. The value-function of physical beauty ceases, in fact, where it begins, in symbolizing something other than itself. It does not enter into the kingdom towards which it points the way, but remains physical, mechanical and unspiritual in its substance and common-sense function, in spite of its occasional power of stimulating idealistic youth to an interest which develops beyond sex-interest in its physical reference.

The seventh step down the ladder is occupied by physical strength, i.e. robustness and muscular development. This is obviously an affair of the body, and its relation to eating, sleeping, and taking exercise is unmistakable. Its relation to bodily excellence generally is clearly less complete than is the case with health, and it is never regarded as an awakener of idealism. The value of thews and sinews is the value of the hewer of wood and drawer of water, i.e. is instrumental and strictly subordinate to higher values, such as health and—more remotely—courage.

The eighth and lowest step is taken by money and material possessions generally. These are not very directly connected with the higher life at all, but only as a medium of exchange in a social group which has evolved up to a certain point. In such a group money is of value as a means for translating the surplus products of labour into food, rest and recreation for the body, schooling and training for the mind and character, etc., and its value is wholly subordinate to such ends. It does not constitute essentially any portion of human life, physical, moral, or mental. It is, further, a fundamental lesson of the education, towards the securing of which the possession of means can partly contribute, that money is valueless *per se*, a definitely lower thing than strength, good looks, or health. There should, therefore, be no illusion as to its distance from the ideal life of philosophic contemplation, which constitutes the standard of value. Money and material possessions represent the very lowest rung upon the ladder which leads gradually upwards towards that life.

Let us sum up our results. The value-scale under consideration passes from the mechanical to the spiritual. On the lower rungs of the ladder are found those elements which remain largely mechanical and, while contributing somewhat indirectly towards the higher life, cannot be taken up directly and completely into that life. Money-making, beyond the securing of the necessary minimum, is never an object of idealistic endeavour. Muscular development and beauty-culture, beyond the attainment of a stage of development which renders the higher life easy and more attractive, are not objects to which the philosophical spirit devotes its best energies. Physical well-being, beyond the stage at which the body, like a well-regulated machine, gives no trouble, simply does not obtrude itself upon the philosophical consciousness at all. Such things are simply taken for granted. Their absence would be a nuisance, but their presence contributes little that is positive, little that could arouse the enthusiastic pursuit of the man whose vision is fixed upon the higher things of life. On the upper rungs of the ladder we find elements which, while remaining partly mechanical, contribute directly towards the higher life, and can be taken up into the idealistic vision as more and more completely coinciding with the activities in which that vision expresses itself. Resolution of character, justice, self-control and the student's devotion to the cause of truth—these obviously constitute essential elements in the life of the spirit ; and the highest of all, wisdom and insight, while resting partly upon that curiosity, that reaching out after novel experiences which is instinctive with humanity, clearly contains all the other spiritual excellences and fuses them together into the ideal life itself. The value of this life of insight, however, rests not only upon this harmony and organic fusion of its elements, but especially and essentially upon its objectivity, the fact that it is based upon the nature of a reality which is all positive, all harmonious, and essentially spiritual. For this insight expresses itself by taking up reality into human life, and thus making that life real and of genuine significance in the ideally real world.

These conclusions seem simple and reliable, as far as they go. Value consists in the development of potentiality and especially in the transmutation of the apparently mechanical into the truly spiritual which is also truly real. But when we look more closely at e.g. the higher goods, we notice a certain difficulty. Each one of these has itself a mechanical basis, and admits of development into higher forms. Thus, courage begins in instinctive pugnacity, passes through the phase of *morale*, and ends in a moral courage resting upon philosophical insight. Temperance begins in an instinctive shrinking from excitement, passes through the phase of obedience to authority, temporal and spiritual, and ends in a rational self-control resting upon philosophical insight. Justice begins in the herd-instinct, passes through the phase of law-observance and law-making, and ends in the perfect social relations of the ideal community envisaged by philosophical insight. Finally, wisdom itself seems to originate in instinctive wonder or curiosity, to pass through a phase of acceptance of text-book " knowledge," and to culminate in philosophical insight into the structure and meaning of ultimate reality. The higher goods, then, originate in instinct, are developed by social pressure, and finally all pass over into philosophical insight into the Idea of Good. The difficulty which this causes is simple, but entirely disconcerting. If at the highest stage of their development these goods all pass over into one and the same form of experience, *viz.* philosophical insight into the Idea of Good, they are identical, and if they are identical, they cannot possibly be compared with one another in respect of value, so as to constitute different rungs upon a ladder of values.

Let us consider this further. The underlying physical mechanisms of the virtues in question are clearly different. The physical basis of courage is not the same as the physical basis of temperance or the physical basis of gregariousness. So too at the level of " opinion," while it is social pressure which, in each and every case, brings about this development, military *morale*, which faces death upon the battlefield, differs from " minding one's own business," and from " co-operating with the government," much as war is different from peace. So, too, conventional respect for law differs from the pupil's docility, much as a law-court differs from a high school. But at the highest level, based upon insight into the principle of realizing the maximum of possible value, whatever the concrete situation, the virtues can no longer be kept apart. The enlightenment, characteristic of this level, concentrates *all* the forces of the organism, those underlying temperance and wisdom no less than those underlying courage and justice, upon the problem of realizing maximal value, and from this ideal point of view the virtues interpenetrate and become identical. The truly enlightened soldier is not merely brave ; he is the champion of justice and truth, and a pattern of temperance and self-control. So, too, the enlightened dialectician, stooping to the task of administration because of the just claims of the community to his devotion, is not only being ideally just, but is also being ideally wise, ideally resolute, and ideally self-controlled. So, finally, the student, penetrating the last veil which stands between his growing insight and the absolute truth of the principle of ideality, is an example of ideal persistency, resolution, and self-control, no less than of wisdom. From the standpoint of the highest enlightenment then it looks as though such a thing as a value-scale must be a commonplace affair, something, possibly, for *le bon bourgeois*, but not taken seriously by the philosopher.[74]

Before drawing such a conclusion, however, let us examine the lower goods also. Health, good looks and strength are all physical in origin, and all depend upon proper nourishment, proper exercise, and proper sleep. The instinctive tendencies connected with seeking nourishment, exercise, and sleep may (a) be left to their own guidance, i.e. may be left to seek their own satisfaction in an unenlightened, brutish way, in which case they are apt to issue in disease rather than in health, and weakness rather than strength.[75] On the other hand (b) they may be subjected to social control, as eating, drinking, and an interest in flute-girls were controlled by social usage in the typical Greek symposium.[76] Or, finally (c) they may be guided by a higher kind of control, whether by the scientific insight of a medical expert,[77] or by the philosophical insight which characterizes Socrates and Plato.[78] When we examine the physical basis of health, good looks, and strength, then, we can discern the presence of the same three levels of idealization which we have already noted in the case of the higher goods ; and if we investigate the lower goods, health, good looks, and strength, in themselves, we note Plato's frequent insistance upon the importance of their being guided by wisdom or rational insight if they are to be truly valuable.[79] From this standpoint, then, these " goods of the body " coincide, both in respect of their physical basis, and in respect of their final ideal. When idealized as completely as possible, the bodily organism becomes a single entity, a unit, just as the higher virtues fuse together and become a unit. The *corpus sanum* is, as such, both strong and beautiful, with a strength and beauty which are superior to the excessive development of muscles alone, or of facial complexion alone, as the well-rounded whole is superior to the one-sided development of a single part.[80]

What are we to say about money? This seems to be a definitely lower thing, and yet, if we pass beyond the lowest level, at which possessions appeal mainly to the acquisitive instincts, and beyond the conventional or social level of value to the highest or rational level, we realize that money, when expended in an enlightened way, as a medium for translating labour into physical culture, by providing quarters, gymnasia, hygienic meals and expert trainers and medical advisers for the military caste, does really enter into the class, " goods of the body." While the members of this class do not personally own and spend this money, it must be recognized that the ideal life depicted in Plato's pages does rest upon a certain minimum of this world's goods, and if, on the one hand, we must confess that the value of money is conventional and indirect, on the other hand we must also insist that, in the ideal community, it enters into, and constitutes an integral part of, the highest life itself.[81]

At the enlightened level, then, the lower goods, including money, constitute a unit, no less than the higher goods. It remains to ask whether there exists a real gap between the lower and the higher goods, or whether, once the highest level is attained, the ideal life as a whole does not constitute a unit, so that even the comparison of " lower " and " higher " goods becomes impossible. Starting with the " higher " goods, our question is, do those who have the higher development of character also, as an integral portion of that development, take nourishment, exercise, and rest in the most enlightened way? To this question, there can be only one answer. It is very clearly stated that gluttony, drunkenness, and sexual excess constitute no portion of the ideal life, whether from the military, the administrative, or the strictly philosophical point of view,[82] and, further, it is an obvious maxim that the candidates for the ideal system of education are to be, from first to last, superior to vulgar temptations in the case of wealth and private possessions.[83] We must, therefore, conclude that the ideal life includes not merely the " higher," but also the " lower " excellences as constituent elements. This conclusion is borne out by explicit statements in the *Laws*,[84] and it is a consistent Platonic doctrine that the highest virtue, *viz.* wisdom or philosophical insight, is the root of all excellence, physical, moral, and mental.[85] The ideal life, then, viewed from above, constitutes a unit.

So, too, when viewed from below, i.e. starting with the goods of the body. It is not possible to attain the maximal development of our bodily powers without bringing philosophical insight to bear. Temperance and self-control are essential to bodily health,[86] and, as Plato puts it roundly, bodily goods depend upon the soul, and the soul depends upon wisdom.[87] That is to say, when once the stage of enlightenment has been reached, the ideal life, whether viewed from above or from below, constitutes a single, organic entity, with an excellence which ideally includes all conceivable excellences.

This conclusion at once brings out prominently the whole difficulty of constructing a value-scale. To the Greeks generally, and to Plato himself in various contexts, it has appeared possible to construct a ladder or scale of goods, passing from those which are, in their own essential nature, more remote from the ideal standard of value, to those which more nearly coincide with that standard. But it now appears that the idealistic spirit can take up into itself, as a genuine portion of the ideal life, not merely such an instinct as curiosity or wonder, which underlies the search after truth, but also such an instinct as the acquisitive tendency, or such instinctive appetites as those connected with taking nourishment, exercise, and rest. For the Platonist, enlightenment or philosophical insight constitutes a kind of crucible or melting-pot in which all the " goods " of the typical Greek value-scale become fused together into a single virtue, which derives its excellences not from the intrinsic nature of the elements which have been taken from the value-scale, but rather from the idealizing principle, the Idea of Good which has transmuted them one and all. To sum up our present conclusions briefly : intrinsic value belongs to our various instinctive dispositions at no level whatever. Not at the lowest or simple instinctive level ; for without enlightenment, these dispositions are just as likely to be harmful as helpful.[88] Not at the intermediate or socialized level ; for the value there is derived from the organizing principle of social pressure, and this is one and the same in all the dispositions which are reorganized under its influence. Not at the rational level; for the value there belongs to the Idea of Good, and this is a single, all-transmuting principle, one and the same in every case. It looks then as though, from the Platonic standpoint, the popular notion of a value-scale would have to be entirely abandoned.

But it is not abandoned. On the contrary, the value-scale under consideration is officially adopted for legislative purposes, i.e. is accepted by Plato as a method for realizing the highest good. How is this conceivable without contradiction? The only point of view which can unite these two diverse-appearing conclusions is the following :—Our natural dispositions possess no value in their own right.[89] But some of them admit of sublimation more easily than others, and can more easily and more fully be taken up into the ideal life. Hunger, thirst, and sex-interest contain elements which remain obstinately primitive, hard to idealize. In fact, they endeavour to pervert reason into their slave.[90] As compared with these, the quiet, sober, and docile disposition which underlies temperance, while dangerously near to weakness of character, is obviously far easier to handle in the work of educating the organism and training it for higher purposes. So too pugnacity, the spirited element in human nature, is easily converted into morale and righteous indignation, the natural ally of reason in its work of reorganizing character ; and apart from curiosity, the disposition to persist in asking questions, we should hardly develop that intellectual life which furnishes the basis for the last and highest reorganization of character. External goods, such as money and material possessions generally, are harder to take up into the higher life than such things as healthiness and sobriety ; for these already, of themselves, constitute portions of our living, and tend to enter into our growing system of purposes. Bodily goods such as strength and good looks, again, are less easily assimilated to the life of reason than is the case with the dispositions underlying temperance, courage, and justice ; and these, in their turn, can be elevated to their place in the life of enlightenment less readily than the dispositions underlying curiosity, which are less mechanical and tend of themselves to awaken and persist in stimulating our higher intellectual development. The Platonic idealism thus confirms the distinctions which constitute the popular scale of values, but alters and deepens the basis upon which the value-distinctions rest. There is nothing about the natural dispositions which makes them intrinsically valuable. Their value consists rather in the degree of their availability as instruments for the reception and expression of values whose source is higher, deriving ultimately from the principle of value itself which Plato names the Idea of Good.

It remains to compare the value-scale just studied with all value-scales in the *Dialogues* which have any degree of affinity with it. We shall first bring together all scales in which " wealth " or " material possessions " are found, then all scales in which " strength " occurs, then all scales in which " physical good looks " have a place, then all scales in which " health " or " physical well-being " has a place, and so on, until the list of goods on our value-scale has been completely compared, item by item, with all such scales. We should then be in a position to sum up our general conclusions in regard to our value-scale taken as a whole.

1. Wealth, i.e. material possessions, has a definite value-position in the following value-contrasts :—

    a. Wealth—body—soul ;

    b. Means to wealth—wealth ;[91]

    c. Wealth—virtue and wisdom ;[92]

    d. Other goods, including wealth—justice in the soul ;[93]

    e. All lesser goods, including wealth—wisdom ;[94]

    f. Wealth—reason ;[95]

    g. Wealth—honour—philosophy.[96]

Of these scales, the first, which constituted the subject-matter investigated in the last chapter, appears to be much the same sort of thing as the present value-scale. For our present scale starts with wealth, proceeds to the goods of the body, then to the virtues, and finally to the goods of the mind, which culminate in wisdom ; and wisdom is understood as the essence of the soul. It would seem, then, that our present investigation is dealing with a more extended form of the value-scale which we have already studied, in a more contracted form, so that the general conclusions reached in our earlier chapter should apply here also. This means that all the lower elements, wealth, good looks, health, etc., become transformed as we advance up the scale, and are taken up without remainder into the higher goods, the highest good of all, viz. wisdom, being the transforming principle which organizes and unifies all the others. It follows also that the conclusions reached in the present investigation apply to the previously studied scale of wealth—body—soul ; so that body is not *per se* a lower thing than soul, and money and material possessions are not *per se* lower than the body. From the standpoint which considers value, they differ chiefly in idealizability, the mental and moral elements in " soul " being more easily raised to the ideal level than the biological instincts especially characteristic of " body," and the organic, as a whole, being more easily sublimated to higher uses than the inorganic, exemplified by material possessions. In themselves, however, i.e. considered apart from the principle of realizing the maximal value, the potentialities of material possessions, of bodily instincts, and of moral and mental dispositions, are valueless. It is the organizing principle which reduces the various tendencies to a common focus, and, by so doing, concentrates and extracts the element of value, building up a totality which represents all of positive value which can be extracted from the experiences in question. It is the organizing principle alone which develops the natural resources of our potentialities which, left to themselves, would simply run to waste and never realize their highest destiny.[97]

The second scale (b) is a simple appendix to the wealth—body—soul scale, and can accordingly be treated as an appendix to the present scale. Money-making is depicted in the Dialogues as largely a laborious activity, tilling the soil, taking infinite pains, undergoing serious risks, some of them honourable, others dishonourable, but all affectively unpleasant, something of a nuisance at best, and with a tendency to distort our value-sense and warp our appreciation of higher things.[98] Of these activities, the more honourable are of value so far as they provide the means for sustenance and education, physical, moral, and mental, and thus have their place in the life of idealism. The ideal community, for example, rests, economically speaking, upon labour, agricultural and industrial,[99] but it is only in so far as economic values are taken up into the sphere of physical, moral, and mental values that they become transmuted into something worth while *per se*. These strictly economic values, then, can be added to our value-scale without inconsistency, and should perhaps, for the sake of completeness, be added, though officially they are usually presupposed in the Dialogues, rather than explicitly taken up into the centre of the Platonic investigation.

The remaining scales in this group need no long investigation. It is easy to see that to rank wisdom, reason, or philosophy as higher than wealth is entirely consistent with the principle, and indeed with the details, of our value-scale. It is also sufficiently plain that to rank justice above wealth is equally consistent with our value-scale, and on such points no further consideration is required. The one point which remains is the case of honour, which is ranked as lower than philosophy, and as higher than wealth (g). Honour or ambition does not occur, in any direct shape or form, in our value-scale, but if we compare the various passages in which honour is mentioned in the Dialogues, it appears to belong to the virtues of the body-soul organism, such as temperance and justice, and to have special affinities with the virtue of courage.[100] To value honour, then, as higher than wealth, though lower than philosophy, is entirely consistent with the principle of our value-scale.

2. We pass on to consider physical strength, which has a place in the following value-contrasts :—

    a. The power which rhetoric gives—strength resulting from training ;[101]

    b. Strength—the spirited element in our nature ;[102]

    c. Strength—temperance ;[103]

    d. Strength—justice and piety ;[104]

    e. Strength—temperance and justice, *plus* wisdom ;[105]

    f. Strength—honour—wisdom ;[106]

    g. Strength—wisdom.[107]

Most of these value-contrasts fit into their obvious places on our value-scale. Strength is in every case understood as muscular development, a definitely bodily thing, and takes its place among the bodily goods, while temperance, justice, and wisdom are understood mainly as attributes of the soul in its higher stage of enlightenment, and thus take their places among the goods of the soul. So too with the unusual cases of the spirited element (b) and honour (f) ; these are both closely connected with the virtue of moral courage,[108] and are thus thought of as belonging to the soul rather than to the body. The basis of comparison, however, in these value-contrasts is, on the whole, not between strength as such and temperance, justice, etc., as such, but rather between unenlightened development, exemplified by the size of the muscles, and the more enlightened activities of the organism, exemplified by the temperate, just, and wise use of the muscles, etc. Strength results from eating, drinking, exercising, and resting, and the value-contrast in which Plato is interested is between (1) the professional strong man, whose muscles are technically developed at the expense of general healthiness and fitness for civic, military, and intellectual activities, and (2) the more ideal citizen, whose potentialities are all harmoniously developed. The meals, exercise, and rest of the ideal citizen are regulated, not only by regard for general physical health, but also especially by regard for all higher duties. The exercises, for example, are partly of a military character, partly, e.g. in the form of dances and marches in honour of local deities, of a civic and religious character also.[109] Plato's ideal citizen thus represents a case of all-round development rather than of technical muscle-culture, and his strength is a consequence of his whole mode of living, so that in the ideal community strength is a part of the higher life, and the value-contrast between strength and the higher life has ceased to exist. In the Dialogues the contrast is between the mere athlete and the ideal citizen.[110] The former represents the culture of body at the expense of health as well as of mind, while the latter represents the complete interpenetration of physical, moral and mental dispositions. The only value-distinction which at all remains in the ideal community is that bodily dispositions are not quite so easily taken up into the higher life as are moral and intellectual dispositions. But as these also, in the end, rest upon bodily dispositions,[111] the difference is one of degree only, i.e. is a difference in the degree of readiness with which they take on ideal character.

3. We pass on to consider physical charm, which has a place on the following value-scales :—

a. the persuasive power of the rhetorician—physical beauty resulting from training ;[112]

b. physical charm—justice and other virtues ;[113]

c. physical charm—wisdom ;[114]

d. beautiful things—the Idea of beauty ;[115]

e. beautiful objects—beauty of soul—beauty of fair practices—beauty of laws—beauty of sciences—the science of the beautiful.[116]

When compared with our value-scale, these value-contrasts all take their place without any real difficulty. Physical charm is clearly ranked below moral and intellectual charm, much as the physical values are ranked below the moral and intellectual values in our value-scale. A study of the authoritative passages shows clearly that there is a tendency, in opposition to the judgment of "the many,"[117] to regard bodily good looks as "nonsense," from undue respect for which the philosophical student needs to be purified.[118] But in the ideal community there is no doubt that the ideal citizen is intended to have all the symmetry of form and beauty of skin which proper food, rest, and well-planned exercise can give him,[119] and it is definitely stated that the good man is superior to the evil man, not only in virtue and propriety of life, but also in good looks, meaning thereby, no doubt, the good looks which go with perfect health.[120] From the standpoint of Platonic idealism, therefore, physical beauty is not something less valuable *per se* than moral or intellectual beauty—for these are all exemplifications of the Idea of beauty,[121] and receive from that Idea whatever value they have come to possess—but rather readily and less completely idealizable. Physical charm has a certain corrupting influence, to a more obvious extent than moral and intellectual charm,[122] and is sometimes a drag upon the soul which is straining towards the higher development of character and insight. In the ideal community, then, the value-distinction rests, not upon what is regarded, in the common Greek value-scale, as an "intrinsic" difference, a difference of kind, but rather upon a difference in degree, viz. in respect of the readiness and completeness with which moral and intellectual, as contrasted with physical excellence, can be taken up into the higher life and become organic parts of that life.

4. We pass on to consider physical health, which is found in the following value-contrasts :—

   a. Means to health—health ;[123]
   b. the power which rhetoric gives—health ;[124]
   c. health—temperance ;[125]
   d. health—holiness and justice ;[126]
   e. health—temperance and justice (with wisdom) ;[127]
   f. health—wisdom ;[128]
   g. health—good fortune.[129]

Most of these value-comparisons take their places without any difficulty along the scale we are studying, in which mere physical well-being is ranked below moral and intellectual excellence. But two cases, perhaps, call for explanation. By the "means to health" (a) are understood mainly unpleasant experiences, such as those connected with surgery and cautery, dieting, and a prescribed regimen. These are obviously accepted, not for their own sake, as though such experiences were valuable *per se*, but rather for the sake of the physical well-being, in which it is expected that they will result. "The power which rhetoric gives," (b), i.e. the power of persuasion which is based upon opinion but not upon knowledge, is contrasted with the medical advice which is based upon scientific insight into the nature of disease and health. It is admitted that the rhetorician can persuade a timorous patient to undertake an unpleasant regimen, when the mere physician might be unable to persuade him. But it is pointed out that persuasion, while valuable as an indirect means to health, is less valuable than the knowledge which prescribes the direct, scientific procedure which will result in actual well-being. The further case of "good fortune" (g) is merely playful, and is applied at first in a popular sense, in dealing with a simple-minded youth, and then explained as equivalent to "wisdom." These value-comparisons, then, one and all, are consistent with our value-scale, and are to be understood in the sense in which body and bodily goods are popularly ranked as intrinsically less valuable than soul and goods of the soul, but by Plato are ranked as less readily susceptible to sublimation, though finally capable of taking their place in the ideal life itself.

5. The next case, courage or manliness, is found in the following definite value-comparisons :—

  a. Bodily pleasures—courage ;[130]
  b. cobbling, cooking, etc.—courage (and wisdom) ;[131]
  c. desire—courage—reason ;[132]
  d. rashness—courage ;[133]
  e. courage—wisdom.[134]

Certain elements here with different names are probably to be equated in respect of meaning. The contexts of the different comparisons show that "bodily pleasures" (a) have much the same significance as "cobbling, cooking, etc." (b), and as "desire" (c), and all are contrasted with "courage" much as "body" in ordinary Greek valuation is contrasted with "soul" or "mind." So too the "rashness" (d) is the bodily or irrational element, as contrasted with the mental or enlightened element in courage considered as a moral virtue. In spite, then, of variations in phrasing, these value-contrasts are to be taken, on the whole, as fitting into their places in our scale. Nothing new is added.

6. The next case, justice, occurs in the following value-comparisons :—

    a. rhetoric—justice ;[135]
    b. wealth—justice ;[136]
    c. family (and life itself)—justice ;[137]
    d. the reputation of justice—the reality of justice ;[138]
    e. actual laws—ideal justice ;[139]
    f. justice—wisdom.[140]

Of these comparisons, those numbered b and f seem to fit at once into their places on our value-scale, but the other comparisons can only be justified in cases of genuine conflict. Thus, where there is a conflict between rhetoric and justice, justice is the more valuable of the two, in the sense in which reality is more valuable than mere appearance. But conflict is not universally necessary. In fact, justice can direct the use of persuasive rhetoric, so that it will serve moral ends.[141] So again with our interest in money and material possessions : while this interest, e.g. in the form of avarice, may definitely conflict with justice, yet the ideally just legislator, embodying his moral judgments in the form of laws, insists that a certain minimum is essential to the development of the model citizen.[142] That is to say, in the ideal community, there is no ultimate conflict between justice and such institutions as a currency, family life, training in the art of self-expression, and legislation. These institutions can all be idealized, and are thought of as differing in value, not when idealized so as to assist the citizens in realizing their full potentialities as citizens, but rather in respect of the degree of readiness with which they can be made to play their part in the ideal life.[143]

7. The next case, temperance or self-control, is found in the following value-comparisons :—

    a. wealth—temperance ;[144]
    b. money and property—goods of the body—goods of the soul (of which temperance is a condition) ;[145]
    c. desires, pleasures and pains—self-mastery ;[146]
    d. beauty of body—temperance ;[147]
    e. health of body—temperance ;[148]

f. temperance—wisdom.[149]

These cases all fit into their obvious places upon our value-scale. The value-oppositions, in all cases, rest upon conflicts which occur at some stage of moral development which falls short of the highest. At the highest level, conflict vanishes. " Wealth " (a) is not really to be banished from the temperate life,[150] " pleasure " (c) is, ideally speaking, a pronounced characteristic of the life of self-mastery,[151] and as to physical beauty (d), the Platonic ideal is definitely to attain to perfection of body as well as of soul.[152] In the same way, temperance and health (e) are closely connected,[153] and temperance and wisdom are almost identified.[154] The conflict and consequent value-contrast is thus not absolute, but holds good only in particular cases which are fragmentary and unideal. In the ideal community the only contrast which remains is the readiness and completeness with which temperance can be taken up into the ideal life, as compared with wealth, pleasure, beauty and health.

8. The last case, wisdom, may well be left over to Chapter X., where we have already planned that it shall receive special consideration.

We have now completed the detailed comparison of the items on the comprehensive value-scale under consideration with all other value-contrasts in the Dialogues in which the same items are found, and should thus be in a position to sum up finally our conclusions as to the meaning of this scale for Platonism. This value-scale appears to be an expanded form of what we have already discussed in more condensed form in the last chapter, viz. the scale of wealth—body—soul. Here, as in the last chapter, we first discovered that, for the typical Greek intelligence, the value-distinctions appeared to be absolute, something obviously acceptable to the cultivated mind, and that even for Plato wealth and the goods of the body appeared at times as definitely " lower " in value than moral and intellectual excellence. In particular, " mind " or " wisdom " appeared to be immeasurably superior to all other goods, if not, indeed, the sole source of their value. But our detailed investigation has shown that all the value-contrasts, out of which the popular scale seems to have grown, admit of comparison only when the basis of comparison shifts during the comparison itself. It is when a less developed x is compared with a more developed y that x is judged to be " lower " than y. That is to say, the true comparison is between the different stages of development, and not between x and y themselves. Platonic idealism recognizes three such stages, (1) the natural or physical basis, unenlightened by intelligence, (2) the conventional or social level of valuation, and (3) the level of philosophical enlightenment.[155] From this standpoint, value depends, not upon wealth as such, or temperance as such, but rather upon the degree of enlightenment with which we use our material possessions and our psycho-physical dispositions.

At the physical level, the dispositions underlying the virtues are neither more nor less valuable than the dispositions underlying bodily goods ; for the sole value-standard at this level is the satisfaction of individual impulse. At the conventional level, socially enlightened acquisitiveness, in the form of commercial life, socially enlightened sex-relations, in the form of conventional family life, and socially enlightened eating and drinking, in the form of banquets and parties, have a definite value for group living, no less than is the case with military morale, and with the law-courts, theatres, and schools. In group living, these various interests are already becoming so welded together that the courts, e.g. are intimately connected with commercial, no less than with domestic life, and that banquets and theatres play a not unimportant part in military, political, and commercial life, no less than in the more restricted family circles. It is true that, at Sparta, military values predominate, at Athens, cultural values, and in Sicily, apparently, the values connected with banqueting.[156] That is to say, different groups emphasize different elements in the value-complex. But where the different elements which enter into life are becoming closely interwoven, any strict *scale* of values is out of the question. The standards of the soldier, artist, or reveller penetrate to the details of living and regulate the times and amounts of eating, sleeping, etc., until social life, as a whole, approximates to unity, and we have a complex, rather than a scale, of values. In the final case, i.e. that of philosophical enlightenment, this intimate interpenetration of the dispositions which go to make up our life-interests is so complete, that any sort of value-comparison is out of the question.

In conclusion, then, this comprehensive value-scale presents three aspects which are of outstanding significance.

(1) From the popular standpoint, it is understood in an almost personal sense, as an exaltation of the philosopher, as contrasted with the politician, soldier, or *viveur*.[157] The philosopher really gets more out of life than the others, who represent ideals which are one-sided, deficient in comprehensiveness. (2) From the more scientific standpoint, it is enlightenment, as contrasted with individual impulse or with social pressure, which is regarded as the real source of value in life. Reason is the profoundest element in our nature, and it is only when reason takes full control that the other elements which enter into our nature can be so organized and welded together as to extract from all of them the utmost which they can contribute to make life what it should be, the perfect harmony which is the reflex of the Divine Life. From this standpoint, the Platonic value-scale is not a comparison of " health " with " temperance " or " wisdom," but depends upon the degree of enlightenment with which these are employed, and consists essentially of (*a*) unenlightened impulse, passing over into (*b*) social pressure, and culminating in (*c*) philosophical enlightenment. (3) Finally, from the practical standpoint which applies the scientific scale to the details of human life, it appears that some of our dispositions lend themselves more readily to philosophical purposes than others. Moral and mental dispositions are more easily and more completely raised to the higher level of enlightenment than is the case with (*a*) such goods as eating and resting, which remain obstinately physical, and (b) such goods as money and material possessions, which obviously remain mechanical and are, at best, perhaps only partially idealizable. The elements compared in our comprehensive scale are retained, and are retained in an order identical with the popularly approved order. But the basis of comparison is different. From the popular standpoint, the value-distinctions were regarded as inhering absolutely in " health," " temperance," etc., as such. Here they are compared in respect of the readiness and completeness with which they can be raised to the ideal level. All three aspects—popular, scientific, and applied—of the value-scale under consideration are found, pretty generally, in the Dialogues ; but the first is chiefly understood as reflecting the ordinary cultivated Greek judgment, and it is only the second and third which seem to express, in any adequate way, the deeper spirit of Platonism.

CHAPTER IX

PRIVATE AND PUBLIC SPIRIT IN PLATONISM

AMONG the value-distinctions which we find in the Dialogues, one of the most frequently emphasized is the distinction between private and public spirit. So various are the contexts in which this occurs, that it seems to cover the whole field of Hellenic living, and to discuss in adequate detail all cases of this distinction is impracticable. For the purposes of the present study, it will perhaps be sufficient if we examine carefully some five "sample" cases, and then, after reaching some kind of generalization on the basis of these detailed investigations, proceed to verify our conclusion by applying it somewhat widely to the variety of cases discussed in the Dialogues. In this way we should be able to discover concretely, as well as abstractly, how and why public spirit is ranked above private spirit in the Platonic value-judgment.

We shall begin, then, by examining in detail the following "sample" cases, selected arbitrarily[1] from the vast field before us :—(1) Eating and drinking ; (2) Farming ; (3) Business and commerce ; (4) Schooling ; and (5) Politics. The aim of our examination is to discover on what grounds community eating and drinking, community farming and business, etc., are regarded as an improvement upon private eating and drinking, private enterprise in farming and business, etc., and eventually to construct a generalization which can be extended so as to cover all types of cases discussed in the Dialogues. We shall then verify this generalization, by applying it to such cases as property, the home, art, science, philosophy, and religion, and if these cases substantiate our generalization, we shall regard it as conclusive for platonism.

1. Eating and Drinking.

The body is naturally subject to the action of physical elements in the external environment, and, in the action and reaction which thus occur, tends to disintegrate. Elements of earth and water, etc., become separated from their proper places in the organism, and are drawn away to their kindred earth and water, etc., in the environment. This continuous breaking down of tissue which results from the daily wear and tear of life would soon cause the body to consume away utterly,[2] if it were not for the opposite processes of replenishment which take place in eating and drinking.[3] The meats and drinks, whether vegetable or animal, which are taken in at meal-times, represent new organic material which can be utilized in the bodily organism so as to build up the tissues which are breaking down. This material is partly broken up in the process of mastication,[4] and is further dissolved in the abdomen by the " internal heat,"[5] thus separating the nutritive material into its elements. In this process of digestion, the elements of earth, water, fire, and air, which have been separated from their original connections in the meat or drink taken into the organism, become thoroughly mixed together, and constitute a rich fluid of great nutritive value. By means of the processes associated with respiration,[6] this fluid is gradually taken up into the circulatory system,[7] and is carried to every part of the body, where it repairs the losses caused by wastage. The particles of the blood obey the cosmic principle of " like to like," the earth-elements filling up the places where earth is needed, the water-elements filling up the places where water is needed, etc., and in this way all waste products are continually replaced.[8]

In this process of breaking down and building up tissue, a certain proportion has to be observed. The elements taken in from the environment should just about balance the wastage of the tissues in the daily wear and tear.[9] Otherwise, difficulties arise. If too little is taken in, the body gradually wastes away ;[10] if a surplus is taken in, then (a) if the body is still in the growing period, this surplus goes to build up the extra tissue required for growth,[11] and what is taken in is properly assimilated. But when the growing period is past (b), the organism is unable to assimilate more than a certain amount of food and drink in excess of what is needed to repair wastage, and unhealthy surfeit brings the attendant penalty of disease in a variety of forms.[12] In the still later period (c) when the body is growing old, its assimilative powers weaken, and it becomes gradually unable to digest the food taken in, unless this is very carefully adapted to its needs.[13] Speaking generally, the digestive processes become adapted to a certain quantity and quality of digestible material, and any great change, either in quantity or quality, upsets the system for a while, although, until the onset of old age, fresh adaptations of the digestive processes are possible, and the organism recovers and attains a new equilibrium.[14]

From the standpoint which considers eating and drinking, then, the organism is regarded as what we should nowadays call an alimentary canal with various appendages. Of itself, the mouth simply takes in food and passes it down towards the abdomen, whenever the organism feels empty and experiences the pangs of hunger and thirst.[15] It is the irrational and concupiscent principle of the soul which experiences the flutter of these desires,[16] and increases in strength in proportion as they are indulged. The natural tendency of the alimentary canal is thus towards the irrational gratification of its instinctive needs, towards unenlightened and uncontrolled excess, eating for eating's sake, gluttony.[17]

This functioning of the alimentary canal is associated with certain advantages for the organism, as well as certain disadvantages. The advantages are (1) the repair of waste tissue, without which the organism could not continue to exist ; (2) the pleasures which accompany the gratification of our instinctive need for food and drink ; and (3) the pleasures which accompany the resulting accession of strength and physical well-being.[18] The disadvantages only arise from excessive or ill-regulated functioning of the alimentary processes, and are of the following nature : (1) the upsetting of the digestive process by improper diet, which may result in sweating, vomiting, diarrhoea, and other pathological consequences. This leads, not to the natural repair of waste tissue, but rather to the breaking down of existing tissue, in a variety of ways.[19] (2) The development of unnatural cravings for improper meats and drinks,[20] and (3) the upsetting of the proper balance of the elements in the soul, the concupiscent element, which is already the largest,[21] battening on the pleasures of the body, and thus growing more powerful at the expense of reason and strength of character. This results in keeping the eye of the soul turned downward upon the swinish pleasures of the table, instead of upward towards philosophy and that guardianship of reason which is best for the organism as a whole.[22]

To obtain the advantages associated with the functioning of the alimentary canal, and to escape the disadvantages, it is essential that proper habits of eating, drinking, and taking exercise should be established. This means (1) that the diet should be suited to the needs of the organism in respect of quality, as well as quantity. Not merely should excess be avoided, but plain fare, bread and meat without sauces or Attic confectionery, and the simpler kinds of wine, should be consumed. In normal health, an occasional variation from this diet will do no harm, but it must be only occasional. Simplicity spells health, variety spells disease. Variety titillates the palate, but ruins the digestion.[23] It means further (2) that proper exercise must be taken daily. If the body is to be kept fit, so that the alimentary canal will function properly, it must be exercised vigorously and systematically. There is a direct relation between regular exercise and good digestion, and a further direct relation between lack of exercise and various diseases of the alimentary canal.[24] This establishment of correct habits will prevent the third of the disadvantages enumerated above. For when the machinery of the body is well-regulated, it will not distract the higher cognitive powers from their proper function of philosophical investigation ; it is only when something is going wrong, as in the case of indigestion and sick headache, or in the far worse case of settled habits of gluttony, that the eye of the soul is compelled to turn downwards.[25]

To establish correct habits, knowledge or insight is necessary, and of knowledge or insight, Platonic thought recognizes three levels. (1) The lowest level is where the individual is left to the uncontrolled guidance of his own impulses, and simply pursues that kind of action which seems likely to procure immediate and unmistakable satisfaction of those impulses. At this level, sweetmeats have a stronger appeal than the simple food which the physician prescribes,[26] and over-eating and under-exercising become the order of the day. When the digestive system becomes seriously upset, the physician is called in to tinker with the bodily machinery, so that the gastronome, after taking a few nauseous drugs, will be able to continue his way of life for a little longer.[27] (2) The second or medium level is where the individual's impulses are controlled

by social standards, as in community eating and drinking.
What is understood by *syssitia* is not anything like our modern
banquets, but rather the regular mess-tables of a hospital
or military organization, or the regular meals of a boarding-
school or college, etc., where the food is simple rather than
elaborate, and adapted to the needs of regular work under
every-day conditions. The *symposia* were more like our
banquets, but even here the drinking tended to be regulated
by community standards, and direct attention was paid to
medical advice.[28] It was not supposed that obedience to
community standards in well-regulated cities[29] would lead to
excess and calling in the doctor, but that systematic eating
and systematic exercise under these conditions would result
in regular health.[30]

In the above, reference has been made to the physician.
In matters of eating and drinking he is always, in the Dialogues,
the technical expert whose science informs him what food or
what drink will produce the best physical organism.[31] He is
the artist who, by means of his science, " disposes all things
in order, and compels the one part to harmonize and accord
with the other part, until he has constructed a regular and
systematic whole, giving order and regularity to the body,
i.e. health and strength.[32] It might therefore be supposed
that the scientific knowledge of the physician represented the
third stage of insight.

Let us consider this. Representatives of the dietetic art
in the Hellenic world are of three types. (a) For persons in
good health, the trainer in the gymnasium can give sound
advice about eating and drinking, as well as about exercising.[33]
But his knowledge is limited to cases of normal health, or
extends, at furthest, to advising about cases which arise in
connection with the earlier ill-effects of rigorous training,[34]
and in abnormal cases it is necessary to call in the physician
proper. Physicians competent to deal with such cases are
of two kinds. The inferior or rule-of-thumb practitioner (b),
whose *clientèle* is recruited largely from the lower classes, can
prescribe a correct regimen in routine cases, but in all cases of
a higher degree of difficulty is not competent either to diagnose
or to prescribe corrct treatment.[35] The highest kind of physician (c) is a genuine specialist in dietetics, therapeutics, and
surgery, and the scientific nature of his art is nowhere ques-
tioned in the Dialogues. He can prescribe for any given case,

and can reason upon causes and effects in relation to health and disease.[36] But his knowledge is restricted, specialized, technical. His study is of the body, and his insight is limited by the circumscribed nature of his field of study. Literature, art and music, pure science, politics, religion, and philosophy fall outside his field, and his insight, scientific though it is, thus falls far short of what one could imagine as the ideal.[37] The knowledge of the physician is thus not representative of the third stage of insight. For this, we must look further.

As contrasted with this departmentalized knowledge of the technical expert, Plato always recognizes (3) a more comprehensive kind of insight, which arises only when the character and intelligence have received the best which a liberal education can bestow. At home in all the fields in which the mere expert tends to remain a stranger, such a mind acquires knowledge of the whole intellectual realm. This liberal education culminates in the self-knowledge which consists in insight into the Idea of Good, i.e. the principle of extracting from any situation its maximum of ideal elements and focussing these into the concentrated unity of the Idea, both in theory and in action. This is the highest conceivable stage of insight,[38] and the man who has reached this level is an excellent "artificer of temperance," etc. This means that he organizes his thought and action, including the taking of food and exercise, in the most ideal way, and thus needs no physician to tell him how to live, unless he has the quite exceptional constitution of a Theages.[39] At this level, correct habits, with their consequent advantages for the organism, become automatic.

So much for eating and drinking generally, as we find them treated in the Dialogues. The special question of the distinction between "private" and "public" eating and drinking remains to be discussed. This distinction arises especially in connection with the different stages of insight. "Private" eating is thought of by Plato in two ways :—(1) from the standpoint of physical health. Eating and drinking in an unsocial way, by oneself, in one's own house, withdrawn from the direct influence of community standards, is thought of by Plato as tending to lapse into the mere gratification of the palate, with a distinct tendency to select food unwisely, to over-eat and under-exercise. Piquant sauces, rich cakes, and the Sicilian style of table tend to abound in such a house.[40] " Private " eating thus, for Plato, means withdrawing from community standards, and withdrawing from community standards means falling below them, with all the physical consequences of such a lapse. (2) From the social and moral standpoint, to withdraw from the community tables means to take sides with the disruptive tendencies of fourth-century democracy, to lose personal contact with the interests of one's fellows, and to live a stranger to the more intimate aspects of citizenship.[41]

" Public " meals, on the contrary, not only make for better health all round, but bring the citizens together like the members of a family or of a college, and, in spite of the diversity of occupations, establish a sense of community morale to an extent which could hardly be realized by other methods. The value of this institution in a century of social disruption, whether for civic or military unity of purpose, can hardly be over-emphasized.[42] The guardians, accordingly, in the ideal community, are " to attend common messes and live together as men do in a camp,"[43] and, in order to obviate the social evils which tend to arise when the sexes are kept rigidly apart,[44] Plato's co-educational ideal is made to apply to the community meals also.[45] The natural tendency of Hellenic women towards seclusion is to be counteracted by regulations which will bring the whole body of adult citizens under the beneficial rule of law and order,[46] and although in later life Plato relaxes somewhat of the strict communism of the *Republic*, and permits the men to sit together at a table by themselves, he insists that the wives and daughters must sit together at a women's table, and that this must be near the men's table.[47] Private eating and drinking, then, are condemned because leaning towards ill-health and withdrawal from the full, concrete life of citizenship, and community meals are adopted as organic portions of the life which aims at the maximal development of human potentialities, physical, moral, social, and intellectual.

2. Farming.

Man, with a physical nature composed of earth, water, fire, and air, requires food ; and the food suitable for his animal nature is organic material taken from animals and plants ;[48] the food of animals, again, comes ultimately from plants. It follows, then, that the production of plant-food, and of whatever animals are most suitable for human food, will be one of the serious arts, and will be of fundamental importance for human living.[49]

Physically considered, plants, like everything else in the universe, are composed of earth, water, fire, and air, and improve or deteriorate in their growth according to the nature of the soil, water, sun-light, and climate in which they find themselves.[50] In the wild state, they grow where they can and as they can,[51] but, in view of their importance for human life, the plants suitable for human consumption are almost everywhere cultivated. These require rich soil with a clayey bottom, so as to keep in the water, a plentiful water supply, and the variety of light, shade, and climate which are adapted to their needs, a combination frequently found in river-valleys.[52] The soil is prepared by ploughing,[53] manure is provided for their roots,[54] weeds and encumbrances of all sorts are stripped off.[55] Their tendency to straggle and run wild is checked, partly by pruning,[56] but especially by selecting only the best seeds[57] and by paying particular attention to the seedlings when they are young,[58] " nursing and rearing the tame parts " and keeping away all harmful food, i.e. in general, seeing that the most favourable conditions are present.[59]

The primary business of the farmer is thus to tend the plants which are suitable for human consumption,[60] seeing that their wants are supplied and that no harm comes to them. His business is essentially empirical, a matter of co-operating with nature,[61] and while in a sense scientific—for the farmer studies the laws and conditions of plant-growth[62]—it contains little of a mathematical and exact nature. The judgment which guides him is not so much a matter of scientific calculation as of guess-work, helped out by the improvement in sense-perception which comes with experience, attention, and practice.[63] For success in this kind of work, college study and intellectual investigation are neither necessary nor desirable. Farming has to be learnt on the farm, by the apprenticeship method,[64] and is a matter of attentive observation and faithful service. The farmer thus belongs naturally to the serf or peasant class, and in the ideal community is ranked, as a matter of course, with the third estate.[65]

With the farmer proper, who tills, sows, and reaps, and provides the food and timber which comes directly from the soil,[66] are associated the shepherd, who attends to the sheep and other farm-animals which are bred for the market, and prepares milk and cheese for local consumption,[67] and the bee-keeper, who, in a country like fourth-century Attica, where the denuded mountains were for the most part capable of supporting only bees,[68] provides honey on a commercial scale.[69] These belong to the same humble and hard-working class as the agriculturist, and the general statements made concerning this class of food-producers apply to all three groups.

We are now in a position to distinguish between farming as a private venture, and farming as a community enterprise. The private farmer looks upon his work, not merely and not mainly as an indispensable contribution to group living, but as a way of making money, and may be more interested in the money-making side of his way of living than in the crops or sheep and cattle as such.[70] In such cases the competitive tendencies may lead him, not so much to positive efforts, to producing better wheat or finer cattle than his neighbours, as to negative efforts, to seeking out ways of hindering them from becoming his rivals. As typical cases of unfair competition, Plato enumerates (1) encroachment upon land, by removing boundary-stones, (2) pasturing cattle upon a neighbour's land, (3) decoying a neighbour's bees when swarming, (4) interfering with a neighbour's water-supply, even to the extent of polluting wells, (5) stealing fruit, and (6) doing damage in the harvesting operations.[71] Under private competition, then, farmers will not co-operate, but by unfair methods discourage their neighbour's efforts, and thus tend not to increase but to decrease production, i.e. to contradict the *raison d'être* of the farming class.

From the strictly ideal standpoint, Plato thinks that farming in all its branches should be a community enterprise, and should not be left to the principle of competition between individuals. The land belongs fundamentally to the community, and ideally the ploughing, harvesting, and marketing should be undertaken by the community rather than by individuals.[72] He does not give details of such an ideal scheme, but the *Laws* contains a " model " which is " second best." Here farming is the basic activity.[73] The land is divided up in such a way that each citizen receives a farm-section of standard productivity, and his family retains this farm-section, subject to good behaviour, in perpetuity.[74]

In the model community, each citizen takes care of his own ploughing and harvesting, and makes the purchases and distribution of necessaries upon his own farm.[75]   But a wheat-pool and publicly owned and administered markets take care of distribution.[76]   No citizen engages in any sort of private, retail business,[77] but, while managing his farm with hired and slave labour,[78] spends part of the year in his city house, and devotes the major portion of his life to the duties of citizenship.[79]   Money-making tendencies are relegated, partly by public opinion and partly by restrictive legislation, to a very unimportant position, and the element of private interest in private gains derived from farming is strictly subordinated to public welfare and the community ideals which set the whole tone in the model community.[80]

The reason for preferring public to private enterprise in farming is largely because the production of food for the community is so vital a necessity that no community can afford to neglect it.   The *raison d'être* of farmers is the production of an adequate food-supply for the group,[81] and community control can provide public-spirited citizens with land, farm-help, artisan assistance,[82] and protection against unfair competition and non-co-operation.[83]   Under such conditions, an adequate food-supply can reasonably be expected.   Under private competition, acquisitiveness is encouraged, interest in private gains stimulates unfair methods of discouraging rivals, and productivity tends to decrease. The community principle, then, is preferable, because it develops the potentialities of the farming class, always in the service of the community, to their maximum, and thus ensures not only an adequate food-supply but also a group of public-spirited citizens—which, from the community standpoint, may be regarded as the greatest good of all.[84]

3. Business and commerce.

Exchange of the products of labour is essential to community living ; and this involves two things, (1) the use of some standard medium of exchange, a currency in terms of which it is possible to equate the products of the different trades,[85] and (2) a special class of middle-men who devote their whole time to the business of buying and selling, with all which this involves.[86]   For Greek thought there was always implied in this (3) a special place for buying and selling, i.e. a community market in the centre of the city.[87]   This market was always a publicly regulated institution, but in respect of the currency and of the business classes a sharp distinction is drawn by Plato between a private and a public spirit.

(1) A currency lends itself easily to certain uses which are in the interest of individuals, rather than of the community. Currency in excess of the modest requirements of daily living can be hoarded[88] and increased by financial manipulations of many kinds.   The exchange of one currency into another, the lending of " capital " at high rates of interest,[89] whether for commercial enterprises[90] or for mortgages on real estate,[91] and the banking system of paying a low rate of interest on deposits which furnish " capital " for more lucrative operations[92] are all methods of accumulating currency.   This accumulation of currency in a few hands, with a corresponding absence of currency in the hands of others, inevitably impairs the unity of the group, dividing it up into rich and poor,[93] i.e. into sub-groups which scheme against each other[94] and steadily deteriorate in ethical and civic quality.[95]   In the end, the rift between classes grows so wide that the class-warfare in which it started[96] terminates in the death or exile of most of the plutocrats and the absorption of the remainder in the party of the successful proletariate.[97]   The accumulation of currency without check[98] thus destroys itself and is self-contradictory, devoid of ideal quality.

As contrasted with this individualistic attitude towards currency, the public-spirited attitude consists in regarding a currency as a mere means of expediting and improving the business connected with community living.   It is essentially a medium of exchange, so that the farmer may exchange his products with the builder, etc., and continue to be a farmer, not accumulate money and " retire."[99]   It is a part of the machinery for distributing food, implements, shelter, etc., in such a way as to develop the civic potentialities of the different citizens and strengthen the community living as much as possible.[100]   Because of the inveterate tendency of human beings to be grasping and avaricious,[101] the commissions charged with administration are to see to it that opportunities for handling and hoarding gold and silver are reduced to a minimum.   The governing classes are not allowed to possess money or to engage in business ; and in the ideal community, business men are not permitted to function as

governors.[102] To sum up : under a system of private enterprise, a currency lends itself to undue accumulation in private
hands, disrupting the community and ultimately defeating
its own *raison d'être*. Directed in a more public-spirited way,
a currency can be used so as to bind the community together
and assist in the maximal development of the economic,
social, moral, and intellectual potentialities of the citizens.

(2) Business men, i.e. the class of middle-men who devote
their lives to buying and selling, whether they deal mainly in
local products[103] or in merchandise imported wholesale from
other communities,[104] tend to develop a marked private-
property attitude towards their profession, i.e. devote themselves to buying and selling for what they can make out of it.
This, while true of the wholesale importer and exporter,[105]
is especially noted in the case of the local retailer,[106] and
results, as a rule, in the development of an undesirable type
of character. Acquisitiveness is a natural human tendency,
and the temptation to make large profits is hard to resist.[107]
Finance, salesmanship, and discreditable trades attract large
numbers,[108] and business men, in general, tend to become
wholly absorbed in the pursuit of wealth, and to have no eye
for the higher things of life.[109]

The consequences of this attitude of private interest
are developed in three relations. (a) In relation to their
equals, business men make poor citizens. Competition in
money-making leads inevitably to quarrels and law-suits
about property,[110] and Plato even speaks of murder in this
connection, and the use of force, as well as of fraud, in increasing one's possessions.[111] All these, however, tend to disrupt
the community. (b) In relation to the poorer classes, whose
numbers are increased by the financial operations of the rich,[112]
the arrogance and blind avarice of the business men[113] awaken,
not only servile flattery,[114] but, as time goes on, resentment
and contempt.[115] In their uncontrolled pursuit of wealth,
the business men upset the balance of the State, and build
up a group of enemies which eventually leads to the overthrow
of the constitution and to the death or exile of the " business
men's government."[116] (c) In relation to the needs of the
community, viz. the completest positive development of
every citizen in the service of the community as a whole,[117]
the business men are too one-sidedly devoted to money-making
to be valuable citizens. As tax-payers they evade their

obligations.[118]   In public service their contribution represents
the absolute minimum.   In warfare they will not make the
sacrifices required for victory.   In education they will not
look after the rising generation properly.   Finally, in civic
contests, sports, and religious ceremonies, which are of great
importance to public morale, their absorption in money-making
effectually prevents them from taking part or giving active
encouragement.[119]   In a word, they are not interested in the
community, as such, at all.

These are sins of omission.   But systematic *pleonexia*
induces other sins also, of a more positive nature.   There is
constant temptation to overcharge for goods and services
rendered, to withhold payment for goods and services received,
to practice malfeasance towards minors, to fleece young men
of property, to embezzle state funds, and generally to pervert
the laws in order to suit private purposes.   As platonism
understands it, this tendency leads inevitably to the complete
overthrow of constitutional government and the establishment
of the direct contrary of the ideal community.[120]   The private
interest, then, of the business man tends towards (1) the
eventual ruin of the business man himself, and (2) the complete
overthrow of the ideals which give to community existence
its meaning.

In contrast with this attitude towards business activities,
Plato sets up (1) an ideal, and (2) a second-best policy.   The
ideal (1) is only briefly mentioned.   If public-spirited men
and women of high character and liberal education could
somehow be compelled for a time to enter the business arena,
e.g. to undertake some retail business on ideal principles,
i.e. in the spirit of enlightened public service, or to manage
a " travellers' rest " in an essentially hospitable way, for a
moderate charge, then, just as in the administration of a state,
so in running a small business, the philosophic spirit would
satisfy the needs of the community, would link the citizens
together, " reducing their inequalities to equality and common
measure," and would raise such occupations to honour and
esteem.   But public-spirited persons of character and education are too rare and precious to the community to be used
for any such purposes.   They are needed for the administration
of the State, as philosopher-kings.   The notion of " philosopher
innkeepers " is ludicrous,[121] and it is necessary (2) to adopt
a second-best policy.   The philosophical guardians use their

insight so as to avert the worst consequences of commercial activities. In the first place, citizens escape the corrupting influences of petty trading by being forbidden to indulge in it. One-third of the produce of the soil is to be disposed of in a public market, managed entirely by public officials, where aliens (who, of course, own no farms) purchase their food.[122] Prices for agricultural implements and all commodities sold are to be fixed, after conference with experts, by the guardians, so as to allow a reasonable profit only.[123] Over-charging and any kind of " bargaining " are to be strictly prohibited.[124] In the second place, citizens are not allowed to handle or possess gold and silver,[125] or to accumulate property in excess of four times the minimum requisite for performing the duties of citizenship,[126] or to leave fortunes to their children.[127] Finally, the business activities in which individuals participate as individuals are to be reduced to a minimum,[128] and are to be undertaken, not by citizens, but by " metics " and strangers.[129] These pay no " foreigner's tax " or " business tax " or " customs duties,"[130] but their residence is contingent upon good behaviour. That is, they must obey all regulations *re* registration of property, fixed and moderate charges, refusal of " credit," etc.,[131] and, last of all, must leave the city after twenty years, and must take their property with them.[132] In all these ways then, *viz.* by public control, by reduction of business men and commercial activities to a strict minimum, and by restriction of these to a temporary and non-citizen class, whose partial corruption will be of slighter importance to the community,[133] an attempt is made to escape the evils of materialism, i.e. law-suits and economic-political divergences which tend to disrupt the community.

As Plato understands it, commercial activities are inevitable in community living, but should be regulated and controlled in such a way as to function as a mechanism which will assist the citizens in what is the real business of citizens, viz. living, as nearly as possible, an ideal human life, in which " big business," wealth, and possessions are the last things to be considered important.[134] Public control is better than unrestricted self-interest, because the latter, instead of furthering the ends which give significance to community existence, tends to destroy the group altogether, and thus to contradict, not merely itself, but also the stable organization of society, which it presupposes.[135] This *pleonexia* brings about deterioration of the soul in the business men, and also disrupts the city, leading directly and inevitably to an intolerable despotism, which is the direct antithesis of orderly, constitutional government.

4. Schooling.

According to Hellenic usage, education was conceived as commencing with life and passing through a series of stages, each of which had a fundamentally moral significance, as fitting the child to develop his potentialities and become a valuable member of the family and community. First parents and nurses, then " tutors " and schools, grounded the child in the rudiments of behaviour and the traditions of the group ; then military service, initiation into fraternities, and taking part in religious, theatrical, and civic institutions generally, fitted the free-born youth to take in public life the part to which his family and wealth entitled him. Of these stages, those connected with military, religious,[136] and civic institutions were essentially of a public nature, while all the rest were private. It was further possible for special training in later adolescence, whether in heavy-armed fighting and field-sports, or in public speaking and the arts of persuasion, to be added, where the family was wealthy. Such special training was always private.

Parents are represented as eager to secure for their sons as much education as possible, especially the private training which could be purchased and would, perhaps, give their sons an advantage over contemporaries who had not enjoyed these special advantages. The idea of the parents is to develop the potentialities of their sons so as to fit these for taking a leading part in civic life.[137] There is also the further notion (frequently expressed) that a child so trained would be the staff of his parents' old age.[138] That is to say, from the parents' standpoint, schooling was mainly conceived as a family venture, an investment expected to bring returns to the family. In a secondary sense it would, of course, be of advantage to the community, but it was thought of mainly as a private, rather than as a public affair.

The nurses and " tutors " were essentially household servants,[139] often foreigners, with a training and outlook which kept them attached to the family, and, as being without a liberal education and without the free-born parent's interest in civic affairs, their mental and moral horizon was even more narrowly private-spirited than that of the parents. So too in the case of the teachers. In the ordinary Hellenic community, the elementary schoolteachers tended to be persons of no especial education or character, who were driven by poverty (like the seventeenth and eighteenth century " ushers " in England) to cleaning the blackboards and floors, and assisting in the A B C work.[140] While they gave attention to manners,[141] their moral horizon was terribly restricted by their poverty. Even in the model city of the *Laws*, they were to be foreigners, attracted by pay,[142] and were thus hardly qualified to serve as patterns of community idealism. Plato expects " tutors " to be subject to the chastisement of any free citizen, if they seem to merit it.[143] The teachers of poetry, of music, and of gymnastics would be in slightly better case, but not much. One and all, they were professionals, driven to the business of teaching by the necessity of making a living, and thus essentially unqualified to bring up their pupils in the amateurish attitude towards the arts which the free-born Greek parent desired for his free-born sons. The whole atmosphere of teaching in the schools and gymnasia was thus private rather than public, an extension of the parent's idea that special advantages could be obtained by those who could pay for them, an investment which would bring results when it came to public life later. So, too, with the higher teachers or sophists. These were foreigners who, for large fees, gave the final finish to this essentially private education, reflecting the ideas of their pay-masters, that the community was a field in which special cultivation produced valuable results to the far-sighted family which made the necessary sacrifices.[144] The whole attitude of those concerned with the detailed technical business of schooling was thus private rather than public-spirited.

The children themselves, brought up in the constant presence of this sharp contrast between the deliberate amateurishness of their parents and free-born citizen friends, and the technical professionalism of nurse, " tutor," and schoolteacher, would inevitably come to regard all persons concerned with the technical side of education as low-born, foreign, slavish or quasi-slavish persons, and to feel that technical dexterity in the content of their training would be *banausic*. To lisp seems more " noble " than to articulate correctly ; to speak and write with grammatical exactitude seems pedantic ; to quote the poets correctly, or to accompany themselves on the lyre in any except an amateurish way, will smack of a narrow professionalism.[145] So, too, in physical exercises, minute attention to the details of athletic training[146] or even of military exercises[147] means going beyond the " gentlemanly-interest " ideal. The youth of twenty takes part in " sport " (i.e. hunting, racing, cock-fighting, wenching, etc,) or " philosophy " (i.e. public speaking, political science, etc.), but his interest is essentially that of the gentlemanly amateur who carries "nothing too far." If, e.g. a youth should be carried away by an interest in philosophy which seemed likely to become permanent, citizens of the type of Callicles would feel inclined to strike him for his slavish disposition.[148] The free-born ideal is to take part in public life, to stand forth and govern, to join a political club[149] and enter politics, seeking for the spoils of political victory in the aristocratic but faction-torn life of the age. In fact, this free-born notion of the social organism as an aristocracy where birth and ability in public-speaking carry off the prizes is essentially a private rather than a public-spirited way of regarding the community. Public life, with its prizes, is to be the arena of a privileged class, who are superior to the drudgery connected with real work,[150] and furnish the officials, directors, supervisors, and political and military leaders, betraying in their habitual ways of thought and action an essentially private-property attitude towards all public institutions.

As contrasted with these fourth-century tendencies, the Platonist desires to infuse into schooling an entirely new spirit, the spirit of public service, which regards the good of the community as the true goal of aspiration, and " private " good as something which attains its most perfect development only when entirely absorbed in the endeavour after public good.[151] With this desire, special measures are taken in the ideal community to root out the private property attitude towards public office, and to implant in the rising generation a public-spirited attitude. The private, family idea which characterizes parents is to be removed by eliminating, not only private property but also the private family, with its relations of exclusive possession between husband and wife, parent and child. Marriage and parenthood become essentially public functions, where service of the community is the dominating principle.[152] Nurseries are to be removed from the family circle, and the children in the new State nurseries and schools are to be in the charge of public officials from the moment of birth.[153] The best schooling which can be provided is to be given, not to the sons of the rich especially, but to all children in the community, so far as intelligence and character tests indicate that they are capable of profiting by such schooling, irrespective of sex and family considerations.[154] The best of the rising generation thus constitute a civil service class which receives a schooling calculated to fit them morally, socially, and intellectually for the work of administration and research. The other children are prepared for the basic industry of agriculture, or for industrial manufacture, or for commerce, law, or medicine, by the usual apprenticeship system,[155] and thus resemble, to a certain extent, similar children in other cities. But the leadership class are deliberately cut off from every opportunity to acquire private possessions, and are so trained as to develop an intellectual enthusiasm for science and research which carries them right out of the usual circle of human interests, and makes them superior to all vulgar temptations to acquire wealth, or power for power's sake, etc.[157] This culminates, at the age of fifty, in the apprehension of the Idea of Good, the scientific principle of extracting the "ideal element," i.e. the utmost of positive value from every concrete situation, and, during the administrative portion of the life which remains to them, this principle is applied to the work of governing the community in the most ideal way which is humanly conceivable.[157] The attitude which these "guardians" take towards public institutions is thus essenti- ally the attitude of public service, entirely unmixed with thought of private advantage, except possibly in so far as service is itself regarded as the ideal which also develops the potentialities of the individual in the best possible way.

It remains to inquire why the public-spirited attitude is ranked higher in value than the private-property attitude towards public institutions which characterized so many of Plato's contemporaries. The reasons suggested in the various contexts are as follows : The competitive, private-property policy (*pleonexia*) is unprogressive, leads nowhere, makes of life a meaningless will-to-power which is essentially ir- rational, unprincipled, contradictory, futile, chaotic, headed straight for "not-being."[158] These expressions are all forms of one and the same objection, viz. that, when measured by the standard of ideality, the private-property attitude towards public institutions is essentially un-ideal, self-contradictory, logically condemned to self-destruction. As contrasted with this attitude, the spirit of public service calls out the utmost of positive value in individual and community alike, and thus approximates to fulfilling the requirements of the ideal principle itself.

As applied to schooling, this means that a schooling which fosters private spirit leads nowhere except towards social chaos, while a schooling which fosters public spirit develops the individual citizen and the community so as to call out the maximum of value which can be attained by men living in social groups. In order to overcome the short-sighted selfishness of family and party spirit of the fourth century, Plato sees no remedy but public education in State-supported and State-controlled institutions, with the family and the political party simply eliminated. So far is he from supposing that private family and private school life could furnish a sound training for public-spirited citizenship, that he regards it as a miracle, a divine interposition, if, under the conditions which prevailed in his time, any individuals have been able to attain to an unbiassed insight into the philosophical requirements of the ideal.[159]

5. Politics.

A number of instinctive tendencies impel men to live together in groups. On the positive side, a typical tendency is sociability, in the absence of over-crowding and competition for food.[160] On the negative side, a gregarious force frequently noted is the desire for self-preservation, whether against wild beasts,[161] or against other human groups.[162] The group once formed, common work and the facing of common problems, such as the constant battle for an adequate food-supply, the constant vigilance against disease, and the constant rivalry with other groups, tend to draw the members of each group more closely together, and give rise to a set of habits and customs which have all the force of written law.[163] For example, the older and more experienced members of the group naturally take the lead, and, under the economic conditions which Plato has in mind, some form of patriarchal system naturally evolves, in which the ruler is, in Homeric

language, the " shepherd," and the people are his " flock."[164]
This type of civic structure arises naturally and inevitably
in relation to the environmental conditions, and is in no sense
arbitrary, " man-made," or questionable,[165] and even in his
highest flights, Plato always comes back to this patriarchal
system, as fundamental.

Politics is thought of by Plato as the " royal " art which
presides over the group as a whole. At the natural and instinctive level, the group is a kind of family, and the father-
ruler provides for his family. But when the group develops in
complexity and becomes politically self-conscious, all kinds
of difficulties make their appearance. Political clubs come
into being,[166] and individuals and parties attempt to manipulate the central authority of leadership, no longer in the
interest of the group as a whole, no longer in a public spirit,
but in a narrowly conceived selfish interest, in a strictly private
spirit, milking the flock for their own personal gain.[167] Let
us consider this contrast between private and public spirit
more in detail.

In the Hellenic communities of Plato's time, the private
attitude in politics was sufficiently in evidence. Oligarchies,
administering the affairs of their communities in the interest
of the governing class, democracies, moderate or extreme, and
unconstitutional despots, all alike using the power of the
group mainly to keep themselves in power, were known
to everybody.[168] Even more obvious was the strife of competing factions, oligarchic and democratic, each seeking to
seize the helm and steer the ship of state in the democratic
direction.[169] In fact, when once the age of political experimentation has been reached, Plato regards this tendency
towards the use of power in a narrowly conceived self-interest
as almost universal in humanity.[170] His objections to it are
two-fold. In the first place, it is blind and stupid. Such
rulers do not know what to do with the community power
when they have attained to a position from which they can
direct it in accordance with their own desires. As administrators, they are devoid of insight into the elements of administrative policy. They have nothing to fall back upon but their
uneducated and barbaric notions of squandering power upon
the gratification of sensual impulses. And it is not only of
the " tyrant " that this is true.[171] The inner ring of wealthy
men who direct policies in an oligarchy are every bit as stupid,

and can think of nothing but adding to their private fortunes, and spending public money on their crude sensual impulses.[172] And as for a democracy, it is a pitiful illusion to suppose that " the many " have more insight than " the few." They are almost incredibly stupid, blundering along with uproar and unreasoning panics and boastings,[173] tolerating as leaders only flatterers who repeat and magnify their own many-headed prejudices, and holding them responsible for the shipwreck of policies for which their own stupidity is essentially to blame,[174] and leading by gradual, but inevitable steps to their own enslavement under a despot who understands when to apply the whiff of grapeshot.[175]   In fact, whether the governors are one, or few, or many, so long as their ideal of administration is this private-property attitude towards the resources of the community, the difference is purely formal.[176] Blind, empty-headed, null, all alike are parasites, a tax upon community production.[177]   The wonder is, that the community can hold together as long as it does, under these wasteful and nonsensical conditions.[178]

In the second place, this absence of vision exhibits the characteristic which one would expect where " Ideas " are absent, viz. inconsistency, the futility of self-negation.   The one-sided oligarchs, with an interest only in money, inevitably build up a rival group of paupers, and disrupt the community so that it falls into two groups, one of the rich, and one of the poor.   These work against one another, and, when the balance is entirely upset by the maladministration of the rich group, the slightest occasion brings about an *émeute*, and the personnel of the administration receives a sudden change, passing from " oligarchs " to " democrats."[179]   But here again there is no essential change in policy, for " freedom " in a democracy is simply a more extreme glorification of the private attitude.   Each citizen pursues " happiness " as he happens to conceive it.   Some make money, others follow their fancies in other equally individual directions, and the disruption of the group into its elements is almost complete. There is no common purpose,[180] and the tendency of the champion of freedom (thus formally conceived) is to enslave himself to some dominant impulse, and thus to contradict his own love of freedom.[181]   As to the unconstitutional dictator, under his *régime* the resources of the group are still more obviously squandered upon private gratifications, and by exile and plain murder the forces which make for stability and organization are steadily eliminated, until the social disintegration is extreme.[182] The dictator himself lives surrounded by foreign mercenaries, fearing for his life in the community which his misuse of power has rendered more savage, treacherous, and inhuman.[183] The stupidity, then, of the private-property attitude towards the administration of community resources leads in every case to its own opposite, and also, by negating the purpose for which administration of resources exists, is steadily wasting the resources and destroying the unity and significance of the community itself. It is the exact contrary of what administration should be, and its changes of governmental form are simply meaningless. Backward or forward it's all one ; upward or down, it's just the same.[184]

As contrasted with this, Plato insists that there can be a public-spirited attitude towards public resources. If there is any sense at all, any meaning that the mind can grasp, in administration as a genuine art, politics must be more than this see-saw game of parties preying upon the resources of the community. It must be possible to administer a going concern without ruining it.[185] Any art which has any grasp of scientific principle improves what it handles,[186] and the art of political science should be able to improve, rather than squander, the community resources which it administers. For this, two things are necessary. In the first place, a truly public-spirited attitude towards public concerns must be developed. For this, there must be (a) rigid selection of the very few persons who have character enough to keep their hands off what does not belong to them,[187] and (b) these persons must receive an education which will liberate them, as far as humanly possible, from the pull of selfish interests.[188] Plato himself goes even further, and (c) will not allow them, as public administrators, to possess private property at all.[189] In the second place, it must be recognized that the Idea of Good—the scientific principle of extracting from concrete situations all elements of positive value and reorganizing these elements so as to constitute a self-consistent unity which has its place in the ideal totality—is the only conceivable principle of intelligent administration.[190] The administrator's business is to bring out all the potentialities, all the undeveloped resources, of his community, and to concentrate into a single focus all tendencies which are of civic value, so as to realize, as far as is possible with his human material, the ideal vision of a Reality which is all positive, all harmonious, a manifold completely permeated by the spirit of unity.[191]

The true art of politics is thus fundamentally concerned with public good, bringing out the social unity of the citizens, their harmonious co-operation in developing the potential resources of the group, and thus, in the activity of ideal citizenship, achieving reality and salvation, the fulfilment of the Divine plan for humanity.[192] For the ideal State, whose pattern is laid up in heaven, and whose outline and details are depicted in the *Republic*, *Politicus*, and *Laws*, is the kingdom of God, who is the ideal patriarch and shepherd of his folk. The philosopher-kings govern as God's ministers and servants,[193] co-operating with Him in realizing the eternal plan—the Idea of Good—by legal enactments adapted, for the time being, to the actual state of social evolution, and perpetually re-shaped to meet changing conditions.[194] As possessing the sacred metal of idealism in their own souls, they neither need nor desire earthly dross, and the private is entirely sunk in the public-spirited attitude towards administration,[195] so that the individual, whether governor or subject, realizes his own Idea and achieves the highest that is in him, by taking his place in that harmonious totality which, in the group of men, is the visible community,[196] and, in the larger environment, is the unseen but ever-real fellowship of spirits with their Maker and Father.[197] In politics, then, public spirit makes for the salvation of States and the realization of their highest good, viz. the progressive development of all their powers in accordance with the Divine plan, whereas the private, self-regarding spirit contradicts itself and disrupts the community and squanders its resources, and thus tends, not towards God's Reality, but towards the bottomless abyss of Not-being.[198]

So far, we have examined in detail five cases of the value-distinction between private and public spirit. We shall now attempt to put together our results and state them in a more general way, going behind the phrases used in particular contexts so as to reach a universal formulation which can be tested by application to cases not yet examined.

As we look over what we have discovered in our special

investigations, three points of the desired universality stand
out somewhat sharply :—(1) Private spirit, in any enterprise,
is thought of as *pleonexia*, unregulated self-seeking, the natural
tendency of every impulse to seek its own immediate satisfaction, regardless of everything except such satisfaction.   Hunger
demands food. Thirst demands drink. This is elementary
and obvious, instinctive, universal, and inevitable, a simple
expression of the nature of impulses. Without in any way
denying that this is natural and universal,[209] the Platonist
objects to the " private " element, i.e. to the absence of
regulation, on the grounds that this necessarily involves
(a) blindness (b) non-coherence, and (c) self-contradiction.

Let us examine these objections more closely. (a) When
unregulated, i.e. unenlightened by reason, impulse gropes
blindly after its own satisfaction. Where it knows and cares
nothing for the needs of the organism of which it is a mere
part,[210] good results, if ever attending these groping efforts,
are a matter of chance, not of reasoned calculation. The
hunger impulse, e.g. is just as likely to lead to satiety and
disease, as to health and strength ; but to select, out of the
multitude of possible objects, those which will most surely
bring good results, requires knowledge and organized experience, and cannot safely be left to the blind promptings of
instinct. This is, perhaps, sufficiently plain, but there is
also a certain degree of enlightenment which, though keen-
sighted in spying out means which will lead to the immediate
satisfaction of instinct, is still blind, in the Platonic sense.
A Callicles, for example, or a burglar or rascally lawyer, can
use his intelligence, not as a controlling force, but as a servant
which will procure a maximum of immediate satisfactions
for individual impulses. But where it is not realized that
each impulse attains its deepest and completest satisfaction
only when contributing to the development of the whole,[211]
and that the universe of reality is essentially a systematic
totality evolving in accordance with its own laws, the intelligence which restricts itself to seeking means for the
satisfaction of individual impulses is ignorant of the controlling
conditions which determine success or failure in the world of
action. Such a life, passing from one *de facto* successfully
gratified impulse to another, may still be blind, out of touch
with things as they are and, upon the whole, meaningless,
devoid of genuine significance, as in the cases of the " brilliant

statesmen," Miltiades, Themistocles, Pericles, *et al.*, who, as the Platonist envisages them, were merely brilliant failures.[212] Tinkering with details which do not matter, and without insight into the ideal principle which alone gives valuable contact with reality, private or selfish gratification of impulse, whether merely instinctive or whether attaining the level of "opinion" at which it converts intelligence into its minister and servant, is simply stupid, likely to fail even in the miserably inadequate aims which it makes its own, and still failing, even if successful in every one of its pitifully dwarfed and stunted ambitions, to establish contact with anything which will give vitality, significance, and reality to its going up and down upon the earth.[213]

The second objection (b) was that private or unrestrained search for immediate gratification exemplified the principle of non-coherence. Let us consider this. The typical faction-torn city of the fourth century passes from oligarchy to democracy and back again, with an occasional tyranny in between, and furnishes an excellent example of unstable equilibrium. The point made by the Platonic critic is that such a polity is devoid of unity, and is really a collection of groups, of rich and poor, of oligarchs and democrats, etc., all conspiring against one another and virtually in a state of war. But when within the same city walls we have this phenomenon of hostile groups devoid of any inner unity of purpose, there is exemplified the disruptive principle of non-coherence. Such a "city" simply falls to pieces.[214] So, too, in the case of smaller social units. Each group or faction or gang, if its elements persist in following the principle of individualistic self-seeking, fails to cohere and falls asunder into its elements. So, also, if we go further and consider the case of an individual man. If his various impulses refuse to recognize the controlling function of the organism as a whole, they fail to cohere, and the individual disintegrates, falling under the dominance, now of this, now of that impulse, and never attaining to concentrated, systematic unity.[215] It is the "privacy" of the various impulses concerned, their refusal or inability to co-operate and recognize the controlling principle of coherence and totality which is logically responsible for the disintegration noted, with its definite tendency in the direction of complete dispersion of energy which constitutes not-being, the antithesis of reality.

The third objection (c) is that private spirit is self-contradictory and thus devoid of ideal quality. In the Dialogues, this is brought out in two chief ways. The first method is to show that disregard for other elements within the same totality leads to the negation of the purposes of those elements. Thus the impulse towards avarice, the concupiscent element, works against the rational element and often against the spirited element as well,[216] and in this unregulated warfare within the individual soul no one impulse is likely to be the victor for long, as it makes no attempt to educate the other impulses or find some common ground, but merely tries to keep them out of control over the action-systems of the organism ;[217] much as a dominant political faction seeks to keep its opponents out of all the spoils of office, or to convert them into unwilling ministers to its own purposes.[218] This refusal to co-operate and find a common, rational ground logically involves a state of warfare. In this *bellum omnium contra omnes*, some one impulse or complex of impulses—e.g. those concerned with wealth, honour, or freedom—assumes control for a time, but inevitably builds up a rival complex of defeated elements which have the common ground of all being excluded from control. The new complex becomes in time too powerful, and the originally dominant group is itself broken up and destroyed.[219] What brings about its destruction is essentially its own exclusive self-regard or private spirit, which, by refusing to co-operate, inevitably builds up a rival organization and thus leads to its own negation. That is to say, private spirit is indirectly self-contradictory.

A second way of showing that private spirit is self-contradictory is to show that it contradicts its own presuppositions. Brigandage, for example, is destructive, and can subsist only when a great deal of productive work is being done by others. It thus presupposes peaceful, stable devotion to productive activities, i.e. the exact antithesis of its own activities. The absurdity of this position can be seen if we assume the amount of successful brigandage in a country to increase beyond a certain point. It would soon appear that killing the goose which laid the golden eggs had destroyed the *raison d'être* of the brigand classes themselves. If the stable society upon which they prey were destroyed as a result of their operations, there would be nothing left

T

for the brigands themselves to do but to turn honest men and devote themselves to co-operative and productive labour. As a philosophy of life, brigandage represents the temporary dominance of the whole by a single part, and is really contradicting, directly, the totality or whole upon the work of which the brigand lives, and, indirectly, as is seen when the wider group becomes disorganized, the principle of destruction contradicts itself, considered as a principle of life. Destruction is, in fact, no principle at all, but rather the negation of principle, deriving any meaning and strength which at any time it seems to possess from the whole, with its positive, constructive principle, which destruction is attempting to negate. It is thus logically condemned to the meaninglessness and nothingness of self-negation, by necessarily assuming as sound, principles which are logically inconsistent with its own activities.[220]

From such examples of *pleonexia* we can realize that, whether merely instinctive or whether perversely intelligent, private spirit is stupid, blind to the genuine nature of the universe ; we can see, further, that it is non-coherent, i.e. falls to pieces and disintegrates, disappearing in the direction of nothingness ; finally we can see that, in the struggle for existence, it is self-contradictory, lapsing into the *bellum omnium contra omnes*, and accepting, in place of a constructive principle of life, parasitism, the negation of principle, and the meaninglessness of not-being.

The second point (2) which stands out when we look over our conclusions, is that public spirit, as the Platonist conceives it, is a force which (a) binds the community together, (b) makes for the maximal development of the potentialities of every member of the group, and (c) thus approximates to the ideal principle of reality.

Let us consider these more in detail. (a) What does it mean, to say that individuals are bound together into a living organism by public spirit ? Plato is very well aware that what binds people together into groups, whether small or large, is primarily a matter of instinct rather than of reasoning. Such gregarious instincts may be negative, community in pain or fear, as fear of wild beasts, for example, leads men to build common walls and to live close together for protection,[221] or fear of other men leads further to preparation for war, with all which this entails in the way of common discipline, common exercises, common meals, common sleeping quarters, etc.[222] Other gregarious instincts, such as sociability,[223] are positive. The chief examples in this group are the strong instincts connected with family life, the joys and pains which bind together husband and wife, parent and child, and, to a lesser extent, brothers and sisters, and other relatives.[224] In connection with the instinctive basis underlying these gregarious tendencies the force of habit also comes into play. Work and play in common, and all the personal associations involved in living together, link people into groups. At this instinctive and habitual level of conduct, common joys and common griefs bind individuals together as nothing else does or can.

In a secondary sense, considerations of self-interest may link men together in partnerships, clubs, or other associations which exhibit community of purpose based upon advantage to all the members concerned. For example, it is to the advantage of a parent that his son should be educated ; it is to the advantage of the son that he should learn how to make a place for himself in society ; and it is of advantage to the sophist that he should have successful, paying pupils. Community of interest thus links these three together. So, too, business partnerships rest emphatically upon the advantage to all the partners concerned in working together ; otherwise they would dissolve partnership.[225] So, too, with secret societies, whether of a political,[226] or of a theological nature.[227] It is community of interest, rather than any elevated philosophical consideration, which links men together in groups of this type. It should also be added that many associations originating in the direct pressure of instinct may be continued not merely because of instinct or habit, but from a consideration that it is to the individual's interest to continue them.[228]

In both these cases, whether it is instinct and habit or whether it is interest and advantage which have bound individuals together into groups, the resulting groups may be either small or large, and may have much or little to do with public spirit. In fact, the family, as ordinarily understood, and the secret club, whether political or religious, are to be banished from the ideal state, precisely because such units, while bound together by the closest ties, are examples, as Plato believes, not of public, but of private, anti-social spirit. So also of the other groups. That they are bound together by instinct, habit, and interest, is obvious. But they may be examples, not of public, but of private spirit. In other words, what binds men together is some community of purpose, but the purpose common to the group may, apparently, be either public or private. The Platonic contention, however, is that public spirit binds together, while private spirit disrupts social groups,[229] and of the disruptive force of a merely private spirit we have already considered a number of examples. The meaning seems to be as follows :— community of purpose does, of itself, bind men into groups. But if the purpose is private, individualistic, anti-social, it tends to destroy the wider group within which alone the special group—family, partnership, or party—has a meaning, and thus tends to fall apart itself. Where public spirit is present, the wider group is preserved and maintained, and the smaller groupings, so far as dependent upon the wider social unit, are furthered. The preservation of the general social order makes it possible to form stable family, commercial, and political ties.[230] Such a public spirit must, however, include the minor purposes which link men together, i.e. must be, not a thin and watery friendship, but a sense of unity which penetrates to the details of the citizen's life, and is present, not merely in political, legal, and commercial activities, nor merely in the temple, theatre, or gymnasium, but in the home itself, regulating marriage, birth, education, and even eating and drinking, taking exercise and rest.

A third type of gregarious tendency, resting mainly upon strictly rational considerations, requires only the briefest explanation here. It consists in insight into the logical implications of community living, e.g. the necessity of putting the whole before the part, of co-operating actively with all positive, forward-marching tendencies in the group, of developing a living and all-pervasive sense of idealism, of membership in the ideal community which is the city of God. From this standpoint it is obvious that public spirit binds men together in the truest bonds of friendship and service, and is that " golden cord " of reason, which is superior to all other links which men or life can forge. Once this cord is present, then the other bonds, instinct, habit, and interest, can safely be utilized to bind men together in public service.

In the second place (b) public spirit, as the Platonist

conceives it, makes for the maximal development of the potentialities of every member of the community. At first sight, this seems strange. We might think that interest concentrated in a narrow field would be more efficient than when dispersed over a wide area.[231] But this is not Plato's meaning. His position is rather that a narrow point of view stultifies itself by not taking into consideration the points of view of other citizens and of the community as a whole. Concentration upon a definite task, as weaver, potter, farmer, or guardian, etc., is essential. But it is concentration in the broad spirit of citizenship, of community with the other citizens in living the ideal life and co-operating with God in developing all the resources of the group, so that the other citizens also attain their Ideas. That is to say, positively, it is public-spirited concentration upon one's individual task which really makes for social efficiency, for full development of every activity of positive value which the individual can contribute to the welfare of the community. Negatively, concentration in such a spirit of co-operation upon one's task eliminates much, if not all, of the waste due to conflict and unending friction, in groups where private, rather than public spirit, directs the citizen's work.

In the third place (c) public spirit is a force akin to the principle of the truly real, the Idea of Good. Reality is conceived as a living organism, God Himself, containing all the forces in the universe which are of positive significance, bound together into the systematic unity of a single, all-penetrating Idea which expresses God's nature. The community attains to reality, or is assimilated to the nature of God, when it also is a living organism, containing all the activities of its citizens which are of positive significance, bound together into the systematic unity of a single, all-penetrating Idea, viz. the ideal city whose pattern is laid up in heaven. That public spirit binds together its citizens into the unity of a living organism, we have already seen (under (a)), and that it makes for the development of all the potentialities of the citizens in a systematic way, we have just discovered (under (b)). It follows, then, that, as thus developing the full civic resources so as to realize the ideal community whose pattern is laid up in heaven, public spirit is assimilating the citizens to reality, and represents the workings of the principle of the truly real, the Idea of Good.

As we look over our conclusions, the third point (3) which stands out clearly is the relation between private and public spirit. At first sight, it seems as though this relation is purely an affair of contrasts :—private spirit is blind, while public spirit shows genuine insight ; private spirit disintegrates, while public spirit organizes, binds together, and builds up ; private spirit is ultimately self-contradictory, meaningless, devoid of ideal quality, while public spirit partakes in a very direct way of the principle of ideality itself. It might seem, then, that private and public spirit are mutually exclusive, and that reality and value belong only to public spirit, private spirit being relegated to the uncertain realm of not-being. This, however, would be a misinterpretation. In particular, it would omit a number of passages which have to be taken into account. It is frequently suggested, e.g. that public spirit includes all that is of value in private spirit, i.e. that private spirit, seeking the good of the individual, can obtain that good most surely when completely absorbed in public spirit, which seeks the good of the social organism as a whole.[232] The whole includes its parts. It is also frequently suggested that private spirit, while ultimately out of valuable touch with the ideal principle, receives whatever power it possesses from the sole conceivable source of power, i.e. the ideal principle. Thus a gang of thieves could not hold together unless they observed the principle of justice among thieves.[233] Concentration of the forces of the organism in a single direction is a manifestation of the ideal principle, even when the direction is unworthy and mis-conceived, as in the case of the rascally lawyer or financier.[234] While, in the abstract, absolute injustice would be absolutely un-ideal, futile, weak, and powerless,[235] the concrete monster of injustice never reaches this end, though approaching it, because in the concrete he still, to act at all, uses powers of organization which, to some extent, exemplify the ideal principle itself.[236]

Taking all this into account, our conclusion as to the relation between private and public spirit must be as follows :— All power and might come from God, the sole reality and sole source of existence and meaning. To exist at all, anything, even private-spirited self-seeking, must have ideal quality, must exemplify the " one-in-many," the principle of organization. It is by concentrating the forces of the organism in a single direction, binding them into the unity of an idea, that anything whatever is accomplished. Selfish and private-spirited activities, no less than noble and public-spirited activities, obey this law. The difference, then, between public and private is not absolute, purely an affair of contrasts. To aim at bodily well-being by a carefully planned diet, exercise, and rest, is to concentrate in a single direction forces which have genuine existence, even though the food, perhaps, belongs to someone else, and even though the exercise and rest, it may be, are taken at the expense of more important activities. So, also, to aim at mental development by a carefully planned course of reading and investigation, concentrates in a single direction a number of genuine forces, even though the aim may be to exploit rather than to serve the community, and even though the student may be blind to the higher implications and social obligations of education.

The forces, then, which are used are the same, whether the spirit in which they are used is public or private ; and the general method, viz. of concentrating these forces into the unity of a single idea, is the same, whether it is a selfish scoundrel or a philosophic guardian who is employing these forces. And further : private spirit, in the sense that the individual is seeking what he takes to be his own good, is always present,[237] even in the case of the student who is investigating the laws of the celestial spheres, or raising his eye so as to contemplate the Idea of Good itself. Public and private spirit, then, are not mutually exclusive. Their difference is the difference between (a) seeking after true and abiding reality by activities which give immediate satisfaction, but are superficial, out of touch with the deeper realities of experience, not thought out in their remoter consequences, and hence, in the long run, unsatisfactory, and (b) seeking after the same true and abiding reality by activities which represent the result of profound mental and moral development and are guided throughout by an acquired insight into the ultimate principle of reality as well as of mind, viz. the Idea of Good.[238] Private spirit tends to lose sight of the whole in its feeling after the parts ; public spirit has the whole ever before its eyes, and is thus able to secure the parts also, each in proportion to the rest and each in its proper place in relation to the whole.[239]

It follows that, where the forces used are the same, and the general method is the same, the important thing is to have the right spirit. Where education and reason have established this spirit, minute regulation of conduct is not only unnecessary but is impertinent.[240] The form of constitution, for example, whether monarchical, aristocratical, or democratical, is a purely formal difference. Given the right spirit, even a formal despotism may be used for good.[241] So, too, in regard to other institutions. Private property can be regarded as a public trust.[242] Private education can develop public spirit. Even retail trade can be handled in a public-spirited way.[243] But such spirit is rare ; and where it is not present, or is present only to a slight extent, regulation by law is necessary, to prevent man's nature from degenerating still further.[244] In the second-best community of actual individuals, it must be recognized that certain institutions and certain social environments are more favourable to the development of idealism than others, and where there is a strong human tendency to regard, e.g. public trusts as private property,[245] and where the governing classes tend to regard the great mass of the citizens as their servants,[246] it makes a very great difference in practice whether the constitution is despotic or democratic. With such conditions in mind, the Platonist legislates so as to weaken the forces and institutions which tend towards fostering individualism and private spirit, and to strengthen the institutions which make for idealism and public spirit.

We should now be in a position to make certain deductions in reference to cases not yet examined in detail. If such deductions from our general conclusion prove to be substantially the same as the position actually taken *re* such cases in the Dialogues, we can regard our conclusion as sufficiently verified. If the evidence in the Dialogues fails to agree with our deductions, or if new evidence appears, our conclusion will have to be modified. We shall examine briefly the cases of (a) private property, (b) the private home and private family life, (c) private-spirited artistic creation, (d) the private-spirited pursuit of science and philosophy, and (e) private religion, as examples which extend sufficiently widely over the portion of the field of experience which has not yet been examined in detail.

(a) In the case of private property we should deduce that, as an institution, it encourages acquisitiveness and tends blindly towards heaping up possessions without the slightest regard for the consequences to other citizens and the community.[247] We should deduce further that a community in which the amassing of private fortunes without restriction is a major interest, is a group which is losing its spiritual unity of purpose and is tending to fall to pieces, whether one considers the relation of one wealthy man to another, or the relation of the wealthy few to the impoverished many.[248] We should deduce further that the unrestricted pursuit of private fortunes, when associated with disregard of the poorer citizens and steady increase in their numbers, eventually builds up a group of enemies who react by violence and eliminate the conservative group, the business men's government.[249] We should further deduce that such self-regarding financial operations, by ruining the farmers, labourers, and everyone except the small inner ring of business magnates, gradually but inevitably destroys the community itself. For the farmer or artisan, when impoverished beyond a certain point, ceases to be able to make his characteristic contribution to the development of the community, not only in food or work, but also in training his apprentices, and the community is thus being steadily reduced to two non-labouring classes, viz. paupers and financial experts, out of which it is impossible to make citizens and a progressive civic community.[250]

It would follow from these deductions that the Platonist would disapprove of the institution of private property in his ideal state, and would either eliminate it altogether, having all natural resources possessed by the community as a whole and managed by public officials,[251] or, if allowing it to remain, would so regulate its acquisition and use as to reduce its influence to a minimum and avert, as far as humanly possible, the socially disruptive consequences which we have enumerated.[252]

In the case of the home (b), similar deductions can be drawn. The private family, with a private home in which private possessions can be stored or lavished upon members of the family,[253] would be regarded as a nest of individualism. As such, it would be blind to the consequences of its anti-social joys and pains to other families and to the social group as a whole.[254] The family and its concerns would come first, the rest of the community would hardly be considered at all. We should deduce further that devotion to this exclusive kind of family would tend to lead to rivalries between families and to disregard of civic duties generally, and thus have a strong socially disruptive tendency.[255] Further, if some one family became dominant in the community, and private spirit so directed its policies that nepotism and the foundation of a dynasty became the order of the day, with family caprice rather than public interest as the ruling motive, we should deduce that such a spirit would in time inevitably create a combination of the dispossessed and disregarded elements, and that the private-spirited family would be ousted from its position, probably not without violence.[256] We should further deduce that a community in which the citizens were excessively devoted to the interest of their families and correspondingly careless of public interests, would in time, as its members withdrew more and more from the ranks of active contributors to civic well-being, cease to exist as a community at all, as there would be no common work or common purpose to hold the different families together. Indirectly, as the disappearance of the community would involve the disappearance of the family also, so far as the family is dependent upon the community, this one-sided devotion to family concerns would involve the ruin of the family and the private home itself.[257]

From the situation involved in these deductions it would follow that the Platonist would disapprove of the private home as a social institution, and would either eliminate it altogether, having all matters connected with the birth and upbringing of a family regulated entirely by public officials acting on behalf of the community as a whole,[258] or, if allowing the home to remain, would so regulate marriage and education, etc., as to reduce their exclusive and anti-social tendencies to a minimum, and convert the home, so far as possible, into an institution for fostering public spirit.[259]

In the case of art (c) we should deduce that the private-spirited artist is concerned essentially with creation of art-products of an effective type, and proceeds blindly with this creation of art for art's sake, without the slightest regard for the social consequences of his art-works—a child-like figure, wholly carried away by whatever is brilliant and effective, and knowing and caring nothing for the ultimate significance of his work.[260] We should deduce further that unregulated production of effective poems and music has a disintegrating result, so far as the community is concerned, leading away from single-mindedness and towards a chaotic plunging into emotional experiences of any and every sort, towards stimulation and excitement. Such would be the tendency of a creativity unrestrained by rational considerations, an effective but meaningless imitation of fragmentary and contextless, planless experiences, what is nowadays called " jazz," rhythm for rhythm's sake, sound and fury signifying nothing.[261] We should deduce further that unrestricted devotion to this restless and unprincipled stimulation would so influence the minds of the citizens as to seduce them from their settled conservative habits, and pave the way for fretfulness, for change, variety, novelty, preparing their minds ultimately for radicalism, treasons, stratagems, and plots, culminating in some violent upheaval in the constitution which hitherto held the community together.[262] Out of men devoted to novelty in their sensations and perpetual stimulation of their emotions by the *art nouveau,* none of the steadfast regard for tradition and the welfare of the group, upon which the existence of a community depends, is to be expected. Unregulated private spirit in artistic creation and appreciation is thus not merely indifferent, but in its consequences hostile, to the spirit which makes a community, and in working against the community is ultimately, by destroying its own *milieu,* working towards its own destruction and disappearance.[263]

From the situation thus deduced, it would follow that the Platonist would disapprove of the institution of art for art's sake, the creation of art-works in an unsocial or antisocial, private spirit, and would either banish artists of this type altogether from the ideal community, entirely doing away with creative novelty in literature and music,[264] or, if artistic creation were permitted, it would be so censored and regulated by law as to reduce the publication of novel, untried, original works to a minimum,[265] and to make what did pass the censor, as far as possible, of use in developing and maintaining public spirit.[266]

In the case of scientific and philosophical investigation (d), we should deduce that, so far as this is carried on in a private spirit, its devotees care nothing for the social consequences of their discoveries and for the welfare of the community, but are interested merely in research for the researching's sake. Something of the greatness and impersonality of scientific law will, it is true, enter their souls, but to human interests they will remain blind.[267] We should deduce further that such devotion to scientific specialization, untempered by any concern for the community, tends to isolate the individual scientists, partly from one another but especially from the great mass of non-scientific citizens, and so far tends to break up the community into two groups, of scientists and non-scientists, with the scientists themselves not cohering, but differing among themselves.[268] We should deduce further that dominance by a group of scientists interested only in research and without regard for the social and economic welfare of their community would eventually build up, out of the dispossessed, non-scientific groups, a combination of enemies bent upon revolution and the death or exile of the private-spirited men of science.[269] We should further deduce that unchecked devotion to specialized research, when joined to a total disregard of the social obligations of citizenship, if widespread, would tend to destroy the sense of belonging together and wishing to work together, upon which the existence of any community depends. In this way, by destroying the *milieu* in which the *savant* pursues his researches, such one-sided devotion to science or philosophy ends by making the further pursuit of scientific or philosophical investigation itself impossible.[270]

It would follow from these deductions that the Platonist would disapprove of the private, anti-social pursuit of scientific or philosophic research in the ideal state, and would either have all knowledge, research, and investigation handled entirely by public research bureaus working in the spirit of public service,[271] or, if permitting private initiative in such matters at all, would so regulate this as to avoid all monkish isolation and academic withdrawal from practical life, together with the personal eccentricity of those who pursue science for the sake of science, and the other socially disruptive consequences enumerated above, and would seek to make such researches, so far as possible, of general advantage to the community.[272]

Finally, in the case of religion (e), we should deduce that a strictly non-social, private-spirited, self-regarding attitude towards religion is blind to the real facts of the situation and lapses inevitably into selfish and stupid superstition.[273] We should deduce further that such selfish superstition tends to lose sight of social solidarity, and to break up the community into groups of sectarian individuals competing against one another for divine favours, distinguishing themselves sharply from the general mass of the uninitiated.[274]   We should further deduce that if any one such religious sect, guided by selfish considerations rather than by interest in the welfare of the whole group, ever became dominant in the community, such an established church, with its exclusive devotion to ceremonies intended to procure for its devotees a private salvation un-shared by the rest of mankind, would provoke a combination among the other sectarians, and possibly also among the general body of the citizens, resulting in its disestablishment and possible expulsion from the community.[275]   We should deduce further that individualistic devotion to private worship and private salvation, if widespread, would be so incompatible with the requirements of citizenship as to substitute, for a thriving community, a number of sectarian competitors for divine favours, incapable of co-operating in any common pur-pose, and would thus tend to destroy the community itself. In this way, since the pursuit of other-worldly salvation pre-supposes a stable social environment of citizens who will at least provide the necessities for life in the present world, the anti-social pursuit of religious aims indirectly makes its own further continuance impracticable, and thus contradicts itself.[276]

It would follow from the situation thus deduced, that the Platonist would disapprove of such irrational, anti-social, superstitious pursuit of religious aims in his ideal state, and would either eliminate private worship altogether, making all worship, prayer, and religious ceremony a matter of strictly public observance, directed by a public service college of priests,[277] or, if permitting some private worship, e.g. of the usual Hellenic family deities, would so regulate religious observances as to make them, as far as possible, expressions of community spirit, and ministering to community welfare.[278]

The above deductions, in which our conclusions are applied to the institutions of property, the home, art, science and philosophy, and religion, are drawn mainly from the first of the three points emphasized above, viz. the part referring to the influence of the private spirit. The attitude towards public spirit is merely adumbrated, and the possible relation between them, in which private spirit would be included in public spirit, has been omitted.   For the sake of completeness, it would be necessary to make detailed deductions here also ; but as comparison of our deductions with the detailed refer- ences to the Dialogues given in the footnotes shows, not only that these references constitute a reasonably complete veri- fication of our conclusions concerning private spirit, but also, in many cases, in their immediate contexts substantiate our general conclusion concerning the influence of public spirit, it is perhaps unnecessary to continue the work of verification further. It remains, however, to compare our conclusions briefly with the conclusions reached in the case of cognate value-distinctions, before attempting a final re-statement.

1. As compared with the value-distinction of body—soul, a very close analogy is to be noted, from three main points of view. In the first place (a) there is a similar shifting of the basis of the value-distinction. The body was sometimes regarded as the enemy of the soul, a downward drag upon its idealism, blindly tending towards excessive preoccupation with the things of this world, i.e. towards an irrational and meaningless materialism. At other times the body was regarded as a fit and proper instrument for carrying out idealistic purposes, being physically, in its sense-organs and muscular reaction-systems, adapted to the Idea of Good, though this adaptation was admittedly susceptible of almost indefinite improvement.[279] In the same way, private spirit is sometimes regarded as the enemy of public spirit, dragging citizens and community blindly towards materialism, and essentially irrational and meaningless. At other times, private spirit, the universal desire to make the most of life, is regarded as essentially akin to the idealistic principle, of which public spirit constitutes, as a rule, a more adequate expression, and is further regarded as capable, after improve- ment, of being completely absorbed in public spirit.

In the second place (b) the body and private spirit seem to be very closely connected. The body is primarily a bundle of instinctive tendencies, each of which seeks its own satis- faction without much regard to the rest, in a somewhat chaotic way which is much in need of the guidance of reason. Under such guidance, cosmos comes out of chaos, and the bodily tendencies learn to function organically in the service of spiritual ideals. In the same way, private spirit is *pleonexia*, the blind tendency of each of our instincts to seek its own satisfaction. Under the guidance of reason, the individual reorganizes these tendencies, and seeks his complete good by using them in the service of higher ideals. The tendency of both towards degeneration, when separated from the guidance of reason, towards absorption in material interests and eventual interests and eventual dispersion of energy in futile, self-contradictory ways which seem headed straight for not-being, is one and the same tendency ; so too the adaptability of both to higher purposes, when rational principles are brought into play, is one and the same adaptability.

In the third place (c) the human soul and public spirit seem to have very much in common. Both act consciously in accordance with the rational principle of making the best of all the resources confided to their care, co-ordinating these into a systematic unity which brings out their utmost of positive value. Both, at their best, are exemplified in the person of the philosopher-king, guiding his community towards the free life of the spirit, which is the true service of God. Both at their best, include within themselves all lower tendencies, assimilated and transmuted so as to embody and express the ideal forms of courage, temperance, justice, holiness, and, in general, the Idea of Good. In fact just as materialism, the blind absorption in things bodily, *pleonexia* or private spirit, represents the natural lapsing of the body when deprived of the higher guidance of reason, so idealism, conscious devotion to making real the ideal life of the spirit, which, in social relations, is called public spirit, represents the natural functioning of the soul when not blinded by materialistic self-seeking. The value-distinction of private and public spirit is thus very closely analogous to the value-distinction of body and soul, and is ultimately, perhaps, to be regarded as a phase of the same distinction.

2. In studying the comprehensive value-scale of wealth—courage—wisdom, which represents an expanded form of the wealth—body—soul scale, we concluded that, while popular thought admits an absolute value-distinction between such goods as wealth, health, justice, etc., for Platonism these are not strictly comparable with one another, the true basis of comparison being rather in terms of three levels of enlightenment. These are :—(a) the level of unenlightened, instinctive desire, (b) the level of conventional, social approval, and (c) the level of philosophical insight. It was also noted that the Platonist tends to retain the popular scale of values,

but on the basis, not of absolute distinctions in value, but rather of relative distinctions in respect of degree of idealizability, moral virtues being more easily elevated to the ideal level than physical appetites. Let us apply these results to our present conclusions. It might seem at first sight as though private spirit should be identified with the lowest level, the level of unenlightened self-seeking, and public spirit with the social pressure which sets the stamp of its approval upon whatever seems to make for the good of the group, the greater value of public spirit thus consisting in organization, comparative absence of contradictions, and comparative approximation to a strictly rational standard. But if we apply these results in the spirit of the investigation which led to them, we shall see that this simple conclusion is specious rather than sound. Self-interest or private spirit can be understood (a) in an instinctive sense, in which case it may be blind to higher issues, and may well, as a principle of action, be futile and self-contradictory. But it can also be understood (b) in a socialized and conventionalized sense, as e.g. a business man, or lawyer or politician, while always pursuing his selfish interests, may keep within the law and may appeal to socially acceptable conventions rather than to simple instincts. It can also be understood (c) as a truly enlightened self-interest, which seeks the highest good for the individual by plunging into studies and a mode of living which will completely reorganize the character upon ideal principles, bringing out in harmonious, systematic interplay all the forces of the individual which are of positive significance. So too public spirit can be understood (a) in the sense of instinctive gregariousness, the tendency to herd with others for protection and for certain pleasures. It can also be understood (b) in the sense of conventional social pressure, the public opinion which enforces conformity, e.g. to religious standards in the case of a Socrates or even of a citizen of Plato's "model" state. Finally it can be understood (c) as the enlightened attitude of the philosophic guardian, who represents the highest development attainable by humanity. For all three senses, in the case of private, no less than of public spirit, there is evidence in the Dialogues.

If we proceed to compare private and public spirit with a clear understanding of what is involved in these different levels, it is obvious e.g that instinctive private spirit will rank as lower in value than conventional public spirit, or than enlightened public spirit, as being more chaotic and contradictory, less well organized, further removed from rationality. Similarly the conventional self-interest which remains within the law but is blind to higher things, is clearly less valuable than the enlightened public spirit which is seeking, with every means in its power—including therein the force of social pressure[280]—to realize the higher things of life. It should also be clear that mere instinctive gregariousness, clinging together, whether for protection or aggression, is less valuable than the self-seeking attitude of the ordinary decent citizen who is deficient, possibly, in respect of the very highest insight, but at least obeys all the regulations involved in social living. So too it is very plain that mob-feeling is inferior in value to the enlightened self-interest of the individual who is seeking to develop his powers in the direction of the ideal life. Plato has little but contempt for " the many " when thus contrasted with " the one " who has attained the level of enlightenment. It should be plain that, at the conventional level which applies social pressure to enforce its standards in education, in religious opinion, and in social living generally, public spirit is far inferior to the insight which guides the Socrates whom it condemns, i.e. to the enlightened self-interest of the highest type of character.

If we try to compare self-interest and public spirit when considered at one and the same level of enlightenment, it appears that value-comparison is difficult, if not impossible. Thus at the highest level we have already noticed that private spirit is completely absorbed in public spirit. The good man and the good citizen are one and the same, viz. the philosophic guardian. So too the self-interest which seeks its ends by conforming to all social standards because the individual, without understanding the *rationale* of the situation, finds it to his interest to conform to social pressure, seems to be much the same as the public spirit which, without insight into the why and wherefore, enforces conformity to its entirely self-interested views upon the individual citizens. The standard of organized force as a method of attaining one's ends, " the interest of the stronger " which constitutes the only standard recognized at this level of enlightenment, is identical for the individual and for the community,[281] and no difference upon which a value-comparison could be based makes its appearance. So too at the instinctive level, where the only value-standard is pleasure in the satisfaction of impulse, it appears difficult to compare in any way likely to lead to sound conclusions, the pleasure attending the satisfaction of hunger or thirst with the pleasure of being one of the crowd.

We must therefore conclude that, from the standpoint now reached, no legitimate comparison of private and public spirit in respect of value is possible. In accordance with the indications of the last chapter, it may be suspected that public spirit, whether at the instinctive or at the social level, lends itself less obstinately to education and elevation to the highest level than does the interest in eating, drinking, or sleeping. That is to say, from a practical point of view, more can be made, without too much trouble, of a man with a tendency towards public-spiritedness, than of a man with a marked tendency towards private-spiritedness. It must be admitted that the Dialogues contain evidence which partially confirms this suspicion.[282] Finally we must confess without reserve that most of the comparisons in the body of the present investigation, dealing, as they do, with situations taken directly from the Dialogues, represent comparisons of public spirit at one of its higher levels of enlightenment, with private spirit at one of its lower levels. It follows, without question, that the true comparison, throughout, is logically not between private and public spirit, as such, but ultimately between a more instinctive and unenlightened attitude, which grasps blindly and foolishly at the good things of life, and a more rational and enlightened attitude which, in the spirit of service and co-operation with the deepest forces in the universe, seeks to utilize the opportunities which life brings so as to raise the whole of human living gradually towards a higher, freer, and more ideal level.

CHAPTER X

MIND AND ITS VALUE

IN a number of passages, mind is said to occupy a somewhat peculiar position in relation to the other values recognized by Platonism, and in fact to be superior to them, one and all. The aim of the present chapter, therefore, is to investigate, in the first place, the meaning of the term "mind"[1] in the Dialogues, and then, by comparing it with other typical values, to discover why this peculiar position of superiority is assigned to mind. We shall begin, then, by putting together all the Platonic statements which refer to the nature and function of mind, using this term in the broadest and most general sense that we find in the Dialogues, and shall proceed empirically, passing by due gradations from the many to the one, in the hope of thus reaching a conclusion which may reasonably be regarded as final.

For the typical Post-Heraclitean Hellenic thinker, physical nature is obviously a texture of motions or, perhaps we should say, of moving particles, A, B, C. . . . . B receives motion from impact with an already moving A and passes on the motion, by impact, to C, and the general texture of the physical universe is thus an affair of motions received and transmitted by impact. To the scientific Greek mind, fertile in hypotheses, this situation suggested a great number of lines of fruitful research and speculation. Amongst others, the question as to the *source* of the motions whose interplay constituted the physical drama, was asked and answered in a variety of ways. The answer which appealed most to the Platonic Socrates, as to Aristotle later, was the suggestion, ascribed to Anaxagoras,[2] that mind is somehow the *fons et origo* of the whole business, the efficient, formal, and final cause of the entire physical drama. At present, we are concerned with the efficient cause only. The efficient spring, or moving cause of the motions whose transmissions constitute the physical world, is mind. The motion ascribed to mind is thus, not transmitted, but original motion, spontaneous or self-motion, pictured as circular motion, continuous movement around a centre.[3] Merely transmitted motion is the criterion of inert matter ; originated or self-motion, the power to originate movements in the material world, expressing itself, primarily, in the form of circular motion, is the criterion of life and consciousness.[4] For Thales, the loadstone is alive because it can move iron, and for Plato and Aristotle, no less than for the average Greek, the planets are alive because of their regular self-motion.[5]

We have now a physical universe composed of moving bodies, A, B, C. . . . These bodies, in physical interaction with other physical bodies, are all receiving and transmitting motions, but some of them, N or M, are capable also of originating motions, primarily circular motions within the space occupied by N or M, but directly transmitted, in any number of the possible forms of motion, to A, B, C.[7] . . . As members of the physical system, N and M are of course liable to all the physical changes which affect A, B, C, perpetually losing or gaining part of the earth, water, fire, and air which constitute their physical substance.[8] As far as A, B, C, are concerned, such gain or loss is associated with no consciousness whatever, but in the cases of N and M, the centres of energy with which these are associated are affected by certain of the changes, and are conscious of the greater gains or losses of substance. Indeed, there tend to develope specialized receptors, sense-organs for appreciating certain types of vibration, for the centre of energy is of course influenced by the instrument through which it transmits its motions.[9] In the same way, N or M tends to develop special transmitters for the transference of the central energy to A, B, C. A particular mind is thus a living centre of energy associated with an instrument for receiving and transmitting energy, and limited, to some extent, by the limitations of this transmitting and receiving instrument.[10]

These two specialized developments of the instrument are related to each other in the closest possible way, so that the origination of motion, although spontaneous, is connected with the motions transmitted, via the receptors, to the vital centre. These motions stimulate responses, and the originated motions thus assume the character of purposive reactions to stimuli. N or M is now regarded as an organism in vital action and reaction with the environment, conscious, to some extent, of environmental stimulation and its own purposive reaction, and distinguishing in the environment (a) inert matter from (b) other organisms endowed, like itself, with spontaneous and purposive reaction-systems.[11] These latter are regarded as possessing life and consciousness, and thus as being capable of entering into a new kind of relationship with N or M.

The stimulations which have value for the organism are not any and every kind of motion, as such. They are specific stimuli, primarily of a biological type, stimulations which set some instinctive action-system in N or M functioning in a way which is important if N or M is to live an earthly life. An organism which is to preserve itself against the comstant strain of environmental wear and tear must meet loss of substance by some way of repairing tissue, i.e. must experience the stimulation of hunger and thirst, and must react by taking out of the environment enough material to build up again the tissue which has been wasted, and thus replenish the stores of energy which keep in trim the instrument through which the vital centre acts. That is to say, the receptors must be especially adapted for the apprehension of everything in the environment which is beneficial or harmful, in the way of food or drink.[12] Similarly, the transmittors must be adapted for the selection and preparation of food and drink, as well as for its proper assimilation. That is to say, the human organism must possess, in germ, the power of utilizing the environment so as to plough land, sow seed, reap the harvest, cook and digest the food, etc. It must also be able to obtain shelter from the climate, in the form of clothing and housing, etc. All this is elementary,[13] and stimulations connected with these simple needs will have immediate and obvious value for the organism, calling forth mechanically, or quasi-mechanically, the appropriate reactions, if the organism is to continue in existence.

In the same way, in relation to M, i.e. in relation to other organisms also engaged in obtaining from the environment sufficient food and shelter to maintain themselves in existence, N will require to appreciate the value, whether positive or negative, of certain social stimuli, and to react accordingly, if N is to continue in existence. Thus fear of wild animals, added to general sociability, the positive tendency, induces men to herd together, to build common walls for protection, and to enter upon the whole complex of social relationships in the way of competition and co-operation which are involved in the situation thus created. The strongest social instincts are those connected with sex and with family life, but the others are also powerful.[14]

As we now understand the matter, minds are living centres of energy associated with complex instrumentalities for appreciating and reacting towards environmental stimulations which have biological and social value for the organism. Out of social life there develop, further, whole systems of political and educational values, which call for further refinements in appreciation and reaction, so that the conscious life of the more highly developed organisms becomes extremely complex, and indeed tends to increase in complexity.

Let us pause here, in order to consider a little more deeply what is involved (1) in the instrumentalities of appreciation, the receptors which select from the environment those motions which have value for the organism and are thus regarded as stimuli, and (2) in the instrumentalities of response, the reaction-systems which translate the spontaneous motive principle into specialized forms of motion minutely adapted to the various stimuli, physical, biological, and social, which have definite value for the organism.

(1) The receptors are thought of especially as the peripheral organs concerned in sensation, the skin, tongue, ear, eye, etc. As all motion is transmitted by physical impact, the reception of motion depends upon changes in the peripheral region of the body being produced by impact and being conveyed inward through appropriate channels. It is obvious that the most fundamental of the senses will be some form of contact-sense, and touch, which is the least specialized of our senses, and the most widely diffused over the surface of the body, is so regarded. This is understood to include, not merely appreciation of impact as such, but also some apprehension of roughness and smoothness, lightness and heaviness, warmth and coolness, which are directly connected with pressure upon the surface of the body causing clear alterations in the skin.[15] All other sensations are specialized forms of this contact-sense, the motions of the external world which have value for the organism being filtered out by means of specially constructed organs which receive these motions and convey them, via movements taking place in appropriate ducts,

to the brain and spinal cord. Thus taste arises out of contacts with the tongue producing changes of roughness and smoothness, of warmth and coolness, and certain chemical changes, which are transmitted to the central organs by movements in the ducts which run from the tongue inwards.[16]   Hearing arises from the impact of air-waves passing their motions through the ear to the brain and cord, via the motions which take place in the appropriate ducts, differences of pitch being directly connected with the differences in the rate of the motions involved.[17]   Vision arises from the impact of light-rays coming, originally, from the sun and being deflected from the surface of some visible body in such a way as to stimulate the kindred substance in the eye, and by means of the resulting changes to pass their motions on to the seat of consciousness within.[18]   Finally, organic sensations, connected with changes in the digestive and reproductive organs, pass their somewhat irregular motions along the " spinal marrow " up to the brain, where they may produce serious disturbances.[19]   Each sense-organ is, in fact, a mechanism for selecting and concentrating certain of the external motions which have value for the organism, bringing to a common focus the light-rays,[20] sound-waves, etc., in such a way that they are brought to the brain and cord in a form which is one instead of many, and orderly instead of chaotic. It is, however, not denied that these external impacts are all more or less violent shocks which, primarily at any rate, interfere with the smooth running of the internal motions.[21]

(2) The transmittors are thought of mainly as outgrowths from the brain. Of these, the chief is the spinal cord, enclosed, like the brain proper, in a protective bony covering. In the case of the cord, this covering is flexible, and is provided with sinews, so as to admit of movement. The whole is further covered by somatic tissue which acts as a protection against violent impacts such as occur, e.g. in falling, and against sudden changes, e.g. of temperature.[22]   By means of the cord, movements originating in the brain are transmitted directly to the thoracal and abdominal segments of the body, controlling, as far as possible, the somewhat unruly motions of the organs located in those segments.[23]   Further transmittors, constructed out of similar tissue and thought of as direct outgrowths from the cord, are the tracts which lead to the extremities of the arms and legs, and are enclosed, like the

cord, in a flexible bony covering provided with sinews and protected by somatic tissue.[24] The final protective coverings of skin, hair, and nails are outgrowths of somatic tissue controlled, somewhat indirectly, by cerebral emanations.[25] The whole system transmits centrally aroused motions to the external world by means of (a) the unspecialized surface of the body, and (b) the specialized instruments found at the extremities, particularly the hands.[26]

A secondary complex of motion-transmittors within the body, only indirectly subject to the control of the brain and cord, corresponds fairly closely to what we nowadays regard as the organs connected by the sympathetic nervous system. Of these, the chief is the circulatory system, with the heart as centre. This is closely connected with the functions of respiration on the one hand, and digestion and excretion on the other, though the abdomen and pelvic organs generally are sometimes classed together as being more irregular in their motions and less amenable to central control than the heart.[27]

Genetically, the whole apparatus thus involved in the reception and transmission of motions develops, in reaction with the environment, out of a single tissue. The cerebrospinal tissue is thought of as constituted by a multitude of micro-organisms which are the ultimate physical seat of life, and it is out of this as yet undifferentiated tissue, by subdivision and growth under appropriate conditions, that the other tissues and the whole body develop to maturity.[28] The mechanism as a whole is so complex that it easily gets out of order, and so delicate that excessive motions, whether in the physical environment or in some inadequately controlled portion of the mechanism itself, temporarily interfere with the central self-motion and make of the body as a whole anything but a single machine. And it is not only in relation to the primitive organs connected with nutrition and reproduction that such disorganizing forces are noted. Where the central self-motion is weak and environmental influences are strong, continuous stimulation may develop almost any system of reaction-tendencies in a one-sided way, so that it will upset the proper balance of the parts and attempt to get control over the organism.[29] Continuous devotion to gymnastics brutalizes ; continuous devotion to music produces effeminacy ; one-sided pursuit of learning results in gaucherie ; etc. The first task of the central self-motion is to acquire control over the whole mechanism, so that the transmittors as well as the receptors will co-ordinate and concentrate the motions which fall within their scope, and thus present an orderly, systematic, and unified front to the relatively unorganized motions in the external world.[30]

This acquisition of central control is brought about by training, physical, moral, and social, aided by all the resources of literature and art. The organism thus comes to develop, out of its original receptors and transmittors, not merely mastery over walking and the simpler physical adjustments, but also systematic dispositions towards friendliness and regard for others, towards dignity, manliness, self-control, and singleness of aim, towards love of the beautiful in every shape and form, a feeling for the value of religion, and some premonitory sense of the value of reason.[31] The organism now functions, not in sections, one part reacting to stimulation A while another part is responding to stimulation B, with little or no connection between the two reactions, but as a united totality reacting, as a single purposive whole, to both stimulations. Motions from the outer world awaken the system as a whole, and the biologically or socially appropriate physical reaction follows with almost mechanical smoothness and regularity, so that consciousness, while highly complex, is still chiefly an awareness of the functioning of the reaction-mechanisms in response to sensory stimulations.

Here, however, it is necessary to notice something further, something which takes us beyond the broadest and most general view of mind as mere consciousness of bodily functioning, and leads to the view of mind as self-consciousness, reflective awareness of its own powers in distinction from the mechanisms of its body. In order for the body to react, it must be supplied with receptors as well as transmittors. But our sense-organs, while responsive especially to motions which are of directly biological significance, are, in the nature of the case, capable of appreciating motions which are only very indirectly connected with the great primary instincts. The eye, in order to be able to detect the visual indications of food, etc., must be able to appreciate colour, whether this is directly connected with food or not. It follows that, after food has been selected, the eye is free to appreciate colour in other connections also. The ear, if it is to catch the auditory indications of food, affection, and danger, must be able to appreciate sounds as such, whether directly connected with biological needs or not.　It follows that, when those needs have been satisfied, a residuum of sound in the environment is left over, which can be appreciated in leisure moments.　The use of our sense-organs is wider than strictly biological necessity requires, and may thus, under appropriate conditions, lead to the reception of experiences which will broaden and deepen indefinitely the range of consciousness.[32]

Again, the synthetic tendency of consciousness, which in relation to the receptors reduces the many stimulations to unity, and in relation to the transmittors produces a unified, organized response, is, as such, necessarily susceptible of a development which far transcends the original needs of day-to-day living.　The ordinary effect of a given stimulus is to pass over into action, by means of the appropriate systematic channels of expression which the organism has developed. It gives rise only to a very simple problem, and the problem is immediately and almost automatically solved.　But certain stimuli produce a different sort of effect.　It sometimes happens that contrary stimulations occur at the same time.　In this case, they cannot pass over into immediate action, but balance and hold each other in suspense, and the tension cannot be relieved until the new problem, the problem of opposition and conflict, has been solved.　This new problem, however, cannot be solved automatically.　Other forces, besides simple sensori-motor reaction, must be brought into play, viz. comparison, deliberation, analysis, and judgment, and the first result of their activity is, not physical reaction, but an intellectual concept.[33]　When two sensations refuse to fit in with one another and flow together into action—and such perplexing difficulties frequently arise out of the fluctuations and contradictions of sensuous experience—we seek a one in this many, a unity which can overcome these differences, a way out of the sensory contradiction, by rising into the conceptual realm.[34]　For example, our sensory intimations of magnitude are subject to well-known illusions, so that an object which in one relation appears small, in another appears large, and in the field of touch an object may appear hard in one relation and soft in another, just as in the field of hearing one and the same sound may appear to different persons to have different degrees of loudness, or may appear to be, now loud, now soft, to one and the same person.　Such fluctuations generate nothing but a baffling sense of confusion, until, by processes of analysis, comparison, and standardization, the mind obtains the concepts of greatness-as-such, which can never be mistaken for smallness, and smallness-as-such, which can never be confused with greatness, etc., etc., thus gradually rising entirely out of the level of sensuous experience and entering the clear-cut level of conceptual experience.[35]

The first opening of the mind to these intellectual notions is purely temporary, and still dream-like in character. Problems and questions lead, indeed, to concepts and stimulate intellectual life and growth. But unless the problems are repeated and occur in a wide variety of forms, the mind easily lapses back into the ordinary twilight awareness of sensori-motor processes.[36] On the other hand, if such problems force themselves repeatedly upon the growing mind, as under the purposive stimulation of an experienced teacher, one of the first results of the newly awakened intellectual consciousness is to become fascinated by the game of conceptual manipulation, "rolling up the many into the one, and unrolling the one again into the many," as Plato puts it, or, like a playful puppy, tearing everything to pieces, and making shreds and tatters out of old beliefs, however venerable, in enthusiasm for the new pursuit.[37] In the case of the highest ideas of all, most men remain permanently in the dreamy or twilight state of consciousness, owing partly to their unfamiliarity with these ideas, partly to the intrinsic difficulty of the subject, and partly to the absence of proper method in the approach to the study of these ideas.[38] Plato himself proposes to turn the mind very gradually into the new direction, building up a firm basis by many years' study of the arts and sciences, before the student is permitted to enter upon the more formal study of dialectic and intellectual gymnastics proper. The already somewhat formal study of mathematics, physics, astronomy, and harmonics is carried through with the definite idea of familiarizing the student with the intellectual world, as well as stimulating him to attack and solve intellectual problems, as such. Given these years of preparation, it is expected that the student will not lapse back into the life of sensation, habit, and convention, but will be stimulated to remain in the intellectual world, pushing on from one problem to another, and seeking eventually a solution of the dialectical problem, the search for an unhypothetical first principle, the principle of ideality itself.[39]

Such concepts, then, as hardness, softness, greatness, smallness, etc., originate, by analysis and standardization, from the challenging perplexities of sensory experience. Another group of concepts also originate from sensory experience, but are not felt at first as giving rise to any perplexities. Such concepts as finger, man, ox, earth, etc., are taken up into the mind by way of sensuous experiences as concrete objects, without any feeling of puzzlement or contradiction. They are taken up unreflectingly, and it is not usual to attend especially to their essence or meaning, as this would be expressed in a scientific definition, because no question arises. Everyday experience seems to be their guarantee. So too of the concepts which arise in ordinary social experience, such as farm, city, work, and the various excellences, physical, moral, and intellectual. These just grow up by the sifting processes of repeated sensation and association, at first without any need for reflective analysis and synthesis, and without the slightest feeling of difficulty. They are concepts at the level of what Plato calls " opinion," i.e. at the ideational level which, with most people, does duty for " mind."[40] But when the intellectual life has once been awakened into thoroughgoing activity, and such conventional concepts of things and duties are subjected to questioning, whether sophistical or dialectical, then all such concepts, including even those which have always been accepted as obvious and not suggesting the slightest difficulty, such as the concept of growth, are found to present unsuspected difficulties and to be riddled with contradictions of a most puzzling and challenging kind.[41]

In these difficulties, it becomes realized that empirical concepts are obtained by mind working through its sense-organs. The content of such concepts as man, ox, shuttle, bed, city, etc., is derived primarily from sensuous experiences, at first of an unreflective type. The sense-organs focus for the mind certain recurring types of sensuous stimulation, reducing these to tactile, auditory, or visual form, so that they come to constitute rudimentary generalizations, unities of a sort. These unreflectively formed generalizations are very imperfect, when judged by the standard of unity, because our sensuous experiences fluctuate to such an extent that we are sometimes at a loss to know to what " object " we should refer them, e.g. whether a distant stimulus is to be interpreted as a living man, or as a scarecrow or some figure made by shepherds.[42] In the face of such puzzles, reflective consciousness is stimulated into activity and applies its methods of standardization, by analysis and synthesis working over these semi-generalizations and reducing the many to the principle of the one, much as in the case of hardness and softness, considered above.[43]

The process does not, however, come to an end with the standardization of sensuous experiences. When once our intellectual life has been awakened into vigorous exercise, reflection proceeds further and develops other ideas, concepts of a more formal type, which result from comparing the various operations of the mind itself. Take, e.g. such concepts as ox, horse, man, etc. On the concrete side, as contents, they originate in sensation. But on the formal side, as concepts, they are meanings or essences, products of an analytic-synthetic process which picks out identities, distinguishes differences, enumerates characteristics, defines, classifies, and systematizes, seeking everywhere some deeper principle of unity which will bring together the apparent manifold in a way which the mind can grasp and understand. Reflection upon these operations of the mind gives us such concepts as identity and difference, unity, duality, triplicity, etc., and conceptuality itself, with all which these ideas imply in their various relations. For it is not only in relation to sensuous experiences that the mind operates in these ways. Concepts also can be compared and counted, identified and distinguished, systematized and transformed in relation to one another and to deeper underlying unities, e.g. in relation to the ideal of systematic consistency and truth.[44] These formal concepts of second intension, then, while originating in relation to sensory contents, apply also to concepts on their formal side, or are strictly universal. They can thus be studied without further reference to sensory objects, and in this way we have the purely formal investigations of mathematics, logic, and dialectic, whose function is to explore the *mundus intelligibilis* from one end to the other, until mind finally comes to rest in its own principle, the principle of conceptualization itself.[45]

This principle once thoroughly grasped, the further work of mind consists in applying it to the formal disciplines themselves. Dialectic, mathematics, etc., are transformed so as to become an adequate expression of the intellectual principle ; that is to say, they are converted into mental instruments for extracting the ideally utmost of meaning-value from the subject-matter to which they can be applied, and for concentrating this meaning-value into the form of a concept which is, as nearly as possible, fit to take its proper place in an ideally perfect system of concepts all grounded in the principle of conceptualization. Thus considered, the work of mind, once the fundamental principle has been grasped, consists in perfecting its own mental instruments and then, through their instrumentality, conceptualizing experience, raising it from the mainly sensuous and emotional level to the level at which its significance becomes completely permeable to intelligence and is reduced, without remainder, to conceptual formulations, all alike grounded in their own principle.[46]

The activity of mind is not, however, devoted merely to the specifically intellectual work of transforming sensuous into conceptual experience. It is an organizing energy which concentrates into consistent and harmonious activity all aspects of life, reducing the many, in every field of experience, to the principle of the one. In the field of practical experience, the individual, torn in different directions by his sensuous and rational impulses, and only very partially assisted by social conventions in his struggle for a genuine individuality, tends eventually to give up the attempt and thus remains many rather than one. But mind, when once he has penetrated to its principle, aids him in organizing all the forces of his character so as to extract the maximal life-value from each in consistent, systematic, and harmonious unity with the maximal positive value of the rest. His various tendencies cease to conflict in the stupid way which is characteristic of them at the instinctive, unenlightened level. His eating ceases to be gluttonous, and his sleeping ceases to be lazy. Enlightened by the vision of life-as-it-should-be, a harmonious texture of impulses all alike rationalized, all like converted into constituent elements of the well-planned life of reason, he so trains and educates his various tendencies that they all contribute to the development of the higher personality, whose every energy, physical, social, moral, and intellectual, is dedicated to the progressive idealization of self and of the world.[47] So too on the wider field of civic life. The principle of mind finds for all the cross currents of civic life their proper place in the ideal city wherein every element of civic value receives its ideally fitting place, all harmoniously working together towards the gradual realization of the civic ideal.[48]

So, again, in the field of art. The creative artist tends to let himself go, to yield to the impulses which inspire him and to create whatever the creative urge suggests to him. Vivid contrasts which stimulate the emotions, sudden changes, rapid fluctuations, exciting situations of any and every description, lend themselves to the purposes of artistic creation.[49] Of themselves, however, such situations, while appealing strongly to the artist's magical powers, are devoid of inner coherence, unity, and meaning. The artist is no philosophical interpreter of life as a totality representing ideally the harmonious result of all the contributions made by individual men and women, but is a pure impressionist, reproducing, in rhythmic forms which make a powerful appeal to human sensibilities, all kinds of images, momentary insights, suggestions of things unutterable, each of which is itself an independent individual and declines to join with the others in constituting a single consistent system which the mind can grasp. The philosopher whose thought has penetrated to the principle of mind has lost, perhaps, his artistic creativity, the power of yielding and giving himself up *sans arrière pensée* to the impulse of the moment. The forces of nature, thunder, lightning, and storms, are coolly judged to be without especial significance, and are not permitted to awaken humble, imitative impulses. The machines created by man, with their ropes, pulleys and wheels, are judged to be what they are, viz. neither more nor less than useful machinery, and awaken no admiring wonder and imitative creation.[50] So also the rise and fall of human fortunes, human hopes and fears, pain, misery, and even death, are apprehended by the philosophical intellect in as dispassionate a manner as possible. The philosopher gives way before their power as little as he can, and despises the artistic stooping to reproduce and embellish such situations in tragedy, as unmanly and irrational.[51] The rational man has thus lost the ability to let himself go and create, and accordingly leaves to others the composition of moonlight sonatas and strange, tragical histories. But he has gained something which the artist never had : the ability to judge. With his new insight into nature and human nature, he can judge, coolly and accurately, which of the various productions of his artistic co-evals contain a measure of truth and are likely to be of value in kindling the imagination of the rising generation to the beauty of idealism in every shape and form. As a censor, he can thus suppress what is harmful and can encourage whatever artistic creations are helpful in preparing the less rational sides of human nature for idealistic development, and can see to it that whatever has value for the community receives community sanction.[52]

So too in the field of religion. We all have in us something that responds naturally to the power everywhere revealed in the world around us and in the workings of the human heart. Rivers, seas, and tempests, the moon, stars, and sun, all the forces of nature seem like workings of spirit, purposive, though with purposes only partly comprehensible in comparison with human infirmities of purpose, regularities which seem like ideal patterns in comparison with our human waverings and uncertainities, periodicities which constitute a moving image of eternity itself, and serve to regulate our human time-measurements. In a word, nature witnesses everywhere to the workings of spirits more powerful and more rational than ourselves, spirits more ideal in every way, Gods.[53] Our untutored attitude towards such beings is one of worship, prayer, and service, and temples, with rituals expressing abasement, penitence, and willing self-surrender which leads to some sort of companionship, are the simple and inevitable outcome of this natural attitude. For to these spirits we are, after all, akin, and they are not only our creators, but also our preservers, the sources of all good to us both in this life and beyond the grave.[54] In default, however, of a clear tradition, our spiritual leaders, the poets, with their uncritical yielding to any strong impulse, have presented us with imaginative pictures which are neither always consistent nor always worthy; and the uninspired priestcraft of the professional ministers of our temples has mingled with the ideal intuitions of the poets institutions and rituals which, whatever their original symbolism, have degenerated into little more than entertainments, to be purchased by the vulgar rich, with an appeal to economic and political artifices which are degrading to God, priest, and worshipper alike.[55] So mingled with earthly dross has the religious tradition become by the fourth century, that spiritual leadership is sought in vain in the temples and holy places of Hellas, and intelligent students are turning hopelessly to atheism and the study of natural science, as a sub-

stitute to fill their need.[56] If we can withdraw for awhile
from these degraded and warring creeds to meditate upon
the essential nature of spiritual experience, and succeed in
penetrating to the principle of mind, we shall make three
important discoveries. In the first place, we shall find
that our original and primitive, natural belief in the universe
as spiritually akin to what is deepest in our own nature is
upheld and strengthened by the fact that mind can attain
satisfaction only in the contemplation of its own principle
as ultimate. In the second place, we shall discover in the
relation between our mental processes and the ideal or perfect mind, the rationale for faith, for the belief that the
task of humanity consists in free co-operation with God
in the work of impregnating reality with reason, and thus
bringing to the birth a more rational universe, a world which
more completely realizes the divinely ideal patterns.[57]
Finally we have, in the principle of mind, a definite principle
for reforming our traditional creeds, and so reorganizing
and purifying their content as, without abandoning their
historical elements, to build up a ritual of prayer and worship
which will be consistent, harmonious and satisfactory to our
deepest needs.[58]

In every field of experience, then, practical, aesthetical,
scientific, and religious, mind reveals itself as the organizing
principle which enables us to make the most of our resources,
and build up, out of our varied and fluctuating experiences,
an approximation to that systematic totality which we envisage as the Divine Experience, ideally real and ideally
satisfying every human need which we can conceive as
legitimate. Further study of the nature of mind consists
in making explicit the relation of the human to the Divine
Mind, and in drawing certain deductions, of which the following are perhaps the most important :—(1) The principle of
mind, viz. the principle of reorganizing the otherwise chaotic
so as to enable it to realize its utmost of meaning-value, and
to reduce it, as far as possible, to the concentrated unity
of the intellectual concept, is formally identical in both
cases. Like the human mind, the Divine Mind is essentially
a principle of order, converting everything in existence to a
more adequate expression of this principle. The ordered
sequences of the heavenly bodies, the apparently capricious
storms and calms which affect the surface of the earth, the

alterations in the internal economy of plants and animals which result in growth and development, in a word, the whole realm of physical law, is an expression of this principle, the idea of good.[59] The backward drag of matter, the tendency of the physical cosmos to lapse towards not-being if the Divine control is relaxed, is paralleled by the obstinate pull of human appetites away from the ideal and towards the brutish. Both alike have need of the constant watchfulness of mind, if the idea of good is to any extent to prevail.[60] (2) Out of this identity of task arises a sense of community, of fellowship and co-partnership of all minds in the real work of the world. The human mind which is struggling with the task of acquiring mastery over the forces of its own body, and reducing this to an instrument for the idealization of its immediate environment, feels a sense of fellowship, not only with other men, but also with the once human and now semi-divine minds which it believes to be wrestling with the task of acquiring mastery over the cosmic forces of some planet,[61] so as to convert this into a more adequate instrument for the idealization of the physical universe. This sense of fellowship extends even further, so as to include, not only the yet more divine minds believed to be working upon yet greater cosmic problems, but also the Divine Mind itself, the ideal principle conceived in living form.[62] For all alike represent the idea of good working at its proper task of converting the environment into its own likeness and image. Finally (3) the centre for receiving and transmitting energy in accordance with the principle of self-motion, which has gradually risen from the sensory to the conceptual level, from the conceptual level to the level of reflective self-consciousness, and from reflective self-consciousness to a thoroughgoing awareness of its fellowship and humble co-partnership with the living principle of value which men call God, discovers that only in such service does it succeed in taking up value, life, and reality into its own processes, and seeks this highest human good in reverent assimilation of itself to God, re-forming its action-systems until they are modelled more exactly upon the Divine patterns, and devoting the rest of its life to filling, as worthily as may be, that place in the world which the Divine plan has prepared for it.[63]

To sum up : The function of sensation is *anamnesis*, the stimulating into activity of the life of mind, the awakening

from the dreams and intimations of sensory and intuitive
experience to the concepts of systematic, scientific knowledge,
culminating in that perfect self-consciousness which is at
the same time apprehension of the principle of ideality,
involving an understanding of the nature of the world and
of God, with consequences, practical, aesthetical, logical,
and religious, of overwhelming importance. Thus understood as spiritual experience, " mind " is the ultimate meaning
of all that has any sort of existence. The chaotic becomes
cosmic, ordered and meaningful, until the whole world is
charged with purpose. These purposes become gradually
conscious of themselves, of one another, of higher purposes,
and finally of the spirit of purposiveness, becoming progressively more spiritual, more permeated with the unity and
rationality of this spirit. This transmutation of fact into
value, of matter into mind, of mechanism into purpose, and
of purposes into a single system of co-operating spirits, is
the characteristic work of Mind, of that ideal experience which
is the sole source of meaning and value wherever and however manifested,[64] taking up into itself and endowing with
its own life all that, apart from this creative spirit, would
remain eternally slumbering in the bosom of not-being.
Thus conceived as ideal spiritual experience, mind is not
merely the efficient cause, but also the formal and the final
cause of all which in any way attains to reality.

So much for the nature of mind. We now turn to the
problem of ascertaining its value in relation to other " goods "
accepted by Platonism, considering in turn the various value-
scales already studied, in order to discover what place is
assigned to mind in each of these scales.

The first to be considered is the scale of soul—body—
wealth. Our investigation of this scale was practically
confined to a study of the human soul, and we identified
this, at its deepest, with spiritual life, understood as the
source of all values which fall within the field of human
experience, taking up into its own system of purposes and
thus endowing with spiritual value such things as body and
wealth, which would otherwise remain outside the value-
scale altogether, in the realm of not-being to which they
naturally belong. Two distinct points of view in Platonism
were discovered. From the first of these, body was considered
as the correlate of soul, the two constituting a single organism,

the material living embodiment of the principle of value called the idea of good. From the second, body was considered as essentially a portion of not-being. In both cases, however, spiritual life, whether associated with a body, or not, was regarded as a form of the principle of value, and its purposes were thought of as endowing with value whatever they touched. In the present chapter, " mind " has been treated in a broader way, as the source of motion in the physical universe generally, in the planets, and in plants and animals, no less than in the human soul. In the human soul, however, " mind," at its deepest, while studied along slightly different lines from the study of soul in the earlier investigation, seems to coincide with " soul " at its deepest. For mind also has been identified by us with ideal spiritual experience, and in the case of the Divine Mind, at any rate, we have met with the conception of its complete transcendence of sensory phenomena, much as in the case of soul, considered from the transcendental point of view.

The conclusions of the present chapter, then, while more widely based, and while reached by slightly different paths, seem to coincide, in principle, with the conclusions of our earlier investigation, and we may reasonably proceed to ask whether " soul " and " mind " do not, for Platonism, ultimately coincide in all respects. In both the ultimate constitutive principle is the idea of good, the principle of idealization in living form. In both this is a kind of enzyme which converts into value all that surrounds it, starting with the body with which it is associated. This body becomes an instrument adequately attuned to the spirit of value, not only in respect of its sense-organs, but also in its complete system of instinctive reaction-potentialities, so that these become formed upon the " ideas " of manliness, self-control, regard for the community and for truth, and in the end are re-formed upon the patterns which express ultimate reality, and thus become instinct with spirituality, completely responsive to the nature of the idealizing principle. In both " soul " and " mind " this development is accompanied by a gradual increase of intellectual awareness, culminating in a vision of the identity, in principle, of the ideal self with the ideal activity which has created the universe, and an acceptance of all that is involved in this vision of the idea of good, including therein a complete devotion of all the powers of the self to the task of making more ideal, in co-operation with God, the physical, social, moral, and intellectual environment. " Soul " includes intellectual excellence, and " mind " includes, not merely intellectual activity as such, but also physical, social, moral, aesthetical, and religious activity, so that, in spite of differences of emphasis in different contexts,[65] the various functions of soul coincide in detail, as well as in principle, with the various functions ascribed to mind. We may therefore conclude that, for platonism, mind and soul are ultimately one and the same, i.e., are expressions of the ideal spiritual life which we envisage as supreme reality or God, and also as that which makes the existence of individual human beings seem worth while, in proportion as they succeed in re-forming their powers and interests so as to enter more fully into fellowship with that ideal spiritual life.

The value of a particular mind or soul, then, will depend upon the extent to which its powers have been re-formed by the idea of good. In principle and ultimately, the idea of good constitutes the essence of mind or soul, and so far the principle of mind is identical with the principle of value. But the various powers of soul or mind, physical, social, moral, aesthetical, religious, and intellectual, may or may not be permeated by this principle, and different minds may thus differ greatly in respect of value. These powers may remain largely at the instinctive level, and may thus be devoid of insight into the demands of the ideal principle. In this case, they are as likely to be misused as to be wisely used. Pugnacity which is not yet moral courage, timidity which is not yet self-control, gregariousness which is not yet regard for what is involved in community living, curiosity and intelligence which are applied to anti-social ends— such powers, like strength and good looks, if not directed by wisdom, i.e. by insight into the ideal principle, may be directly harmful to the pugnacious or timid individual, no less than to his social environment.[66] Again, these powers may be socialized, so that the individual takes his value-standards from the social *milieu*, hating what the community hates and loving what the community loves. Pugnacity becomes military morale, timidity becomes civic docility and " followership," gregariousness becomes a child-like faith in the competence of assemblies, whether legal or political, and, speaking generally, the individual becomes wholly absorbed in the citizen. Organization and regulation play a greater part in his life, and, in proportion as the ideal principle of organization unifies and harmonizes his various tendencies, the value of his life, both to himself and to the community, becomes steadily greater. But popular opinion fluctuates ; assemblies not infrequently reverse their decisions ; and unless resting upon genuine insight into the nature of reality, legislation, even though it has the support of a numerical majority of those entitled to vote, is liable to error. The highest stage of value is reached only when the various powers of the mind are completely re-formed and integrated by the most comprehensive and the most penetrating wisdom to which humanity can attain. When the mind is completely made over in accordance with the ideal patterns which the supreme Mind has followed in constructing the cosmic frame, then the principle of value becomes, as nearly as possible, embodied in human form, and the individual mind takes on the value which belongs, in its own right, to all which partakes of the supremely real. At the highest conceivable stage of its development, then, when mind is thought of as taking on the character of the ideal spiritual experience, its value is clearly supreme, and the privileged position assigned to mind in the Dialogues becomes understood. It is the highest of conceivable values, thought of as approximating to the source of value itself.

So much for the value of mind considered in relation to the value-scale—soul—body—wealth. We now pass to consider its value in relation to the comprehensive scale beginning with wealth, strength, and beauty, passing through the various social excellences, and ending with temperance and wisdom. What we are at present studying under the name of mind is clearly to be identified with what, in this earlier investigation, we studied under the name of " wisdom," particularly so far as this was understood as somehow including all lower excellences. In our earlier study, we discovered that values were divided into two groups : (1) a lower or human group, and (2) a higher or divine group, the higher being the source of values in the lower group. We further discovered that the higher or divine group was thought of as coming under the leadership of mind. From this it would follow that mind or wisdom is thought of as divine rather than as human, and as the " leader " or chief good of the whole scale, and in some sense the source of value in all the lower " goods," including not merely the human but also the divine group. That is to say, mind or wisdom is the source of value, not only in the case of health and strength, but also in the case of courage, justice and temperance. This means that ultimately wisdom or the philosophic life, i.e. human life directed by philosophic insight into the nature of reality, takes up pugnacity, gregariousness, and timidity into itself, and transmutes them into organic portions of the ideal life. Similarly it takes up into itself even such physical activities as those concerned with eating and drinking, exercising and taking rest, so that these also become transmuted into portions of the same ideal life. It is, in fact, precisely in this reorganization of our living so as to give to each element in our living a full measure of positive value, not only in relation to all the rest, but also and especially in relation to the nature and claims of ideal reality, so that our human living becomes a reflex of the Divine Life, that wisdom of mind exercises its characteristic function. Our present conclusions, then, which regard mind as ideally coinciding with the ideal spiritual life, fit in with our previous conclusions, and mind or wisdom is in both cases identified with this ideal life, and the principle of mind or wisdom is identified with the source of all values, divine no less than human.

It remains to consider the value of mind in relation to the value-distinction of private and public spirit, to which we have also devoted especial study. In this investigation we discovered that, while the fundamental law of all action is to organize the elements in any given situation so as to make them work together, and thus to bring out the maximal realization of the given potentialities, there is a very real distinction between organization in a narrowly understood self-interest, and organization in a comprehensive spirit of regard for the whole. To organize one's powers for the exploitation of one's neighbours differs sharply from the organization of the same powers for the service of the ideal community, in spite of the recognized fact that both involve application of one and the same principle of organization. Organization is the source of strength, but organization in a narrow sense, in conflict with the nature and claims of the universe as a whole, is plainly stupid and self-destructive. We saw, further, that regard for the self and regard for the community, at their highest stages of development, both involve regard for the same metaphysical totality. That is to say, in the end, self-interest and interest in the community tend to coincide in accepting the claims of an ideal totality envisaged as including all its parts in proper relation to one another and to the whole. But this principle is identical with what we have discovered, in our present investigation, to be the principle of mind, viz. the reorganization of the elements constituting any given situation, in such a way as to bring out their maximal contribution to the ideal totality which is the ultimately real, and thus to develop their maximum of value and reality. It follows, then, that it is really mind, with its principle of organization, which is the source of all meaning and value in life, whether private or public, and further, that the life of mind, at its highest conceivable level as ideal spiritual experience, is not merely the most valuable life conceivable, but also the source of all values in physical, social, aesthetical, scientific, and religious situations, i.e. is what Plato calls the idea of good in living form.

Before accepting these conclusions, which are deduced, in the main, from what we have discovered of the general nature of platonism considered as a logical system of thoughts, let us pass in review the chief passages in the Dialogues in which the value of mind comes up for explicit discussion, in order to discover whether these passages substantiate our conclusions, or not. These passages fall naturally into four main groups, as follows :—

1. It is well known that with the hands or with the whole body a man can accomplish a very little, as compared with what he can accomplish by intelligence and strength of mind, or, as it is expressed elsewhere, all human activities depend upon the soul, and the soul depends upon wisdom, which is the source of everything fair and good.[67] From this it follows that wisdom and knowledge are naturally regarded as the most valuable of human pursuits, and that the cultivation of the mind is held in peculiar and especial honour.[68] Finally, when this cultivation of the mind has been carried beyond a certain point, it is the unanimous judgment of all cultivated persons that wisdom and in-

telligence are better and more desirable than other human goods, that the life of wisdom is the pleasantest, as well as the most reasonable, kind of life, and that wisdom undoubtedly ranks among the highest conceivable values.[69]

2. In the second place, it is felt that mind is a natural ruler, while the body, as being devoid of insight, is naturally subject to the control of mind or wisdom.[70] Causes devoid of intelligence always produce, it is maintained, mere chance effects, without order or design, and the inferior activities of the soul, e.g. those concerned with eating, drinking, and sex, or those concerned with the acquisition of money, are largely bodily, and thus, if left to themselves, act foolishly rather than wisely, quarrelling with one another and tending towards extremes, with all the evil consequences inseparable from this way of living.[71] In contradistinction to this, mind co-ordinates behaviour and organizes whatever activities come under its beneficial control, introducing harmony and unity in the place of conflict, and thus increasing the efficiency of the behaviour concerned.[72] In fact the essence of wisdom is to take counsel for the whole, to consider what is absolutely for the interest of the whole organism, disposing all for the best, and putting each particular element in its proper place in relation to the rest.[73]

3. In the third place, it is felt that mind somehow brings us into direct and vital contact with " true being," so that our lives become more real in proportion as they become more imbued with the spirit of mind.[74] Through wisdom we escape from the world of opinion into the world of true knowledge, and apprehend the essences of things as they are, absolute, eternal, and immutable, and govern our lives accordingly, so that our fluctuating and wayward urges of subjective feeling gradually take on stability and objective control, and become converted into a genuine portion of the world which alone is truly real.[75]

4. Finally, it is believed that the life of wisdom is somehow the ideal life which the Gods have prepared for man, the natural life of the soul from which we have fallen and become separated by reason of our sensuality. It is believed that we can return to this life if we are earnest in our love of wisdom, and feed our souls upon their true food, viz. the contemplation of the ideal principles in accordance with which the Divine Artist has constructed the starry heavens

and the ordered movements of the physical cosmos, i.e. ultimately the contemplation of the divine principle of ideality itself. It is in this life of wisdom that human perfection, according to the divine plan for humanity, consists, and, in following this plan, we are not only prudent, consistent, and in accordance with nature, but partake also of fellowship with the divine life itself.[76] Mind and God are thus ideally identified,[77] and to enter upon the life of mind is thus to enter upon the most valuable activity which we can conceive, the spiritual activity which constitutes the ideal life of God.

These passages, which clearly confirm our previous deductions, represent Plato's explicit judgment upon the value of mind, and it only remains to sum up finally his position. Mind is, in principle, the idea of good, i.e. the living principle of ideality and value, whose function is to transmute into ideality and value whatever it organizes. In the physical universe, this principle finds expression in the orderliness and system which mark the movements of the planets and characterize physical law generally. In the human realm, this same principle finds expression in the gradual tendency towards orderliness, system, and objectivity, which become explicit as man progresses from the life of instinct to the life associated with social institutions, from social institutions to the researches of science, and from science to a study of the ideal principle itself. Here the principle of mind breaks through to self-consciousness,[78] and henceforth man seeks to co-operate with this divine principle in idealizing his immediate environment, physical, social, and intellectual, and thus takes his true place in the universe, the place provided for him in the divine plan. The value of mind, thus understood, is beyond question. Spiritual life, in ideal form, is itself the highest conceivable value, and is the principle of all other values ; for other activities and things in general acquire value and meaning only in proportion as they are taken up into the life of mind, become imbued with its spirit, and are gradually assimilated to its principle.

CHAPTER XI

THE DIVINE, AND ITS VALUE

IN the *Laws*, values are divided into (1) lower or human values and (2) higher or divine values, and it is declared that the lower or human class has no value *per se*, but only so far as it is controlled by the higher or divine values, while the higher class possesses value in its own right, as well as being the source of value in the lower sphere. This official position in the *Laws* is substantiated by a great many statements of somewhat similar tenor scattered up and down the Dialogues.[1] It is the object of the present chapter to investigate the meaning of " the divine " in platonism, with a view to throwing light upon this fundamental value-judgment.

The passages in the Dialogues which deal with " the divine " fall, of themselves, into four main groups :—(1) The passages which deal with the natural religious feelings of humanity, the untutored sense of divinity which furnishes the natural *Anlage* of religion, (2) the passages which deal with conventional or standardized religion, the actual creeds and rituals devised by poetic fancy and professional priest-craft to socialize and institutionalize the primitive religious sense, (3) the passages which indicate the path by which the philosopher raises himself by thought to a position superior to the position assumed by " opinion " which accepts without question the results of poetic intuition and priestly organization—for the philosopher seeks to discover the ultimate essence of religion, its meaning and ideal power in the scheme of things, and (4) the passages which indicate how, in the philosopher's judgment, the creeds and rituals ought to be transformed so as to approximate more closely to the ideal which reason has revealed. In studying what we find in the Dialogues, we shall follow this natural grouping.

1. The natural religious tendencies.

Looking about him, man sees everywhere natural forces

in operation, the sun, moon, and stars, with their risings and settings, their eclipses and equinoxes, influencing the course of the seasons and the fertility of the soil, aiding or thwarting man in his various purposes according as those purposes conform or fail to conform to the nature of the changes brought about by the movements of the celestial bodies.[2] So, too, the earth, with its mysterious fecundity, its rivers, lakes and oceans, its mountains, forests, and quiet valleys, seems to possess powers which may make or mar its human inhabitants, according to the wisdom or lack of wisdom with which they adapt themselves to its requirements.[3] The motions of these natural forces have their periodicities, which are either so regular as to establish the time-standards, the day, month, year, etc., used by men to regulate their goings and comings upon the earth, or else, like the sudden storms and calms, are so incalculable as to appear capricious, whimsical, spontaneous. Faced with this situation, the natural animism of primitive man, whether Hellene or Barbarian, inevitably concludes, with Thales, that all things are full of spirits, spirits with greater power and intelligence than human beings, and the analogy of man's relation to the domestic animals seems obviously true. Just as animals are naturally the property of men, and men protect and improve their property, so we men are naturally the property of higher spiritual forces, and these divine forces protect and dispose of their property as seems best to them.[4]

With these views, men inevitably desire to have the friendship of these superior powers, and thus attempt to propitiate them by sacrifice, prayer, and ritual.[5] It is perfectly natural to vow altars and sacrifices when delivered from danger, or to offer up a prayer before undertaking any important venture.[6] The underlying motive is to win these powers to one's own side, to have them share in these undertakings, so that the danger and the victory will be to some extent a common danger and a common victory. As religious feeling develops, the desire for divine friendship takes the form of man attempting to assimilate his nature to what he takes to be the divine nature; for friendship is based upon community of feeling.[7] Man thus attempts, in general, to live a more godlike life by being more temperate and just and wise, and, in particular, to model his development upon some one of the higher spirits to whom he feels himself peculi-

arly akin.   The warrior forms his character upon the attributes
of Ares, the philosopher upon the attributes of Zeus.[8]   But
the further development of this tendency towards working
out details of worship, and details of theology, belongs to
later stages of religious evolution.   To the earlier stage belong
only a general appreciation of the omnipresence of higher
beings, and a desire to approach these with worship and
prayer, so as to enter into some sort of fellowship with them,
which will lead to a greater measure of success in this life
and possibly after this life.[9]   Of itself, this tendency leads
naturally towards the development of a theology, with temples
and rituals, and priests and interpreters—which we shall
proceed to study under the head of " conventional religion."

2. Conventional, or socialized and institutionalized religion,
    comes into being under the influence of three main groups
    of men :—
    a. The poets, whose inspired feeling leads them to clothe
       their religious intuition in symbolic forms with quasi-
       human shapes and attributes.
    b. The priests and interpreters of God's ways to man.
       These, as a special class of technical theologians, pre-
       pare rituals of prayer, worship, and sacrifice to the
       spirits clothed in definite form by poetic intuition,
       and also interpret the oracles, omens, and visions in
       which the spirits seem to communicate obscurely with
       individual worshippers.
    c. The scientists, who make a special study of all the
       forces of nature, investigating the exact movements
       of the stars, the precise changes of the seasons, and the
       antecedents and consequences of all changes, physical,
       biological, or social, which seem of importance to
       humanity.   All these classes make their contributions
       to religious development within the general field of
       social evolution, which brings together different groups
       of believers, and makes it possible for some one group,
       such as the Athenians after the confederation treasure-
       chest was brought from Delos to Athens, to build
       especially fine and numerous temples, to establish
       especially elaborate ceremonials, to sanction local
       cults or to import especially famous cults from abroad.[10]
The first fact which strikes the attention of all who seek

to go beyond the common basis of religious feeling, and inquire more exactly into the nature of the divine element, is the difficulty of investigation in this field. Everywhere men find belief in divine powers, but opinions differ as to the divinities, and to be absolutely certain that one is in possession of truth in this field of inquiry seems to transcend human power. A very little reflection leads to the conclusion that God alone is wise.[11] But a little further reflection suggests that, while God alone is in possession of ultimate truth in this, as in other fields, godlike men, men who have become the friends of God, and are in some sort of communion with the higher spirits, may have notions which, though only human and therefore fallible, result somehow from their communion with the divine, and may thus be accorded a certain measure of reliability.[12] Certain visions which occur in dreams and trances, the whispering of trees in some especially sacred grove, certain happenings which seem like signs and warnings, while obscure, are naturally interpreted as direct communications to especially favoured individuals. In all ages, poets have regarded their intuitions as falling within this general class, and have accordingly claimed to be divinely inspired " sons of God," and a certain degree of spiritual leadership has been freely granted to their somewhat mysterious powers.[13] It is felt that while men, like other animals, have a strong feeling for movement as somehow expressing the joy of living—spontaneous movement being the characteristic criterion of what is alive—they have an even stronger feeling for rhythmic movement, the ordered sequences and recurrences which are at the root of music, poetry, and dancing and find natural expression in the choric dance.[14] " The Muses " are felt to be an especial gift of God to man, and their cultivation has two main functions :—(1) to furnish holidays which provide recreation from the labour undergone by men in the battle of life, and (2) to provide sacred festivals in which man may enter, via the choric dance in its various forms, into some sort of fellowship with the higher spirits. It is felt that at such festivals the gods themselves stir us into life and movement, and we follow them in dances and songs in which they are in some sort our companions.[15] The choric dance is a community rehearsal of the history of the powers and actions of the particular deity in whose honour the festival is instituted, especially in relation to the trials and suc-

cesses of the community, and concludes largely with thanks
for past favours and present prosperity, and with prayers
for a continuance of the same, or for deliverance from evils.[16]
These rhythmic activities lift men out of their ordinary day-
to-day existence, and intensify the sense of companionship
with higher spirits, making the Gods, who join in the revels,
almost human, and the men almost divine, and thus draw them
both nearer together. In these experiences, the poets have
the special function of singing the praises of the God, naming
him, reciting his powers, his past history, his relations with the
community, and constructing the prayers with which the
community approach him. The musician provides an appropriate accompaniment in the form of (a) a chant suited to the
sense as well as to the form of the words, and (b) rhythmic
movements of the body adapted to the music and the sense
of the theme. It is thus of vital importance that the poets,
who trust themselves to the inspiration of the Muses or of
the Gods themselves, whose praises they are singing, should
hymn those praises aright, and should compose prayers which
will not merely state the needs of the community, but will
also be such as the God would regard as proper for him to
grant.[17]

For the most part, it appears to be felt that this inspiration can be trusted. It is the higher spirits themselves who
give life or the power of self-movement, the delight in movement as evidence of life, and the especial delight in rhythmic
movement which heightens the life-sense. Similarly it is
felt that the higher spirits are ultimately responsible for the
inspiration which establishes festivals at which these divine
gifts are used in honour of the divine givers, and in which the
worshipper and the source and object of worship enter into
some sort of community of life-sense, through rhythmic
movement of the voice and whole body.[18] The trustworthiness of this inspiration is believed to extend even, in certain
cases, to all the more universal principles revealed to the
poetic intuition. The relation between the divine powers
with their righteousness, and human beings with their groping moral sense, is largely apprehended aright by the poets.
For example, Hesiod's view that human heroes receive a sort
of deification after death, is accepted as a divinely inspired
truth.[19] The principle, enunciated by Homer and Hesiod,
that righteousness is looked upon by the higher powers with

favour and blessings, is a similar truth.[20] So too the insistence of tragic and epic writers on the unholiness of incest and on the divinely-appointed punishments in the next world for parricide, are approved as " most true tales."[21] So also in the case of the dancing and music which are associated with the poetry in the sacred festivals. It is felt that there are " natural " melodies and dance-movements, i.e. rhythms which express adequately, from the human standpoint, the chief divine truths, and that rhythms which possess this "natural truth and correctness " may possibly be discovered by inspired artists, and, when discovered, should be established forever, *more egyptiaco*, by the legislative authority of the State.[22]

On the other hand, as the divine truths revealed to intuition are expressed in human symbols, and as the poets themselves are human and therefore anything but infallible,[23] Plato is inclined to think that the theology which rests upon simple faith in artistic inspiration is, at best, of the nature of a parable, and, at its worst, of the nature of mischievous falsehood. For the great masses of people are not able to discriminate, and separate the false with certainty from the true.[23] And, further, the conditions of publication in a Hellenic community are scarcely favourable to the most delicate search for divine inspiration. When poets are forced to compete before popular audiences, with all the clamour and uproar inseparable from such conditions, the still, small voice to which the artist should listen is likely to be overwhelmed, and the artist is far more likely to say smooth things which he thinks will please his audience, than to labour attentively at discovering the divine truths to which inspiration, of itself, does perhaps point the way.[24]

Finally, a careful and not malicious study of the successful " publications " of the better-known poets of Greece shows, among many undeniable excellences, a number of flaws inseparable, perhaps, from the poetic creativity which follows blindly any strong impulse, and accentuated, in all probability, by this competitive method of publication. Thus what poets enunciate as " truths revealed by inspiration " are frequently contradictory. And this does not mean merely that one poet contradicts another on important points, such as the existence and character of the Gods and their relation to men, but that almost any given poet frequently contradicts himself. For

example, a poet, like Homer or Hesiod, whose dicta are regarded by the Greeks of the classical period as a sort of " gospel
truths," while teaching that the Gods are righteous, does not
hesitate to ascribe to them all manner of obviously unrighteous
actions, such as theft,[25] lust,[26] deceit,[27] cruelty to parents,[28]
and warfare.[29]   Again, while teaching that the Gods are
ideally just, many a poet does not scruple to ascribe to
them, in all seriousness, a weakness for " rich libations " and
" incense and meek supplications," so that, if approached
with proper sacrifices and the ecclesiastical equivalent of
backshish, they will not merely pardon the wealthy criminal
who thus shares with them a portion of his stolen goods, so
that they become his partners in crime,[30] but will pervert
the course of justice so as to bring misery upon perfectly
innocent persons, who happen to be the personal enemies of
the wealthy criminal.[31]   Similar contradictions are narrated
of demi-Gods and heroes.   Heracles, the reputed son of a
God, is represented as stealing,[32] and Achilles, the reputed
son of a Goddess, and the greatest of all the Homeric heroes,
is represented in anything but an heroic light, and as anything
but respectful to one of the Gods.[33]

As Plato points out with unwearying logic, to represent a
God as ungodlike, or a hero as unheroic, or good as the source
of evil, is to fall into a self-contradiction which reflects anything but credit upon the degree of truth which the poet
claims for his " inspired intuitions."[34]   Furthermore, different poets contradict one another freely in respect of the
highest truths, many having reached such a pitch of sophistication as to doubt, on the basis of an inadequate study of life
and nature, whether there are any other higher beings at all,
and not merely to doubt, but stoutly to deny the existence
of any such beings.   They regard these as pure fictions introduced in the supposed interest of priestcraft and statecraft.[35]
Others, who do not fall completely into this extreme class,
retain sufficient of natural piety to believe in the existence
of superior powers, but, seeing the impious apparently prosper-
ing and criminals, in certain cases, attaining to political power,
they fall into the natural error of confounding material prosperity with blessedness or divinely-sent happiness.   Being
unwilling to believe that the Gods are the authors of the
blessings which seem to follow, in certain cases, upon unrighteous conduct—for this would make the Gods, who are

Y

essentially righteous, favourers of unrighteousness—by a perfectly intelligible error of reasoning, in order to retain (1) their belief in the existence of divinely righteous powers and (2) their knowledge of what they take to be the facts of life, they keep the Gods and human life in two separate, logically watertight compartments, and believe that the Gods " have no thought or care of human things," i.e. believe that the righteousness or unrighteousness of human beings is a matter of complete indifference to these righteous powers, and that they are luxurious, heedless, and idle—i.e. possess a most ungodlike nature.[36]

From such consideration of the evidence, it would seem to follow that " poets are not always quite capable of knowing what is good and what is evil," and that when they create, e.g. prayers to be used in addressing the Gods, they may through inadvertence succeed in having the citizens pray for the opposite of good, and ask for evil instead of real blessings.[37] So, too, in creating lullaby-songs which mothers sing to their children, the poetic interest in the merely effective may lead to the creation of a version of the unseen world which may scare the children and make them afraid of the dark.[38] In the same way, their versions of the " verities of the afterlife " may lead to gruesome descriptions of it as a charnel-house, and to imaginative phrasings which may raise a shudder of fear and abhorrence even in adults.[39] Their descriptions of banquets and love-affairs may be of a kind not calculated to encourage temperance and self-control;[40] their treatment of painful and grievous experiences may encourage effeminacy and cowardice;[41] and their praises of the rewards which await the righteous, may induce regard for consequences, rather than for justice itself;[42] so that, in general, the effect of poets upon those who take part in these festivals, whether as actors or as spectators, may be anything rather than what a censor who has an eye to moral qualities would approve.[43]

It is not necessary that poets should give expression to these effective but morally undesirable characteristics, but in actual fact the great masses of people—whose judgment is not sound, though their numbers, under the Hellenic system, influence the final vote which sets the stamp of community approval or disapproval upon the poet's productions—tend to be attracted peculiarly by the more brilliant kind of poetry which is not unduly restrained by ethical consideiations, and there is thus a direct social demand for inferior poetry.[44] It follows that the festivals in honour of the higher powers are frequently entertainments which appeal to the groundlings of the pit, and are thus not always directly consistent with the avowed aim of such festivals, viz. to hymn aright the praises of the God, and to enter into some kind of fellowship with Him. The fellowship may be there, but the tendency of the poets, under these conditions, is to pull the Gods down to human level, rather than to raise the mortals to the skies. Considerations such as these suggest inevitably that poets are, in fact, the mouthpieces rather than the leaders of their age and social surroundings,[45] and while, by their dicta, they help to crystallize and give semi-permanent form to certain theological ideas, these ideas tend to be somewhat distorted by the social medium through which they are, for the most part, received, though it is not denied that, in the end, their inspiration may come from the higher powers who are guiding the community of which the particular poet happens to be a member.[46]

2. Prophets, interpreters, and priests.

Prophecy, with its incantations, mysteries, oracles, and omens, seem to span in a singularly direct way the gap which divides God from man. The prophetic medium is in some sense possessed and obviously inspired by forces beyond normal, rational control. He falls into a trance, or at least into an unusually vivid dream, and in this state of abnormal sensitivity to psychic influences sees apparitions of good or evil omen, or hears " voices " uttering dark sayings, and returns from his mystical journey with messages which appear to have symbolic significance for the fortunes of those who consult him.[48] The most obvious examples of such professional mediums were met with at Delphi and Dodona, but many a Hellene, at some time or other in his life, would undergo similar experiences. In the mysteries, after purification and sacrifices, a somewhat similar state of mind was induced by ceremonial dances, silence, darkness, followed by flute-music ;[49] and the presentation of the mystical symbols, which formed the central portion of the mysteries, was interpreted, in amazed rapture,[50] as an initiation into the company of the Gods of the under-world, with their magical powers in the way of granting atonement for sin, and security in the after-life.[51] Great influence was attributed to prophecy, not merely by the prophets themselves,[52] but generally, and such mediums were frequently consulted when peculiar problems, especially problems connected with death and the after-life, arose.[53] The institution of sacrifices in connection with mystic rites, the consecration of images, altars, oracles, and temples, occurred historically in Hellas largely as results of such mediumistic utterances, which were regarded as communications from the Gods.[54]

While the importance of these communications was almost universally acknowledged, it was early observed that many of them were highly obscure and required interpretation. The medium himself, when out of his trance, was not always able to explain the message he had received, and thus arose a special class of official interpreters, popularly confused with the mediums, but by Plato sharply distinguished from them on the ground that the interpreters, as such, never fell into a trance, but used all their waking abilities, in a perfectly normal way, to explain as scientifically as might be such phenomena as dreams, oracles, eclipses, the flight of birds, etc., in order to decide, like Joseph in the Old Testament, whether they signified past, or present, or future good or evil to those to whom the vision had come.[55] These public interpreters were associated with the chief Hellenic oracles and also, when they had been approved by the Delphic authorities, with the temples in certain of the larger cities, and held office for life.[56] Their work was not confined to the explanation of obscurities in oracular messages from Delphi,[57] or to the solution of peculiar problems arising in connection with death and the after-world, but they could give official advice as to what prayers and sacrifices should be instituted in connection with burial and in honour of the Gods of the underworld, and could give similarly official advice as to the religious aspects of certain trials, especially where deaths by violence were concerned.[58]

Associated with these interpreters, as curators of the temples and ministers of the Gods, were the priests proper. Of this class, some members were appointed annually, as in the case of the king archonship at Athens, while others held office for life, and in yet other cases the priesthood passed from father to son.[59] The chief function of the priests was to give the Gods gifts from men, in the form of acceptable sacrifices, and to pray, on behalf of the community, for blessings in return, in accordance with the ceremonial forms prescribed by rule or tradition. Their function as curators of the temple buildings and superintendents of temple ritual included certain other powers, such as the power of excommunication, the exclusion from participation in the sacred rites of impure persons, whose presence would have polluted the prayers and sacrifices.[60] They were also entrusted with the duty of dispensing hospitality to certain types of visitors from other communities, and acted as judges of minor offences committed by or against such guests.[61] Unlike the interpreters, they were hardly to be regarded as theological experts, but merely occupied for a time the dignified and solemn position of official ministers presiding over official ceremonies in honour of the Gods worshipped by the community. At the same time, in spite of this lack of expert knowledge, they were like the prophets and interpreters in being, as Plato expresses it, " swollen with pride and prerogative " as being the recognized representatives of the Gods in their relation to men.

In addition to the above " official " theologians, whether expert or not, there were many unauthorized persons, prophetic mediums and priests, the hierophants of *private* mysteries, who went to the houses of the wealthy, offering, for a fee, to purify them from personal or ancestral guilt, to interpret signs, to foretell the future, and, if desired, to call down evil, by incantations and magical devices, upon the enemies of their paymasters.[62] They came in response to a natural demand,[63] but their resemblance to the sophists, who were also private and unauthorized persons, selling spiritual goods in accordance with the ideas of their paymasters, is too much for Plato's judgment, and he roundly declares this whole class to be clever and unscrupulous infidels, monstrous natures who should either be put to death at once, or at least be imprisoned for life, and when dead be cast unburied beyond the borders so as not to pollute the country.[64]

c. Science, from the religious standpoint of the average man, tends to be regarded with suspicion. It seems impious and offensive to inquire too nicely into the ways of the higher powers. Physics and astronomy, for instance, are thought— not without a side-glance at Anaxagoras—to lead directly towards atheism,[65] and it can hardly be denied that the in-

quisitive temperament is usually different from the temperament which accepts and worships. At the same time, it seems
reasonable to suppose that the teachings of science, which
is interested in truth, may perhaps be preferable to the
teachings of poetry and art generally, which is interested
mainly in imaginative make-believe, and to Plato the study of
science in general and of astronomy in particular is regarded
as an essential element in the training of governors. It is
important for them to know the facts of nature, so that, e.g.
in censoring a poem which hymns the praises of the Gods, they
will be able to know whether the poet is hymning the attributes
of the particular deity aright, i.e. telling the truth about the
motions of the starry heavens.[66] Again, the study of nature
introduces objectivity and serenity into the mind of the
student. Reverent contemplation is not alien to religious
feeling, and the scientist contributes to the institutionalized
religion of the community certain elements which come from
no other group.[67] These elements affect, directly at any rate,
the leaders rather than the populace, but indirectly, by means
of the influence of these leaders, a new orientation is introduced
into religion. A spirit of serious and impartial observation of
fact gradually takes the place of an often frivolous and personal
interpretation of literary evidences,[68] a sense that the scientific worker is gradually penetrating into nature's secrets
takes the place of the facile and thoughtless acceptance of an
unintelligible mixture of feeling, fancy, and tradition, and
the scientist, more than anyone else, points the way to that
search for something deeper than the traditional creeds,
which is the especial task of the philosopher.

As these various forces all work in the process of social evolution, it is not one alone which leads to the hope of change
and progress in religion. It is not the poet who is the believer,
while the scientist is the sceptic. The confusions and contradictions of the poets lead to the feeling that the way of
lyrical inspiration cannot be followed implicitly ; it is not
denied that there is something behind the poet's intuitions,
but it is obvious that the poet, as such, is hardly a reliable
guide. In the same way the prophetic medium rarely understands his own message. It is not doubted that his psychic
experiences have some genuine meaning ;[69] but this is usually
obscure, sometimes unintelligible, and it is felt that its correct
interpretation requires all the resources of scientific method,

There thus arises, in connection with all the sources of institutionalized religion, a feeling that the traditional objects of religious worship, the traditional legends, and the traditional ceremonies cannot possibly be regarded as final. They represent parables, allegories, symbols of religious truth; but the key has been lost,[70] and their manifest defects call for reform in the light of some deeper insight, if the religion of the community is not to degenerate into playful fancy or mere ritual, the mechanical observance of forms whose meaning has been hopelessly lost, and in which the blind are led by the blind. The need of the times is thus for some deeper source of insight.

3. The path by which the philosopher gradually attains to this deeper source of insight is, in the main, the path of scientific method. He is convinced that the poetic source of inspiration is unprogressive, and is likely to lead in the future no further than it has led in the past: viz., to imaginative glimpses of the spiritual world which are fitful, unco-ordinated, and hard to feel sure of. He is also convinced that from psychic experiences of the mediumistic sort, as such, nothing further is to be derived, except, possibly, by a more scientific control and method of interpretation.[71] But from science, with its progressive development in knowledge and insight, something may reasonably be expected, something of technical value in the search for truth.

The first element which contributes to the philosopher's search is a well-formed moral nature. The ideas of courage, self-control, social considerateness, piety, etc., must have become, by years of practice under suitable conditions, intimate and fundamental elements in his character. Possessing the divine attributes of holiness, justice, courage, and prudence, he will thus be as like God as education and social experience can make him.[72] What he learns from the study of science is something further, something which takes him beyond a merely human and social point of view, into the world of objective law and scientific generalization, until he is at home in the intellectual realm as such. In this way he trains what Plato calls the eye of his soul, until it takes on something of the divine attribute of wisdom.[73] His training culminates in a grasp of the ideal of scientific truth, the principle of so co-ordinating and reorganizing the generalizations in which he expresses the results of his researches as to extract from them, in the unity of the " idea," their maximum of meaning-value. This grasp of the nature of the principle of ideality is the technical contribution which science makes to the philosophic research. The principle is further studied, and is seen to be of universal scope and application. In science it is the ideal of truth as a consistent, systematic totality of conclusions based upon research. In social ethics it is the ideal of a community in which every citizen realizes the completest development of his potentialities in the service of the group as a whole. In art, it is the ideal which Plato calls " the science of beauty everywhere." In religion it is the ideal of a spiritually perfect life, representing the maximal development of all spiritual powers in harmonious, concentrated unity. It remains to expound this more in detail.

This ideal, " the divine," is thought of as goodness, the perfection of goodness, the idea of good in living form,[74] expressing its nature by doing its own characteristic work, viz., applying in action its principle of combining the many into the one and resolving the one into the many, and thus bringing order into chaos and creating all good things and only good things.[75] The attributes which flow from this divine principle are courage, temperance, justice and wisdom.[76] Omniscient and omnipotent,[77] " the divine " devotes itself to the creation and preservation of these and other forms of the ideal principle in what would otherwise be the world of " not-being," unenviously assimilating everything to its own nature, and thus bringing into being a progressively more ideal universe.[78] In this eternal conflict between " the good " and not-being, God is not alone.[79] The divine principle, while fully possessed by God alone, is in some degree imparted to other orders of spiritual beings, to the spirits which guide the movements of the heavenly spheres, i.e. to the lesser deities and to certain translated mortals, and to man.[80] In man, this divine principle of organization constitutes the essential element in his humanity, and is the root of all his excellences, physical, moral, and intellectual.[81] Overflowing of itself into action and thus " doing its own work," i.e. performing its characteristic function of bringing about the maximal realization of potentiality, this divine principle is, in relation to bodily impulses, self-control,[82] in relation to hostile forces, courage or community morale,[83] in commercial and social relations, justice,[84] in relation to the established religion, piety,[85] and in relation to situations calling for the exercise of intelligent judgment, wisdom, practical and speculative.[86]   What are popularly regarded as " God's gifts to man," viz., our creation,[87] preservation and guidance towards good,[88] art,[89] law,[90] virtue, moral and intellectual,[91] and religion,[92] similarly spring from the divine principle.[93]

How do these divine gifts become ours ?   In different contexts, two methods seem to be indicated, which, in the end, are perhaps regarded as one and the same method.   In one group of contexts it appears that courage, temperance, justice, and wisdom become ours by means of an education, both practical and theoretical, which culminates in a vision of the ideas, the reverent contemplation of the ideal realm which is to be sought beyond the heaven of the fixed stars.[94] In this contemplative vision there is no sensuous admixture. The entities envisaged are " colourless, shapeless, intangible," and the vision is specifically intellectual, a matter of " pure " reason.[95]   This intuition, however, is no cold, remote and solitary intellectual exercise, but is fundamentally joyous, a feast of reason, a replenishment of the soul, our proper food which nourishes the highest part of our nature, the divine element in us,[96] and in such experiences we recognize the essential kinship between our higher nature and the ideas of temperance, wisdom, and the rest.[97]   The divine gifts, then, become ours by our being so trained as to develop in our every-day living the practical side of the ideas which we come to contemplate in their pure form.   We know from another context[98] that reverent contemplation, for Plato, involves imitation, the attempt to assimilate ourselves to what we contemplate.   Thus, by assimilating ourselves to the principles revealed by our trained reason, we give the idea of good, free play in our lives, and by living the life of idealistic endeavour become " holy, just, and wise," taking up into our nature, as far as human beings can, these attributes of divinity.[99]

The second method is referred to in the group of contexts which describe the nature and action of Platonic *eros*.   Love, with its four-fold nature as prophetic, initiatory, poetic, and erotic,[100] is regarded as a divine release of the soul from custom and convention, the true source of inspiration,[101] the mediator who spans the chasm dividing man from God.[102] Mythology apart, this means that love is the idealistic spirit which leads men to seek the good under the manifold forms of its appearance, physical, moral, and intellectual,[103] until they attain to a vision of the ideal realm and its principle which is recognized as divine and as leading to friendship and community of nature with " the divine."[104]

These two methods, if we allow for differences of emphasis incident to the differences of context, are in principle one and the same. In both it is the value-judgment which is analysed until its implications are shown to extend to a search for the ideal world and its ground, the idea of value, the divine principle of ideality.[105] In both our value-sense passes over into philosophy, and in both this dialectical development is felt as an awakening of the soul to its kinship with the fundamental values of the divine life. In both it is felt that God and man are essentially identical in nature and that it is by living the life of idealistic endeavour that the divinity within us flowers into a resemblance of the Divinity in whom and through whom alone can all that is achieve meaning and value. Our value-sense thus penetrates beyond the accidental surroundings of human life, material, sensuous, emotional, and social-conventional, and comes to rest in the contemplation of an ideal experience, an experience which includes these elements, takes them up into itself and transmutes them into its own meaning and value, but in origin and destiny transcends the empirical content which it includes and transforms.

4. The philosophic reform of creed and ritual.

This philosophic vision, when applied to actual life, gives new insight into the lower levels of religious experience. (a) At the lowest level, we had the instinctive feeling after higher powers, expressed in vague and mysterious feelings of reverence before the powers of nature. This is now seen to be part and parcel of the nature of our value-judgment, our reaching out after " good," after something permanent and real amid the changes of life, projected in an animistic way into the starry heavens, the mighty deeps, in a word, into the natural world revealed to sensuous experience. Vaguely, but genuinely, the whole field of sensuous phenomena is felt to be " full of Gods." To the thinker, it might *a priori* seem possible to take towards this level one of two attitudes :—(1) It might seem reasonable to decide that this tendency towards amateurish theology is a subjective projection of a misunderstood value-judgment, an illusion which vanishes when the nature of the value-judgment is rightly understood. Actually, man is faced with situations demanding intelligent choice. To people the forests, rivers, and clouds with imaginary and capricious "spirits" is to multiply the difficulties of the actual situation without really leading to the one thing needful, viz., intelligent choice between alternative lines of conduct. The man of insight will thus tend to make a clean sweep of theology, regarding it as superstition harnessed in the service of vested interests,[106] and will devote himself to making clear and intelligent judgments of value, unimpeded by the imaginary phantoms which get between his intelligence and the realities of the actual situation. On the other hand (2), the thinker might decide to retain the theological tendency which seems to form a natural portion of the value-judgment, and, without giving up the ideal of intelligent choice between clearly envisaged alternatives, might retain the mystical feeling that the world is fundamentally spiritual and contains depths to which the eye of sense, however enlightened by scientific training, remains, perhaps, a foolish stranger.[107] Plato unhesitatingly adopts the second attitude. For him, the judgment that "all things are full of Gods," however vague, expresses a truth which it is the business of philosophy, not to explain away, but to expound, to analyse and develop into its full significance in the philosophic vision. The philosophic reformer, then, in dealing with this level, will try to improve the intellectual quality of the belief in spiritual powers which are concerned with the whole of human life, partly by feeling and expressing respect for the kernel of truth which it contains,[108] and partly by keeping always in close contact with this feeling in his reform of the official creeds and rituals.

The second of these lower levels (b) was represented by popular religion with its traditional deities, traditional creeds, and traditional rituals established by poets, prophets, and other social leaders. A little analysis shows convincingly that the creeds and rituals which at this level have survived the lapse of time are riddled with absurdities and contradictions, and thus hardly commend themselves to the enlightened intelligence which is seeking truth. While the mechanisms of this level are far more complex than the animistic feelings of the previous level, the alternative which faces the thinker is substantially the same as before. (1) He might reasonably declare the whole of traditional religion to be a meaningless farrago which should be relegated to the intellectual scrap-heap, the man of enlightenment devoting himself, perhaps like Democritus, to positive scientific investigation.[109] On the other hand (2), it is equally reasonable to believe that, while the details of the popular polytheism represent, in certain cases, aberrations due, largely, to the social *milieu* in which religious leaders have been compelled to express themselves, the religious feeling of reverence for the spiritual forces of the universe on all occasions of life is, however inadequately expressed, a profound truth. The thinker will devote himself to purging the popular polytheism of its absurdities and contradictions, seeking, however, to retain whatever of traditional belief can be retained ; for a religion is not compounded *in vacuo,* and traditionality, as such, has a certain value in this field.[110] Plato again unhesitatingly adopts this second alternative, and it is with his suggestions for the construction of an ideal popular religion that we are here especially concerned. In two different contexts he draws up a list of fundamental norms to which the religious leader is compelled to conform. The poet, while using, of course, forms which appeal to the popular imagination, i.e. clothing his ideas in sensuous imagery, especially of the visual type, must always represent the divine nature as it truly is, i.e. as human reason at its best discovers the divine nature to be. God must be represented as :—(1) good and the source of all human good, and never as the author of evil ;[111] (2) truthful and unchanging ;[112] (3) steadfast and uncomplaining ;[113] (4) dignified and self-controlled ;[114] and (5) incorruptible.[115] So, too, godlike heroes are to be represented always in a heroic light, as brave, temperate, and not given to lamentation or unreasoning passion.[116] So, too, in the *Laws* it is explained that artists should compose prayers, hymns and encomia suited to the occasion, to the community, and to the divine nature, composing in the spirit of justice, goodness, and beauty, and carefully avoiding, whether in thought, in word, or in action, anything of ill omen ;[117] the music to be in the more severe or classical style, eschewing all sensationalism and the vulgar sweetness of " popular " rhythms and melodies.[118] Only when such norms are obeyed, can we be certain that the compositions will be, both in form and in content, adequate expressions of their idea.

And, further : in the model city, religion, if it is to be adapted to the comprehension of the citizens, should outwardly and visibly touch some phase of life at every moment. Prayers, processions, sacrifices, and rituals take up a great deal of the waking time of the citizens who are trying to live a godlike life in the " city of God."[119] Geographically, every section of the city is to be under the care of some civic deity in his civic temple ; [120] and every aspect of life is to be conceived as being under the spiritual guidance of some definite representative of the divine nature.[121] Philosophically speaking, the Divine plan has a divinely appointed place for each citizen,[122] and the whole machinery of imaginative symbolism is to be called into play to make this an integral portion of the minds of the citizens. Plato is well aware that the Gods of popular religion are imaginative creations, the products of a natural human tendency to clothe thoughts, dreams, and ideals in images,[123] and he wishes to make a very full use of this natural tendency. For the philosopher, while understanding and utilizing this mechanism, does not regard its results as pure illusions. Zeus, Hera, Apollo, and the rest are representations, in imaginative terms which citizens can take up into their lives, of the essential nature of God, and Plato does not, for a moment, contemplate doing away with such imaginative aids to religion. All he is concerned with, is that the imagination which represents the Godhead under such forms shall do so in accordance with rational norms, so as to represent the divine nature as it truly is. The pictorial method of representation is symbolic, allegorical, not final. But what is symbolized may be true and, within the limitations of pictorial expression, adequate. All that is needed to realize this is philosophic censorship, the direction of the philosopher-king.[124] It is for this reason that Plato writes as though " the God," Zeus, Apollo, etc., were Himself directing the inspiration which composes hymns and religious ceremonies in His honour.[125] In this Plato is perfectly serious. His philosophical meaning is that " the divine " does, in actual fact, work through psychological mechanisms and awaken in men such reflections of the divine nature as those mechanisms can produce :—visual images in the poet, concepts in the scientist, the idea of good, with all which this involves, in the philosopher. It is one and the same truth which is expressed in the forces of external nature, in the picture-language of the temples of popular religion, in the work and play of social life in the community, in the intellectual researches of the scientist, and in the final vision of the philosopher.[126] The inspiration, then, which guides poet or medium is not illusory ; but the mechanism needs control and direction, if it is to be rational ; and Plato's ideal for popular religion is thus to make the fullest use of the popular and traditional mechanisms and symbols, so controlled and directed that they will express the truths revealed by philosophy, which are the Divine Truth, in the clearest form which man can grasp.[127]

It is in this spirit that every law in the model city is given specific religious sanctions. Fraud, theft, assault, murder, disregard of family obligations, etc., are of course treated as offences against the community, and, as such, are associated with specific civic penalties, such as a fine, imprisonment, degradation, exile, or capital punishment. But they are also regarded as species of impiety, offences against the God who presides over the market-place, the God who protects strangers, the God who watches over boundaries, the God who protects kindred, etc., and, as such, require religious purification in addition to civic punishment, especially in the case of the greater crimes.[128] In this, Plato is acting in accordance with Greek feeling, which everywhere recognized a Zeus (or Apollo) Patroos, a Zeus Herkeios, Phratrios, Xenios, etc., and naturally linked together justice and piety on the one hand, and injustice and impiety on the other.[129] But Plato goes further in his enactments, and explicitly rejects the objections of conscientious atheists.[130] In the model city, every citizen who keeps the hearth also, as a matter of course, like Cephalos, administers the sacred rites,[131] and atheism, in all its forms, is entirely eradicated.

In the same spirit, every dance-form, every melodic sequence, and every hymn-type which is approved, is dedicated to some God or Goddess. Not only are all other forms regarded as unconsecrated, but innovating musicians are definitely liable to a suit of impiety.[132] In such ways, then, it is made very plain to the citizen that in the city of God " the divine " is present in every phase of life, and that each and every member of the community, in marrying and in educating his children, in planting, sowing, reaping and marketing his crops, in participating in the tasks of government no less than in taking part in religious ceremonies proper, is participating

in the Godlike life, co-operating with " the divine " in realizing,
in the world around him, the ideals of the spiritual life.

So much, then, for the nature of " the divine." It
remains to treat very briefly of its value in Platonism. The
conclusion stands out at once, that " the divine " is not one
value which can be related to other values on a scale of higher
and lower, but is rather value itself, the ideal source of all the
values which fall within our experience. In the physical
world, value is realized in proportion as chaos gives way to
cosmos and all the potentialities of elements which would
otherwise remain apart from a world of " being " become
realized in a single orderly system. But bringing the one in
relation to the many, i.e. bringing systematic order out of
chaos and thus releasing the various potentialities of earth,
water, fire, and air, so that they constitute a single universe,
is precisely the function of " the divine," which is thus the
source of all physical values.[133]   In the animate, and especially in the human world, value is realized, both in the
individual and in the group, in proportion as the various
instinctive tendencies are so reorganized as to work together
harmoniously, thus realizing to the full the various potentialities of the organisms concerned.[134]   But the principle
thus involved is the divine principle of the city whose pattern
is " laid up in heaven," and the ideal of maximal realization
of potentiality on the part of every individual in the service
of the whole is the divine plan for humanity,[135] so that, here
also, the source of all animate and human values is " the
divine." Finally, in reference to the ideal world, in passages
which seem to recognize a distinction of higher and lower,
it is very clearly stated that " the divine " is the source of
all lower values, whether at the level of opinion or of true
insight.[136]   Speaking universally, then, we may conclude
that all order, meaning, and value, wherever and however
manifested, have their source in " the divine," which expresses
unenviously its own nature by bringing to bear its own principle of so reorganizing whatever comes under its influence
as to call out its maximal realization of potentiality in relation
to the whole. This influence is not empirical, in the sense
of physical and mechanical, *in pari materia* with the motions
and impacts of masses. It is rather an ideal impulse calling
forth the innate idealism of the soul, The Divine, as such,
appealing to the divine element within us for recognition,

love, worship, and free co-operation.[137] Value thus belongs, not to the sensuous world *qua* sensuous, but primarily to the ideal world envisaged by rational contemplation, to that Ideal Experience which becomes actual in the empirical realm, in part, through our co-operation, and thus raises the empirical more nearly to the level of the divine which is the level of value.

CHAPTER XII

IN what has preceded, we have investigated the chief value-scales discussed in the Dialogues, drawing, in each case taken by itself, whatever conclusions appeared to follow from the evidence considered. In what follows, these limitations of particularity will be removed, and we shall attempt to consider the evidence as a whole and draw whatever conclusions seem justified in general.

As we look over the great mass of evidence which we have already sifted, seeking a unity in this manifold, the first universal fact which stands out against the great variety of detail is that proverbial value-distinctions, such as " justice—health—wealth," " public—private," etc., represent traditional value-judgments, and have in Platonism a status akin to the status of the traditional deities. That is to say, everyone forms value-scales of one sort or another and relates these somehow to the traditional valuations accepted by the group of which he is a member, precisely as everyone develops religious convictions of one sort or another, and relates these somehow to the traditional representatives of " the divine." Thus understood as a product of social evolution, value-scales have the kind of significance which, in Platonism, attaches to public institutions as opposed to merely private and individual experiences. They rest upon a broader basis than the fluctuating value-judgments of individuals, and penetrate further into the nature of experience than is possible for the relatively unorganized individual feelings after value, and, as relatively more comprehensive and more profound, constitute norms or social standards by reference to which the individual citizen can estimate his moral status.[1]

The second fact which stands out with equal universality and equal clearness, is the immense variety of attitudes actually taken towards these traditional value-judgments. Such social norms may be accepted or rejected, half-heartedly or whole-heartedly, and that unthinkingly, half-reflectively, or after mature consideration. Representatives of each of these attitudes abound in the Dialogues, in the persons of Ion, Meno, Protagoras, Callicles, and the other interlocutors of the Platonic Socrates, and at first sight the variety of attitudes appears so bewildering as to escape classification. But, for the Platonist, such attitudes fall naturally and of themselves under one of four main heads. First (1) comes the varying and fluctuating individual value-judgment, which knows that this tastes sweet or bitter here and now, and either unthinkingly or deliberately denies objective validity to all generalizations which go beyond the individual and rest upon social experience.[2] Next (2) comes the acceptance, whether unthinking or reflective, of these group norms as expressing final truth, or at least final truth for man.[3] Next (3) comes the attitude of rationalistic criticism of all group standards, culminating, at best, in the philosopher's search for a deeper basis of truth in the ideal world. Finally (4), this insight once attained, we have the return to the cave, associated with an attitude of sympathetic reform, so as to retain, from the new position, whatever is of value in the social norms, whether for the guidance of the average citizen or for the stimulation of philosophic thought in the dialectical student.[4]

The third universal fact which is now, perhaps, beginning to stand out clearly, is that the Platonist is not primarily concerned with this or that traditional value-scale. It is the attitude rather than the norm, which especially interests him, and the arrangement of values which he especially champions is not primarily a classification of " goods," but rather a classification of attitudes towards such goods, in terms of the degree of philosophical insight manifested by this or that attitude. What the Platonist is concerned with is that there should be an advance from (1) the attitude of subjective individualism to (2) a social and institutional standpoint ; that there should be a further advance from (2) the social and institutional attitude to (3) a critical and philosophical attitude of insight into the principle of value ; and finally that there should be (4) a regression from contemplation of the ideal to actual life among human beings, with the avowed aim of enabling other human beings, as far as possible, to advance in the direction of the same philosophic insight and then take their part also in the great work of spreading the new enlightenment. Platonists are thus missionaries of the life of idealistic endeavour, and convert to the service of their cause whatever existing institutions can be utilized in spreading their new gospel. Of such institutions, the existing value-scales are among the more important ; for many of them tend, of themselves, to emphasize the value of righteous conduct as opposed to the acquisition of material possessions, and almost all acclaim " mind " as " the king of all."

Let us consider the nature and aim of this new gospel, in order to realize the difference which its adoption makes to the interpretation of the traditional norms. In every phase of experience, man seeks value, and, in order to avoid self-negation, the throwing away with one hand what he is finding with the other, he aims at consistency and at extracting from his various experiences their common and universal value-elements. Reflection upon what is involved in this value-seeking leads inevitably to the ideal of a non-contradictory experience in which all value-potentialities are harmoniously and completely realized. This ideal of maximal realization of potentiality is the " idea of good " which the Platonist proceeds to apply to every phase of experience, and it is plain that certain value-judgments are logically implicit in the acceptance of this ideal principle. For example :—insight into this principle is clearly superior in value to ungrounded opinions as to what constitutes " the good," not only for the individual citizen, but especially for the administrator who is charged with the guidance of the community.[5] Other forms of the same value-judgment everywhere present in the Dialogues are the exaltation of intellectual at the expense of sensuous and emotional experience, of philosophy at the expense of the pursuit of pleasure or power, of soul at the expense of body and wealth, of the one universal idea at the expense of the many fluctuating particulars, of order as opposed to chaos, of reality at the expense of sensuous appearance, etc. Such value-distinctions are implicit in the Platonic position,[6] and so far as the actual value-scales which pass current in the community resemble these value-distinctions, they are seized upon by the Platonist and are shown dialectically to be of a piece with the Platonic position as a whole and to imply, e.g. that the way of salvation is to be sought through philosophy, which alone can realize God's plan for humanity and can raise human life out of the meaningless treadmill and ruinous see-saw of the political game.

The social norms which coincide in detail with these ideal valuations are in this way enlightened as to the identity of the principle which they vaguely presuppose with the ideal principle which the Platonists are advocating. But there are in the community two other attitudes towards values, the treatment of which is more difficult. There are (1) value-attitudes which to a vague agreement as to the principle join a definite disagreement in matters of detail, setting pleasure or power or wealth, for example, higher on their scale than temperance or justice or wisdom. With this unenlightened hedonism and materialism the valuations implicit in platonism immediately lock horns, and subject to logical analysis the sophistry in which such views find their expression and technical defence. The vagueness in respect of the principle is first cleared up. It is not difficult to show dialectically that any genuine value-scale, whatever its details, implies acceptance of the ideal principle of value, viz. the principle of maximal realization of potentiality in a single consistent system.[7] It is then shown, with somewhat more difficulty, that the individualistic self-seeking championed by the sophist is inconsistent with this ideal principle, and that it is thus logically necessary, either to give up belief in the principle, or to accept the deductions of the Platonist in matters of detail. It is enough for the sophists to get a glimpse of the dialectical abyss of not-being beneath their feet, for the boldest and most aggressive of them to desert their position and accept, somewhat hurriedly, the whole position indicated by their Platonic interlocutors, with whom they have in common at least a faith in the power of reason to discover the true life-values.[8] The materialistic hedonist is thus not a final enemy, but is converted to platonism and submits to the rectification of his scale of values until it coincides with the Platonic valuations.

The remaining attitude towards values (2) occasions greater difficulty, for it disagrees with platonism, not only in details, but even in principle, so that it is hard to find any common ground from which to proceed. The representative of this standpoint is the sceptic, who either contents himself with a practical equation of all empirical values,[9] or even goes further and attacks the intellectual integrity of the ideal world itself, and views without shrinking the intellectual abyss to which such unbelief admittedly leads.[10] Where all belief in value-scales of any sort has vanished, it is doubtful whether persuasion, however reasonable, can effect anything, and if conscientious endeavour fails to effect a cure, such cures are in the end treated by the Platonist as pathological perversions, to be cut out of the community life by a surgical operation.[11]

After the hedonist has thus been converted to the true faith, and the sceptic, if proved to be beyond all reasonable hope of conversion, has been eliminated from the community life, the various empirical value-scales are standardized so as to express more nearly the ideal valuations implicit in platonism. A single comprehensive scale of values, passing from material possessions up through physical and moral excellence and culminating in intellectual excellence, is officially established in religion and in law and incorporated into the community life.[12] In this way the Platonist hopes to join hands with the elements of good which are present in the habitual value-judgments of each and every citizen, and thus to raise every phase of the community life more nearly to the spiritual level at which life begins to acquire significance, reality, and true value.

PART III

THE HIGHEST GOODS IN PLATONISM

CHAPTER XIII

PLEASURE, WEALTH, HEALTH

SO far, we have investigated the setting in which candidates for the position of highest good are found. If we now turn to the Dialogues and ask directly what candidates actually put in a claim to this position, we find the following :—(1) Pleasure, (2) wealth, (3) health, (4) power, (5) happiness, (6) the life of the " guardian " or ideal statesman, (7) immortality, (8) goodness of character, (9) temperance, (10) justice, (11) genius, (12) religion, (13) science, (14) philosophy, (15) mind, (16) civilization, (17) the community, (18) intelligent self-knowledge on the part of the community, (19) law and order, (20) measure or the mean, (21) the idea of good, (22) the comprehensive or composite life, (23) the excellence or preservation of the whole, (24) God. Each of these goods is explicitly accepted as fulfilling the requirements of the ethical ideal, in some cases immediately, and in other cases only after discussion. In what follows, we shall scrutinize the claims of each one of these candidates, with an attention to detail proportioned to the amount of evidence contained in the Dialogues, in order to discover, in each case, how far and for what reasons it is regarded as a " highest " good, an adequate expression of the value-ideal.

(1) Pleasure.—The casual reader of the Dialogues receives the impression that, for platonism, pleasure is a satisfaction of our bodily nature which is of no positive value, something to which our spiritual nature is supremely in-

different or even hostile, in proportion as pleasure clogs and fetters the soul which is seeking to soar into the upper regions, and rivets it firmly to materialism and sensualism. It is, of course, noted that there is an occasional advocacy of the claims of pleasure, but the general impression is that this is sophistry, or, at best, " Socratic hedonism," but not genuine platonism.[1] Absolutely opposed to this impression are (a) the undeniable hedonism of the *Protagoras*, (b) the admission of at least certain types of pleasure into the composite life which constitutes the *summum bonum* in the *Philebus*, (c) the contention in the *Republic* that the philosophic life is the pleasantest, and (d) the recognition in the *Laws* of the absolute universality of our pleasure-sense and of its legitimate claims upon all of us. Faced with this opposition, we shall reconsider all passages referring to the subject of pleasure, without any bias except in the direction of evolving some consistent theory which shall be just to all the evidence, and shall not be unduly influenced by individual passages of a striking nature, where ethical feeling leads to especially sharp contrasts.

Approached in this impartial spirit, the passages from the Dialogues seem to fall naturally into four main groups : (a) purely psychological passages, which have nothing to do with ethical valuations ; (b) passages expressing value-attitudes towards pleasure-pain characteristic of man as a social animal ; (c) passages expressing the philosopher's attitude towards pleasure-pain ; and (d) passages suggesting how the social and conventional pleasures might be reformed in the light of this philosophical reflection. In dealing with the subject, we shall follow this natural grouping.

(a) The psychology of pleasure.—Pleasure-pain, as an experience, arises in connection with every form of animal and human activity, whether sensory, motor, or organic. The eye is formed for seeing, the ear for hearing, etc., and the simple functioning of each of our sensory organs in accordance with its characteristic structure is associated with pleasure. Excessive stimulation, as when the unprotected eye is subjected to strong sunlight, is painful, and deficient stimulation, as when the light-adapted eye is plunged suddenly into darkness, is confusing and unpleasant ; and there is a sense in which any effective stimulation of our sense-organs is a disturbance, a violence which interrupts the even flow of the inner motions characteristic of the organ. But where the degree of stimulation merely calls forth an outflow of energy which is within the capacity of the organ, so that its reaction represents a recovery of balance and the attainment of a new equilibrum, this characteristic reaction is always experienced as pleasure.[2] We may take pleasure in simple sensations, in bright colours or pure tones, as such, without reference to anything further such as a picture or symphony. So, too, touching, tasting, and smelling, of themselves, may give simple but undeniable pleasures, quite independently of the social or anti-social setting in which these and other sensory pleasures may be experienced.[3]

Again, from the motor point of view, all animals take a natural pleasure in self-motion, however spasmodic. The frisking of limb or tail heightens their sense of being alive.[4] And finally, from the organic point of view, the assimiliation of material which fills up the gaps left by the wear and tear of life, in the digestive process which restores the proportion of the bodily elements (earth, water, fire, air) to one another and thus renews our bodily equilibrium, is accompanied by pleasure ; and the return from disease, which has disturbed the proportion of earth, water, fire, and air in the body, to health, in which the natural equilibrium is completely restored, is extremely pleasant.[5]

In addition to the above, there are the pleasures which arise from co-ordination. All animals take a natural pleasure in self-motion, however spasmodic and irregular ; but human beings take also an especial pleasure in the ordered measures of the dance, in the kindred rhythm-patterns of music and poetry, and generally in the introduction of unity, meaning, and a principle of order into the otherwise manifold, meaningless and chaotic. This introduction of order is the characteristic work of mind, and we take great pleasure in the characteristic functioning of these synthetic processes, so far as they are successful in overcoming obstacles and reducing the environment to their own order-patterns, whether these are concrete sense-patterns, or the less concrete and more formal patterns which appeal to a more generalized sense of rhythm and order, or the action-patterns which we call ethical, or the more formal and general patterns of mathematics, logic, dialectic, and metaphysics. In all of these, pleasure is taken,[6] although it cannot be denied that, in certain cases, the simpler, more directly instinctive and sensuous activities may come into conflict, either with one another, or with more developed activities such as those associated with ethical or intellectual interests.

(b) Social value-attitudes towards pleasure.—At the natural level, men, women, and children seek pleasure from any and every source, indiscriminately and without much consideration of consequences. Perhaps they are not seeking pleasure, as such, but are rather trying to live out their lives, to set functioning their sensory and motor apparatus, and, as a consequence of this unreflective activity, of course they enjoy the heightened sense of life which accompanies this discharge of energy along organic channels.[8] But, under the influence of social living, certain types of activity and certain types of pleasure become standardized, as objects of community approval. Eating and drinking become, to some extent, community functions. Friendship between individuals becomes an institution hedged about by community usages. Pugnacity develops into sport-rivalry or possibly into military organization. Curiosity becomes, to an increasing extent, a matter of community-regulated study and research. And as social living naturally assumes that the particular social group is a self-legislating unit, so that its members must bow to the will of the majority,[9] and as, further, such groups tend to form especially when the occupations of the day are over, and nothing remains except social enjoyment and pleasure, an interest in social pleasure, as such, tends to develop, and some more or less definite theory of social hedonism, or a quasi-Epicurean type, naturally makes its appearance. Once this theory has definitely attracted minds by its persuasiveness, the various activities in which individuals and groups express their ideals come to be evaluated, by this relatively idle and reflective community, in terms of their potentialities for producing pleasure, especially pleasure of this social type. The pleasure taken in music, in dancing, in literature, in painting, in banqueting, and in disputation or dialectic, is largely of this social type,[10] and in fact, if the after-dinner mood is made the judge, it is likely that characteristic after-dinner activities will be valued as the highest.

Speaking generally, the attitude of any community towards pleasure-pain is to approve all pleasure-pursuits which tend to strengthen the group, whether for peace or for war, and to disapprove all pleasure-pursuits which seem likely to weaken the community in any way. Just which pursuits are approved and which disapproved, varies largely as the type of group organization varies. Thus, the pleasures approved of in a typical oligarchy are the business man's pleasures, the pleasures associated with working hard, saving carefully, accumulating property by methods which fall approximately within the law, avoiding unproductive expenditures, whether personal or communal.[11] The pleasures disapproved of are expensive and unproductive pleasures, such as those associated with mere indulgence of appetites, or with sport, or with military honour, or with disinterested research, whether scientific or philosophic. The natural appetites of hunger, thirst, and sex are kept down with an iron hand, except where someone else can be found to pay the cost, in which case they are indulged in with a crudity and at the same time a thoroughness which are only found in the absence of sound education.[12]

So too in a democracy of the Athenian type, the attitude towards pleasure-approval is connected with " freedom," i.e. with absence of regulation and control, whether rational or otherwise. All pleasures are definitely equated in value, and the nothing-too-much rule in interpreted as meaning that the proper democratic attitude towards the pursuit of happiness is to allow no one pleasure to become the ruling passion for long, but to compel each in turn to give way to the next. With a splendid disregard for inconsistencies, the citizen in a democracy pursues happiness via the pleasures associated with liquor and revelry, via the pleasures associated with an active career as a politician, a military officer, a commercial magnate, etc., everything by starts, but nothing long. No pleasures lose their voting power. All are equally enfranchised, and disapproval is meted out only to the consistent, selectively systematic pursuit of activities which develop definite character and culminate in something exclusive, such as trained leadership in politics, trained leadership in warfare, expert leadership in research, etc. In the land of the free, nothing kingly is tolerated.[13]

So, again, in a government of the despotic type : pleasure-pursuits which tend towards stability, law and order, and constitutional government are steadily eliminated, and the more unruly appetites lift up their heads. The pleasures of debauchery are most highly approved, and the titillation of the emotions in the tragic drama comes a close second. A community in the hands of a despot is on the down grade which leads, with increasing velocity, to disintegration and not-being, and it is pleasures of the disintegrating type which are approved of in such a community.[14]

Each form of social organization thus, out of all pleasure-pursuits, standardizes a certain selection and, by means of social pressure, sets these before its citizens as the most desirable, i.e. as constituting the highest good for these citizens. No community sets before its citizens as an ideal, i.e. as their highest good, the seeking after pleasure, as such. For mere pleasure has neither character nor organized structure, but is a process. As Plato puts it, it is *genesis*, not *ousia*. It is wealth, power, freedom, etc., which are regarded as substantial goods, and the pleasure-processes associated with these take on value-character from the value of the substantial goods with which they are associated. At the same time it is not, of course, denied that some of these goods may well be associated with more pleasure, whether in quantity or in quality or in both, than others, and that it might thus be possible to find a " highest " good which would be associated with the greatest possible quantity and quality of pleasure.[15]

(c) Philosophical criticism of these socialized attitudes.— The criticism of pleasure which we find in the Dialogues is directed mainly against the pleasures pursued by individuals, as such, rather than against the pleasures which they pursue as citizens of some definite type of social group, and the criticism of groups is directed against the concrete ends which these pursue, rather than against the pleasures associated with such ends. Nevertheless, as the criticism of the different types of social organization is made with the aim of ascertaining how the typical oligarch or democrat compares in respect of pleasantness of life with the typical philosophic guardian, it is possible to make certain deductions which are substantiated by the evidence provided in the Dialogues.

In trying to understand this evidence, we come upon a certain difficulty, which arises from an attempt to prove two things which are, perhaps, not entirely consistent. It is shown (1) that pleasure is not, and cannot be, a good in itself, as it is a characteristic process which obtains its meaning and value from the substantial entities with which it is associated ; it is not an " idea," and does not belong to the ideal realm, the " true above," but remains attached to the only partially real world of change and decay, the Heraclitean flux inherent in the sensuous. On the other hand (2), it is not proposed to concede to the sophists that philosophy as depicted in the Dialogues is not, in actual fact, a pleasurable kind of pursuit, and does not, in fact, compare favourably in respect of pleasure with power or sensuality. Plato maintains that philosophy is the pleasantest life, and that, judged by the standard of pleasantness, the life of his philosophic guardian is superior to any other kind of life advocated or practised in his time.[17] This appears to concede the hedonist position, though giving it a new turn and content, and, by this apparent concession, seems to throw a shadow of doubt upon the (thoroughly platonic) contention that pleasure is somehow unreal and unimportant. If, on the one hand, we regard the doctrine that pleasure is unsubstantial as the fundamental position of platonism, then a certain air of unreality undoubtedly surrounds the attempt to demonstrate that the life of the philosopher exceeds in pleasure the life of the *viveur* or of the power-seeker. For it seems paradoxical to assert that the philosopher is not concerned with pleasure at all, and indeed in eating, drinking, and sex-relations is not at all carried away by pleasure, but lives a somewhat ascetic life, and also to maintain that the *viveur*, who does take pleasure in such activities and devotes himself deliberately to a life of enjoyment, does not, after all, get more pleasures out of life than the ascetic, who takes no especial pleasure in such natural activities and rather shuns than pursues them. We should expect Plato, in strict logic, to say :—" The sensualist does, in fact, enjoy a succession of individual pleasures, and his life is, in fact, a procession from enjoyment to enjoyment ; but, as there is no order or consistency in his way of living, while his life is undeniably a succession of pleasures which, as psychological processes, titillations of his nervous system, are real enough, he is missing something more valuable. On the whole, his life, considered as a totality which should be rational and consistent, is a succession of failures to connect and establish contact with the things which make of life something truly worth while. The philosopher misses, in comparison, a very large number of these insignificant neutral titillations ; but his life is a success on the whole, and enjoys genuine satisfaction, because it is consistent and is throughout in touch with the deepest reality. The choice is between (a) a meaningless and frivolous existence which enjoys a succession of sensuous pleasures but misses the deeper realities of life, and (b) a meaningful and truly valuable existence which co-operates with God in doing the real work of the world. But in such a choice, the criterion of value cannot possibly be a neural reaction such as pleasure, which is a subjective heightening of the life-sense which may be present just as much in the *viveur* as in the philosopher, and is far too superficial and too universal to be made a touchstone by which questions of such importance can be decided."[18]

If, on the other hand, we regard Plato as thoroughly in earnest in demonstrating that the philosophic life is the pleasantest, we should expect his position, in strict logic, to be as follows :—" All living beings enjoy pleasure, as a heightening of their sense of being alive, in proportion as they succeed in overcoming obstacles and utilizing external stimulations as a means of calling forth a harmonious reaction of their own motor processes so that these emerge triumphant in their own characteristic activity. There is thus a proportion between the degree of harmony and organized character, on the one hand, and the degree of pleasure experienced, on the other. To a man of definite character, the pleasure associated with eating, drinking, and the satisfaction of other sensuous appetites is slight in comparison with the pleasure associated with a complex reaction—such as the successful daily performance of his characteristic work as farmer, carpenter, or student—which calls forth the harmonious co-operation of all his action-tendencies in the direction of realizing his peculiar character. To a man of no definite character, the more simple appetite-satisfactions seem like great pleasures, because he knows nothing higher with which to compare them. They are genuine enough as far as they go, but they do not go very far, because they awaken no well-developed organization of action-tendencies in harmonious relation to the essential nature of the universe, but remain superficial, out of touch with what is worth while. From this standpoint, the most pleasurable existence will be that of the most highly organized character, who reacts in such a way as to call forth *all* his energies, physical, moral, and intellectual, in harmonious inter-relation and in harmonious relation to the genuine forces of the cosmos. But the life which is devoted to this maximal realization of potentiality is the life whose principle is the idea of good, i.e. is the philosopher's life. The philosopher's life, then, as being the most comprehensively and thoroughly and objectively organized, is the pleasantest. To such a man, a meal, a drink, or a walk, e.g. is not the feverish snatching after a momentary pleasure, coming in between two reachings-out after entirely heterogeneous pleasures. His life is not an aggregate, but is an organized totality, and each moment in it is not an isolated shoot of pleasure, but pulsates with the life of the whole, and is coloured by the hedonic tone of the whole. In this way, where the pleasantness of the whole enters into each moment, the pleasure which continues to tinge the hedonic colouring of each moment is more comprehensive, more smooth-flowing, more consistent than the isolated pleasures of the sensualist, which are pleasant indeed, but are jerky and disconnected, and are somewhat overcast by the shadow of impermanence and insecurity which is always found in the absence of order and system. While, then, all men enjoy pleasures, in proportion as they are successful in their various activities, the philosopher, whose activities are organized in terms of the ideal principle of extracting from every phase of experience its maximum of consistent meaning-value, enjoys the greatest possible quantity and quality of pleasure."[19]

(d) Suggested reforms of socialized pleasures.—In accordance with the difference between these two views, two widely differing types of reform are suggested by the platonic representatives of philosophic insight. On the one hand, we find it roundly asserted that the pleasure-seeking tendencies which, under the name of " the concupiscent element," constitute the largest portion of the human soul, are not amenable to rational considerations at all, but naturally and inevitably compete with reason for control of the action-systems of the organism, and seek to subject the rational and spirited elements to the service of instinct. These irrational tendencies are pronounced uneducable, and the only way in which they can be handled effectively is to prevent them from tasting pleasure, and thus to interfere with their natural growth and keep them as weak as possible. They must further be kept in their place by force *ab extra*, and the spirited element is here enlisted in the service of reason, in order to see that the pleasure-seeking tendencies are kept in due subordination.[20]   It is, in fact, along these lines that reform is suggested.   The philosopher despises the unruly mob of pleasure-seeking tendencies connected with hunger, thirst, sex, self-adornment, etc., and severs himself, as much as possible, from these instinctive activities which are the great concernment of most men and make up some three-fourths of embodied human existence.   Withdrawing himself from the world and the flesh to the shelter of his college walls, he preserves his purity from contamination and devotes himself to the solitary contemplation of ultimate truths in the ideal realm.   Approval of this other-worldly attitude occurs in a great variety of contexts, and is thus to be regarded as characteristically platonic.[21]

On the other hand, many passages indicate directly enough that the pleasure-seeking tendencies can, at least to some extent, be trained and educated so as to recognize and accept the ascendency of reason, not as a merely external force, but as akin to something within their own nature.   In the first place, the spasmodic tendencies towards self-expression in any and every kind of motion can, in human beings, be brought under the direction and control of rhythm and harmony, so that we take pleasure in dancing and in the measures of the dance combined with song.   But any kind of rhythm is already an example of order and law, and, further, certain types of rhythm are, in the nature of things, appropriate to the expression of certain types of character.   It is a peculiarity of human nature that we take pleasure in whatever rhythmic forms are habitual for us, and it is therefore a simple matter of censorship acting in concert with experts, to see that the more effeminate and less desirable types are suppressed, and that the rhythmic forms used in education, in ceremonial and processional dances, are all representative of the more desirable types of character.   In this way our pleasure-pain sense gradually takes on a kind of harmoniousness and measured-ness, and acquires the natural rhythms of a well-regulated life. Words, melodies, and dance-rhythms all exemplifying the approved character-types, we insensibly take up into our characters, (a), in the dances approved for peaceful occasions, the virtues of temperance and holiness, and (b), in the dances approved for warlike occasions, the virtues of courage and discipline inseparable from military morale.   When we further remember how the choric dance links together all members of the community, we realize how the sense of community, which is the basis of the virtue of justice, develops, and, when we further remember the meaning-element embodied in the words of the approved songs, we can understand how it is that Plato can regard this training in music and gymnastic as leading naturally towards an appreciation of the beauty of reason itself, and so preparing us for the acquisition of the virtue of wisdom.[22]

In the second place, it is definitely stated that the desires which together constitute the concupiscent element of the soul vary in the degree to which they can be enlightened. Some of them, at any rate, are of a worthier nature, and can not only themselves listen to the voice of reason, but can also, somewhat like the spirited element as a whole, exercise a measure of control over the less worthy desires, so that these grow weaker, or even cease altogether from troubling. Finally, it is also clearly stated that the concupiscent element, taken as a whole, can be so educated as to come to an agreement with the rational element, namely that the rational element should rule over the whole organism, and that the concupiscent element should refrain from opposing such duly constituted authority : in which case the concupiscent element, no less than the rational element, partakes of the virtue of temperance.[23] From this evidence, then, it is plain that the physical instincts are not always a drag upon the philosopher, but can, to some extent, be so trained as to enter into the philosophic life itself. From this standpoint, it is suggested that the pleasures associated with eating, drinking, sex, etc., should not be abandoned as uneducable expressions of the wild-beast element in man, but should be re-formed by the philosopher re-entering the cave and so training himself as well as his fellow-citizens that they all approximate to the perfection of body as well as of soul. This means that eating, drinking, etc., should and can become community, rather than merely individual, functions, and should illustrate the spirit of service rather than of individualistic pleasure-seeking, and the spirit of enlightenment rather than the soul-darkening lusts of the flesh. One eats and drinks so that the bodily harmony will subserve the symphony of the soul, as the good citizen eats so as to preserve that health of body which is a *sine qua non* for the rest of the higher life.[24] It has been pointed out that, according to the *Philebus*, only the pleasures of aesthetical joy in pure colours, forms, odours, tones, and the joy in knowledge, which all rest on pure relations, on measure and law, with the pleasure peculiar to this, and do not sway up and down between too-much and too-little, like the other pleasures—only such pure pleasures can enter into the good life, which is based upon law and order.   But it is of course to be understood that, as stated in other Dialogues, all the " necessary " appetites with their attendant pleasures enter directly into the philosopher's life.[25]   It is really the spirit of sensualism to which the Platonist is opposed.   He does not, in the end, advocate extreme asceticism or cynicism.   The reform suggested is thus a reform of the spirit, substituting the philosophic spirit for the materialistic and sensualistic attitude towards the various activities in which the body has a share.

(2) Wealth.—That money and material possessions may be utilized so as to assist in living the ideal life, is admitted by everyone, and, when so utilized under the guidance of wisdom or philosophic insight, obviously constitute a " good." But the materialistic impulses incident to humanity (*pleonexia*) tend to omit this reference to wisdom or insight, and to regard possessions as somehow good in themselves ; and that material possessions constitute the chief or highest of goods is the central portion of the business man's creed.   Such believers rest their case partly upon the psychological disposition of acquisitiveness, which is not only strong in humanity when taken by itself, but also, by its connection with the sensuous desires, becomes representative of what, in the majority of men, is the largest portion of the soul.[26]   Thus, it is perfectly in accordance with normal tendencies for a man to acquire considerable possessions, and to spend his money largely in building a magnificent home, and obtaining for his women-folk all the luxuries which money can purchase, turning his home into a veritable nest where he can lay up treasures upon earth and can entertain his friends lavishly with all that can delight eye, ear, palate, or touch, living, as nearly as possible, what he imagines to be the life of the great king.   In sketching the outlines of this millionaire's paradise, Plato emphasizes sometimes the thrift, and at other times the luxury.   But that the ideal of great possessions has an immense fascination for humanity, and that the typical business man of ancient Greece fed his soul with images of wealth and luxury, with the hope

of being, one day, a kind of sultan, is brought out very clearly in the Dialogues.[27] In such day-dreaming, a veritable idealism is involved, but it is an idealism which attributes altogether magical powers to cold cash and real estate, and Plato is concerned to show that the aspirations of humanity cannot be finally satisfied with this simple, though concrete, content of the life which is seeking to attain the highest conceivable good.

For platonism, material possessions only acquire value in relation to human purposes, and the only direct function of cash is in connection with the mechanism of economic living, namely, in order to facilitate the exchange of the products of labour. It is the development of the soul which is the really valuable human activity, and it is only so far as possessions, by providing a sufficient basis for spiritual activity, including e.g. an education which will reveal the moral limitations inherent in the thirst after great possessions, can assist in the development of the soul, that they acquire any sort of positive value. Even so, the value which they acquire is purely secondary, valuable as an instrument, not valuable in itself. In fact, Plato likes to say that, as the chief function of possessions is to minister to the needs of the body, and the chief function of the body is to minister to the needs of the spirit, namely, to enable the spirit to contemplate the ideal realm, spiritual needs come first in value, bodily needs second, and the claims of wealth to be regarded as an object of reasonable human endeavour come third.[28] The exact figures (first, second, third) are, of course, insignificant, as the entities compared are not quantities and are not even *in pari materia*, but the figures are used here, as in the mathematical formulation of the happiness-relation of the tyrant as compared with the philosopher, simply in order to illustrate in a graphic way the great value-distance between the ideals compared. For platonism, possessions have no value *per se*, and could not possibly be a highest good. But when wisely acquired and used, they enter into the mechanical side of social organization, and thus partake of the value of social organization ; much as a card-indexing system has no value in itself, but, by facilitating certain mechanical processes, may even enter, to a certain extent, into the investigation of scientific or philosophical truth, and may thus share in the value which attaches to such investigations, though never attaining to a very high level of value. It is thus the substition of the philosophic, in place of the materialistic, spirit which lends to wealth and materialistic possessions whatever value they can legitimately claim.

(3) Health.—Our third candidate for the position of highest good is health or bodily well-being. The many, the physician, and the patient undoubtedly regard health as the highest good and as supreme among life's values, their conclusion being based largely upon a contrast with disease.[29] If the body is seriously diseased, all the good things of life are out of the question. The patient may not eat or drink what he likes and when he likes, but must, in all such matters, give up the natural right of self-determination, and must act in accordance with the orders of his physician.[30] Nauseating draughts and a regimen of exercise and rest which may at first completely upset his system, not to mention the more painful measures of cautery and amputation, are among the regular prescriptions to which he must be prepared to submit himself.[31] He cannot taste properly. Perhaps he sees and hears things which his healthier friends assure him are not there to be seen and heard. And not only his senses may be disordered.[32] Sometimes he cannot think, cannot use his mind at all. As to really devoting himself to philosophical contemplation, the simplest sick headache interferes with that ; and a man who is really an invalid can devote himself to nothing but valitudinarianism, the unceasing pursuit of a well-being to which he may never attain.[33] Useless to himself and to the community, with no part or lot in the ideal world of true existence, such a man might just as well not be alive, and it is perfectly in accordance with Hellenic feeling, when Plato suggests that weakly infants should be put quietly out of the way, and views death, even for adults, if they are chronically incapacitated for definite work, with indifference or even approval. When the physical basis of life is upset, it is patent that the good life is out of the question, and the representatives of philosophical insight are at one with the many, the physician, and the patient in admitting that bodily well-being is at least a *conditio sine qua non* of the ideal life.[34]

But here the agreement ends. For ancient medical theory, health results from the due proportion of the four bodily elements, earth, water, fire, and air, while disease results from upsetting this proportion. Eating too much adds too much " earth " to the compound ; drinking too much adds too much " water " and tends to put out the " fire," etc.[35] To restore a man from sickness to health, all that is needed is to re-establish the proportion ; hence the medical prescription of emetics and cathartics, or the knife and the hot iron. This simple theory of the physician's function is criticized by the philosopher. He admits that health depends upon maintaining a certain proportion between the four elements in the human organism ; but, as he understands it, this proportion is the effect of the ideal principle of the " mean," a principle which, unless interfered with *ab extra*, tends to maintain itself against minor disturbances from without or from within. The physician has correctly noted that excesses constitute a major disturbance, which throws the organism off its balance for the time being ; but he has failed to note that the medicines which he prescribes themselves constitute precisely such major disturbances. While not denying that these prescriptions are sometimes successful in attaining their immediate object, the platonist feels that the method is wrong in principle, and that the resulting shock is so dangerous to the organism as a whole that such medicines should be used only in extreme cases.[36]

According to the more thorough-going theory which Platonism advocates, the organism has a kind of balance-wheel, a " governor " which regulates its various motions for the best. Any disturbance, even an ordinary sensory stimulation, interferes with the smooth running of this balance-wheel to some extent.[37] A radical change of diet, or the medicines prescribed by the physician, constitute serious disturbances of this principle of self-motion. If such disturbances are continued, the balance-wheel can learn to adapt itself and so regain its equilibrium at the new level, but every such change constitutes a strain upon its powers.[38] The mechanism by which this balance-wheel or governor regulates the movements of the body for the best is by the best kind of movement, viz., circular self-movement. It " regulates " disturbing motions by a more or less gentle, shaking movement, which upsets and dissolves the disturbing motion, reducing it eventually to its own (circular) type of motion, and finding for it a place of its own in the organism as a whole. This is done by gymnastic exercise and regular hygiene. Such mild exercise as we indulge in in dancing, field sports, and military " setting up " exercises, is self-directed motion, and, if not carried to excess, strengthens the control of the central self-movement principle of the " mean," and assists e.g. the processes connected with digestion. It differs from the physician's " pill " in that it represents the self-directed movement of the organism as a whole, while the pill or potion represents an external stimulation of a single portion of the organism, which tends to upset the balance of the whole by only " exercising " a part.[39]

The position taken by platonism, then, is that the organism should be moved and directed always as a whole, from within if possible, but at any rate always as a whole. Consider, e.g. the case where the organism is so upset that the regulating principle of self-motion is definitely thrown off its balance, as in the case of a young baby upset by the " stream of nutrition," or of a middle-aged academician so wrapped up in mathematical pursuits as to live a sedentary and dyspeptic existence. In such cases, drugs are dangerous. The controlling principle can only stand a certain number of shocks, and a variety of strong stimulations may result in chronic ill-health or even death. In such cases the Platonist advises external exercise, but exercise of the whole body. For the baby, he advises the rocking motions with which, from time immemorial, nurses have soothed their cries and little upsets.[40] For the dyspeptic academician, he advises the equivalent motion, so far as consistent with academic dignity, viz., an ocean voyage, in which the " surging " motion of the Greek sailing vessel will see that the academician is moved as a whole and leaves his mathematics alone for a time, or land-travel in a Greek carriage along a Greek road, which is of almost equal potency in shaking the organism as a whole and assisting it in getting rid of whatever is troubling it.[41] No one-sided functioning is permitted. The organism as a whole, including mind as well as body, is to be exercised, the exercise being preferably directed from within, and then health, the condition in which the internal principle of self-movement exercises full control over the whole body, will result.

One further point. For the philosopher, the matter does not stop here. Human beings are not isolated organisms, but are always parts of wider wholes, social, physical, and metaphysical. Consequently, in the model city, the games and exercises are not purely individual concerns, but are community affairs, like the eating, drinking, studying, and all that

man does.   Babies are taken for daily walks by their nurses—
to some appropriate temple, which will be sufficiently remote.
Community playgrounds, under the control of regularly
appointed playground matrons, are established for the younger
children.[42]   The older boys and girls receive regular training
until they are proficient in riding, archery, dancing, etc., and
can take part in religious processions and ceremonial dances,
as well as in the military marches and dances in full armour,
etc.[43]   Older persons, in danger, perhaps, of becoming one-
sidedly intellectualistic, not only take part in ceremonial
observances—there are three hundred and sixty-four regular
public processions each year in the model city—but learn to
copy, if they are wise, the regularity of the central self-motive
principle so conspicuous in the case of the heavenly bodies
and, as the platonic physicist believes, in the universe as a
whole.   Some understanding of the great principle of circular
central self-movement, which regulates the body as a whole
for the best, i.e. is a bodily analogon of the idea of good, is the
metaphysical basis for the value which the Platonist attaches
to health.[44]   Like the stars in their courses, and like the whole
universe in its self-directed revolutions, the human organism
must be controlled as a whole by the divine principle of self-
directed circular movement located in the brain.   This principle, if it is to direct its organism to perfect healthiness, will
avoid, as far as possible, all external and accidental shocks,
such as come from bright lights, loud noises, blows, and sudden
falls, or from the knife, hot iron, and pharmaceutical mon-
strosities of the general practitioner.   On the positive side,
it will attend especially to what ensures its well-being, viz., the
internal contemplation of the ideal realm.   In this daily
exercise it finds its true food, and is spiritually strengthened
and made glad.[45]   The spiritual growth thus ensured is accompanied by applications of the ideal principle of the good to all
problems which arise, of which the proper care of the body is
one.   But from the standpoint thus reached, while bodily
health is important, it now appears to be only one of the
philosopher's interests, and has become merged in something
higher and more comprehensive.

     In dealing with citizens who have not yet attained to this
level of insight, the philosopher appeals to something less
recondite than celestial harmonics and idealistic metaphysics.
Everyone knows that ill-health results frequently from intem-

perance. If, then, temperance is not only a necessary condition, but also an obvious part of the causes which effectively
produce healthiness, temperance must be a higher sort of
thing, something superior to health in value.[46] Everyone
knows, too, that excessively robust healthiness sometimes
induces selfishness, thoughtless disregard for the sensibilities
and needs of others, and also makes for carelessness about
strict temperance.[47] Resting on this common knowledge,
then, the philosopher establishes by law a value-scale in which
health is ranked with the " goods of the body " and is placed
definitely below such goods as e.g. temperance or self-control.
He further teaches that the chief function of bodily well-being
is to subserve the symphony of the soul. That is to say,
when healthiness is finally attained, it is not to be regarded
as a final good, as something ultimate in the field of value,
but rather as a new base from which to make a renewed step
forwards towards solving the moral problem of living an ideal
life.[48] Its value for the Platonist seems, at times, almost
negative, as though healthiness merely keeps the body from
obtruding its needs upon the mind and thus hindering the pure
contemplation which is the real concernment of man.[49] As
a rule, however, well-being of body forms a sufficiently recognized element in the ideal life. The student of the ideal always
keeps his body in perfect training, and several years of his
education are largely given over to physical culture of one
sort or another. As healthiness results from an orderly style
of living, the philosophic student, whose living is a pattern
of orderliness, always enjoys excellent health, and always
regards it as a good. To such a student it *is* a good.[50] But,
while admitting metaphorically that spiritual healthiness and
spiritual well-being constitute an element of supreme value,
the Platonist never regards a merely bodily well-being—if,
indeed, such a thing is possible without spiritual well-being—
as a highest good. Such a belief, though often voiced in the
Hellenic world, he regards as an error due either to pathological
causes or to ignorance arising out of neglected education.

CHAPTER XIV

POWER

TO the Plato-student, the concept of " power " presents many difficulties. Sometimes it is spoken of as a good to its possessor, and even as the highest good. Once it is used, tentatively but with a certain seriousness, as a definition of existence. At other times it is regarded as morally valueless, or even as positively dangerous to the development of character. Who does not at once recall the treatment of the Napoleonic ideal exemplified in Archelaus, Ardiaeus, and the great king of Persia, not to mention the demonstration that the power-seeking soul " does least of all what it wills," but cowers behind locked doors, alone with its insatiable desires, friendless and hopeless, trusting mistrustfully in its bodyguard of faithless foreign hirelings ? And yet, while many passages indicate philosophic shrinking from any exercise of power,[1] it is undoubtedly Plato's earnest faith that salvation for mankind is to be sought only by concentrating all such power in the hands of philosophers, whether we consider the " golden " class of the ideal republic or the " nocturnal council " of the model city. The magistrates in both communities are certainly philosophers, and are certainly intended to exercise power of every sort, including the power of life and death, in a decisive manner.[2]

The object of the present chapter is to examine all Platonic statements about power, with a view to making perfectly clear, in the first place, its essential nature, and, in the second, why it is sometimes regarded as the highest good. The passages in which the Dialogues refer to the subject of power fall naturally and of themselves into the following groups : —

(1) passages which treat of power in general ;
(2) passages which treat of mechanical power ;
(3) passages which treat of psychological power ;
(4) passages which treat of political power ;

    (5) passages which treat of moral power ;

    (6) passages which treat of intellectual power ;

    (7) passages which investigate the ultimate source of power ; and

    (8) passages which treat of the realizability of power.

In our investigation, we shall follow this natural grouping.

    (1) In general, power is regarded as identical with energy, the force or potentiality evidenced in the demonstrable changes and alterations of internal constitution, of external shape, or of direction and speed of motion, whether of parts or of wholes. Two correlative species are recognized, (a) active power, as when A produces changes in B, C, and D, and (b) passive power, as when B, C, and D undergo alterations on coming into effective contact or community with A. It is changes in the phenomenal world which most obviously provide evidence of energy, force, or power, and it is causal energy which furnishes the Dialogues with their most natural illustrations, although the Platonist by no means confines himself to the physical, non-moral world.[3]

    (2) *Mechanical power.* In order to understand the Platonic position in regard to the phenomenal world, we shall follow Plato's advice and shall approach the details of the phenomenal world only after grasping the general outlines of his position.[4] The central distinction is between " being " and " becoming." " Being " is essentially the realm of the ideal patterns, which are products of the principle of " the limit " applied to the otherwise " unlimited " or infinite. Thus applied, the principle of " the limit " concentrates the maximal meaning-values of whatever " infinite " is concerned in a unified form or " idea," which the mind can grasp because it is constructed in accordance with a principle which is the principle of mind itself.[5]

    Let us consider a given infinite : e.g. mathematical extension of two or three dimensions. If the mind is to understand this at all, its meaning-values must be concentrated in some unified way which the mind can grasp. Let us take two-dimensional space first. Our problem is, to find some intelligible principle for concentrating, in a regular, unified way, the meaning-values of two-dimensional space. These meaning-values are concentrated by constructing unified or closed plane figures, and they are concentrated in a way which the mind can understand, if the closed plane figures are of strictly regular form, e.g. enclosed by straight lines in accordance with a definite principle, as triangle, square, rhombus, etc. The simplest conceivable regular rectilinear closed figure is the triangle, and this may accordingly be regarded as the ultimate unit out of which all regular surface-figures admitted by Plato, whether as simple planes or as the terminations of three-dimensional solids, can be constructed.[6] The principle of triangularity, then, i.e. the rule in accordance with which all regular rectilinear closed figures, whether as planes or as the surface-terminations of regular solids, can be constructed in a way which the mind can understand, is the ideal pattern which most adequately represents the application of " the limit " to mathematical extension in two or three dimensions. Let us take a second example. If we assume motion (in such an extension) as = a given infinite, we shall find that the principle of circularity, in virtue of the closed circumference, concentrates the meaning-values of motion, while the unity of the figure, and the regular equidistance of the circumference from its central point, satisfy the condition of intelligibility. The principle of circularity, then, is the ideal pattern which represents adequately the application of the unifying principle of " the limit " to motion, considered as otherwise infinite or unlimited.[7]

If, now, we wish to construct a pure theoretical physics, as a science of mathematical bodies moving in a three-dimensional extension, it is plain that it is with the ideal patterns of triangularity and circularity that we shall approach our problem. The " bodies " recognized as ultimate in such a science will be the regular mathematical solids whose surfaces are built up out of rectangular triangles in a regular way : viz., tetrahedrons, octahedrons, eikosahedrons, and cubes. The " motion " recognized will be circular motion, possibly modified to a calculable extent by considerations of size, shape, and spatial arrangement of the solids whose intelligible motions are being thought out in such a science. The solids will be thought of as completely enclosed and compressed within a spherical space revolving upon its axis with perfect circular motion,[8] and will consequently cohere in such a way that all will partake of this general revolution. But the influence of the circularity-principle will not be confined to the outer surface of the sphere, so as to penetrate within only in virtue of the compression and consequent cohesion of the solids.

Wherever possible, circular motion will take hold upon groups of solids, converting them into coherent spherical masses revolving upon their own axes, while of course each such revolving mass will continue to be carried in its particular orbit, with some definite and perfectly intelligible relation to the central axis of the whole sphere.[9]

If we wish to proceed yet further with our construction of pure theoretical physics, we can deduce subordinate laws of change by considering the application of the compression to our solids. If we remove the assumption of an all-comprehending circular motion, and think of the solids as occupying a space which is strictly infinite and with no compelling principle of coherence (as on the hypothesis of Democritus), the emergence of organized worlds would obviously be a matter of pure chance. But if we assume a principle which sweeps all the solids into a single compressed spherical space and thus compels coherence,[10] we can see that such compression, applied to a loosely organized aggregate of solids differing in size, shape, and internal coherence, will bring about certain changes.

For example, the smaller solids, such as tetrahedrons, will at first fit into the interstices between the larger solids. But, as the compression increases, either (a) the smaller bodies will be squeezed out, until ultimately all the cubes constitute a spherical mass in the centre, surrounded by a spherical envelope of eikosahedrons, which in turn will be enclosed by a spherical ring of octahedrons surrounded by a final ring of tetrahedrons;[11] or (b) the smaller solids will be unable to escape, and the larger compounds may then be broken up. The solid which has the fewest surfaces and sharpest angles (the tetrahedron) will exhibit the greatest resistance under pressure, while a solid such as the eikosahedron, some of whose angles are very obtuse, will rather easily be split up into more elementary forms. (At the same time, a large mass will sometimes compress a few of the smaller elements into its own shape.) The final effect of such a grinding process is to resolve all the solids concerned, including eventually even the tetrahedrons, into de-triangled, shapeless space, until, as the pressure relaxes, the triangular principle of crystallization again succeeds in compounding regular solids.[12] The continuous interplay of these two tendencies (a and b), which both arise from the same principle of a compressing circular motion, necessarily occasions continuous alteration in the shape, size, and spatial inter-relations of the various solids concerned.

Beyond working out the mathematical inter-relations of typical solids brought together by circular motion, and calculating the varieties of motion in a universe constituted by solids of the types defined, a strictly theoretical physics cannot go, and all knowledge derived from such deductions is, of course, purely formal. It starts with " ideas," continues through " ideas," and in " ideas " it ends. All that the mind really apprehends in such a science is the ideal principles of triangularity and circularity, i.e. the unifying principle of the idea as such, in its applications to intelligible space and intelligible motion. Whether there is empirically such an entity as " space " containing empirical " bodies " which actually " revolve," " collide," and " combine," remains to be discovered by other methods.[13]

Let us now consider the world of " becoming." It is difficult to speak intelligibly of a world of *pure* becoming, from which the unifying principle of mind is *ex hypothesi* excluded. For to read meanings into a situation defined as meaningless, is to fall into contradiction. Apart from the unifying principle, the control of universal law disappears, the world falls asunder into a lawless, boundless, shapeless, and structureless chaos, and the only meaning we can attach to " pure becoming " is irregular, confused, unco-ordinated, fluctuating processes of an a-logical type. More positively, pure becoming is pictured as a spatial receptacle which is capable of taking on sensuous characteristics, becoming here watery, there fiery, here airy, there earthy : either separately or in combinations, so that the substratum becomes smoky, steamy, or muddy. Such characteristics, in the absence of form and number, are irregular and impermanent, and present only faint traces of the sense-perceivable " four elements " of Empedoclean science, viz., water, fire, air, and earth.[14] Of these faint traces it is hardly possible to say anything definite without falling into contradictions, but of the substratum or universal receptacle which admits indifferently of any sensuous qualities, it is possible to say more. This unchanging frame in which " the sense-perceivable " appears and fluctuates is a three-dimensional space which is viewed as a physical " image " of mathematical tridimensional extension.[15] This image or copy partly resembles its archetype or original, and partly differs from it.

Its intelligible meaning-values are substantially the same as the meaning-values of mathematical extension. This means that physical space-values can be expressed in terms of tetrahedrons, octahedrons, etc., and physical motion-values can be expressed in terms of the principle of circularity. But physical space is not merely intelligible ; it contains also sense-perceivable values, an earthy, watery, fiery, or airy quality which can be appreciated by our sensuous nature but can perhaps never be reduced without remainder to completely intelligible principles.[16] Space (the "receptacle") thus furnishes an intermediary, in virtue of which the unifying intelligence is enabled to introduce its principles of triangular crystallization and circular motion into what would otherwise remain chaotic, and is enabled to build up a physical cosmos, spherical and moving on its axis, and its sensuous characteristics related somehow to the surface-terminations of unified physical masses approximating to the regular solids of pure theory. This sense-perceivable image of the intelligible cosmos is apprehended by the mind as a texture of approximately regular solids interacting in virtue of an all-comprehending circular motion, but has the additional feature of sense-perceivability—appreciated as a part of life, but never quite grasped by the pure intellect—and the slightly disturbing difficulty arising from the fact that an "image" never exhibits an entirely pure case of the intelligible laws, but falls short, to a not precisely calculable extent, of our intellectual expectations.[17]

In spite of this gap between the intelligible archetype and its sensuous copy—which means that any given physical change illustrates the conclusions of theoretical science only in proportion as the empirical "elements" concerned *exactly* embody the ideal principle of the tetrahedron, octahedron, etc.—the development of empirical science indicates plainly enough that the general assumption of an underlying identity of the spatial conclusions of theoretical physics and the observed spatial behaviour of sensuous phenomena is justifying itself. Let us consider a few examples. Theoretical physics discovers that three out of the four regular solids are constructed by a principle of organization which terminates always in surfaces compounded of triangles of one and the same type-form (rectangular isosceles). It deduces that these solids, having the same base-form, are relatively interchangeable ; that, under specific pressures, an octahedron or an eikosahedron can be reduced to tetrahedronal form ; or that a number of tetrahedrons can be converted into octahedrons or eikosahedrons ; and, further, theoretical physics establishes exact mathematical ratios between these three forms. So much for pure theory. Sensuous experience shows us " water " being converted into " air " by the action of " fire " in fairly definite proportions which approximate to the calculated proportions in which theoretical eikosahedrons become converted into octahedrons by the action of tetrahedrons.[18] Here is at least a striking analogy. Again, pure theory calculates that, in exact proportion as tetrahedrons and octahedrons are squeezed out of the interstices between eikosahedrons, the eikosahedrons fit together and become uniform, compressed into a closely packed solid mass. Sensuous experience shows us " water," in exact proportion as warmth (" fire ") and " air " are eliminated from it, similarly becoming uniform and packed together into a closely compressed solid mass, namely, " ice."[19] Here is another striking analogy. Again, the tetrahedron is theoretically the smallest, sharpest (most acute-angled), and accordingly most mobile of the mathematical solids, while sensuous experience shows us " fire " as the most " penetrating," most " cutting," and most " rapid " of the recognized empirical elements. The smallest particles, therefore, of which the " fire," " air," " water," and " earth " of Empedoclean science are compounded, are reasonably enough regarded by the Platonist as sensuous images of the tetrahedron, octahedron, eikosahedron, and cube, respectively, of pure theoretical physics.[20]

It would be possible to continue indefinitely in this direction, and to draw innumerable parallels between the conclusions of strictly theoretical science and the observed alterations in the realm of sense-phenomena. In this way we could construct an applied physical science, as a system of deductions grounded in the essential nature of reason and at the same time applying to the empirical world of sensuous experience, deductions both transcendentally and empirically real. Thus grounded, such applied science would be deeper than the mere empiricism of the star-gazing amateur, and might furnish an occupation worthy of the philosopher himself. But such an occupation, though highly intellectual, is regarded by Plato as secondary, as learned trifling suitable for one's leisure hours only. For there is always something fanciful about such parallel illustrations from the empirical world. Sensuous experience is too uncertain, too fluctuating and impermanent, to satisfy the requirements of the idea, and inductive observation is accordingly too infirm as a prop upon which to rest when we seek to explore the field of knowledge and discover new laws. Genuine discoveries are made by the "pure" scientist alone, and the method of pure theoretical science is, not observation, but deduction.[21] The true astronomer ceases to feast his eye upon the starry heavens above, and studies the rational law within, solving problems concerning "pure" motion in mathematical extension, with the aid of circles and tangents.[22] The true student of harmonics withdraws from the ingenious instruments for increasing or lessening the tensions of vibrating strings, with whose aid empirical practitioners dispute about audible differential-tones, and devotes himself to the mathematical solution of problems in purely theoretical harmonics, with relative indifference to the empirical audibility or inaudibility of the pure tones and ideally perfect scales about which he reasons.[23] What is really understood in any such applied science is thus the mathematical or formal element, the principle of triangularity or circularity, with whose aid mind is dealing with direct constructions of its own principle of unification.[24]

So much for Platonic physics, pure and applied, in general outline. We should now be in a position to understand what "mechanical power" means in such a system. The physical universe is regarded as a vast machine constructed by circular motion bringing together elementary solids of definite mathematical types, and "mechanical power" refers to the changes of shape, size, relative position, and motion, of such elements in such a machine. The motive power is transmitted from one solid to another in accordance with mathematically ascertainable and formulatable laws; but, while "mechanical" *qua* within a "machine"-like universe, the circularity and triangularity, in terms of which all details of such power-transmissions are understood, are not themselves mechanical, but mental, and originate from the unifying principle of mind. For the Platonist, then, the ultimate source of mechanical power, and the ultimate principle used in its explanation, is not (as with Democritus) "blind" mechanism, but mind.[25]

(3) *Psychological power.* The nature and development of mind have been treated fully elsewhere.[26] In the present place, therefore, it is necessary only to re-state briefly those portions of the Platonic psychology which bear directly upon the question of power.

The organism of a conscious being is, for Plato, a physical instrument constructed, like all physical instruments, out of elementary physical solids. Unlike most physical objects, however, it is peculiarly adapted to serve as an instrument for the realization of the potentialities of life and mind. Essentially a brain, growing out into a spinal cord which in turn grows out into all parts of the body which, like the brain and cord, are enclosed in bony tissue and are protected from direct contact with the outer world by further outgrowths of somatic tissue, skin, and hair, the human body is constructed entirely out of modified cerebro-spinal organisms. These have a firmly knit structure, compounded out of especially smooth solids of the four regular types, and are controlled by a circular motion, in the sphere-shaped brain, which is precisely analogous to the circular motion of the spherical planets, and to the all-comprehending circular motion of the spherical universe. Circularity being the ideal principle which mind applies to the control of motion, we should expect the motions within the empirical brain and its extensions, so far as these obey the voice of reason, to approximate to this ideal principle. The empirical function of this circular brain-motion is, to control the various movements within the body and eventually to control the movements of the extremities of the body, which are in direct interaction with outside forces. The circular cerebrations thus act as a sort of gyroscope or steadying governor in the mechanism of the bodily movements, and control the subordinate functions of nutrition, growth, and reproduction.[27] And further : movements, whether originating within or without the body, which succeed in penetrating to the circular cerebrations, gives rise, not only to controlled reactions, but also, in certain cases, to sensation. Out of sensations, especially if these conflict and suspend the bodily reaction, arises the further development of the conscious life of mind : the genesis of concepts, of reflective logical standards, and eventually of the principle of conceptuality itself, the ideal of systematic organization, applied not only to intellectual values but also to moral, physical, aesthetical, and religious situations. The life of the mind, when complete self-realization has been attained, consists primarily in the contemplation of concepts in the light of the principle of conceptualization, i.e. consists in a quasi-circular movement in which thought reflects upon itself and its own constructions.[28] It consists, secondarily, in apprehension of the various situations which arise, in assimilation of these to its own ideal principle, i.e. in spreading the " circular " or unifying principle so as to select and concentrate the environmental values, so that these cease to belong to the relative chaos from which they are extracted, and begin to play their part in the building up of the ideal cosmos which is the characteristic creation of mind.[29]

The quasi-circular brain-movements are a material image of the ideal motion of thought in its self-reflective activity, and " psychological power," i.e. the power of mind in its pure contemplation of the ideas, exemplifies itself precisely to the extent to which its body constitutes an instrument so trained as to obey perfectly the central control of the brain of which it is an outgrowth. Via the instrumentality of such a body, a particular mind gradually changes its immediate environment from its relatively chaotic state to a state more nearly expressive of the principle of an ideal cosmos, and thus co-operates with other particular minds, human, stellar, and cosmic, in their common task of administrative guardianship.

(4) *Political power.* Gregariousness, coupled with fear of wild animals and other dangers, induces men to live together in groups. Such groups, under the pressure of further common dangers and needs, both internal and external, naturally develop some kind of central authority, in whose hands the direction of the activities of the community, in peace or in war, is concentrated.[30] Such concentrated authority, the power to direct the activities of the community as a whole, is what is meant by political power. In Platonism it is necessary further to distinguish *de jure* or ideal political power from *de facto* or empirical approximations to ideal political power.

In the Greek city-states of Plato's time, political power was the object of contention on the part of factions, oligarchic or democratic, with the unconstitutional dictator lurking always as a possibility in the background. Such groups, or individuals, if they rise to the direction of community affairs, make the maintenance or continuance of their own power their first aim, exiling or destroying competitors, and legislating always in the narrowly understood interest of their supporters. Thus a democratic government aims, first and foremost, at making the political world safe for the democratic party, appointing deserving democrats to all positions of influence or authority, and carefully excluding from power all oligarchs and aristocrats.[31] *En revanche*, the other parties exclude democrats from all important positions, and fill all offices of state with their own appointees. Knowing, as they do, the difficulty of maintaining themselves permanently in office against consolidating opposition, such parties make the most of their brief hour, and utilize public resources largely for their own purposes, subordinating the interest of the community as a whole to what they understand to be the interest of their own party. Under such a system, the *de facto* community power is wielded by a succession of well-organized minorities, and is seldom, if ever, exercised in the public interest, although, if any party is to maintain itself in office, this power must always be exercised in the apparent interest of the largest and best organized group.[32]

As against these one-sided exercises of political power, Plato develops the logical implications of the part-whole relation. He maintains that the principle of regard for the interests of one's party should be extended so as to cover the whole community, of which the party is only a part. For to plunder the whole in the supposed interest of the part is, ultimately, to destroy the part along with the whole. Ideally speaking, then, political power, the direction of the resources of the community, should consider always the interest of the community as a whole, both in its internal and in its external relations, and should be so exercised as to develop the potentialities of all classes of citizens in the best possible way, consistently with the harmony and unity of the whole.[33] The general principle governing the construction of an ideal community is worked out in the *Republic*, but the " model city " of the *Laws* makes some of the details clearer. There Plato establishes a definite number of citizenships in relation to the normal harvest-value of the land controlled by the group, preserves a suitable ratio between farmer-citizens, artisans, labourers, and professional classes, so arranges the incentives and rewards of work that each class is suitably productive along its own line, and is content to continue rendering its particular contribution to the community. He further corrects all social and economic inequalities, and all irregularities of population and of moral conduct, in such a way as to maintain the " model " community, as a whole, at a standard level of living-value.[34] The creation and preservation of these proportionate relationships implies great natural intelligence and special training on the part of the officials, and, whether we consider the magistrates of the *Republic*, or the " nocturnal council " of the *Laws*, we find that the foundations of political power, in the ideal sense, are always to be laid in intelligence. It is mind, with its organizing principle of so rearranging whatever it handles as to bring out its values in a systematic and unified way, which is, for platonism, the ultimate and only true and abiding source of political power.[35]

(5) *Moral power*. The moral virtues of courage, temperance, and justice are frequently referred to as sources of power, and a careful examination of such passages[36] indicates the sense in which this is understood. Courage has the power of issuing in courageous acts and of making men whose actions are habitually of such a kind, courageous. Temperance issues in temperate acts, and makes the habitual performer of such actions, himself temperate. Justice is similarly a potentiality or disposition residing in the soul, which issues in just acts and makes the habitual performer of such actions, himself just. i.e. each of these virtues is a psychophysical disposition to perform actions of a certain type. By training, this disposition becomes a settled habit, and can be further organized so as to have a social, rather than a merely individual, significance. Pugnacity, e.g. can be converted into military morale in the service of the community and its ideals ; the disposition towards quietness can be converted into the docility and " followership " of the good citizen in relation to the community leaders ; the gregarious disposition can be converted into the virtue of social considerateness which brings about civic union and harmony. The highest development, in each case, comes when insight into the principle of ideality takes the place of social pressure as the formative influence, and the psychophysical dispositions become so reorganized as to furnish an adequate instrumentality for the realization, in the social world, of moral influence and power.[37]

On what does the " power " of these virtues depend ? At the dispositional level, each is an organization of action-tendencies which, if unorganized, would result merely in undirected, spasmodic, and meaningless movements. e.g. pugnacity, the basic disposition underlying courage, is an organization, for purposes of attack, of a number of muscular contractions, increase of respiratory and vaso-motor activity, accelerated heart-beat, etc., co-ordinated by their relation to the thoracal segment of the spinal cord, which grows immediately out of, and acts under the direct control of, the brain.[38] Apart from the co-ordinating mechanism, the grasping tendency of the hand and arm muscles would lead merely to spasmodic contractions, of no purposive significance whatever. So too acceleration of heart-beat and blood-flow, of itself, i.e. unco-ordinated with the other manifestations of pugnacity, would be valueless. It is from the organization of these various functions in the service of a single purpose, that the bodily disposition obtains its power, its ability to produce results in the space-time world. So too if we consider the trained courage of the soldier, grafted upon the pugnacious disposition by the Spartan discipline.[39] It is from the further organization of muscles and action-tendencies which comes from the training, that the courage of the soldier obtains its higher degree of value. And when the final development of philosophical insight into the idea of good comes, so that the individual rallies all his forces to the support of whatever realizes this idea, it is from the further organization brought about by the ideal principle, that moral courage obtains its power. Apart from the direction which comes from the idea of good, courage is of no particular value, and may even be an evil, acting at cross-purposes with the virtues of temperance and justice.[40]

If, then, we may regard courage as typical of the moral virtues, the power of any given virtue depends, primarily, upon the degree of organization of the psychophysical disposition through whose instrumentality the virtue expresses itself ; secondarily, upon the further organization of this disposition in relation to other dispositions which are of moral and social significance ; and, ultimately, upon insight into the ideal principle of organization, which co-ordinates all these dispositions into a single moral influence which represents the idea of good in its social reference.

(6) *Intellectual power.* Sensation, memory, and imagination are faculties which work through definite bodily mechan-

isms. The sense-organs are selective mechanisms which pick out, from the environmental motions, those which have visual, auditory, tactile, etc., significance for the needs of the organism, and convey these, in condensed and concentrated form, to the seat of consciousness.[41] By thus reducing visual, auditory, tactile, etc., stimulations to concentrated unity, these mechanisms carry through a kind of rudimentary generalization, and thus exhibit, so far as such mechanisms can, the principle of ideality which concentrates and unifies meaning-values. Memory is the retention of the sense-percept in a less fluctuating and relatively permanent form, and imagination and " opinion " arise from the synthesis of memory-images with new percepts, in a way which carries further the principle of concentrating and unifying sensuous meanings in the form of empirical generalizations. Out of the conflicts among inconsistent sensuous meanings, arises the standardized intellectual concept, and ultimately the whole formal apparatus of logical methods, categories, and ideals, with clear insight into the nature and implications of formal consistency. This is " dialectic," the final flowering of that pure reason which contemplates the realm of ideas in relation to their principle. This principle lies slumbering in the original sensuous curiosity and dogmatic philodoxy of the average man, and comes to full wakefulness only in the purely rational search after truth which characterizes the philosopher. Intellectual power thus consists in that selection and concentration which gives us, in place of obscure, chaotic, and fluctuating sensations, clearcut ideas whose nature, inter-relations, and principle are entirely apprehensible by mind, and the principle which makes this power possible is the principle of selection and concentration of meaning-values, i.e. the idea of good.[42]

(7) *The ultimate source of power.* If we look over what we have so far investigated, we find that, while changes in the phenomenal world provide the most obvious examples of power-manifestations, such changes are to be understood as sense-perceivable " images " of strictly calculable proportion holding between mathematical entities whose " forms " are ultimately constructed by the unifying principle of mind. The power which regulates and controls phenomenal changes is thus the power of mathematical implication and ultimately of mind, which expresses its own unifying principle in mathematical structures, and creates, out of what would otherwise

be a chaos of meaningless movements, a cosmic system in which all the possibilities of movement are realized, so far as is compatible with the principle of consistent unity. This is true of the astronomical universe, of the individual living organism, of the social organism, of moral and social development. Selective concentration so as to realize the maximum of meaning-value possible within a single universe, is the principle upon which, in all these cases, power depends. This principle, which in each case so selects and concentrates the available meaning-values as to transmute a relative chaos into an organic portion of the ideal cosmos, is the idea of good.

These conclusions must now be compared with the statements which we find in the Dialogues *re* the ultimate source of power, in order to determine whether they are confirmed or whether, perhaps, they require modification.

In the first place, there are many passages which explain that "combining many things into one," i.e. so organizing or arranging elements that they constitute a unified system, is the way in which power is manifested. This is true of the world of nature,[43] of the world of art,[44] of individual development,[45] of social living, whether from a military,[46] or from a civic standpoint,[47] of philosophical development,[48] of heroic and divine government,[49] and of the metaphysical cause.[50] That is to say, the application of this principle of organization, introducing unity, order, and system into what would otherwise be chaotic, is universal in its scope and manifests the operation of genuine power.

In the second place, there are many passages which state unequivocally that "the good" is the ultimate source of power. Thus it is when concerned with the good that love has the greatest power and is the source of happiness and harmony ; it is by their relation to the good that all other things acquire genuine value ; it is the idea of "the best" which God follows in His administration ; and the good is the *ratio cognoscentis*, the *ratio cognoscendi*, and the *ratio essendi*.[51] This "good" is the principle which rearranges the elements of any given situation so as to bring out its utmost of positive value. In a "chaos," the value of each element and of the whole is lost, owing to the absence of order and arrangement. In converting such a chaos into a cosmos, "the good" is the principle of realizing the maximal development of potentiality, (a) of the whole, by so rearranging the elements that they cease to conflict with one another in a purposeless *wirrwarr*, and (b) of each element, which, in such a cosmos, " does its own work," i.e. fulfils its own characteristic function, in the best possible way.[52]   As this is the principle of ideality which selects values and concentrates them into the unity which is an " idea," its universality and objectivity will be apparent without further proof.

A third group of passages states that the soul is the source of power.   This statement is understood in two main senses. In the first place, the soul is the " self-mover," and the world-soul, in particular, originates and maintains the spherical revolution in which all the otherwise irregular motions of pre-cosmic space are gathered together and reduced to an orderly texture of movements, thus giving rise to a physical " image " of the ideal system of interacting mathematical solids, and so creating the system of celestial mechanics in which mechanical power is manifested.[53]   The star-souls similarly revolve upon their axes, approximating, as far as possible, to the regular revolutions of the world-soul, and the human souls, in their turn, regulate their cerebrations, as well as they can, according to the patterns set by the stars, from which they have descended and to which they may one day return.   That is to say, the physical universe is regarded as a sphere in which an organized hierarchy of souls perform " each his own work " of converting the otherwise chaotic environment into an organic portion of the ideal, all-embracing cosmic system, in which all is directed by the purpose of realizing maximal spiritual value.[54]   In the second place, soul, defined as a " cause endowed with mind, which works things fair and good," is thought of mainly as the spatial spear-head of mind, so that it is mind which is ulti-mately the ruling power, the true master-creator in the uni-verse.[55]   Understood as a spatial organism by whose means mind operates in the empirical universe, the soul is regarded as " naturally improving and governing the body," and the philosopher-kings are entrusted with supreme social power, as being especially prepared " souls " who are to govern and improve the human flock entrusted to their care.   The study of philosophy thus becomes an essential part of the education of all souls intended to wield such social power.[56]

The above three groups of passages, looked at more closely, are seen to be three ways of expressing one and the same meaning.   The ultimate source of power, for Platonism, is mind applying its inherent principle of " the good " to an environment which, apart from such reorganization, is chaotic and valueless, but, when so reorganized, constitutes a systematic totality in which the greatest quantity and quality of value of which it is susceptible is realized. This mind is at times referred to as " God," " Zeus," and " the ultimate cause " ; but, whatever its name, it coincides in all respects with the principle of selection and concentration of meaning-values which we have seen to be at work in the astronomical, organic, moral, social, and intellectual realms, and the passages now studied thus confirm our earlier conclusions, without significant modification.

(8) *The realizability of power.* How far can mind convert chaos into cosmos ? Does Platonism solve this problem entirely, at least in principle, so that any untransmuted residuum is to be explained as a mere factual detail, a fluctuating sensuous variation which will some day be reduced without remainder to law and order, a " particular " which will be completely resolved into a nexus of strictly intelligible " universals," a " brute fact " which will some day lose its " brutish " and factual character, and be completely made over into " value " ? Many Plato-students say, yes : the problem is solved finally, at least in principle. The ideal world is the complete and ultimate truth of the empirical world of everyday experience. After the principle of ideality has " done its work," nothing remains over, and the picture of a precosmic chaos is an imaginary, mythical creation of Plato's genius, poetically suggestive but with no ultimate scientific status.[57] An idealism like Plato's, which is " one long dialogue with materialism," and has finally resolved " matter " into " not-being,"[58] cannot logically concede the existence of an essentially non-ideal residuum. Mind can only admit the existence of mind as ultimate, unless it wishes to commit intellectual suicide.

In this difficulty, let us turn to the evidence in the Dialogues. The individual character is built up on a basis of mechanisms which are instinctive, the " necessary " appetites concerned with hunger, thirst, and sex, as well as a more general tendency to seek organ-gratifications for the sake of the " pleasure " involved.[59] These, like all bodily mechanisms, are primarily instrumentalities for the selective concentration, (a) of the stimuli concerned with these needs, and (b) of the appropriate reactions, and thus exhibit, at the physical level, the principle of "the good." Although exemplifying this principle, they are, however, somewhat primitive and tend, with most men, to remain primitive. In fact, we find in the Dialogues what look like two different attitudes towards these mechanisms. On the one hand, it is stated roundly that they cannot be sublimated. They constitute a lawless, wild-beast element in our nature which is innate, very extensive, and highly complex.[60] Of this "concupiscent" element, some portions can be tamed and educated, but other portions can not, because these have no share in reason and consequently are deaf to rational appeals and unable to appreciate rational motives.[61] It is possible to interfere forcibly with the growth of these irrational portions of the soul, but it would be unreasonable to expect active co-operation on their part, or even passive acquiescence.[62] If left to themselves, they tend inevitably toward uncontrolled excess, i.e. to gluttony, intoxication, and lust, in a way which ruins the organism which they use as their instrument.[63]

Irrational as these appetites are, it is, however, still possible to do something with them. Force has been mentioned. A man can abstain totally from rich cakes, from the second bottle, and from Syracusan and Corinthian indulgences. His motive may be hedonistic, social, medical, philosophical, or simply miserly ; but enforced abstinence is perfectly possible, and tends eventually to weaken the strength of his irrational appetites. If, however, to an irrational impulse an equally irrational force is opposed, as when a man abstains from one sort of indulgence mainly in order to secure another sort, or merely to avoid the expense, no real progress is made. To exchange one indulgence for another is a species of barter by which no one ever acquires genuine mastery over his appetites.[64] Social pressure, again, can do something. The institution of community meals introduces a social control which refuses to tolerate gluttony and drunkenness, and at least discourages undue interest in the flute-girls. Laws against immoderate wealth and dishonourable excesses, physical hygiene and the inculcation of traditions of temperance and self-control, with proper regard for the higher values, can do more.[65] So, too, much can be done by a strictly medical regimen. At its lowest, this is nothing better than force— the unreasoning commands and prohibitions suitable, possibly,

in dealing with slaves—and to Plato it always seems that there
is something slavish in having to yield up one's free-born right
of self-determination to the prescriptions of a medical tech-
nician, with his crude use of knives, hot irons, and nauseating
drugs.[66] At its best, however, medical treatment deals with
mind as well as body, reasons upon causes and effects, and
educates the patient as a whole. At this level, medical science
passes over imperceptibly into philosophy ; and, as disease
is normally the consequence of bodily excesses, it would appear
that education and philosophy can do much with the bodily
impulses. For the reasoning upon causes and effects terminates in an attempt to reorganize the bodily impulses so that
they constitute an approximation to an ideal whole, in which
each impulse secures its appropriate quantity and quality of
gratification, consistently with the similar gratification of
every other impulse in a totality in which the maximum of
positive value is being realized.[67]

If this is true, then either the primitive impulses are
completely repressed or at least redirected *ab extra*, or else
they do, after all, contain sufficient of a rational element to be
appealed to on rational grounds and taken up into the rational
life, not as so much crude lumber, mechanically necessary but
spiritually null, but as an organic portion of the life of reason.
Health, which depends upon observing a law of rational
proportion in one's eating, drinking, exercising, and resting,
realizes to a maximal extent, the potential values of the body,
and thus certainly exhibits the fundamental principle of " the
good " ; but for our present purposes it is necessary to decide
whether this principle is introduced wholly *ab extra*, or whether
it is internal and belongs intrinsically to the " motion " of
which such activities as eating, exercising, and resting are
specific determinations.

It is difficult to establish Plato's meaning with certainty
here. Eating, drinking, etc., like all physical mechanisms,
exemplify to some extent the principle of selective concentration resulting in the maximal realization of potentiality,
and indeed clearly derive their efficiency and power from this
principle ; for it prevents their motions from being so irregular
and disorderly as to interfere with the proper development of
the organism as a whole.[68] And further : the elementary
triangles and the texture of motions out of which all bodily
forms are constructed plainly exhibit the working of the same

principle. It might well seem, then, that " the good " is the sole source of power, wherever and however manifested, and as though, in consequence, any mechanism which derives its efficiency from this principle must be inherently susceptible of obedience to the idea of good, and is thus to be regarded as intrinsically rational. But, on the other hand, there is so much evidence in the Dialogues that " the good " is an essentially transcendental principle, to which this world, at best, can only furnish a physical analogon, an " image " which definitely falls short of its "archetype," that we must, in the end, conclude otherwise. The passages which state that there is something " incapable of reason " in our bodily impulses, and that ideals can never be entirely realized in this empirical world, [69] cannot be explained away. They are plainly meant to be taken seriously. So too the pre-cosmic irregularities of the *Timaeus* are not purely fanciful, but indicate, in spite of the efforts of most commentators to explain them away, an inherent incapacity of the pre-cosmic constituents of motion to take on more than the external surfaces and main directions of the ideal cosmos. Behind those surfaces and within the main streamings of motion there lurks always something which is not quite tamed, a barbarism which is not quite hellenized. The universal laws are obeyed, but beneath the serene appearance of universality and reason there exists always something which remains particular, a-logical, primitive, chaotic. [70] The universe can never be so completely transmuted that it can be trusted to run itself, but the ideal stands continually in need of active service and spiritual co-operation in its " undying conflict with the forces of evil."[71]

Power, then, or the creation of value by the best possible reorganization of what otherwise remains chaotic, is an eternal process. It has no end which can be completely realized. As Plato puts it, " there must always remain something which is antagonistic to good." It is, however, the idealistic spirit which gives meaning to every activity in which life expresses itself, and is most completely found in the life of research and administration exemplified by the philosopher-king, the hero or demi-god, the deities of Greek mythology, and the Master-workman who is the eternal Father of all. In the co-operative conversion of fact into value, each individual expresses the principle which is the source of power, and his life so far, and so far only, acquires genuine significance. Taken universally, then, "power" is the principle of "the good" in the process of self-realization, and is thus identical with the highest good in relation to a world which is in time. In relation to such a world, however, no final end can be attained. The process of such power-exercise is unending.

CHAPTER XV

HAPPINESS, AND ITS ETHICAL VALUE

THAT all men naturally and inevitably desire happiness, and that the term "happiness" is somehow final as a formulation of the object of desire, has only to be mentioned in the Dialogues to secure immediate and universal acquiescence. But as to what constitutes this happiness which all desire, opinions differ. All believe that happiness comes from the acquisition or possession of good things, but as to what things are good, and how far, and why, there is little agreement. Many seek happiness by the road which simply acquires as much and as many as possible of such "goods" as real estate, fine houses and furnishings, fine clothes and foreign travel, with all the luxuries and friendships which money can purchase.[1] Others seek their happiness by a more explicitly psychological or physiological road, eating, drinking, and love-making in such a way as to make of their lives one sensuous gratification after another, using their bodily organisms as seives or channels for the passage of a maximal number of such gratified stimulations.[2] Others, again, seek happiness by way of power and leadership in the community, with the idea that members of the inner ring which controls policies are able to do what they wish without restraint from others, and that happiness somehow comes to those who are free to do whatever they desire. To those who follow this pathway, some quasi-Napoleonic figure, such as Archelaus or the "great" king of Persia, represents the type of happiness.

The Platonist, however, regards all such roads, as commonly understood, as failing to lead one, with perfect sureness, to anything worthy the name of happiness. It is perfectly possible for a man to acquire a fine house and all that goes with it, and still to miss happiness. On the other hand, it is equally possible for a man to have no private possessions, but to live "as men do in a camp," and, in spite of the absence of such possessions, to attain to the highest human happiness. So too it is possible to pass one's life in the Sicilian style, revelling and banqueting and titillating every sense one has, and yet never to attain to anything truly worth while. On the other hand, it is equally possible never to imbibe large quantities of wine, or to taste Attic confectionery, or to visit the damsels of Corinth, and yet to live the happiest of human lives. So again, in the third place, it is not only possible to live a quasi-Napoleonic life without being really happy, but Plato attempts to demonstrate that, in proportion as he succeeds in grasping the reins of power, the irresponsible dictator becomes progressively less happy until he reaches the acme of human misery. On the other hand, it is perfectly possible for a man never to commit a single act of arbitrary power, and still be a pattern of human happiness. The suggested methods of attaining happiness have, therefore, omitted something from their calculations, and that something is the matter of character. To the man who is himself " good," such things as food and drink, possessions, and leadership may be true goods, that is to say, may be taken up into his life and constitute organic portions of the ideal life, whereas to the man who is not himself " good," such things may turn out to be evils, and may bring misfortune and ruin upon their possessor.[3]

Let us consider more closely what is meant by calling a man " good." In the first place, he must be temperate or self-controlled. The temperate life runs less to excess, whether in pleasure or in pain, than the intemperate life, and on the whole has a favourable balance of pleasure. It is also superior in rectitude or excellence, and in reputation. The Dialogues consistently maintain that this victory over the passions is essential to happiness, and that, the more self-controlled a man is, the more happy he will be.[4] The temperance in question may be the social virtue which comes from habit and attention, independently of philosophical reflection. This helps to perfect our innate love of the good, and makes for social friendliness and harmony, and easily expands into justice and religion.[5] This temperance, however, which is based merely upon habit, unless expanded so as to include wisdom also, is not perfectly satisfactory. It may invite aggression from rough neighbours, or may at all events lead to a species of smugness which abstains from certain forms of pleasure mainly in order to obtain a greater amount of other pleasures, and thus hardly rises above the level of hedonistic psychology to the genuinely ethical level.[6] For its full development, then, as an element in the ideally good character, temperance needs the enlightened guidance of wisdom or philosophical insight.

In the second place, courage is a necessary element in character. This is based upon the psychological disposition toward pugnacity, and is developed by habit and training into the Spartan type of morale, which faces death upon the battlefield in defence of the community and its ideals. To the Greek mind, this is the typical expression of courage, but in the Dialogues it is always pointed out that battlefields represent only one out of the many occasions when courage may be and should be exercised. In perils by water, in sickness, and a thousand such occasions, in pleasures no less than in pains, even in such activities as judging a public dramatic contest, there is need of manly resolution and strength of character.[7] For the finest development of this virtue, something more than habitual discipline is needed, viz., wisdom or philosophical insight into values. For the highest kind of courage is the strength of character which supports " the good " in its undying conflict with the forces of evil, including among these forces certain secret places in one's own character no less than the assaults of openly declared enemies.[8]

How is this connected with happiness ? The character which is devoid of resolution is unable to make headway against temptation, whether from without or from within, and falls an easy prey to every suggestion of pleasure-pain, and his life is a succession of battles in which he always loses, a succession of moral failures. Here a pleasure is enjoyed, there a pain is avoided, but always his personality is infirm of purpose and suffers degradation. Part of Plato's picture of the misery which attends irresponsible power applies here, although in the whole picture other vices, as well as cowardice, are present. On the other hand, strength of character used in the service of the higher values makes life consistent and purposeful, superior to momentary temptations no less than to fears, and by its aid our life acquires unity, rectitude, and genuine significance in the ideal scheme of things. But these are obviously organic elements of the happy life.[9]

In the third place, justice is an essential element in the

character of the good man. Man is a social animal and finds satisfaction in community living, as such. He ceases to live as a mere individual, and learns to live as a member of the group, bound to his fellow-members by all the ties, whether of pleasure or of duty undertaken and shared in common, which community living involves. Social pressure urges each citizen to undertake some definite function in the community life, whether as producer or distributor or as official, and to devote his chief powers to his chosen work. It also urges him to refrain from meddling with the work of his fellow-citizens who are undertaking other functions, either by direct interference or indirectly by undertaking a multiplicity of functions and setting himself up as a competitor.[10] With most men, social virtue is a matter of habit and social pressure, but it is possible also to guide one's social activities by direct philosophical insight into the rationale of group life ; to regard, i.e. the work which one does as a citizen as definitely one's chosen activity, the free and joyous realization of one's own potentialities as a citizen of the ideal community envisaged by the intellect as the goal toward which progressive actual communities are trying to work their way. This intelligent development of his potentialities for community service on the part of the individual himself includes both resolution of character and restraint or self-mastery, and constitutes justice in the full sense.[11]

Thus understood, justice or social virtue is very closely connected with happiness. The just citizen not only realizes his own potentialities in a harmonious way and is thus at peace with himself, but also enjoys the comradeship which links together all good men, and is at peace with his fellows. That is to say, he not only lives the kind of life which he has freely chosen, but, if he is thoroughly at one with the ideals of his fellow-citizens, he also enjoys the undeniable pleasures which belong to the social side of life. He is at home in the actual, no less than in the ideal universe, and, so far as these tend to coincide, he succeeds in living the naturally happiest and fittest of the lives which are humanly possible.[12]

Social happiness is always dependent upon justice or social virtue. Some men attempt to live an anti-social, individualistic life, giving no positive service themselves, and robbing the community of some of the contributions of its other citizens. This is injustice. If, now, social pressure, e.g. in the form of legal condemnation and punishment, succeeds in restoring to such a man his value-sense, so that, after making restitution, he devotes himself to the positive duties of citizenship, he too attains to a measure of the happiness enjoyed by the perfectly righteous man. To precisely the same level he can never attain, because the consequences of his former misdeeds inevitably place him in a different position toward himself no less than toward the community.[13] If, however, on the other hand, he succeeds in maintaining his position above the law, and succeeds in escaping punishment and repentance, such an individualist lives an unhappy life. With the forces in the community which make for orderly and constitutional government he is necessarily in a state of permanent warfare. His only friends are the other anti-social elements in the community and his foreign mercenaries, in whom he can repose no real confidence. And finally, he is not at peace with himself. The elements within him which make for law and order are kept down by the *force majeure* of some powerful appetite, and he is headed straight for psychological, as well as for moral, chaos. Alienated from himself, no less than from his fellow-citizens and from the ideal realm which is the only source of abiding satisfaction, his life, even though he may succeed in overcoming each external obstacle as it arises, is, as a whole, a complete failure, and he is necessarily, not happy, but supremely miserable.[14]

In the fourth place, holiness or a sense of religious values constitutes an integral portion of the good character. This, like justice, is a social excellence, expressing man's relation, however, not so much toward his fellow-men as such, as toward spiritual beings generally, and particularly toward the community representatives of the spiritual life, such as the gods of the established religion. At the same time, the religious attitude of worship and service is clearly extended to include national heroes, who lived and died in the service of the community ideals, and even certain living men, such as parents and " divinely inspired " persons such as poets, prophets, lawgivers, and priests.[15] And further, in view of the fact that most civil and criminal offences in the model community are associated with specific punishments for impiety in addition to the civic penalties, it appears that the religious attitude, in the City of God, is intended to cover the observance of law generally, and that all occasions of life, including not merely birth, education, marriage, sickness, and death, but commercial, judicial, and social relations, are, for the Platonist, within the scope of the religious value-judgment.[16] It is thus hardly correct to define Platonic holiness as a part of justice, i.e. the part concerned with the gods as distinct from the part concerned with one's fellow-citizens, justice in the wider sense being understood as complete social virtue.[17] The general position of the *Laws* is rather that religion is the more inclusive concept, and applies to all the relations of life, while justice is rather a civic support of the religious value-judgment, enforcing with the organized power of the community the decrees which the religious man naturally accepts and which it is impious to disobey. It is thus more correct to regard justice and religion as closely allied. Justice, i.e. social virtue resting upon the organized power of the community, passes over into religion when the community is regarded as the earthly reflex of the ideal pattern laid up in heaven ; and religion, i.e. the attitude of acceptance and worship of ideal powers, passes over into justice when it becomes necessary to deal with men who refuse to recognize the religious sanctions of the unseen world.

How is this religious attitude connected with happiness ? The religious man regards himself as the servant of God in all his thoughts, words, and actions, and endeavours, as far as in him lies, to assimilate himself to God, to develop the divine element within him until it dominates his whole nature, and he becomes as like God as a human being can.[18] In so doing, he fulfils the function assigned to humanity in the divine plan, co-operating with God in applying the idea of good to the idealization of his limited environment. The divine plan applies the idea of good to the whole, realizing for each part its maximum of positive well-being in relation to the other parts and to the whole, and man, so far as he fulfils the function assigned to him, attains to his maximum of positive well-being, i.e. attains to as much of happiness, both here and hereafter, as a human being well can.[19] The impious man may seem for a time to be successful here below, but he is not at home in the ideal realm, and ultimately has no part or lot in the ideal whole toward the realization of which all things which have a share of positive reality are gradually working together ; whereas the righteous soul becomes more and more adapted to its true, ideal home, and dwells eternally, as Plato puts it, in the company of the gods, secure of happiness.[20]

Finally, wisdom or philosophical insight forms an in-gredient in the good character. This is the most divine element in man, the eye of the soul which develops, not by bodily *askesis*, but by intellectual exercises which gradually liberate it from all bodily interferences, whether from the sense-organs or from the emotions, until it envisages, as clearly as may be, the intellectual realm of the ideas from one end to the other, and rises to the contemplation of the principle of ideality itself, as the principle of realizing, in every concrete situation, its maximum of significance and value in relation to the whole. Grasping the finality of this principle, and its identity with the divine principle in accordance with which the cosmos is created and ordered, the wise man devotes himself to making over his habitual ways of thinking and acting. This he does until the pugnacious dispositions which characterize his organism develop into ideal fortitude and resolution, his dispositions toward quietness and avoidance of excitement develop into ideal temperance and self-moderation, his social feelings develop into ideal justice, his instinctive feelings toward superhuman forces develop into the ideal religious attitude, and his instinctive inquisitiveness develops into ideal science and philosophy.[21] When all the dispositions inherent in his organism have thus become enlightened and raised, as nearly as possible, to the ideal level, his whole life, in detail as well as in principle, becomes gradually instinct with wisdom, not only in relation to his own organism, but also in relation to his social and physical environment. In every situation which arises, whether in his public or in his private relations, he now brings to bear a group of action-tendencies which have been so developed as to produce the ideally most suitable and most valuable reaction of which the circumstances admit.

Thus understood, wisdom is very definitely related to happiness. The so-called goods of life, viz., wealth, noble birth, health, good looks, power and honour in the community, are apt to confuse our judgment and make us think that they are good in themselves and that we cannot have too much of them. The wise man, however, after due reflection, comes to the conclusion that in themselves they are neither good nor bad, but that, human nature being what it is, not only too little of such " goods," but also too much is an evil, and that, as is obvious in the case of eating and drinking, in all external good the mean state, something between the two extremes, represents what is best for us, if we are to live a happy life. Further, the use of such goods, even in such moderate amounts, must always be controlled by wisdom, and this is true, not only of external goods, but also of all moral and mental qualities.[22] It follows, that, ultimately, the wisest and the happiest lives coincide in all respects ; for wisdom consists in so living as to extract from all the elements which enter into our experience, their maximal value, and happiness consists precisely in the life of maximal well-being, i.e. the life which realizes the greatest possible quantity and quality of true value.

The type of the ideally happy man, for Platonism, is thus, not Croesus, Napoleon, or the *viveur*, but the philosophic guardian, i.e. a member of the " golden " class living and working in the ideal community depicted in the *Republic* and approved in the *Laws*. Born under eugenically as well as morally ideal conditions, and so trained from the moment of birth as to develop all his faculties, aesthetic, moral, religious, and intellectual, in the service of a community which is envisaged as patterned upon the divine model, the philosophic guardian becomes the human embodiment of the idea of good, the channel through which this divine principle moulds both individual and community into the semblance of divinity and thus makes real upon earth the kingdom whose pattern is laid up in heaven. The life which such a man lives is a human pattern of the happy life, and the legislation in which he gives concrete expression to his insight into the ideal principle serves as a human standard, both for judges who administer that legislation and for private citizens who are seeking the way of happiness.[23]

The superhuman pattern of happiness closely resembles this human model, with its two sides of philosophic contemplation and administrative guardianship. The good man who, after bodily death, is translated to the abode of intermediate spirits—goes aloft to rule a star, as Plato puts it—carries on the same function of administrative guardianship. Freed from the sensuous haziness and emotional confusion of earthly experience, his vision of the ideas is more clear and more sure. Contemplation, however, even of the idea of good, does not content him. He proceeds, as before, to apply this idea in the sphere of activity suitable to his state of existence, and, in proportion to the improvement in his powers of insight, his administrative guardianship shows improvement. On earth, his control over motion was uncertain and irregular. In his new sphere, his control over stellar motions is certain and regular, so regular, in fact, that these motions furnish a pattern to guide and correct the irregularities of spirits who are still earth-bound.[24] His happiness, like his activity, is thus still the happiness of a philosophic guardian. And if we look higher, at the life of the gods depicted poetically in Plato's pages, we find it a further extension of the same ideal. The lesser gods are represented as essentially ministers appointed to apply the idea of good to some particular section of the cosmic system. Their powers of contemplation of the eternal ideas are, no doubt, greater, but what they learn in such contemplation they apply to doing " each his own work " of administrative guardianship.[25] Full justice is done to the administrative side of this divine activity in the further demonstration that the gods do not live an idle life, neglecting the spiritual universe which they have helped to create, and even in the case of the entity represented in Platonic literature as *Deus summus*, i.e. the Master-artificer of the *Timaeus*, there is no question that his activity is fundamentally administrative, the application of the idea of good to the cosmos in general, the details being left to his ministers.[26] The blessed life, then, in which gods and men share, consists in applying the principle of ideality to the gradual elevation of the less ideal elements in the environment until they, too, are fitted to take their appointed place in the ideal plan which realizes the greatest possible quantity and quality of value. The happy life is, in brief, the principle of " the good " in conscious, self-directed activity.

One difficulty remains to be explained. In certain moods, Plato writes as though the two aspects of (1) contemplation and (2) administrative guardianship were diverse, and it cannot be denied that the expressions of this mood have worked themselves into many characteristic Platonic passages. Thus it is the external enforcement of the community which is said to induce the philosopher to leave his beloved seclusion and apply himself to the ungrateful task of educating the beasts in the den into some semblance of humanity. His sense of justice accepts their verdict, but only because he owes his education to the community.[27] If he had somehow succeeded in obtaining his liberating education by himself, or by the aid of his family or of some teacher, independently of community assistance, it is very directly implied that he would have been justified in refusing the position of administrator, or that, at best, his motive in accepting would have been in order to avoid being misgoverned by someone not adequately educated in political science.[28]   The many passages conceived in this vein are logically inconsistent with the depiction of the divine nature and goodness as essentially devoid of envy and as of itself so acting as to make the rest of the world good, in its own image.   The spirit of goodness of course overflows into good actions.[29]   So too they are inconsistent with the demonstration, in the *Laws*, that the gods are not idle and neglectful of human concerns, living a life apart.   What one would expect, after studying the logic of the Platonic position, is that insight into the idea of good would, of itself, lead to the idea working itself out in action, and would thus bring about an acceptance, freely and from self-determined motives, of the tasks of administrative guardianship.   An educated man, in so far as he is educated, inevitably spreads education around him.   To do so is the free, self-determined expression of his nature.   To withdraw into selfish seclusion, and to use his powers for the good of the community only upon external compulsion or when appeals are made to his economic or political interests, is to fall short of the ideal of education. Like Achilles sulking in his tent, he makes one doubt whether he has really beheld the vision, and one can understand his position only by assuming the presence of certain " human " weaknesses, i.e. certain still unidealized elements, in his character.   A completely ideal guardian would of course act ideally, and would not withold his services.

By Platonic happiness, then, we shall understand the logical consequence of the Platonic position as a whole, i.e. the life which devotes itself, freely and joyously, to the maximal development of the value-potentialities in itself and in the environment, in accordance with the ideal vision.   The philosophic vision is a dialectical apprehension of the principle of value, as the principle of bringing to light, in every concrete situation of life, its maximum of value in harmonious, consistent, systematic unity with the other values of life.   For the application of this vision to the actual details of empirical living, experience is needed, an experience partly sensuous,[30] but chiefly, for Platonism, an experience which, by the processes of analysis, comparison, and standardization, has been raised to the level of scientific psychology, both individual and social. Such situations as are involved in low birth, or in high birth, in a typical Hellenic community, such situations as are involved in robust health, or in chronic invalidism, such situations as are involved in the possession of great wealth, or in subjection to actual poverty—these, and a hundred other typical situations, are separated out by analysis, and their consequences for the development of the soul are carefully considered, both in isolation and in circumstances involving combination with other similar situations. The general conclusion from such a study is that, in the case of all natural and acquired gifts of the soul, the extremes of excess and deficiency are to be avoided, and the mean state is to be pursued : for this is the way of happiness.[31] Excess in such natural gifts, physical, moral, and intellectual, leads almost inevitably to insolence, self-importance, and an arrogant assumption of superiority which, as in the notorious case of Alcibiades, culminates in disorder and downright injustice, with their usual harvest of contentions and hatreds.[32] Deficiency in such gifts leads, on the contrary, to meanness and a quasi-slavish poverty of spirit, from which nothing of genuine value is to be expected.

Psychological determinations, however, while important in their place, viz., in connection with working out the concrete details of the happy life, do not, of themselves, explain the principle of that life. The search for pleasures which are constituted out of organ-satisfactions, as such, is of merely subjective significance, empty and meaningless when out of touch with that reality which alone gives meaning and value to the functioning of our psychophysical mechanisms. The life of philosophical guardianship, on the other hand, is rich in satisfactions which are throughout controlled by contact with objective reality. This life attains to reality in the fullest sense, and derives its own reality and value from the idea of value, the ultimate principle which enables the human guardian to bring out the value-aspects of all elements in his own character and in the social and physical milieu in which he has been stationed by the Divine Guardian. In this " blessed " life, pleasure is indeed an element, but not a constituent element, as such. In Aristotelian terminology, pleasure is an inseparable accident (or even a property) of the blessed life, but does not constitute its essence. Its essence is constituted by the idea of good, the ultimate principle of value.

Platonic happiness is thus primarily of metaphysical, rather than psychological, significance. It remains to ask in what sense it is of ethical significance, in what sense it constitutes a " highest " good. The answer to this question consists in showing (1) that nothing else, such as possessions, pleasure, or power, can be conceived as an essential constituent of the ideal life, and (2) that the blessed or happy life just considered represents the good life par excellence, the best and finest life which our thought can construct, a life which is the idea of good itself, so far as this can be realized in our psychophysical mechanisms, and that, in idea, the " blessed " life and the ideal life coincide in all respects. The ethical life, e.g. seeks to realize value ; but what could be more valuable than the life which consistently realizes the maximal value-potentialities of its organism, and applies the principle of value itself in all its thoughts, words, and works ? The ethical life seeks a firm basis in objective values ; but what life could be more firmly based than the life which rests upon the principle of ultimate reality and forms itself entirely upon the nature of the world which is real in the deepest sense ? So too the ethical life seeks spirituality ; but what life could be more spiritual than the life which assimilates itself reverently to what reason reveals as the nature of the divine, and thus enters, as directly as may be, into the divine life itself ? Whatever point of view one takes, one finds that the " blessed " life depicted by Plato satisfies the demands of the ethical ideal, and the final conclusion which we reach is that Platonic " happiness " and the ethically ideal life are completely coincident.

CHAPTER XVI

IMMORTALITY, AND ITS ETHICAL VALUE

TO the average Hellene of Plato's time, no less than to the average modern civilized man, life as he found it seemed good. He too had his instincts to drive him on to found a family, acquire a residence, fine clothing, friends, servants, a bank account, and the means of travel and enjoyment of beauty, whether natural or artificial. He too had a dash of poetry in his composition, and an interest in the things of the mind, which coloured his otherwise sensuous disposition and made his grasping after pleasure and power seem a less crude thing than it appears to more critical eyes. If he thought at all about physical death and a possible after-life, his mental processes were vague and a little discouraging. The religious traditions created by his poets had it that there was an after-life, but so pale, bloodless, and shadowy, that the gibbering ghosts in the realm of shades would give anything for the meanest position on the " real " earth.[1] In addition to tradition, the ancient Hellene, like the modern inquirer, had, of course, his spiritualism, particularly if he could afford to pay for it. But if he was of a thoughtful turn of mind, he found this unsatisfying ; for its messages seemed to be either a naïve tribute to his position and power and supposed desires, promising an eternity of feasting and merry-making, or else were so obscure and uncertain as to task the powers of trained experts to find an interpretation of them.[2] Of one thing only he was sure : that life as he knew it through his senses and emotions was good ; and that, if he were to look for a " highest " good, this could be found only in more of what he knew to be good, *i.e.*, in continuing to satisfy his senses and emotions, possibly in a somewhat more artistic way. Everything else was uncertain tradition or poetic fiction, to be taken seriously only by those unfortunates who had come face to face with the thought that they must die and leave this pleasant place.[3]

To the Platonist, however, such a view of life, whether in this world or in the next, appears grotesquely distorting. Sensuous emotion, with its many-facetted interplay of lights and shadows, even when guided by the artistry of a great rhetorician, such as Homer and his fellow-poets, or Pericles and his fellow-statesmen, is, after all, a thing of surfaces, all lengths and breadths, but with nothing behind in which the intellect can rest. And the thought which cannot penetrate to something deeper than mere continuity of such existence, has hardly begun to discover the real surface of the problem of immortality. Such unreflective mental processes, in fact, scarcely reach the level one would expect of an adult human being, but represent little more than protracted adolescence posing as the central thing in life. In such matters, the average Hellene, like the average modern, refuses to grow up. He remains in a play-world of images. But to the Platonist it is plain that, without sustained philosophical reflection, the true depths of life cannot even be suspected, much less scientifically sounded ; and it follows that all such illusions of the image-world are resolutely to be put on one side.[4]

What, then, does Platonism understand by immortality ? It is, of course, an " idea." The easiest way of approach to its meaning is to say that it is the kind of life lived by the " immortals," i.e. the kind of life lived by Zeus, Hera, Athene, and the other gods, and shared in, though to a slightly lesser extent, by the demigods recognized by Greek mythology. We shall proceed to examine the chief characteristics of this life of the immortals, and shall then ask how far it realizes the absolute idea of immortality, and, finally, how far human beings can partake of this absolute idea.

" The kind of life lived by the immortals " is a phrase which suggests different things to different men. To the student of Homer and Hesiod, " the immortals " live a very human sort of life, quarrelling, love-making, revelling, laughing, dreading and deceiving one another, and keeping up perpetual intrigues on behalf of the causes or persons whom they regard, quite capriciously, with favour. Sometimes they resemble a group of sportive nobles at the court of some " merrie monarch " of human history. At other times, they are far more like a group of children who have been " naughty," and wonder what the All-father will do to them, when he finds out what they have accomplished in his absence. They are distinguished from human beings in two ways :— (1) By their greater relative power, and (2) by the fact that they are deathless and ageless, and seem to enjoy perpetual youth or perpetual maturity. The student of Homer has no hope that men will ever, except under the rarest of circumstances, enjoy this kind of immortality. Kings and nobles can imitate it in their life on earth, but after death the greatest and noblest of them seem to pass to the realm of pale phantoms, which appears as the fitting reverse to the picture of the immortals.[5]

To platonism, " the life of the immortals " suggests something very different. The immortals, as the philosopher understands them, constitute a perfect society, in which quarrels, intrigues, deceit, and any kind of friction are entirely out of place. Each has his own work to do, and fulfils his especial function in harmonious co-operation with the rest.[6] The inspiration for this work is drawn from contemplation of the eternal ideas in the intellectual place, which lies altogether outside the merely physical universe. It is especially the ideas of courage, temperance, holiness, justice, and wisdom which inspire them. These ideas they contemplate with a clearness and steadiness unknown to mortals, and feed on them in their hearts with joy and thankfulness, deriving from this nourishment the renewal and refreshment of their spiritual life.[7] The divine essence is, in fact, precisely holiness, justice, and wisdom—which means that the acts of such beings are always patterns of virtuous action. They act always in accordance with the principle of " the best," i.e. realize, in every situation, its maximum of possible value ; for the divine plan, in general, is so to act as to reduce the many to the principle of the one, i.e. to construct, out of the relatively chaotic universe, a single systematic totality of elements in which there is a definite place for each element, and each element realizes its maximal value-potentialities in harmonious co-operation with all the rest. It is by reorganization, re-arrangement of the elements in question so that barren conflict and conditions which interfere with the development of potentiality are removed, that progress is made towards the ideal value-system.[8] At the same time, while so acting, they are not turning themselves into slaves to some external power, but are living out their own innermost nature, in free self-determination. The living principle of justice, considered as a principle of action, of itself, and without external compulsion of any kind, issues in just acts, as the love of beauty, which guides the hand of the artist from within, issues in beautiful art-works. So too the living principle of holiness issues in actions which are holy, the principle of wisdom in actions which are wise, and, speaking generally, the divine principle of " the best " issues naturally and freely in the direction of realizing the divine plan.[9] In realizing this plan, then, the divine spirit is realizing itself, and the natural overflow of the divine spirit upon men and upon the world gradually forms men and the world more nearly according to the divine pattern and spirit. The world becomes more orderly and better adapted to furnish the environment and temporal home of spiritual life ; and human beings, under the divine influence, tend to become more holy, just, and wise. That is to say, immortality, understood as the life of the immortals, tends, in accordance with its own essential principle, to share itself unenviously with mortals, so far as these are capable of entering into the divine heritage offered to them.[10]

One way of explaining this is to say that the immortals are essentially creative. They create order out of disorder, beauty out of ugliness, cosmos out of chaos, and so rearrange what is without value, in its particular context, as to bring value into being, a value which is not merely the value of the elements rearranged, but is at the same time the divine value, or an approximation to the divine value. That is to say, the principle of immortality issues in, or creates, immortality. All values originate with the immortals, but, in proportion as they assist men to realize the qualities of the immortal life, viz., holiness, justice, and wisdom, men too in their turn become imbued with the creative spirit and overflow naturally into actions which are holy, just, and wise, and thus themselves become creative of values, passing on this same creative spirit to other men, whose holy, just, and wise actions pass it on still further. In a word, so far as men become imbued with the divinely given spirit of immortality, they share this with their fellows and with the rising generation, and thus gradually assist in winning over the world to immortality.[12]

This life of the immortals has two sides or aspects. On

the one hand (1), they contemplate the eternal ideas in the heaven beyond the physical heaven, i.e., in the intellectual place, and so far live right outside the space-time world of sun, moon, and stars. From this point of view, the immortals appear to be essentially intellectual beings, spirits living a life of pure contemplation and worship, and an ingenious philology can find, even in their human appellations, traces of a belief that the chief immortals are all forms or aspects of mind.[13] It is, indeed, difficult to think of such spirits as having their true home anywhere else—for what more natural than that the "intellectual place" should be the homeland of an intellectual spirit?—and it would be easy to think of them as declining to live anywhere else—e.g., as declining to descend into the space-time arena and busy themselves with the concerns of inferior spirits such as human beings. But this activity in the space-time world, which constitutes (2) the other side or aspect of their life, is not something in which they have no concern, but is a portion of the "work," in doing which they realize themselves, and Plato always insists upon this activity in the space-time world.[14] A casual reader of the Dialogues might suppose the whole space-time world to be relatively unreal, a mere appearance, entirely separable from the ideal world. But this is not really the platonic view. That view is, rather, that the space-time world is a copy or image of the intellectual world, i.e., *is* the intellectual world considered as pouring out its spirit of order and meaning upon what would otherwise be sensuous chaos. It is the intellectual world mirrored in sense-perceivable imagery, with all which this implies.[15] The form of the physical universe, e.g., the form of the planets, and the form of the human brain—these represent the ideal form of the sphere, working in an alien medium and shaping this into an image of itself.[16] Again, the movements in the physical universe, from the apparent regularities of the starry heavens to the more spasmodic movements of a dancing child or frisking lamb, all represent the ideal principle of perfect circular revolution, applied to a closed group of aggregates compounded of regular mathematical solids of specific types, and realized approximately in a world which is fundamentally sensuous. So too astronomical time, with its days, lunar months, solar years, and "great year"—when all the cycles of all the planets are so completed that each has again resumed its original position in the system—is a reflection, in the sense-perceivable world of physical motion, of the absolute duration and the ideal motion which characterize the intelligible world.[17] It is the nature of the divine to pour forth its own spirit, and the order, regularity, and law of the space-time world is the natural and inevitable outcome of the spiritual world, mirrored, however, in an alien medium, whose sensuousness refracts and distorts, to some extent, the divine rays.

Such, in general, is the life of the immortals, as conceived in platonism. It remains to ask, how far this attains to the absolute ideal of immortality. To answer this question, we must first establish a certain distinction, corresponding to the distinction recognized in platonic literature between *deus summus* and *di immortales*. The first of these terms corresponds to the idea of good, while the second corresponds to the particular ideas. *Deus summus*, i.e., the Master-workman of the *Timaeus*, like the idea of good in the *Republic*, represents the absolute, the *ne plus ultra*, the principle of ideality, as such. This is the ultimate source of all order, system, meaning, and value, and in its natural overflow it is the creative principle par excellence. It does not create not-being or fluctuating chaos, but creates especially the spirit of creativity, pouring out its own spirit, primarily upon the *di immortales*, and secondarily upon human beings, endowing them all with the power of unifying the manifold and so creating order and value, so far as this is compatible with their relative finitude.[18] This represents the absolute ideal of the immortal life, the immortal creation of immortality. The inferior deities or *di immortales*, while thoroughly imbued with this same spirit of creativity, are relatively finite. Hera, Apollo, Poseidon, and the rest, have specific and limited functions, as compared with the " demiurge," God, as such, who is absolutely unlimited in his functions. These " immortals," then, being themselves created, are not, like the absolute spirit of creativity, immortal *per se*. It is the absolute spirit of divinity which is the source of their power and the assurance of their immortality, and they are essentially, from the lowest to the highest of them, ministers of this spirit.[19] That is to say, speaking philosophically, these " ministers " represent the absolute spirit considered as concentrated upon some specific task, just as each " idea " represents the principle of ideality turned in some specific direction, and as limited and particularized by that specificity. But the living principle itself is unlimited, and is absolutely universal, the eternal father of *all* that is good.

How far can man participate in the immortal life? There are many ways of approaching the platonic answer to this question. We might say, e.g., that, so far as man consciously fits himself for the place prepared for him in the ideal cosmos of spirits, he participates *ipso facto* in the immortal life. For he is developing all his powers as thoroughly as he can, and is co-operating with other men of good will in using those powers for the common good, and not only with other men, but with the higher spirits also, so that he is becoming, at least to that extent, one of their fellowship. In this way he participates directly in the life of the immortals, regarding himself, in thought, word, and deed, as the servant and minister of God, and regarding all other men as his colleagues and fellow-servants.[20]

Another way of approaching the platonic answer is to say that man becomes immortal so far as he regards this earthly habitation with its sensuous flux as alien and evil, and seeks to fly to the true homeland of the spirit by assimilating himself to divinity, i.e., by withdrawing from a mainly sensuous life and endeavouring to become holy, just, and wise, until he succeeds in taking up these " ideas " into his nature and becoming as godlike as possible. So far as he is thus successful in taking on the attributes of the immortals, he rises above the average level of everyday humanity, and his nature participates directly in immortality.[21]

Another way of approaching the answer is to say that man's nature is complex. On the one hand, it is physical, an affair of earth, water, fire, and air mixed in certain proportions and subject to the fluctuations which are a part of the world of physical motion. On the other hand, he has in him the germ of an organizing power, which is at first overcome by the influx of the nutritive forces which take hold of his body. Whether he becomes immortal or not depends upon which side wins in the ensuing struggle. If the bodily forces win, so that his actions are always the direct resultant of the fluctuating environmental stimulations, and the man is thus a mere part of the physical world, with no power to look before and after and direct himself according to which he thinks right, he hardly rises to the human level at all, and certainly belongs to the realm of not-being rather than to the realm of ideal being. If, however, his organizing power wins out, so that he acquires mastery over himself in the first place, and over the environment in the second, creating everywhere images of beauty, temperance, and justice, he has clearly begun, while still living here below, to partake directly of true life. Anyone who thus succeeds in dominating circumstances to the extent of " doing his own work," i.e., performing consistently and with free self-determination some definite function which is of value to the community, so far participates directly in the life and work of the immortals.[22]

Yet another approach is to maintain that soul, as such, is immortal. Soul, as the principle of life, belongs essentially to the world of true being rather than to the world of not-being ; and, further, as the originating principle of motion, at least of all motion of the orderly, " circular " type, it is the source of all order and system in the physical world.[23] Its true home is with the eternal " ideas," to which it is akin, and the world-soul, which is the most perfect type of a created soul, is regarded as directly divine—forming, together with its body (the physical universe) a " blessed god," self-sufficient for its own purposes, like the personified " nature " of the poetically-minded scientists. As divine, it lives, like the other created gods, the *di immortales*, an immortal life, with an immortality dependent upon the All-father. That is to say, the world-soul is a direct overflow of the creative idea of good. So too in the case of human beings : the essential element in their souls is of directly divine origin, a similar overflow of the creative idea of good, containing, as its immediately divine heritage, the germ of unity, law, and order, i.e., the characteristic principle which expands into the life of the immortals. The soul is thus naturally, in its own essence, immortal, i.e., is begotten akin to the source of holiness, justice, and wisdom, and belongs, in its own right, to the ideal family.[25]

Yet another way of showing how the soul participates in the immortals' life appears when we attend to the number and situation of the created souls. In accordance with a motif whose roots lie far back in mythology, as well as in philosophy, Plato tends to regard the number of created souls as limited. Their number is determined by the number of the physical stars, the "instruments of celestial time," in which the souls were orginally planted, and to which they may some day return, if only they succeed in overcoming the material forces under whose influence they have somehow fallen. The true destiny of the souls is thus to govern their own stars, as the world-soul governs the universe.[26] That is their immortal destiny, and their sojourn in an earthly body should be regarded as a temporary aberration, a stooping from their heavenly home, a putting on of mortality, from which they may one day recover and resume their eternal function, particularly if they live a holy, just, and wise life here below. If we regard this descent as a kind of planetary orbit, we might say that each soul has a different orbit, or rather succession of such orbits, but that a time may one day come when all the different orbits will be completed at the same instant, and all the souls will be with their stars, and a spiritual great year will begin in which the immortal fellowship of all souls in carrying on their work of converting not-being to true being will be manifest.[27]

This last view contains mythological elements which it is difficult to include without remainder in true platonism. The contrast of physical stars and earthly bodies, for instance, is a distinction of degree rather than of kind. Perhaps we can, with more justice to the evidence as a whole, sum up the general platonic position as follows :—

The life of the spirit is the one thing worth while, and is divine in origin, function, and destiny. Its mission is to extend itself over the realm of material chaos, to reduce this to law and order and, as nearly as possible, to its own type of being. The world as we come to know it represents an original or primaeval chaos overlaid with principles of spiritual origin, and in process of being reduced to law and order. Human beings are partly of divine, and partly of material, origin, and experience directly in themselves this cosmic conflict between good and evil, between the forces of the spirit and the backward pull of matter towards disintegration, not-being, chaos. In virtue especially of their intelligence, they are able to look before and after and rise above the sensuous pressure of immediate impulse, and to form vague and hazy conceptions of the eternal ideas which prevail in the spiritual life. So far as they attain to sufficient clearness in this contemplation, and are able to apply the resulting knowledge to the making over of their own lives and of their environment, physical and social, human beings —especially in the form of philosophic administrators, but to a lesser extent also as priests, poets, farmers, shoe-makers, day-labourers, etc.—are able to participate directly in the life of the spirit. That is to say, they experience directly the sense of spiritual fellowship with one another and with higher spirits, and, in the light of that experience, play a man's part in the cosmic conflict in which the true work of the world consists. Man can in this way rise superior to the materialistic life which looks askance at the thought of anything higher than the senses and instinctive emotions, and can enter upon the true life which is the only life worth living.

At this point an objection may and should be raised. That man can participate in spiritual living is, of course, granted. And that he *so far* participates in the life of the immortals is, of course, also granted. But does not a difficulty remain? Is not the fundamental distinction between mortals and immortals left precisely where it was? For, surely, what distinguishes them is that, however they may co-operate in spiritual living, the immortal is deathless, while the mortal obviously comes to an end and dies. Does the immortal remain immortal, and the mortal remain mortal, or does platonism urge that co-operation in spiritual living somehow overcomes the gap, so that the mortal who lives the higher life somehow survives the obvious fact of a physical death and participates in the deathlessness of the immortals, as well as in their holiness, justice and wisdom?

In order to answer this question intelligibly, it is necessary first to make precise the nature and limitations of terrestrial time. For, if we may assume the existence of something which in some sense is not subject to the visible disintegration of the body which obviously belongs to the space-time world, it may well be that this something is not directly subject to the conditions of terrestrial time, and that, consequently, an attempt, e.g., to inquire into its status five hours after physical death, as compared with its status five hours before physical death, is entirely futile. It may well be that its status, even if admitting of a before and after, does not admit of the species of before and after which can be measured in terms of a human chronometer, whether ancient or modern. What we call " Greenwich time " depends upon the motions of the heavenly bodies, so far as these influence the duration of day and night, month and year, upon the earth. But the motions of the heavenly bodies are not such that one day is of absolutely the same duration-length as another day, or one year of absolutely the same duration-length as another year. Consequently, as contrasted with these varying and fluctuating amounts of absolute duration which in reality correspond to the unchanging symbols of time-measurement which we use, there arises the thought of an absolute or perfect duration, in which there are no variations of rate, but one unit is absolutely equal in duration-length to any other unit, although it comes either before or after that other unit. For the Platonist, Greenwich time is an imperfect and fluctuating copy or image of true duration, and it is in true or ideal duration that the immortal life is lived. Spiritual progress cannot be measured by the movements of a Greek water-clock, but has its own moments, its own hours, and perhaps its own great year.[28]

Granting all this, we may still ask : if spiritual life expresses itself by using the physical body as its instrument for spiritualizing its environment, what happens to spiritual life when the physical body disintegrates, as it obviously does at physical death ? Dialectically speaking, there are many conceivable alternatives. The position taken by Plato, after due discussion of these alternatives, seems to be as follows :—When the body perishes, the spirit withdraws for a period to the intellectual place, and there, in company with the immortals, it renews, through contemplation unclouded by physical needs, its refreshing vision of the greater " ideas." Eventually it descends into another physical body, and again plays its part in the great conflict between good and evil. In this kind of eternal alternation between its heavenly home and this place of mortal union with a succession of physical instruments which inevitably wear out after a while, it lives its immortal life ; much as the philosopher-king—whose earthly life is a facsimile of the immortal life, so far as a human being can partake of that life while here on earth—withdraws from the task of administration in order to renew his vision of the idea of good, so as to return with renewed spiritual insight to his administrative duties. It is suggested that a human being who has lived a particularly heroic and philosophical life, or succession of such lives, may be raised to higher rank in the spiritual world, and so may be elevated above the necessity of further physical births and physical deaths, but this remains only a suggestion.[29]

In this alternative union and separation of spirit and body, just how much is mortal and how much is immortal? The usual view of the commentators is that "the rational element" is immortal, while the sensuous, instinctive, and emotional elements of experience, and also the elements of character which, like courage and self-mastery, rest partly upon bodily dispositions, are all evanescent. That is to say, when once the organizing spirit which stooped from its heavenly home and called them all into some semblance of being has departed on its further way, all these elements of empirical experience sink back again into their original status of not-being. Some authorities believe that the spirit retains something from its sojourn on earth, e.g. retains the cognitive essence of all its experiences. The details of this type of view are worked out with great clearness and in-genuity by St. Thomas Aquinas, in his account of "beatified spirits."[30] But all seem agreed to make a somewhat sharp distinction between spirit and body, and to regard every-thing bodily as falling back again into the abyss of not-being which is its original and only home. For this distinction and this conclusion, there is undeniable evidence in the Dialogues.[31] But if one is willing to consider the whole of the evidence, and concentrate upon this question all which belongs to the general position of platonism, it is perhaps possible to go a little deeper.

The function of spiritual experience, according to platonism, is to convert not-being into being, to change chaos into cosmos, to transmute fact into value, to rearrange material conditions in such a way that the germ of the spirit which is overlaid and overwhelmed by unfavourable con-ditions may develop and flower into perfect spiritual life, and may thus play its part in the work of spiritualizing the universe. Groups of pioneers go out into the wilderness, and in less than two full generations of men, where the ox-trails used to meet at the junction of two rivers, there is a large city, not only growing grain for trade with the motherland, but developing schools and colleges of its own, which send out teachers and preachers and other pioneers of the spiritual life in their turn. This is the work of the human beings who participate in the life of the immortals, and it is a growing thing. The work done by one generation makes it easier for the next generation to carry on the task. For the second generation finds farms where the first found only homesteads. The second generation finds banks and schools and a municipal organization, where the first generation found nothing beyond a loose agreement about leadership, and some sort of vigilance committee.[32] The spiritualizing agencies thus do something more than just mark time in an eternal conflict with foemen who can be neither converted nor destroyed.

It is conceivable that there is a limit beyond which the chaotic element will always remain chaotic, making an ordered living, to that extent, precarious. The process of hellenizing humanity may not succeed in overcoming some ultimate residuum of barbarism. But, until that limit has been reached, what might be regarded as " materialistic " agencies can certainly be harnessed in the service of idealism, and can thus contribute very directly to the process of spiritual-izing the universe.[33] For example : food, drink, exercise, and rest can so strengthen the body as to make it a useful instrument for studying philosophy and for carrying out philosophical purposes ; much as courage, which has a definitely physical basis, can be used as the natural ally of the philosophical principle in the soul.[34] So too money and material possessions can be used for educational purposes, and in the model community a certain minimum of such possessions is regarded as a *sine qua non* for living the life of ideal citizenship.[35]

The question, then, as to whether these material elements are merely humble contributors which, at best, cancel out and leave the way clear for higher, purely spiritual forces, is, on the whole, to be answered in the negative. Bodily health and strength enter directly into the higher life of service, and the material possessions which make possible health and strength, and education, physical, moral, and intellectual, also enter directly into the higher life of service. And, further, the undoubted self-interest incident to humanity —which is often regarded as " materialistic "—can be identified with the interest of the group, or even of the ideal life, so that a citizen may pursue his own best interest in devoting himself to a life of service.[36]   In other words, the spiritual principle so reorganizes material elements and converts them into spiritual agencies, that they become themselves instrumental in carrying further the work of spiritualizing the universe. Health, once established, goes on of itself.   An institution like a public educational system or a good civic constitution, once definitely established, tends, of itself, to continue. Such institutions require a guiding hand from time to time, but on the whole it is fair to say that they have taken on ideal colouring and belong, not to the fluctuations of not-being, but to the realm of true being.   The temporal realm can thus take on eternal characteristics, and what is mortal can, to that extent, put on immortality.[37]

If, then, in the light of these conclusions, we again ask, how much of a man can share in immortality, we must now answer : as much of him as can be so reorganized as to serve as the instrument of the idea of good.   This includes, not only his intellect, but also his moral dispositions, his courage, temperance, justice, and piety, so far as these are informed by wisdom, and also his physical activities, the eating, drinking, exercising, and resting upon which his health, strength, and good looks depend, so far as these, in their turn, are subservient to his moral and intellectual improvement.   The elements, then, out of which the physical universe is constituted—the fire, water, earth, and air which enter into his organism and keep it healthy and strong for its higher life— can themselves enter into the higher life ; and this means that so far there is nothing in the world, psychological or physical, for which there is not some place in the eternal plan, a place, the filling of which means sharing in the eternal plan of the immortals, i.e., partaking, to that extent, in the immortal life itself.

Put briefly, then, the platonic view is that immortality is identical with spiritual life, i.e., the function of hellenizing barbarism, transmuting fact into value, converting material into spiritual.   This spiritual life is realized through finite centres of experience, all endowed with the characteristic power of making one out of many, i.e., selecting values and concentrating them into the unity of portions of a single consistent system.   The union of such a spiritual centre

with any given material body is a transitory affair, and the
eternal function of the spirit in such a union is to turn its
temporal body into a more perfect instrumentality for
spiritual purposes.   A single soul can transmute a succession
of material bodies to such purposes, much as a teacher can
awaken spiritual insight in a succession of pupils, with whom
his temporal contact is even more transitory.[38]   But whatever the fate of the bodies with which it is, for the time being,
associated, the organizing centre itself endures throughout
all temporal changes, and is creative, divine, and immortal ;
not, indeed, *per se*, but, like the *di immortales*, in virtue of the
outpouring of the divine spirit which called it into being.
In the intervals between its separation from one temporal
body and its union with another, it passes through a contemplative phase in which it renews its vision of the ideal
world—a vision which was perhaps growing dim in its latest
incarnation.   Its rebirth is a fresh descent into the cave,
in which it has a further opportunity to live out and realize
in this mortal sphere the ideals with which it has enjoyed
communion in the intellectual place, and it thus continues to
play its part in the eternal plan of spiritualizing the universe.[39]

It remains to ask two questions :—(1) how far is this kind
of view philosophically satisfactory, and (2) how far is immortality in this platonic sense a " highest " good ? To the first
question, the answer is difficult. Plato's view, while persuasive and acceptable, perhaps, to the moral consciousness,
is not the only hypothesis dialectically conceivable. Granted
e.g. that spiritual life, of itself, overflows in the direction of
spiritualizing the universe, there is no sound logical reason
for regarding the number of finite centres as fixed—either in
relation to the number of physical stars (which also does not
need to be regarded as fixed for all time), or in any other
relation.   If this assumption is given up, the further assumption of a succession of incarnations—connected with their
recurrence of a " great year "—and of the permanence of each
one of the (numbered) centres, also falls to the ground.

What remains is the faith that a divine overflow cannot
die or come to an end, and that what is genuinely creative
cannot be subject to its logical contrary, viz., not-being.
As Plato puts it, the cardinal point in any faith in values is a
thorough-going belief in the essential priority of spiritual life,
of its independence upon material conditions conceived as

per se inert and incapable of originating any rational kind of motion.[40] But this faith is dialectically compatible with belief in the extinction of the finite centre, as such, at bodily death, even though its *work* survives in the whole ; and, although the whole would be the poorer for the extinction of one such finite centre, it might well be enriched by the creation of another centre which, working upon the basis erected by past generations, might well carry further the work in which the life of the whole expresses itself. The specific doctrines urged in the Dialogues are thus not dialectically compelling, even if we concede the general platonic position as a matter of reasonable faith. It should, perhaps, be added that, in platonism, the emphasis is not upon the specific doctrines, not, e.g. upon the persistence of the finite centre, but rather upon the work, i.e. upon participating in the ideal justice, holiness, and wisdom of the immortals.[41]

Thus understood, how far (2) can immortality be regarded as the highest good ? The answer here is not difficult. To realize one's powers to the utmost in co-operation with other spiritual agencies in raising the whole world to a higher level of spiritual value, is to develop oneself and at the same time to make, to the well-being of the whole, the greatest contribution of which one is capable. It is not possible to conceive of a " good " which could be higher. Platonic immortality, i.e. the life based upon holiness, justice, and wisdom, and the ideal life, i.e. the most valuable kind of life which human reason can conceive, coincide in all respects. It follows that, so far as a finite centre of experience can participate in the immortal life, it is, so far, succeeding in realizing the highest conceivable human good.

CHAPTER XVII

GOODNESS OF CHARACTER AS THE HIGHEST GOOD : TEMPERANCE, JUSTICE

GOODNESS of character has been described elsewhere, and has been analysed into such factors as courage, temperance, justice, holiness, and wisdom, and, as so analysed, has already been pronounced the central element in the blessed or happy life which is, according to platonism, the chief good.[1] In the same way, the factors of holiness, justice, and wisdom—understood, not as excluding, but as of course including courage and temperance—have appeared to constitute the essential attributes of the immortals. When found in man, they are regarded as an assimilation to the nature of the immortals, and the "immortality" in which the holy, just, and wise man, so far, participates, is equated unhesitatingly with the chief good.[2] In equating the functioning of good character with the blessed life, whether we call this blessed life "happiness," or whether—as being the life, not only of the philosophic human guardian, but also of the *di immortales* and of the Father-artificer who is the source of their immortality—we prefer to call it "immortality," is immaterial ; for they are one and the same. It is, then, obvious that goodness of character, understood as functioning in the best possible way, is identical with what, under the heads of "happiness" and "immortality," we have already accepted as a reasonable formulation of the highest good. All that we need to add in the present place is that this supreme value of goodness of character, whether in the citizen, in the magistrate, or in the ideal ruler, is repeatedly and explicitly recognized in the Dialogues.[3] In the present chapter, therefore, accepting these results as established, we shall examine more closely into the claims of single elements of character to be accepted as satisfactory formulations of the highest good. The claims of courage to be so accepted are mentioned only to be set aside, and courage is given the fourth place, ranking after temperance, justice, and wisdom.[4] But temperance and justice are frequently accepted as formulations of the essence of the chief good. In what follows, therefore, we shall consider their claims in some detail.

1. *Temperance as the highest good.* The Greek word *sophrosyne* is used in many senses in the Dialogues, and in many of these significations it would be plainly absurd to regard it as the highest good. Indeed, in a number of these cases, it is stated very explicitly that it is an inferior form of goodness. Thus, as an instinctive bodily disposition towards quietness, shrinking from notoriety, avoidance of any form of excitement, as in the case of Charmides, it is merely a graceful attitude suitable for a refined and modest Greek youth in the presence of his elders. In other contexts, this same bodily disposition is declared to belong to the feminine, rather than to the masculine, side of human nature, and it is definitely stated that effeminacy of this type almost inevitably provokes aggression. The modesty and restraint of a Socrates exposes him to the crudest insults in the free democratic city of Athens, and a community too tender-minded to fight is simply inviting its more tough-minded neighbours to reduce it to some form of vassalage. Unless directed by wisdom, such a bodily disposition is at least as likely to prove hurtful as helpful, and it is deliberately maintained that it is in wisdom, rather than in temperance, that the root of genuine excellence is to be sought.[5]

In another group of contexts, it is the scope, rather than the bodily nature of the virtue which is adverse to any lofty claims. It is to eating and drinking and sex-relations that the term is especially applied. Sometimes dress and bearing or deportment are included as well. In such a signification the term is obviously too restricted, too narrow, to be regarded as a supreme value. And even here there is a tendency to disparage the over-modest attitude which shrinks, e.g. from eating and drinking in public—the attitude characteristic of the secluded *femme d'intérieur* of Athens. Plato seems to feel that those who avoid public standards are likely to fall below them and to exhibit, not a superior, but an inferior degree of respect for law and order. In any case, such shrinking prevents them from playing their full part in the community life, and the community is the poorer for their withdrawal. The remaining half of the group has to do the work of the whole.[6]

In all such cases, there can be no question of regarding *sophrosyne* as a form of the highest good. But these are all popular conceptions, and are not especially characteristic of the platonic conception of *sophrosyne*. There are, however, in ordinary Hellenic feeling, two lines along which an approach to treating this virtue as a supreme value seems natural enough. The aims characteristic of Hellenism at its best are peculiarly well expressed in the two Delphic mottoes :—(a) nothing too much and (b) know thyself. The former of these expresses the restraint which we admire in Greek art of the classical period, and this motto was used over the whole country as a guide to character-formation. The avoidance of excess in any direction, and the seeking of the middle pathway as a guide through life is formulated by tragedian and historian,[7] long before Plato taught the doctrine of the " limit " and Aristotle the doctrine of the " mean," as expressing the secret essence of all excellence. To the Hellenic mind, this saying formulated that characteristic of *sophrosyne* which we call " moderation in all things," and temperance thus easily took on some of the attributes of a supreme good. So also the second proverb or slogan expressed the reflective self-knowledge inseparable from the higher development of character. This aspect of temperance is especially treated in the *Charmides*, and it is clear from this treatment that self-knowledge, as an ideal, is the equivalent of the supreme value of wisdom elsewhere acclaimed as the ideal guide throughout life. Reflective knowledge of values, of one's own powers, and of the value of the claims made by and upon others—what more valuable guide to true success in life could be conceived by the Hellenic mind ?

The value of self-knowledge and wise restraint were not merely accepted by Hellenic feeling, but formed part of the stock-in-trade of the more successful popular lecturers who made their appearance at Athens during its period of imperial expansion. Characteristically, these lecturers are represented as appealing especially to the adolescent in his phase of natural development toward a consciousness of self and of the world, and as undertaking to supply technical and professional assistance toward the development of a mature self-consciousness.[8] But they are also represented in Plato's pages as not being able to go much beyond the beliefs and desires of their *clientèle*. The moderation they taught was a hedonistic avoidance of certain types of excess, mainly, however, in order to obtain other pleasures, and in order, by keeping healthy and prosperous to secure a maximum of pleasurable moments in life. This hedonism was a balancing of pleasure against pleasure, and pain against pain, and supported the claims of " temperance " by an appeal not, in the end, on a different level from the appeal by which the intemperate *viveur* justified his unrestrained pursuit of pleasure-sensations from any and every source.[9] But this lawless and indiscriminate pursuit of pleasure-sensations, of that characterless " happiness " which Plato regards as an ideal peculiar to democracy, is logically the contrary of temperance, moderation, and restraint, and Plato contemptuously treats such hedonism as a shadow-play to amuse children, or as a game with counters,[10] although to all professional teachers of ethics, as well as to the typical man of the world, such hedonism, when a mathematical calculus is tacked on to it, appears as the " saving " principle of life.[11] In the Dialogues, this contrast between sophistic *sophrosyne*— = unprincipled seeking after a maximum of pleasurable experiences—and Socratic *sophrosyne*— = self-control guided by wisdom—appears almost as a personal contrast, with democracy and its representatives, whether statesmen or lecturers, on the one side, and Socrates, with his philosophy of the ideal community, standing, alone and unafraid, on the other.

Again and again, Plato comes back to this element of self-control and self-knowledge partly expressed in the popular conception. There is, he teaches, in human nature an eternal conflict going on, and, according to the issue of that conflict, men may be described as mastering themselves, or as sinking into slavery to themselves. Is this conflict for mastery correctly described as a conflict between opposing pleasures, or is it not rather something much more profound ? On the first of these alternatives, there would really be no rational ground for the distinction ; for any situation in which pleasure A mastered pleasure B, or in which pleasure B mastered pleasure A, might with equal reasonableness be described as a victory over pleasure or as a defeat by pleasure.[12] The platonic treatment of this difficulty is precisely analogous to the platonic treatment of the conflict between sensations in the field of cognition. This conflict is solved by rising to a level higher than that of competing and fluctuating sensations, viz., the ideal level of concepts in which reason can rest, as in its own home.[13]   So here, in the affective field, when there is conflict and contradiction and competition for control, on the part of pleasurable experiences, a solution of this conflict can be reached only if we rise altogether above the pleasure-weighing level to the ideal level of clear-cut concepts which admit of logical proof and disproof. Temperance, or rational self-control, belongs, for the platonist, to this higher level. The pleasure-seeking tendencies are put in their proper place, as all alike belonging to the lower self. This is a psychological fact, but has not attained to the level of ethical valuations. Self-mastery is then described as an agreement between this " concupiscent element " which constitutes so large a part of the mechanisms inherent in the embodied soul, and the " rational element " which contemplates the systematic principles of the ideal realm. The agreement is, that idealism shall direct, and the pleasure-seeking tendencies shall obey its rule and carry out, as far as possible, its directions. Only in this way can blind conflict and the futile waste of contradiction be avoided.[14]

The groping after a " better," inherent in popular experience, thus becomes knowledge of the ideal realm and its principle (the idea of good), and temperance, like every other virtue, reaches its highest development by passing over into wisdom or philosophic insight. When conduct is directed by the idea of good, so that, in every situation which life brings, a maximum of positive value is sought, much as a good musician realizes the maximal tonal potentialities of his instrument, restraint or control ceases to be an external or negative force, and temperance passes over into the positive self-unfolding of the potentialities of the organism as a whole, and is thus indistinguishable from complete excellence, i.e. from the ideal life. In this sense, temperance—usually associated with justice in the Dialogues—becomes a human reflex of the divine life, and is regarded without hesitation as the highest good.[15]

If, however, we allow " temperance " to pass over, without remainder, into the ideal life which applies the divine principle of realizing the maximal value-potentialities contained in concrete situations, we must freely admit that platonic *sophrosyne* has passed beyond what the average Greek understood by this term, and has become idealized to an extent which makes it indistinguishable from ideal justice, ideal piety, ideal wisdom, and, in a word, ideal character. This is fully recognized in the Dialogues,[16] and we must therefore sum up the platonic doctrine by stating that, while, at the level of natural bodily disposition, or at the conventional level recognized by " opinion," temperance is a separate and one-sided excellence, and is never regarded as good in itself, at the highest or philosophical level, temperance has so altered as to be hardly recognizable. When re-formed by insight into the idea of good, temperance expands and broadens as well as deepens, and thus passes over into the life of idealism which transcends both natural disposition and conventional opinion and suggests a goodness so high that it is only realizable, perhaps, in the world of divine patterns envisaged as in " heaven."

2. *Justice as the highest good.* Justice, in the Dialogues, is usually connected with life in organized communities, and is regarded as a *sine qua non* of such life. Men naturally seek to live together in social groups, partly for mutual protection against dangers, whether from wild animals or from other human beings, partly for security against hunger, etc., and partly for the purposes of social life. Co-operation of some sort is involved in such life from the beginning, co-operation in building protective walls, in facing common dangers, in solving common problems connected with hunger, disease, pests, etc. ; and out of such co-operation there inevitably arises a collection of community usages and some sort of organization of the members of the group for deliberation, for the establishment of policies, and for the administration of community policies and community resources.[17] In social living, as such, then, there is implied the ideal of social solidarity, with all which this involves, such as community of purpose, community of feeling, community of action, i.e. a community which links together the diverse potentialities and interests of individuals and so stimulates them that, as members of the community, they live a finer and fuller life than they could live otherwise. The absolutely ideal community would thus be one in which each citizen realized his maximum of potentiality in harmony with his fellow-citizens and in the service of the whole, especi-ally if he further believed that such a life was the realization of the divine plan for humanity, and that his community repre-sented the city of God whose pattern was laid up in God's heaven.

Justice, then, as Plato understands it, is the virtue of social life, of man in relation to his fellow-man, the virtue of citizenship, of membership in an ideal community. In every relation of life it involves the substitution of public spirit for private interest : in the constitution of the family, in education for the rising generation, in eating and drinking, in farming, in business life, in politics, in law, art, science, and in religion. The just citizen is the man who sinks his private self wholly in the welfare of his community, and thereby attains to the larger, better, more worthy and more enjoyable self of the citizen. As a loyal member of his community, he is able to develop his powers more whole-heartedly and more completely than if he had remained unable to find a cause large enough to call for the employment of his full energy. He finds himself in the community work, finds, that is to say, his ideal place in the divine plan for humanity, and thus attains to the greatest measure of reality which is possible for him, i.e. the completest possible realization of his " idea," whether as farmer, business man, day-labourer, or governor or ambassador, in harmonious co-partnership with his fellow-citizens, and in a spirit of followership directed by divine guidance. In order to discover how the platonic conception of justice enters into the details of the citizen's life, we shall consider, somewhat more particularly what is involved in (1) the realization of the citizen's " idea," (2) the co-partnership with his fellow-citizens, and (3) the relation to his divine leader.

(1). That justice consists in each citizen realizing his " idea," as farmer, or statesman, or teacher, in the community, should be plain. The community is thought of as an institution containing precisely so many vacancies for citizens, i.e. a definite number of farmerships—agriculture being the basic activity—a definite number of priestships and administrative positions, etc., much as a college may contain so many fellowships, so many scholarships, etc., in accordance with its available income. The ideal life of the community is only realized, when each of these citizenships—whose proportions to one another as well as to the available sources of livelihood have been very carefully planned—is working to capacity.[18] This must not be understood in a too narrowly economic sense. The art of farming supplies food for the community, but the number and quality of the farms are such that moderate industry in their management will keep the community

plete peace and harmony with the world in general and the enemy country in particular. Officially, the city may be at peace : yet individual citizens may be carrying on private wars of their own. So too in internal relations : the city may have officially condemned one of its citizens to exile or death ; but the independent sovereign individual may remain with his friends and refuse to concede the position assumed by the city ; and it seems to be no citizen's business to protest. There is, in short, too great a spread between the collective and the distributive aspects of democratic citizens. The futility of self-negation involved in this absence of unity is brought out very clearly in the Dialogues,[26] and, in contrast with it, the advantages of unity and co-peration of the citizens are duly emphasized.

Of these advantages which attach to co-operation, the majority mentioned in the Dialogues are treated in a negative way, i.e. in contrast with the disadvantages which attach to unrestricted individualism. Individualism is blind, and defeats its own ends by destroying the community life upon which it is, after all, dependent. For example, excessive individualism prevents the farmer from realizing his " idea," i.e. from producing an adequate food-supply ; it prevents the business man from realizing *his* " idea," i.e. from making more and more money ; it prevents the would-be Napoleon from enjoying permanently that " power " after which he grasps so eagerly ; etc., etc. If farmer, merchant, etc., are really to play their parts in an approximately ideal community, they must sink their natural feeling for private gain at each other's expense in the more educated feeling for public welfare, in which all can share without detriment to one another. The logic of this position is simple and inexorable. Politicians must cease to play politics, and the different parties must genuinely work together for the welfare of the whole, or there will be no whole ; and, if no whole, there will be no parts. In peace, as in warfare, unity is strength, and division is weakness, and justice, the essential excellence of social living, is fundamentally a principle of strength.[27] A sense of unity, then, of being so bound up with the success or failure of the other citizens as to rejoice when they rejoice, and to grieve when they grieve, analogous to the sense of unity and to the co-operation which binds together the members of a family, is so important for the citizen, that Plato is willing to abolish even the institutions of the private family, and party politics, and private education, in order to develop this public spirit which places first the living sense of unified citizenship, and views every problem, feeling, and action from the stand-point of the beloved community. In such a sense of unity, and in such a feeling of being so bound up with the social life of all other members of the community, that the citizens feel, think, and act together, as a single organism, justice, as Plato conceives it, consists.[28]

(3) Following the divine leader. The ideal community depicted in the *Republic*, *Politicus*, and *Laws* is thought of as the city of God, the city in which God is the ideal Patriarch. The philosopher-kings, and other magistrates who in turn bear rule, act as His ministers in everything, while the citizens in general feel that they are puppets, whose life is entirely in His hands, and believe, further, that this is the best for them. Their attitude is one of worship and living service,[29] and the whole life of the ideal community is so organized that the citizen's relations to " the divine " come home to him on every occasion. He feels that he is, as far as in him lies, always co-operating with God in the work of realizing the divine plan of idealizing the environment ; raising to the level of the ideal world, as far as possible, what would otherwise belong to the world of not-being ; bringing out and concentrating the ideal elements in the life and in the world around him, so as to bring the world nearer to God's Reality, the Heaven beyond the fixed stars, the " intellectual place " where the " ideas " have their divine home. This sense of co-operation is realized not only at birth, marriage, and death, but in the lesser things too : in every-day business relations, in eating and drinking, in taking a walk, in lying down to rest ; in going abroad, and in returning home ; in offering and in receiving hospitality ; in meeting a stranger and in greeting a friend. His feeling of companionship with higher powers and submissive acceptance of their guidance is thus universal.[30]

It might be thought that this attitude of followership should be called " piety " rather than " justice ; " and it must be admitted that " piety " or " holiness " is the term frequently used to connote this aspect of the ideal life. But Plato-students are in substantial agreement that piety and justice are very closely connected, and that *dikaiosyne* has a definitely religious tinge—so much so that Plato-students sometimes translate the term by *Gerechtigkeit* or righteous-ness,[31] with a full understanding of what this term involves. In accordance with the evidence, then, we take the position that, for Plato, the ideal life, considered on its social side, includes the relations of man with higher beings, as well as with his equals, and that " justice " or "righteousness " is the virtue or excellence of the whole of this aspect of the ideal life. The evidence goes further, and includes, not only man's attitude toward God, but also God's attitude toward man. If a man co-operates with God, or seeks to do so, he will find that God is co-operating with him, and that he can count upon divine assistance. The " justice of Zeus " consists in this, that the just and righteous become more just and righteous, more and more like their ideal pattern and divine Friend.[32]   To him that hath, more is given, and his assimilation to the divine nature in spite of the empirical and earthly elements which cling to his mortal nature, is a growing thing, and he can count upon divine support.   So, on the other hand, the unrighteous become progressively less fit for living in the ideal community, more and more adapted for living only with thieves and cut-throats, and the mythical stories which, in the after-world, separate completely the unrighteous from " the place of righteousness " express a profound truth.   In the language of the puppet-myth, it only remains for God to shift the pieces in His game, sending the better to the better place and the worse to the worse place.[33]   God's justice pro-vides an ideal place for each of us.   If we seek steadfastly to attain to it, we can count upon divine co-operation.   If we steadily reject God's helping hand, we, in the end, cease to have any part or lot in the ideal community, in which alone genuine reality is to be found.

Two smaller points remain to be discussed.   (a) The first is the relation between ideal justice and the concrete laws everywhere in evidence in actual communities.   The second is the identification of injustice with *polypragmosyne*, the doing of many things.   Let us consider these in turn.   Social living, of itself, gives rise to certain customs and usages which have all the force of laws.   In order to solve the day-to-day pro-blems which confront the community, some sort of centralized authority, whether patriarchal or otherwise, inevitably grows up, and the decrees of such authority have all the force of laws.[34]   Respect for the customs and laws of the community is essential to the production of the best sort of citizenship, and on this point the virtues of temperance and justice coincide. The necessity of such law and order, if human life is to rise above the brute level and become civilized, is properly stressed by Plato, although he always points out that it is in relation to man's brute nature, rather than to his ideal nature, that concrete laws are a necessity. If men were all spiritual, all mind, and were all educated and genuinely intelligent, minute regulation of conduct would be simply impertinent, if not harmful. And the view held in fourth-century Athens, that men can be made moral by resolutions of the Assembly, tinkering with details but missing the essential fact that a spiritual nature is the necessary foundation for the higher development of character, is properly ridiculed in the Dialogues.[35] But, given man's dual nature, while idealism appeals to the ideal or spiritual element in him, law and order can be of great, though secondary, assistance to him in his upward struggle against the brute elements in his own nature, as well as in the social environment. For they act, partly by repressing such elements, and partly—if the laws enacted are a little in advance of what the citizens have reached in the way of moral development—by representing patterns which can be used idealistically as models for imitation, and as precepts or maxims to be learnt by heart, challenging the citizen to live up to their demands.[36] If this idealistic challenge fails of its effect, the final appeal to force—suppressing the lower elements of our nature and eliminating from the community life everything which falls below the established moral minimum—is definitely and unhesitatingly brought into play.[36a] Plato's ideal community is not so much adapted to the needs of human beings as actual individuals, but begins with " citizenships," i.e. with a type-form already elevated, in moral tendency, somewhat above the average. Merely average actual human beings are, indeed, present in the model city, but they are aliens, who are only accorded, as a rule, temporary residence, and do not attain to the rights of citizenship, as long as they remain at the level of average humanity.[37] Laws, then, are a necessary institution in community living, but their function and justification, for platonism, is moral. Their appeal to the holders of citizenships is primarily moral and ideal—that is why the laws have " preludes " attached to them—and only secondarily and as a last resort are they a matter of sheer physical force. It should be noted that, just as soon as physical force has to be applied in all seriousness, and not as a temporary correction intended to be understood as a species of admonishment—i.e. understood still in a fundamentally moral sense—the individuals to whom it is applied are regarded as falling below the moral minimum expected of citizenship-holders, and are usually excluded from their citizenship in the model community.[38]

(b) The second point to be considered is the connection between injustice and "doing many things." That the individual who fritters away his energies by attempting to do so many different things that he succeeds in none would not qualify for a citizenship in the ideal community—in which every citizenship is counted upon to contribute something definite, to realize some distinct "idea"—is intelligible enough. Such an individual does not reach the level of ideal living at all, and thus cannot possibly exhibit justice in the platonic sense. But we should hesitate, at the present day, to call such a man "unjust." The democratic citizen, everything by starts and nothing long, with whom we, as well as Plato's contemporaries, are familiar, seems to illustrate this type. He fails, of course, to attain to the ideal level, but we should hardly regard him as falling so low as to be ranked as definitely anti-social, positively unjust. When, however, injustice and "doing many things" are equated in the Dialogues, something more is meant. Plato means that the unjust man is a busy-body, and meddles with other people's affairs, occupying the position which *they* should be occupying in the community, and mismanaging other people's businesses. It is when the individual whose "citizenship" calls for shoe-production insists upon governing the community without adequate preparation, and governs it badly, that injustice occurs. For the community is the poorer in two ways : the position of cobbler is left vacant, and the idea of the governor is not realized. So too when the man who should be mending pots and pans, for which he is perfectly qualified, thrusts himself into philosophy, for which he is not qualified, a wrong is done to both "ideas," and the community as a whole, which rests upon a carefully calculated balance of these and other "ideas," suffers accordingly.[39] This is why, in the ideal community, the philosopher consents to take over the work of administration, for fear lest some unworthy person may grasp at power and, by mismanaging what is part of the philosopher's specific " idea," may ruin the community.   He consents, we read, " because he is a just man," i.e. because he recognizes the principle that the ideal life requires each citizenship-holder to realize his own " idea," to fulfil his specific function, and neither to encourage nor to permit others to usurp functions for which they are not fitted.   Justice, then, is the name given to the ideal life on its social side, and whatever interferes with such realization of definite ideals which are of value to group life, is called injustice.[40]

In the light of the above conclusions, it is not difficult to see why justice is spoken of as the highest good.   It is identical with the ideal life, considered in its social aspect, i.e. is the finest kind of life which a public-spirited citizen with some feeling for religion can be expected to live, and is exemplified in the career of the philosopher-king, who certainly represents Plato's philosophical ideal.   Like temperance, at its highest it seems to pass beyond what can be accomplished by actual human beings ; and, again like temperance, at its best it seems to coincide with goodness of character, which we have already accepted as a reasonable formulation of the highest good.

UNDER the head of "genius," Plato understands the human being of altogether exceptional natural ability, whose appearance in any community is unpredictable and is regarded as a gift from the hand of God. Such exceptional men are of the greatest value to any community which succeeds in obtaining their services, particularly if they have received from their community an education corresponding in value to their degree of natural ability. That is to say, while recognizing that such men make their appearance in all sorts of communities, " bad as well as good," Plato insists that it is not the Sophist, but rather the select nature which has been educated so as to fit the position of " philosopher-king " in his ideal community, which, to his mind, constitutes the highest good. The value of such a person to the community consists partly in the excellence with which he performs the especial tasks of administration, and partly in his spreading around him, as far as possible, his own peculiar gift : passing on his powers, through education, to a selected group of the rising generation, and thus training successors who, when their turn comes, will succeed, not only in carrying on the work of administration proper, but also in solving the at least equally important problem of educating worthy successors. Such a person is perfectly good and wise, perfectly temperate, courageous, and religious, and represents, in every respect, the type of the ideally perfect character. As such, he is, of course, intended as a portrayal of the highest conceivable good in human form.[1]

The subject of " religion " has been treated of elsewhere in some detail.[2] In the present context, it is necessary, after a brief *résumé*, only to show how far, and for what reasons, religion is regarded as constituting the highest good.

Psychologically, the natural disposition of piety develops in connection with man's experiences when brought face to

face with the forces of nature. His own tendencies towards
self-expression are thwarted, and, at the same time, his admiration is challenged, by the superiority and inevitability of
these forces. This situation he naturally interprets animisti-
cally, as a conflict of wills or persons akin to himself. The
stars in their courses, the earth with its fertility and barren-
ness, the storms and calms of the ocean, the regularity and
order of nature which furnish man with standards of orderly
behaviour, and the incalculable changes which appear to him
like human caprice : into all such phenomena he imag-
inatively projects a self with wishes and feelings like his own,
but with powers infinitely greater. His natural tendency
to worship such powers, and to seek their companionship
and friendship, leads directly to the building of temples, the
establishment of rituals, and the development of priestcraft,
with all which these imply ; while his projective imagination,
of itself, issues in poetical constructions which name and
describe these higher powers, and weave about their names a
tissue of legend and myth which receives allegorical interpretation, and becomes closely interwoven, not only with
spiritualistic experiences and their interpretations, but also
with the traditions and rituals of the temples. The whole
concrete fabric of religion is thus a complex imaginative projection of human frustrations and human hopes when con-
fronted with forces beyond immediate and direct human
control. And further : when such projected beings become
the objects of prayer and intercession in connection with
historical as well as with natural events, e.g., with wars as
well as with pestilences and famines, etc., the " Gods of
Olympus " become surrounded with national and even local
halos ; so that the general tissue of Greek religion, with its
Athene, Poseidon, and Apollo on the one hand, and its " vulgar
Polyhymnia " and its " rascally Hermes " on the other, comes
to represent a species of autobiography of the Hellenic race,
with its failings as well as its virtues, its trials as well as its
triumphs, magnified to a more than human stature and
significance.[3]

Faced with this concrete legendary projection of traditional ideals and thwartings, reflective rationalism, whether
sophistical or dialectical, readily seizes upon incongruities,
unworthinesses, and fantastical survivals of primitive barbarism. The mythologizing is not all of a piece and cannot

possibly be accepted implicitly by any thinker who respects the laws of consistency.   What should be done with it ? Should it be dismissed as purely subjective, the product of a too-credulous imagination resting upon nothing stronger than superstitious ignorance on the one hand and the enlightened self-interest of priest or ruler, on the other ?[4]   Or is there, perhaps, something objective underlying these fabrications of the human imagination, something which is necessarily refracted and distorted when expressed in imaginative terms, but, beneath these figurative refractions and distortions, remains genuine and of the utmost importance ?   Plato accepts the second alternative.   For him, popular religion is a natural, and inevitably distorted representation, in terms of anthropomorphic imagery, of the philosophical truth that the universe is fundamentally spiritual, a group of minds co-operatively at work upon the problem of transmuting material into spiritual, enlisting mechanism in the service of idealistic purposes and reducing the whole world, as far as possible, to the level of mind itself.[5]   The actual religious tissues invented by poet and priest require, doubtless, to be made over in accordance with a more philosophic insight into the nature of the universe and its fundamental problems, so that temple-worship and official spiritualism, in their details as well as in their general spirit, shall function as the handmaid of philosophic insight.   *Theologia ancilla philosophiae.*   Men need to be reminded, in connection with every detail of their living, of the essentially spiritual nature of life and of the universe, so that their life will be made as philosophic as possible.   That is to say, every citizen of the model community depicted by Plato will live in such a constant atmosphere of the reformed mythology, that his underlying kinship with every member of the ideal fellowship of spirits, in which each and all are endeavouring, with all their forces, to fill worthily the place prepared for them in the ideal plan, will inescapably be brought home to his feeling, imagination, and will.   But, while essentially illuminated by philosophic insight, platonic religion is not constructed *in vacuo*.   Traditionalism is fundamental in religion, and the most scrupulous respect is paid to each local legend and each form of worship which has grown up with the community, so far as it can be incorporated in the new rationalism.   Platonism is not abstract but as concrete as possible.[6]

Thus understood, how far can a philosophically reformed religion be regarded as constituting the highest human good ? Life in accordance with the ideal plan which provides a place for every individual to realize his potentialities in harmony with all his fellow-individuals is the finest kind of life which the philosophic intelligence can think out, both in principle and in detail. Such a life, of course, constitutes the highest good for humanity. Ideal religion, as conceived by platonism, *is* this ideal life, expressed in imaginative projections which constitute the only idealistic appeal which most men can appreciate. The new religious life is, then, identical with the highest human good conceived by the philosopher, so far as this can be expressed in terms of the projective imagination with its poetry, its rituals, and its necessarily anthropomorphic constructions.

Science, or scientific knowledge, is based upon instinctive curiosity, i.e. upon the natural impulse to touch, feel, and handle for ourselves all objects which are unfamiliar and at the same time attractive. This impulse is primarily sensuous rather than intellectual, and is, in large part, satisfied by sensuous experience. When we have reached out after an unfamiliar object, and have handled it, listened to it, eaten it, or otherwise exercised our sense-organs upon it, the instinctive cognitive urge of our nervous system is usually satisfied, and seeks to go no further. As Plato puts it, most of us are " philodoxers," lovers of " opinion," i.e. of seeings, hearings, and touchings *en masse*, and such gratifications of our cognitive sense-organs, like other organ-gratifications, represent the natural termination or conclusion of our reaction to sensory stimulation.[7] In fact, we should probably never seek to go further, if we could always succeed in obtaining this kind of organ-gratification. But it so happens that the gratification is sometimes withheld, while the stimulus continues to stimulate ; e.g. when contrary stimuli affect the nervous system at one and the same time—and Plato believes that such situations frequently appear in the changes and fluctuations of sensory experience—there may arise tendencies to opposite reactions ; and these may hold each other in suspense, so that no gratification is experienced, and the stimulation reaches no immediate termination. In such cases, if the suspense is not to continue indefinitely, it is necessary to rise to the conceptual level by seeking a " one " in this " many," a concept or group of concepts which will overcome and resolve the conflict which persists at the sensory level of experience.[8]   Such concepts or ideas are, in the first place, generalizations which unify the characteristics common to a number of sensuous experiences, as the concepts of horse, ox, man, bed, shuttle, etc., sum up and express, in a unified form which the mind can grasp, the meaning-elements extracted from certain fluctuating sensuous experiences.   When we reflect further upon this situation, a second group of more formal ideas arises, such as identity, difference, unity, duality, etc., and the logical ideal of a single consistent systematization of experience as a whole.   This last is the " idea of good," the ultimate intellectual principle in grasping which mind finally apprehends itself and discovers that it has attained the conclusion of its knowledge-quest.[9]

Of scientific knowledge, Plato distinguishes certain types. In the first place, there is the empirical science of the " so-called Pythagoreans," which consists in making sensory generalizations, especially with the help of sensory observation and experiment.   The method is strictly inductive, and aims at discovering elements and establishing precise relations between the elements discovered, in every field of experience. To this Plato objects that sensuous experience is too fluctuating as a basis upon which either exact elements or precise relations can be established.   Upon such a basis, no science can be erected.   Take, for example, the science which the Pythagoreans have made peculiarly their own :   mathematics. Mathematical elements, such as the unit and the dyad, and mathematical relations such as the precise ratio between the sides of their venerated right-angled triangle, are not established by sensory observation and experiment, and cannot possibly be so established.   To suppose that induction upon such a basis could lead to anything worthy the name of science, is to show that the " so-called Pythagoreans " really remain at the level of " opinion " and have not reached the level of exact knowledge at all.   This criticism has been misunderstood, but it is clearly sound in principle.[10]

As contrasted with this empirical groping known as Pythagorean " science," Plato gives us the outlines of a slightly different type of knowledge, which is both scientific and empirical.   After the dialectician depicted in the *Republic* has penetrated to the ideal principle of knowledge, he turns back again to the assumptions and hypotheses with whose assistance he has been working his way upward, and, in the light of his new principle, transforms these assumptions or hypotheses into subordinate principles deductively connected with his highest principle. This is, of course, not empirical, but is pure deductive science. So too in the *Timaeus* we find the outlines of a pure deductive science of physics, which investigates the interrelations of mathematical solids of definite type-forms, thought of as compressed into a single revolving spherical space. In this case, not only the outlines are constructed, but the deductions are worked out with suggestive approximations to detailed knowledge. Empirical science proper arises when analogies between these pure deductions and the observed behaviour of sense-phenomena are discovered ; when, e.g. the observed behaviour of water turning into ice or steam in proportion as heat is withdrawn or applied coincides in detail with the deduced interrelations of octahedrons, tetrahedrons, and ikosahedrons.[11] And it is not only among the phenomena of nature that such analogies can be discovered. In the field of social phenomena, a similar empirical science is possible. The finished dialectician can work out a pure deductive science of politics, constructed entirely in the realm of " ideas." The concept of city or community is analysed into the interactivity of citizens, each contributing something essential to community life, and with as many types of citizen as there are typically distinct essential functions of citizenship. The dialectician thus deduces the presence of such elements as farmerships, artisanships, warriorships, distributorships, priestships, etc., and calculates their proportional and functional interrelations in a single self-sustaining community of five thousand and forty families. All this is " pure," non-empirical science. Empirical political science proper arises when analogies between these pure deductions and the observed phenomena of human beings in society are discovered, i.e. when the observed behaviour of actual flesh-and-blood men and women coincides in detail with the deduced behaviour of the corresponding conceptual constructions. In the case of political, as of natural science, such analogies are frequent, and their discovery and establishment furnishes a highly intellectual occupation, a species of game by playing which the philosopher can amuse his hours of leisure, when he is resting from the more strenuous work of strict deduction.[12]   But actual men and women differ from the ideal concepts quite as much as the actual sense-perceivable world of nature differs from the intra-spherical deductions applied to ikosahedrons, etc., so that this empirical science, though superior to Pythagorean groping because grounded in the ideal world, is precarious in its applications to a region in which fluctuation takes the place of permanency.   As science, such analogies cannot be taken very seriously.[13] But while the study of natural science is optional for human beings, political science, however precarious its empirical applications, is obviously a necessity for reflective human beings compelled by the exigencies of their empirical nature to live together in social groups which, in varying degrees, fall short of the calculated ideal.   This practical necessity,[14] however, does not alter the fact that, from the standpoint of logical validity, both branches of empirical science are upon the same level, and consist in the search for analogies between the ideal realm of pure rational deduction and the fluctuating sense-perceivable phenomena among which our actual empirical life is spent.

There are thus, in platonism, three types of scientific knowledge :   (1) the empirical generalizations which constitute the " science " of the so-called Pythagoreans ;   (2) the pure deductive rationalism of the dialectician, which consists in working out the logical inter-implications of pure concepts and thus constructing an absolutely intelligible world ;   and (3) the empirical science proper, which is constituted by the analogies discovered between the positions of the pure scientists and the behaviour of sense-perceivable phenomena.   It is not to be supposed that the empirical behaviour of the sense-perceivable phenomena constitutes, in any sense which the Platonist would regard as important, a criterion by which to test the validity of the pure deductions of the dialectician.   These, like the operations of the pure mathematician, stand upon their own feet.   For the Platonist, it is the empirical applications which are precarious and not entirely scientific.   The only justification for undertaking such applications in a serious spirit is practical, not theoretical, necessity ;   i.e. the need of making human life as rational as possible, as nearly as possible a concrete embodiment of the pure idea of good, the principle of maximal realization of potentiality.   When, then, it is stated that scientific know-

ledge constitutes the highest good, we must understand that
the Pythagorean type of empiricism is finally rejected, and
that it is only to the two platonic species of science that the
value-judgment applies. Of these, further, it is pure, rather
than empirical, science which is regarded as the highest good ;
though the empirical applications are sometimes included as
logically implicit, for a human being, in the pure science.
In saying, then, that scientific knowledge is the highest good
for man, it is meant that the knowledge of the dialectician,
applied to human affairs, is the highest good. But to say this
is to resolve scientific knowledge into what platonism understands by " philosophy " ; and to this we accordingly now
turn.

That philosophy is regarded by Plato as the highest of
human goods, is obvious to every reader of the Dialogues.
In the philosopher-king of the *Republic*, Plato depicts a character intended to be ideally perfect from start to finish.
Physically, he is all that could be desired : beautiful, healthy,
strong in body, trained in all manly sports and exercises,
and recognizing always the limitations of a merely physical
excellence. Morally, he is all that could be desired : possessing not only the physical dispositions which underlie courage,
temperance, justice, piety, and wisdom, but also so trained
socially and intellectually that moral action is not merely a
habit, but is always a matter of principle with him. Intellectually, he is all one could hope for in an ideal character :
for he is saturated with the literature and traditions of his
race, and has been trained for many years in the sciences until
finally he has attained to the deepest metaphysical insight.
Thus equipped, he is, for the future, a free citizen of the whole
intellectual realm, and is enabled to devote his whole powers
of action to the practical side of political science, refreshing
himself, at intervals, with deep draughts of speculative investigation. With such a character, the genius of criticism
itself could find no fault. He is a perfect soul in a perfect
body. The only weakness about the pictures—if platonism
would regard it as a weakness[15]—is that it is, if anything, too
perfect. Such characters are not actual.

So too philosophy itself is a study which rests upon and
includes everything of value in other studies and practices,
and culminates in direct insight into the principle of value,
as such. This insight implies possession of the power to

improve indefinitely the principles and methods of every field of investigation and action, and, as a further corollary, implies willingness to use that power for the betterment of humanity, partly by administration, and partly by education. Here, too, the only possible objection is that Plato's depiction is too ideal for ordinary humanity. It is not merely a study he depicts, but a life ; and, for him undoubtedly, philosophy is the way, the truth, and the life. It is consciously delineated as the highest of goods, and this is so completely understood by every reader, that it is unnecessary, in the present place, to do more than indicate the evidence upon which this universally admitted fact rests[16] before passing on to the investigation of mind.

The nature of mind has been made the subject of detailed investigation in an earlier chapter. In the present section we shall confine ourselves to rearranging the main results of the previous investigation in such a way as to throw light on the question as to the value of mind. How far, and for what reasons, does the philosopher regard mind as the highest good ?

For platonism, mind is under all circumstances a principle of order, which so analyses and synthesizes its data, as to extract from them their utmost of meaning-value. Thus, given a number of sense-impressions, fugitive, chaotic, contradictory, and, to that extent, meaningless, mind, applying its characteristic procedure, reduces the whole situation to a texture of clear-cut concepts, partly sensory, as in the case of hardness, softness, loudness, etc., and partly formal, as in the case of sameness, difference, unity, duality, etc., all so rearranged that each comes to have its definite place in that all-comprehending totality of consistent meanings which is the ultimate logical ideal. Again, given a chaotic welter of conflicting human interests, the procedure followed by mind can untangle the apparently hopeless confusion, by analyzing out the conceptual elements of individual and social psychology involved in the situation, and by constructing and applying the ideal of harmonious co-operation, the model or pattern which represents perfect community of feeling, thought, and action. In this way mind provides a definite, meaningful sphere of activity for each one of the interest-elements revealed by the analysis, so that each can proceed to do its own work in harmony with the rest.[17]

In this procedure, mind is never purely arbitrary or fanciful. The analysis follows lines of cleavage which it finds indicated in the data. Mind takes an element out of one context, in which its potentialities are counteracted or suppressed, and puts it into another, in which co-operative stimulation helps it to realize its maximal value, much as a child, experimenting with the pieces of a jig-saw puzzle, fits them together into a perfect picture, in which there is a meaningful place for each piece. Apart from this procedure of mind, there is chaos, in which a minimum of meaning-value is found. After mind has taken hold of the situation, there is an approximation to a cosmos of meaning and value, to which each of the rearranged elements contributes something, and realizes, in that contribution, its own nature and characteristic function.[18] All that mind does is to experiment with the data until those data realize their own potentialities within a single consistent totality of meaning and value. In such experimentation, mind keeps in the closest possible contact with its data, and its procedure is, so far, as objective as an experiment can well be.

The value realized, then, is the value of the elements. But this is not the whole truth. For these elements, if left to themselves, cannot and do not realize this value which is somehow theirs. Without the addition of some principle which can compel unity, and can thus bring the elements together in their most suitable contexts, their value-potentialities remain forever unrealized, slumbering eternally in the bosom of not-being. A mindless chaos of Democritean atom-whirls in which pure chance rules, is purposeless, a blind unmeaning fixture before which the heart and soul of man recoils. A fortuitous concourse of atoms might conceivably produce haphazard effects, without order or design, but could never generate true values. The successful advance of experimental science itself indicates that the space-time phenomena of our experience obey the logical principle of unity inherent in mind, and Plato regards the atoms themselves as products shaped by mind. They are not, as Democritus supposes, ultimate, unanalysable elements, but are complexes whose unity and regularity are to be ascribed to the principle of unity, and their movements are to be explained, not by reference to pure chance, but as logically deducible consequences of the axial revolution of a perfect sphere—also the product of mind

—which contains and compresses them all. The physical universe with which we come into positive contact by means of our sense-organs, is to be understood as a sense-perceivable image of a perfect, mind-constructed pattern, and its sense-perceivable changes are to be explained in terms of intelligible deductions from the nature of this pattern.[20] If, then, we wish to understand the order, meaning, system, and value which we find in the world we experience, we shall regard as secondary all investigation of a hypothetical " matter " which is essentially chaotic and meaningless, and shall regard as primary the investigation of the principle of order, meaning, and value, i.e. the ruling principle of mind. It is mind, with its ideal of a single ultimate totality of elements perfectly co-ordinated so as to realize the maximum of conceivable value, which is the true source of the law and order found in the world around us.[21]

One further point. The creativity of mind is not exhausted or even most adequately expressed in the reorganization of lifeless matter so as to make the best of its natural resources. In so acting, mind is at the same time making, of its material environment, surroundings suitable for its own further activity, and instruments to assist it in its divine mission of spiritualizing the universe. Its own body, in the first place, when made over so as to respond perfectly to the control of the central self-motion in the brain, is used directly, as a kind of first convert, in further missionary activity. The farmer who uses this, and his other instruments, in tending the things that grow for food, while seeing that the earth, water, warmth, and air which his corn and wheat need for their best development are provided for them, and that they are properly pruned and protected against weeds and other adverse conditions,[22] is really using his farm, not as an end in itself, but as a means. In reclaiming the wilderness, or in making two blades of wheat grow where one grew before, he is extending human civilization over a wider area of the earth's surface, and, while providing food for his own family and for the community, he is, at the same time, strengthening his own and his neighbours' will to advance further. That is to say, while applying the idea of the best in a thoroughly objective way, mind is at the same time making of the universe a more adequate home and instrumentality for mind itself.[23]

And there is something even further. Mind has been

viewed by us as a kind of enzyme which goes out into the world and reduces to its own type of organization, as far as possible, whatever it meets there.   But as long as it meets only lifeless matter, it can succeed only in impressing an image of itself, a circular movement which is a physical copy or imitation of the reflective activity of pure thought.[24]   When it meets, not lifeless matter, but other minds, it creates more directly in its own image.   The mature gymnastic trainer does more than build up muscles and strengthen the digestion.   He appeals by mind to mind, and creates the gymnastic spirit, pouring out his own spirit upon his pupils.   So too the better sort of physician does not confine himself to an unreasoning pre-scription of the approved remedies, but questions, explains, philosophizes, and educates his listeners, creating the thought-ful physician's spirit, as far as his human material admits, so that his apprentices become doctors, and even his more intelligent patients almost become educated to an appreciation of the medical art.[25]   So too the mature farmer creates farmers of his apprentices, the mature lover creates lovers and spreads the gospel of love, and the mature sophist pours out the sophistic spirit upon his pupils and creates sophists,[26] Socrates creates a Plato, and Plato an Aristotle.   The ulti-mate source of this creative spirit is the divine mind.   In the life of the gods depicted in Plato's pages, the divine artist, while leaving the shaping of details to his ministers—them-selves outpourings of his spirit—himself pours out his own creative spirit in " contriving the good in his creations," e.g. in creating the germ of intelligence, the power of realizing the one in the many.   This power is what makes a human being human—i.e. he may one day blossom out into a philosopher-king ; but, even if degraded into the service of vice and crime, this human quality always contains something which reminds us of its high origin and destiny.[27]

Mind, then, creates mind, as a missionary bishop creates, not only converts, but converts who, as they become mature, themselves become missionaries and assist in spreading the gospel.   The spirit of creativity creates the spirit of creativity in an ever-widening circle, and the aim of this spirit is the progressive spiritualization of the universe.   To this creative outpouring of the spirit, all minds, from the poet and law-giver to the simplest peasant, contribute after their kind, and are to some extent aware of their community of effort in this onward march.   But it is in educating and training the select material provided by the rising generation, so as to bring this in its turn to philosophical self-consciousness and to the will to undertake the task of leadership in directing the development of the spiritual resources of the community, that mind becomes most clearly aware of its own function and mission.[28] That is the inner logical ground for the large place occupied by the subject of education in the writings of Plato, and that is why the ability to educate others is regarded by Aristotle as the real test of scientific maturity.

There is a certain danger of misapprehension here.   It might be thought that the objective world has vanished from the philosopher's ken, and that nothing remains but a society of introverted minds, a community suffering from an epidemic of " inwardness." This would be unjust to the evidence, taken as a whole.   The vast majority of men in the platonic, as in other communities, are engaged in activities connected with farming, manufacturing, and distributing.   The " silver " class, selected for civil and military service, is relatively small, and the number of potential philosophers, in the highest sense, is always regarded as extremely small.   Furthermore, the life of the " golden " class itself is at least as objectively oriented as that of the other classes.   The chief difference is in the careful selection of its personnel and in the more intensive cultivation of personal and social excellence in this class. The one occasion in the life of this class which might seem to approach the ascetic withdrawal from the world and an introspective absorption in self, is when the almost-philosopher finally seeks to obtain the vision of the good.   Many scholars to-day, as in Neo-platonic times, interpret this mystically, and it cannot be denied that there is evidence which supports this interpretation.[29] When it is remembered, however, that it is after a period of about fifty years of training in the literature, traditions, and activities of the community, associated with long-continued and intensive study of science,[30] that the philosophic student is encouraged to reflect upon the ultimate principle of being and of knowing, it should be recognized that the groundwork, upon which the value of the reflective process will, of course, depend, is as objective as could well be provided by education ; and when it is further remembered that insight into the principle is followed by its application, not only to the philosopher himself, but also to the task of administering the affairs of the community, there should be no possibility of further misunderstanding. More concretely, the platonic republic, like other communities, while resting upon a broad basis of agricultural and industrial activity, prides itself upon the advanced culture and flowering of the spirit which appears in the small class of its leaders. The chief difference consists, not in there being a small class which might conceivably be regarded as parasitic and useless, but in the special education which makes the platonic leaders peculiarly valuable and useful to their community. Their training and insight have made them, not more etiolated and subjective than the leading classes in other communities, but more objective in every way, and more bound up with the development of their community, more definitely a part of its success or failure. Part of Plato's complaint against the oligarchic and democratic communities of his day is precisely that the leaders in such communities tend to separate the thought of themselves and their own interests so completely from the thought of the well-being of the communities which look to them for leadership and direction, and he has done his best to remedy these conditions in his ideal republic.[31] The philosopher-king is thus not the presiding official of an institution which exists in order to teach teachers to teach teachers to teach teachers . . . but is the representative of mind in its characteristic effort to raise to its own level of order, unity, system, and the self-conscious life of the spirit, whatever, in its environment, is to any extent capable of being so raised, and, in so acting, mind is aware that it is acting for the best, not only of itself, but also of its environment.[32]

Thus understood, how far, and for what reasons is mind regarded as the highest good ? In the first place, it is the primary source of goodness, wherever manifested, the creative activity which calls into being the values which would otherwise remain forever in the state of not-being. Mind is the source of motion in the physical universe. That is to say, mind is the original source of the perfect or circular motion which unifies and compresses space-time phenomena into a physical image of the ideal cosmic system : so that the stars in their courses approximate to the ideal motions contemplated by mind, and physical time comes into existence, which is an image, in the world of motion, of that eternal duration of the intellectual place beyond the heaven of the fixed stars, in which the contemplative spirit feeds upon the mind-renewing Ideas.[33]   So too in the psychological realm : it is mind which makes of our dispositions something worth while, and develops their natural resources to the highest pitch of excellence of which they are susceptible. In art, commerce, politics, science, and religion, mind is the primary and ultimate source of all values. It removes hindrances, banishes conflicts, creates harmony and order, and thus makes it possible for everything which has the potentiality of value, to realize that potentiality.[34]

This is enough, of itself, to give to mind a high place in the rank of goods. But it is not enough to make it appear that mind holds the *highest* place. We think nowadays readily of a university or industrial corporation. The president, or administrative head, is the ultimate source of value, in a certain sense ; for he removes hindrances, banishes conflicts, creates harmony and order, and develops the value-potentialities of his institution or corporation to the highest pitch of realization. And it is true that his services usually receive the highest compensation. But we often feel that the value of the institution really depends more upon the abilities of the personel whose services the institution can attract and hold, than upon the smooth running of the administrative machinery ; and in some of the most distinguished institutions the administrative headship is little more than a routine position, held for a year or two by the senior men in rotation. In consequence, we should hesitate to regard administrative headship, as such, as the highest good. Plato exhibits a somewhat similar hesitation, and tends, at times, to regard the life of the contemplative scholar as higher in value than the life of administrative leadership, and to admit that his scholars might grudge the time taken from investigation in order to attend committee meetings and keep the machinery running.[35]   But, on the whole, he regards the presidential position as calling for the full utilization of the highest powers of knowledge, judgment, and leadership, so much so that men of presidential calibre, even in his ideal community, would be extremely few. For the presidential position is never a matter of routine, but is a position of genuine leadership which should be entrusted, not to the senior man, but to the man whose whole life has shown him to possess the finest character and the deepest as well as the most comprehensive mind.[36] Mind is therefore regarded, by the Platonist, as the highest of goods.

It remains to discuss briefly two questions :—(1) the relation of " mind " to " soul," and (2) the relation of the individual mind to the mind which is regarded as the highest good. (1) In different contexts, Plato recognizes different levels of mind and of soul. Sometimes " soul " is the wider term, including the functions of nutrition and reproduction, and the mechanical side of all the social and personal dispositions.[37] As contrasted with this, " mind " is used in a strictly intellectual reference, as the non-mechanical source of that wisdom and sound judgment which brings value to our various dispositions. In this sense it is said that " all things hang upon the soul, and the soul depends upon wisdom," etc.[38] At other times, it is pointed out that the intellect itself may be misused, as by the rascally lawyer, money-maker, or burglar.[39] But, at its best, " soul " and " mind " are undoubtedly intended to coincide in all respects ; and we have accordingly, in treating of " mind " as the highest good, not scrupled to treat it as identical with " soul " at its best.[40]

The highest good being " mind," then, the question (2) may well be asked :—whose mind—yours or mine, or just mind in general ? To this question, the answer is relatively simple. The mind which is the highest good is, of course, an ideal pattern, ideal mind, never the actual mind of a particular human individual. Particular human beings may approximate to this ideal, may make their lives gradually take up into themselves more and more of this ideal, so that their every thought, word, and action becomes instinct with wisdom. In this sense, a particular human individual—such as the philosopher-king—might conceivably become a human pattern of wisdom. But the ideal pattern would always be something more than human beings had actually experienced. Over and above the best we have seen and heard, there always remains for thought the idea of a still more absolute perfection, and the " mind " which is the highest good belongs, of course, in the realm of absolute ideas.[41] Again, for the Platonist, man is only one of an order of spiritual beings which extends, not merely below, but also above his own level of capacity ; and the most perfect human pattern of wisdom would thus fall short of an ideal of wisdom which would serve as a pattern, not merely for men, but for spiritual and rational beings, as such. The mind which is the highest good is thus God's mind, the ideal Experience which we regard as including human experience, at its best, and also as transcending it in dignity and value. It is in this sense, as the living essence of ideal spirituality, that mind, for the Platonist, constitutes the highest good.[42] As for the individual human being, it is *his* highest good to develop his mind as far as he can, so that he can enter as fully as possible into this Experience in which alone true reality is to be found.[43]

CHAPTER XIX

I N many contexts, "moderation" and "the moderate,"
the "mean" and the "limit," are highly praised as
principles which make art and conduct valuable, and
in a few contexts they are definitely stated to be the
highest good. This is, of course, especially true in the *Philebus*,
but the *Laws* are full of such contexts, and they are found
scattered up and down all the later Dialogues, including the
Republic. In order to obtain a concrete idea of what is to be
understood by this term, we shall therefore deal with the whole
field investigated in these later Dialogues, and shall inquire
what is meant by " the mean," in the world studied by natural
science, in medical science and art, in the art of music, and in
human conduct. From such an investigation we should be
able to discover the general sense of the term, and in particular
to discover why it is identified with the highest good.

The world studied by natural science has been investigated in detail elsewhere.[1] In the present context it will,
perhaps, be sufficient to extract from our various discoveries
the portions which bear directly upon the principle of " the
mean." Pure rational science, as Plato understands this,
has for its task the construction of a strictly theoretical universe, in terms of mathematical solids whose regular surfaces
are compounded out of right-angled triangles, and whose
motions are conditioned throughout by the principle of circularity. The triangle and the circle, however, are mental
constructions in which the mind applies its own fundamental
principle of the " limit " or " mean " to an otherwise unlimited
and chaotic " extension " and " motion." The principles and
details of the theoretical universe thus constructed derive
their whole significance from the principle of the " mean."[2]
Empirical science, as Plato understands this, proceeds by
discovering analogies between the deductions of theoretical
physics and the observed behaviour of sense-perceivable

442

phenomena.   There is, e.g. an analogy between the deduced behaviour of the theoretical tetrahedron and the observed behaviour of " fire " ;   and a further analogy between the octahedron and " air," between the ikosahedron and " water," and between the cube and " earth."[3]   But in all such empirical science, what is really understood by the mind is the formal or mathematical elements, i.e. ultimately the mental principle of the " mean."   In the world studied by natural science, then, it is the function of the principle of the " mean " to super-impose a mind-made system of geometric patterns upon a primitive chaos, and thus to reduce this chaos to order, and to endow it with meanings, laws, and a system which the mind can grasp because, in apprehending them, it is ultimately apprehending its own principle.

Let us now consider medical science.   The human body, with which medicine is especially concerned, consists of quasi-atomic elements of fire, water, earth, and air, arranged in accordance with a certain formula or law of proportion.   A different formula, applied to similar elements of fire, water, earth, and air, would give us a different animal or a plant.[4] Such an organism, in perpetual interaction with the fire, water, earth, and air which constitute its inorganic environment, loses parts of its substance, and, even if its special formula or pro-portion is preserved, would, of itself, dwindle away in the wear and tear of daily life.[5]   However, by the processes of eating and drinking, organic material containing fire, water, earth, and air is taken into the alimentary canal.   There it is split up into its elements, which are then conveyed, in quasi-fluid form, via the mechanisms of the circulatory sustem, to the different parts of the body, and all deficiencies of earth, water, fire, and air in these parts are made good from the new material.   So long as the proportionate relationship of the specific human formula is preserved, the human being remains healthy, his organism grows—or at least maintains its *status quo*, and the atoms of earth, water, fire, and air are controlled and kept in their appointed places.[6]

In this case, by the " mean " Plato understands the formula or principle of proportion which controls the elemen-tary atoms of earth, water, fire, and air, and keeps each in its appointed place, or at least, if one disappears, replaces it with another from the material taken into the alimentary canal. This controlling principle does its work by means of properly regulated motion, i.e. primarily by circular motion originating in the cerebral hemispheres and spreading gradually into the circulatory system. A second method of doing its work is by exercise of the body as a whole, in such a way as to shake the whole system. By means of such motion, the waste elements in the organism tend to be removed, and the new material being conveyed throughout the circulatory system becomes fitted into its place, fire-elements fitting into tetrahedronal vacancies, water-elements fitting into ikosahedronal vacancies, etc., and the whole becomes properly welded together in the intervals of rest and sleep.[7]

What occurs in the absence of the mean ? Suppose that one takes too little exercise and too much sleep, as in the case of the professional wrestlers of whom Plato so strongly disapproves.[8] In this case, the food taken into the alimentary canal is not sufficiently dissolved and is not sufficiently conveyed through the circulatory system, while the waste products are not properly carried off. The body does not succeed in absorbing the new material, and a plethora results, which upsets the balance or proportion of the bodily elements. An excess of watery elements produces dropsy. An excess of fiery elements produces fever. Serious excess of all elements produces severe indigestion, which is always followed by wasting away, as the mean-principle has become enfeebled and is unable to master the entering streams of food and drink.[9] In brief, when the principle of the mean is overcome, the body tends to fall apart. The various elements refuse to combine, and fight with one another. The flesh comes away from the bones, the marrow of the bones disintegrates, and the body begins to fall to pieces, tending by degrees towards chaos and not-being.[10]

Faced with this situation, scientific medicine endeavours to restore the principle of the mean to full control. If the process of degeneration in the direction of chaos or not-being has not gone too far, the physician educates his patient, philosophizes, in fact, and gives him a rational understanding of the nature and importance of the mean. He urges his patient to observe the regularity of the stars in their courses, and to take these as a pattern by which to correct his own irregularities, especially in connection with his circular cerebrations. If this circular brain-motion can be restored, all the rest, viz., self-determined gymnastic exercise, and the observance of hygienic measures in eating, drinking, exercising and resting, will follow as a matter of course.[11]   If, however, the process of degeneration has reached such a point that the patient is incapacitated, and cannot possibly carry out a regimen of self-directed gymnastic exercise, the physician prescribes an ocean voyage, or carriage riding, which will provide the whole body with gentle but persistent movement, and will enable the organism gradually to get rid of the noxious waste products and to absorb properly a carefully balanced diet, until the principle of due proportion is again restored.[12] If, however, the processes of degeneration have gone so far that the body can hardly be treated as a whole, the physician has to take extreme measures.   In order to arrest the decay due to an overbalancing of the earthy or watery elements in the body, he has recourse to emetics and cathartics, or to the scalpel and cauterizing iron, by local operations removing whatever elements are present in extreme form.   These expedients of scientific medicine are purely negative in themselves.   They are dangerous and weakening to the system, and must always be followed by the previous positive measures for restoring the original principle of the mean.   For it is not when disproportion has been removed by force, but rather when proportion has extended its sway gently but persistently over all the bodily elements, that health is genuinely present and can continue of itself, without further assistance from the outside.[13]

In the case of scientific medicine, then, absence of the mean is synonymous with disintegration, chaos, not-being, while the presence of the mean signifies proportion, law, order, control, and reason.   These put each element in its place, so that all continue to work together for the good of the whole. There is a further suggestion that, as the circular cerebrations of man resemble the circular orbits of the stars and the circular revolution of the universe as a whole, the scientific physician, in removing irregularities and thus restoring the principle of circularity to its control over human motions, is co-operating with the deepest purposes of nature, in its especial work of rearranging material elements so as to realize their potentialities to the full.   And further : as this rearrangement not only seeks the maximal development of material co-operation among the elements concerned, but also furnishes the best conceivable basis for the development of spiritual life, aesthetic,

moral, religious, and intellectual, the physician believes, and
believes reasonably—i.e. philosophically—that scientific medicine is working directly towards the realization of the highest
good.[14]

Let us pass to consider the art of music. Sounds, considered absolutely, are infinite in range and variety. The
air-waves produced by the singing voice, or by blowing into
some such instrument as the flute, or by plucking a string of
varying tension, are what the Greeks call " infinite." That
is to say, between what we call A and what we call B, it is
possible to produce an indefinite number of intermediate tones
which pass into one another by imperceptible gradations, as
when a flute-player is trying empirically to produce a note of
determinate pitch by placing his finger over more or less of the
vent-hole, or as when a harpist or lyre-player is fiddling with
the tension of his vibrating chords until he produces the precise
note towards which he is groping. It is all a matter of more
or less, of approximating empirically to what the trained ear
of the artist regards as just right.[15]

In this absolute range, however, of an infinity of tones
varying by imperceptibly minute gradations, there are, as far
as the human singing voice is concerned, certain ranges which
differ from each other in extent and quality. The singing
voice of a young man differs characteristically from the singing
voice of a young woman both in range and in quality, and there
are a definite number of such vocal ranges recognized and
standardized in ancient music, corresponding roughly to the
range of a soprano, contralto, tenor, and bass voice in modern
music.[16] And further : within each such range, the human
voice, while capable (like the flute) of producing an indefinite
number of sounds, tends, in fact, to express and to dwell with
peculiar satisfaction upon certain very definite sounds,
separated from one another by ascertainable intervals. This
gives rise, within each vocal range taken by itself, to a characteristic progression of tones which, when duly standardized,
is called a natural scale. These scales differ from one another,
not only in respect of terminal points—as the bass register
differs from the soprano register, for example—but also in
respect of the intervals. The intervals of a characteristic bass
scale, e.g. proceed according to the following proportions :

while the characteristic intervals of a soprano scale are different, proceeding as follows :—

17

In producing a definite note on one of these scales, whether by the singing voice or by means of some musical instrument such as a flute or lyre, the musician feels after his note, toning down a sound which is too high, or toning up a sound which is too low, until he strikes the pitch which his practised ear assures him is just right. This process of feeling his way towards the right note and avoiding any of the innumerable possible gradations to either side, is regarded as seeking the "mean," and to apply the principle of the mean, in Greek music, thus means primarily to produce the characteristic note in a given natural scale.

There is something further to be considered. Not only are such interval-series within the natural vocal ranges an integral part of music as the Greeks understand it, but it was early observed that it is natural for the human voice to express certain dispositions in a characteristic way. This is a matter of rhythmic patterns rather than of pitch, as such. Rhythmic distinctions are also, taken absolutely, infinite, but, relatively to human dispositions, fall into fairly definite patterns. The manly character expresses itself naturally in marching rhythms; the feminine character expresses itself naturally in certain characteristic dance-rhythms ; and the human dispositions towards courage, temperance, piety, etc., have each a natural rhythm, while a loose and abandoned disposition has a natural affinity with rhythms which approximate towards formlessness.[18] It is found that certain of these natural rhythms seem to go naturally with certain of the natural vocal ranges. But, as the number of recognized human dispositions is far greater than the number of natural vocal ranges, and some of these dispositions seem to cut across the rhythmic patterns appropriate to the natural scales, a number of extra scales have been artificially created, by slightly relaxing or tightening up the natural scales, or even by mixing them up in a form which combines all of them into a single (chromatic) scale and thus robs music of the definite characteristics associated with the definite separate scales.[19]

The function of music being to accompany the dance and song, it goes almost without saying that the rhythmic patterns adopted in a given musical composition will be identical with the rhythmic patterns of the dance which the musician is accompanying. That is to say, if the dance is anapaestic, the accompaniment will be anapaestic ; and if the dance follows the rhythm called "enoplion," the music will be set in the enoplion rhythm, so that, to each movement and accent of the foot, a definite movement and accent will be provided by the accompanist, with a one-to-one correspondence. It follows also that, as the dance rhythms and the song rhythms coincide, at least in principle, the notes of the singing voice will correspond exactly with the syllables and accent of the words which are to be sung, one note to one syllable, and that, where there is an instrumental accompaniment, the notes of the lyre will be identical in pitch, length, and stress, with the notes of the voice. The Greek composer does not set the words to music, but sets music to the words, and his music follows the words, not only in the correspondence of one note to each syllable, but in every other possible way as well.[20] Thus, if the song is warlike, it will be in enoplic or at least in marching rhythm, and the music will be in the corresponding natural scale or harmony, using the note-intervals and the vocal range appropriate to young men in war-like mood. That is to say, it will be set in the so-called "Dorian mode." A hymn of praise and thanks, again, will be set in ceremonial rhythms appropriate to the occasion, and the music will be in the "Phrygian mode," using the note-intervals and vocal range appropriate to peaceful citizens in a temperate and pious mood.[21] According to the stricter usage in what, with the ancient Greeks, took the place of our "classical music," this unity between (a) the words expressing appropriate sentiments, (b) the dance-rhythms expressing the same sentiments, (c) the vocal melody, and (d) the instrumental accompaniment, was always observed, and each musical composition was thus true to its "idea" or natural type.[22] The attainment of this unity was regarded as an expression of the " mean," which avoided the infinity of possible divergences and selected the one point of identity in the various elements which together made up a musical composition, and thus brought order and meaning into what might otherwise, i.e. apart from some such unifying principle, be a disorderly and chaotic jumble of words, rhythms, and tones, without the slightest inner connection with one another, and with no direct relation to any definite sentiment or meaning.[23]

In applying this principle of the mean, whether to the scales as wholes, or to the individual notes of voice or lyre, or to the unison-effect of voice and accompaniment, in connection with rhythm and meaning, the last court of appeal was always the artistic musician, with his practised ear and hand. One artist agreed with another artist about such matters as pitch, scale, and rhythm, etc., and thus the agreement of experts had introduced a certain definiteness and standardization of natural types into ancient music. It was empirical, but still there was agreement.[24] From the point thus reached, two lines of development were possible. Greek music actually followed, to a great extent, (1) the path of empiricism,[25] but Plato would prefer that musicians should follow (2) the path implied in their agreement with one another, and should reflect upon what is involved in the essential naturalness of the scales, and the interesting fact of their standardizability.

Let us consider, in the first place, the path actually followed by Greek music. Faced with a number of scales, all appropriate to special situations, but all capable of being relaxed or toned up to meet varieties of situation not precisely corresponding, at least in their entirety, to the standard scales, the musicians inevitably experimented with their scales, producing a large number of new ones, and eventually incorporating all the notes recognized (after a few minor changes) into a single all-inclusive scale. They further experimented in the direction of harmony, giving up the earlier independence of the standardized scales, and permitting boys and men, for example, to sing together in a chorus which combined the soprano register with the bass register. As boys and men could not well sing notes of identical pitch, they were allowed to sing notes an octave apart, and this became a regular feature of choral music, thoroughly understood and regarded as a typical form of Greek composition.[26] They experimented further in having men and women sing together, and in trying out intervals less than the octave, such as the third and fourth.[27] So far, representatives of the two registers, while differing in pitch, would continue to sing note for note, following always the same rhythm and accent. But further experimentation tried out an accompaniment which would play notes differing in number from the notes of the voice part, and would thus interfere, as it might seem to an amateur, with the absolute rhythmic simplicity of musical composition. This variation on the part of the accompaniment might be similar in pitch to the voice part, or, in certain cases, might be either higher or lower. Finally, there was a tendency for the instrumental accompaniment to go still further, and break away entirely from the words, and even from the dance rhythms, and to endeavour to establish itself as an independent art.[28] Such complications went beyond what the gentlemanly amateur could follow, but were regarded as not inartistic or inappropriate for trained musicians ; and in all such cases Greek musicians recognized, as the law or " mean " which prescribed to them their limitations and their possibilities, the trained ear of the musical expert.[29]

But there was a further tendency, due largely to the accident of musicians competing before a popular audience, for such experts to submit their own judgment of what was legitimate and appropriate in their art to what the musically untrained populace would greet with unrestrained applause. Variations, trills, and other meretricious ornamentations of melody and rhythm became the order of the day, and then, farewell to the old " classical " type of music ! The standard is no longer anything even approximately absolute, but is the mere capricious pleasure-reactions of the popular audience. The old, distinct type-forms go. All the rules go, and nothing is left but a characterless jumble of tones and rhythms corresponding to the boundless confusion of modern, fourth-century democracy. The ancient art has been swallowed up by the new chaos which its experimentation and novelty-seeking has helped to bring about. The bounds are loosed, and " the one " has become lost in " the many."[30] This suicide of art has been brought about by the artists themselves. The artist has two sides to his nature : the one, truly artistic, concerned with apprehending and applying the principle of the mean ; the other, human, seeking the flattery and applause of his essentially inartistic though enthusiastic fellow-men. It is this social motive which induces him to stoop to innovations and meretricious experimentations, doing away with this rule and with that, until none are left. When all have gone, art has gone too, and the one-time artist has degraded himself to the level of the inartistic multitude. He has become one of the mob, and has forgotten how to envisage and how to use the principle of the mean. This is the path of development actually followed by empirical musicians in Greece, and terminates in senseless imitation of any striking noises, such as the moaning of the wind, the rolling of thunder, the bellowing of oxen, the wailing of children, the hoof-beats of horses, the creaking of waggon-wheels, the screeching of ship's pulleys, or of other badly oiled machinery.[31]

In explicit contrast with this actual development, Plato emphasizes the objective rather than the subjective aspects of music. What is it which makes a " natural " scale natural ? Surely it rests, not upon a merely subjective reaction such as pleasure, but upon the artist's apprehension of distinctions which really exist objectively, *in rerum natura*. The relations to one another of the intervals which constitute any given scale can, as the " Pythagoreans " discovered long ago, be expressed as mathematically exact proportions of chord-tension, and when all the scales have been thus expressed, it is possible to compare their inter-relations, no longer (as with Aristoxenus or Archytas) in terms of such a fluctuating standard as minimal audible distinctions, but in terms of their standardized and exact mathematical correlates, such as $1:2$, or $9:8$, and out of such numerical ratios to construct a single theoretical or perfect system of all musical scales. Such scales can be finally standardized, not at all in terms of the audible properties of sensuous tones, but in terms of the absolutely intelligible properties of numbers.[32] And further : as man and the cosmos are smaller and larger portions of one and the same natural system, and exhibit in other respects the operation of the same fundamental laws, it is to be expected that the musical intervals which are natural to man will correspond to musical intervals which are natural to the cosmic organism. From this it will follow that, as the mathematical expression of the tetrahedrons, octahedrons, etc., of which a man's body is composed is in principle identical with the mathematical expression of the elements which go to make up the macrocosm, so the final mathematical expression of (intelligible) human scales will coincide in principle with the mathematical expression of the system of cosmic scales. In this case, it will be reasonable to take the position that the musical artist is, in practice, feeling, by sensuous means, after the absolute music of the cosmos which the philosopher can apprehend in intelligible terms. This absolutely intelligible scale is at least partially realized in the motions of the planetary system, the intervals between the notes of the absolute scale being exactly proportioned to the distance of one planetary orbit from its next neighbour, and the proportions of these distances being identical with the proportionate intervals which separate the notes on the standardized scale perfected after intellectual reflection upon human music.[33] So also the rhythmic forms which approve themselves to the genuine artist are approximations to the objective rhythms of the universe apprehended by the intellectual insight of the philosopher. It follows, then, that true music—music which is not just playing with tones and rhythms—should be a representation, in melodies, scales, and rhythm-forms which can be appreciated by the sensuous nature of man, of the mathematically intelligible dance of the stars in their courses, courses which are a visible copy of the invisible and purely intelligible laws of the absolutely ideal universe created by God and understood directly only by a mixture of human logic and divine inspiration.[34]

It should not be supposed that the philosopher is a better artist, however, a better creator of musical forms which please the human ear than the creative artist who is not a philosopher. On the contrary, Plato is perfectly aware that sober logic and creative art are seldom, if ever, united in a single human personality.[35] The dialectician attains to insight into the system of intelligible laws, of which the starry heavens are a sense-perceivable copy or image. But his severely non-sensuous method of inquiry makes him at home in a universe which is primarily intelligible, and the perfect scale and intelligible harmony, which he lovingly apprehends as characterizing the intelligible world, are not directly reproducible upon human instruments of music. His scale and his harmonies are, in a word, unplayable, and the absolute or ultra-cosmic music which he apprehends in principle, and venerates, is (to human ears) inaudible.[36] On the other hand, the

creative artist, while partly feeling that he is trying to reproduce ideal strains which he is discovering rather than inventing,
does not permit himself to waste his energies in attempting
to play the unplayable, but contents himself, as best he can,
with throwing together, in a way which partly satisfies his
artistic sense, sounds and rhythms which represent a compro-
mise between actuality and the demands of the ideal. His
scales fall short, to some extent, of the perfect system apprehended by a Plato. His melodies come short of the beauty
of the unheard ideal. But his music can be danced to, can
be chanted, and can be enjoyed by mortals ;[37] whereas
transcendental music can be neither heard, sung, danced to
empirically, nor apprehended in a more than symbolic intuition
by any save the most intellectual of mankind. And even by
them it is apprehended only in idea, and not at all in a way
which could reasonably be called " music."

Faced, then, with this acknowledged contrast between
creative art and philosophic insight, platonism draws the only
possible conclusion : viz., that the creation of music in the ideal
community is to be a matter of co-operation. The artist
creates what he can, but is compelled to submit his creations
to the censorship of the dialectician. The dialectician, in
consultation with experts, lays down certain norms or standards, in the way of scales, rhythms, and melodic patterns
adapted to induce in the citizens who play and hear such music,
courage, temperance, piety, justice, and a feeling for the beauty
of wisdom. These virtues represent the essential elements
of character approved for members of the ideal community,
and the dialectician sees to it that the new standards, which
have, as he understands it, metaphysical objectivity and
metaphysical justification, are conformed to by all compositions which receive his *imprimatur*.[38] In this co-operative
effort, both artist and philosopher are guided throughout by
the principle of the mean. It is this principle which introduces unity, law, and order into the individual notes, the
individual scales, the individual rhythms, and the composition
as a whole, on its technical side ; and so far the principle is well
understood by the artist. In what follows, the artist does
not need to understand ; but it is fully apprehended by the
philosopher. It is because the principle of the mean is also
the principle of order, not only in the actual cosmos, but also
in each member of the ideal realm of which the actual cosmos

is a sense-perceivable image, that the art of music acquires, in becoming the thorough-going application of the principle of the mean to the realm of sounds and rhythms, a significance which is not merely physical, and not merely human, but is metaphysical and divine in meaning and function.[39]

Let us pass to consider human conduct. In this field, " the mean " is used in a sense analogous to the sense in which it is used in the arts. The Dialogues assume that, if life has any meaning, it is an art, and that the artist in life, as in medicine or music, will avoid extremes and will seek and find the middle path, i.e. what expert artists agree to regard as just right. Too much power, too much wealth, too much pleasure, etc., lead inevitably to that very inartistic state called by the Greeks " *hybris*," that ill-bred insolence which is always provoking divine nemesis.[40] Too little power, too restricted means, too little enjoyment, on the other hand, make a man unmanly, deficient in proper self-respect, inefficient and incapable of asserting himself as a freeman should, slavish.[41] The mean state in respect of possessions, noble birth, personal beauty and strength, and in all natural and acquired gifts of the soul, represents the ideal, if one is to live the happy life of the good citizen.[42]

In giving expression to these views, the Dialogues simply follow the universal Hellenic axiom, " nothing too much," not only expressed on the pillar at Delphi, but receiving a hundred different formulations in tragedy and history, in poetry and myth, and in every form of Greek literature. What platonism adds to the popular belief, beyond Plato's personal view that fourth-century democracy represents an almost mean-less chaos, is a justification of this belief in terms of the ideal theory. The " idea " represents the application of the principle of the mean or limit to a specific field of experience, so that to observe the mean is to follow the principle of the idea, i.e. to partake of the ideal life. In this way, one who is observing the mean is *ipso facto* living the ideal life or realizing the highest good, with the further feeling that his life has not only personal and popular sanctions, but has also a metaphysical basis and is being formed upon the objective principle of ultimate reality.

If we now look over all the cases we have studied, we find that in all of them, in the physical universe no less than in science, art, and conduct, the mean or objective standard of measurement is identical with the principle of the idea.   The idea is, in fact, the application of the principle of the limit to the otherwise unlimited or chaotic, in such a way as to reduce it to unity, law, and order, and by so unifying it to develop its meaning or value-potentialities to the highest degree.   In a chaos, potential elements, meanings, and values, not being interconnected in any rational way, do not become developed, but remain eternally slumbering in a state of not-being. Unifications so interrelate them that they do not conflict and cancel out, but develop their positive value-potentialities in a single, mutually supporting system.   The principle of this unification is the limit or mean, and, when it is stated that " the mean " is the highest good, what is meant is that the principle of the idea is the source of all idealization, of all elevation of fact to value, in a word, that the principle of the mean is identical with the principle of the best, or idea of good, and is thus the source of all organization and re-arrangement of materials so that the maximal value or highest good is developed and comes into being.[43]

CHAPTER XX

CIVILIZATION, THE COMMUNITY, COMMUNAL SELF-KNOWLEDGE,
LAW AND ORDER, THE COMPREHENSIVE OR COMPOSITE LIFE,
THE EXCELLENCE AND PRESERVATION OF THE WHOLE, GOD, AS
HIGHEST GOODS

T HE first four of these candidates for the position of highest good can be examined together, as the contexts in which these terms appear show that they all four have one and the same general reference, and are to be understood as phases of one and the same highest good.

In the first place, civilization or ordered social life is contrasted with life which is uncivilized, wild, unordered, chaotic. It is like the contrast between a cultivated and an uncultivated plant, or between a trained and a wild animal. The wild plant grows where it can and as it can. It straggles, puts out all kinds of shoots, and disperses its energies without, as a rule, making more than a bare living in its incessant struggle against weeds, poor soil, poor water, too much or too little sunshine, and other adverse circumstances. The cultivated plant, on the other hand, receives rational treatment which applies to it the idea of good, i.e. arranges its circumstances and its growth for the best. It is given just the right kind and amount of sunshine, water, earth, and air, is kept free from weeds, and is pruned and properly assisted and directed, so that it realizes its potentialities to the utmost.[1] In the same way, uncivilized life, a life without law and order, is like the life of wild animals herding together in a none too rational way. There may be survival, but the circumstances are largely adverse. Such a life is a constant struggle for the bare subsistence minimum, and is marked by a complete absence of almost everything which makes life seem, to a civilized man, worth living.[2]

In contrast with such a life, let us consider the development of a civilized community. Formed, originally, to protect human beings from wild beasts and other dangers, even more than for sociability, the city wall which brings men and women together around a common geographical centre naturally develops a number of institutions which are new. Their primary motive is, no doubt, their value for group survival, but their subsequent development is influenced by idealism, i.e. by the self-conscious attempt to make communal institutions subserve the best life.[3]   For example, the problem of securing an adequate food-supply brings the members of such a group together, necessitating co-operation and calling out whatever natural resources in the way of leadership happen to be present in the group.   So too fear of warlike competitors for food and control over the natural resources of the locality, of itself, necessitates military organization of the members, and their disciplined obedience to a leader in whom they have confidence.   Again, disease, especially if it takes the form of an epidemic, necessitates group control and co-operation under expert guidance, if the group is to survive ; and fear of floods and storms necessitates further similar co-operation.   In all these ways, then, there arises naturally and inevitably a thorough-going co-operation and the establishment of leaders who can bring about, with the help of this co-operation, what is best for the group as a whole, in connection with farming and distribution,[4] in connection with war and diplomacy,[5] in connection with public health,[6] and in connection with emergencies of all sorts.[7]   This co-operation and obedience to duly established leaders, of itself, involves the creation of rules of organization and also the inculcation of special measures, on the part of the leaders, to ensure the attainment of the purposes for which they have been entrusted with power. Out of these rules and measures grows up inevitably a group of community usages and administrative decrees which have the force and function of laws, and are, in fact, the source of whatever law and order becomes established in the community. A community directed by wisely devised laws is efficient in attaining its objects, as contrasted with an undisciplined and unorderly mass of savages, and it is clearly realized in the Dialogues that law and order make for the realization of the best life, and are thus an important element in the highest good of the community.[8]

This function of law and order in social life resembles the function of law and order in the life of the individual, and in the non-social, physical universe. Apart from law and order, both world and individual fall apart into a lawless, boundless, shapeless, and structureless chaos, with movements which are confused, unco-ordinated, fluctuating processes of an a-logical type. In the absence of form and number, life, whether social or individual, becomes irregular, impermanent, unorganized, meaningless. At best, it goes backwards. At worst, it does not go at all, but is entirely devoid of unity and character. Law and order, then, are a condition *sine qua non* of any kind of life, whether social or individual.[9]

Are law and order, however, good in themselves ? Do all social systems, provided they partake of law and order, *ipso facto* and to that extent partake also of the highest good ? The answer is not far to seek. Plato arranges the different communal types in a series, according as they exhibit less or more of order. At the bottom he places unconstitutional despotism, a type of social organization in which an individual rules with a minimal regard for constitutional law and order.[10] Slightly above this he places what he understands as " democracy," where contempt for law and order is almost universal, each individual living as he happens to choose, with complete disregard for the good of the whole. In such a community there is no unity of purpose whatsoever, whether for peace or for war, for business or for religion. Each does as he likes, man, woman, and child, and the very animals in the streets, and, if they agree in anything, it is in intolerance of any sort of leadership, wise or otherwise. In the land of the free-and-equal, everyone is his own king.[11] Slightly above this Plato ranks oligarchy, the community run by a business men's government. In such a community, there is respect for all laws which have to do with business efficiency, and complete contempt for all laws which have to do with other sides of life. The citizens of such a community are pictured as mean, pettifogging scoundrels, so completely absorbed in private gain that they gradually allow the constitution to go to ruin. But at least they do respect property and the laws concerning property.[12] Above this, again, is ranked aristocracy of the military type, concerned primarily with honour, and to a somewhat lesser extent interested in wealth. Here there is respect for far more laws, and these cover a far wider range of subjects than we find respected in the business men's community. Sports, military exercises, and war are prosecuted with efficiency and with thorough-going respect for all the rules of the great game. But in this, as in the other communities, there is complete absence of genuine insight into the true *rationale* of law and order, and a strong tendency to satisfy self-interest rather than to work for the good of the community as a whole. A military dictatorship is not a perfect type of constitution.[13] Finally, above all the rest Plato places his ideal republic, in which the laws are established and administered by philosophic wisdom, in the person of his philosopher-king. Here there is the maximal conceivable respect for law and order, as they are grounded entirely in reason. [14]

From this brief review of the evidence, it would appear that law and order, as such, *are* good in themselves, and that a community, in proportion as it develops more regard for law and order, becomes progressively more like the ideal pattern of what a community might be. Law is a method of introducing unity and system into what would otherwise be social chaos, and is the only intelligent method of bringing about a state of affairs in which the value-potentialities of the citizens become capable of development, instead of just cancelling out or being frustrated.[15] But there is something else to be considered. In the tyrant's city, value-development is at a minimum. The value-potentialities of all the better types of citizenry are hindered from developing, and such citizens tend to be eliminated by violence, leaving in their places only the predatory and criminal types, whose value is mainly negative.[16] Yet there are laws, even in the tyrant's city. In the philosopher's city, on the other hand, value-development reaches the maximum, and the values developed are all positive. The development, in both cases, thus depends upon the same method, viz., the method of law and order. On what, then, does the difference in the results depend ? The answer is simple. Law, while always a method of introducing order and system, may be imposed by a force which is blind to the ideal aim of maximal development of potentiality. The primitive origins of law are unconscious custom and unreflective administrative procedure. But in the inferior types of community, the legislators, while possibly reflective and self-conscious, may be unenlightened and almost completely blind to ideal aims. In such communities, the laws originate in the conscious reflection of a narrowly self-interested adventurer, whether despot, business man, or military dictator. Social groups governed in this way can hardly be regarded as " communities " in any strict sense, and it is something of a miracle that they hold together as long as they do.[17]

The best type of law-making, however, makes its appearance only when the law-makers are thoroughly enlightened and awake to the ideal needs of the community ; and this occurs only when philosophers are called to governing positions, or when governing bodies become imbued with the spirit of genuine philosophy. In this case, a philosophically self-conscious type of community comes into being, and in this the laws are based upon the principle of reason, which brings out the maximal realization of all positive value-potentialities of all the citizens. This philosophically self-conscious community represents civilized life at its best. It has a definite place for every citizen who is capable of making positive contributions to the common well-being, and coincides, both in principle and in detail, with the life of ideal justice, and ideal temperance, considered above.[18] That is to say, civilized life, arising out of self-conscious observance of a law and order based upon philosophical insight into the ideal principle of value, represents the application, to human life, of the pattern community-idea " laid up in heaven," and is thus the ideal good in its social reference, i.e. is the highest human good.

So much for the community-ideal, as a candidate for the position of highest good. We now pass to consider the ideal of the comprehensive or composite life. This ideal is developed in explicit contrast with such one-sided ideals as the life of mere pleasure and the life of mere intellect. It is felt that all such ideals are abstract and fall short of the highest conceivable good, for the very simple reason that, valuable, no doubt, as each is in itself, a life which is more inclusive would obviously be even more valuable. It is not only children who cry " give us both ! " Animal pleasure, apart from reflective self-consciousness, memory, and anticipation, is unmistakably less valuable than pleasure *plus* reflective self-consciousness ; and intellectual contemplation without emotional satisfaction of any description is unmistakably less valuable than intellectual contemplation *plus* all kinds and amounts of reasonable satisfaction which can well be combined with the intellectual life—such as the satisfaction which goes along with the enjoyment of music.[19] In explicit contrast, then, with all such abstract and one-sided ideals, Plato develops the conception of a concrete and complete life, including all features of embodied existence in such quantity and quality as can in consistency be combined as portions of a single, non-contradictory totality of experience. The dominant characteristic of such a life is the formal ideal of developing maximal value in a single, all-comprehensive system, i.e. is the rational principle of organization, " the mean " or principle of value as such, the principle of so combining elements of potential value as to develop the potentialities of each to their maximum, with full justice to the potentialities of all other elements conceived as working together in a single system.[20]   As a formal ideal, this principle is irreproachable, and coincides with what is elsewhere called the idea of good, the principle of ideality and value.

The concrete filling in of this formal outline constitutes the composite or comprehensive life, and includes the following enjoyable experiences :—(1) satisfaction of the " necessary" appetites, i.e. taking reasonable meals at suitable times, under social conditions which enhance the sense of community existence and its value,[21] and living a sex-life suited to citizens of an almost ideal community,[22] (2) the satisfaction associated with the prosecution of some socially valuable profession or activity in the community,[23] (3) the enjoyment of art in all the forms approved by reason for citizens of an ideal community,[24] (4) the satisfaction taken in being a member of a law-abiding and reverential community,[25] and (5) the satisfaction which comes from intellectual activity in all the forms approved for members of the ideal community.[26]   In a word, this composite or comprehensive life includes beauty, goodness, and truth, and the virtues of holiness, temperance, justice, courage, and wisdom.[28]   It is identical with what is called the blessed or happy life, which we have elsewhere recognized as the highest human good, and is thus to be regarded as a new formulation of the same ideal.[29]

We pass now to consider a new candidate for the position of highest good.   That " the preservation and well-being of the whole " ranks higher in value than the preservation and well-being of one or two parts only, is stated as a principle in relation to various fields of experience.   In the political field, for example, it is shown repeatedly that the good of the community, taken as a whole, is superior in value to the good of a mere portion of the individuals who together compose that whole. Thus, the Thrasymachean ideal of *pleonexia* as the art of life—i.e. the ideal of master-morality on the part of natural supermen as contrasted with their natural inferiors, i.e. as contrasted with the simple citizens who admire the strong rulers who have made themselves masters of the whole community—is considered and refuted by reference to the necessary logic of the part-whole relation. The whole includes its parts, and for a part to set up as the whole is to destroy the organization upon which the well-being of the whole depends. To destroy the whole, however, is to interfere with the well-being of its parts also, so that, in the long run, the attempt of the part to set up as the whole is a form of suicide. A band of brigands can subsist only provided (1) that the whole social organism (of which they are a part) is allowed to subsist in its own way. For, if no one were allowed to devote himself to farming, manufacture, or commerce, there would be nothing of which one robber could rob another. To destroy the whole, therefore, is to destroy the possibility even of brigandage. A second proviso is (2) that the robbers must themselves accept the principle of the superior value of the whole, as compared with the independent development of the parts, in its application to their own organization. For if the members of the band take to robbing one another, the band will speedily fall apart into its elements, and will not be strong enough to prey upon the population or even to protect itself against organized police raids. *Pleonexia*, then, by offending against the obvious logic of the part-whole relation, is a form of self-stultification.[30]

The absurdity of this position is illustrated further by showing what happens to the victorious despot after he has applied the whiff of grapeshot to the democratic mob in the city of the free. This " supreme lord and master of life and death " who has rooted out all honest and patriotic opposition with the sword, finds that he has necessarily surrounded himself only with those who are left—viz., thieves and murderers, in whose society he can take no pleasure or pride, and on whose loyalty he can repose no trust. Accordingly, the more successful he is in rooting out the good, the more precarious he finds his existence to be becoming among the faithless scoundrels who remain. In destroying the whole, he too has destroyed the parts, including himself also. Triumphant despotism is thus self-destructive, and successful murder is a form of suicide.[31]

Again, in constructing the ideal community, the greatest care is always taken to arrange conditions in such a way that the ideal ruler shall never be tempted to set his own personal well-being above the well-being of the community as a whole. Not only does his whole education tend to free him from the fascination which the prospect of wealth and power seems to exercise over most men, developing an intellectual love of the ideal world of order and system in place of the usual more sensuous interest in pretty things and cash values, but he is not permitted, by the conditions of his caste, to gratify in any way the natural itch to acquire and heap up possessions.[32] It is also carefully explained that the thought of his own personal happiness must never be permitted to weigh more heavily than the thought of the welfare of the whole group, and in all such reflections reference is made to the compelling logic of the part-whole relation. His happiness is to be sought in becoming an organic portion of the well-being of the whole community.[33]

Again, in the case of artistic creation, it is obvious that parts have to be strictly subordinated to the whole, as otherwise something hopelessly inartistic would result. It is the idea of the whole which exercises the controlling influence and determines just what proportionate treatment should be allotted to each part, and it is the resultant proportionality or symmetry which makes both whole and parts beautiful.[34] This is easily seen if we compare an artistic with an inartistic painting, or an artistic with an inartistic rhetorical composition. The inartistic workman puts together his elements just anyhow, without order or system, and with grotesque over-emphasis or under-emphasis. He will paint the eye of a statue (which should be, e.g. black) bright purple, because he likes that colour, and does not see that he is completely spoiling the artistic effect of the statue as a whole.[35] Or in rhetorical composition he will begin at the end, or in the middle, dealing boldly with his topics in any order in which they happen to strike his fancy, and he does not observe that in this way he is making nonsense of his theme, considered as a whole.[36] The artist, on the other hand, by bringing together what would otherwise be *disjecta membra* into the unity of a single idea, in such a way as to make the most of each and all of them in relation to the persons with whom he is entering into communication, is attempting to do, in play, something akin to what the philosopher is doing in earnest, i.e. playing his part in constructing an ideal totality of meaning and value, and it is this insight into the demands of the ideal totality which lends to artistic creations whatever value they may succeed in expressing.[37]

Again, in the case of medicine, the rule-of-thumb practitioner prescribes hit-or-miss treatments which affect a part only. His emetics and cathartics, his scalpel and his cauterizing iron give local stimulations, and are not designed to deal with the needs of the organism as a whole. His prescriptions do, indeed, produce the desiderated local effects, but, owing to his neglect to consider the organism as a whole, he sometimes succeeds also in killing his patient *secundum artem*. The really scientific physician, on the other hand, never prescribes this violent local treatment, unless it is clearly called for by the situation as a whole. He considers the patient as a whole, including mind as well as body, and prescribes a regimen of exercise, diet, and rest from this standpoint. That is to say, he prescribes a whole way of life, rather than mere local stimulation. Like the ideal artist, the ideal physician seems to be a sort of philosopher, reproducing, in his special medium, the essential characteristics of the macrocosm or ideal totality, and it is this insight into the demands of this totality which gives to his prescriptions the value which they possess in truth.[38]

Finally, we may consider the part-whole relation from the standpoint of logic and metaphysics. For platonism, it is plain that the part-whole relation is a formula which expresses the principle of the idea as such. To gather together, into the unity of a single comprehensive whole, parts which would otherwise not be brought together, and would thus never acquire the meaning and value resulting from such rational synthesis—this is the way in which the principle of ideality functions. Whether it is the ideal city constructed in the *Republic* and *Laws*, the ideal rhetorical composition constructed in the *Phaedrus*, the ideal cosmos constructed in the *Timaeus*, or any other platonic idea, the method is the same. In each case, the " parts " are inter-related by reference to the idea of the whole, an ideal totality in which the maximal values of the parts are brought out so that they, too, acquire ideal significance. It is in relation to the statue that the part properly sculptured and painted becomes an eye, and thus realizes the eye-idea. It is in relation to the community as a whole that the farmer becomes a complete farmer, or completely realizes the farmer-idea. So too the carpenter becomes a genuine embodiment of the carpenter-idea, the guardian becomes a genuine embodiment of the guardian-idea, etc.[39] That is to say, the ideal totality of metaphysics, consisting of all positive elements of value so inter-related as to bring out their full value-potentialities in this single, all-inclusive totality, is the dominant idea. It is in relation to this metaphysical ideal that all subordinate ideas acquire their true meaning, and all concrete actualities acquire value just in so far as they fit into the places logically prepared for them in this metaphysical ideal. It is with this ideal before his mind that the philosophic guardian directs his own life, no less than the lives of the citizens who entrust themselves to his leadership, and it is only in this way that the highest good for human beings can be approximately realized.[40] To say, then, that the preservation and well-being of the whole is the highest good, is simply to express, in words appropriate to their special contexts, the principle of ideality which is called the idea of good.

We pass now to consider the passages which represent God as the highest good. Zeus, Hera, and the other figures of popular mythology, so far as we accept the account of their doings given by the poets, cannot, of course, be regarded as in any sense perfect beings. For the poets represent them with human weaknesses and human passions, as somewhat cowardly, unwise, unjust, and anything but self-controlled.[41] The philosopher, however, regards these popular figures as imaginative expressions, adapted to particular localities, of the principle of ideal divinity,[42] and insists that the ideal immortals are holiness, justice, wisdom, and self-control personified. The life of these ideal representatives of the principle of divinity constitutes a pattern of the perfect life, the God-like life which, both in principle and in detail, coincides with the blessed or ideally happy life which we have elsewhere accepted as the highest human good.[43]

A difficulty is sometimes felt in connection with Plato's picture of the " demiurge " or Divine Artist-creator in the *Timaeus*. It is difficult to identify directly (1) the demiurge

and (2) the idea of good. There is no question that the
" principle of the best," in accordance with which the Divine
Artist creates the world, is identical with the idea of good, i.e.
with the principle of so rearranging the elements of what would
otherwise be a meaningless chaos, as to fit them into their
places in an ideal cosmos of maximal meaning and value.[44]
But it has seemed difficult to identify the Artist with the
principle in accordance with which He acts. For the one is
personal, and the other is impersonal.

This difficulty has, perhaps, more meaning for the present-
day critic than it had for Plato himself. If we remember that
almost every one of Plato's ideal constructions consists of
" ideas " or " impersonal principles," we shall perhaps be able
to understand, not only why, for Plato, no difficulty is felt in
identifying God with the divine principle, but also that it
would seem incorrect for him to do anything else. The
" model city " in the Laws consists of 5040 citizen-ships, i.e.
blanks to be filled, of course, by human beings ; but Plato's
reasoning applies to the ideal blanks, and explicitly not to
actual persons.[45] Similarly, the philosopher-kings of the ideal
republic are " ideas," not actual persons, and Plato is always
aware that there is a gap between what his reasoning can attain
to, and sense-perceivable actualities.[46] But, in spite of this,
his reasoning considers actualities only in so far as they coincide with the ideal counters constructed by his reason. The
guardian is the human personification of the " ideas " of
courage, temperance, holiness, justice, and wisdom,[47] and God,
the Divine Guardian, is, similarly, the ideally perfect personification of these same " ideas," i.e. especially, and as a
matter of course, the perfect personification of the idea of
good.[48] As absolute perfection, God could not be thought
of as anything less than the absolute idea.

If, then, we are justified in regarding " the divine " as the
living principle of value, an ideal experience which proceeds
by transmitting the otherwise chaotic and meaningless into
a form of itself, the living principle of spiritual energy radiating
spiritual energy in such a way as to convert into spiritualizing
agencies all with which it comes into contact,[49] we can see,
without further difficulty, that this is the finest conceivable
experience, and is thus to be accepted as a formulation of the
highest conceivable good.

CHAPTER XXI

CONCLUSION : THE PLATONIC HIGHEST GOOD

THE aim of the present chapter is to put together, so far as possible, all that we have discovered in our previous investigations, so as to formulate a conclusion which shall not only be just to the whole of the evidence, but shall also place us in the position of the dialectician, who can move freely up and down the whole ideal realm, trusting securely in the power of the ideal principle into which he has acquired an insight which is adequate.

We have discovered, in the first place, that the general criterion of good and evil advocated in the Dialogues is the conception of an ideally perfect life. Whatever feeling, thought, or action constitutes an organic portion of this life, conceived as the concrete application of the formal ideal of a consistent totality of maximal meaning and value, is accepted as " good." Whatever feeling, thought, or action fails to fit in coherently, and so contradicts the essential purpose of this ideal principle of value, is rejected as " evil."[1] Insight into the nature and demands of this ideal criterion enables the dialectician to understand the positive value expressed in such more generally employed criteria as " universal assent," " written law," " the hedonistic calculus," " aesthetic quality," " expediency," " social value," " orderliness," " objectivity," etc., and also to appreciate the limitations of such semi-popular criteria, when divorced from his dialectical insight and accepted simply, as somehow reliable in themselves.

With this discovery in mind, we have investigated the various value-scales discussed in the Dialogues, that is to say, the various standardized value-judgments which occupy somewhat the status of formulations of proverbial wisdom in ancient Greece. Some of these appear to be merely superficial. Of the rest, some are flatly opposed to the platonic criterion of value, either in detail or at least in principle, while others—e.g. those which place " mind " or " philosophy " or " the godlike life " first—more nearly fit in with the platonic

467

ideal. Our investigation has disclosed that the representatives of philosophic insight in the Dialogues tend to re-interpret these popular value-scales until they coincide, both in principle and in detail, with the demands of the ideal criterion. Underlying this reinterpretation is the dialectician's assumption that any sound value-comparsion is, at least implicitly, of a piece with the platonic position, and can be shown, by a little dialectical ingenuity, to involve explicit acceptance of that position. The treatment of these value-scales is thus analogous to the previously considered treatment of the popular criteria of good and evil. Divorced from the dialectician's insight into their true implications and limitations, and accepted simply, as somehow reliable guides to life *per se*, such value-scales are at times misleading, precisely as a literal acceptance of written law is at times misleading. But understood as the dialectician understands them, they can safely be used in the philosopher's task of raising gradually to the ideal level whatever half-developed tendencies in that direction he finds ready to his hand in the social environment.

With this further discovery in mind, we shall now turn to the problem of a " highest good," as this meets us in the Dialogues. We have investigated the claims of some twenty-four claimants to the position of a highest good, and shall now proceed to select the characteristics which are common to these claimants, with especial emphasis upon such as are obviously least acceptable to platonism. Having thus reached, if at all possible, a general conclusion as to the concept of a highest good in platonism, we shall proceed to verify this conclusion by comparing it, not only with the teaching of the *Philebus*, but also with the cases of " mind " and " philosophy," which are obviously acceptable formulations of the chief good.

As we look over the candidates examined above, we find only two respects in which each and all of our results agree. In the first place we find (1) a popular standpoint rejected in favour of a more philosophical standpoint. This popular standpoint appears to have two levels, (a) individual and (b) social. The individualist regards all so-called goods as being somehow good in themselves, independently of the character of their possessors, and believes that the highest good for the individual consists in acquiring possession, whatever the means adopted, of some one or more of these goods.

From this standpoint, fine houses, fine clothes, elegant vehicles, and a good bank account seem good in their own right, and anyone who succeeds in acquiring a fair quantity of these goods is regarded as enviable and (so far) truly happy. Even a cutpurse or burglar, so far as he is successful in his profession, succeeds in realizing this ideal; but unqualified admiration is reserved for the unconstitutional dictator, who has succeeded in stealing the whole community, including the citizens as well as their property, and including also the whole machinery of making and administering the law.[2] So too with " goods of the body," such as good looks, health, and pleasure. These too are regarded, at this level of the value-judgment, as valuable in their own right, independently of the way in which they are acquired and used. In fact, at this level, anything regarded as " good " is thought to have its value in itself.[3] The materialistic individualist simply aims at acquiring for himself and his family as much and as many of such goods as he can, and believes firmly that in so doing he is realizing his own highest good, and that, in fact, no loftier ideal can even be conceived.

The social level (b) of this popular standpoint appears at first sight to be different from the individual level, and even opposed to it. Some of the " goods " which seem valuable to the individual would seem to be neither good nor bad from the standpoint of the community. For example, no community, as such, is especially and peculiarly interested in such " goods " as personal good looks, or personal immortality, which seem, at least on the face of them, to be specifically concerns of the individual. What the community is especially concerned with, is the excellence and preservation of the community itself, its increase in wealth, in power, and, in certain cases, in pleasure, and certainly in law and order, so far as these further the interests and ideals of the community. It is further concerned with goodness of character, genius, religion, scientific research, philosophy, civilization, etc.,[4] so far as these can be utilized in preserving or extending the power of the community. This obviously contrasts with the way in which the individualist is interested in these same goods, namely, in so far as they seem to forward his own aims and bring to him personally wealth or pleasure or power.

But while individual and community are thus undoubtedly opposed to each other, for the philosopher there is another

and a profounder standpoint from which they are in fundamental agreement. Both regard the " goods " with which
they are concerned, as good in their own right, and both
believe that the highest good is to be attained simply by
acquiring possession of as much and as many of these " goods "
as possible. The opposition between individual and community is thus like the opposition between one individualist
and another individualist. That is to say, given a certain
amount of " goods," A believes that happiness consists in
his acquiring possession of as many as possible, so that as few
as possible are left for B, while B believes that happiness
consists in *his* acquiring possession of as many as possible,
so that as few as possible are left for A. Individuals seek to
enrich themselves at the expense of the community, and the
community seek to enrich itself at the expense of individuals.[5]
There is complete agreement on the fundamental point that
life is essentially competitive, " pleonectic," predatory. It
follows that any kind of society can only superficially be at
peace and in harmony. Beneath the surface a constant
struggle is going on, and it is almost a miracle that any kind
of social existence continues, even for a single generation.
The fundamental tendency is obviously disruptive and essentially anarchic, and thus contradicts, as the philosopher sees
it, the most elementary conception of social living.[6]

As contrasted with this popular standpoint, whether
individual or social, we have (2) the philosophic standpoint
proper. For the philosopher, none of the " goods " of this
world possess value in their own right. He points out occasions where wealth, good looks, pleasure, health, and even life
itself, are evils to their possessors,[7] and insists upon the inherent contradictoriness of the individualistic or predatory
tendency. Value resides in character rather than in things,
and in taking the right attitude towards the acquisition and
use of things. Temperance, courage, justice, and wisdom
are essential to the right use and enjoyment of such goods,
and only to him who is holy, just, and wise are the things of
this world truly goods. The question of value is, in fact,
directly proportioned to the degree of insight. Where the
insight is little, the value is little. Where the highest level
of insight has been reached, the highest degree of value is
enjoyed; and the man who sets this standard of value clearly
before his eyes lives the most valuable life, whether it is his

own house which he is setting in order, or the community which entrusts itself to his skilled guidance. In either case, his insight teaches him to realize the maximum of value of which the situation admits.[8]

What is this insight ? It is the vision of an ideal system of elements, each with a definite and positive function, so arranged that, while each realizes, as completely as possible, its own function, these functions are so adapted to one another that all, taken together, are co-operating to realize a single, all-comprehending, systematic totality of value. The interpenetration of whole and parts is thought of as so complete that each element, while preserving its distinctness from each other element, is permeated by the spirit of the whole, and represents the concentration of all the forces of the ideal totality in some particular direction ; while the whole is entirely realized in the ideal functioning of all of its particular manifestations, its parts or elements, and indeed the spirit of the whole is completely realized in the ideal functioning of any one of its elements. It follows that, so far as any element fulfils its function in the ideal system and plays its part in the spirit of realizing the good of the whole, it is thereby realizing its own highest good.[9] For an administrator, so to govern as to bring out the potentialities of the citizens so that they fit in together in the realization of the varied yet harmonious life of the ideal city which is the idea of good applied to social living—i.e. wise leadership—is the highest good. For the average citizen, so to obey the laws and co-operate with the efforts of the government to improve social and civic conditions, as to make his definite contribution to the life of the group, as farmer, manufacturer, industrial worker, or official—i.e. wise followership or " temperance "—is the highest good. Each member of the community realizes his highest good by " doing his own work " as administrator, farmer, manufacturer, etc., in the spirit of ideal citizenship, i.e. with the " form of good "—i.e. this formal ideal of a system of maximal value which contains a place for the work of each citizen—as applied to his own concrete problems, continually before his eyes.[10]

There is thus one and only one highest good : to apply, always and everywhere, the ideal form of goodness, i.e. so to arrange the empirical elements of every concrete situation that they cease to conflict and thus to destroy one another's potential value, and begin to work together and thus to become true elements of that ideal situation in which all positive values are fused together into a single harmonious systematic totality. While, however, there is, ultimately, only this one highest good, it will necessarily take many shapes and names, according to the varieties of concrete situation in which it is realized. To realize this ideal on the battlefield, or in some sudden emergency, will usually be praised as " bravery " ; to realize the ideal in one's business relations will usually be praised as " justice " ; to realize the ideal in one's church relations will usually be praised as " piety " or " religion " ; and, in one's eating and drinking, as " temperance." But, whatever the variation of nomenclature, and however different the situation may appear to be : to the philosopher who sees the one in this many, the highest good is always to do the ideal thing, to apply the form of goodness and, by its aid, to transform the empirical situation into an organic portion of the ideal system, the harmonious actualization of all positive values.

When the philosopher, having attained to this insight, turns his attention upon the world of actual human ideals, what does he find ? He finds an immense variety of claimants contending for the position of highest human good : from money, good looks, health, and pleasure, to self-control, reason, science, and philosophy. Faced with this variety, he takes, sometimes one, sometimes another, attitude. In the first place (1) he picks out and emphasizes those formulations of the ideal which most nearly resemble his own. For example, such formulations as " soul," " mind," " reason," " knowledge," " insight," " philosophy," " wisdom," etc., as currently accepted and regarded as ideals worthy of whole-hearted devotion, so nearly coincide with his own beliefs, that he scarcely scruples to acclaim them without further definition.[11] In the same spirit, such formulations as " wealth," " pleasure." " personal beauty," etc., which, as currently understood, seem almost the exact antithesis of the philosophic ideal, he tends to reject without a too-nice examination of their qualifications.[12] Hence the tendency to accept without much discussion such value-fo   " soul—body—wealth," " wisdom—temperance—courage—health, etc.," and the frequent treatment of   est " good as occupying the topmost position on some such ladder of " goods." But the acceptance of such value-scales, with their implications and ramifications reaching far down into merely popular thought, is not *der Weisheit letzter Schluss*, and the philosopher thus sometimes takes a less conventional attitude and faces the concrete problems more directly. From this standpoint (2), he sees that in the pursuit even of wealth or pleasure there may be a genuine idealism involved, a veritable attempt to make the most of life. There are occasions and situations in which the pursuit of wealth or pleasure does constitute the content of the ideal good,[13] though the spirit in which such " goods " are usually pursued certainly needs enlightenment. It follows that the philosopher's business is less to reject or simply condemn such pursuits, and rather to enlighten the seeker after wealth or pleasure, so that he may come to see the true nature of the ideal principle, and the consequent limitations, as well as the right and proper function, of such formulations of the ideal principle as " wealth " or " pleasure." From this standpoint, the philosopher does not simply accept or reject the conventional valuations, but, by his questioning dialectic, endeavours to change the relatively unenlightened attitude of the average man, which is dangerously close to a completely blind materialism, into the enlightened attitude of the philosopher who not only sees good everywhere, but sees also how far and under what conditions the transcendental ideal may be realized with the means and motives at his disposal in this empirical world. The ideal can be realized only in so far as these empirical means and empirical motives become shot through with a more transcendental insight and thus lose their merely empirical character, and become veritable channels for the transcendental purposes to make their way into the chaos of this empirical world and transmute it into a more close approximation to the perfect order and harmony of the ideal realm.[14]

Connected with this two-fold attitude on the part of the philosopher is a certain difficulty in platonism, namely, as to the relation of ideal and actual worlds. On the one hand, the philosopher tends to withdraw from the actual world, because it is not ideal, and devotes himself to solitary contemplation of a world which is ideal, but not actual.

The actual world seems to him unreal, empirical, chaotic, unsatisfactory to the demands of reason, fluctuating, sensory, emotional, confused, not being: actual, but meaningless. Similarly the ideal world satisfies all the demands his reason can make: it is perfect, beautiful, systematic, permanent, clear-cut, intelligible, transcendental—though not actual. Following this tendency, the philosopher lets the world and the flesh go on their own way, content if, behind his college walls, he can pursue, without being disturbed, his strictly academic interests, assimilating himself to the ideal world in his own way, and eschewing all but absolutely necessary contacts with empirical actualities. This tendency is connected with the attitude which accepts philosophy or wisdom as the highest good and simply rejects pleasure, wealth, and power, without further investigation. From this standpoint, the transcendental realm of " ideas " in which mind is at home is absolutely and entirely distinct from the empirical realm in which the philosopher is condemned, thanks to his incomprehensible attachment to an empirical body, to sojourn for a season. The relation between transcendental and actual is thus the relation of logical contraries, of being and not-being, which are mutually exclusive.[15]

On the other hand, the deeper philosophical tendency to transmute the relative chaos of the empirical world into something more closely approximating to the ideal realm, is connected with a somewhat different view of the relations of the two worlds. While containing elements whose material constituents can, perhaps, never be entirely idealized,[16] the empirical world, in so far as it exhibits order, law, and system, is not the absolute chaos for which philosophers have sometimes taken it, but is the ideal world of order and meaning, refracted and distorted in an alien medium, but still there, clearly visible to the scientific and philosophic intelligence. The physical universe as a whole is an almost perfect sphere, and its motion is almost perfect axial revolution. The planets are similar spheres, and their motions are almost perfect axial revolutions in orbits which are almost perfect circles.[17] So too the minutest elements which, taken as aggregates, are named "earth," "water," "fire," and "air," are almost perfect cubes, ikosahedrons, octahedrons, and tetrahedrons, respectively, and their empirical combinations and separations are to be analysed, almost without remainder, into the consequences of the spherical motion of the whole, thought of as compressing, in definite ways, these definitely shaped solids, whose structure is ultimately reduced to combinations of the principle of rectangular triangularity. The circle and the triangle are, in fact, ideal figures which exhibit the ideal principle of the limit applied to the otherwise unlimited motion and extension in definite ways which the mind can fully grasp, and, by the aid of the pure geometry which the mind constructs, the physical world ceases to be regarded as an absolute chaos and appears as a sense-perceivable copy or image of the ideal, i.e. as the ideal realm itself in sense-perceivable form.[18] So too biological and psychological phenomena exhibit the same principles of law and order, and it is thus possible for the philosopher to live an almost ideal life without entirely quitting " this mortal place." From this standpoint, the relation of actual and ideal worlds is one of almost complete interpenetration, and the task of the philosopher is to co-operate, with the fullest understanding, with this tendency towards interpenetration, and thus to actualize, as far as he can, the ideal, but especially by enlightening others so that their actions also can be motivated by the same insight into principle.[19]

It remains to compare these conclusions with the platonic statements concerning mind or philosophy as the highest good, and then to see, further, how far these results satisfy the requirements of a highest good set forth in the *Philebus*. Mind, considered as the highest good, is the organizing principle which converts chaos into cosmos. This is not, of course, the imperfect and fluctuating approximations to mind found in particular human beings, but is understood absolutely, as the Divine Mind, the ideal experience which is identical with reality in its ultimate sense.[20] This can be considered abstractly, in separation from the world, as the organizing principle can be distinguished from the chaos which it organizes ; or it can be considered as united with the world, as the organizing principle in its actual functioning ; and it is in this latter sense that it receives its most concrete significance and importance. Understood in this sense, mind is the principle which rearranges the meaningless chaos of the world, until this assumes the form of definite elements moving in accordance with definite laws, exemplifying the principle of perfect self-motion, not only in a general way, viz., in reference to the axial revolution of the universe taken as a whole, but carried, so far as possible, into the detailed movements, not only of large organizations such as the planets and smaller complexes

such as the human brain, but also into the detailed structure
of the quasi-atomic ultimate constituents of the physical
universe ; thus realizing the motion-potentialities ideally
inherent in these elements but held in frustration by the actual
lack of order and system.   As the principle which brings out
into actualization the value-potentialities which were slumbering in the physical universe at the chaotic stage, mind is the
source of the highest good of the physical system at the ideal
stage.   So too in the social and intellectual spheres ; as the
principle which makes actual the value-potentialities inherent
in those spheres, mind is the ultimate source of their highest
good.   Speaking universally, mind is the ultimate source of
all positive value-development, and is thus the ultimate
principle of value, the " idea of good."[21]   For the physical
universe, the prevailing of this principle means that a chaos
which is factual but meaningless and valueless becomes an
ordered system in which each element has a meaningful function and the whole realizes as much value as possible.   For
the individual human being, the prevailing of this principle
means that in place of drifting along at the mercy of his chaotic
desires and the chance stimulations coming from without, the
individual deliberately chooses to devote his reorganized
powers to playing a man's part in co-operating with the ideal
forces which are making for order, system, and the maximal
realization of positive value.

How does this compare with what we have already
concluded as to the nature of the highest good ?   Mind,
considered as a mere principle of organization, apart from its
actual field of operation, corresponds to the view of the ideal
realm as distinct from the actual world, discussed above, and
to the notion, so often expressed in platonism, that the highest
good for man consists in abstract contemplation of this ideal
realm.   The concrete view of mind as transforming the chaos
of the world into an ordered system in which no value-potentialities are lost, but are all developed as much as possible,
corresponds to the view of the ideal and the actual world as
gradually interpenetrating, discussed above, and to the notion
that the highest good for man consists in his devoting his
powers to furthering this interpenetration.

This comparison shows that the account of mind (at the
philosophic level) as the highest good exhibits the same general
characteristics established independently in our examination

of the claims of pleasure, wealth, power, happiness, immortality, etc., and we can therefore regard our former conclusions concerning the nature of a highest good as, so far, confirmed. It remains to compare these conclusions with the position adopted by Plato in the *Philebus*.

In this dialogue, it is stated that any highest good must be (1) universally desirable, i.e. what all men would choose without hesitation, if the issue were clearly set before them, (2) complete and entire, i.e. needing no further addition to make it valuable, and (3) perfectly sufficient, i.e. a well-rounded whole.[22] It is further shown that these demands are satisfied by a life which is full and concrete rather than one-sided and abstract, and richly empirical rather than formal or purely transcendental, and is organized in accordance with a principle of consistency, harmony, and objectivity. What is fundamental in such a concrete, empirical life, is, of course, " measure," i.e. the organizing principle. The rich detail of empirical living, if it is to form part of a " highest " good, must be so rearranged as to constitute a single, consistent, harmonious, systematic totality in which nothing of positive value which can possibly be fitted in is omitted or is left in conflict with other positive values.[23] This principle of rearrangement coincides in all respects with the " idea of good," and it follows that the highest good is the complete life which expresses the adequate functioning of this principle.

This, however, is the life which we have been describing as " happiness," as " immortality," as " the life of mind." What we learn from the *Philebus* is thus a simple confirmation of our conclusions. The one item of new information which emerges from careful scrutiny of the *Philebus* is that the abstract, other-worldly contemplation to which the Phaedo and, at times, the *Republic* incline, is now definitely rejected as being formal and one-sided, while the concrete idealization of the present world is accepted as the only adequate expression of the highest good.[24] Our final conclusion is thus that the highest good for the universe consists in the ideal functioning of the whole so as to realize the maximum of value-potentiality inherent in its elements, and that the highest good for a particular human being consists in so living as to constitute a consciously organic portion of this whole, and, in so living, to realize his own deepest happiness and well-being.

NOTES

INTRODUCTION

1 : This is not intended as simply destructive criticism of the various scholarly studies referred to in succeeding notes. A student has, of course, a perfect right to confine himself to a single aspect of a large subject, or to a few special passages in the Dialogues, if he so wishes. The object of the criticism is to point out that the existing monographs do not solve the more general problem in which the present writer is interested, and that there is thus room for the present study.

2 : G. Grote, *Plato and Other Companions of Socrates*, London, 1888, Vol. II, pp. 208, 305-309, 314. C. Piat, *Platon*, Paris, 1906, pp. 249, 253, 255, 258.

3 : Th. Hartmann, *De diis Timaei platonici*, Wratislaw, 1840, p. 35. P. Höfer, *Bedeutung der Philosophie für das Leben*, Göttingen, 1870, pp. 34-35. B. Jowett, *The Dialogues of Plato*, New York, 1911, Vol. II, p. 6. H. Meyer, *Geschichte der alten Philosophie*, München, 1925, pp. 185-186. Ueberweg-Praechter, *Gundriss der Geschichte der Philosophie*, Berlin, 1909, Vol. I, p. 175. Ed. Zeller, *Plato and the Older Academy*, E. T., London, 1888, pp. 436-438, 442-444.

4 : H. Meyer, op. cit., pp. 186-187. R. L. Nettleship, *Philosophical Lectures and Remains*, London, 1897, Vol. I, pp. 374, 384, Vol. II, pp. 10, 81. C. Ritter, *Platon*,[2] München, 1923, Vol. II, pp. 556, ff. E. Trommershausen, *Darstellung . . . der Ansicht Platons uber das Wesen der Seele . . .*, Bonn, 1873, p. 44. W. Wundt, *Ethik*, Stuttgart, 1886, Vol. I, p. 244. Ed. Zeller, op. cit., p. 461.

5 : G. P. Adams, *Idealism and the Modern Age*, New Haven, 1919, pp. 11-12, 66, 75, 153, 198, 215, 236. J. I. Döllinger, *Gentile and Jew in the Courts of the Temple. . . .*, E. T., London, 1862, Vol. I, p. 322. A. Fouillée, *La philosophie de Platon*, Paris, 1869, pp. 76, 78, 233, 234 n. R. Hirzel, *De bonis in fine Philebi enumeratis*, Leipzig, 1868, p. 54. P. Höfer, *Die Bedeutung der Philosophie für das Leben nach Plato. . . .*, Göttingen, 1870, pp. 31, 36. Fr. Jodl, *Geschichte der Ethik*,[2] Berlin, 1906, pp. 71-80. B. Jowett, op. cit., Vol. II, p. 6. H. Meyer, op. cit., pp. 188, 196-197. R. L. Nettleship, op. cit., Vol. I, pp. 374, 384, Vol. II, pp. 218, ff. Ueberweg-Praechter, op. cit., pp. 176, 180. Th. Wehrmann, *Platonis de summo bono doctrina*, Berlin, 1843, pp. 62, 84-85, 96, 103-106, 111, 113, 147-148, etc.

6 : P. Höfer, op. cit., pp. 59-60. J. Martineau, *Types of Ethical Theory*, Oxford, 1886, Vol. I, pp. 67, 85. R. L. Nettleship, op. cit., Vol. I, pp. 360-362. Ueberweg-Praechter, op. cit., p. 175. Marie V. Williams, *Platonic Theory of Knowledge*, Cambridge, 1908, pp. 62-65, 67, 87.

7 : W. A. Butler, *Lectures on the History of Ancient Philosophy*, New York, 1879, Vol. II, pp. 113, 116, 250, 266, 268. E. Frank, *Plato und die sogennanten Pythagoreer*, Halle, 1923, pp. 14, 109, 117 n. U. v. Wilamowitz-Moellendorff, *Platon*,[2] Berlin, 1920, Vol. I, pp. 420, ff., 455, 636, 640, 651, 759, Vol. II, p. 209. Cf. J. Adam, *The Republic of Plato*, Cambridge, 1907, Vol. II, pp. 169-170, *etc.*, and A. E. Taylor, *Plato, the Man and his Work*. New York, 1927, pp. 231, 232, 285-289.

8 : H. Bonitz, *Platonische Studien*,[2] Berlin, 1875, pp. 221-222, J. I. Döllinger, op. cit., Vol. I, pp. 308-310. A. Fouillée, op. cit., pp. 338, 441. J. Martineau, op. cit., Vol. I, pp. 67, 85. G. Schneider, *Platos Auffassung von der Bestimmung des Menschen*, Gera, 1883, pp. 12, 14, 15. Ueberweg-Praechter, op. cit., pp. 176, 180.

9 : A. W. Benn, *The Greek Philosophers*, London, 1882, Vol. II, pp. 229, 234. A. Fouillée, op. cit., pp. 44 ff., 456, 467-468.

10 : P. Natorp, *Platos Ideenlehre*, Leipzig, 1903, pp. 8, 9, 27-28, 47-49, 171, 173, 186, 189 f.

11 : J. E. Erdmann, *History of Philosophy*, E. T., London, 1910, Vol. I, pp. 109-110. J. A. Stewart, *Plato's Doctrine of Ideas*, Oxford, 1909, pp. 29, 59, 91, 100. F. A. Trendelenburg, *De Platonis Philebi consilio*, Berlin, 1837, pp. 16-17.

12 : E. Halévy, *La théorie platonicienne des sciences*, Paris, 1869, pp. 145, 246, 337. Cf. B. Jowett, op. cit., Vol. II, p. 134.

13 : J. Burnet, *Greek Philosophy, Part I.*, London, 1921, p. 336. W. A. Butler, op. cit., p. 146. J. I. Döllinger, op. cit., Vol. I, p. 308. P. Höfer, op. cit., pp. 12-17, 31, 36. H. Sidgwick, *Outlines of the History of Ethics*,[5] London, 1906, p. 39. E. Trommershausen, op. cit., p. 59, n. 1.

14 : These views, promulgated not only with the erudite virtuosity expected of Plato-scholars, but also with a persuasive logic or dialectic, are associated especially with the names of Professor John Burnet and Professor A. E. Taylor. For the present writer's attitude towards their contentions, see Proceedings of the Sixth International Congress of Philosophy.

CHAPTER I

1 : *Prtg.* 319d, 322c-d, 323a, c ; *Lach.* 194d, f.; cf. *Euthyd*, 287a.

2 : *Prtg.* 324d, e, 325a, 328a-b ; *Lach.* 196d ; *Rep.* 518c, 527d, e ; *Laws* 863e f., 950b-c ; cf. *Crito* 47c-d ; *Phileb.* 64d.

3 : *Prtg.* 325b-326e ; cf. *Rep.* VII, and *Laws, passim.*

4 : *Prtg.* 322d, 323.; *Rep.* 382a-c, 404e f., 444, 535e ; *Soph.* 227d f.; *Polit.* 302a-b ; *Tim.* 86b f.; *Laws* 958a ; cf. Nettleship, *Lectures and Remains*, Vol. II, pp. 90 ff.

5 : *Prtg.* 319d. Auermann (*Platons Cardinaltugenden*, p. 12), resting upon the judgment of Steinhart, Hermann, Schleiermacher, and Ast, regards this as un-Platonic, a view adopted uncritically by Protagoras. Credé (*Kritik der Lehre des Protagoras*, pp. 33, 36-37) similarly denies that empirical sensation furnishes a basis for Plato's idealism, and insists—as most commentators do—that

Anamnesis and a strictly transcendental standpoint are representative of Plato's real views.

6 : *Prtg.* 319e f.; *Meno* 93c ff.

7 : *Prtg.* 322c-d, 323a, 324e ; *Rep.* 351b f.

8 : *Polit.* 308e f.; *Laws* 862e f., 957e ; cf. *Gorg.* 525b-d.

9 : *Euthyphr.* 7d f.; *Rep.* 505b ff., 534b-c ; *Phaedr.* 250a-b, 263a ; *Polit.* 277d, 285e f.

10 : *Rep.* 504b f., 532-533d ; *Parm.* 136b-c ; *Polit.* 285a-b, 286a ; *Phileb.* 16d-e ; *Laws* 965b-c.

11 : *Crito* 47b-d, 48a ; *Rep.* 488, 493b-d, 514-515d, 557a ff.; *Laws* 661a, 964d.

12 : *Rep.* 492-495a ; *Laws* 659a-b, 950b-c.

13 : *Rep.* 489a-c ; *Laws* 627d f.

14 : *Rep.* 473d, 499b e f., 500e ff.; *Polit.* 276b-c.

15 : *Rep.* 502a-c, 540d f.

16 : *Rep.* 500c, 516e ff., 519d f., 540a-b.

17 : Cf. *Prtg.* 319d.

18 : *Prtg.* 352d-357e ; *Meno* 82c-85e ; *Rep.* 336b ff.; *Theaet. passim* ; *Parm.* 137b-c.

19 : *Gorg.* 460e f., 466 ff.; *Theaet.* 150b f.

20 : *Prtg.* 337a, 338e ; *Phaedo* 102a ; cf. J. E. Erdmann, *History of Philosophy*, E. T. Vol. I, p. 99 ; Gomperz, *Greek Thinkers* E. T. Vol. II, p. 306 ; Grote, *Plato and the Other Companions of Socrates*, 1888, Vol. I, p. 399 ; Nettleship, op. cit., Vol. II, p. 217.

21 : *Charm.* 160d, e, 166c-e ; *Theaet.* 154d f., 157c-d, 166-168c.

22 : *Rep.* 533 f.; *Soph.* 230b-d.

23 : *Rep.* 532e.

24 : *Lysis* 217e ; *Meno* 89b ; *Rep.* 395c, 396a-c, 409a-c, 491d f.; *Laws* 728b, 816e.

25 : *Rep.* 409b, 484c, 490a-b, 498e, 501a-c, 538c-e ; *Laws* 653b-c.

26 : *Rep.* 581c ff.; *Theaet.* 166e f.; *Laws* 663c-d.

27 : *Rep.* 595b ff.; *Laws* 658e f., 801d.

28 : *Laws* 765d f.

29 : *Theaet.* 166e f.; *Laws* 661b, d, 662, 945b ff.

30 : *Rep.* 379b f., 492e f., 509b, 612e ff.; *Phileb.* 39e ; cf. *Eryx.* 397e f.

31 : *Rep.* 450b, 519c ff.; *Soph.* 230d-e ; *Laws* 811d-e.

32 : Cf. *Laws* 643e f., 658e f.

33 : *Rep.* 408d f., 538c f.; *Phileb.* 62a-b ; *Laws* 951a-c ; *Epist.* 322d-e ; cf. Campbell, *The Theaetetus of Plato*, pp. lii-liii.

34 : *Rep.* 328e, 539c-d, 540a-b, 582a ; *Laws* 658e, 715d-e, 765d, 802b, 951a-c.

35 : *Rep.* 395c f., 409, 491d ff.; *Laws* 728b, 816d f.

36 : *Rep.* 409c-d ; cf. *Laws* 655d f.

37 : *Rep.* 405b-d, 519a-b, 553c ff.; *Theaet.* 175c-d ; *Laws* 697b, 831c-e.

38 : *Meno* 99e f.; *Rep.* 484d, 539c-d ; *Polit.* 308e ff.; *Laws* 659d, 951b-c.

39 : *Rep.* 428e, 441e, 577a-b, 581b ff.; *Laws* 688a-b, 689d.

40 : *Prtg.* 342b-d, 352b ff.; *Rep.* VII, *passim ;* *Laws* 659a.

41 : Plato is no absolute ascetic, cf. *Phaedo* 64d-e, 67a ; *Rep.* 571e f.; *Phaedr.* 256c-d ; *Laws* 648 ff.

42 : *Rep.* 441d-e, 442c-d, 443d-e.

43 : *Meno* 88b f.; cf. *Eryx.* 393d-e.

44 : *Rep.* 428b-d ; cf. *Alc. I,* 106d.

45 : *Rep.* 428 f., 441e.

46 : *Menex.* 246e ; *Rep.* 420b f., 442c.

47 : *Rep.* 462a, 464b f., 519c ; *Polit.* 285a-b ; *Laws* 693b-c, 903b f.

48 : *Rep.* 411e, 518d-e ; *Phaedr.* 247d ; *Polit.* 309c.

49 : *Polit.* 294 ; *Laws* 875c-d.

50 : *Rep.* 473d, 581b ff.; *Polit.* 294a ; *Laws* 711e f.; cf. *Hipp. Maj.* 296a.

51 : *Rep.* 487c-d, 489d, 490d, 494a, 495c f., 500b, 535c-d, 539d ; *Polit.* 299b-d.

52 : *Rep.* 472b f., 474b-c, 501.

53 : *Rep.* 459-461a ; *Tim.* 18d-e ; *Laws* 783d-785b.

54 : *Rep.* 375a, 459d, 460c, 461c ; *Tim.* 19a ; *Laws* 789, 790d-e.

55 : *Rep.* 375e f., 485, 486c-e, 490a-b, 494b, 503c, 535b-e.

56 : *Phaedo* 68c ff.; *Crito* 47c f.; *Rep.* 375 ff., 485e f., 487a, 490b f., 496b, 535a, 536a-b.

57 : *Rep.* 376c ff., 401b f., 460c-d.

58 : *Rep.* 484d, 539e ; *Phileb.* 62b.

59 : *Rep.* 532-535a.

60 : *Rep.* 517b, 532b.

61 : *Rep.* 508d f., 511c-d, 517b-c, 518c ; *Tim.* 29e f.

62 : *Rep.* 486a, 500c, 516c ff., 540d-e, 604c, 608c ; *Polit.* 294b ; *Laws* 875a.

63 : *Rep.* 510b, 511b-c ; *Phaedr.* 265d-e ; *Tim.* 27e f.; *Parm.* 136b-c ; *Polit.* 285b f.; *Phileb.* 16d-e ; *Laws* 965b-c.

64 : *Symp.* 211a ; *Rep.* 477, 484b f., 508d f., 511c d, 517b-c, 518c, 520b, 534 ; *Phaedr.* 250b.

65 : *Rep.* 486a-b, 487a, 490b-c, 491 ff., 535.

66 : *Gorg.* 486d-488b ; *Rep.* 413c f., 503a, e, 537a-b, d, 539e ; *Laws* 649d f., 735, 571c-d, 831a, 966b.

67 : *Rep.* 582 f. (with Jowett and Campbell's notes) ; *Phileb.* 65a f.

68 : *Symp.* 211a ; *Rep.* 509b, 540a ; *Phileb.* 30c-d.

69 : *Rep.* 500b f., 508d f., 511c-d, 517b-c, 518c ; *Phileb.* 59d.

70 : *Rep.* 473c (with Jowett and Campbell's note) ; *Theaet.* 173 f.

71 : *Rep.* 500d, 501b-c, 519c—521b.

72 : *Rep.* 497b-d ; *Polit.* 294, 299e f.; *Laws* 769b f., 875c-d.

73 : *Rep.* 378e ff.; *Laws* 801c f., 811c-e, 858c f., 957c-e.

74 : *Polit.* 305b-d ; *Laws* 627d f., 728a-b, 880d f.

75 : *Menex.* 247d ; *Rep.* 415, 495b ; *Theaet.* 175a-b.

76 : *Laws* 965a-b. For the " tests," see references in note 66 *supra.*

77 : *Rep.* 428e f., 431c-d, 491b, 499e ff., 540a-b, d ; cf. *Theaet.* 186c ; *Polit.* 293a, 297c. Plato usually writes of the *full* guardians as being very few in number, although of the "auxiliaries," in a city presumably of about 5,040 families (*Laws* 737d, but cf. *Rep.* 423b-d), there must have been at least 1,000 (including both men and women) who succeeded in reaching the middle rungs of the educational ladder (*Rep.* 423a, with Adam's note ; *Polit.* 292e).

CHAPTER II

1 : The Dialogues treat of mental and moral, as well as of
bodily health (*cf. Rep.* 444e ; *Tim.* 86b f.; *Soph*, 228-230 ; *Polit.*
310a ; *Phileb.* 26), but we are concerned here only with health
as a representative of the class " goods of the *body*." The mental
and moral treatment is, in fact, strictly analogous to the physical
treatment, dialectical refutation taking the place of cathartics,
and an appreciation of law and order taking the place of the due
proportion of earth, water, fire, and air in the body.

2 : *Gorg.* 487e f.; *Rep.* 341e, 342b, d ; cf. *Eryx.* 404d.

3 : *Ion* 531d f.; *Hipp. Min.* 373d ff.; *Prtg.* 345a-b ; *Rep.*
438e ; *Polit.* 283c f.; *Laws* 816d-e.

4 : *Symp.* 186d, 188a.

5 : *Tim.* 82.

6 : *Cratyl.* 419b-c ; *Tim.* 86a.

7 : *Prtg.* 353c-d ; *Gorg.* 518c-d ; *Symp.* 188b ; *Rep.* 404d-e,
405c-d, 559b-c ; *Laws* 691c ; cf. *Eryx.* 397a.

8 : *Tim.* 82-86a.

9 : *Soph.* 228a.

10 : *Tim.* 84c.

11 : *Tim.* 83e f.

12 : *Rep.* 556e ; *Tim.* 82b, 87c ; *Phileb.* 31c-d ; *Laws* 691c.

13 : *Prtg.* 354a-b; *Gorg.* 479a, 522a ; *Rep.* 406d ; *Tim.* 84e.

14 : *Cratyl.* 405a-b ; *Rep.* 467c ; *Phaedr.* 268a-b ; *Soph.* 227 ;
Tim. 85e.

15 : *Rep.* 407d, 567c ; *Soph.* 226d, 227a, d ; *Polit.* 293.

16 : *Rep.* 444d ; *Tim.* 88e ; *Phileb.* 25e f., 31d.

17 : *Laws* 723a, 857c.

18 : *Laws* 720b-c.

19 : *Laws* 723a, 857d.

20 : *Phaedr.* 270b f. ; *Laws* 720d.

21 : *Charm.* 156e f.; *Rep.* 403d.

22 : *Symp.* 188a ; *Rep.* 591d ; *Phileb.* 25e.

23 : *Rep.* 444d ; *Tim.* 87c, 88e ; cf. *Meno* 77a.

24 : *Rep.* 591d ; *Phileb.* 31c-d.

25 : *Gorg.* 505a ; *Rep.* 444c ; *Tim.* 88b.

26 : *Gorg.* 452a.

27 : *Lysis* 217 ff.; *Rep.* 583c-d.

28 : *Lysis* 218e f.; *Gorg.* 451e ; *Rep.* 357c, 367c-d ; *Laws*
728e.

29 : *Charm.* 164b-c ; *Phaedo* 66a ; *Rep.* 403d, 491c ; *Phileb.*
55b ; *Laws* 661, 728d f.

30 : *Lach.* 195c f.; *Euthyd.* 289a ; *Phaedr.* 268b-c.

31 : *Gorg.* 477a-b, 479b-c, 480d, 505a ; *Rep.* 406b f.; *Laws*
661c.

32 : *Symp.* 186b ; *Rep.* 583c f.; *Theaet.* 159c f.

33 : *Rep.* 583c ff.

34 : *Rep.* 591b-d.

35 : *Phaedo* 66a ; *Rep.* 500d, 501b-c, 509b, 519c-521b.

36 : *Phaedo* 66b-67a ; *Rep.* 406b f., 559b-c, 571 f.

37 : *Meno* 87a ; *Euthyd.* 281a-b, 289a ; *Rep.* 504e, 618e ;
Phileb, 63e ; *Laws*, 661a f.

38 : *Prtg.* 351a; *Rep.* 491 c f., 495b.

39 : *Rep.* 591b-d; *Phileb.* 25e, 26b; *Laws* 691c, 728e; cf. *Amat.* 134a f.

40 : *Rep.* 330b; *Laws* 744e f.

41 : *Symp.* 185a; *Rep.* 362b, 553d, 554c, 555c f.; *Laws* 742c, 773c, 928b f.

42 : *Rep.* 552d, 556d, 575b; *Laws* 831e, 884 f.

43 : *Rep.* 343d-e, 551e, 554a-b, 555a, 572c; *Laws* 743b.

44 : *Prtg.* 310d, 311b f., 328b; *Gorg.* 467d; *Rep.* 370e f., 552a, 553c, 564e; *Laws* 804c-d, 831d-e, 849a f., 919b f.

45 : *Euthyd.* 281d-e.

46 : *Gorg.* 451e; *Symp.* 185a.

47 : *Gorg.* 466b-492c *passim;* *Rep.* 344a-c, 359c f.; cf. *Theag.* 124e; *Alc. II,* 141a f.

48 : *Rep.* 343d-e, 362b-d; *Laws* 743.

49 : *Rep.* 551e, 554a-b, 555a, 572c; *Laws* 953c-d.

50 : *Rep.* 330a-c. The limits for honourable money-making are indicated in the *Laws* (744d f., 855b, 856d).

51 : *Rep.* 518c f., 550e f., 553c-d, 562b; *Laws* 831c f.

52 : *Rep.* 330c, 421d, 552c; *Laws* 679c, 728e, 741e, 832a-b; *Epist.* 317c-d.

53 : *Rep.* 553c-d.

54 : *Rep.* 422, 551d-e; *Laws* 832a-b.

55 : *Rep.* 422e f., 551d, 556c f.

56 : *Rep.* 520e, 556e f., 562b.

57 : *Euthyd.* 279c ff.; *Rep.* 504e; *Phileb.* 64d-e, 63e; *Laws* 631c, 697b, 743d.

58 : *Rep.* 331b, 552a; *Laws* 744d-e, 855b, 856d.

59 : *Meno* 87a, 88d-e; *Euthyd.* 279c, 281 f., 292e; *Rep.* 619a; *Phaedr.* 279c; *Epist.* 355a-c.

60 : *Laws* 631c, 697b, 870b.

61 : *Rep.* 330, 591e.

62 : *Phaedo* 78a; *Theaet.* 167d; *Laws* 743d.

63 : *Rep.* 343d; *Laws* 743a-c, 953c-d.

64 : *Meno* 87e f.; *Euthyd.* 279c-280d, 289a; *Rep.* 520e, 586d-e; cf. *Eryx.* 397e f.

65 : *Rep.* 619a, d-e; *Laws* 661b-d, 744d f., 773b f., 836a, 920c, 926a-b.

66 : *Laws* 653d-e, 815e f.

67 : *Hipp. Maj.* 297e ff.; *Tim.* 67a; *Phileb.* 54d-e; *Laws* 645d f., 673e f.; *Epist.* 326c-d, 335b-c.

68 : *Prtg.* 353c f.; *Rep.* 403a, 571b f.

69 : *Rep.* 571c; *Phileb.* 60a, 67b; *Laws* 653d f., 732e f.

70 : *Laws* 670d-e, 672c-d, 673d.

71 : *Phileb.* 51b f.; *Laws* 653e ff., 673c f., 815d.

72 : *Rep.* 398c ff., 424b f., 607c-d; *Laws* 656 ff.

73 : *Rep.* 401a, etc.

74 : *Rep.* 401d f., 486d-e, 500b f.; *Phileb.* 12c-d, 63e; *Laws* 653, 663.

75 : *Rep.* 498e f.

76 : *Phaedo* 97c; *Rep.* 583a; *Phaedr.* 247c f.; *Phileb.* 50e ff., 65 ff.

77 : *Prtg.* 358a; *Laws* 732e f.; cf. G. Entz, *Pessimismus und Weltflucht bei Plato,* pp. 11-12, 20, 103-104.

78 : *Phileb.* 12c f.

79 : *Prtg.* 351c-d ; *Gorg.* 499c ff.; *Rep.* 505c-d.

80 : *Rep.* 438a ; *Phileb.* 13b-c, 60a.

81 : *Gorg.* 491e ff.; *Rep.* 343c ff., 560e f.

82 : *Rep.* 365a f., 538c f.; *Laws* 655c f.

83 : *Prtg.* 353d f.; *Rep.* 559a-c, 573d f., 575a, 586a f.

84 : *Gorg.* 507e ff.; *Laws* 733 ff.

85 : *Prtg.* 356d f.; *Gorg.* 506e ff.; *Phileb.* 64d-e ; *Laws* 734c f., 792c-d.

86 : *Gorg.* 507e ; *Rep.* 585b ; *Tim.* 65a, 67a ; *Phileb.* 42c ff.

87 : *Rep.* 402e f.; *Phaedr.* 238e, 239c ff.; *Tim.* 64d f.

88 : *Rep.* 583e ff.; *Phileb.* 31d f.

89 : *Rep.* 584d f.; cf. Schopenhauer, *Welt als Wille und Vorstellung,* IV., 57.

90 : *Phaedo* 64c, 65a ; *Rep.* 609d f.

91 : *Phaedo* 65 ff.; *Rep.* 509d ff.; *Theaet.* 151e ff.; *Tim.* 109.

92 : *Rep.* 518c f., 581e ff.

93 : *Rep.* 480a, 485a-b, 583e, 586a ; *Phileb.* 31a, 54a f., 65d ; cf. R. G. Bury, *The Philebus of Plato,* pp. xlii-xliv.

94 : *Symp.* 211a ; *Rep.* 490a-b, 581e ff.; *Phaedr.* 250b ; *Phileb.* 51b ff.

95 : *Rep.* 485d, 605a f., 611d f.

96 : *Phaedo* 64 ff.; cf. Windelband, *Platon,*[2] pp. 20, 127 ff.

97 : *Rep.* 571 ; *Phileb.* 63d-e.

98 : *Prtg.* 356e f.; *Gorg.* 499d ; *Rep.* 424e f., 462a, 559d f., 586e f.; *Laws* 653b-c, 655d f., 733e f., 792c-d. It is, of course, only to the good man that pleasure is at any time a true good (*Rep.* 587e f.; *Phileb.* 40c ; *Laws* 661b).

99 : *Prtg.* 356e f.; *Rep.* 585d f.; *Phileb.* 64d, 65d, 66c.

100 : *Phileb.* 31a, 32d., 54c f., 60a-b, 63d-e.

101 : *Rep.* 602d f.; *Phileb.* 26b. 31d f., 33a-b ; *Laws* 674c, 733 ff., 792c-d, 793a ; cf. R. G. Bury, op. cit., p. xliii.

102 : *Meno* 84d, 85b f.; *Phaedr.* 250 ff.; *Phileb.* 38b ff.; *Epinom.* 976a-b ; cf. *Phaedo* 96b ; *Theaet.* 194c f. For a modern account of these same processes, cf. Wundt, *Logik,* Band I, pp. 10-69.

103 : *Theaet.* 187a, 189e f.; *Soph.* 263e f.; *Phileb.* 38e.

104 : *Phaedr.* 250a-b ; *Theaet.* 187 ff.; *Soph.* 260e, 263b f., 264d.

105 : *Charm.* 159a ; *Theaet.* 194d ; *Soph.* 263d, 264a-b ; *Phileb.* 39b ff., with Bury's notes. Cf. Halévy, *La théorie platonicienne des sciences,* p. 89 ; Beare, *Greek Theories of Elementary Cognition,* p. 268.

106 : The sphere of *doxa* (usually rendered by *Urteil* in German expositions, cf. H. Barth, *Die Seele in der Philosophi Platons,* pp. 202 ff.) has a certain analogy with what modern logicians call " judgments of experience," though running over into what are called " judgments of imagination " and even " transcendent judgments." (Cf. Lodge, The Division of Judgments, *Journal of Philosophy,* Vol. XV, 1918, pp. 544, 548). It is, however, erroneous to render it simply by the term " judgment." For the idea of judgment nowadays (e.g., in Lotze, Bradley, Bosanquet, Creighton, Hibben, etc). is a *reflective* reconstruction of sensory experience in the light of certain clearly

understood *intellectual standards*. But of clearly understood intellectual standards there is, in *doxa*, explicitly no trace. In fact, the distinction between *doxa* and *episteme* resembles rather Kant's distinction between *Einbildung* and *Verstand*.

107 : *Theaet.* 171a, 189a, 199b ; *Parm.* 142a, 155d, 164b, 166a ; *Soph.* 263b, 264d ; *Laws* 653b, 851b.

108 : *Phaedr.* 275a ; *Theaet.* 201a-c ; *Tim.* 28a-c, 51d f.

109 : *Meno* 85c ; *Rep.* 476c, e, 477b f., 484c, 505e, 506c, 508d.

110 : *Symp.* 207e ; *Meno* 97e f.; *Rep.* 509d f., 515a-b, 518d-e ; *Phaedr.* 275a ; *Soph.* 230b.

111 : *Meno* 86a ; *Phaedo* 96b ; *Rep.* 479e ; *Polit.* 277e, 285b ; *Laws* 965b-c ; cf. Bury, op. cit., p. xlvii.

112 : *Rep.* 476, 479d f.; *Theaet.* 207c ; *Tim.* 51e.

113 : *Theaet.* 187d ff., 194e ; *Soph.* 260b-c, 263b, d, 264d.

114 : *Symp.* 202a ; *Rep.* 413a ; *Theaet.* 171a, 189a, 194b-d, 199b ; *Tim.* 37 ; *Phileb.* 39a.

115 : *Cratyl.* 420b-c ; *Phileb.* 37d-e, 38d.

116 : *Meno* 97b-c, 98b-c ; *Theaet.* 201a-c ; *Laws* 631c, 632c, 953a-b ; *Epist.* 311d-e.

117 : *Crito* 46d f.; *Rep.* 505d ; *Polit.* 309c.

118 : *Rep.* 412c ff., 429c f., 484b f ; *Polit.* 308d.

119 : *Rep.* 537c, 518c, 519b-d ; *Polit.* 285b ; *Laws* 951b, 965b ff.

120 : *Rep.* 518d ; *Polit.* 309c-d ; *Laws* 966c f.

121 : *Phileb.* 40b, e. Many writers believe that Plato teaches a quasi-Kantian " priority of the practical reason," largely because the highest " idea " is " the good," i.e. not (they think) a specifically intellectual principle. Their belief is hardly, however, consistent with such passages as *Phaedr.* 237d-e, 238b ; *Laws* 631c, 653a, 875c-d. The general tenor of the Dialogues is undoubtedly that it is important to have opinion *right*, because right conduct depends upon rightness of opinion, and not *vice versa*.

122 : *Rep.* 490 ff.; cf. *De Justo* 375b-d ; cf. Bury, op. cit., pp. xlii-xliv.

123 : *Meno* 97b-c, 98b-c.

124 : *Prtg.* 358c-d ; *Rep.* 382a f., 441e ff.

125 : *Symp.* 210d f.; *Meno* 97e ; *Rep.* 485c ff.

126 : *Meno* 98a ; *Phaedr.* 275d-e.

127 : *Rep.* 537e f., 538c.

128 : *Rep.* 538a ff.

129 : Reflection does not maintain the traditional standards without alteration, although it frequently recognizes the fundamental correctness of the principles accepted even by popular thought. Cf. Nettleship, op. cit., pp. 3-4, and, for concrete applications, see *infra*, ch. XI, pp. 327, 331-334 ; ch. XII, pp. 337-341 ; and ch. XXI, pp. 468, 472-473.

130 : *Rep.* 538d f.

131 : *Rep.* 539a f.

132 : *Crito* 46d f.; *Theaet.* 194d-e ; *Phaedr.* 237d-e, 238b, 253d ; *Polit.* 309c-d ; *Phileb.* 41e f.; *Laws* 864a ; *Epist.* 311d-e.

133 : *Theaet.* 191d ; *Phileb.* 33c f., with Bury's note.

134 : *Theaet.* 191e ; *Tim.* 64b-c ; *Phileb.* 34a. The symbols, used in the interest of intellectual clarity, are, of course, not platonic.

135 : *Tim.* 43c f.; *Phileb.* 39a.

136 : *Theaet.* 163e ; *Tim.* 64b ; *Phileb.* 33d f.

137 : *Theaet.* 198d, 199a-b, 200b-c ; *Phileb.* 19d, 34a ; *Laws* 783c, 811a.

138 : *Theaet.* 182a f.; *Tim.* 43c f.

139 : *Cratyl.* 437b.

140 : *Tim.* 26a-c. The "age" refers, of course, to the association, not to the man ; for men, as they grow older, form weaker associations (*Lach.* 189c). From memory *plus* sensation arises opinion and (later) knowledge (*Phaedo* 96b ; *Phileb.* 38b f.; *Laws* 645e ; cf. Bury, op. cit., pp. 81-82).

141 : *Meno* 85d ; *Phaedo* 73b f.; *Phileb.* 34b-c.

142 : Cf. *Gorg.* 501a.

143 : *Charm.* 159e ; *Meno* 71c ; *Theaet.* 194c-d ; *Epinom.* 976b.

144 : *Theaet.* 194c-195a ; *Tim.* 43c f., 64b f. Disturbance of the proportion of the bodily elements, such as occurs in intoxication, impairs memory (*Laws* 645e).

145 : *Meno* 88 ; cf. *Epist.* 344a f. On the other side, cf. *Rep.* 487a ; *Phileb.* 21b-d, 60d-e ; *Laws* 896c-d ; *Epinom.* 989c.

146 : *Charm.* 159a ; *Phileb.* 38b ff.

147 : *Meno* 86a ; *Phaedo* 96b ; *Rep.* 479e, 524 ff.; *Polit.* 277e f., 285b ; *Laws* 965b-c ; cf. Bury, op. cit., p. xlvii.

148 : *Rep.* 486d, 487a, 490c ; *Laws* 709e, 710c ; *Epinom.* 989c ; *Epist.* 340d. For the educational value of rote memory, in connection with a content of philosophical value, cf. *Laws* 811a f., 957c, and for the connection of memory with the inspiration which comes from *anamnesis*, cf. *Phaedr.* 249c ff.

149 : *Theaet.* 194c-d. Intellectual acumen is dealt with by Plato under many Greek names (*oxytes, anchinoia, eumatheia, xunesis*), the contexts of which, however, sufficiently justify the treatment of them, in the text, as referring to one and the same complex of mental processes.

150 : *Charm.* 159d f.; *Lach.* 192a-b ; *Theaet.* 144a-b ; *Epinom.* 976b-c.

151 : *Cratyl.* 412a-b ; *Theaet.* 147a-b.

152 : *Phaedr.* 249b.

153 : *Phaedr.* 249b-c ; *Polit.* 277e f.

154 : *Rep.* 383c f.; *Laws* 809a f.

155 : *Rep.* 521c ff., 535b ; *Laws* 747b-c.

156 : *Theaet.* 144a-b ; *Epist.* 327a f., 339e.

157 : *Rep.* 487a, 490c, 494b f., 503b, 535b ff.; *Laws* 710c.

158 : *Rep.* 409a c, 519a ; *Laws* 747c.

159 : *Meno* 88 ; *Rep.* 518e f.

160 : *Rep.* 498b, 500b f.; *Epist.* 340c-d.

161 : For other dangers of "cleverness," when unballasted by sound moral qualities, cf. *Rep.* 503b f.; *Polit.* 306c f.; *Laws* 747b-c, 964e.

162 : *Tim.* 70a-d.

163 : *Lach.* 196e f.; *Prtg.* 350a f.; *Laws* 963e.

164 : *Prtg.* 350b f.; *Rep.* 375a f., 516e ; cf. Shorey, *Unity of Plato's Thought,* p. 11 n.

165 : *Laws* 633b-d.

166 : *Rep.* 375b f.; *Laws* 791b f.

167 : *Rep.* 412c ff., 429b f.
168 : *Rep.* 376a f., 386a-b, 403d, 410b f.; *Polit.* 309c.
169 : *Gorg.* 491b ; *Cratyl.* 413e f.
170 : *Phaedo* 68d f.; *Laws* 631c, 734c f.
171 : *Lach.* 190e f.; *Rep.* 386b ; *Theaet.* 177b ; *Laws* 944e f.
172 : *Lach.* 191d f.
173 : *Meno* 81d ; *Euthyd.* 275c-d ; *Phaedo* 69b-c ; *Rep.* 537 ;
Theaet. 157d, 177b ; *Laws* 633b f., 659a, 792c f.
174 : *Lach.* 192e ff.; *Prtg.* 350a f.
175 : *Apol.*, *passim* ; *Laws* 646e f., 649b-c.
176 : *Phaedo* 68d f.; *Rep.* VI-VII, *passim.*
177 : *Lach.* 192c-d ; *Meno* 88a-b ; *Polit.* 307b f.
178 : *Menex.* 247d f.; *Laws* 792c f.
179 : *Charm.* 159b, 160e, 161b, 163a ; *Gorg.* 504d ; *Phaedo*
68c ; *Phaedr.* 256a-b ; *Polit.* 306b ff.; *Tim.* 72a ; *Laws* 710a, 831e.
180 : *Rep.* 503b-c ; *Polit.* 306c ff.
181 : *Symp.* 216d ff.; *Phaedo* 68c f.; *Rep.* 329a f., 430e ;
Laws 733e f.
182 : *Rep.* 549c f.; *Polit.* 306b ff.
183 : *Rep.* 559 ff., 571e ; *Epist.* 326b f.
184 : *Rep.* 485d-e, 496b f., 549b f.
185 : *Polit.* 307e f.; *Laws* 696b, 710a.
186 : *Gorg.* 491d-e ; *Rep.* 412c ff., 429c f., 484b ff.; *Phaedr.*
237d f.; *Laws* 968a ; *Epinom.* 977c-d.
187 : *Charm.* 157a ; *Crito* 47d ; *Rep.* 538c.
188 : *Charm.* 167a, 170d, 171f.; *Gorg.* 491d-e ; *Symp.*
216d ff.; *Rep.* 430e f.; *Phaedr.* 237d-e.
189 : *Rep.* 375c f., 410b ff.; *Polit.* 308e, 309b ff.; *Laws* 773c,
802e.
190 : *Rep.* 519e f.
191 : *Rep.* 498b-c, 540a-c.
192 : *Rep.* 431d f.; *Phaedr.* 238c ; *Polit.* 309 ; *Laws* 710a.
193 : *Charm.* 164d ff.
194 : *Rep.* 430e-432a, 442c-d.
195 : *Gorg.* 508a ; *Rep.* 402a, 500c-d ; *Phaedr.* 237d f.
196 : *Rep.* 376b-c, 410d-412a, 487a, 503c f.; *Polit.* 309a-b, d.
197 : *Polit.* 307e, 309a ; *Laws* 696d.
198 : *Phaedo* 68c-d.
199 : *Gorg.* 504d, 507b f.; *Meno* 88a-b ; *Phaedo* 69a-b ;
Phaedr. 256a-b ; *Laws* 673e, 693b-c, 711b f., 733e f.
200 : *Prtg.* 322c-d, 323a, c, 324e f.
201 : *Prtg.* 323c, 325b, 327a ; *Gorg.* 525b f.; *Rep.* 351c f.;
Polit. 308e f.; *Laws* 862e f., 957e.
202 : *Theaet.* 167c ; *Laws* 864a ; *Epist.* 335d.
203 : *Prtg.* 325c ff.; *Rep.* 492b ff.
204 : *Rep.* 338d f., 343b f.; *Theaet.* 172a f.; *Laws* 714c ;
Epist. 334c f., 336d ff.
205 : *Apol.* 24d-e ; *Laws* 957a f.
206 : *Crito* 50c ff.
207 : *Polit.* 305b-d ; *Laws* 627d f., 658e f., 888d, 945b ff.,
957d.
208 : *Rep.* 331d ff., 419-421c, 443c f., 465e f., 519e f.
209 : *Rep.* 462-464b.
210 : *Rep.* 505 ff.

211 : *Symp.* 210d f.; *Rep.* 490b-c, 500 f., 517c.

212 : *Cratyl.* 412c f.; *Rep.* 444d, 508d f., 511b, 532a f., 534b f.; *Laws* 757b f.

213 : *Meno* 88b f.; *Laws* 864a ; *Epist.* 335d.

214 : *Rep.* 357b ff.

215 : *Rep.* 351a f.

216 : *Rep.* 358e ff.

217 : *Rep.* 362e ff.; *Laws* 889e f.

218 : *Rep.* 358a-c, 367a, c, 368b ; *Laws* 714c f.

219 : *Prtg.* 322b ff.; *Rep.* 433 ff., 443b ff., 462 ff.; *Laws* 937d-e. On the other side, T. Maguire (*Essays on the Platonic Ethics*, pp. 11-13) insists that the four virtues, and especially the virtue of justice, are, in the first instance, internal, " essentially non-social."

220 : *Tim.* 29e f.

221 : *Rep.* 444d, 505 ff., 508d f., 511b, 534b f., 612b ff.; *Laws* 757b-d.

222 : *Laws* 653d f., 673c.

223 : *Polit.* 283b f.; *Tim.* 47c-d ; *Phileb.* 26a-b ; *Laws* 657c, 672c, 815e f.; cf. Wilamowitz-Moellendorff, *Platon,*[2] Vol. II, p. 308.

224 : *Laws*, 653e f., 673c-d. This is denied in the *Oxford History of Music*, Vol. I, p. 43.

225 : *Rep.* 397b, 398d, 400d.

226 : *Rep.* 392c ff.; *Laws* 669d f.

227 : *Ion* 532e f.; *Cratyl.* 423c f.; *Laws* 889d.

228 : *Rep.* 372e f., 397c, 399c f., 404d-e.

229 : *Phaedr.* 277c f.; *Laws* 719b f., 801b f.

230 : *Phaedr.* 245a, 265b ; *Laws* 719c.

231 : *Euthyphr.* 3c ; *Phaedr.* 234d, 238c-d, 241e, 244 ff.

232 : *Rep.* 492 ff.

233 : *Rep.* 372b, etc.

234 : *Rep.* 372e f., 394d f., 399d-e ; *Laws* 962d f.

235 : *Rep.* 395d f., 397a, 398e ; *Laws* 816d f.

236 : *Rep.* 393d, 601b.

237 : *Rep.* 397d, 401d f., 411a-b, 605a, 607c ; *Tim.* 47c-d ; *Laws* 656 ff.

238 : *Rep.* 604d ff.; *Laws* 719b-c.

239 : *Rep.* 424b f.

240 : *Gorg.* 501d ff.; *Rep.* 424d, 562b ff.

241 : *Rep.* 605b, 607a. Artists have nothing to do with civic justice, and are thus, at best, superfluities in the ethical community (*Rep.* 373a-c, 398a, 399e).

242 : *Rep.* 607d f.

243 : *Rep.* 601c ; *Phaedr.* 260c f., 262a-c, 274e f., 277c f.; *Laws* 719c.

244 : *Phaedr.* 245a, 265b.

245 : *Rep.* 377b f., 378e ff., 383c, 386 ff., 392b ff., 401b f.; *Laws* 817d-e.

246 : *Rep.* 389d ff., 397d, 413e ; *Laws* 801b f.

247 : *Prtg.* 326a-b ; *Symp.* 197b-c, 201a ; *Rep.* 376e ff., 395b f., 401b ff., 425a ; *Laws* 670d, 671a, 673a, 815e f.

248 : *Rep.* 396c f., 399 f.; *Laws* 814e ff.

249 : *Rep.* 424b f.

250 : *Symp.* 210e ff.; *Rep.* 476c f., 479e f.; *Phaedr.* 248d,

249 f., 260d f., 273d f., 277b f.   The artist, *as a rule*, knows the many beautiful things, i.e. the " appearances," (*Rep.* 476b, 479a-b, 598 ff.) but does not really understand their principle, the " idea " of beauty (*Phaedr.* 248d-e, 251a, 260c, 262a f.; *Laws* 889d), in spite of the suggestions of *Euthyphr.* 6e ; *Rep.* 472d, 484c.

251 : *Symp.* 218e ; *Phaedr.* 249d ; *Tim.* 47c-d.   The Dialogues imply at times that artistic creation which does not serve the community spirit is bad *as art*, and that, as creative art functions by introducing law and order into the otherwise chaotic and meaningless (*Gorg.* 503e ; *Laws* 653d f.), the most ideally artistic creation would introduce the Divine law and the ideal order, so that the philosopher with his clear vision of the " idea " would be the ablest creative artist (*Euthyphr.* 6e ; *Symp.* 212a-b ; *Rep.* 425a, 484c-d, 501a f., 595b ff., 602 ff.; *Phaedr.* 244 ff., 259d, 260e ; *Laws* 858d f.).   But Plato's knowledge of the actual processes of artistic creation (see notes 229-231, 235, 243) is inconsistent with this, and the function of actual art-production is, in general, regarded as strictly subordinate to a non-creative, non-artistic, philosophical insight.

252 : *Rep.* 373d f., 422d ff.; *Laws* 709a f., 766d ff.

253 : *Rep.* 421b ff., 464c ff., 520c f., 546 ff.

254 : *Rep.* 470 ff.; *Laws* 709.

255 : This is especially noted in the cases of Crete and Sparta (*Crito* 52e ; *Hipp. Maj.* 283e ; *Rep.* 544 ff.).   It is also maintained that the constitution is a reflection of the character of the citizens (*Rep.* 544d ; *Laws* 766d ff.), and many writers regard this as the more fundamentally Platonic position (cf. e.g. T. Maguire, *Essays on the Platonic Ethics*, pp. 11-13).

256 : *Laws* 624a f.; *Minos* 313 ff.

257 : *Gorg.* 482e ff.; *Menex.* 245b f.; *Rep.* 550d f.; *Laws* 889d f.

258 : *Rep.* 343b ff.; *Theaet.* 167c, 172a f.; *Laws* 714b ff.; *Epist.* 334c f., 336d ff.

259 : *Rep.* 343b-c.   For this there were, no doubt, historical reasons.   The victory over the Persians, followed by the conversion of Delian League into Athenian Empire, made inevitable an imperialistic tendency in legislation.

260 : *Rep.* 521a-b, 550c ff.; *Laws* 715b.

261 : *Rep.* 419 ff., 466a f., 519e f.

262 : *Rep.* 423b f., 462 ff., 520a ; *Laws* 858d f.; *Epist.* 337c-d.

263 : *Gorg.* 465c ; *Cratyl.* 388e ff., 437e, 438d f.; *Rep.* 500b f., 508c f., 520c, 540a-b ; *Laws* 715b ; *Epist.* 337c-d.

264 : *Apol.* 17d ; *Lach.* 196b ; *Rep.* 405a f., 492b f., 518e ; *Phaedr.* 272d f.; *Theaet.* 172c ff.; *Laws* 743c.

265 : *Rep.* 425b ff.

266 : *Polit.* 293 ff., 300c f.; *Laws* 875c f.

267 : *Hipp. Maj.* 284d ; *Laws* 645a-b, 766d ff., 875c f., 880d-e ; *Epist.* 322d-e.

268 : *Rep.* 497b f., 500b f.; *Polit.* 294a f., 299e f.; *Laws* 875d.

269 : *Tim.* 64a f.; *Phileb.* 51b, d-e, 52a, d f.; *Laws* 653d f., 673c-d, 815e f.

270 : *Rep.* 375e f., 474b-c, 475b ff., 485b f., 490a f.;   cf. *Hipp. Maj.* 297e ; cf. *Amat.* 133c.

271 : *Prtg.* 353d ; *Hipp. Maj.* 297e-298a, d f.; *Rep.* 764b ;
Phileb. 54e ; *Laws* 653a, d f.
272 : *Rep.* 522c-526c ; *Theaet.* 155d ; *Tim.* 47a f.
273 : *Rep.* 476b, c, 479e.
274 : *Rep.* 475d ff., 484b f., 490a.
275 : *Rep.* 475b ff., 485 ff., 526b-c.
276 : *Phaedo* 96b ; *Theaet.* 194c f.; *Phileb.* 38b ff.
277 : *Rep.* 524 ff.; *Polit.* 277e f., 285b ; *Laws* 965b-c.
278 : *Rep.* 477a-b, 484b, d, 485b, 486d-e, 510b ff.; *Soph.*
253c f.
279 : *Gorg.* 484c ; *Euthyd.* 288d f.; *Tim.* 88b-c.
280 : *Phaedo* 64 ff., etc.
281 : *Gorg.* 486a f.; *Rep.* 487d, 489d, 490d, 495c f.
282 : *Rep.* 497d f., 503c f., 537e ff.; *Polit.* 299b-d.
283 : *Gorg.* 484c ; *Menex.* 234a ; *Rep.* 487c, 498b.
284 : *Gorg.* 487c f.; *Rep.* 487c-d, 489d, 516e ff.
285 : *Gorg.* 485b ff.; *Rep.* 496b-c, 519c.
286 : *Rep.* 488 ff., 495c f., 535c f.
287 : *Rep.* 489d ff., 498a f.
288 : *Phaedo* 68c f.; *Rep.* 496b f., 520a f.
289 : *Rep.* 519c f., 539e f.
290 : *Rep.* 503e f., 537b f.
291 : *Rep.* 540a f.
292 : *Phaedo* 68c f.; *Rep.* 500b f.
293 : *Rep.* 500d f., 505a-b, 540b f.
294 : *Rep.* 477a-b, e, 484b, d, 485b, 486d-e ; *Soph.* 253c f.;
Laws 903b f.
295 : Cf. Nettleship, op. cit., Vol. I, pp. 244, 287 ; W. A.
Thompson, *The Gorgias of Plato*, pp. xx-xxi. As the evidence for
what follows rests wholly upon what has preceded, references
already given will not be repeated.
296 : *Rep.* 505b-c.
297 : *Tim.* 90b f.

CHAPTER III

1 : *Prtg.* 322c f.; *Symp.* 204e f., 206a ; *Rep.* 413a, 438a,
505d-e ; *Phileb.* 20d.
2 : *Phileb.* 60a f.
3 : *Euthyphr.* 7d f.; *Rep.* 505b ff.; *Phaedr.* 250a-b, 263a ;
Polit. 277d, 285e f.
4 : *Laws* 957a f.
5 : *Rep.* 497b f.; *Polit.* 294a f., 299e ; *Laws* 875c-d.
6 : *Polit.* 305b ; *Laws* 627d f., 945b ff.
7 : *Laws* 811a f., 858e, 957a f.
8 : *Laws* 627e f., 728a f., 880d f.
9 : *Polit.* 294a-b, 300c f.; *Laws* 875c f.
10 : *Laws* 653a.
11 : *Prtg.* 353 ff.; *Rep.* 505c f.; *Phileb.* 12c f.
12 : *Prtg.* 353d ff.
13 : *Prtg.* 358a f. T. D. Goodell, *Plato's Hedonism*, pp.
25, 30, 33, states roundly that only a superficial reader can find

scientific hedonism in the *Protagoras*, and insists that the references to the " art of measurement " are purely figurative. If he is right, how many well-known Plato-students must be " superficial readers ! " But this view is hardly consistent with the evidence, which surely substantiates the usual interpretation.

14 : Cf. *Rep.* 587b f.

15 : *Rep.* 522c ff.

16 : *Phaedo* 69a f.; *Rep.* 581d ff.

17 : *Symp.* 211c f., *Rep.* 485d, 490a-b ; *Phaedr.* 250b-c ; *Phileb.* 51c ff.

18 : *Lys.* 216d ; *Alc. I*, 116a ; *Symp.* 201c ; *Soph.* 228c ; *Phileb.* 64d f.; *Laws* 773a.

19 : *Rep.* 401a, 444e.

20 : Cf. Fouillée, *La philosophie de Platon*, p. 353 ; Natorp, *Platos Ideenlehre*, pp. 172-173 ; A. E. Taylor, *Plato the Man and his Work*, pp. 230-231.

21 : *Rep.* 588a.

22 : *Gorg.* 503d f.; *Symp.* 212a-b, 218e ; *Rep.* 425a, 484c-d, 501a f., 596 ff., 602 ff.; *Phaedr.* 249d f., 260e ; *Laws* 858e f.

23 : *Phileb.* 66a.

24 : *Rep.* 400d-e, 352e ; cf. Fouillée, *op. cit.*, p. 365 n.

25 : *Rep.* 477a, 335c f.

26 : *Euthyphr.* 13b-c ; *Gorg.* 477a, 525b ; *Meno* 87e ; *Rep.* 519e, 618e.

27 : *Meno* 99e f.; *Rep.* 456e ; *Phaedr.* 278a ; cf. *Peri Aretes* 379a-d ; cf. *Eryx.* 393d-e.

28 : *Rep.* 590c-d, 613a.

29 : *Rep.* 421a, 508d f.; *Laws* 966b f.

30 : *Meno* 87d-89a ; *Euthyd.* 292b. So too, of men, the mere fact that a man's actions have benefitted or harmed others does not, as such, make the actions good or evil, respectively. The further question remains to be asked, as to the disposition of the agent, etc. (*Laws* 862a f.).

31 : *Rep.* 605 ff.; *Phaedr.* 277b f.; *Laws* 719b f., 801b f.

32 : *Rep.* 618c f.

33 : *Rep.* 397d-e, 413e ; *Laws* 715a f., 875a f.

34 : *Rep.* 412d-e, 428e ff.

35 : *Rep.* 473d-e, 479d, 501e, 519c ff.

36 : *Rep.* 423e f.

37 : *Rep.* 423b f., 462 ff.; *Laws* 942c.

38 : *Rep.* 420d f.; *Laws* 831c f., 875a-c.

39 : *Rep.* 521a, 547a, 551d, 556e ; *Laws* 715b f., 832c.

40 : *Rep.* 351c f., 422e, 562b f.; *Laws* 728b f.

41 : *Rep.* 462 ff.

42 : *Rep.* 419 ff., 519c ff.

43 : *Rep.* 462b f.

44 : *Rep.* 551d, 556e ; for platonic criticism of the usual *vae victis* policy, cf. *Laws* 715a f.

45 : *Rep.* 500b f.; *Laws* 903b f.

46 : Uncritical faith in the standard of " social solidarity " belongs to the level of " opinion " as opposed to " knowledge." This last rests upon insight into the " idea of good." (*Rep.* 505d-e.).

47 : *Rep.* 338c ff., 343b ff.

48 : *Gorg.* 483b ff., 507 f.

49 : *Epist.* 326c-d.

50 : *Charm.* 159b, etc.; *Phaedo* 68c ; *Rep.* 503b-c ; *Polit.* 307a ff.; *Laws* 710a, 733e f.

51 : *Crito* 50c ff.; *Rep.* 412c f., 424e f., 431d f., 518d ; *Polit.* 308d ; *Laws* 851b.

52 : *Gorg.* 508a ; *Rep.* 485c f.

53 : *Rep.* 490b, 493e f., 500b ff., 508e f., 510d ff.; *Laws* 897c, 898 f., 967d-e.

54 : *Rep.* 349b ff., 619a ; *Polit.* 283e ff.; *Phileb.* 25a f., 66a ; *Laws* 903b f.

55 : *Polit.* 307e, 309a.

56 : *Meno* 88b ; *Rep.* 441e f.

57 : *Rep.* 527c ff.; *Laws* 898 f.

58 : *Gorg.* 506d-e ; *Phaedo* 68e f.; *Rep.* 484c f., 534b f., 540a f.

59 : *Phileb.* 20d, 66a f.

60 : *Apol.* 28d f., 37e f., 41c f.; *Gorg.* 508c f.; *Crito* 48 ff.; *Phaedo* 67e ff.; *Rep.* 505 ff.; *Polit.* 294 ff.; *Laws* 875c f.

61 : *Gorg.* 466b, 469c, 470d f.; *Rep.* 344a f.

62 : *Gorg.* 483a-b, 486a f.; *Rep.* 364a-b, 365c-d.

63 : *Gorg.* 484a, 492e f.; *Laws* 661b.

64 : *Gorg.* 466b-c, 468e, 469c, 492c ; *Rep.* 362b-c ; cf. *Theag.* 124e ; cf. *Alc. II*, 141a f.

65 : *Rep.* 520e f., 581e ff.

66 : *Rep.* 500d f., 519c ff., 540b-c.

67 : *Gorg.* 491e ff.; *Rep.* 566d ff., 587e ; *Polit.* 294b ; *Laws* 715b.

68 : *Gorg.* 466b ff., 508d f.; *Rep.* 572d ff.

69 : *Rep.* 421c f.; *Laws* 744d f., 855b, 856d.

70 : *Rep.* 502a-c, etc.

71 : *Phaedo* 65 ff.; *Rep.* 517c-d, 604c ; *Phaedr.* 250c ; *Polit.* 294a f.; *Phileb.* 60b f.

72 : *Rep.* 486a, 500b f., 520e f., 540 ; *Polit.* 303c.

73 : e.g., as opposed to "halfness" of character, *Laws* 647c-d, 806c.

74 : Cf. *Phaedr.* 249b-c.

75 : *Rep.* 499b.; *Laws* 653a, 896b.

76 : *Phaedo* 68d ; *Rep.* 387d.

77 : *Rep.* 581d ff.

78 : *Rep.* 351 ff.; *Soph.* 227e f.; cf. *Eryx.* 397e f.

79 : *Rep.* 567e ff.; *Theaet.* 176b-c ; *Laws* 728b-c.

80 : *Rep.* 586a, 605 ff.; *Phileb.* 39c ff.

81 : *Theaet.* 154d f.; *Soph.* 230b f.

82 : *Gorg.* 460e f., 509a ; *Rep.* 335d f., 350c.

83 : *Rep.* 498e.

84 : *Prtg.* 361a f.; *Soph.* 253b f., *Polit.* 285b f.; *Laws* 965b f.

85 : *Rep.* 531c f.; *Parm.* 136b-c ; *Soph.* 259e ; *Polit.* 277e f.; *Phileb.* 16d-e.

86 : *Phaedr.* 249b ; *Soph.* 254b f.

87 : *Soph.* 250 ff.

88 : *Rep.* 490b-c, 611e ; *Phaedr.* 249e f.; *Theaet.* 185d f.

89 : *Rep.* 529b f., 531a f. ; *Theaet.* 157a f., 185b ff. ; *Soph.* 248a.

90 : *Euthyphr.* 3c ; *Rep.* 401d f., 604d ff.; *Phaedr.* 244 ff., 265b ; *Laws* 656 ff., 719b f., 801b f.

91 : *Rep.* 402c, 618c f.; *Parm.* 136b f.; *Theaet.* 186a f.; *Soph.* 253b f.; *Phileb.* 16d f.

92 : *Rep.* 490b f., 532a-b.

93 : *Rep.* 475b, 485a f.

94 : *Symp.* 205e ff.; *Rep.* 496b f.

95 : *Rep.* 402c, 618c f.

96 : *Rep.* 422 ff., 551d, 556e f.   So also " justice " consists in each element in the state being true to its own " idea," the " ideas " in question constituting a perfect system (*Rep.* 433 ff.).

97 : *Rep.* 351b ff.

98 : *Rep.* 354c.

99 : *Gorg.* 462e, 509a, 527b f.; *Rep.* 338e ff.; *Theaet.* 150b f.

100 : *Euthyd.* 300d, 301b, 303a, d f.; *Parm.* 135b f.; *Theaet.* 161e.

101 : *Rep.* 508c f.; *Parm.* 131c ff.; *Soph.* 241e, 251d ff.

102 : *Rep.* 472c f., 484c f., 510d-e ; *Phaedr.* 247c f.; *Parm.* 132d ; *Soph.* 247a f.

103 : *Parm.* 136b-d ; *Polit.* 285b f.; *Phileb.* 16d-e.

104 : *Theaet.* 156e, 163b f.; *Phileb.* 33d.

105 : *Soph.* 247d-e.

106 : *Rep.* 522c ff.

107 : *Cratyl.* 437b ; *Theaet.* 163e f.

108 : *Phaedo* 96b ; *Phileb.* 38 b.

109 : *Meno* 97a f.   Opinion may be based upon our own sensory experiences, or upon the experiences of others imparted to us in words (*Tim.* 51d f.; *Theaet.* 201a-c).

110 : *Meno* 97c f.; *Symp.* 202a ; *Theaet.* 187d ff.

111 : *Polit.* 278d-e.

112 : *Parm.* 131e ; *Polit.* 277e f.; 285b.

113 : *Rep.* 510b f., 511c-d, 533d.

114 : *Rep.* 484c f., 531e, 533b-c, 534c ; *Phaedr.* 250a-b.

115 : *Rep.* 511b ff., 531c, 532 ff.; *Phaedr.* 247c f.; *Parm.* 132d ; *Soph.* 254b f.

116 : *Rep.* 508c-d, 517b-c, 527d-e ; *Phileb.* 58a.

117 : *Rep.* 518c f., 534b f.

118 : Cf. *Laws* 903b f.

119 : *Rep.* 472c f., 500b ff.

120 : *Rep.* 490b, 540a f., 613a-b ; *Phileb.* 40b-c ; *Laws* 661b f.

121 : *Rep.* 373d f., *Laws* 709, 766d ff.

122 : He is never fully successful (*Rep.* 473a), for the material in which he seeks to embody the ideal does not fully admit of this. The best he can do is to establish a legal system which will do for the time being. It will need constant revision (*Polit.* 294a f., 299e f.; *Laws* 769b f.).

123 : *Phileb.* 12c f.

124 : This statement does not seem perfectly consistent with *Gorg.* 503e ; *Rep.* 349d f.; *Phaedr.* 244 ff., 260e. cf. *supra*, ch. II, note 251.   Perhaps the inconsistency exists only at the level of " opinion "—at which level the actual artists are found. Ideally speaking, no doubt the completest beauty and the completest goodness coincide.

125 : The actual beholder, of course still at the stage of
" opinion." The philosopher in the strict sense is not led astray
by what, to the actual beholder, looks like beauty—otherwise he
would be unable to fulfil his function of moral censorship (cf.
Rep. 475c ff.).

CHAPTER IV

1 : The general method of interpretation consists in omitting
altogether the evidence concerning the instincts and habits, in
insisting that the true Platonist always cuts loose entirely from
" pleasure " and from every sort of sensory or even social experience, and in believing that in *anamnesis* we have the clear and
final platonic answer to this question (cf. Adam's notes to *Rep.*
476a, c). The reference to *anamnesis* is doubtless important,
but surely it is a mistake in method to omit or seek to explain
away the very considerable body of evidence *re* pleasure and
sensory experience.

2 : *Phileb.* 20d, 60a-b ; *Laws* 732 f. The Greek words *to
gignoskon* signify cognitive awareness of all sorts, including what
we should call sensory perception, as opposed to more specifically
intellectual processes.

3 : *Rep.* 437e f.

4 : *Laws* 653a-b.

5 : *Hipp. Maj.* 297e ff.; *Phaedr.* 239c-d ; *Tim.* 67a ; *Phileb.*
54d-e, 63e.

6 : *Laws* 653d-e, 815e f.

7 : *Prtg.* 353c f.; *Rep.* 403a, etc.

8 : *Prtg.* 354c ff.; *Laws* 732e f.

9 : *Soph.* 228b-d ; *Laws* 782.

10 : *Laws* 653d f., 672c-d, 673c-d.

11 : *Phileb.* 26a, b ; *Laws* 814e ff.

12 : *Rep.* 401d f.; *Laws* 656 ff.

13 : *Charm.* 159b ; *Lach.* 196e f.; *Prtg.* 322c ff., 350a f.;
Tim. 70 ; *Laws* 963e.

14 : *Prtg.* 322d. The " social " element, as essential to
justice, is denied by Maguire, *Platonic Ethics*, pp. 11-13.

15 : *Rep.* 375e ; *Tim.* 64 ; *Phileb.* 54e ; *Laws* 653d f.

16 : *Phaedo* 97c ; *Rep.* 523c f.; *Theaet.* 147d f.

17 : Cf. *Rep.* 498e.

18 : *Symp.* 204e f., 206a ; *Rep.* 505d ; *Phileb.* 20d.

19 : *Prtg.* 322c ; *Rep.* 378 ff.; *Theaet.* 176a ; *Laws* 716c f.

20 : *Rep.* 532b, 583a, etc.

21 : *Prtg.* 356d f.; *Rep.* 425a, 585b f.; *Laws* 673c f., etc.
It should, perhaps, be noted that the feeling after the pleasant
is also a feeling after law and order (*Phileb.* 31d ff., 42c ff.), inasmuch as pleasure is the affective side of the recovery of equilibrium on the part of an organism which has been disturbed,
but is coming back to its proper form and balance. It is only
excessive pleasure which is lawless (*Rep.* 402e, *etc.*). But it
remains true that the law-element in pleasure is very general,
indefinite, and unspecialized.

22 : *Rep.* 511b f.

23 : *Symp.* 204e f., 206a ; *Rep.* 402e.

24 : *Rep.* 518c f., 533d f.

25 : *Rep.* 519b, 571b f., 586a-b ; *Phaedr.* 247b.

26 : *Rep.* 492a ; *Laws* 765e f.

27 : *Meno* 89b ; *Rep.* 492e f.; *Polit.* 309c-d ; *Peri Aretes* 379c-d.

28 : *Prtg.* 319e f.; *Gorg.* 455e f., 503c-d, 515d f.; *Meno* 93c f.

29 : *Rep.* 613a-b ; *Phileb.* 39e.

30 : *Rep.* 558b ; *Theaet.* 167b-c ; *Polit.* 309c-d, 310a ; *Laws* 951b-c ; *Peri Aretes* 379a-b.

31 : *Symp.* 209 ; *Rep.* 491b, 495a-b ; *Laws* 710b, 765e f.

32 : *Meno* 99 f.; *Rep.* 492a ; *Laws* 710c-d, 803c f., 875c.

33 : *Rep.* 491b, 495b.

34 : *Rep.* 586a-b ; *Phaedr.* 250a-b ; *Laws* 875b.

35 : *Rep.* 492b f.; *Laws* 659a-b.

36 : *Rep.* 412d f., 430a f.

37 : *Prtg.* 324d f.; *Rep.* 492d, 494e.

38 : *Prtg.* 322b, e, etc.

39 : *Rep.* 479a-b ; *Laws* 655b f.

40 : *Rep.* 411a-c, 424b f.; *Laws* 655c f.

41 : *Euthyd.* 276b, d, 303b ; *Rep.* 493d-e ; *Laws* 659a-b. This influence of the community is not a mere matter of the often despised " many," for in the " model city " Plato would himself compel artists—using as compulsion the legal enactments and legal force of the social group—to produce only art-works which embody community ideals (*Laws* 801c-d, 829d-e, etc.), so much so, that many writers regard the " model city " as a veritable *Zwangsanstalt* (cf. Wilamowitz-Moellendorff, op. cit., vol. I, p. 723).

42 : *Euthyphr.* 7d f.; *Rep.* 505b ff., 534b-c ; *Phaedr.* 250a-b, 263a ; *Polit.* 277d, 285e f.

43 : *Laws* 691, 711e f., 713c, 716a f., 975a.

44 : *Rep.* 351c f., 422, 562b f.

45 : *Rep.* 492b.

46 : *Rep.* 492c, 493d-e.

47 : *Rep.* 430a, etc. Plato himself takes full advantage of the power of the state in enforcing upon the citizens generally, as well as upon artists, community standards of conduct (*Menex.* 238c ; *Rep.* 538b f.; *Laws* 829d-e, 941b ff.; *Epist.* 322d-e).

48 : *Prtg. passim* ; *Rep.* 493a-c.

49 : *Prtg.* 334e ; *Euthyd.* 272a, 289c f., 304b-c, 325b-c ; *Rep.* 337c f., 498e ; *Theaet.* 154d-e.

50 : *Prtg.* 320c ff., 328e f.; *Gorg.* 449b-c ; *Euthyd.* 282d-e, 288a, 303e.

51 : *Rep.* 528b-c.

52 : *Prtg.* 342d f.

53 : *Rep.* 500d, 519c ff.

54 : *Cratyl.* 400c ; *Rep.* 364e f.; *Laws* 782c.

55 : *Rep.* 427b-c ; *Laws* 738b f., 759c f.

56 : E.g. belief in the existence of the Gods, and in the priority of soul over matter (*Laws* 966b ff., etc.).

57 : *Rep.* 468e f., 540c.

58 : *Rep.* 462 f.; *Laws* 942b-c.

59 : *Apol. passim* ; *Meno* 94e f.; *Rep.* 492c-d, 494e, 496d-e.

60 : *Rep.* 597e, 599a, d, 600e, 602c.

61 : *Gorg.* 491e ff.; *Rep.* 517d, 520c f., 586c ; *Polit.* 303c ; *Laws* 715b.

62 : *Rep.* 484c f., 531e, 533b-c, 534c.

63 : *Rep.* 364b ff., 377d ff.; cf.Windelband, *Platon*⁵, pp. 127 ff

64 : *Rep.* 493.

65 : *Rep.* 476b f., 479d-e.

66 : *Rep.* 438a, 505d f.; *Phileb.* 20d, 60c.

67 : *Euthyd. passim ; Rep.* 538c f.

68 : *Rep.* 422d f.

69 : *Rep.* 369e f., 462, 519e f.

70 : *Phaedr.* 249b ; *Polit.* 277e f., 285b.

71 : *Rep.* 472c-d, 500b ff.

72 : *Prtg.* 326a-b ; *Rep.* 389d, 396c f., 399a-b, e f.; *Laws* 814e ff.

73 : A certain identity between the ideal vision of beauty (*Symp.* 210e ff.) and the ideal vision of truth (*Rep.* 511b f.) has frequently been pointed out in the literature. Cf. e.g. Fouillée, *La philosophie de Platon*, p. 353 ; Natorp, *Platos Ideenlehre*, pp. 172 173 ; Taylor, *Plato the Man and his Work*, pp. 230-231 ; Wilamowitz-Moellendorff, *Platon*², Vol. I, pp. 388-391.

74 : *Gorg.* 491b ; *Cratyl.* 413e f.; *Phaedo* 68d f.; *Laws* 646e f.

75 : *Charm.* 170d, etc.; *Gorg.* 491d-e ; *Rep.* 431d f., 519e f.; *Laws* 710a.

76 : *Cratyl.* 412c f ; *Symp.* 210d f ; *Rep.* 462 ff., 508d, 612b ff.; *Laws* 757b f.

77 : *Cratyl.* 430 ff., 438a-b, 439a ; *Rep.* 490b, 540a-b, 613a-b ; *Phileb.* 40b-c.

78 : *Rep.* 364b ff., 277d ff.; cf. Windelband, op. cit., p. 142. Wilamowitz-Moellendorff, on the other hand, insists that Plato's personal religion was a purely personal, internal affair ; *er wollte nicht reformieren* (op. cit., Vol. I, pp. 412-414, 420 ff.). According to the *Laws* (966b ff., etc.), what is "essential" is that men should believe in the existence and thorough-going goodness of God, and in the immortality and supreme importance of the soul. How far " God " is to be equated with the " idea of good " has always been in dispute among Plato-students. On philological grounds, the two terms are, apparently, to be distinguished. On philosophical grounds, the terms, when somewhat specially defined, may reasonably be equated (cf. Taylor, op. cit., pp. 40 ff.). Conformity to religious principles, and conformity to the ideal world seem, in platonism, to coincide in all respects. Cf. *infra*, chs. xi, xvi.

79 : *Prtg.* 353 ff.; *Rep.* 505c-d ; *Phileb.* 12c f.

80 : *Laws* 647e ff.

81 : *Rep.* 484c f., 500d f.; *Laws* 653b f. This appears to be contradicted by *Rep.* 501b f., as well as by the usual interpretation. The demand, however, for a *tabula rasa* is to be understood, as Adam's appendix V to *Rep. VI* indicates, as a picture of the " idea " loosed from the actual world. Where *actual* men are in prospect, these accept willingly the guidance of the reformer, and he is the " artificer of virtue " in them by the way of *orthe doxa*, i.e. by training their habitual modes of thought and action.

82 : *Rep.* 459d, 460b, d f.; *Laws* 783d ff.

83 : *Laws* 792e.
84 : Cf. *Menex.* 238c.
85 : *Rep.* 460c f.; *Laws* 789e ff.
86 : *Rep.* 605c f.; *Laws* 792a-b.
87 : *Laws* 792c f.
88 : The details are not clearly worked out. *Rep.* 377a f., and 383c seem to indicate that " music " in the sense of " fables " (composed by poets, and properly censored before being used by mothers and teachers) would be taught *before* " gymnastic "—i.e. presumably up to the age of six, when the sexes are separated and the children go to school (*Laws* 794c). They indulge in outdoor games and sports of an infantile character, from the age of three to the age of six, in charge of " playground matrons " (*Laws* 793d f.). From six to ten, their teachers instruct the boys in horsemanship, archery, etc. From ten to thirteen they learn to read and write ; from thirteen to sixteen they learn to accompany themselves upon a simple musical instrument (*Laws* 809e f.). Up to the age of eighteen, all members of the rising generation, separated into proper age and sex groups, take part in the annual community sports (flat racing, horse racing, etc). After eighteen, this is no longer compulsory for young women (*Laws* 833c f.), but the men continue to compete in military sports till an advanced age.

89 : *Rep.* 377b, 378d, 399d, etc.
90 : *Rep.* 378-402 *passim*, 522a-b.
91 : *Rep.* 377a, 403d.
92 : *Rep.* 404.
93 : *Rep.* 411c f.
94 : *Rep.* 498b, 559b, 591c-d.
95 : *Rep.* 519a, 536d.
96 : *Rep.* 519b, 571b f., 586a-b ; *Phaedr.* 247b.
97 : *Rep.* 535b ff.
98 : *Rep.* 537b f.
99 : *Rep.* 522d-e, 525b-c, 530e f.
100 : *Rep.* 531e ; cf. 498a-b.
101 : *Rep.* 523b ff., 526, 527d f., 533c ff.
102 : *Rep.* 531c ff., 537c.
103 : *Rep.* 540e f.
104 : *Rep.* 405b-c, 409, 519a-b ; *Theaet.* 175c-d ; *Laws* 831c-e, etc.
105 : *Rep.* 462 ff., 484 f., 490.
106 : *Rep.* 409a-b ; *Theaet.* 173d f.; *Epist.* 322d-e.
107 : *Rep.* 409c-d, 484d ff., 574d f.; *Theaet.* 175c f.
108 : *Rep.* 412b, 466e f., 537a.
109 : *Rep.* 537b-d.
110 : *Rep.* 538c ff.
111 : *Rep.* 539e.
112 : *Rep.* 540.
113 : *Rep.* 537c ff.
114 : *Rep.* 518e f., 521c ff.
115 : *Rep.* 510b f.
116 : *Rep.* 531e, 533c.
117 : *Rep.* 511b-c, 527b f., 533b f.; *Phaedr.* 250b.
118 : *Polit.* 277e f., 285b.

119 : *Rep.* 534b f.

120 : *Rep.* 506b f., 533. Most writers on this subject either regard apprehensions of " the good " as an " inexpressible intuition " (e.g. Wilamowitz-Moellendorff, op. cit., Vol. I, pp. 421-424 ; Frank, *Platon u. d. sog. Pythagoreer*, pp. 108-109), or else endeavour to demonstrate that it is a " logical necessity " that " the good " should be ultimately unintelligible (cf. Lafontaine, *Le plaisir d'après Platon et Aristote*, pp. 159-160). From the philosophical standpoint, the position taken by Natorp is preferable to the usual explanation of *obscurum per obscurius*.

121 : *Rep.* 533d.

122 : *Rep.* 508b f. The principle is also the *ratio cognoscendi* and the *ratio essendi* (*Rep.* 508d f.).

123 : *Prtg.* 322, cf. 320e f.; *Gorg.* 491e f.; *Symp.* 211c f.; *Rep.* 458d, 558e ff.; *Phaedr.* 250d f.; *Laws* 782b f.

124 : *Rep.* 571 ff.

125 : *Gorg.* 491d f.; *Rep.* 343c ff., 365b ff., 538c f.

126 : *Gorg.* 470e ff.; *Rep.* 517b ff., 579.

127 : *Rep.* 583 ff.

128 : *Rep.* 582 f.; *Laws* 627e.

129 : *Rep.* 498e, 500d, etc.

130 : *Soph.* 253b f., 254b-c, 256d-258b, d f.

131 : *Rep.* 351c f., 588c ff.; *Laws* 903b f.

132 : *Rep.* 540, 590d ff.

133 : *Euthyphr.* 3c ; *Phaedr.* 244 ff.

134 : *Rep.* 372e f., 395d f., etc.

135 : *Gorg.* 462b, ff.; *Rep.* 595e ff.

136 : *Symp.* 212a-b ; *Rep.* 425a, 472d, 484a-d, 501a f.; *Phaedr.* 259d, 260e ; *Tim.* 47b, d ; *Laws* 858d ff.

137 : *Phileb.* 30c-d.

138 : *Phaedo* 84a-b ; *Rep.* 496c f., 590d ff., 621c-d ; *Theaet.* 176 f.; *Tim.* 90b f.; *Laws* 716a f.

139 : *Meno* 99 f.; *Rep.* 492a ; *Laws* 710c f., 803c f., 875c.

CHAPTER V

1 : *Rep.* 472c.

2 : The evidence is contained in chapter III, *supra*.

3 : The evidence is contained in chapter IV, *supra*.

4 : *Rep.* 484c f., 532a, 534b ; *Phaedr.* 247e, 277b ; *Parm.* 135a f.

5 : *Rep.* 529c ; *Parm.* 130d.

6 : *Phaedo* 103c f.; *Tim.* 51b f. Against this interpretation, cf. Lewis Campbell, *The Sophistes and Politicus of Plato*, p. lxix n.; Marie Williams, *Essays on the Platonic Theory of Knowledge*, pp. 14-15. Burnet, *Greek Philosophy*, *Part* I, pp. 256-257, thinks that the ideal theory breaks down here.

7 : *Phaedo* 79a. In *Phileb.* 17b f., " sounds " are classified. In *Rep.* 510 f., it appears that " ideas " of animals and things (generalizations abstracted from sensory experiences) belong to the " third stage of intelligence." The view of Wilamowitz (developing further a hypothesis suggested by Campbell and

carried further by Natorp), that the *Parmenides* merely contains material for practice in dialectic within Plato's school, *eine wahre Seminarstunde*, Plato's real views being expressed in the *Timaeus* (51b f.). justifies the position taken in the text. This *Seminar* view, however, is rejected by Burnet and Taylor.

8 : *Parm.* 130c ; *Theaet.* 186a f., 190c ; *Phileb.* 15a. The "ideas" of "mastery" and "slavery" (*Parm.* 133e) would seem to imply the ideality of "man."

9 : *Rep.* 507b, 510 f.

10 : *Cratyl.* 389b (though cf. Wilamowitz, op. cit., Vol. I, p. 345) ; *Rep.* 480a, 596a-b.

11 : *Rep.* 618b f.; *Theaet.* 176b ; *Laws* 697b, 733 f. "Health" and "strength" are stated to be "ideas," and it is implied that "disease" is so regarded (*Phaedo* 65d, 105c).

12 : *Rep.* 584a f.; *Phileb.* 54a f.

13 : *Prtg.* 353b ff.; *Rep.* 509a ; *Phileb. passim.*

14 : *Phileb.* 20b, etc.

15 : *Phileb.* 20a.

16 : *Rep.* 618b.

17 : *Rep.* 476a, 618c-d ; *Phaedr.* 277b f.; cf. Aristotle, *Met. A* 990b 11-13.

18 : *Rep.* 526a-b, 587c-e ; *Theaet.* 185c-d.

19 : *Rep.* 520c, 592a.

20 : *Phaedr.* 247d ; *Theaet. passim ; Soph.* 247a ; *Phileb.* 20a-c, etc.

21 : *Rep.* 507b, 520c, 540a ; *Phaedr.* 277d ; *Theaet.* 176a, e f.; *Soph.* 247a ; *Phileb.* 15a, etc.

22 : *Phaedo* 65d f., 75c f., 76d f., 100b.

23 : *Symp.* 210, etc.

24 : *Phaedo* 105d ; *Rep.* 472d f., 529b-c, 585b f.

25 : *Phaedo* 74a f., 78d, 100b, 102b f., 103d f., 105b ; *Theaet.* 185d-e ; *Soph.* 254d ; cf. *Laws* 903b f. Writers like J. A. Stewart (*Plato's Doctrine of Ideas*, pp. 123-124) regard these as "native categories of the mind."

26 : *Rep.* 508d f.

27 : *Rep.* 462 ff.

28 : *Symp.* 210.

29 : *Phaedo* 80d f.; *Rep.* 383c, 500d, 501c, 613b ; *Theaet.* 176 ; *Tim.* 28c, 29e ff.; *Laws* 716b f. Like many modern commentators, Frank (op. cit., p. 109) regards the "idea of good" as essentially inexplicable, *mysterium summum.* Wilamowitz (op. cit., Vol. II, p. 209) says that scientific dialectic can never apprehend it ; it remains a matter of *doxa.* To the present writer it appears to be a perfectly intelligible formulation of the principle of idea-ness *überhaupt,* somewhat as it appears to Natorp.

30 : *Rep.* 510d, with Adam's notes, and his "appendix I" to Bk. VII, esp. pp. 159 ff. I take it that the "mathematical square" is a generalization which still contains empirical elements, the lower level of the "idea" as contrasted with the same generalization when, after its formal element has been emphasized in relation to the ideal of complete consistency, the empirical content is transcended, and only the strictly logical or ideal content remains. Cf. Aristotle, *Met. A* 990b 11-13, who certainly implies that all objects of scientific study are "ideas."

31 : *Rep.* 476a ; *Phaedr.* 277b f.; *Theaet.* 176a, e f.; *Soph.* 257c f.; cf. Fouillée, *La philosophie de Platon*, pp. 140-143.

32 : *Phaedo* 74a f., 78d, 100b, 102 ; *Parm.* 129a, d-e, 131a-d ; *Theaet.* 186b ; *Polit.* 284b f.

33 : *Ion* 531d f.; *Hipp. Min.* 373d ff.; *Prtg.* 345a-b ; *Rep.* 438e ; *Polit.* 283c f.; *Laws* 816d-e.

34 : *Phaedr.* 265e ; *Soph.* 251d ff.

35 : *Tim.* 83c. Cf. Fouillée, op. cit., pp. 101, 102.

36 : *Parm.* 135b-c ; *Theaet.* 161e ; *Soph.* 259e f.; *Phileb.* 63, where it is stated that to isolate classes is not possible.

37 : *Rep.* 510c f.

38 : *Rep.* 476a, 618c f.

39 : *Laws* 963c ff. Cf. Burnet, op. cit., p. 176.

40 : This " idea " is not mentioned by Plato, but is used here for illustrative purposes. The conclusions thus reached may be verified by comparison with the " virtues " which overlap in a somewhat similar way.

41 : Cf. Natorp, op. cit., p. 47 ; Windelband, *Platon*[5], pp. 105-106.

42 : *Rep.* 533b-d, 534c ; *Parm.* 131e ; *Polit.* 277e f., 285b.

43 : Or, how " temperance " is related to " courage "—this is the way in which the question generally suggests itself to Plato (cf. *Polit.* 306 ff.).

44 : *Parm.* 129 ff. The interpretation of this is still disputed among Plato-students.

45 : *Soph.* 253b f.

46 : *Rep.* 508d f., 511b-c, 532 ff. In *Laws* 693, " wisdom," " temperance," and " friendship " are equated ; cf. Fouillée, op. cit., p. 181.

47 : *Laws* 903b f.; cf. Fouillée, op. cit., pp. 233, 234 n; cf. Halévy, *La théorie platonicienne des sciences*, p. 246.

48 : *Rep.* 422e f.; *Laws* 712e f., 714b ff.

49 : *Rep.* 420d f., 462 ff., with Adam's note on 462b 9.

50 : *Rep.* 431d f.

51 : *Rep.* 415a, 421c, 434c ; *Laws* 903.

51a : Cf. Windelband, op. cit., p. 159.

52 : *Phileb.* 26a-b ; *Laws* 672c-d, 673d.

53 : *Rep.* 571b f.

54 : *Rep.* 553c-d, 574 ff.

55 : *Rep.* 364b ff.

55a : *Rep.* 439d ff.

56 : *Polit.* 306 ff.

57 : *Rep.* 409c f.; *Theaet.* 173a-b.

58 : *Gorg.* 461e f.; *Rep.* 557b-c, 561b f.

59 : *Rep.* 558d f.

60 : *Phaedo* 68e f.; *Rep.* 554.

61 : *Rep.* 555a-b ; *Laws* 831c-d.

62 : *Rep.* 343d f., 555e f.; *Laws* 743b f.

63 : *Rep.* 560 f.

64 : *Rep.* 561c.

65 : *Rep.* 561d f.

66 : *Rep.* 573a f.

67 : *Rep.* 577d f.

68 : *Rep.* 554d.

69 : *Rep.* 462c-d, with Adam's notes.
70 : Cf. *supra*, Chapter IV, pp. 105-122.
71 : *Phaedr.* 249e f.
72 : *Prtg.* 326a-b ; *Rep.* 376e, 396c f., 399a f.; *Laws* 314e ff.
73 : *Rep.* 533b f.
74 : The negative kind of control remains, consisting in not permitting any one impulse to encroach too long upon the " equal " rights of other equally egoistic impulses (*Rep.* 561b f.).
75 : *Rep.* 472c-d, 498e f.
76 : *Laws* 903b f.
77 : *Gorg.* 466b, 468e ; *Rep.* 343c f.
78 : *Rep.* 592b ; *Parm.* 132e f.; *Tim.* 28e f.
79 : *Phaedr.* 249b ; *Polit.* 277e f.
80 : *Rep.* 509c ; *Tim.* 27e ff.
81 : For the evidence, and discussion of its significance, cf. *supra*, Chapter III, pp. 73-77 (consistency).
82 : *Rep.* 472b f., 508e f., 517b-c ; *Parm.* 133b f.
83 : It is difficult to be quite certain as to the platonic position here. Cf. Schleiermacher, *Introduction to the Dialogues of Plato*, E.T., pp. 387-388 ; cf. Frank, op. cit., p. 241. On the other side, cf. Rep. 424a-b, and C. Ritter, *Platon*, Vol. II, p. 558, who contradicts absolutely the statement in the text. Nettleship, op. cit., Vol. II, p. 140, says (correctly) that the idea of progress is " very seldom " touched upon. Change is, of course, recognized.

CHAPTER VI

1 : *Crito* 47 ; *Rep.* 618e ; *Theaet.* 176e f.; *Laws* 728b.
2 : *Laws* 627e f., 728a, 880d f.
3 : *Polit.* 294a f., 299e f.
4 : *Meno* 87e f.; *Rep.* 586d-e, etc.
5 : *Meno* 87d ff.; *Laws* 862, etc.
6 : Cf. *supra*, Chapter IV.
7 : *Rep.* 582 ff.
8 : *Rep.* 408d f., 538c f.; *Phaedr.* 271e ; *Laws* 951a f.; cf. *Epist.* 322d-e.
9 : *Tim.* 90b f., etc.
10 : Cf. *supra*, Chapter III, pp. 78-81.
11 : Cf. *supra*, Chapter IV, pp. 98-104.
12 : *Laws* 903b ff.; cf. also *supra*, Chapter V.
13 : It is noteworthy, how little (as compared with modern psychologists) Plato has to say of the part played by adolescence in our moral development. It is not, of course, entirely omitted, but the evidence is scattered and is never brought into exact focus.
14 : The arguments of Trendelenburg, *De Platonis Philebi Consilio*, pp. 17-22 n. 42, denying the equation " idea of good = God," consist partly of proof that no Greek writer would predicate the term *eidos* of the term *theos*. But the philological expression is irrelevant to the question of ultimate philosophical identity, and, like Schleiermacher and Natorp, we are attempting to see behind the laws of predication in Greek to the deeper philosophical significance of the thought. Cf. Taylor, op. cit., pp. 442-443.

CHAPTER VII

1 There are, of course, very many special monographs on the platonic conception of *psyche*, and upon its relation to *soma*. But as they concern themselves, for the most part, with philological problems, seldom attempting to go behind the Greek phrases to the more profound philosophical aspects of platonism, and as, further, not one of the previous writers is at all seriously concerned with the value-scale of soul-body-wealth, the present investigation is not a repetition of work already done.   The ingenious elaboration of a fairly complete doctrine from the Socratic term *epimeleia psyches* (as the whole duty of man), by Professors Burnet and Taylor, is of more than merely philological significance, but runs along lines which hardly bring it into relation to the present investigation.

1a : *Phaedo* 105c-d ; *Laws* 895c ; cf. H. Barth, *Die Seele in der Philosophie Platons*, pp. 285 ff.

2 : *Prtg.* 353c ; *Rep.* 403a, 558e ff., 580e ; *Soph.* 228b f., 283d ; *Laws* 782d.

3 : *Rep.* 442a.   This way of treating the subject is thought to be specifically Aristotelian (and un-platonic) by A. S. Pringle-Pattison, *The Idea of Immortality*, pp. 63 ff. (though cf. p. 206).

4 : *Phaedo* 66b f.; *Rep.* 404d, 586a f.; *Epist.* 326e f.

5 : *Rep.* 370 ff.; *Laws* 707e, cf. 709a-b, 766d f.

6 : Cf. Wilamowitz-Moellendorff, *Platon*[2], Vol. I, p. 663.

7 : *Laws* 648 ff.

8 : *Rep.* 586a ; *Laws* 673e f.; *Epist.* 325e f.

9 : *Symp.* 206c ; *Rep.* 404d ; *Laws* 839a, e f., 840d.

10 : *Rep.* 573c ff.; *Laws* 835e ff.   Cf. Wilamowitz op. cit., Vol. I, p. 46.

11 : *Rep.* 571b, 574d ff.

12 : *Rep.* 571c f.   Adam (note on 571c 14) explicitly denies this ; but it is a function of the " concupiscent element " and is " an original part of *every* one " (571b 10), and while it is sometimes completely mastered, or at least weakened, this is regarded as rare (b 11-13). Cf. further *Rep.* 442a ; *Phaedr.* 256c-d ; *Laws* 837b f., 838e f., 840d, 841d.   And further, the words *mete endeiai dous* (571e), show that even the ideal man is supposed to concede something to the concupiscent element, so that it will cease from obtruding its wants upon him.

13 : *Rep.* 458d-e, 461a ; *Laws* 838b, 841.

14 : *Rep.* 461b-c, 571e f.; *Laws* 930b-c ; cf. Aristotle *Pol.* 1335b 37-38, with Newman's notes.   Newman (*The Politics of Aristotle*, Vol. III, p. 476, note on 37) omits to notice that *hygieia* is mentioned in connection with young widows by Plato (*Laws* 930c), though not, of course, with older persons. Wilamowitz represents Plato as self-repressive (op. cit., Vol. I, p. 723)—but is not this what Wilamowitz would call " Pauline Christianity " rather than genuine platonism ?

15 : *Symp.* 206a, 210 ff.

16 : *Symp.* 178e f.; *Rep.* 464a f., 468b f.

17 : *Rep.* 458e, 459e f.

18 : *Phaedo* 94b ; *Phileb.* 34e f., 39b, 40a-b.

19 : *Phaedo* 99a f.

20 : *Rep.* 571b, 573a-c, 586a-b ; *Tim.* 71d.

21 : *Rep.* 519a f., 611c f.

22 : *Rep.* 412c ff.

23 : Cf. *supra*, Chapter IV, pp. 98-104.

24 : *Charm.* 159b ; *Phaedo* 68c f.; *Rep.* 503b-c, 549c f., 559a f.; *Laws* 733e.

25 : *Polit.* 306c ff.

26 : *Lach.* 196e f.; *Prtg.* 350a f.; *Tim.* 70a f.; *Laws* 963e.

27 : *Lach.* 190e f.; *Phaedo* 68d f.; *Laws* 646e f.

28 : *Prtg.* 322b ff.; *Rep.* 433 ff.

29 : *Rep.* 402b ff.; *Laws* 941b ff.

30 : *Rep.* 375 f., 410b ff., 503c ; *Polit.* 306c-311c ; *Theaet.* 144a-b.

31 : *Rep.* 484b ff. For leadership, i.e. for appointment to the higher magistracies, philosophic insight proper is necessary (*Rep.* 534c f.; *Laws* 964c ff.).

32 : *Rep.* 462b ff.; *Laws* 951b f.

33 : *Rep.* 540b, 591c f.

34 : *Phaedr.* 253d ; *Laws* 864a.

35 : Chapter II, *supra*, pp. 31-38.

36 : *Rep.* 532b.

37 : *Rep.* 511b-c, 533b-c.

38 : *Phaedo* 79c ; *Rep.* 508b f.; *Phileb.* 38b ff.

39 : *Rep.* 517b-c, 540a-b ; *Polit.* 309c ; cf. Natorp, *Platos Ideenlehre*, pp. 140d ff.

40 : *Tim.* 70 ff., cf. 56c, 68e.

41 : *Polit.* 306b ff.

42 : *Rep.* 485c f., 500c-d ; *Tim.* 47b f.; cf. *Phaedo* 79d.

43 : *Rep.* 508d f., 540a-b.

44 : *Tim.* 71a ; *Phileb.* 65c.

45 : *Phaedo* 81c f.; *Rep.* 519a-b, 611e f.; *Epist.* 326b.

46 : *Phaedr.* 246b, 247b, 248a-b, 253c ff.

47 : *Rep.* 553c f.

48 : *Rep.* 492b f., 494e.

49 : *Phaedo* 79 f.; *Rep.* 610.

50 : *Phaedo* 66b ff., 81b f., 82e f.; *Cratyl.* 400c.

51 : *Phaedo* 106d f.; *Alc. I*, 130c. This position is often in the literature regarded as the final expression of platonism (cf. Piat, *Platon*, p. 237 ; A. S. Pringle-Pattison, *The Idea of Immortality*, p. 34). Burnet, *The Socratic Doctrine of the Soul*, pp. 11-13, 25, 27, regards this as Socratic rather than specifically Platonic.

52 : *Meno* 81c-d ; *Phaedo* 72e, 75c f., 77a, 92d.; *Phaedr.* 245c f., 247 f., 250c.

53 : *Phaedo* 64 ff., 79c-d, 82d ff.; *Theaet.* 172 ff.

54 : *Phaedo* 67 f., 80e f., 84b, 114c ; *Phaedr.* 246b, d, 248e f.; *Tim.* 42b.

55 : *Rep.* 387d, 496b f., 500b f., 581d, etc.

56 : *Phaedr.* 246c, 248c-d ; *Laws* 828e, etc. The account of creation in the *Timaeus* merely states that souls should be implanted in bodies by necessity (42a), and that men were to be created so that the universe should be truly universal and not remain imperfect (41b-c), the reason for having a complete universe

being in order that all things should be good and nothing bad, which is a logical consequence of the definition of the Divine Nature (29e f.).

57 : *Apol.* 31e f.; *Rep.* 496b-e. Cf. Windelband, *Platon*[5], p. 162.

58 : *Rep.* 499b-c, 500d, 519c ff.

59 : *Rep.* 498c, 540b.

60 : Cf. Wilamowitz-Moellendorff, op. cit.,Vol. I, pp. 441-442. G. Entz, *Pessimismus und Weltflucht bei Platon*, pp. 81 ff., 173-175, believes that the evidence of the Dialogues shows that Plato was personally an adherent of the Orphic-Pythagorean movement. Burnet and Taylor, on the other hand, believe that the evidence shows that *Socrates* was probably an adherent of this movement, but that *Plato* was emphatically *not*.

61 : Cf. Natorp, op. cit., pp. 127, 187 ff., 171 ff.; J. A. Stewart, *Plato's Doctrine of Ideas*, pp. 52-53, 55-56.

62 : *Rep.* 561c-e.

63 : Cf. *supra*, Chapter V, pp. 148-152.

64 : *Rep.* 462c-d, 519e f., etc.

65 : *Symp.* 186d, 188a ; *Rep.* 556e ; *Tim.* 82 ff.; *Soph.* 228 ; cf. Adam's note on *Rep.* 444d, 24.

66 : *Rep.* 444b f., 609 f.

67 : *Rep.* 534c ; *Phaedr.* 253d ; *Laws* 864a.

68 : *Rep.* 402d, 443c, 444d.

69 : *Charm.* 156e f.; *Rep.* 498e f.; *Polit.* 301e ; *Tim.* 87d. This is apparently denied by Adam, *The Republic of Plato*, Vol. II, p. 442 n., who refers to *Phaedo* 114c, and believes the ideal to be for the soul to do without a body.

70 : *Gorg.* 504b f.; *Meno* 87e f.; *Rep.* 443e f., 518e f., 609 f.; *Phaedr.* 270b-c ; *Tim.* 82 ff.

71 : *Phaedo* 76c ; *Tim.* 34d f.; *Laws* 892a f., 966d f.

72 : *Meno* 88 ; *Phaedo* 65 ; *Rep.* 532 ; *Phaedr.* 247c ; *Tim.* 90a , *Laws* 896e f.

73 : *Phaedo* 65d f.; *Euthyd.* 295b, e ; *Phaedr.* 246 ff., 278.

74 : *Phaedo* 82d f.; *Phaedr.* 247b f.; *Soph.* 248a.

75 : *Prtg.* 313d f.; *Phaedo* 84a f.; *Phaedr.* 248b-c.

76 : *Laws* 896a, 897c.

77 : *Phaedo* 99a f.; *Rep.* 484c f., 540a-b ; *Theaet.* 176e.

78 : *Symp.* 209 ff.; *Rep.* 443c f., 591c f.

79 : *Phaedo* 79d f. The passages in which change is predicated of the soul (*e.g. Symp.* 207e f.) refer to the *embodied* soul, not to soul considered (as we are here considering it) apart from body.

80 : *Phaedo* 80a-b ; *Phaedr.* 248a.

81 : *Meno* 81b f.

82 : *Phaedo* 98c f. So, too, students of St. Thomas Aquinas feel that the disembodied human spirit, as compared with a still embodied human spirit, is a pale shadow of virtuality, a knowing and willing which are clear indeed, as being unclouded by sense and emotion, but are restricted in content to ideas derived from sensuous experience in the embodied state. It appears to be better for the soul to have been embodied than not. Cf. *Summa Theologica*, P.I, Q.Q. LXXVI, LXXVII, LXXIX, LXXXIV, LXXXV ; cf. also Bosanquet, *Logic*, Vol. II, p. 255, and *Value*

and Destiny of the Individual, p. 61.   On the other side, however, is an explicit statement in the *Laws* (828d) to the effect that the soul receives *no* benefit whatever from its association with a body.

83 : Adam maintains (*Rep.* 608d n.) that the soul would not lose "its essential individuality."   One can understand, in Thomistic fashion, that the soul, while originally pure virtuality, might acquire an individuality in its embodied phase (by building up cognitive generalizations different from the cognitive content of other embodied spirits), and that after bodily death it might retain this distinguishing content.   But if the immortal part of the soul is to be limited to the *logistikon* (Adam, *Rep.* 611b n.), and if complete independence of bodily conditions is the goal (*Phaedo* 114c), it is hard to see how the soul, in its "essence," can have individuality.   Adam himself writes elsewhere (*Rep.* 546a, 4n., and appendix, Vol. II, p. 287) " Soul, viewed merely as the vital principle, is one and the same in every organic creature (cf. *Tim.* 77b)."   It appears, in its "higher" part, whether before, during, or after life on earth, to be an organizing principle, the principle of ideality, which could take on an invidual colouring only from that to which it is applied, being "an artificer of justice, temperance," etc., within the fields of choice presented by appetitive, social, and philosophical situations.   Cf. K. Justi, *Die aesthetischen Elemente in der platonischen Philosophie*, pp. 177-178.   Considered strictly apart from body, however, as we are at present considering it, the soul appears to be strictly universal, pure virtuality, essentially capable of application to individual cases, but not in its " essence " itself individual.—These difficulties are not, of course, confined to platonism, and can indeed hardly be regarded as solved by any present-day philosophical school.

84 : *Gorg.* 465d f.; *Phaedr.* 246a ; *Laws* 896e ff.

85 : *Cratyl.* 400b ; *Phaedo* 80 ; *Rep.* 353d ; *Tim.* 34d f.; *Laws* 961d f.

86 : *Cratyl.* 399d f.; *Phaedr.* 245c f.; *Laws* 892, 894e f., 896a-b.

87 : *Symp.* 183e ; *Rep.* 611 ; *Phaedr.* 271a. Cf. Trommershausen, *Das Wesen der Seele*, p. 73.

88 : *Tim.* 71a ; cf. *Charm.* 160a ; *Gorg.* 465d f., 513d f.; *Phaedo* 99a f.; *Rep.* 439a f.; *Phaedr.* 271e f.

89 : *Phaedo* 79a ff., 94c f., 114c.

90 : *Laws* 896 ff.

91 : *Rep.* 369c-d.

92 : *Rep.* 369b ff.; *Laws* 742a, 846d f., 918b.

93 : *Rep.* 370e f.; *Laws* 742b, 758e ff., 915d ff.

94 : *Rep.* 416d f., 419 f.; *Laws* 949 f.   Vocational training for agriculture and manufacture seems to be left to some kind of apprenticeship system (*Rep.* 421e, 466e f.), i.e. is not specifically developed by state-endowed institutions.   So too professional training in law and medicine seems to be left to a similar system (*Laws* 720b).   It is liberal education for public service on some one of the governing commissions, military, commercial, or directly administrative, which is in the foreground throughout the discussion.

95 : *Rep.* 371b f., 421c ; *Laws* 920b f.

96 : *Rep.* 420e ff., 462b f. Emigration and immigration are permissible only as emergency measures. They never receive unqualified approval.

97 : *Rep.* 421c f., 552b f.; *Laws* 831e.

98 : *Rep.* 420d ff., 550c ff.; *Laws* 919b-c.

99 : *Rep.* 417, 422e f., 551d f.; *Laws* 744d.

100 : *Rep.* 552e, 554b, 559d ; *Laws* 870a f.

101 : *Rep.* 416c f., 419, 422d, 464c ; *Tim.* 18b ; *Laws* 739c f.

102 : *Laws* 737c f., 740a f., 741b f. The regulations for the productive or farming classes are taken from the " model city " of the *Laws*, as details are, for the most part, missing in the *Republic*.

103 : *Laws* 855a f., 856c f., 877c f., 923 ff.

104 : *Laws* 708c, 735e f., 740e, 928e f.; cf. A. S. Pringle-Pattison, *The Idea of Immortality*, pp. 50-51.

105 : *Rep.* 550e f.; *Laws* 742e f., 744d f.

106 : *Rep.* 460a ; *Laws* 721, 740c f.

107 : *Laws* 736b-c. Plato is very reluctant to admit immigration, even in extreme cases (*Laws* 741a).

108 : *Rep.* 472b f.; *Laws* 739c f., 746a f.

109 : *Rep.* 420d f., 466a-b. Plato is not interested in quantity-production, which would simply create wealth with all its corrupting influences.

110 : *Gorg.* 491e ff.; *Rep.* 548a-b, 555a-b, 580c f.; *Laws* 714a, 875a-c.

111 : *Rep.* 553b f.; *Laws* 831c f.

112 : *Rep.* 521a, 551a f., 552d.

113 : *Rep.* 347b f., 416c ff.; *Laws* 691c f., 712a.

114 : *Rep.* 404c f., 561b f., 573 ff.

115 : *Rep.* 556b f.; *Laws* 695e f.

116 : *Gorg.* 504b ; *Rep.* 404c, 410b. The " rule " is, of course, the maximal harmonious satisfaction of bodily needs in subordination to higher requirements (*Rep.* 558e f., 591b-d).

117 : *Rep.* 343d f., 550e f., 555 ; *Laws* 743a f., 831c f.; *Epist.* 355b-c.

118 : *Rep.* 556b f.; *Laws* 695e f.

119 : *Supra*, pp. 195-198.

120 : *Prtg.* 326c, 328b ; *Phaedo* 78a ; *Theaet.* 167c-d ; *Laws* 826d.

121 : *Rep.* 528c ; *Laws* 953b f.

122 : *Rep.* 371b f.; *Laws* 742a, 862 ; *Epist.* 355a f.

123 : *Phaedo* 82b ; *Rep.* 518e f., 591b f., 619d. See, however, *infra*, Chapter VIII, pp. 235-237, where this statement is modified.

124 : *Rep.* 560 f.; *Laws* 714a, 715a-b, 728e, 875a.

125 : *Phaedo* 64e ff.; *Phaedr.* 248c.

126 : *Phaedo* 66c, 81 ff.; *Rep.* 572c ff.; *Epist.* 326b f.

127 : *Phaedo* 64c ff., 79c f. 82c-84b.

128 : *Phaedo* 66d ; *Rep.* 416e f., 547b, 521a.

129 : *Phaedo* 66b f.; *Rep.* 571c f., 591b f.

130 : *Phaedo* 82b f., 83e f.

131 : *Phaedo* 65b f., 78e f., 83a f.; *Rep.* 532a-b, 533c-d.

132 : *Rep.* 571c f., 591b f.

133 : *Rep.* 591d ; *Laws* 744e f., 746a.

134 : *Phaedo* 67c f., 84a-b, 114d-e ; *Rep.* 611b f., 618c f.; *Phileb.* 55b.

135 : *Prtg.* 313a ; *Hipp. Min.* 372e f.; *Rep.* 403d f., 527b, d-e, 585d f.; *Laws* 726 ff., 870a f., 891e f., 895a f., etc.

136 : *Laws* 728a, 967d f.; cf. *Epist.* 355a-c.

137 : *Tim.* 77a-b ; *Phileb.* 29b f.; *Laws* 896e f., 898c f., 899b.

138 : *Rep.* 560a f.; *Tim.* 47a f.; *Phileb.* 26 ; *Laws* 897b-c.

139 : *Gorg.* 478d f.

140 : *Rep.* 353e f., 366b f., 591b f.; *Soph.* 247a ; *Laws* 660e f., 663c.

141 : *Rep.* 430e f., 519a f.; *Tim.* 42a f.

142 : *Phaedo* 79c f., 82d f., 99d f.; *Rep.* 527d-e.

143 : *Phaedr.* 246a f., 248a, 249c f.

144 : *Meno* 88 f.; *Rep.* 441d f., 513a, 585b f., 590d f.; *Phaedr.* 248c f.

145 : *Rep.* 521c ff.; *Theaet.* 167b.

146 : *Rep.* 518d f.

147 : *Phileb.* 29 f.

148 : *Laws* 788d f.

149 : *Charm.* 165c ; *Lys.* 217 ff.; *Alc. I*, 126a-b ; *Gorg.* 452a, 464a f.; *Rep.* 407d f., 409e f., 583c-d ; *Tim.* 82 ff.; *Laws* 661a, 646b f.

150 : *Rep.* 521a, 553c f., 554e, 562b ; *Laws* 631c-d, 697e, 705e.

151 : *Rep.* 364b f., 612b f., 614a, 618b f.; *Laws* 661a f., 913b.

152 : *Phaedo* 68b-c ; *Rep.* 543 ff., 582e f.

153 : *Phaedo* 68e f.; *Rep.* 554c-d, 589e f.

154 : *Meno* 87e f.; *Euthyd.* 279b ff., 292 ; *Phaedo* 69a f.; *Rep.* 586d f.; *Laws* 631c.

155 : *Polit.* 309 ff.; *Laws* 631b f.; cf. Shorey, *The Unity of Plato's Thought*, p. 11 n.

156 : *Rep.* 521a f.; *Laws* 831b f., 875a.

157 : *Prtg.* 354a f.; *Gorg.* 467d f.; *Rep.* 357c f.

CHAPTER VIII

1 : *Laws* 631b f.

2 : *Prtg.* 351a ; *Gorg.* 456d-e ; *Rep.* 410b, 486d.

3 : *Rep.* 591b f.

4 : *Rep.* 491c ; *Laws* 631c, 661a f.

5 : *Rep.* 371e. It might seem that, because it is for money that the labourer works, money is more valuable, more of an end-in-itself, than strength. But the superior personal value of strength is brought out in other contexts (e.g. *Rep.* 556b f.).

6 : *Lach.* 181e f.; *Rep.* 403e f.; *Laws* 830a f.

7 : *Rep.* 404a f., 375a f., etc.

8 : *Rep.* 464c ; *Tim.* 18b ; *Laws* 758e ff.

9 : *Rep.* 416d-e, 419, 422d ; *Laws* 742a.

10 : *Laws* 788c ff.

11 : *Phileb.* 26b, 64d-e.

12 : *Laws* 631c.

13 : Cf. A. Ruge, *Die platonische Aesthetik*, pp. 14-15. In

virtue of the reflected power of love, this applies also to the beloved, whose charms first awakened the idealism of the lover, for enthusiasm is catching. Cf. *Symp.* 210 f.; *Rep.* 476b f.; *Phaedr.* 250d ff.

14 : *Prtg.* 354a f ; *Phaedr.* 270b, etc.

15 : *Gorg.* 451e f., 467c ; *Rep.* 367d ; *Laws* 661a. The philosophical representatives criticize the value placed upon health by the patient and his medical adviser (*Lys.* 217 ff.; *Lach.* 195c f.; *Rep.* 583c-d ; *Phaedr.* 286b-c), but this is in relation to higher goods, not (as here) in relation to lower goods such as strength and good looks.

16 : *Rep.* 404a f.

17 : *Phaedr.* 239c-d.

18 : *Meno* 77a ; *Tim.* 87c, 88b, e ; *Phileb.* 26a, 31c-d.

19 : *Lys.* 217a ; *Rep.* 351 ff.; *Soph.* 227e f.; *Phileb.* 66a ; *Laws* 647c-d, 806c.

20 : *Theaet.* 159c f.; *Phileb.* 45a f.

21 : *Phaedo* 67a ; *Rep.* 406b f., 571a f.

22 : *Rep.* 591c-d. The case of Theages (*Rep.* 496b-c) is exceptional.

23 : *Rep.* 495b ; cf. Xenophon, *Memorab.* V, i, 3, 4.

24 : *Rep.* 491 f.

25 : *Meno* 87 f.; *Euthyd.* 281a-b ; *Rep.* 486d f., 495b, 586d-e ; *Tim.* 47c-d ; *Laws* 661b.

26 : *Meno* 88a f.; *Euthyd.* 280a ; *Phaedo* 97c f.; *Rep.* 505d-e.

27 : *Lach.* 196e f.; *Prtg.* 350 ; *Tim.* 70 ; *Laws* 963e.

28 : *Rep.* 412e ff., 429b f., 518e ; *Polit.* 309c.

29 : *Phaedo* 68d f.; *Laws* 646e f.

30 : *Laws* 631b, d.

31 : *Laws* 963e.

32 : *Tim.* 71a, d ; *Phileb.* 65c.

33 : *Prtg.* 322c ff.

34 : *Prtg.* 326c ff.; *Crito* 50c ff.; *Polit.* 305b f.

35 : *Polit.* 309 ff.

36 : *Laws* 631c.

37 : *Rep.* 420b ff., 434a f.

38 : *Rep.* 372a.

39 : *Rep.* 592.

40 : *Rep.* 462 ff., 505 ff., 590e ff.

41 : *Prtg.* 323c f.; *Rep.* 518e f.

42 : *Rep.* 351a f., 433 f., 441c-d, 442e f.

43 : *Charm.* 159b, etc.; *Phaedo* 68c f.; *Rep.* 485d-e, etc.; *Polit.* 306c ff.; *Laws* 733e f.

44 : *Rep.* 412c f., 431d f., 484b ff.; *Laws* 710a, 964 ff., 968a.

45 : Very many Plato-students take this position, but the evidence seems insufficient, and *Rep.* 442c-d appears definitely contradictory to this interpretation.

46 : *Rep.* 485e, 487a.

47 : *Rep.* 410b f.; *Polit.* 308e f.

48 : *Phaedo* 68c f.; *Rep.* 484c-d, 501b, 540a-b.

49 : *Rep.* 519e f., 592.

50 : *Rep.* 346e f., 520e f.

51 : *Polit.* 306 ff.; *Laws* 631c.

52 : *Prtg.* 358c ; *Gorg.* 507e f.; *Rep.* 375c f., 401e f., 410d ff., 500c-d, 539d.

53 : *Polit.* 294a f., 299e f.; *Laws* 875c-d.

54 : *Rep.* 498c, 520e f., 540b ; cf. *Phaedr.* 248b-c. Wilamo-witz-Moellendorff (*Platon²*, Vol. I, pp. 489 ff.) maintains that Plato burned to take his place in the political arena at Athens, and was bitterly disappointed to find himself *nur noch Lehrer*. The evidence in the Dialogues seems to insist that the philosophical doctrine known as platonism can hardly be interpreted as an expression of its founder's personal desires, if the contentions of his biographer are to be accepted here.

55 : *Rep.* 409, 484d, 539e f.; *Laws* 659d, 951a f.

56 : *Rep.* 518e ; *Phaedr.* 246c, 248b f.

57 : *Rep.* 500c f.; *Phaedr.* 250a f.

58 : *Tim.* 90a, etc.

59 : *Phaedo* 74b f.; *Polit.* 285b f.; *Laws* 965b f.

60 : *Rep.* 409c f., 491d f., 495a-b, 518d f.; *Theaet.* 172e ff.

61 : *Meno* 88d ; *Euthyd.* 281b, d ; *Phaedo* 69b-c.

62 : *Rep.* 508d f.

63 : *Alc. I*, 133b-c, 134d ; *Phaedo* 84a-b ; *Phaedr.* 247c ff.; *Tim.* 90a ; *Laws* 896e f.

64 : *Phaedo* 65c f., 66e f.; *Rep.* 532a-b, 540a-b ; *Theaet.* 176 f.

65 : *Rep.* 375e ; *Tim.* 64a f.; *Phileb.* 54e ; *Laws* 653d f.

66 : Cf. *supra*, Chapter VII, pp. 186-187.

67 : *Rep.* 476b f., 479e, 522c ff.; *Theaet.* 155d ; *Tim.* 47a f.; *Phileb.* 38b ff.

68 : *Gorg.* 484c ; *Euthyd.* 288d f.; *Rep.* 524 ff.; *Polit* 277e f.; *Tim.* 88b-c.

69 : *Phaedo* 64 ff.; *Rep.* 591d f.

70 : *Meno* 88 ; *Euthyd.* 281b, d ; *Phaedo* 69b-c ; *Rep.* 518e f.

71 : *Rep.* 441a-b ; *Tim.* 71a, d ; *Phileb.* 65c.

72 : *Meno* 81d ; *Rep.* 535a f.; *Theaet.* 157d, 177b ; *Laws* 630a-b.

73 : *Tim.* 70d f., 71d.

74 : *Meno* 72c f.; *Rep.* 441e f., 519c, 540a ; *Polit.* 310e f.; *Laws* 630a-b, 660e f., 963a f., 965c f.; cf. Burnet, *Greek Philosophy Part I*, p. 176 ; cf. P. Höfer, *Die Bedeutung der Philosophie für das Leben nach Plato*, p. 34 n. 44.

75 : *Rep.* 404e, 586a f., 588e f., 609c.

76 : *Prtg.* 347c f.; *Symp.* 213e ; *Laws* 641b, 671d f., 673d-e ; cf. Lucian, *Saturn.* 4 Vol. III, p. 387 R.; cf. Plutarch, *Symp.* 1, 1, I, 4, 5.

77 : *Symp.* 176c-d, 214b.

78 : *Rep.* 410b-c, 591c.

79 : *Meno* 88 ; *Euthyd.* 281b, d ; *Phaedo* 69b-c ; *Rep.* 518e f.; *Laws* 644a.

80 : *Rep.* 420c f., 588a.

81 : *Phaedo* 78a ; *Rep.* 421d f., 552b f.; *Theaet.* 167c-d ; *Laws* 737b f., 740a f., 741b f.

82 : *Phaedo* 64d f., 68e f.; *Symp.* 176d ; *Rep.* 398e, 403 f.; *Laws* 674, 775b f.

83 : *Rep.* 421e f., 485e, etc.

84 : *Rep.* 505a f.; *Laws* 631b, d, cf. 906.

85 : *Meno* 88 ; *Euthyd.* 279d f.; *Laws* 661b f., 896c f.;

cf. *Alcinous, Eisagoge*, Ch. XXIX *ad fin.* (*ap.* Hermann, *Platonis Dialogi*, Vol. VI, p. 183).

86 :   *Charm.* 157a ;   *Rep.* 404, cf. 586a f.
87 :   *Meno* 88e ;   *Laws* 896e f.
88 :   *Meno* 87e f.;   *Euthyd.* 281b f.;   *Polit.* 307e f.
89 :   *Phaedo* 65e ff., 83 f.;   cf. *Euthyd.* 292b, d.
90 :   *Rep.* 519a-b, 553d ;   *Tim.* 71a, d.
91 :   *Prtg.* 354a f.;   *Gorg.* 467d ;   *Rep.* 357c f.
92 :   *Rep.* 491c, 521a.
93 :   *Rep.* 618e, etc.
94 :   *Meno* 87e f.;   *Euthyd.* 279 f.;   *Phaedo* 69a-b ;   *Rep.* 586d f.;   *Laws* 631c.
95 :   *Phaedo* 68e f.;   *Rep.* 554c f., 589e f.
96 :   *Phaedo* 68b-c ;   *Rep.* 543b ff., 582d f.
97 :   *Rep.* 500c f., 505a-b, d f., 508d f.
98 :   *Gorg.* 467d ;   *Rep.* 370e f.;   *Laws* 831c f.
99 :   *Laws* 737b f., 740a, 741b f.
100 :   *Menex.* 246c f.;   *Phaedo* 68c, 82c ;   *Rep.* 545 ff., 581 ff.; *Laws* 870c, cf. 859d f
101 :   *Gorg.* 452b.
102 :   *Rep.* 410b f.
103 :   *Laws* 696b.
104 :   *Gorg.* 456e f.;   *Laws* 661a f.
105 :   *Rep.* 591b f.;   *Laws* 644a, 711d-e ;   cf. *Epist.* 320b, c.
106 :   *Menex.* 246d f.;   *Rep.* 545 ff., 581 ff.
107 :   *Alc. II*, 146e f.;   *Meno* 87e f.;   *Laws* 686e.
108 :   *Menex.* 246e ;   *Phaedo* 68c ;   *Laws* 870c.
109 :   *Rep.* 404a-b, 537a ;   *Laws* 796c-d, 799 f., 832e ff.
110 :   Cf. *Rep.* 403e f.
111 :   *Rep.* 518d f.
112 :   *Gorg.* 452b.
113 :   *Charm.* 154d-e ;   *Menex.* 246e ;   *Rep.* 591c.
114 :   *Meno* 87e f.;   *Euthyd.* 281a-b.
115 :   *Rep.* 476b f.;   *Phaedr.* 250b f.
116 :   *Symp.* 210 f.;   218e.
117 :   *Laws* 661a f.
118 :   *Symp.* 211e.
119 :   *Rep.* 401 ff.
120 :   *Rep.* 588a ;   cf. *Phaedr.* 239c-d.
121 :   *Hipp. Maj.* 292d ;   *Rep.* 402d.
122 ;   *Rep.* 491c, e f., 494b ff.;   *Phaedr.* 239c-d.   Cf. Wilamowitz, *op. cit.*, Vol. I, pp. 44 ff.
123 :   *Prtg.* 354a f.;   *Gorg.* 504b-c, 467c ;   *Rep.* 357c ;   *Phaedr.* 270b ;   *Laws* 789d.
124 :   *Gorg.* 452a.
125 :   *Rep.* 591c ;   *Laws* 744a.
126 :   *Laws* 661b.
127 :   *Rep.* 591b.
128 :   *Euthyd.* 281a f.
129 :   *Euthyd.* 279 f.
130 :   *Phaedo* 114e.
131 :   *Gorg.* 491a f.
132 :   *Rep.* 440b ff.;   *Tim.* 69e ff.
133 :   *Lach.* 196d f.

134 : *Prtg.* 349e ff.;   *Meno* 88a f.;   *Phaedo* 68c, d, 69b f.; *Polit.* 309c.

135 : *Gorg.* 465c f.

136 : *Meno* 78c f.; *Rep.* 336e.

137 : *Crito* 54b.

138 : *Rep.* 367c f.; 612b f.

139 : *Rep.* 426d f., etc.; *Polit.* 293 ff.; *Laws* 875c f.

140 : *Meno* 88a f.

141 : *Gorg.* 504d f.

142 : *Rep.* 522a ; *Laws* 744d-e.

143 : Cf. *Meno* 72c f.; *Rep.* 441e f., 519c f., 539e f.; *Polit.* 308d ff.; *Laws* 630a-b, 660e f., 963a, 965c f.; cf. Höfer, *Die Bedeutung der Philosophie für das Leben nach Plato*, p. 34, n. 44.

144 : *Critias* 121a ; *Laws* 636a.

145 : *Alc. I*, 134b ; *Meno* 78c f.; *Laws* 710a, 743d f.

146 : *Rep.* 430e, 559b ; *Laws* 673e f., 835e f., 840a f.

147 : *Charm.* 158a-b ; *Symp.* 216d f.

148 : *Laws* 744a.

149 : *Meno* 88 ; *Phaedo* 68c f.

150 : *Laws* 870b-c.

151 : *Phileb.* 12d, etc.

152 : *Rep.* 402d.

153 : Cf. *Rep.* 372e f., 404c f., 505c f.

154 : *Prtg.* 333b.

155 : Cf. *supra*, Ch. IV, pp. 88-99 ; cf. Hans Meyer, *Geschichte der alten Philosophie*, p. 195.

156 : *Rep.* 404d, with Adam's note ; *Epist.* 326 ff.

157 : *Phaedo* 64d ; *Rep.* 581c ff.; *Laws* 660e f., 662c ff., 733 f.

CHAPTER IX

1 : (1), (2) and (3) have not hitherto received special treatment at the hands of Plato-students.   (4) and (5) were selected on account of their obvious importance.   They have not been treated by others from this standpoint.   These five, together with the six further cases used in verification, cover approximately the whole field of platonic thought.

2 : *Tim.* 56c f., 77a f.

3 : *Tim.* 81a.

4 : Cf. *Tim.* 81c f.

5 : *Tim.* 79a, 80c f.

6 : *Tim.* 78d f.

7 : *Tim.* 77c f., 80d f.

8 : *Symp.* 207d-e ; *Phaedo* 96e f.; *Tim.* 82c f.

9 : *Phileb.* 29e.

10 : *Tim.* 81b.

11 : *Phaedo* 96c f.

12 : *Gorg.* 517c f.; *Rep.* 405d, 407d f.; *Tim.* 82 ff.

13 : *Tim.* 81c-d.

14 : *Laws* 797e f.

15 : *Rep.* 585b ; *Laws* 782e.

16 : *Rep.* 439a f.; 442a f.

17 : *Tim.* 70d-e, 72e ; cf. *Phaedo* 94b-c. A natural check is supplied by the mechanism of the intestines, which ensures that certain of the waste products of metabolism are carried off very slowly (*Tim.* 73a).

18 : *Gorg.* 499d-e ; *Rep.* 558e, 559b.

19 : *Gorg.* 518b f.; *Rep.* 404a f., 407d f.; *Tim.* 82a ff.

20 : *Rep.* 571b, 574e.

21 : *Rep.* 442a.

22 : *Phaedo* 81c f.; *Rep.* 586a-b, 590d ff.; *Tim.* 70e, 73a ; *Laws* 645d f.

23 : *Rep.* 404b ff.

24 : *Prtg.* 354a ; *Rep.* 404a f.; *Tim.* 88d f.; *Laws* 646c f., 788e ff. It is admitted that the *first* effect of gymnastic exercises may be unsatisfactory.

25 : *Rep.* 407c, 571d f., 591c f.; *Tim.* 72e f.

26 : *Gorg.* 464d f., 521e f.; *Rep.* 404.

27 : *Rep.* 405 ff., 585e f.; *Laws* 646c f.

28 : Cf. *Symp.* 176, 213e, 214b ; *Laws* 640.

29 : Such as Athens and the Hellenic cities generally, with their *meden agan* standard, as opposed to the way of living which was proverbial in Sicily and in Magna Graecia generally (cf. *Rep.* 404d ; *Epist.* 326b f.).

30 : Cf. *Laws* 646b, 783b, 789c, 842a-b.

31 : *Ion* 531e ; *Prtg.* 314a ; *Gorg.* 464d, 517e, etc.

32 : *Gorg.* 504a.

33 : *Alc. I*, 107e f.; *Prtg.* 326b-c ; *Crito* 47a f.; *Rep.* 406a, cf. 389c.

34 : *Gorg.* 452b ; *Laws* 646d.

35 : *Rep.* 459c ; *Laws* 720c f., 722e, 857c.

36 : *Phaedr.* 270b f.; *Laws* 720d-e, 723a, 857d.

37 : Cf. *Lach.* 195c f.

38 : *Rep.* 519c f., 540c f.

39 : *Rep.* 405 f., 496c. In the ideal community, sickly infants would not be reared, so that such a case could hardly arise (*Rep.* 459d-e, 460c, 461b-c. Cf. Aristotle, *Pol.* 1262a 5). Cf. Adam, *The Republic of Plato*, Vol. I, pp. 357-360.

40 : *Rep.* 404d ; *Epist.* 326b f.

41 : *Rep.* 552b ; cf. *Laws* 762b f., 781.

42 : *Laws* 625e f., 633a, 780b f., 942b.

43 : *Rep.* 461d-e ; cf. *Laws* 762b f.

44 : *Laws* 636b f.

45 : *Syssitia koina echontes, Rep.* 458c-d.

46 : *Laws* 780e f.

47 : *Laws* 806e ; cf. Aristotle, *Pol.* 1265a 9. Plato understands that Greek feeling views such regulations as impracticable (*Laws* 781c, 839d), but insists that, where the ideal to be attained is so important, Greek feeling should learn to change.

48 : *Tim.* 77a ; *Phileb.* 29.

49 : *Rep.* 369d ; *Laws* 889d.

50 : *Symp.* 188a-b ; *Rep.* 491d ; *Laws* 845c ; cf. *Hipparch* 225c.

51 : *Tim.* 77a f.

52 : *Critias* 111c f.; *Laws* 680e f.

53 : *Rep.* 370c ; *Critias* 112b.

54 : *Prtg.* 334a-b ; *Theaet.* 149e.

55 : Cf. *Rep.* 611d f.

56 : *Rep.* 333d, 353a, 589b.

57 : Cf. *Rep.* 459a-b.

58 : *Euthyphr.* 2d ; *Laws* 765e.

59 : *Symp.* 185c f.; *Rep.* 589b.

60 : E.g. vegetables, fruits and cereals; also pasturage for cattle, and tree-wood for timber (*Rep.* 372b-c ; *Critias* 111c, 114e f., 117a, 118b ; *Laws* 848a, 849c-d, etc.).

61 : *Laws* 889d.

62 : *Lach.* 198d-e ; *Laws* 906a.

63 : *Phileb.* 55d f.

64 : *Rep.* 420d, 421e (which apparently applies to farmers as well as to potters) ; *Tim.* 23a-b.

65 : *Rep.* 547d ; *Phileb.* 55d. In the " model city " the farms are owned and " managed " by the citizens, but the work of ploughing, etc., is, of course, done by practical farmers, who belong to the serf class.

66 : *Critias* 111c ff., etc.

67 : *Rep.* 343b, 345c f., 359d-e ; *Polit.* 267b-c, 268a-b ; *Laws* 735a-b.

68 : *Critias* 111c.

69 : *Laws* 842d ; *Epist.* 361a.

70 : Cf. *Rep.* 341d f., 343b, 345c ff.

71 : *Laws* 842d ff.

72 : *Laws* 739e, 849b.

73 : *Laws* 842c, 949e.

74 : *Laws* 745c, etc.

75 : *Laws* 740a, 847e f.

76 : *Laws* 849b f. The aim is not to make money for the farmers by keeping out the middle-man, but to preserve them from the morally deleterious effects of personal contact with retail trade.

77 : *Rep.* 371d ; *Laws* 848d, etc.

78 : *Rep.* 371e ; *Laws* 742a, 806d.

79 : *Laws* 806d, 807c-d, 846d, 847a. This is not apparently regarded as conflicting with e.g. *Rep.* 397d f., although the citizen-farmer, with his city home as well as his country home, and his civic, as well as his agricultural, interests, appears (like the philosopher-king) to be somewhat of a dual personality.

80 : *Laws* 849c f. Plato expects that there will be some interference with boundaries, and that some pilfering will take place. But this is because the " model " city is only a second-best.

81 : *Euthyd.* 291e f.; *Rep.* 369c-d, 370a ; *Laws* 842c.

82 : *Laws* 740a, 848d f.

83 : *Laws* 842d ff.

84 : *Rep.* 456e, 462 ff.

85 : *Rep.* 371b ; *Laws* 742a.

86 : *Rep.* 371c, 434c-d ; *Laws* 918a.

87 : *Laws* 849b f., 915d.

88 : *Rep.* 548a.

89 : *Rep.* 555e ; *Laws* 742b-c, 921c.

90 : *Laws* 846e.

91 : *Rep.* 555d.

92 : Cf. *Laws* 646e.

93 : Not " capital and labour," but retired capitalists and idle paupers, both falling outside the classes employed in socially useful work (*Rep.* 421d f., 552b f.; *Laws* 744d, 831e, etc.).

94 : *Rep.* 551d, etc.

95 : *Rep.* 550d ff.

96 : *Rep.* 551b-c.

97 : *Rep.* 557a.

98 : *Rep.* 562b, etc.

99 : *Rep.* 420d ff., 550c ff.

100 : *Rep.* 371b f., 434c-d ; *Laws* 742 f.

101 : *Apol.* 36b ; *Laws* 831c, 918b f.

102 : *Rep.* 397d f., 416d f.; *Laws* 741e ff., 919c f.

103 : I.e. mainly farm produce, and simple manufactures produced in connection with the farms, cf. *Laws* 849c, and Ritter's *Kommentar* on 846d.

104 : *Rep.* 371a-b ; *Soph.* 223c f.; *Laws* 952e f.

105 : *Laws* 705a.

106 : *Laws* 918b ff., cf. 847d.

107 : *Laws* 870a, 918c-d.

108 : *Symp.* 184e f.; *Rep.* 553c-d ; *Laws* 743e (with Ritter's note).

109 : *Laws* 831c f.

110 : *Rep.* 573e ff., 405a ; *Laws* 729a, 743c-d, 745a.

111 : *Rep.* 344a-b, 552d ; *Laws* 870c.

112 : *Rep.* 555c f.

113 : *Rep.* 555e ; *Laws* 728e.

114 : *Rep.* 465c ; *Laws* 729a.

115 : *Rep.* 422b f.; 556c f.

116 : *Gorg.* 515d f.; *Rep.* 556e f.

117 : *Rep.* 420b ff.

118 : *Rep.* 343d, 551e ; *Laws* 743a f.

119 : *Rep.* 343d-e, 551e, 552c, 555a, c ; *Laws* 831b f.

120 : *Symp.* 185a ; *Rep.* 344a f., 362b, 550d, 554c, 555c, 568d f., 573d ff.; *Laws* 742b-c, 773, 918e f., 921a f., 928 f., 941c f.

121 : *Laws* 918a, d.

122 : *Rep.* 371c-d ; *Laws* 848b ff.

123 : *Laws* 920b-c.

124 : *Laws* 917c, 921a-b.

125 : *Laws* 742a.

126 : *Laws* 746a. This is admittedly somewhat impracticable.

127 : *Laws* 729a, 922c ff.

128 : *Laws* 919c, 952e f.

129 : *Laws* 920a. It is Phoenicians and Egyptians who are thought of as peculiarly money-loving (*Rep.* 435e).

130 : *Laws* 847b.

131 : *Laws* 745a, 914c, 915d, 925e.

132 : Exceptions (e.g. for distinguished public service) might conceivably be permitted (*Laws* 850).

133 : *Laws* 919c.

134 : *Laws* 697b-c, etc.

135 : *Rep.* 562b.

136 : *Laws* 808c f. Greek usage, however, admitted a

partly " private " attitude towards religion (a) in the case of the " private and ancestral Gods " (*Laws* 717c, 785a), and (b) in the case of initiation into the Mysteries (cf. *Rep.* 364b f.). But in the main, as in the case of Socrates, the citizen was expected to accept the deities recognized by his city, and confine his religious devotion to them (*Laws* 909d f.).

137 : *Prtg.* 325c ff., etc.

138 : Cf. e.g. Heliodor. *Aethiop.* I, 13 ; Eurip. *Medea* 1033, *Supp.* 923, *Alcest.* 663 ; Sophocl. *Ajax* 570 ; Aristoph. *Acharn.* 678 ; Dio Halicarn. 8, 51.

139 : *Lys.* 208c ; *Laws* 790a. It is not entirely clear whether the " playground matrons " are freewomen or slaves (cf. *Laws* 793e f.). The commentators seem to interpret the text in such a way as to regard them as free-women. This would have been considered altogether exceptional at Athens. Mothers who lose their own babies (*Rep.* 460d, with Adam's note), and free-born women impoverished by the wars (Demosth. *Adv. Eubulid.* 1309, 1313 ; cf. also Plutarch, *Lycurg.* 16) sometimes act as nurses ; but this is rare.

140 : Cf. Demosth. *De Coron.* 313 ; Lucian, *Necyom.* 17 (Vol. I, p. 480 R.).

141 : *Prtg.* 325d f.

142 : *Laws* 804c-d.

143 : *Lys* 223a ; *Laws* 808e.

144 : Cf. *Prtg.* 326c, 328b-c.

145 : *Gorg.* 485b.

146 : *Rep.* 404a.

147 : *Lach.* 182d ff.; cf. Herodot. *Histor.* VI, 11-12.

148 : *Gorg.* 485c-d.

149 : *Apol.* 36b ; *Gorg.* 482e ff.; *Rep.* 365d ; *Theaet.* 173d.

150 : Cf. *Prtg.* 318d f.

151 : *Rep.* 462, etc.; *Laws* 903b f.

152 : *Rep.* 457c ff. Even in the second-best city of the *Laws* service of the community is the dominating idea (*Laws* 773 f.; cf. *Polit.* 310b f.). Nettleship (*Lect. & Rem.*, Vol. I, pp. 358-359) thinks there is an inconsistency here between Plato's principles and his detailed deductions. But cf. the concluding paragraph of the present chapter.

153 : *Rep.* 460b f.

154 : *Rep.* 415b, with Adam's note.

155 : *Rep.* 421e, 466e f.; *Laws* 720b. Not many lawyers or doctors would be required in the ideal community (*Rep.* 405 f.).

156 : *Rep.* 500b f.; *Theaet.* 172d ff.; *Tim.* 47b f.

157 : *Rep.* 540a-b, 591e f.

158 : *Rep.* 562b f., etc.; *Laws* 715b.

159 : *Meno* 99b f., etc.; *Rep.* 492e f.; *Polit.* 301e f.

160 : *Laws* 678c, e f.

161 : *Prtg.* 322b ; *Laws* 681a.

162 : *Rep.* 365c-d, 373d.

163 : *Rep.* 373d f.; *Laws* 709a f., 766d ff.

164 : *Rep.* 343a-b, 345c f.; *Polit.* 261c ff.; *Laws* 680b, d-e.

165 : *Polit.* 271e ; *Laws* 624a f.; cf. *Minos* 313 ff. Cf. Wundt, *Ethics*, Vol. I, p. 238.

166 : *Apol.* 36b ; *Gorg.* 482e ff.; *Rep.* 365d ; *Theaet.* 173d.

167 : *Rep.* 343b f.; *Laws* 715a f.
168 : *Gorg.* 466b f.; *Rep.* 550c ff.; *Laws* 714c f.
169 : *Rep.* 338d f., 488.
170 : *Laws* 875b f.
171 : *Gorg.* 479 f.; *Rep.* 576b ff.
172 : *Rep.* 551c, 552d-e, 553c f., 555c f.; *Laws* 831c f.
173 : *Rep.* 492b, 564c-d ; *Polit.* 292d-e ; *Laws* 659a-b.
174 : *Gorg.* 515d f., 519a-b ; *Rep.* 426c f., 492b f.
175 : *Rep.* 565c ff., 569b-c.
176 : *Polit.* 292c f.
177 : *Rep.* 416a, 422a, 548a f., 550c f.
178 : *Meno* 99b f.; *Rep.* 492e f.; *Polit.* 301e f.
179 : *Rep.* 422e f., 556d f.
180 : *Rep.* 557b ff.
181 : *Rep.* 562b, 563d f., 565d, 572c ff.
182 : *Rep.* 573d ff.
183 : *Rep.* 579b f.
184 : *Laws* 715b f.
185 : *Gorg.* 515d f., 519a-b.
186 : *Rep.* 345c ff.; *Polit.* 296e f.
187 : *Rep.* 416a ; *Laws* 875a f.
188 : *Rep.* 416b-c.
189 : *Rep.* 416d f., 419 ; *Tim.* 18b. Cf. Nettleship, op. cit., Vol. I, pp. 358 f.
190 : *Rep.* 540a-b ; *Polit.* 293b f.; *Laws* 903b.
191 : *Rep.* 519e f.; 590d f.; *Soph.* 253c f.; *Polit.* 296e f., 310e f.
192 : *Meno* 99a f.; *Polit.* 305d, 311b f.; *Tim.* 90a.
193 : *Polit.* 271e 275b, ; *Critias* 109b ; *Laws* 713a, 715c f., 907a. Bonitz, *Platonische Studien*, pp. 222, 224, sees this contained (implicitly) even in the *Euthyphro*.
194 : *Rep.* 497b-d ; *Polit.* 294a, 299e f.
195 : *Rep.* 416e f.; *Laws* 875a.
196 : *Rep.* 420d f.; *Polit.* 293c-d, 296e f., 305d, 311b f.
197 : *Laws* 715c ff., 903b ff.
198 : *Rep.* 543d ff.; *Laws* 875.
(199 No. 209, nothing is omitted).
209 : *Phileb.* 60a ; *Laws* 732e f.; cf. *Epist.* 335b-c.
210 : *Laws* 903b f.
211 : *Gorg.* 500a f., 503d f., 506d-e, 507d f.; *Rep.* 420b f., 466b-c, 519e f., 586a f.; *Laws* 806c.
212 : *Gorg.* 503b f., 515c ff.
213 : *Rep.* 409c f., 585b f.; *Theaet.* 173a-b, 175c f.
214 : *Rep.* 422e f.; *Laws* 945c-d.
215 : *Rep.* 351c f.; cf. Isocr. *Panath.* 226.
216 : *Rep.* 437b ff.
217 : *Phaedo* 68e f.; *Rep.* 554, 561b f.
218 : *Rep.* 553c-d ; *Laws* 715a-b.
219 : *Rep.* 444b.
220 : *Rep.* 351c ff.; cf. Nettleship, op. cit., Vol. II, pp. 40-41.
221 : *Prtg.* 322b ; *Laws* 681a.
222 : *Rep.* 415d-e, 416c f., 461d-e ; *Laws* 633a, 762b f., 780b f.
223 : *Laws* 678c, e f.
224 : *Rep.* 458c-d ; *Phaedr.* 256c-d ; *Laws* 636c.

225 : *Prtg.* 328b ; *Rep.* 333b f.
226 : *Rep.* 365d ; *Theaet.* 173d ; *Laws* 856b ; cf. *Epist.* 333e.
227 : *Rep.* 364b f.; *Laws* 909d ff.
228 : Cf. *Rep.* 359a.
229 : *Laws* 875a.
230 : *Crito* 50b f.
231 : Cf. Aristotle's criticism, *Pol.* 1262b 14-24.
232 : *Laws* 875b.
233 : *Rep.* 351c f., 352c-d.
234 : *Rep.* 409c-d, 519a f., 553c-d ; *Theaet.* 173a-b.
235 : *Gorg.* 466d-e ; *Meno* 77c ; *Rep.* 351a, e, 577d-e.
236 : *Rep.* 609b d., 610d-e.
237 : *Prtg.* 358a ; *Symp.* 206a ; *Rep.* 505d f.; *Laws* 732e f.
238 : *Rep.* 505a f., 586a-b.
239 : *Gorg.* 503d f., 506d-e, 507d f.; *Rep.* 420b f., 466b-c ;
Laws 903b f.
240 : *Rep.* 423e f.; *Polit.* 293 f.; *Laws* 875c f.
241 : *Polit.* 292c f.; *Laws* 709e ff., 712a.
242 : *Laws* 740a.
243 : *Laws* 918a f.
244 : *Laws* 766a f., 874e, 875d.
245 : *Rep.* 521a, 554c f.
246 : *Rep.* 343b, 463b, 547c.
247 : *Rep.* 550d ff.
248 : *Rep.* 550e f., 551d.
249 : *Rep.* 555d f., 556e f.
250 : *Rep.* 421d f., 552d.
251 : *Rep.* 416d f., etc.; *Laws* 742a.
252 : *Laws* 746a, 919c, 952e f., etc.
253 : *Rep.* 548a f.
254 : *Rep.* 550d.
255 : *Rep.* 464c-d, 550e.
256 : Cf. *Rep.* 551a-b. This particular deduction is not
completely verifiable from the Dialogues, though there are many
scattered hints, which indicate its general coherence with platonic
doctrine.
257 : This deduction is also not completely verifiable. But
it is substantiated in principle by *Rep.* 464c-d, 548a-b, 550c f.
258 : *Rep.* 460a f.; *Laws* 739b f.
259 : *Laws* 740b f., 923 ff., etc.
260 : *Ion* 533d ff.; *Rep.* 600e f., 604d ff.; *Phaedr.* 254a ;
Laws 719b-c.
261 : *Gorg.* 501d ff.; *Rep.* 395d f., 397a f.; *Laws* 660a-b,
669c f.
262 : *Rep.* 424b f., 586b-c.
263 : *Rep.* 397d f.
264 : *Rep.* 424b f., 595a, 605b, 607b ; *Laws* 656c f., 798e ff.
265 : *Rep.* 401b-c ; *Laws* 719b-c.
266 : *Rep.* 399a f., 401c f.; *Laws* 659d ff., 800 ff., 814d ff.
267 : *Gorg.* 484c ff.; *Rep.* 487d f., 489d, 490e ff., 495c f.
268 : Cf. *Rep.* 496b f., 500b f., 520a-b.
269 : One thinks in this connection of the Pythagorean
society at Kroton, and its downfall about 450 B.C. (Cf. Burnet,
Early Greek Philos.[2], sect. 40), but there is no reference to this in

the Dialogues, though it is consistent with *Rep.* 494a, and with the treatment of Socrates as a " gad-fly."

270 : Cf. *Rep.* 495b.

271 : Cf. *Rep.* 497e f., 528b f.

272 : *Rep.* 530a f., 530e f., etc.

273 : *Rep.* 362c, 363, 364b f., 365d f.; *Laws* 716e f., 885c f., 905a-b, 908 f., 948c.

274 : *Phaedo* 69c-d ; *Rep.* 365a, 366a ; *Laws* 909d f.; cf. also *Euthyd.* 277d-e ; *Rep.* 364b. There is no direct evidence of hostility between rival sects, though Plato himself seems to wish to destroy the " private and unauthorized " mystery-mongers who go to the doors of the rich (*Rep.* 364b f.; *Soph.* 223d f.; *Laws* 908b ff., 933).

275 : There is no real evidence for this deduction, though cf. *Laws* 885b-c, 887a, 888e, 908 f.; cf. note 269, *supra.*

276 : *Laws* 908c, 910b. Such references as *Rep.* 365a, 366a, etc. indicate that this impiety is a kind of injustice, which is itself destructive of the social order (cf. also *Rep.* 351c f.).

277 : *Laws* 909d f.

278 : *Laws* 717b, 785a, etc.

279 : Cf. *supra*, Ch. VII, pp. 186-191.

280 : *Rep.* 468e, 538b f., 540c ; *Laws* 801c-d, 829d-e, 941b ff., 966b ff.

281 : Cf. *Rep.* 492 f., etc.

282 : Cf. *Rep.* 412d f., 485 f., 490b-d ; *Tim.* 19a.

CHAPTER X

1 : In spite of Beare's *caveat* (*Greek Theories of Elementary Cognition*, p. 8), the writer hopes to remove some of the obscurities which undeniably exist in this field. What is here treated as " mind " is in the Dialogues expressed indifferently by such nouns as *dianoia, nous, phronesis, psyche, sophia,* and by a whole host of verbs and phrases, which pass into one another in one and the same context.

2 : *Phaedo* 97b-c ; *Cratyl.* 400a ; *Laws* 967c f. Aristotle (*Met.* 984b 16 ff.) is aware that Anaxagoras is not the first to make this suggestion.

3 : *Tim.* 34a, etc.; *Laws* 895b f., 897c f. For Anaxagoras, cf. Ritter & Preller, *Historia Philosophiae Graecae*, sect. 155.

4 : *Cratyl.* 400a-b ; *Soph.* 247d-e, 248e f.; *Laws* 895c.

5 : *Laws* 886a f., 898c f., 966e f.

6 : *Cratyl.* 413d ; cf. Ritter & Preller, op. cit., sect. 160b.

7 : *Laws* 893b ff., with Ritter's notes (894a is better explained by Frank, *Plato u.d.sog. Pythagoreer*, p. 102).

8 : *Tim.* 42a, 56c f., 77a.

9 : *Theaet.* 182a f., 184d ; *Tim.* 43b f.; *Phileb.* 33c f. For Anaxagoras, cf. Ritter & Preller, op. cit., sect. 155.

10 : *Phaedo* 79b, etc.; *Rep.* 455b.

11 : *Phaedo* 99a f.; *Tim.* 46c-d.

12 : *Tim.* 42a, 77a f.; *Phileb.* 34d f.

13 : *Rep.* 369c f.; *Laws* 678e f., 782d f.

14 : *Prtg.* 322b ff.; *Rep.* 369b ff., 458d ; *Laws* 678c ff., 781e ff.

15 : *Tim.* 61d f., 64a ; cf. 37a ; *Theaet.* 154b, 190d.

16 : *Tim.* 65d f.

17 : *Tim.* 67b, 80a-b.

18 : *Rep.* 507d f.; *Tim.* 45b f. The intra-ocular rays correspond roughly, in function, to what modern psychology calls the *Eigenlicht.*

19 : *Rep.* 571c f.; *Tim.* 43b, 44b, 70a f., 91a f.

20 : This must not be understood literally. Plato does not pay attention to the function of the lens, or of the retinal image.

21 : *Tim.* 43a ff.; *Phileb.* 33d. Each sense-organ has, of course, its own specific type of self-motion, so that the sensation-mechanism can be described as a meeting of *two* motions (*Theaet.* 182b).

22 : *Tim.* 73b ff.

23 : *Tim.* 69b ff., cf. 91c-d.

24 : *Tim.* 75a f.

25 : *Tim.* 76a f.

26 : Cf. *Laws* 794d f.

27 : *Tim.* 70b f., 77c ff.

28 : *Tim.* 73b f., 91a f.

29 : Cf. *Rep.* 444b f., 561b f., 572d f., 586e f.

30 : *Gorg.* 503d ff.; *Rep.* 443c f., 591d f.

31 : *Rep.* 378 ff., 386-402 *passim*, 522a-b.

32 : *Tim.* 46e f.

33 : *Rep.* 523b ff.; *Theaet.* 184e ff.; *Polit.* 278 f.

34 : *Phaedo* 65b ff.; *Rep.* 603d ; *Theaet.* 187a.

35 : *Phaedo* 100e ff.; *Rep.* 524c f.; *Theaet.* 154 ff.; *Parm.* 129 ff.; cf. Natorp, *Platos Ideenlehre*, pp. 140-142.

36 : *Meno* 85c f., 86a f.; *Rep.* 475d f.; *Theaet.* 150e.

37 : *Euthyd.* 275c ff.; *Rep.* 497d f., 537e ff.; *Phileb.* 15d f.

38 : *Phaedr.* 250b, d-e ; *Polit.* 277c, 285e f.; *Phileb.* 17a.

39 : *Rep.* 521c ff., 533c ff.

40 : *Meno* 85c, 97b f.; *Rep.* 476c ff.; *Tim.* 51d f.; *Phileb.* 39c f.

41 : *Phaedo* 96 f.; *Rep.* 537e f.

42 : *Theaet.* 193b f.; *Phileb.* 38c f.

43 : *Polit.* 277e f. 285b.

44 : *Phaedo* 74a f., 78d, 100b, 102b f.; *Theaet.* 185d-e ; *Soph.* 251d ff.

45 : *Rep.* 510d f., 517b f., 525d f., 532a ff.

46 : *Rep.* 511b-c, 540a-b. The ascent seems to be accomplished by withdrawal from sensuous and emotional experience, and by concentration upon the formal elements in experience until their principle is grasped, in a process which resembles etiolation. After this comes the descent, i.e. the arduous task of idealizing human experience, making it over in the light of the ideal principle. Some distinguished Platonists (e.g. Adam, op. cit., Vol. II, p. 71, and E. Frank, op. cit., pp. 14-16, 65, 107, etc.) misapprehend the meaning of this descent, and regard platonism as essentially etiolation.

47 : *Rep.* 462b ff., 517b-c, 591c f.

48 : *Rep.* 519e f., etc.

49 : *Ion* 533d ff.; *Rep.* 603c ff.; *Phaedr.* 245a-b ; *Laws* 719b-c.

50 : *Rep.* 396b, 397a, 596c ff., 600e f.

51 : *Rep.* 395d f., 603e ff.

52 : *Rep.* 376e ff., 389d f., 400d ff.; *Phaedr.* 245a, 265b ; *Laws* 660a, 801c, 814e ff., 817d-e, 936a.

53 : *Cratyl.* 397c f., 408d ; *Tim.* 37c ff.; *Laws* 821b f., 886a, 899, 901c ff.

54 : *Euthyphr.* 12e ff.; *Phaedo* 79c f., 108c ; *Laws* 715e f., 801c ff., 887c f.

55 : *Alc. II*, 149e f.; *Rep.* 363 ff.; *Laws* 716e ff., 905c ff.

56 : *Apol.* 26c f.; *Laws* 821a, 886d f., 889 f., 967.

57 : *Phaedo* 66a, 79b f.; *Rep.* 490, 500b ; *Tim.* 46c, 48a, 90b f.; *Soph.* 249 ; *Phileb.* 23d, 28c f.

58 : *Rep.* 379 ff., 427b f.; *Laws* 738b f., 799.

59 : *Tim.* 28 ff.

60 : *Rep.* 439 f., 608e f.; *Polit.* 269c f., 272e f.; *Tim.* 70e f.

61 : *Tim.* 41d-e, 42b f.; *Laws* 898e f., 966d f.

62 : *Gorg.* 507e f.; *Rep.* 612e f.; *Phaedr.* 247 f.; *Tim.* 41a ; *Phileb.* 39e f.; *Laws* 716c f.; cf. Nettleship, *Lect. & Rem.*, Vol. I, p. 238 (4).

63 : *Rep.* 540a-b ; *Theaet.* 176 ; *Laws* 903b f.

64 : *Tim.* 30a ff.; cf. Natorp, op. cit., pp. 99, 107 f., 112, Cf. Barth, *Die Seele in der Philosophie Platons*, pp. 301 ff.

65 : " Soul " tends, perhaps, to be regarded as what later ages call " spiritual substance," and " mind " as " spiritual activity inhering in spiritual substance." Cf. e.g. *Rep.* 435b ff. 580e f.; *Soph.* 247a-b, 249a f.; *Tim.* 30b ; *Laws* 961d. But in Plato's writings the one term often passes into the other, in one and the same context.

66 : *Meno* 87e f.; *Polit.* 307e f.

67 : *Meno* 88e f.; *Polit.* 259c ; *Tim.* 46d.

68 : *Prtg.* 352b-c ; *Phaedr.* 241c ; *Phileb.* 59d.

69 : *Rep.* 528e f., 581d ff.; *Phileb.* 11c, 66b.

70 : *Cratyl.* 400b ; *Phaedo* 80 ; *Rep.* 353d ; *Laws* 896e ff.

71 : *Rep.* 439a f., 518d f., 553c ff., 580e f.; *Tim.* 70d f.

72 : *Rep.* 444d f., 590d.

73 : *Phaedo* 97c f.; *Rep.* 431c, 439c f., 441d f., 442c ; *Laws* 690a, 875c, 903b f.

74 : *Rep.* 486e, 490a-b, 500b f., 534.

75 : *Phaedo* 65d f.; *Rep.* 479e, 585b f.; *Theaet.* 185c ff.

76 : *Euthyd.* 295b, e ; *Phaedo* 82d f., 84a f., 99a f.; *Rep.* 532, 540a-b ; *Tim.* 37, 90a f.; *Laws* 653a.

77 : *Laws* 896e f., 966d ff.; cf. *Cratyl.* 400a ; *Phileb.* 22c, 30d.

78 : *Rep.* 509b, 540a-b.

CHAPTER XI

1 : *Laws* 631b. P. Bovet, *Le dieu de Platon*, pp. 53-82, maintains that the concept of God has no place in the platonic philosophy, until we come to the later Dialogues. Then (pp. 133 ff.) we find the conception of God as a " perfect soul," which

is the " author of the world," and observe that this conception is so bound up with the platonic dialectic that it may reasonably be regarded as the creation of that dialectic. The position of Burnet and Taylor is not, in essentials, different from this, but is, if anything, strengthened by their view that the earlier Dialogues represent Socratic, not Platonic, opinions. In attempting, without bias, to put together the references in the Dialogues, the present writer does not find himself compelled by the evidence to draw these sharp distinctions.

2 : *Cratyl.* 397c ; *Laws* 821, 885e, 886d, 887d f.

3 : *Cratyl.* 408d.

4 : *Phaedo* 62b, 80a ; *Polit.* 271e f.; *Tim.* 42c ; *Laws* 644d f., 713d f., 803b f., 902b ff., 906a, 907a.

5 : Cf. *Laws* 930e f.

6 : *Laws* 887d-e, 909e f.; cf. *Tim.* 27c f.

7 : *Euthyphr.* 14a f.; *Lys.* 214 ; *Phaedr.* 255a.

8 : *Phaedr.* 252c f.; *Theaet.* 176a f.; *Laws* 716c f.

9 : *Apol.* 41c f.; *Phaedo* 63b f., 81a ; *Rep.* 612a f.; *Laws* 887c f.

10 : *Laws* 738b f., 798a-b.

11 : *Apol.* 23a ; *Cratyl.* 401d f.; *Phaedr.* 278d ; *Laws* 641d.

12 : *Cratyl.* 425c ; *Phaedo* 85c ; *Tim.* 53c-d.

13 : *Ion* 535e f.; *Rep.* 366a ; *Phaedr.* 244d, 265b ; *Laws* 682a.

14 : *Phileb.* 51b f.; *Laws* 670d ff.

15 : *Laws* 653c f.

16 : *Laws* 815d.

17 : *Rep.* 398d, 399e ff.; *Laws* 801a f.

18 : *Ion* 535d ff.; *Laws* 682a, 804a-b.

19 : *Rep.* 468e f.

20 : *Rep.* 613a ; *Laws* 803e.

21 : *Laws* 838b-c, 880e f.

22 : *Laws* 657a-b, 799a f.

23 : *Rep.* 378b-c ; *Tim.* 28d f.

24 : *Gorg.* 501d ff.; *Rep.* 492b f., 493d f., 501b-c ; *Laws* 659a f., 700c f.

25 : *Rep.* 334a-b ; *Laws* 941b.

26 : *Rep.* 390b-c.

27 : *Rep.* 379e, 381c f., 383.

28 : *Rep.* 358c, 378.

29 : *Euthyphr.* 6b ; *Rep.* 378c f., 379e.

30 : *Rep.* 364d-e, 365e f., 390d ; *Laws* 906d f., 909a f., 948c.

31 : *Rep.* 364b f., 380a f.

32 : *Gorg.* 484b ; *Laws* 941b.

33 : *Rep.* 388a f., 390d f.

34 : *Rep.* 380c, 388e f., 391c f., 392d.

35 : *Laws* 885c f., 886d, 889d f.

36 : *Laws* 899d ff., 901a f.

37 : *Laws* 801a f.

38 : *Rep.* 381e.

39 : *Cratyl.* 403b f.; *Rep.* 386c f.; *Laws* 904d.

40 : *Rep.* 389e f., 390c f., 391c f.

41 : *Rep.* 603d ff.

42 : *Rep.* 363a f.

43 : *Rep.* 395c ff.

44 : *Rep.* 397c f.
45 : *Rep.* 492b ff.;   *Laws* 637c-d.
46 : Cf. *Rep.* 425d, 492d.
47 : *Symp.* 202e f.
48 : *Phaedr.* 244b ;   *Tim.* 71d f.
49 : *Crito* 54d ;   *Euthyd.* 277d f.;   *Laws* 815c.
50 : *Phaedr.* 249e f.
51 : *Phaedo* 69c f.;   *Rep.* 364c f., 366a.
52 : *Polit.* 290c f.
53 : *Euthyphr.* 4c f.;   *Laws* 870d, 872c f.
54 : *Laws* 738b f.
55 : *Ion* 538e f.;   *Phaedr.* 244c ;   *Phileb.* 67b.
56 : Cf. *Laws* 759d f.
57 : *Laws* 759c.
58 : *Euthyphr.* 14a-b ;   *Laws* 865c-d, 871b-c, 958c-d.
59 : *Polit.* 290c f.;   *Laws* 759a f.
60 : *Laws* 799b, 800a-b, 868d-e, 871a f.
61 : *Laws* 953a f.
62 : *Rep.* 364b f.;   *Laws* 933.
63 : *Laws* 909e f.
64 : *Soph.* 223d f.;   *Laws* 908b ff., 933.
65 : *Apol.* 26d f.;   *Laws* 821a f., 886d f., 889b f., 967.
66 : *Laws* 821b f., 941b f.   Benn's view (*The Greek Philoso-*
phers, Vol. I, p. 234) that Plato's own theology was " a sort of
star-worship," while supported by such references as these, is not
consistent with the evidence adduced *infra* (cf. notes 74-108).
67 : Cf. *Rep.* 500b f., 525b ff.
68 : Cf. *Prtg.* 347b f.;   *Rep.* 596c ff.;   *Laws* 719c.
69 : *Symp.* 202e f.;   *Phaedr.* 244b ;   *Tim.* 71d f.
70 : *Rep.* 378c f.
71 : *Tim.* 71e f.
72 : Cf. *supra,* Ch. IV, last half.
73 : *Rep.* 518c f., 521c ff.
74 : *Symp.* 208b ;   *Rep.* 381a ;   *Phaedr.* 246d-e ;   *Theaet.*
176 ;   *Polit.* 273a f.;   *Tim.* 29e f.;   *Laws* 887b-c, 900c f., 967a.
75 : *Rep.* 379b, 380b-c ;   *Soph.* 265b f., 266b f.;   *Tim.* 46,
68.
76 : *Apol.* 23a ;   *Rep.* 501b-c, 613a f., 617d-e ;   *Phaedr.*
246d f.;   *Theaet.* 176e ;   *Tim.* 42c ;   *Laws* 717d f., 900d, 902e ff.
77 : *Cratyl.* 391d ;   *Phaedo* 80a ;   *Rep.* 382c ;   *Tim.* 68c ;
Laws 641d, 709c, 901d f.
78 : *Phaedr.* 253b-c ;   *Soph.* 265b f., 266b f.;   *Tim.* 29e f., 46c.
79 : *Laws* 906a f.
80 : *Tim.* 39d ff., 68d f.
81 : *Rep.* 353b f., 449a, 540a-b ;   *Phaedr.* 249b-c, e.
82 : *Charm.* 161a-b, 163d-e ;   *Rep.* 442a-b.
83 : *Rep.* 429c f., 442b-c.
84 : *Rep.* 335c, 433 f., 441d f.;   cf. *Laws* 863e f., 913b.
85 : I.e. that portion of justice which is concerned with the
Gods (*Euthyphr.* 12d-e).
86 : *Meno* 88e f., 98e ;   *Rep.* 428d f., 442c, 518c f.
87 : *Cratyl.* 396c f.;   *Polit.* 270a ;   *Tim.* 41b ff.
88 : *Apol.* 33b-c ;   *Rep.* 468e f.;   *Polit.* 271d f.;   *Tim.* 42c-d,
71d f.;   *Laws* 757e, 903b f., 907a f.

89 : *Prtg.* 321c f.; *Phaedr.* 245b-c ; *Polit.* 274c-d ; *Laws* 653c f., 804a-b, 921d.

90 : *Rep.* 425d ; *Laws* 634d, 644e f.

91 : *Prtg.* 322 ; *Symp.* 179a, 202e f.; *Rep.* 366c, 492d ; *Polit.* 269d ; *Laws* 631, 713d f., 757c f.

92 : *Laws* 803e f.

93 : Cf. *Euthyphr.* 14e ; *Rep.* 375b.

94 : *Rep.* 532 f.; *Phaedr.* 247c f.

95 : *Phaedo* 65d f., 79c f., 82d f.; *Phaedr.* 246d ff.; *Soph.* 248.

96 : *Phaedo* 80a-b, 84 ; *Phaedr.* 248.

97 : *Phaedo* 79d, 84b ; *Phaedr.* 248b-c ; *Tim.* 90a.

98 : *Rep.* 500b.

99 : *Theaet.* 176.

100 : *Phaedr.* 245b-c, 265b.

101 : Cf. *Symp.* 180a ; *Laws* 653c-d, 804a-b.

102 : *Symp.* 202d-e.

103 : *Symp.* 205d f., 208e ff.; *Rep.* 402c, 618c-d.

104 : *Symp.* 179a f., 210e f., 212a.

105 : *Rep.* 505a-b, d f.

106 : *Laws* 886d f., 889b f.

107 : *Phaedr.* 245c ; *Laws* 890d.

108 : *Laws* 887d f.; cf. Burnet, *Greek Philosophy*, Pt. I, p. 12.

109 : *Laws* 889 f. *Laws* 886a-b shows that the rejection of traditional religion which is under discussion is not to be dismissed as a mere excuse for hedonism.

110 : *Rep.* 427b-c ; *Laws* 738b f., 759c-d, 828a, 909e.

111 : *Rep.* 377e f., 379 ; *Polit.* 271c f., 273b.

112 : *Rep.* 380c f., 383a ; *Polit.* 269c-d.

113 : *Rep.* 388b f.

114 : *Rep.* 389a, 390b-c ; *Laws* 717d f., 900d.

115 : *Rep.* 390e f.; *Laws* 905d, 910b.

116 : *Rep.* 387c ff. *passim.*

117 : *Laws* 800b f.

118 : *Rep.* 395c ff., 399e f.; *Laws* 802c f.

119 : *Laws* 803e f., 809c-d, 828.

120 : Cf. *Laws* 745b f.

121 : *Polit.* 271c f.; *Laws* 920d f., 935e.

122 : *Laws* 903b f.

123 : *Laws* 889b f., 890d, 909e.

124 : *Rep.* 377b f., 386 ff., 401b ff., 600e ff.; *Laws* 656c 660d f., 682, 719b-c, 801c f., 817, 829c f.

125 : *Phaedr.* 265b ; *Laws* 653d f., 657a-b, 665a, 672b f., 804a.

126 : *Ion* 533e ff.; *Apol.* 22b-c ; *Meno* 99c-d ; *Laws* 682a, 890d, 909e.

127 : *Phaedr.* 249e f.; *Polit.* 277c-d. This treatment of popular theology is paralleled by the treatment, in the Dialogues, of popular proverbs (Nothing too much ! ; Know thyself ! etc.). These express in condensed form the wisdom of certain phases of experience, but are frequently distorted from their original meaning and may be made to look ridiculous (cf. *Prtg.* 342b ff.; *Rep.* 538c f.). Plato uses these as vehicles of communication with his readers, much as Socrates used popular concepts as starting-points. But such proverbs and concepts are utilized by Plato to express philosophical meaning in a symbolic form, thus leading

beyond the popular stage to the stage of philosophical reflection. There is a negative element in passing beyond the merely popular standpoint (cf. the Socratic " torpedo ") ; but the main emphasis is upon the further advance (*Phaedo* 67, 82c f.; *Soph.* 230b f.). Cf. Windelband, *Platon*[5], p. 142. This position is denied by Wilamowitz-Moellendorff, *Platon*,[2] Vol. I, pp. 412-414, who insists that Plato's religion centres in contemplation of ideal good, and is a purely personal affair : *er wollte nicht reformieren.*

128 : *Laws* 741d f., 745b, 854b f., 879c f., 880e f., 884 f., 913 f., 916e f., 927a f., 931, 941d f.

129 : Cf. *Euthyphr.* 5d-e ; *Prtg.* 323e f.

130 : *Laws* 885c f., 887a, 907d ff.

131 : *Rep.* 328c, 331d ; *Laws* 878a.

132 : *Laws* 799b f.

133 : *Soph.* 265c-d, 266b ; *Polit.* 273d ; *Tim.* 30a f., 53a f., 68c f., etc.

134 : *Rep.* 462 ff., 505, 540a-b ; *Tim.* 69b ff. *passim.*

135 : *Rep.* 590d f., 592b ; *Tim.* 29e f.; *Laws* 903b ff.

136 : *Meno* 87c f., 99c f.; *Laws* 631b f.

137 : *Rep.* 416e f.; *Polit.* 271e, 275b, 293c f.; *Critias* 109b-c ; *Laws* 713af., 715c f. 907a.

CHAPTER XII

1 : *Laws* 728a f., 858e f., 880d-e.

2 : *Prtg.* 353a ; *Theaet.* 156 f., 159 f., 166e.

3 : *Rep.* 476b f., 479e, 492b ff.

4 : *Laws* 811b f.; cf. *Rep.* 519d ff., 538c f., 540a f.

5 : *Rep.* 484b ff., 505e f., 518d ; *Laws* 951b, 965 ff.

6 : It should be added that Plato himself betrays at times a tendency to over-emphasize the distinction. The relation which seems to express, without over-emphasis, all that is logically involved in platonism has been pointed out, in considering the value-scales in detail, in the preceding chapters.

7 : *Gorg.* 509a, etc.; *Rep.* 504.

8 : *Prtg.* 356d f.; *Gorg.* 482c f.; *Rep.* 350 ff., 358b. Plato does not himself insist that all the details are to be accepted literally.

9 : *Gorg.* 491e f.; *Rep.* 561.

10 : *Euthyd.* 301b-c ; *Parm.* 132 ff., 135a f.; *Soph.* 254 ff., 259e f.

11 : *Laws* 908e f.

12 : *Laws* 631b f.

CHAPTER XIII

1 : Cf. Schleiermacher, *Introduction to the Dialogues of Plato*, E.T., p. 95 ; Zeller, *Plato*, E.T., pp. 611-612 ; Shorey, *Unity of Plato's Thought*, pp. 20, 23-24 (modified by p. 22) ; J. W. van Oordt, *Plato and the Times he lived in*, p. 72 ; Wilamowitz

Moellendorff, *Platon*, Vol. I, pp. 630 ff.; Vol. II, pp. 266 ff (modified by p. 276). Natorp, *Platos Ideenlehre*, pp. 17, 19, regards the hedonism as Protagorean, and as contradicting the Socratic position. Grote, *Plato and the Other Companions of Socrates*, 1888, Vol. II, pp. 208 ff., appears to be the only scholar who regards the hedonism as definitely Plato's own. Cf. however, n. 8, *infra*.

2 : *Rep.* 357b-c, 475d f., 515c f., 516e f.; *Tim.* 45b f., 47c-d ; *Laws* 732e f.

3 : *Rep.* 436a f.; *Tim.* 67a ; *Phileb.* 51b f., 63e.

4 : *Phileb.* 51a f.; *Laws* 653d-e, 815e f.; cf. Lafontaine, *Le plaisir d'après Platon et Aristote*, pp. 1-53.

5 : *Lys.* 217 ff.; *Prtg.* 353c f.; *Rep.* 403a, 437b f., 438e f., 583c-d, 591d ; *Tim.* 87c, 88b, e ; *Laws* 661a.

6 : *Phaedo* 97c ; *Rep.* 398c ff., 493e f., 583a ; *Phaedr.* 247c f.; *Phileb.* 51 f.; *Laws* 653e f., 656 f., 670d f., 673c-d, 815d f.

7 : *Phileb.* 12c f.

8 : *Prtg.* 358a ; *Laws* 732e f. G. Entz, *Pessimismus u. Weltflucht bei Platon*, pp. 11-12, 20, thinks this a projection of Plato's own uncritical joy in pleasure in his youth.

9 : *Parm.* 136e ; cf. *Prtg.* 335d ff., 348b-c ; *Gorg.* 506a f.; *Hipp. Min.* 373a f.; *Phaedo* 53b ; *Symp.* 215e f.; *Rep.* 327c, 368c, 449b f.; *Soph.* 217b f.

10 : Cf. *Symp.* 176 ff. *passim.*

11 : *Rep.* 553c f.; *Laws* 831c f.

12 : *Rep.* 554 f., 558d f.

13 : *Rep.* 560b ff.

14 : *Prtg.* 353d ff.; *Rep.* 572e ff.; cf. *Epist.* 326c-d.

15 : *Rep.* 584 ff.; *Phileb.* 12c f., 31c ff., 54 f.

16 : *Phaedo* 66b f., 69b-c, 81b f., 83d f.; *Rep.* 584d f., 587a ; *Phileb.* 31a, 32d, 54c f.

17 : *Rep.* 466a f., 583b, 585b f., 586e, 588a ; *Laws* 662e f. For the inference which follows, cf. Lutoslawski, *The Origin and Growth of Plato's Logic*, p. 311.

18 : Cf. *Phaedo* 64d f.; *Rep.* 402c f., 439c-d, 571b f.; *Tim.* 71a-b ; *Phileb.* 12c f.; cf. Jodl, *Geschichte der Ethik*, Vol. I, pp. 574-575 ; Nettleship, *Lectures and Remains*, Vol. I, p. 305.

19 : Cf. *Prtg.* 356d f., 358a ; *Rep.* 581d ff.; *Phaedr.* 247b f.; *Phileb.* 12d ; *Laws* 653a, 732e f.

20 : *Rep.* 402e f., 439c f., 441e f., 571b f.; *Phaedr.* 254d ff.; *Tim.* 70e f., 91b f.

21 : *Apol.* 31e ; *Gorg.* 508c f., 515 ff.; *Phaedo* 64 ff.; *Rep.* 496, 516e ff.; *Theaet.* 173c f.; *Epist.* 322, 324b ff., 330c f.

22 : *Prtg.* 325e f.; *Rep.* 376c ff., 522a ; *Laws* 653 ff., 799 ff.

23 : *Phaedo* 68e f.; *Rep.* 399 ff., 441e f., 518e, 571b f.; *Laws* 659d f.

24 : *Rep.* 410 ff., 498b, 591b f.

25 : Natorp, *Platos Ideenlehre* pp. 324, 328, is writing with reference only to the *Philebus* (cf. 51c-d). For counterbalancing passages from other dialogues, cf. *Prtg.* 353c ff.; *Phaedo* 64e 1, 67a 4 ; *Rep.* 464, 466a f., 558e f., 561b-c, 571e f., 581d ff.; *Laws* 653 f., 658e f., 663b f., 670d.

26 : *Euthyd.* 279c ff.; *Meno* 87e f.; *Rep.* 330, 580e f.; *Laws* 742c ff., 782d f., 831c f.

27 : *Rep.* 461d, 419 f., 553c ff.; *Phileb.* 40a.

28 : *Euthyd.* 280d f.; *Meno* 88d f.; *Rep.* 371b f., 419 f., 521a ; *Laws* 631c, 661a f., 697a f., 728 f., 742, 870, 913 ; cf. *Epist.* 355a f.

29 : *Lach.* 195c f.; *Lys.* 217a-b, 218e f.; *Gorg.* 452a ; *Rep.* 357c, 583c-d.

30 : *Rep.* 405a, c, d ; *Laws* 720c, 723a, cf. 887c.

31 : *Prtg.* 354 ; *Gorg.* 479a ; *Rep.* 406d ; *Tim.* 84e ; cf. *Soph.* 227a-b.

32 : *Theaet.* 159c f., 166, 190c ; cf. *Symp.* 186b.

33 : *Rep.* 406b ff.; *Laws* 728.

34 : *Laws* 639, 734d.

35 : *Symp.* 186d, 188a ; *Tim.* 82 ff.

36 : *Rep.* 405c-d ; *Tim.* 89b-d.

37 : *Tim.* 43a ff.; cf. *Phileb.* 33d f.

38 : *Rep.* 404a ; *Tim.* 70d f., 81b f.; *Laws* 646c, 797e f.

39 : *Tim.* 88c f.; *Laws* 789 f.

40 : *Tim.* 81b f., 88d-e ; *Laws* 798e, 790c-d.

41 : *Tim.* 88a, c, 89a ; *Laws* 789d. It is not supposed that the exercise prescribed will be too violent.

42 : *Laws* 794a f.

43 : *Laws* 794c ff.

44 : *Tim.* 88c-d, 90c-d.

45 : *Phaedo* 82d f., 84a, 99a ff.; *Rep.* 540a-b ; *Phaedr.* 247b f.

46 : *Prtg.* 353b f.; *Rep.* 444d ; *Laws* 743e f.

47 : *Rep.* 411c f.; *Laws* 679b-c, 691c-d, 701e.

48 : *Rep.* 591b-d ; *Laws* 631b f., 728c f.

49 : *Rep.* 571d f.

50 : *Eryx.* 397e f.; *Laws* 661a f., 808e.

CHAPTER XIV

1 : *Gorg.* 466ᴅ ff., 521 f.; *Rep.* 496b f., 498b-c, 499b, c, 576 ff., 615c f.; cf. *Theag.* 124b ff.; *Alc. II*, 141 f.

2 : *Rep.* 473c-d ; *Polit.* 308e f.; *Laws* 908 f., 946d f., 968 f.

3 : *Phaedr.* 270d ; *Soph.* 247d f., 248b ; *Laws* 893 ff. Cf. J. Souilhe, *Etude sur le terme DYNAMIS dans les dialogues de Platon*, pp. 148-149.

4 : *Tim.* 46d f., 68d f. Commentators differ somewhat hopelessly in their interpretations of almost all the evidence considered in the present section, in matters of principle as well as of detail. Thus Archer-Hind regards Th. Martin's *Etudes* as insignificant on the philosophical side, while E. Frank regards Archer-Hind (along with Eva Sachs) as too materialistically minded to comprehend Plato's physical science. Rodier and Natorp (with many others) think the difficulties of interpretation are due to Plato's mixing up " myth " with " science." Frank insists that the " mythical " form is the only proper form (on platonic principles) for handling *exakte Naturwissenschaft*, and consequently takes very seriously much which other commentators treat lightly. None of the commentators known to the

writer would accept fully the interpretation given in the present section.

5 : *Phileb.* 26b f.; cf. Fouillee, op. cit., pp. 146 f.; Natorp, op. cit., pp. 340 f.; Burnet, *Greek Philos., Pt. I.*, pp. 323, 329, 332. From the standpoint which makes numbers of the " ideas," the limit is " one " and the unlimited is the " indefinite dyad."

6 : *Tim.* 53c f.; cf. Rodier's commentary on the *De Anima*, pp. 217-218. In Herodotus' time, as appears plainly in his geographical descriptions, the square was taken (in Greece) as the unit for mensuration purposes—doubtless also in Anaximander's famous " map "—but by Plato's time, Pythagorean geometry had substituted for the square the simpler figure of the right-angled triangle—perhaps borrowed from Egypt—which has remained the unit for mensuration purposes down to the present day.

7 : *Phaedr.* 245c f.; *Tim.* 34a, b ; *Laws* 893c ff., 897c f. Many commentators point out that, as the circle in a sense " contains " all the regular figures (triangle, square, etc.) which can be inscribed in it, the principle of " circularity " is really the ideal pattern in terms of which both extension (triangles and their compounds) and motion are to be understood.

8 : *Rep.* 529d f.; *Tim.* 32c f., 53d ff., 58a f.

9 : *Rep.* 616b f.; *Tim.* 36d, 38c ff., 40a f.; *Laws* 822a-b.

10 : *Tim.* 32d, 58.

11 : Cf. C. Ritter, *Platon*, Vol. II., p. 349.

12 : *Tim.* 54 f., 56c f., 58 ff., 60e f. ; cf. Archer-Hind, *The Timaeus of Plato*, pp. 202-204 (note on 56d).

13 : *Rep.* 511b-c, 529 f.; *Tim.* 27e f., 46d f., 51d f.; cf. W. A. Butler, *Lectures on the History of Greek Philosophy*, Vol. II, pp. 66-67, 121 ; Natorp, op. cit., pp. 201 ff.

14 : *Tim.* 29b-d, 30a, 51a f., 52d f., cf. 53d, 69b, 73b.

15 : *Tim.* 49a, e, 50b f.; cf. *Rep.* 529d f. Most commentators (e.g., Baeumker, *Das Problem der Materie in der griechischen Philosophie*, pp. 155, 177 ff., 184 ff.; Natorp, op. cit., pp. 348 ff.; Archer-Hind, op. cit., pp. 170 ff., 182-183) *identify* this " image " with its " original." Burnet (*Gk. Phil., Pt. I*, p. 344) goes further, and regards " space " as " only one aspect of continuity, and not an essential one." E. Frank, op. cit., pp. 14-16, 117 f., 163 ff., 195, regards the " image " as strictly scientific, but the ideal numbers—i.e. presumably (R.C.L.) oneness, twoness, threeness, fourness—as so much metaphysical speculation, the aberrations of a too-philosophical intelligence.

16 : *Tim.* 28, 30a, 52 f.; cf. *Theaet.* 156d f.; *Rep.* 529b-c ; *Parm.* 130c-d ; cf. Marie V. Williams, *Six Essays on the Platonic Theory of Knowledge*, p. 86. The interpretation of most of these passages is still in dispute. E. Frank regards the platonic universe as the product of an essentially irrational creativity. Not only are the " secondary motions " inherent in physical space irrational, but the " ideas " are products, and " the good " itself is ultimately a riddle to which there is no answer (op. cit., pp. 104, 109, 117, 372, 295 n). Very many commentators, including all those who, like Fouillée and Wilamowitz-Moellendorff, believe in a supra-intellectual " intuition," agree with this last clause.

17 : *Rep.* 473a, 508e f., 516b ff.; *Tim.* 51d, 52c ; *Parm.*

133b f.; cf. *Phaedo* 90 ff. Burnet (op. cit., p. 349) believes that " the gulf . . . has been bridged," at least in principle.

18 : *Tim.* 54c f., 55d ff. " Earth " is omitted here, because its mathematical archetype (the cube) is constructed out of rectangular *isosceles* triangles, which are not interchangeable with the rectangular *scalene* triangles which furnish the basic form for the archetypes of " water," " air," and " fire."

19 : *Tim.* 58a-b, 59e.

20 : *Tim.* 56 f., 61d f.

21 : *Phaedo* 99d f.; *Rep.* 475c ff., 529b-c ; *Tim.* 59c-d. Cf. Frank, op. cit., p. 39 ; Natorp, op. cit., pp. 140-145, 153, 234-235, 269, 301. For the modern standpoint, cf. Wundt, *Logik³*, Vol. II, p. 31. Those who emphasize the implications of the *Timaeus* passage *re* the precariousness of physical science, as contrasted with what they take to be the proper study of mankind, viz., political science, fail to observe that, in the logic of platonism, political science and physical science are strictly parallel, not only in value but also in their limitations. In fact, empirical applications of the principle of the ideal city are, if anything, more precarious than empirical applications of the principle of the ideal cosmos, and this is duly recognized by Plato.

22 : *Rep.* 529 f.; *Tim.* 46d-e, 68e f.; *Laws* 822a ; cf. Jowett, *The Dialogues of Plato* . . ., Vol. IV, p. 103 ; Natorp, op. cit., pp. 203-204.

23 : *Rep.* 531, 617b ; cf. *Phileb.* 56a; cf. Natorp, op. cit., pp. 208-209. So, too, the modern pure " logistician " leaves to empiricists the problem of finding possible applications for his symbols. E. Frank oscillates between regarding the platonic attitude as *grossartig*, and condemning it as a *spekulatives Hirngespinst*. He tends to ascribe what is *grossartig* in platonism to the influence of Archytas, and the more regrettable *Spekulation* to a fatal slipping towards the position of Speusippus (op. cit., pp. 13-16, 39, 58, 65, 132, 165, 266).

24 : *Prtg.* 356d f.; *Rep.* 511c, 602d-e ; *Polit.* 284c f.; *Phileb.* 24 ff., 55e ff.; cf. Natorp, op. cit., p. 34.

25 : *Phaedo* 97c ff.; *Tim.* 46d f., 68d f.; *Laws* 896e ff.

26 : *Supra*, Ch. X.

27 : Growth is due to the assimilation of appropriate material taken in from the environment to counterbalance tissue which has been broken down in the wear and tear of life (*Tim.* 56c f., 77 f., 80c f.; cf. *Phaedo* 96c f.; *Symp.* 207d-e). Reproduction takes place by the ejaculation of cerebro-spinal micro-organisms into a suitable environment, in which they mature and subdivide in such a way as to give rise to another brain with its characteristic outgrowths, controlled by a new beginning of circular movement (*Tim.* 86b f., 91).

28 : *Rep.* 511b-c, 532b, 533b-c ; *Laws* 898a-b.

29 : *Rep.* 517b-c, 540a-b ; *Tim.* 29e f.; *Laws* 903b f.

30 : *Prtg.* 322b ; *Rep.* 369b f.; *Laws* 678e ff., 709.

31 : *Rep.* 343 f., 557a ; *Laws* 714d f.

32 : *Meno* 99b f.; *Rep.* 548 ; *Polit.* 292d f., 301e f.

33 : *Gorg.* 515 f., 519a-b ; *Rep.* 345c ff.; *Polit.* 296e f.; *Laws* 875.

34 : The ideal Republic and the model city are both " ideal "

constructions, and it is not expected that either of them could be directly realized in empirical communities of flesh-and-blood men and women (*Rep.* 472d f.; *Laws* 739c f., 746). Empirical applications of the ideal, here as in the case of physical science, are precarious.

35 : *Rep.* 517b f., 540a f.; *Laws* 903b f.

36 : *Hipp. Min.* 375d f.; *Symp.* 188d ; *Rep.* 351d-e, 366e, 429b.

37 : For discussion of the evidence on which this rests, see *supra.* Ch. II, pp. 38-45.

38 : *Prtg.* 350 ; *Lach.* 196e f.; *Tim.* 70.

39 : *Rep.* 375a, 412c ff., 518e ; *Laws* 653b f., 971b f.

40 : *Lach.* 192c-d ; *Meno* 88a-b ; *Polit.* 307b f.

41 : Cf. *Tim.* 34b, 44e, 69c ; *Laws* 896 f. Whether consciousness is located within the brain, or whether the brain is rather to be located within consciousness, on the (explicit) analogy of the world-soul, need not be determined here.

42 : *Rep.* 477b f., 484b-c, 508e, 518c f.

43 : *Tim.* 68d f.; *Phileb.* 16c f.

44 : *Rep.* 420d ; *Phaedr.* 265d f.; *Phileb.* 17b f.; *Laws* 668e, 669b f., 903c.

45 : *Rep.* 441d ff., 519c, 586e, 590d ff.; *Laws* 864a.

46 : *Laws* 687a-b, 942c.

47 : *Rep.* 462 ; *Polit.* 310e f.; *Laws* 739b f., 965b ff.

48 : *Phaedr.* 266b ; *Polit.* 285b ; *Phileb.* 15d f.

49 : *Polit.* 271d f.; *Laws* 903 f.

50 : *Phileb.* 16c f., 30c-d.

51 : *Phaedo* 99 a-c ; *Symp.* 188d ; *Rep.* 505a, 508e f., 518c ; *Tim.* 46d f.

52 : *Tim.* 52d f.; *Laws* 903b f.

53 : *Phaedr.* 245c f.; *Tim.* 34 ff.; *Laws* 896 ff.; cf. Frank, op. cit., pp. 14, 100, 104.

54 : *Phaedr.* 247a ; *Tim.* 41d f., 69b f., 88c f., 90a f.; *Laws* 896e ff.

55 : *Tim.* 46e, 47e ; *Phileb.* 30c f.

56 : *Gorg.* 465d f.; *Cratyl.* 400b ; *Phaedo* 80 ; *Rep.* 353d, 403d, 540a-b ; *Phaedr.* 246a ; *Laws* 965c ff.

57 : E.g. Nettleship, *Lectures, etc.*, Vol. II, pp. 195 ff., 209-211 ; Natorp, op. cit., pp. 201-202, 205, 216, 350-351, 357-358, 367 f.; Burnet, op. cit., p. 349 ; Archer-Hind, op. cit., pp. 15, 28 ff. (contradicted, however, p. 92, n. 1.)

58 : I.e. into a space filled only by the movements of immaterial points, according to Frank (op. cit., pp. 56, 58, 97-98, 101, 102, 369, 278 n.), who does not, however, believe that no unidealizable residuum remains (*ibid.*, p. 117).

59 : *Rep.* 558e f., 580e ; *Laws* 782d f.

60 : *Rep.* 442a, 571b f., 588c, 589b, 591b ; *Tim.* 70d.

61 : *Tim.* 71a ; *Phileb.* 65c-d ; *Laws* 645d f., 782e f.

62 : *Phaedo* 81 f.; *Rep.* 519a-b, 552e, 554a, c, d, 589b ; *Phaedr.* 253c ff.

63 : *Gorg.* 518c f.; *Rep.* 407d f., 439d, 586a f.; *Tim.* 72e.

64 : *Phaedo* 68e f.; *Rep.* 554 f.

65 : *Prtg.* 347c f.; *Symp.* 176e ; *Laws* 836a, 838b ff., 841c.

66 : *Rep.* 405 ff.; *Tim.* 89b f.; *Laws* 720.

67 : *Phaedr.* 270b-c ; *Tim.* 87c, 88b f.; *Phileb.* 25e, 31c-d ; *Laws* 857d.

68 : *Tim.* 43 f., 48a, 69b, 87d ff.

69 : *Phaedo* 98 ff.; *Rep.* 472d f., 508e f.; *Parm.* 133b f.; *Tim.* 51d f.

70 : *Theaet.* 176a ; *Polit.* 273b ; *Tim.* 30a, 52d f., 69b ; cf. Frank. op. cit., pp. 99 ff., 104, 372 n. 295.

71 : *Polit.* 272e f.; *Laws* 906a ; cf. Fr. Jodl. *Geschichte der Ethik*, p. 580. This is not necessarily inconsistent with *Laws* 904b.

CHAPTER XV

1 : *Rep.* 419e f., etc.

2 : *Gorg.* 493 f.; *Rep.* 586.

3 : *Euthyd.* 280e f., etc.

4 : *Charm.* 176a ; *Phaedo* 81a-b ; *Rep.* 579c f., 606d ; *Laws* 733d f.

5 : *Phaedo* 82a-b ; *Symp.* 188d f.; *Rep.* 580c.

6 : *Phaedo* 69a ; *Polit.* 307e f.

7 : *Lach.* 191d f., 194a ; *Euthyd.* 275c-d, etc.

8 : *Phaedo* 67e f.; cf. *Rep.* 439d ff.

9 : *Gorg.* 470e ; *Phaedo* 81a ; *Laws* 734d.

10 : *Rep.* 397e, 462 ff.; *Laws* 847a.

11 : *Rep.* 590e ff.; *Laws* 631c.

12 : *Symp.* 188d ; *Rep.* 618e f.; *Laws* 662d f., 829a.

13 : *Gorg.* 473b f., 478c f.

14 : *Rep.* 576e, 579e, 580c, 589c, etc.

15 : *Cratyl.* 398a ; *Rep.* 427b, 469a, 540b-c ; *Laws* 717b f.

16 : *Laws* 745, 885b f., 887, etc.

17 : Auermann's thesis (*Platons Cardinaltugenden vor und nach Abfassung des Euthyphron*)—that holiness, as a " cardinal " virtue, disappears after the *Euthyphro* has tucked it away in its proper pigeonhole (as a sub-form of the cardinal virtue of justice)— while accepted without question in the later literature (e.g. by Piat, *Platon*, 1906, p. 257 ; Wilamowitz, op. cit., 1920, Vol. I, p. 206 ; Vol. II, pp. 77-79 ; H. Meyer, *Geschichte der alten Philosophie*, 1925), is not consistent with the general position taken in the *Laws*. His definition of " service of God " as *Selbstveredlung und Menschenbildung* (p. 27) is also far too narrow when compared with the *Laws*.

18 : *Theaet.* 176b f.; *Laws* 716d f.

19 : *Rep.* 500e ; *Laws* 664b, 732d, 903b ff.

20 : *Apol.* 40e ; *Phaedo* 81a-b ; *Phaedr.* 250b ; *Tim.* 90b f.; *Laws* 905b-c.

21 : For a more minute discussion of the evidence upon which the above rests, cf. *supra*, Ch. II, pp. 50-53.

22 : *Euthyd.* 281e f.; *Meno* 87e ff.; *Rep.* 618c f.; *Laws* 691c f.

23 : *Polit.* 305b-c ; *Laws* 627e f., 728a-b, 880d f.; cf. Hofer, *Die Bedeutung der Philosophie für das Leben nach Plato*, pp. 46-47.

24 : *Tim.* 41d f., 47b-c ; cf. *Laws* 747e.

25 : *Phaedr.* 247a f.; *Polit.* 271d ; *Critias* 109b ; *Laws* 903b.

26 : *Tim.* 28 ff.; *Laws* 904 ; cf. K. Justi, *Die aesthetischen*

Elemente in der platonischen Philosophie, pp. 156-159. For what follows, cf. Wundt, *Ethik,* 1886, p. 243.

27 : *Crito* 50d-e ; *Rep.* 520. Höfer, op. cit., pp. 59-60, denies that this opposition is to be found in the Dialogues.

28 : *Rep.* 347c ; cf. *Polit.* 301e f.

29 : *Rep.* 335c f.; *Tim.* 29e f.

30 : *Rep.* 408e f., 539e f., 582a f.; *Phileb.* 62a f.; *Laws* 951a-c ; *Epist.* 322d-e.

30 : *Rep.* 408e f., 539e f., 582a f.; *Phileb.* 62a f.; *Laws* 951a-c ; *Epist.* 322d-e.

31 : *Rep.* 402c f., 618b f.

32 : *Rep.* 494b f.; *Laws* 691c, 728e f., 792c-d.

CHAPTER XVI

1 : *Rep.* 386c f. Studies of platonic immortality usually confine themselves to an examination of the " proofs," or else treat the evidence as throwing light upon the disputed question of Plato's *philosophische Entwickelung.* So far as the writer knows, no study of the subject from the present standpoint (which is, however, platonic) has appeared. There is a suggestive hint in Natorp, *Platos Ideenlehre,* p. 127.

2 : *Ion* 538e f.; *Rep.* 363c-d, 364b-c ; *Phaedr.* 244c ; *Laws* 759c f.

3 : *Rep.* 330c f., 419 f., etc.; cf. J. van Oordt, *Plato and the Times he lived in,* pp. 262-263.

4 : *Phaedo* 65d f.; *Rep.* 476b ff., 505e f.; *Phaedr.* 247c.

5 : *Rep.* 377e f., 379d-391e.

6 : *Rep.* 378b f.; *Phaedr.* 247a ; *Critias* 109b f.; *Laws* 941b.

7 : *Phaedo* 84a f.; *Phaedr.* 246d f., 248b f.; *Theaet.* 176b, c.

8 : *Polit.* 271d f.; *Tim.* 69b f.; *Laws* 903b ff.

9 : *Phaedo* 100d f.; *Tim.* 29e f.; *Soph.* 247a.

10 : *Phaedr.* 247a ; *Laws* 713c f.; cf. L. Prat, *Le mystère de Platon, Aglaophamos,* p. 28.

12 : *Cratyl.* 403d ; *Symp.* 209, 210c f., 212a ; *Tim.* 30a f., 41a-b ; *Laws* 721b-c, 773e f., 776b.

13 : *Cratyl.* 396b-c, 398b, 403a, 404b, d, 407b-c ; *Phaedr.* 247c f.

14 : *Rep.* 612e f.; *Laws* 899b ff.

15 : *Tim.* 28e f., 37c f., 47e f., 48e, 52d ff.

16 : *Rep.* 519d f.; *Tim.* 33b, 34a f., 36d f., 44d, 62c-d, 73c-d·

17 : *Tim.* 37d f., 39d f.

18 : *Phaedr.* 265d ; *Tim.* 41a, b, 68d-e.

19 : *Tim.* 41c, 43a, 44d, 69c-d.

20 : *Rep.* 463b ; *Polit.* 271e, 275b ; *Laws* 713a, 715c f., 707a ; cf. R. A. Tsanoff, *The Problem of Immortality,* pp. 297, 365.

21 : *Phaedo* 107c-d ; *Rep.* 613a-b ; *Theaet.* 176a f.; *Laws* 713e.

22 : *Symp.* 212d ; *Rep.* 590e-592b ; *Tim.* 43b f., 69c ff., 90a f.

23 : *Phaedr.* 245c f.; *Tim.* 34a ; *Laws* 895b f., 897c f.

24 : *Tim.* 28e ff.

25 : *Phaedo* 84a f.; *Rep.* 611d-e ; *Tim.* 32c f., 41c ; *Polit.*

273e ; cf. A. S. Pringle-Pattison, *The Idea of God.* p. 181 ; *The Idea of Immortality*, p. 152.

26 : *Tim.* 41d f.; *Laws* 899a f., 967a f.

27 : *Rep.* 617e ; *Tim.* 38e-39e.

28 : *Tim.* 37d ff.

29 : *Phaedo* 114c ; *Rep.* 498c, 520e f., 540b ; *Phaedr.* 248b-c, 249a, c.

30 : *Tim.* 69c-d ; cf. *Summa Theologica*, Pt. I, QQ. LXXVI, LXXVII, LXXXIV, LXXXV.

31 : *Phaedo* 64 ff., 75c f.; *Rep.* 609e f.; *Theaet.* 172 ff.; *Tim.* 41c-d ; cf. E. Trommershausen, *Das Wesen der Seele*, p. 75.

32 : *Rep.* 501a f., 540e f.; *Laws* 683d f.; cf. the treatment of education in the " Cretan or Cnosian colony " in the *Laws*.

33 : *Rep.* 442a, 472e f., 519a-b, 571b f.; *Theaet.* 176a ; *Tim.* 30a, 52d f., 69b, 70d f.; *Polit.* 273b ; *Laws* 645d f., 782e f.; cf. E. Frank, op. cit., pp. 99 ff., 104, 372 n. 295.

34 : *Rep.* 410 f., 498b, 591c-d ; cf. Höfer, op. cit., pp. 31-32.

35 : *Laws* 744d f., 746a.

36 : *Symp.* 206a ; *Rep.* 505d f.; *Laws* 732e f., 875, 903b f.

37 : *Rep.* 590e f.; cf. *Symp.* 206e f., 207d f., 209c f., 212a.

38 : *Phaedo* 80 ff., 87b f.; *Phaedr.* 278a-b.

39 : *Phaedo* 74e f., 76c f.; *Phaedr.* 248c f., 249e f.; *Tim.* 41c, 69c-d.

40 : *Phaedr.* 245c f.; *Tim.* 53a f.; *Laws* 966c, 967d.

41 : *Phaedo* 107c f., etc.; cf. Natorp, op. cit., p. 127 ; C. Ritter, *Platon*, Vol. II, p. 133.

CHAPTER XVII

1 : Cf. *supra*, pp. 383-390.

2 : Cf. *supra*, pp. 396-403, 409.

3 : *Menex.* 247d ; *Rep.* 465e, f. 498e f., 501b f., 543d, 580b-c ; *Polit.* 294a, 301a-b ; *Laws* 729d f., 817, 823a, 829a, 964 ff.

4 : *Laws* 630 f., 667a, 688a, 963.

5 : *Euthyd.* 279b ff.; *Meno* 88b f.; *Phaedo* 69a-b ; *Polit.* 307e, 309a ; *Laws* 631c-d.

6 : *Rep.* 552b ; *Laws* 762b f., 780e f., 806e.

7 : Aesch., *Pr. V.*, 887-906 ; *Per.* 724-725, 744-752, 820, 827-828 ; cf. 362, 532 ff.; *Agam.* 468-471, 921 ff., cf. 335-384, 947 ; Sophocl., *Philoc.* 517 f., 601 f.; *Oed. Rex* 379 f., 1281 f.; Eurip., *Bacch.* 999 ff.; Solon, 7 ; Theognis, 153, 751 ; Pindar, *Pyth.* 10, 31, 69 ; Herodot., *Hist.* I, 32, 34 ; III, 40 ; VII, 46.

8 : *Prtg.* 316c, 318a, 328b.

9 : *Phaedo* 68e f.; *Rep.* 560d-e.

10 : *Phaedo* 69b ; *Rep.* 561a f.

11 : *Prtg.* 356e f., 358a-d ; *Gorg.* 491e ff., 507.

12 : *Phaedo* 69a ; *Rep.* 560a ; *Tim.* 43b f., 69c ff., 90a f.

13 : *Phaedo* 65b ff., 100e ff.; *Rep.* 521c ff., 524c f., 533c ff., 603d ; *Theaet.* 154 ff., 187a.

14 : *Rep.* 442c-d.

15 : *Symp.* 209a ; *Phaedo* 68c f.; *Rep.* 484c-d, 501b, 540c-d ; *Polit.* 308e f.; *Laws* 729d-e, 730e, 840c.

16: For discussion of the evidence, see *supra*, Ch. VIII, pp. 233-234.

17: *Prtg.* 322b; *Rep.* 373d f.; *Polit.* 261c ff., 271e; *Laws* 624, 678c, e, f., 680b, d-e, 681a, 709.

18: *Rep.* 420c ff.; *Laws* 737c f., 739e f., 741b f., 855a f., 877c f., 923 ff. The "1,000 warriors" of the ideal Republic (*Rep.* 423a) would make their community about equal to the "5040 lots" of the model city of the *Laws*.

19: *Rep.* 461d-e, cf. 458c-d; *Laws* 636b f., 806b f., 846d f.

20: *Rep.* 369d, 420e f., 552, 555d, 559c-d, 564b f.

21: *Rep.* 433, 441d f., 443b f., 613a f.; *Laws* 757c f., 903b ff.

22: *Meno* 99b f.; *Rep.* 473c-d, 548a-c; *Polit.* 292c f., 301e f.

23: 99b f.; *Rep.* 473c-d, 548a-c; *Polit.* 292c f., 301e f. For further discussion of the evidence, see *supra*, Ch. IX, pp. 256, 259-260.

24: *Apol.* 36b; *Prtg.* 318d f.; *Gorg.* 482e ff.

25: *Rep.* 422e f.

26: *Rep.* 557c f.

27: *Rep.* 351 f.

28: *Rep.* 462 ff.

29: *Phaedo* 62b; *Polit.* 271e, 275b; *Critias* 109b; *Laws* 644d f., 713a, 715c f., 803c f., 902b, 907a.

30: *Gorg.* 507e f.; *Rep.* 612e f.; *Phaedr.* 247 f.; *Tim.* 41a; *Phileb.* 39e f.; *Laws* 903b ff.

31: Cf. e.g. Windelband, *Platon*[6], 1920, p. 152; Wilamowitz-Moellendorf, ff., *Platon*, 1920, Vol. I, Ch. XII; Hans Meyer, *Geschichte der alten Philosophie*, 1925, pp. 202 ff.

32: *Rep.* 612e f.; *Theaet.* 176b f.; *Laws* 716b-d, 757b f.

33: *Laws* 728, 903d.

34: *Rep.* 343a-b, 345c f.; *Polit.* 261c ff., 271e; *Laws* 624, 680b, d-e, 709a f.

35: *Rep.* 425 f., cf. 405a f.; *Laws* 875c-d.

36: *Laws* 627e f., 728a f., 811a f., 858e, 880d f., 36a. Cf. e.g. *Rep.* 538b f.; *Laws* 801c-d, 829d-e, 854, 908e f., 941b ff., 966b ff.

37: *Laws* 846d f.. 850, 919c f.

38: *Laws* 877a f., cf. 847a, 854e, 856c f., 862e f., 864e, 867c f., 868d f., 869d, 871a.

39: *Rep.* 397e f., 417a, 429e f., 495c f.; *Laws* 847a-b.

40: *Rep.* 351b f., 519d ff.

CHAPTER XVIII

1: *Lach.* 199d-e; *Rep.* 466a f., 484c, 498e ff., 540a-b; *Theaet.* 176a; *Polit.* 294a, 301a-b; *Laws* 951b f., 964 f.

2: *Supra*, Ch. X, pp. 304-305, and Ch. XI *passim*.

3: *Cratyl.* 397c f., 408d; *Rep.* 364b f.; *Tim.* 37c ff.; *Laws* 715e ff., 801c ff., 886a, 887c f., 899.

4: *Rep.* 377d ff.; *Laws* 886b f., 889b f.

5: *Laws* 890d.

6: *Rep.* 427b-c; *Laws* 738b f., 759c-d, 828a, 909e.

7: *Rep.* 475d ff., 523a-b.

8 : *Phaedo* 65b ff.; *Rep.* 523b ff., 603d ; *Theaet.* 184e ff.; *Polit.* 278 f.

9 : *Phaedo* 74a f., 78d, 100b, 102b f.; *Rep.* 510d f., 517b f., 521c ff., 532 ff.; *Theaet.* 185d-e ; *Soph.* 251d ff.

10 : *Phaedo* 99d f.; *Rep.* 475c ff., 525d-e, 529b ff.; *Tim.* 46d-e, 68e f.; *Phileb.* 56. For the misunderstanding, cf. Frank, *Plato u. d. sog. Pythagoreer,* pp. 13-16, 65, 132, 165, 266.

11 : *Rep.* 511b-c ; *Tim.* 54c f., 55d ff., 58a-b, 59e, 61d f.

12 : *Rep.* 472b f., 475e f.; *Tim.* 59c-d ; cf. Frank, op. cit., pp. 39, 58.

13 : *Phaedo* 99d f.; *Rep.* 529b-c ; *Tim.* 29e, 30b, 48d-e, 55c-d, 56b, 72d-e ; *Laws* 745e f.; cf. 781a-d, 839b ff.

14 : *Rep.* 492d f., 496c f., 519c f., 539e f.; *Laws* 803b.

15 : *Rep.* 472c f., 473a, 487a, 592b ; *Laws* 739, 807b f.

16 : *Rep.* 487a, 489c, 500c f., 505a f., 540a f.; cf. Bonitz, *Platonische Studien,* pp. 260 ff.

17 : For discussion of the evidence, see *supra,* Ch. X, pp. 297-307.

18 : For discussion of the evidence, see *supra,* Ch. V, pp. 152-155.

19 : *Tim.* 30a, 48b, 52d f., 58a, f., 69b.

20 : *Tim.* 48e f., 50b f.; cf. *Rep.* 529d f.

21 : *Tim.* 46c f., 47e f.; *Laws* 966d ff.; cf. Natorp, *Platos Ideenlehre,* pp. 47 f.

22 : *Rep.* 353a, 369d, 491d, 589b ; *Tim.* 77a ; *Laws* 842b ff., 889d.

23 : *Symp.* 186c-e 188a-b ; *Critias* 115b f., 117a f., 118b f.; *Laws* 678e ff., 737c f.

24 : *Phaedr.* 245c f.; *Tim.* 33b, 34a, 58a, 89e f.; *Soph.* 249 ; *Polit.* 269c f.; *Laws* 895b f., 897c f.

25 : *Symp.* 186 ff.; *Rep.* 408d f.; *Phaedr.* 270b f., 276e f.; *Laws* 720d, 857d.

26 : *Prtg.* 312 f., 315a ; *Gorg.* 449a-b ; *Rep.* 419d f.; *Phaedr.* 255b f.

27 : *Rep.* 518c f., 527d f., 611b f.; *Phaedr.* 249b-c, e ; *Theaet.* 185d-e ; *Tim.* 41c f.

28 : *Symp.* 209 ff.; *Rep.* 540a-b.

29 : Cf. e.g. Wilamowitz - Moellendorff, *Platon,* Vol. I, pp. 422 ff.; E. Frank, op. cit., pp. 16, 91, 108 f., 117.

30 : Frank, op. cit., pp. 13-16, 65, 107, 163, 165, thinks it was not " science " which was studied, but *abstruseste Zahlenspekulation.* This interpretation, however, seems one-sided and exaggerated and, in particular, fails to do justice to the universality of the concept of " the good."

31 : *Gorg.* 466b f.; *Rep.* 338d f., 416, 548a-c, 550c ff.; *Tim.* 18b ; *Polit.* 292c f., 301e f.; *Laws* 714c f., 831c f., 875a f.

32 : *Meno* 99 ; *Rep.* 473c f.; *Tim.* 90c ; *Polit.* 305d, 311b f.

33 : *Rep.* 532 ; *Phaedr.* 247c ; *Tim.* 47e f., 58a. 90a ; *Laws* 896a, 897c.

34 : *Laws* 961d f.; cf. *supra,* Ch. X, pp. 301-305.

35 : *Rep.* 520 f.

36 : The reference is, of course, primarily to the philosopher-king (*Rep.* 487a). In the *Laws,* where a council of the best men governs (*Laws* 951d f., 961, 962c f., 968a-b, 969b-c), the highest

office, requiring the very greatest abilities, is held by the minister of education (*Laws* 765d), and this position corresponds, in function, with what we have regarded as the most important function of the philosopher-king in the *Republic*.

37 : For discussion of the evidence, cf. *supra*, Ch. IV, pp. 106-108 ; Ch. VII, pp. 177-184.

38 : *Meno* 88e f.; *Rep.* 523d, 524b ; *Tim.* 30b ; *Laws* 961d.

39 : *Gorg.* 456c f., 460d f.; *Rep.* 343d f., 409c f., 553c f.; *Theaet.* 173a-b.

40 : " Soul " is treated as identical with " mind " or " intellect " in the following passages : *Phaedo* 79d ; *Rep.* 508d ; *Theaet.* 185d f., 187a (compared with *Rep.* 603d) ; *Tim.* 43c f. (compared with 64b) ; *Phileb.* 33d f., 39a.

41 : *Phaedo* 80b, d f.; *Rep.* 532 ; *Phaedr.* 247b f.; *Tim.* 90 ; *Phileb.* 22c.

42 : *Tim.* 27e ff., 41 f., 47b f., 51e.

43 : *Rep.* 474e ff.; *Laws* 965 ff. It might further be asked : is the divine mind " personal," or is Plato a " pantheist " ? This has been disputed, chiefly in connection with the problem of identifying or distinguishing " God " (the divine mind) and the " idea of good." See G. Rettig, *Aitia im Philebus die persönliche Gottheit des Plato, oder Plato kein Pantheist*, Bern, esp. p. 26, 1875, and *De pantheismo qui fertur Platonis commontatio altera*, Bern 1886, esp. pp. 11, 12. Burnet believes that Plato's God would be a personal consciousness (*Gk. Philos, Pt. I*, pp. 337, 338), and Taylor distinguishes between the technical question whether Plato would himself have predicated the term *theos* of *to agathon* (which he denies, like Trendelenburg), and the deeper philosophical question, which he answers in the affirmative, like Burnet (see A. E. Taylor, *Plato*, 1927, pp. 441 ff.).

CHAPTER XIX

1 : Cf. supra, Ch. XIV, pp. 362-368.

2 : *Phaedr.* 245c f.; *Tim.* 34a-b, 53c ff., 58a f.; *Phileb.* 26d, cf. 16c, 17d ; *Laws* 893c ff., 897c f.

3 : *Tim.* 54c f., 55d ff., 59e, 61d ff.

4 : *Symp.* 188a-b ; *Tim.* 77a f.

5 : *Tim.* 56c f., 77c f., 82c f.

6 : *Symp.* 207d, 208b ; *Phaedo* 96c f.; *Rep.* 491d f.; *Phileb.* 29e ; *Laws* 845c.

7 : *Tim.* 78e f., 80c f., 88d f.

8 : *Rep.* 404 f.

9 : *Gorg.* 517c f.; *Rep.* 405d, 407d f.; *Tim.* 81b ff.; *Laws* 797e f.

10 : *Rep.* 556e ; *Tim.* 82-86, 87c ; *Soph.* 228a.

11 : *Rep.* 500c ; *Phaedr.* 270b f.; *Tim.* 47b f.; *Phileb.* 31c-d (compared with *Rep.* 591d) ; *Laws* 720d.

12 : *Tim.* 89a-d.

13 : *Tim.* 87c f., 88b, 89b f.

14 : *Gorg.* 452a ; *Symp.* 186c f., 188d · *Rep.* 500c ; *Tim.* 47 ; *Phileb.* 29e ; *Laws* 661a.

15: *Rep.* 349d f.; *Phileb.* 17b, 56a.

16: *Laws* 802d f., cf. 654e f., 669b f. But *Rep.* 398e f., seems to imply that Mixolydian, Syntonolydian, etc., are "female" scales, while Chalaro-ionian and Chalarolydian are "male" scales. The Dorian are male scales, perhaps also the Phrygian (there is no doubt about the Phrygian scale being "manly" in the literature, but I do not find an unambiguous expression in the platonic text). Further, *Laws* 664b ff. seems to imply that there are different scales suitable (a) for young boys; (b) for young men; and (c) for old men. There is no reference intended here to the "four forms from which the scales are constructed" (*Rep.* 400a 6). I follow Monro (*apud* Adam), in regarding these "forms" as the ratios 2 : 1, 3 : 2, 4 : 3, and 9 : 8, as many recent interpreters do.

17: I have here followed H. E. Woolridge, *Oxford History of Music*, Vol. I, p. 17. Westphal's reconstructed scales (*apud* Adam) all differ in the order of their intervals. A comparison of the intervals of Plato's scale (*Tim.* 35b f.) with the intervals in the systems of Archytas and of Aristoxenus is made by E. Frank, op. cit., p. 155. The technical details connected with the actual Greek scales are difficult, as Plato is well aware, when he leaves them to the experts (*Rep.* 399a, 400a, c). Modern experts disagree also, and it is doubtful if anyone would accept the interpretation which I have ventured to suggest, although it keeps very close to the evidence of the Dialogues.

18: *Rep.* 399e, 400b, with Adam's notes; *Laws* 654e f.

19: The Dorian scale is (conventionally) associated with martial music (such as the marching song *aget'o Spartas euandro* . . . attributed to Tyrtaeus). The Phrygian scale is associated with hymns and peace-time processions. The Chalaroionian and Chalarolydian scales are conventionally associated with drinking songs. Adam does not regard the "Panharmonion" as a chromatic scale, but as a form of composition like the XIX Century "fantasia," which modulates into any key, according to the feeling of the musician. The evidence is perhaps hardly conclusive.

20: *Rep.* 400.

21: *Laws* 814e-816d.

22: *Rep.* 397b-c, 398d, 424b f.; *Laws* 700a-b; cf. 656c ff., 669b f. 812d f.

23: *Rep.* 399c f., 404d f.; *Laws* 669d f.

24: *Rep.* 349e.

25: *Phileb.* 56a; cf. *Rep.* 530e f.; *Laws* 660b-c.

26: Cf. Woolridge, op. cit., Vol. I, p. 4, who traces this back to the time of Pindar.

27: Woolridge, op. cit., Vol. I, pp. 3-6, following Aristotle (*Prob.* xix, 18, 39; cf. Athenaeus, *Deipn.* xiv, 36) states without qualification that Greek music had not proceeded beyond combining vocal parts for boys and men, in notes set an octave apart, with a corresponding accompaniment, and insists, in particular, that until " at a much later date " the intervals of the fourth and fifth became recognized as intervals at which parts for two voices (or for voice and accompaniment) could be set, no musical progress from the chant to polyphony was possible.—The evidence of

Laws 669c f., and 812d f., however (cf. England's notes *ad locc.*), shows clearly that experimental innovations had actually been made along these lines, and that these were sufficiently well known for Plato to discuss them in some detail, and with partial approval ; and the passage from Aristotle (*Prob.* xix, 18) implies very definitely that *other* " antiphonies " (i.e. the fourth and the fifth) had been tried out before being rejected in favour of the consonance of the octave.   These rejected intervals were thus known to Greek music, and were used (cf. *Tim.* 80b), although it appears to be true that they did not become accepted as approved principles for regular musical composition.

28 : Further experimentation combined " manly " sentiments with (conventionally) " feminine " rhythms, and " freeborn " sentiments with (conventionally) " slavish " rhythms, and vocal parts for men and animals, etc.   (*Laws* 669c f.).

29 : These " frills " are to be omitted from the " short course for amateurs " (three-year course) on the ground that such students have time only for fundamentals (*Soph.* 253b ; *Laws* 660b-c, 812d f).

30 : *Rep.* 397b-e, with Adam's note on e 29 ; *Laws* 658 f., 700c, 701a f.

31 : *Laws* 700d f.; cf. *Rep.* 396a-b, 397a f., which refers to what we should call " vaudeville exhibitions " and to the kind of " music " which performers extract from the Saxophone. Frank, op. cit., p. 9, claims that this is what we nowadays understand as genuine music.—*Some* persons do, undoubtedly.

32 : *Rep.* 400a, 530 ; *Phileb.* 17b f.

33 : *Tim.* 35 ff., 43c f.; cf. *Rep.* 617b, on which Adam writes : " A choir of eight Neo-Pythagoreans would have had no difficulty in rendering the music of the spheres on a small scale."

34 : *Rep.* 401b f.; *Tim.* 47d f.; *Phileb.* 62c.

35 : *Ion* 533d ff.; *Phaedr.* 245a.

36 : *Rep.* 531c ; cf. Theo Smyrn., 72-75, *apud* Adam ; cf. Adam, *The Republic of Plato*, Vol. II, pp. 165-166. For the " inaudibility," cf. *Rep.* 529d (to which Plato refers 530b-c, *dianoiai lepta, opsei d'ou*) ; cf. Frank, op. cit., pp. 13-15.,

37 : *Rep.* 399 f., 425a ; *Phaedr.* 265b ; *Phileb.* 62b-c ; *Laws* 653d ff., 659d f., 661b f., 668 ff.

38 : *Rep.* 377b, 401b f.; *Laws* 800 f., 817d, 829d.

39 : *Rep.* 401b, 402c, 602a-b ; *Polit.* 283c ff.; *Phileb.* 15 ff., 26a, d, 30c f.; *Laws* 669e f.

40 : *Rep.* 349d f.; *Laws* 691c.

41 : *Gorg.* 485b f.; *Laws* 701e, 728d f.

42 : *Rep.* 619a-b ; *Laws* 679a-b, 792d f.

43 : *Rep.* 602d f.; *Phileb.* 64d f., 66a.   The identification of " measure " with the " limit " which is the principle of the " idea " occurs *Phileb.* 15 ff., esp. 16c, 17d, 19b, 26d ; cf. Trendelenburg, *De Platonis Philebi Consilio*, pp, 16-17 ; Nettleship, *Lect. and Remains*, Vol. I, p. 329 ; Piat, *Platon*, pp. 95, 96 ; Natorp, op. cit., p. 331 ; Marie V. Williams, *Platonic Theory of Knowledge*, pp. 30-31, 35-36, 38, 41-42.   On the other side, cf. Karl Justi, *Die aesthetischen Elemente in der platonischen* Philosophie, p. 109 n. 2.

CHAPTER XX

1 : *Euthyphr.* 2d ; *Prtg.* 334a-b ; *Symp.* 186c-e, 188a-b ; *Rep.* 353a, 370c, 491d, 589b ; *Tim.* 77a f.; *Critias* 111c f.; *Laws* 680e f., 765e, 845c, 889d.

2 : *Laws* 765e f., 874e f.; cf. *Hipp. Maj.* 284d.

3 : *Prtg.* 322b ; *Laws* 677e ff., 951 f.

4 : *Rep.* 369d ff., 371b f.; *Laws* 680e f., 740, 742 ff., 842c ff.

5 : *Rep.* 373d ff.; *Laws* 681a f., 685c f.

6 : *Gorg.* 452a-b ; *Symp.* 176c f., 186c f., 214b ; *Rep.* 605 ff.; *Laws* 741a.

7 : *Laws* 709c f.

8 : *Laws* 712a, 715b f., 765e f.

9 : *Tim.* 52d f., 69b ; *Polit.* 269c f., 272e f.; cf. *supra*, Ch. II, pp. 47-50, 54-55 ; Ch. III, pp. 65-68.

10 : *Rep.* 565c ff.

11 : *Rep.* 557 ff.

12 : *Rep.* 550c ff.

13 : *Rep.* 544 ff.

14 : *Rep.* 458b ff., 541, 543 ; *Polit.* 293d f.; *Laws* 739.

15 : *Laws* 874e f.

16 : *Rep.* 575a f.; *Theaet.* 176e f.; *Laws* 728b-c.

17 : *Meno* 99b f.; *Polit.* 292c f., 301e f.; *Laws* 712e f., 715b f., 832b f.

18 : *Rep.* 433 ff., 462 ff., 540 f., 580b ff.

19 : *Rep.* 549b ; *Phileb.* 11e, 20b-22d, 27d-e, 60c f.

20 : *Phileb.* 59d-e, 61b ff., 63b f.; cf. Hirzel, *De bonis in fine Philebi enumeratis*, p. 54 ; Höfer, *Die Bedeutung der Philosophie für das Leben nach Plato*, p. 16.

21 : *Rep.* 558d f.; *Phileb.* 62e f.; *Laws* 625e f., 633a, 780b f., 942b.

22 : *Symp.* 178e f., 206c ; *Rep.* 458d ff.; *Laws* 835e ff.

23 : *Rep.* 423c, 462e ff.; *Laws* 846d f.

24 : *Phileb.* 51b f., 53a f., 62c.

25 : *Phileb.* 63d f.; *Laws* 806c ff.

26 : *Rep.* 524d ff.; *Phileb.* 52a-b, 57c f., 66b ; *Laws* 817e ff., 964b ff.

27 : *Phileb.* 64b, d f.

28 : *Rep.* 377c ff., 427d-e, 484 ff.; *Phileb.* 55b ; *Laws* 791b ff.

29 : *Phileb.* 64d f., 66a. P. Shorey, *The Unity of Plato's Thought*, p. 17, regards Plato's enumeration of elements here as "fantastic" and not "scientific."

30 : *Rep.* 351c f., 352c-d, 548 ff.; *Polit.* 292d f., 301e f.; *Laws* 875.

31 : *Rep.* 577c ff.; *Theaet.* 176e f.; *Laws* 728b-c.

32 : *Rep.* 416, etc.; *Tim.* 18b ; *Laws* 875a-b.

33 : *Rep.* 466a f., 519e f.; *Laws* 903b f.

34 : *Phileb.* 64d-e.

35 : *Rep.* 420 f.

36 : *Phaedr.* 264b ff.

37 : *Phaedr.* 265d f., 270e ff., 276 ff.; cf. *Laws* 682a.

38 : *Phaedr.* 270b f.; *Tim.* 88d f.; *Laws* 902d, 903d.

39 : *Rep.* 420b ff., 466a-b.

40 : *Rep.* 540a f.; *Laws* 903b ff.

41 : *Rep.* 377d ff.

42 : *Rep.* 377b f., 386 ff., 401b ff., 600e ff.; *Laws* 682a, 801b f., 889b f., 890d, 909e.

43 : *Rep.* 378b f., 383c ; *Phaedr.* 246e f.; *Theaet.* 176b, c ; *Laws* 715e f.

44 : *Rep.* 597b f.; *Tim.* 29e f., 53a f.; *Laws* 903b ff.

45 : *Laws* 739c-e, 746a f.

46 : *Rep.* 472b f., 508e f., 517b-c ; cf. *Parm.* 133b f.

47 : *Rep.* 487a f.

48 : *Rep.* 379b, 380c f., 501b-c ; *Tim.* 68d ; *Laws* 716c f., 900c ff., 906a-b, 907a.

49 : *Tim.* 27e ff., 41a, c f., 69b f.; *Laws* 903b ff.; cf. *Apol.* 33c ; *Symp.* 209-212a ; *Rep.* 379c f., 612d f.; *Phaedr.* 246d f., 248c f., 252c ff.; *Polit.* 271d f., 273a f.

CHAPTER XXI

1 : *Rep.* 618b f., etc.

2 : *Gorg.* 470d, 472a, 484a ; *Rep.* 344a f.; cf. *Alc. II,* 141 ff.

3 : *Gorg.* 483 f.; *Euthyd.* 279 ff.; *Rep.* 357b ; *Laws* 661a-b.

4 : *Gorg.* 484c ff.; *Rep.* 497, 519c f.; *Laws* 951b-c.

5 : *Gorg.* 483b f.; *Rep.* 338d f., 343b f., 548a-c ; *Laws* 875. Conscription of capital by the system of " liturgies " was sufficiently well known at Athens, even before Plato's time.

6 : *Rep.* 351c f., 550c ff.; *Polit.* 302a ; *Laws* 714, 715b.

7 : *Euthyd.* 279d f.; *Meno* 87e f.; *Rep.* 491b f., 495b, 586d f.; *Laws* 631b f., 661b f.

8 : *Rep.* 484c, 501a-c, 540a-b, 591 f.; cf. Bonitz, *Platonische Studien,* p. 134.

9 : *Rep.* 420d f.; *Polit.* 293c-d ; *Laws* 903b ff.

10 : Cf. Fouillée, *La philosophie de Platon,* pp. 51, 70, 90. It is not " *doing* his own *work,*" understood literally, which constitutes the highest good, but rather the spirit in which he does *his own* work. To use this phrase as a definition of the highest good, we must interpret " his own " as referring to the work of the " true " self whose real home is with the " ideas," as a member of the ideal community whose pattern is laid up in heaven.

11 : *Euthyd.* 282c ; *Cratyl.* 400a ; *Rep.* 505b f.; *Phileb.* 30d, etc.

12 : *Rep.* 422a, 550e ; *Laws* 697b f., 705, 728c f., 831c, 919b f.

13 : Cf. *supra,* Ch. VII, pp. 208-209, 211 ; Ch. VIII, p. 235.

14 : Cf. *supra,* Ch. IV, pp. 103-105, 113 121. Cf. Gomperz, *Greek Thinkers,* E.T., Vol. II, p. 364. For what follows, cf. Windelband, *Platon,* p. 91.

15 : *Phaedo* 64 ff., 78d ff., 82e f.; *Rep.* 496d, 610 ; *Theaet.* 173c ff.

16 : This is disputed, e.g. by Burnet, *Gk. Philos. Pt. I,* p. 349. On the other side, cf. E. Frank, op. cit., p. 117.

17 : *Tim.* 36d, 38c ff., 40a f., 53d ff., 58a f.; cf. *Rep.* 529d f., 616b f.; *Tim.* 32c f.; *Laws* 822a-b. How far Plato believed in an axial revolution for e.g. our earth, is disputed by scholars.

18 : *Phaedr.* 245c f.;   *Tim.* 34a-b, 53c f.;   *Phileb.* 26b f.; *Laws* 893c ff., 897c f.

19 : *Cratyl.* 403d ;   *Symp.* 209, 210c f., 212a ;   *Tim.* 30a f.; *Laws* 721b-c, 773e f., 776b.

20 : *Phileb.* 22c-d, 28d-e, 30b-c.

21 : For the evidence and its discussion, see *supra*, Ch. X, pp. 312-314.

22 : *Phileb.* 60c, 61a, 67a.

23 : *Phileb.* 61b-66a; cf. J. Beare in *Hermathena* No. XXIV, 1898, p. 179.

24 : *Phileb.* 60c ff.

BIBLIOGRAPHY

For complete bibliography, consult the latest edition of Ueberweg's *Grundriss*. The partial bibliography which follows consists of books referred to for specific reasons.

ADAM (James).—The Republic of Plato, edited with critical notes, commentary, and appendices. Cambridge, 1905.

ADAMS (George Plimpton).—Idealism and the Modern Age. New Haven, 1919.

AUERMANN (Gustav).—Platons Cardinaltugenden vor und nach Abfassung des Euthyphron. Jena, 1876.

BARTH (Heinrich).—Die Seele in der Philosophie Platons. Tübingen, 1921.

BENN (Alfred William).—The Greek Philosophers. London, 1882.

BEARE (John I.).—Greek Theories of Elementary Cognition, from Alcmaeon to Aristotle. Oxford, 1906.

BEARE (John I.).—The Philebus of Plato. In Hermathena, No. XXIV, Dublin, 1898.

BONITZ (Hermann).—Platonische Studien. Berlin, 1875.

BOVET (Pierre).—Le dieu de Platon, d'aprés l'ordre chronologique des dialogues. Paris, 1902.

BURNET (John).—Early Greek Philosophy.[2] London, 1908.

BURNET (John).—Platonis Opera recognovit, brevique adnotatione critica instruxit. Oxford, 1899-1913.

BURNET (John).—The Socratic Doctrine of the Soul. London, 1917

BURNET (John).—Greek Philosophy, Part I. Thales to Plato. London, 1921.

BURY (Robert Gregg).—The Philebus of Plato, edited with Introduction, Notes, and Appendices. Cambridge, 1897.

BUTLER (William Archer).—Lectures on the History of Ancient Philosophy, edited by W. H. Thompson. New York, 1879.

CAMPBELL (Lewis).—The Theaetetus of Plato. Oxford, 1861.

CAMPBELL (Lewis).—The Sophistes and Politicus of Plato. Oxford, 1867.

CAMPBELL (Lewis) and JOWETT (B.).—Plato's Republic, edited with Notes and Essays. Oxford, 1894.

CREDÉ (Hartmann).—Die Kritik der Lehre des Protagoras in Platons Theätet. Offenbach a, M., 1880.

DÖLLINGER (John J. I.).—The Gentile and the Jew in the Courts of the Temple of Christ : an Introduction to the History of Christianity. E.T., London, 1862.

ENTZ (Gustav).—Pessimismus und Weltflucht bei Platon. Tübingen, 1911.

ERDMANN (Benno).—Logik, Band I. Elementarlehre.

ERDMANN (J. E.).—History of Philosophy, Vol. I. E.T., London, 1910.

FOUILLÉE (Alfred).—La philosophie de Platon : exposition, histoire, et critique de la théorie des idées. Paris, 1869.

FRANK (Erich).—Plato und die sogenannten Pythagoreer : ein Kapitel aus der Geschichte des griechischen Geistes. Halle, 1923.

GOMPERZ (Theodor).—Greek Thinkers ; a History of Ancient Philosophy. Vol. II. E.T., London, 1905.

GOODELL (T. D.).—Plato's Hedonism. In American Journal of Philology, Vol. XLII, 1921.

GROTE (George).—Plato and the Other Companions of Socrates. Vols. I, II. London, 1888. Vols. II, III. London, 1892.

HALÉVY (Elie).—La théorie platonicienne des sciences. Paris, 1896.

HARTMANN (Theophilus).—De Diis Timaei Platonici. Vratislaviae, 1840.

HIRZEL (Rudolfus).—De Bonis in Fine Philebi Enumeratis. Lipsiae, 1868.

HÖFER (Paul).—Die Bedeutung der Philosophie für das Leben nach Plato dargestellt. Göttingen, 1870.

JODL (Friedrich).—Geschichte der Ethik als philosophische Wissenschaft. Stuttgart, 1906.

JOWETT (B.).—The Dialogues of Plato, translated into English, with analyses and introductions. New York, 1911.

JOWETT (B.) and CAMPBELL (Lewis).—Plato's Republic, edited with Notes and Essays. Oxford, 1894.

JUSTI (Karl).—Die aesthetischen Elemente in der platonischen Philosophie. Ein historisch-philosophischer Versuch. Marburg, 1860.

KRANICHFELD (Gulielmus Rudolphus).—Platonis et Aristotelis de Hedonei Sententiae, quomodo tum consentiant, tum dissentiant, perquirendo inter sese comparatae. Berolini, 1859.

LAFONTAINE (Albert).—Le plaisir d'aprés Platon et Aristote. Etude psychologique, métaphysique et morale. Paris, 1902.

LODGE (Rupert Clendon).—On a recent Hypothesis concerning the Platonic Socrates. In Proceedings of the Sixth International Congress of Philosophy. New York, 1927.

MEYER (Hans).—Geschichte der alten Philosophie. München, 1925.

NATORP (Paul).—Platos Ideenlehre. Eine Einführung in den Idealismus. Leipzig, 1903.

NETTLESHIP (Richard Lewis).—Philosophical Lectures and Remains, edited with a Biographical Sketch, by A. C. Bradley and G. R. Benson. London, 1897.

NEWMAN (W. L.).—The Politics of Aristotle, with an introduction, two prefatory essays, and notes critical and explanatory. Oxford, 1887-1902.

PIAT (Clodius).—Platon. Paris, 1906.

PRAT (Louis).—Le Mystère de Platon. Aglaophamos. Paris, 1901.

PRELLER and RITTER.—Historia Philosophiae Graecae[8]. Gothae 1898.

PRINGLE-PATTISON (A. Seth).—The Idea of God, in the light of recent philosophy. Oxford, 1917.

PRINGLE-PATTISON (A. Seth).—The Idea of Immortality. Oxford, 1922.

RITTER (Constantin).—Platon. München, 1910.

RITTER and PRELLER.—Historia Philosophiae Graecae[8]. Gothae, 1898.

RODIER (Georges).—Aristotelis De Anima.

RODIER (Georges).—Etudes de philosophie grecque ; avec une préface de M. Etienne Gilson. Paris, 1926.

RUGE (Arnold).—Die Platonische Aesthetik. Halle, 1832.

SCHNEIDER (G.).—Platos Auffassung von der Bestimmung des Menschen. Gera, 1883.

SCHLEIERMACHER (Friedrich).—Introduction to the Dialogues of Plato. E.T. London, 1836.

SHOREY (Paul).—The Unity of Plato's Thought. Chicago, 1903.

SHOREY (Paul).—The Interpretation of the Timaeus. In the American Journal of Philology, Vol. IX, 1923.

SIDGWICK (Henry).—Outlines of the History of Ethics for English Readers[5]. London, 1906.

SOUILHE (Joseph).—Etude sur le terme DYNAMIS dans les dialogues de Platon. Paris, 1919.

STEWART (J. A.).—Plato's Doctrine of Ideas. Oxford, 1909.

TAYLOR (A. E.).—Plato, the Man and his Work. New York, 1927.

THOMPSON (W. A.).—The Gorgias of Plato, with English Notes, Introduction, and Appendix. London, 1905.

TRENDELENBURG (Fredericus Adolphus).—De Platonis Philebi Consilio. Prolusio Academica. Berolini, 1837.

TROMMERSHAUSEN (Ernst).—Darstellung und Beurtheilung der Ansicht Platons über das Wesen der Seele und ihr Verhältniss zum Leibe. Bonn, 1873.

TSANOFF (Radoslav A.).—The Problem of Immortality : studies in personality and value. New York, 1924.

UEBERWEG-PRAECHTER.—Grundriss der Geschichte der Philosophie. Band I. Berlin, 1909.

VAN OORDT (J. W. G.).—Plato and the Times he lived in. Oxford, 1895.

WEHRMANN (Theodorus).—Platonis de summo bono doctrina, ratione et antiquorum sententiarum et Aristotelis judicio habita. Berolini, 1843.

WENKEL.—Plato's Lehre über das höchste Gut oder die Glückseligkeit. Sondershausen, 1857.

WILAMOWITZ-MOELLENDORFF (Ulrich von).—Platon. Berlin, 1920

WILLIAMS (Marie V.).—Six Essays on the Platonic Theory of Knowledge, as expounded in the later dialogues and reviewed by Aristotle. Cambridge, 1908.

WINDELBAND (Wilhelm).—Platon[5], mit Bildnis. Stuttgart, 1910.

WUNDT (Wilhelm).—Ethik : Eine Untersuchung der Thatsachen und Gesetze des sittlichen Lebens. Stuttgart, 1886. (E.T. Vol. I., The Facts of the Moral Life).

WUNDT (Wilhelm).—Logik[3]. Stuttgart, 1910.

ZELLER (Eduard).—Plato and the Older Academy. E.T., London, 1888.

INDEX OF NAMES

547

INDEX OF SUBJECTS